I0823852

LOUISA S. McCORD

Poems, Drama, Biography, Letters

THE PUBLICATIONS OF THE SOUTHERN TEXTS SOCIETY

Michael O'Brien, Chair of the Editorial Board

An Evening When Alone:
Four Journals of Single Women in the South, 1827–67
Edited by Michael O'Brien

Louisa S. McCord: Political and Social Essays
Edited by Richard C. Lounsbury

Civilization and Black Progress:
Selected Writings of Alexander Crummell on the South
Edited by J. R. Oldfield

Louisa S. McCord: Poems, Drama, Biography, Letters
Edited by Richard C. Lounsbury

LOUISA S. McCORD

Poems, Drama, Biography, Letters

EDITED BY RICHARD C. LOUNSBURY

University Press of Virginia
Charlottesville and London

THE UNIVERSITY PRESS OF VIRGINIA

First published 1996

∞The paper used in this publication meets the minimum requirements of the American National Standard for Information Sciences—Permanence of Paper for Printed Library Materials, ANSI Z39.48-1984.

Library of Congress Cataloging-in-Publication Data
McCord, Louisa Susanna Cheves, 1810–1879.
Louisa S. McCord : poems, drama, biography, letters / edited by Richard C. Lounsbury.
p. cm.—(Publications of the Southern Texts Society)
Includes bibliographical references and index.
ISBN 0-8139-1653-4 (cloth : alk. paper)
1. McCord, Louisa Susanna Cheves, 1810–1879—Correspondence. 2. Women authors, American—19th century—Correspondence. 3. Gracchus, Gaius Sempronius, 154–121 B.C.—Drama. 4. Rome—History—Servile Wars, 135–71 B.C.—Drama. 5. Women—Southern States—Correspondence. 6. Women—Southern States—Poetry. I. Lounsbury, Richard Cecil. II. Title. III. Series.
[PS2355.M6A6 1996]
818′.309—dc20 95-36193
CIP

Printed in the United States of America

Publication of this book has been supported by a grant from the National Endowment for the Humanities, an independent federal agency.

Iterum

Dis Manibus

L. S. M.

Nutrix. Abiere Colchi, coniugis nulla est fides
nihilque superest opibus e tantis tibi.

Medea. Medea superest.

Contents

Preface

"It is to me more than an amusement,—it is an absolute comfort, an almost necessity, to put my fancies upon paper."[1] The mixture of ambition and deprecation is typical of Louisa S. McCord. That ambition caused her to essay many genres. To historians of the antebellum American South, her vigorous, even violent contributions to periodicals—these have been collected in *Louisa S. McCord: Political and Social Essays* (Charlottesville, Va., 1995)—are important and often consulted. But her contemporaries and the generation succeeding her own knew her as much for her poetry and for her play, *Caius Gracchus,* and in these she herself placed her hopes for literary fame. What she wrote in Southern journals was for her state and her region. As poet and tragedian Louisa McCord allowed her voice to speak more elusively, ambiguously, privately.

The private voice is heard most clearly in her letters, nor is the public voice silent there, wrathful with the abominable Mrs. Stowe or upbraiding a Northern political economist gone wrong. Known thus far only to those researching in archives, the letters are the closest we can come to Mrs. McCord. They are written with the energy and the eye for telling detail that we should expect of the essayist, but now exercised among family griefs, the cruel last illness of her father, endangered eyesight, the constant worries of the plantation mistress. We listen to her as she writes to the sculptor Hiram Powers a few days after the Ordinance of Secession in South Carolina; we listen to her bitterness and her unsubdued anger during Reconstruction. This later correspondence is supplemented by writings composed after the war. Both her accounts of the sack of Columbia and her recollections of her father were meant to preserve an accurate memory where the truth was too likely to fail. She wrote briefly, modestly (only of what she herself had seen)—too briefly, we may feel, tantalized by the little left us.

Louisa McCord created a venturesome, various, not seldom ardent and

1. Louisa S. McCord to William Porcher Miles, May 2, 1848. (See chaps. 9 and 10 below for Louisa McCord's letters.)

sometimes hectic, body of work. Offering an interpretation of that work, suggesting some readings of it, the Afterword is challenged to treat both her immediate personal and political experience and her larger cultural experience. The former will be sought in responses to her by her contemporaries, friendly, dispassionate, inimical; in her fervent opinions on women, political economy, and slavery; in the religious views that so strongly affected her sense of the world about her; there will be something of her family life and affections (above all for her father). Her cultural experience—disclosed foremost through her experiments in genre and method—must require the Afterword to reach further than might be expected, at first, when approaching a writer and a woman who passed most of her life within a single region: to learn from the Roman poet Lucretius Louisa McCord's quality of mind; to seek Herrick, Gray, Goldsmith, and Crabbe in her poetry, Shakespeare in her tragedy, Edmund Burke in her polemic; to apply to her texts rhetorical analysis got from Cicero and Quintilian; to compare her exile and her choices with the exile and choices of the earl of Clarendon; to elicit from Herodotus' portrait of Xerxes the consequences and the punishment of her pride. In short, the Afterword is designed to tell why hers was "a great, a longing, a hungering intellect,"[2] an intellect in which there is much to like, much to fear, and most to admire.

In the preface to *Louisa S. McCord: Political and Social Essays* I was glad of the opportunity to thank those who have assisted me throughout my study of Louisa McCord. But I should like to add here mention of those contributing specifically to this volume. Helping in the search for persistently evasive McCordiana were Suzanne Maberry at the University of Arkansas and Carey Roberts in the South Caroliniana Library. Miriam Pierce made a preliminary draft of *Caius Gracchus* in computer form. Preparation of the correspondence and the poems owes much to Rebecca Billings, William Cole, Patti Lyn Gordon, Katherine Stosich, and Patrice Crandall. No less than for the earlier volume, I relied upon the diligence and good humor of Kathleen Hansen and John Higginbotham, with the rest of the Interlibrary Loan department, at the Harold B. Lee Library. Karen Macfarlane helped to make the index. Subventions toward publication were received from the following at Brigham Young University: Scholarly Publications; the Women's Research Institute; and the Charles E. Merrill Monograph Fund in the College of Humanities.

2. "Enfranchisement of Woman," in *Louisa S. McCord: Political and Social Essays*, p. 110.

Abbreviations

Chesnut	C. Vann Woodward, ed., *Mary Chesnut's Civil War* (New Haven, 1981)
De Bow	*De Bow's Review*
Duke	Manuscript Department, William R. Perkins Library, Duke University, Durham, N.C.
FOLS	Louisa McCord Smythe, *For Old Lang Syne: Collected for My Children* (Charleston, S.C., 1900)
Fraser	Jessie Melville Fraser, "Louisa C. McCord," M.A. thesis, University of South Carolina, 1919
Huntington	Henry E. Huntington Library, San Marino, Calif.
LC	Library of Congress
LSM	Louisa Susanna McCord
PHS	Historical Society of Pennsylvania, Philadelphia
PSE	Richard C. Lounsbury, ed., *Louisa S. McCord: Political and Social Essays* (Charlottesville, Va., 1995)
SCHM	*South Carolina Historical Magazine*
SCHS	South Carolina Historical Society, Charleston
SCL	South Caroliniana Library, University of South Carolina, Columbia

SHC	Southern Historical Collection, University of North Carolina, Chapel Hill
Simms, *Letters*	Mary C. Simms Oliphant et al., eds., *The Letters of William Gilmore Simms*, 6 vols. (Columbia, S.C., 1952–82)
SLM	*Southern Literary Messenger*
Smithsonian	Archives of American Art, Smithsonian Institution, Washington, D.C.
SQR	*Southern Quarterly Review*
Smythe	Louisa McCord Smythe, "Recollections of Louisa Rebecca Hayne McCord (Mrs. Augustine T. Smythe)" (typescript), South Caroliniana Library, University of South Carolina, Columbia
VHS	Virginia Historical Society, Richmond

LOUISA S. McCORD

Poems, Drama, Biography, Letters

Louisa Susanna McCord, bust by Hiram Powers, 1859
(*Courtesy of Lenora Cheves Brockinton*)

Chronology

1810 Born December 3, in Charleston, South Carolina, the second daughter and fourth of the fourteen children of Langdon Cheves (born September 17, 1776) and Mary Elizabeth Dulles Cheves (born May 27, 1789); is named Louisa Susanna after two daughters of her mother's aunt, Ann Heatly Reid Lovell, all of whose children died young. The son of Alexander Cheves, who emigrated from Scotland to Charleston in 1762 and became a trader to the Cherokees, Loyalist exile, and merchant in Charleston, Langdon Cheves is a prosperous lawyer, former attorney general of South Carolina, and lately elected to the United States Congress. Mary Cheves' father is a merchant in Charleston (he retires to Philadelphia in 1812), her mother a daughter of William Heatly, a planter with extensive holdings in St. Matthews Parish, about fifty miles north of the city.

1814 Langdon Cheves, now Speaker of the House of Representatives, returns from refuge in Germantown, Pennsylvania, to Washington, burned by the British in late August, where Cheves' congressional colleague William Lowndes, weary of political speculations, finds relief in Mary Cheves' parlor and "Louisa and Sophia propose no projects of a bank."[1]

1. Lowndes to Elizabeth Brewton Pinckney Lowndes, Nov. 6, 1814, William Lowndes Papers, LC.

1819 Langdon Cheves is appointed president of the Bank of the United States by President James Monroe. He moves his family to Philadelphia, where LSM and her elder sister Sophia are sent to William Grimshaw's school for young ladies, among whom LSM first confronts hostility to slavery; the sisters' manner of dress, "dark merino dresses high necked and long sleeved, and high, heavy, ugly boots," excites disdainful comment in contrast to the lighter fabrics, lower necklines, short sleeves, and slippers favored by their schoolmates—until their credit is repaired by a visit to the school from Mary Cheves arrayed in the height of fashion, her golden hair crowned by a chinchilla cap, a chinchilla pelisse enfolded about a frock of the most delicate muslin.[2] LSM studies French with Charles Picot and his wife, émigrés from France. According to family tradition, has been detected hiding behind the door, taking notes and working problems, while her brothers are being tutored in mathematics in the next room; her father therefore has decided that henceforth she should be instructed also in subjects taught more usually to boys.

1822–29 The architect William Strickland builds for Langdon Cheves a house on Washington Square in Philadelphia. Three stories high and of conspicuous splendor, it is soon known for its hospitality and for the brilliance of its guests, among them Hugh Swinton Legaré. When appointment to a commission investigating rival claims under the Treaty of Ghent takes Cheves more and more to Washington, he establishes his family on an estate of 73 acres, soon enlarged to 194, just outside Lancaster, Pennsylvania, where Lancaster's congressman, James Buchanan, is a frequent guest.

1829 The Cheves family returns to South Carolina (December). After sister Sophia is married on December 1, 1830, and because the health of Mary Cheves, never strong, is being enfeebled by her numerous confinements, LSM assumes more and more the management of the family household, which from 1830 begins to spend its summers, and from 1832 the whole year, at Pendleton in northwestern South Carolina, a village popular for its cool breezes and distance from the ma-

2. Smythe, p. 100.

laria of the coast. There LSM and her mother join the Social Library Society.

1833 Langdon Cheves purchases 1,530 acres adjacent to the plantation of LSM's sister Sophia and her husband Charles Haskell near Abbeville; this land is bestowed upon LSM, who brings to it thirty-eight slaves given her in 1830 by her grandmother Sophia Heatly Dulles and entrusts it to her brother-in-law's management. At Pendleton, LSM is set by her mother to making clothes for the domestic staff: "Louisa who had never before had any such business to attend to sat to work and cut and made a frock Coat (they call [them] Jackson Coats) and pantaloons in a day, sometimes 2 Coats a day and sometimes more[,] and the work I will answer for not to give way before the cloth. [I]n fact she made all the clothes for the men and children including shirts to all[,] with a few days work from an old woman hardly worth counting."[3]

1834 Near Portman Shoals, eight miles west of Pendleton, on the Seneca River, Langdon Cheves builds an ample, rambling house "to hold all the family and[,] in case of need, a dozen or two more." It is thirty-five miles to the Haskell plantation. "John and Louisa came down on horse back, and stayed with us for ten days. They both looked very well, and Louisa seemed quite pleased with their quiet winter in Pendleton"—quiet, but not idle, John teaching Latin to their younger brother Charles, LSM instructing Charles and younger sister Anna in English, French, writing, and arithmetic, and having charge of the illness of a servant whose mother has just died: "L[ouisa] is," her grandmother observes, "an uncommon Girl[;] I dont know how the [family] would make out without her."[4] From Mary Cheves' aunt Ann Lovell, who dies on October 16, Langdon Cheves inherits large properties, among them the plantation Home Place, now renamed Lang Syne, in Orangeburg County near Fort Motte, about thirty-five miles south of Columbia. Cheves intends Lang Syne for his eventual retirement.

3. Mary Cheves to Ann Heatly Reid Lovell, Nov. 28, 1833, Ann Heatly Reid Lovell Papers, Duke.

4. Sophia Cheves Haskell to Ann Heatly Reid Lovell [Spring 1834], ibid.; Sophia Dulles to Joseph Heatly Dulles, June 21, 1834, Langdon Cheves I Papers, SCHS.

1835 Joins the family of James Hamilton, Jr., nullifier governor of South Carolina (1830–32), for a summer tour to New York City, Newport, and Ballston Spa, near Saratoga Springs.

1836 Amid plans to travel, with "Louisa as my companion," to seek medical advice in Philadelphia, thence to "the Falls, the Lakes, Canadas, etc. etc. . . . and thus dispose of the summer as much to her gratification as possible, for she did not reap much last summer," Mary Cheves dies at Lang Syne (April 5). LSM remains in charge of the plantation's management. "I feel as I wander about the house and have to take her place in a thousand things as if I were doing wrong all the time."[5]

1839 With her father, older brother Alexander, and sister Anna, spends the summer at resorts in western Virginia. "I have surmounted a summer at the Springs, which thank Heaven *est finie* and I am again released f[ro]m playing belle, which, nolens volens, seems some how or other to be my destiny when I go into company. Next time I go to matronise Miss Anna in the gay world, I vow it shall be in a cap, or some such distinguishing mark of old age. . . . I'll pin a piece of paper with '*aged twenty-nine,*' on my shoulder, and if that don't scare off the young seventeen-year-olders who come to flirt with me, the dear knows what will." At Asheville, North Carolina, during the journey home, the Cheves family finds Langdon Cheves' former pupil and old friend Robert Young Hayne mortally ill. "We staid to see him die" (September 24).[6] On Christmas Eve, LSM's younger brother Langdon Cheves, Jr., marries Charlotte McCord, eldest of the eleven children of David James McCord. Recently a widower, his wife having died in early August,[7] McCord (born January 13, 1797), a former newspaper editor and member of the state legislature, is a lawyer and president of the Bank of the State of South Carolina in Columbia, renowned for his fiery temper and ardent politics at least since his nullifier days.

5. Mary Cheves to Alexander Cheves, Feb. 26, 1836, Langdon Cheves I Papers, SCHS; LSM to Sophia Cheves Haskell, April 8 [1836].

6. LSM to Langdon Cheves, Jr., Portman Shoals, Oct. 7, 1839.

7. "Mrs. McCord is dead. She died in confinement. Poor children. I pity Charlotte." Francis Lieber to Matilda Lieber, Aug. 22, 1839, Francis Lieber Papers, SCL.

1840 Is married to David James McCord (May 20); held at Lang Syne, the wedding, as sister Anna, baffled of beaux, complains, is "about as quiet an affair as could well take place."[8] There are three children of the marriage: Langdon Cheves (born April 17, 1841, in apartments above his father's bank in Columbia), Hannah Cheves (born September 18, 1843, at Fortress, a Sandhill village preferred by those summering from Fort Motte), and Louisa Rebecca Hayne (born August 10, 1845, in Pendleton). Son Cheves, "a fine intelligent lad, but whose health has from an infant been uncertain, and her greatest cause of anxiety,"[9] is stricken with a disease of the hip for his first two years and must use crutches for some years thereafter; his suffering, LSM thinks later, contributes to the firmness and composure characteristic of him throughout his life. LSM supervises her daughters' education carefully, in Columbia sending them three afternoons a week to the home of a Frenchwoman for practice in conversation, herself daily reading aloud to them in French as well as English, and at Lang Syne receiving regular shipments from John Pennington's bookshop in Philadelphia, many of the books ordered for the children being in French or German.

1841 Passing in their carriage through Lexington, South Carolina, the McCords recognize Matilda Lieber, a friend from Columbia, enjoying on a piazza the cool air of an August morning: "I was much pleased in having a momentary chat with Mr. and Mrs. McCord who with their infant were on their way to Pendleton, she looking miserable[;] she has been in very bad health."[10] With his family gathered at Lang Syne, Langdon Cheves divides his property among his children (November). LSM, asked to cede the land near Abbeville given to her in 1833, receives the title to Lang Syne. Its library—located in a separate building until, in 1852, it is transferred into a room added to the main house—becomes the McCords' workroom, their identical writing tables standing on either side of

8. Anna Cheves to Anna Dulles, May 24, 1840, Dulles-Cheves-McCord-Lovell Papers, SCHS.

9. Sophia Cheves Haskell to Eleuthera Du Pont, Nov. 11, 1856, Langdon Cheves III Papers, SCHS.

10. Matilda Lieber to Francis Lieber, Aug. 5, 1841, Francis Lieber Papers, Huntington.

the fireplace. The room is plainly furnished with bookcases homemade of pine (except one, more handsome, bought by LSM for her husband) and carpets woven on the plantation, and of the books many are bound by David James McCord, who also makes frames for the engravings placed on the mantelpiece; large windows open upon trees, among them a sycamore, its base surrounded with violets, and sweetbrier and lilacs. It is an agreeable isolation. "Such is the spirit of the day, that I seem no longer to belong to the community. My only companion is my wife, whose opinions, taste, reading, and prejudices are all in my own line."[11]

1845 Edward Dagge Worthington, physician, of Sherbrooke, Quebec, traveling for his health after service in the British army and practice in Edinburgh, visits Lang Syne (November) and stays for two months, an admirer of the plantation's order and of his hostess's horsemanship. When pneumonia breaks out he accompanies LSM during her regular morning inspections of the slaves' quarters. "Then she would take me off for a gallop through the open to some high point commanding a view of the country. . . . She was a tall *queenly* woman, and a very queen at heart; motherly and kind. She treated me as though I were an over grown boy."[12]

1848–54 Period of LSM's most intense literary activity. Publications include her translation of Fréderic Bastiat's *Sophismes économiques*, published as *Sophisms of the Protective Policy* in 1848, with a foreword by David James McCord and an introductory letter by family friend Francis Lieber, professor of history and political economy at South Carolina College; a collection of poems, *My Dreams*, dedicated to her father and published in 1848; dedicated to her son, *Caius Gracchus*, a tragedy in five acts, appearing in 1851; fugitive poems contributed to Paul Hamilton Hayne's *Southern Literary Gazette;* and essays—which quickly gain for their author a reputation for energy, hard-driving argument, and invective—published in the *Southern*

11. David James McCord to William Campbell Preston, Lang Syne, May 8, 1842, Preston Family Papers, VHS.

12. Worthington (1820–95) to David Ross McCord, 1894, in *FOLS,* pp. 4–5.

Quarterly Review, *De Bow's Review*, and *Southern Literary Messenger*. Building upon the translation of Bastiat, the essays concerning political economy uphold its intellectual claims against what LSM identifies to be the pernicious nostrums of competitors like socialism and communism. Other essays discuss the role and place and, especially, the duty of women; and, most numerous, slavery. An embattled and resourceful sequence of these last is initiated when William Gilmore Simms, editor of the *Southern Quarterly Review*, deciding that Harriet Beecher Stowe is best answered by another woman, invites LSM to review *Uncle Tom's Cabin*, "that abominable woman's abominable book. . . . It is one mass of fanatical bitterness and foul misrepresentation wrapped in the garb of Christian Charity."[13]

1849 Builds house in Columbia on a lot of one and a half acres at the northwest corner of Pendleton and Bull streets. Lays out a handsome garden with walks and, as soon as pipes carrying water are laid down in Columbia, many fountains. The house stands across the street from South Carolina College, of which David James McCord has served three four-year terms as a trustee (1829–40) and old friend William Campbell Preston is now president; the McCord family quickly becomes part of college life.

1850 Spends summer with family and brother Hayne at Narragansett Bay, Rhode Island; a journey to Niagara is cut short when in Boston son Cheves is struck by a heavy wagon and temporarily lamed. Making a tour of the Southern states with a wealthy friend also recuperating from illness, James Burrill Angell, lately graduated from Brown University in Providence, is entertained to tea by LSM in Columbia (late autumn), who, although "extremely cordial," tells her young guests, "We ought to fight you of the North."[14] On December 19 the two Northerners travel from Charleston to Lang Syne to spend the Christmas holidays with the McCords; the prosperity (Lang Syne now has 137 slaves), meticulous manage-

13. LSM to Mary Dulles, Oct. 9, 1852.

14. "We pray for the independence of the South, at any sacrifice of existing conditions and relations, as the greatest blessing that heaven could confer upon our beloved and almost

ment, elegant mansion, and splendid grounds are recorded by Angell in his *Reminiscences*, published in 1912.[15]

1851 At White Sulphur Springs in western Virginia, author of *Swallow Barn* John Pendleton Kennedy encounters "several South Carolinians . . . ridiculously distempered with nullification and Disunion." David James McCord, predicting civil war, "is the most moderate of them—though I am told his wife, who has lately written a tragedy called 'Gracchus,' is not." At Red Sweet Springs, LSM meets diarist Jane Caroline North. "Mrs. M'Cord paid us a visit this afternoon. Aunt Harrie did not see her as she was lying down, with a headache—She made me quite a long visit—she is a masculine clever person, with the most mannish attitudes and gestures, but interesting and very entertaining. Mrs. [Langdon] Cheves[, Jr.,] is her step daughter and sister in law—her children are made to call her Aunt, Mrs. M'Cord not believing in the relationship of half sister—so I was told at least."[16]

1852 Summer finds the McCords restless in Columbia, the campus nearly deserted, the town emptied of most of its society. "I am glad to hear that you are all enjoying yourselves so well at Nar[r]agansett. What would I not give for a walk on the beach . . . with my brats tumbling along before me[?] I am almost sick of this horrid little place Columbia. I hope that Mr. McC. will get his fill of it some day. For surely I cannot see where the society he dreams of is. For myself, I do not care a fig for the society, but I long for a climate where a family can keep healthy and grow strong." Son Cheves' state of health continues worrisome; David James McCord "certainly does not look well, but I cannot see what is the matter with him. I verily believe he is just sick, for want of company and a little excitement of some kind or another. He will have it that this is a

---

prostrate country." *PSE*, "Diversity of the Races; Its Bearing upon Negro Slavery" (published in April 1851), p. 174.

15. Pp. 56–61.

16. Kennedy, Journal, 7 (July 14, 1851–June 1, 1852): entry of July 29, 1851, John Pendleton Kennedy Papers, Peabody Institute, Baltimore; North, "Journal of an Excursion to the Virginia Springs, No. 2," entry of Sept. 12, 1851, in O'Brien, *An Evening When Alone*, p. 174.

charming place; but apparently it is charming for me to stay in, and for him to go away."[17]

c. 1853 Has portrait painted by William Harrison Scarborough, a Tennessean, who, having moved to South Carolina in 1830 and married to advantage, has settled in Columbia in 1843 (he is LSM's neighbor in 1865). The portrait does not find favor with the sitter, in general unsympathetic to representations of herself, on one occasion standing by, and smiling at the wreckage afterward, when her children toss out of a window a bust of her by Clark Mills, "a humbug,—a mere plaster-dauber, too ignorant even to be called an imposter."[18]

1855 Sally Baxter of Boston and New York visits Lang Syne (April): friend and correspondent of William Makepeace Thackeray, she has met the McCords while a guest of Francis and Matilda Lieber in Columbia and is full of praise for Lang Syne, which "is considered rather a model place even in South Carolina where there are so many fine ones," and commends to her father LSM's review of *Uncle Tom's Cabin*. "You must understand that the Cheves and McCord family is as much the stronghold of the slavery party as the Adams faction is of the Abolitionists. Mrs. McCord is hotly engaged in the strife and almost all her feeling and intellect seem to be expended on that one topic, and she and her husband warmly espouse the cause in every paper and periodical to which they can get admission."[19] Death of David James McCord (May 15). "Mamma and we little girls did not go to the church, but I recollect her taking us by the hands and walking very fast down to the bottom of the long garden path, where we could watch the procession going down the street and out of sight round the corner to Trinity Church."[20] Adducing LSM's considerable property held in her own right, David James McCord's will (dated February 21 the year previous) leaves nothing to his wife or to his three children by her. Francis Lieber reports to his son Oscar frictions between LSM and

17. LSM to Mary Dulles, Aug. 25, 1852.

18. LSM to Hiram Powers, July 29, 1860.

19. Sally Baxter to George Baxter, April 15, 1855, in Hampton, *A Divided Heart*, pp. 20–23.

20. Smythe, p. 19.

her stepchildren, two of whom refuse to call on her after their father's death; it is said that she means to cheat them of their inheritance. Oscar Lieber replies that "Langdon Cheves[, Jr.,] regards her as insane—the most charitable opinion that can be held of her actions" and, remembering David James McCord's kindness to him, concludes: "Poor old man, to think that he should have been so utterly without a friend in whom he was permitted to confide in all things. She must be a wicked woman indeed!"[21] After her husband's death LSM's health becomes cause for worry: in particular, symptoms of severe eyestrain grow more troublesome. Traveling to Philadelphia, loses her wedding ring into the sea.[22]

1856–57 Langdon Cheves has in 1852 retired to a house in the Sandhills near Columbia, convenient for visits, where he indulges his McCord grandchildren. Declining health in body and, more, in mind, and a stroke suffered after the death of his son Charles at the age of thirty, now require him, even against his will, to be removed to LSM's house in the city. "It is very painful and makes me feel like a jailer." Despite appeals to relatives, in particular to her brother Langdon Cheves, Jr., who has charge of their father's financial affairs, LSM is left largely alone to care for the old man. In the garden and near the greenhouses and their flowers beloved of his grandson Cheves McCord, LSM causes to be built a cottage of four rooms and a piazza: intended originally as a refuge "to go to if needed, and to hide my children when he is as he has lately been," it is converted into private quarters for her father.[23] Impelled by medical warnings that her eyestrain may result in blindness and that her son's vision appears to show incipient cataracts, and although she must call upon the reluctant help of her brother Langdon to assume the care of their father dur-

21. Lieber to his parents, May 31, 1855, Francis Lieber Papers, SCL.

22. "The summer after my father's death she was sitting on the steamer with her hand hanging over the rail, and the finger being very thin her wedding ring slipped off and was lost. I remember the look on her face as it went." Smythe, p. 76.

23. LSM to Langdon Cheves, Jr., Jan. 16, March 7, 1856. "[Later in the war] fuel too began to fail—coal was not to be had, and with the scarcity of men and horses it was hard to get wood and what we got was green and worthless. One by one fires were given up and we went about much of the time in a striking costume of old faded calico dresses, and a blanket shawl pinned over our shoulders. . . . The little coal we had was saved and doled

ing her absence, LSM takes her children to spend the summer at Narragansett Bay, joined by her Dulles relations from Philadelphia; surprising the others present, breaks down and weeps at scenes of Charles Dickens' *David Copperfield* being read aloud in the family circle. Health not improving, travels with children to the White Mountains in New Hampshire; with the coming of winter, worsening eyesight constrains her to pass her days in a darkened room.[24] A Scotsman, his melodious conversation and love of reading soon making him a favorite of the family, is employed as a nurse replacing Langdon Cheves' servants, whose influence LSM suspects to encourage her father's agitation of mind, their behavior grown more unruly after their master has affirmed a desire to emancipate them; their leader is arrested, then sent down to Charleston to be sold out of the state "and in such manner as to prevent his return. This is a painful business to me, but my life or that of my children may depend upon proper action and I cannot hesitate." Her brother Hayne (born 1829), for many months ill of tuberculosis—"he belonged to me so young and so long, I cannot but feel that it is my child"—has died in Florence (August 14, 1856), news kept from their father, his mind collapsing into senile dementia; he dies June 26, 1857. A death mask is made by a workman summoned from Charleston by Langdon Cheves, Jr.; LSM never sees it. Besides certain residuary property to be shared equally with her sisters and possession of those slaves hitherto given to her conditionally, her father's will bequeaths to her "my house servant Priscilla, also,

---

out to keep alive the flowers in the greenhouse. They were so associated with your Uncle Cheves who was a great lover of flowers that we could not bear to let them go. After his death his man Tom returned to his old place as gardener and through all the trouble the garden and greenhouse were kept up as though their young master and lover were expected to come back to them. But at last the day came when Tom had to say that there was only coal enough to make the fire once more. It was a bitter cold evening and I well remember the look on Mamma's face and on poor Tom's as she said, 'Well, Tom, keep it up as long as you can.' The fire was lit but burned out before morning. . . . The doors of the two greenhouses were locked and we left them like graves. I never entered them again." Smythe, p. 55.

24. "I believe I wrote to you of Louisa. . . . Her health is not good, and her eyes are so much affected in some way, that she is entirely prohibited the use of them; not even to expose them to a strong light, night or day. It is a great trial, but the danger is so great, that she submits I believe in great measure to these directions." Sophia Cheves Haskell to Eleuthera Du Pont, March 24, 1857, Langdon Cheves III Papers, SCHS.

my house and the land whereon it stands in the Sand-Hills near Columbia, with my Library, Carriage and Horses, and the Household and Kitchen Furniture." In the summer of 1857, again in search of health, with her children LSM visits White Sulphur Springs, Sweet Springs, and Old Sweet Springs in Virginia, among her fellow guests being John Slidell and Judah P. Benjamin, and Francis W. Pickens in pursuit of Lucy Holcombe. At the end of the year, her "eyes continue almost useless."[25]

1858–59 A quarrel over the paternal estate between brothers Langdon and John and sister Sophia and her husband Charles Haskell begets ill will and resentments crowned by a lawsuit before the equity court of appeals in Charleston (May–June); LSM, although "quite willing to appear anywhere and do what is right in spite of blind eyes and straw flats pulled over them," is caught in the middle of the dispute.[26] Upon urgent advice from Dr. Eli Geddings, professor of surgery at the Medical College of South Carolina, on July 7 LSM sails from New York for Europe, on the paddle steamship *Persia* into Liverpool, accompanied by son Cheves and daughter Louisa and paying the expenses of her personal physician, John W. Powell, to attend the family. Tours Britain and Ireland, including Aberdeen, where she locates some Cheves connections, and the Orkneys, where at an inn daughter Louisa sees for the first time, and reads, *Uncle Tom's Cabin*.[27] In Paris, consults Jules Sichel and other ophthalmologists, who prescribe a course of treatment and the nurse of Empress Eugénie. Albeit a marked improvement follows in her son's health and her own, from now on LSM must wear specially tinted spectacles. Rents an apartment on the Champs Elysées, engages two ser-

25. LSM to Langdon Cheves, Jr., Dec. 18, Jan. 25, 1856; Langdon Cheves, "Last Will and Testament," Nov. 6, 1854, Langdon Cheves I Papers, SCHS; LSM to Langdon Cheves, Jr., Dec. 26, 1857.

26. LSM to Langdon Cheves, Jr., Feb. 5, 1858.

27. "Mrs McCord writes me from London discont[ent]ed with every thing even the climate of London!!! She has seen lots of sights[,] all Ireland Scotland and England, and poor lady it is all vanity and vexation of spirits. The garden culture of England has not enough green to show it off[;] Poets Corner at Westminster is a dirty hole,—how can England do any thing having no negro slavery[?]" William Campbell Preston to Francis Lieber, Oct. 20, 1858, Francis Lieber Papers, SCL.

vants, a coach and pair with coachman, and a music master for the children, and attends the opera. Enters society, where an acquaintance from school days is the Princess Murat;[28] and John Smith and Caroline Martha Hampton Preston, friends from Columbia now resident in Rome, and Dr. Alfred Stillé and his wife, cousins from Philadelphia, are visiting also. Is entertained frequently at the house of the Virginian John Young Mason, American minister plenipotentiary to France, and is presented with son Cheves at the court of Emperor Napoleon III.[29] In late winter, travels in leisurely fashion to Italy. Arrives in Rome in time for Carnival. Meets Cardinal Bofondi(?),[30] who assists the McCord party in the minutiae of sight-seeing, among these the loan of a burly Irish priest to keep at bay the goat-skinned inhabitants of the Campagna; interview with the papal secretary of state, Cardinal Antonelli. Is granted a private audience with Pius IX. At the beginning of Lent, leaves Rome, and travels to Naples and in southern Italy, and ascends Vesuvius, before returning to Rome for Holy Week and happening upon John Taylor Rhett, nephew of Robert Barnwell Rhett, among the crush of tourists surging up the marble staircase into the Sistine Chapel for *Misereres*. In Florence, sits to sculptor Hiram Powers, who also entertains the McCord family at his home, once a monastery, which, as he informs LSM, is haunted by pertinacious monks (late April–May). With Napoleon III moving his armies into

28. Carolina Georgina Fraser, daughter of Thomas Fraser, a commander of British and Loyalist troops in South Carolina during the Revolution, and Ann Loughton Smith Fraser, descended of one of Charleston's oldest families, was married in 1831 to Lucien Murat, then living in exile at Bordentown, N.J., second son of Joachim Murat and Napoleon Bonaparte's youngest sister Caroline, fleetingly king and queen of Naples.

29. "I was delighted at seeing my Mother for the first time in full evening dress. She wore a beautiful black moiré antique dress . . . trimmed with a profusion of black lace, some of which I have. It was in the days of hoop-skirts and the skirt of the dress was trimmed down the sides with panels of lace flounces, headed with ruchings of pansy colored ribbon. The neck was low, which rather shocked me, and was surrounded with a fall of lace and beautiful velvet pansies. Her hair was dressed too with pansies, and as I remember she was a splendid looking woman. . . . I remember being quite impressed with the fact that Mme. Poron [the dressmaker], who usually 'received' at home in state and superintended the work of her assistants, came in person to see *this* dress put on. I can see my dear young brother still, in his court dress, with his sword at his side, practicing court bows in our parlor, before they set off for the presentation and ball at the Tuileries." Smythe, p. 27.

30. See *PSE,* app. 4.

Italy against an Austrian invasion of Piedmont, LSM returns to Paris by way of Marseilles; thence to London, where she sees Queen Victoria on her way to open Parliament. Sets out for the Netherlands and Germany, this part of the journey abbreviated by an ankle sprained at Schlangenbad, near Wiesbaden. Tours Switzerland and the Alps: Lucerne, the Rigi, Grimsel Pass, Interlaken, Geneva, Chamonix, Bern. After a third visit to Paris, departs for home on the *Persia*, out of Liverpool, being greeted as she disembarks in New York (October 26) by news of John Brown's raid on Harpers Ferry, Virginia. In Columbia the McCords find their house "in beautiful order—the silver standing bright and shining on the sideboard just where Mamma had forgotten it when she went away." The "last Christmas gathering at Lang Syne" is especially resplendent and populous: LSM's uncle and aunt Dulles with their three youngest children, Haskells, Thornwells, Barnwells, Reynoldses, and visitors from the neighborhood. The library, being "big and long," is chosen to house the dancing; there is a tournament, at which LSM's nephew Alexander Haskell, mounted on a handsome and unpredictable mare, cuts a fine figure, having "borrowed from Mamma a beautiful long white ostrich plume which had belonged to her mother."[31]

1860 In January, disposed to acquiesce in whatever settlement of her father's estate her brothers and sisters and brothers-in-law may decide upon, yet "as regards negroes I cannot consent to receive any more, for I am almost out of my senses with those that I have, and with my now permanently established defective vision, am entirely unfit for learning anything about planting concerns. Those that I have now, I must keep, only till Cheves is ready (which with *his* drawbacks of vision etc. will not be for years) to take them. To embarrass myself with more would be wretchedness to them and death to me."[32] Near Cashiers, in the Blue Ridge country of western North Carolina, where, "having horses, servants, and everything with us," the McCord family reckons to spend a few weeks of the summer, daughters Hannah and Louisa fall sick of typhoid

31. Smythe, pp. 38–39.

32. LSM to Langdon Cheves, Jr., Jan. 18, 1860.

fever; soon, under the care of a physician brought from Anderson, the most accessible large town, they seem to be convalescent—a convalescence almost amiable: from Alexander Ross Taylor, master of opulent plantations near Columbia and now resident with his family about four miles away, comes a daily emissary on horseback "carrying a basket with everything in it that could be wanted for the sick or the nurses. I was just able to be lifted out of bed and laid on a lounge in the piazza, and I remember the way that piazza looked with the dishes, bottles, etc., etc., ranged along it to keep cool and fresh. Wild turkeys and pheasants mixed up with gruel, beef tea, jelly, old brandy—*everything*."[33] But Hannah suffers a relapse, is gravely ill. LSM summons from Columbia Dr. Powell, who, having assessed the danger, returns home and orders a wagon to be built with a mattress fitted into its floor. "He took his own fast horses with this wagon and, feeling that snow would soon be on the ground, and it would then be impossible to bring Hannah over this road, he took her just as she was, and made a bed in the wagon, and with Mamma holding her head and my brother seated by him, he drove at full speed forty miles over the mountains" south to Walhalla in South Carolina, where a bed with springs has been prepared in a railroad car for the rest of the journey home.[34] Anticipating secession, LSM composes songs, one to the tune of "Gaudeamus," another adapting Robert Burns' "Scots Wha Hae wi' Wallace Bled," sung by the students of South Carolina College. When word arriving from Charleston of the Ordinance of Secession is announced by the pealing of the town bell (December 20), Columbia is a frenzy of bells, cannons, clamor; LSM joins the celebrations, riding with her daughters and future daughter-in-law in her new open carriage, a Brett lined with white silk just delivered from the James B. Brewster Company in New York, its quarters hung with banners bearing inscriptions in honor of secession. After dark, the city lit by bonfires, a crowd of merrymakers, with band, serenade

33. Smythe, p. 40. "Yesterday was such a lucky day for my housekeeping in our hired house. Oh, ye kind Columbia folk! Mrs. Alex Taylor, née Hayne, sent me a huge bowl of yellow butter and a basket to match, of every vegetable in season. Mrs. Preston's man came with mushrooms freshly cut. And Mrs. Tom Taylor's with fine melons." *Chesnut,* p. 629 (entry of Aug. 2, 1864).

34. Smythe, p. 40.

the McCord house, refusing to depart until LSM makes them a speech. "We are," she writes on Christmas Eve, "in the midst of a revolution. Our spirited little State has declared its independence . . . and now waits the result. A bloodless revolution (an unheard of event in history) can scarcely be expected; and yet some of us hope that such may be. . . . Even a Woman has the right to wake up when revolution is afoot, and when our Sons (even boys) throw aside their Greek, Latin and mathematics to practice rifles and study military tactics."[35]

1861–65 During the war, becomes famous for her energy, coolheadedness, unremitting labor, and outspoken dedication to the Confederacy, as such conspicuous in the diaries of close friend Mary Chesnut. Expecting, unlike many, the conflict to be long, turns over Lang Syne to the cultivation of provisions; outfits at own expense a company of Columbia Zouaves under son Cheves' command; manages tirelessly the hospital established in buildings of South Carolina College and a ward in her own house;[36] derides profiteers, blockade-runners, fashionable ladies who suppose nursing to be an opportunity for capturing admirers, and the "drill sergeants or military old maids" masquerading as generals of the Confederacy. "Mrs. Preston and I whisper. Mrs. McCord scorns whispers."[37]

1861 Going down "to see where the company with which Cheves is, was likely to be located," arrives in jubilant Charleston "just as the white flag was raised on Fort Sumter";[38] dines that evening with Mary Chesnut (April 13). In Columbia, becomes first president of the Soldiers' Relief Association (later relinquishing the office when pressed by nursing duties at the college hospital) and of the Soldiers' Clothing Association (July).

35. LSM to Hiram Powers, Dec. 24, 1860.

36. "I remember once saying to my husband[,] 'St. Julien, two ladies were here today, who said they wondered at your letting Mrs. McCord manage your Hospital.' He answered abruptly, 'The more she manages the better, every bit of her that isn't enthusiasm is common sense.'" Harriott Rutledge Ravenel to Louisa McCord Smythe, Jan. 2, 1899, in *FOLS,* p. 18. The hospital in the college was set up in June 1862, intended to last the summer only, that it might receive the overflow of wounded from Charleston and the coast; in October the arrangement was renewed, and remained in force to the end of the war.

37. *Chesnut,* p. 361.

38. LSM to Langdon Cheves, Jr., April 20, 1861.

On October 14 son Cheves marries Charlotte Reynolds, daughter of James L. Reynolds, professor of moral philosophy and sacred literature and criticism at South Carolina College. In order to be closer to her son and other Columbia men who after the Federal attack on Port Royal (November 7) have been moved to the coast, LSM brings her family for the winter to Charleston, staying at the Charleston Hotel and later, to her daughters' consternation, at the more sumptuous, but more staid, Mills House. From the roof of the house of a Reynolds kinsman, where they have taken refuge, the McCord family watch the fire of December 11–12 destroy much of the center of the city, five churches being lost including Charleston's largest, the Cathedral of St. John and St. Finbar: its steeple, two hundred feet high, topples "in one tall column of fire, just as a pine tree cut down falls its full length."[39]

1862 In April a dispute over the naming of a new Confederate gunboat: "Dr. Gibbes—Mrs. Pickens's knight errant (knight errand, odd-jobber, says Mrs. McCord) and bodyguard in one—wants to call it Lucy Holcombe. We wanted to call it Caroline, for our old darling Mrs. Preston—but after Mrs. McCord's outburst we were mum. No Lydia Languish for her. 'No Lucy Long-tongue business for me. If we are to have a female name, let it be "she-devil," for it is the devil's own work it is built to do.'"[40] LSM's nephew John Haskell is severely wounded in the arm (it must be amputated); the wife of his brother Alexander dies in childbed, wrongly convinced that her husband is dead; Edward Cheves, only son of LSM's brother John, is killed in the Seven Days while serving as an aide to General Alexander Lawton (late June). "His sister kept crying, 'Oh, mother, what shall we do—Edward is killed!' But the mother sat dead still, white as a sheet, never uttering a word or shedding a tear. . . . While Mrs. McCord was telling me this terrible trouble in her brother's family, someone said, 'Alex Haskell died of grief!' 'Stuff and nonsense. Now you come with your silly sentiment. Folly! If he

39. Smythe, p. 47.

40. *Chesnut,* p. 329. Lydia Languish, character in Richard Brinsley Sheridan's *The Rivals* (1775), is besotted with the romantic expectations inculcated by sentimental comedy.

is not wounded, he is alive. Poor John may die of that shattered arm in this hot weather. Alex will never die of a broken heart.'"[41] Son Cheves is wounded at Second Manassas (August 29). Coming to Richmond, LSM learns from McCord cousin William Porcher Miles, Charleston's representative to the Confederate Congress and chairman of its Committee on Military Affairs, that the government has appropriated all trains and suspended the granting of passports. Ignoring these obstacles, hires special train, finds her son lying among other wounded in a church at Warrenton, and takes him back to Columbia, where he responds well to his family's nursing.

1863 Having returned to active duty before his wounds are fully healed, son Cheves dies suddenly in Richmond from a head wound thought not to be serious (January 23).[42] His only child, born less than two weeks later (February 3), is named, though a daughter, Langdon Cheves McCord after her father and great-grandfather. "A gentle sad letter [came] from poor Lou to your Aunt Charlotte announcing the birth of Lottie's baby, a fine little girl. This was of course a disappointment to all especially to Aunt Louisa and Lottie. . . . I hope your Aunt will be helped to bear her trouble by the necessity of supporting and caring for the two girls now entirely dependent upon her."[43] In July, LSM's brother Langdon Cheves, Jr., and nephew Charles Haskell are killed at siege of Battery Wagner in Charleston Harbor, a second nephew, Charles' brother William, at Gettysburg. "My girls seem to feel as if their brother was lost a second time. Poor children, these shocks

41. *Chesnut,* p. 406.

42. "Mamma was at the hospital—Lottie was with her mother—I was taking a music lesson from little Miss Garnett while Hannah was sitting chatting with Annie Hampton. I remember it all so well and yet I don't remember it for I cannot tell who brought the dispatch. I know that the boy who had it was searching for Mamma over at the hospital and in some way Lottie got it first—then it was brought to us and Mamma got it last of all—it was from Cousin William Miles and said that Cheves was dying. . . . All seemed blackness and confusion after that—the next thing I remember was a carriage at the door and Alex Haskell who had been at home wounded was putting her into the carriage and about to step in after her as he was to go on with her when someone handed her another dispatch. Cheves was dead." Smythe, p. 53.

43. Sophia Cheves Haskell to Sophia Haskell the younger, Feb. 8, 1863, Langdon Cheves III Papers, SCHS.

are very trying to them. This fearful war brings to our daughters a sadder fate than to their slaughtered brothers."[44]

1865 On Friday, February 10, word is brought to LSM at her home in Columbia that the enemy is at Orangeburg, a day's journey away. Flight from the city has begun. Having arranged for Hannah and Louisa to accompany Mary Chesnut, about to join the refugees, now LSM decides to keep her daughters with her. She has buried stores and valuables and ordered the staircase ascending to the back piazza on the upper floor to be removed, and the piazza enclosed, thus sealing off the rear of the house—a precaution which "gave the neighbors a good laugh at Mrs. McCord's fortification as they called it."[45] As the Federal army under William T. Sherman enters Columbia (February 17), soldiers pillage first shops and businesses, then private residences. Standing in the way of invaders who, having ransacked the main floor of her house, strive to move upstairs where her children are secluded, LSM is seized by the throat, and her son's watch, once her father's, torn from her dress. The plunder is interrupted by a staff officer sent to claim the McCord house for the headquarters of General O. O. Howard, deputed by Sherman to maintain order in the city. LSM and her daughters, together with her sister-in-law Rachel Cheves and Rachel's daughter Mary Elizabeth (they have sought refuge with LSM after the fall of Savannah),[46] continue to occupy the upper floor, although urged to flee by a lieutenant who, taking pity on them, has sent up to them by a servant a warning of what is to come "written upon a torn sheet of my dead son's note book, which, with private papers of every kind, now strewed my yard."[47] "As we stood on the upper piazza looking at the flames around, we could distinctly see first one, and then another, of the houses in the environs

44. LSM to Sophia Cheves Haskell, July 16, 1863.

45. Smythe, p. 59.

46. "I rec[eive]d the missing letter that Louisa wrote me before you went up[;] it expresses all that I expected from her well known kindness of feeling and nobleness of character." John Richardson Cheves to Rachel Cheves, Charleston, Feb. 11, 1865, Rachel S. Cheves Papers, Duke. John Cheves was in charge of a field hospital with the army of Gen. William Joseph Hardee, who commanded the Department of South Carolina, Georgia, and Florida.

47. Chap. 7, "The Burning of Columbia," p. 245.

of the town, and *quite out of reach of the fire,* blaze up, and burn down."[48] The McCord house survives the burning of Columbia;[49] but, after General Howard departs, the troops detailed to protect the house from looting loot it themselves, so completing the destruction of McCord family papers and most of the library; a like fate, "when the negroes were turned loose by Sherman upon my plantation residence with orders to destroy and ruin in any way they liked best," befalls the library and its contents at Lang Syne, the house itself being spared.[50] A few weeks before Sherman's approach, a woman claiming to be from Atlanta and destitute has been welcomed and given work as a seamstress in the homes of LSM and the Reynoldses. Now, as the invaders are departing from Columbia, this woman, richly dressed, reappears at the McCord house escorted by Federal soldiers, who, as the family watches, draw forth LSM's silk-lined carriage from the carriage house, where it has been stored beneath linen covers since the McCord horses were donated to the Confederacy;[51] after the soldiers have hitched to the carriage the horses brought with them, the woman gets in and, waving back at her benefactors, drives away in the train of the Federal army. Rachel Cheves and her daughter decide to move into a nearby house shared with the mayor of Columbia and others whose homes have been destroyed, for "we are anything but comfortable where we are and it requires all the patience and amiability one is capable of to live here and avoid violent scenes daily about

48. Rachel Cheves to James L. Reynolds [April? 1866], Rachel S. Cheves Papers, Duke. The letter encloses a draft of a statement, invited by Reynolds and John LeConte, describing Rachel Cheves' experiences of Sherman's troops in Savannah and Columbia.

49. "The house was twice set on fire and would of course have been burned had it not been for Gen[eral] Howard's regard for his own reputation. He couldn't afford to have his headquarters burned. But it was most evident the determination of the soldiers to burn it. They said over and over (to the servants) that it would burn. Burning cotton was found in the most extraordinary places, and Gen[eral] Howard would say in his suave manner that it was remarkable how the cotton was blowing about. On one occasion when a ball of it was found burning in the back entry, my Mother answered him, 'Yes, General, very remarkable, through closed doors,' and he said no more." Smythe, pp. 63–64.

50. LSM to Langdon Cheves III, April 6 [1876].

51. "When the call for horses was made, Mrs. McCord sent in her five bays. She comes now with a pair of mules—and looks *too* long at my ponies. If I were not so much afraid of her, I would hint: those mules would be of far more use in camp than my ponies. But they will seize the ponies, no doubt." *Chesnut,* p. 681 (entry of Dec. 2, 1864).

nothing at all."[52] On June 27 LSM's daughter Louisa is married to Charlestonian Augustine T. Smythe, to whom the same day LSM conveys, for the sum of five dollars, title to Lang Syne and the neighboring plantation of Goshen (formerly owned by her brother John, then by her uncle Joseph Heatly Dulles); also, in a separate transaction, a tract in the Pine Lands near Lang Syne. Smythe goes down to Fort Motte, to a Federal gunboat anchored there in the Congaree River; after taking the oath of allegiance to the restored Union, he is able to reclaim Lang Syne and the other lands conveyed to him, a total of about 3,315 acres. LSM talks of exile, a course adopted by her stepson Russell McCord, who departs for Brazil. In order to sell the Columbia house, which against her family's advice she insists on doing (September 23), LSM, also, is compelled to take the hated oath to the Union, persuaded finally by the father of her son's wife, Dr. Reynolds, who undertakes to submit to the oath along with her. "One of the saddest sights I ever saw was that couple walking arm in arm to the Provost Marshall's office, my mother in her shabby black dress and her rusty crêpe veil. It was like a pitiful, pitiful funeral."[53]

1866–68 LSM with daughter Hannah lives intermittently at Lang Syne, grim and ruinous; for a time with the Reynoldses, then at a boardinghouse, in Columbia; also at Abbeville, near to her father's birthplace and to Sophia and Charles Haskell; there are visits to Smythe relations in Charleston.

1867 Makes sworn affidavit to a committee of Columbia citizens, James Parsons Carroll chairman, appointed (April 22) "to collect evidence as to the burning of the city on the night of February 17, 1865."[54]

1869 Daughter Hannah is married to John Taylor Rhett (March 2). When a South Carolina Monument Association is founded with the aim of building a memorial to the state's soldiers lost in the war, LSM, chosen its first president, composes a public

52. Rachel Cheves to John Richardson Cheves, March 2, 1865, Rachel S. Cheves Papers, Duke.

53. Smythe, p. 79.

54. Carroll, *Report of the Committee Appointed to Collect Testimony in Relation to the Destruction of Columbia, S.C., on the 17th of February, 1865* (Columbia, S.C., 1893), p. 3.

appeal for subscriptions addressed not only to the bereaved but also to "all who cherish the name of Carolinian and cling with a fond love to whatever is left to us of our 'good old State.'"[55]

1870 In March, sends to Hiram Powers in Florence to inquire after the bust of her father commissioned—and, as she believes, completed—before the war; the letter, apologizing for the delay in writing—"truly it has seemed to me often, that I belonged to life no longer"—astounds Powers with its resentment of Northern victory: "Her letter is well written, but I fear that her head is not all right. Trouble has touched her reason."[56] Responds indignantly (April) to a character of Langdon Cheves published in the *XIX Century* as part of a series of "Reminiscences of Public Men" by Benjamin F. Perry. In June, resigns the presidency of the South Carolina Monument Association, refusing to cooperate (as her position demands) with "a powerful faction in our State, which seeks for her the degradation of negro equality," its motive being to attract votes of former slaves so as to unseat the Radical Republican government. "South Carolina is fast becoming to me, but as one great grave of the great past;—One proud memory which must pass away before the sweeping tide of corruption. . . . May *God* grant that some great head and heart shall yet arise to the rescue! But I see them no where."[57] On December 1 Lang Syne, together with Goshen and the tract in the Pine Lands, is sold, all except the family graveyard where David James McCord is buried.

1871–75 "By the sad results of our War, and our crushed out Liberties, now with no settled home, and much a wanderer,"[58] LSM lives largely away from South Carolina, mostly at various places in Canada, among them Cobourg and St. Catharines, whose location on Lake Ontario makes them attractive for summer

55. Chap. 10, "Letters and Documents," p. 381.

56. LSM to Powers, March 20, 1870; Powers to Sidney Brooks, May 2, 1870, Hiram Powers and Powers Family Papers, Smithsonian.

57. LSM to the Board of Managers of the South Carolina Monument Association, June 17, 1870.

58. Chap. 10, "Letters and Documents," p. 393.

visits from her family, and Drummondville, Quebec, accessible to Montreal where she has McCord relations. From Charlottesville in Virginia expresses her dismay at Federal measures to suppress insurgency in South Carolina—"this Ku Klux inquisition despotism, will it not probably stretch its arms through the State?"—and her contempt for Carolinians who "get on their knees to lick the boots of Grant's drunken soldiery."[59] "To a people who have once been proud and great, and great because they were proud, a change in the national spirit is the most terrible of all revolutions."[60] In Drummondville, despite sullen times when she admires suicide, LSM can enjoy an excursion by sleigh to the Drummondville Falls but feels she must avoid sleigh rides on a Sunday, even if the weather is fine and the sun glittering on the snow, lest she be thought "a dissipated old character," and so attends church instead.[61]

1872 Daughter Hannah dies (November 24), six weeks after the birth of her second child. "Poor, dear Hannah had a long, fearful illness! God only knows the depth of her sufferings. I almost felt resigned when I closed the tired, wandering eyes. She was delirious nearly the whole time. She found it hard to leave those she loved."[62]

1873 Having "read carefully the testimony offered for the defence" against British subjects seeking redress before the Mixed Commission appointed, in accordance with the Treaty of Washington (May 8, 1871), to investigate claims for damages incurred during the late war, LSM deposes in Charleston

59. LSM to Augustine T. Smythe, Nov. 14 [1871].

60. Edmund Burke, *First Letter on a Regicide Peace* (1796), in *Writings and Speeches* 9:188. An unidentified newspaper clipping—too brief to determine its context—found in the Langdon Cheves I Papers, SCHS, quotes this passage from Burke (but reading, "to a people once proud and great, and great because proud"), thus introduced: "There is something very terrible in all this. It looks as if the heart of a once proud people was broken, and goes far to verify what Mr. Burke long ago said." There is an annotation to the clipping in LSM's hand: "Referring to France[;] Alas! to ourselves S[outh] C[arolina]. Dec. 1871."

61. LSM to Augustine T. Smythe, March 29, 1874; to Louisa McCord Smythe, Feb. 8 [1874].

62. [Sophia Haskell the younger?] to Rachel Cheves, June 27, 1873, Rachel S. Cheves Papers, Duke.

(May 3) an account of her experiences at the time of the burning of Columbia.[63]

1876 Although at first reluctant, and diffident of the result—"I wish you had thought of asking it of me a half dozen years ago"—at the request of nephew Langdon Cheves III, LSM writes a memoir of her father, carried down to his early career as a lawyer, and meditates a more ambitious memorial, in verse and prose, complementing the obelisk raised at last, "eight months after date of contract," in Charleston's Magnolia Cemetery.[64]

1876/77 Retires to Charleston, making her home with daughter Louisa and her husband Augustine T. Smythe at 25 Legaré Street.

1878 The war having arrested Hiram Powers' work on his bust of Langdon Cheves, LSM renews the commission, now to Hiram's son Preston Powers. The task is complicated, as before, by the want of reliable images to guide the sculptor: "When I sat to your Father, I indulged the faint hope, that he might retain from the family likeness, (which was said to be considerable in me, such as Woman may bear to Man) some far off glimmer of the grand head."[65]

1879 Purchases the house adjacent to the north of the Smythes (January 1) and plans extensive renovations with contractor (early November). An ailment diagnosed as "Gout in the stomach," which having troubled her for some time seems to have left her by late September, recurs abruptly; and after five days of suffering great pain, finally in agony, LSM dies (November 23) and is buried in Magnolia Cemetery next the graves of her father and son. "I do feel," her daughter writes, "in spite of husband children and all, very much alone—like the last of my own people."[66]

63. Chap. 7, "The Burning of Columbia," p. 241.

64. LSM to Langdon Cheves III, July 11 [1876].

65. LSM to Preston Powers, April 21, 1878. Hiram Powers had died on June 27, 1873.

66. Louisa McCord Smythe to Sophia Cheves Haskell, Charleston, Dec. 4 [1879], Langdon Cheves III Papers, SCHS. This letter is printed in *PSE,* app. 2.

Note on the Texts

My Dreams (Philadelphia, 1848), LSM's volume of poems, and her tragedy *Caius Gracchus* (New York, 1851) were unusual among the writings published during her lifetime in that they each bore the author's name. Her poems published in the *Southern Literary Gazette* and the *Southern Literary Messenger* were identified by the initials "L. S. M." Under the title "Later Poems" are collected two poems printed in Epes Sargent, ed., *Harper's Cyclopaedia of British and American Poetry* (New York, 1881). LSM's authorship of the unsigned "Langdon Cheves: Review of 'Reminiscences of Public Men,'" which appeared in the *XIX Century* 2 (April 1870): 885–88, is confirmed by the distinctive style, access to personal details, and other internal evidence. "The Burning of Columbia" comprises two accounts that LSM composed of her experiences during the Federal occupation of Columbia. In accordance with articles 12–17 of the Treaty of Washington between Great Britain and the United States (May 8, 1871), a Mixed Commission was appointed to investigate and adjudicate claims (apart from the so-called *Alabama* claims) for damages incurred, by both British and American citizens, between April 13, 1861, and April 9, 1865. Testimony and evidence for the claims were submitted to the commission, which met first on September 26, 1871, and for the last time on September 25, 1873. On May 3, 1873, at the British Consulate in Charleston, LSM made a deposition before Consul Henry Pinckney Walker. Walker certified on May 13 "that the deponents whose depositions are hereto annexed [including that by LSM] were duly by me sworn to tell the truth, the whole truth, and nothing but the truth; that said depositions were reduced to writing as nearly as practicable in the language of the witnesses; and that the said depositions were read to deponents respectively before being by them subscribed, and thereupon that the deponents respectively signed the same." (A search of the case files of British claimants, held in the National Archives, Washington, D.C., has yielded no manuscript of the deposition.) A second account by LSM, written c. May 1867, was in the form of a sworn affidavit before a committee appointed, with James Parsons Carroll as chairman, to gather evidence relevant to the burning of Columbia. The approximately sixty affidavits assembled by the committee disappeared from the city council archives at some time during the Republican administration of Columbia (1870–78). Two fragments of LSM's affidavit survive.

LSM's "Memoir of Langdon Cheves," her fragmentary notes related to its composition, and an untitled draft of a poem in honor of Cheves, are published here for the first time, from a holograph in the Langdon Cheves I Papers, SCHS.

On March 9, 1912, John Bennett (1865–1956), whose source was presumably his wife's mother, Louisa McCord Smythe, informed his friend Yates Snowden that "Mrs. Louisa McCord wrote a song for Carolina College just before Secession, which was sung, by the student-body publicly—and was circulated through the audience on printed slips:—the air being 'Gaudeamus.' She also wrote another, for like purpose, to the air of 'Scots wha hae wi Wallace Bled.' Can you recover a copy?" Snowden (1858–1933), a professor and historian at the University of South Carolina, in preparing his entry to a competition to choose a song for the university, was searching for models and predecessors. On March 31, thanking Snowden for sending him "several Odes to Carolina," Bennett added that "I hope you'll recover Mrs. McCord's, for their historical interest." In a letter dated the same day Snowden reported: "No returns as yet to my communication as to Mrs. McCord's songs. Might they have been published in the Columbia newspapers? Does Mrs. Smythe know of no copies extant?"[1] LSM's two songs remain elusive. They may have been written to be sung at the college commencement on December 3, 1860, but a detailed account in the Charleston *Courier* mentions no songs or singing;[2] and while a song printed

1. John Bennett to Yates Snowden, March 9, 1912, Snowden-Bennett Collection, SCL; Bennett to Snowden, March 31, 1912, and Snowden to Bennett, March 31 [April 1], 1912, in Anderson, *Two Scholarly Friends,* pp. 46–47.

2. Charleston *Courier,* Dec. 5, 1860. LSM's nephew Alexander Haskell, besides receiving a gold medal for the best essay on a Greek subject ("The Sophists"), was valedictorian and also delivered the closing address, entitled "The Greek Classics."

in the *Courier* appears to answer to Bennett's description, its circumstances make this implausible.[3]

Because no manuscripts are known to survive of LSM's published writings, the printed text forms the basis of the text furnished here. Substantives are preserved throughout; but accidentals—marks of punctuation, paragraphing, and so on—are modified when reading is measurably eased thereby, the editor striving, however, to be as conservative as possible: for example, LSM's 1873 deposition, marked by long strings of semicolons in legal fashion, more accurately conveys the narrative structure when punctuated more variously and more in accord with LSM's usual practice. Emendation has been in general resisted (exceptions are clearly declared), although LSM noticed that she had "suffered enough from the impish fraternity of the printing-office to learn a most sympathizing fellow-feeling towards our co-sufferers in that line"; and we are told of *My Dreams* that its author "never liked it to be seen on account of the mistakes made in the printing."[4] No attempt has been made to reproduce features of the original typographic design. Typographical errors which are clearly such, and do not represent an oddity of usage or habit that may be LSM's, are silently corrected. When there is doubt in any change, a note alerts the reader. A note written by LSM is designated by [LSM] at its conclusion. Of LSM's two favorite sources of quotation, Shakespeare is cited by act, scene, and line number as given in the New Arden Shakespeare, and the Bible in the Authorized (King James) Version.

LSM's poems and *Caius Gracchus* are presented in accordance with conventions adopted by modern editors of poetry and plays. Lineation is added. The design of *Caius Gracchus* is derived from the model of the New Arden Shakespeare, which is both efficient and pleasing to the eye. Stage directions are retained from the first edition, as being LSM's own; on the rare occasions where the use of stage directions is not consistent (for example, *exeunt* appears customarily, but not always, at the end of a scene), the missing direction is added in double square brackets (e.g., [[*Exeunt.*]]).

3. On Oct. 18, 1860, the *Courier* published a song entitled "Men of Carolina! Hear!" to be sung to the air "Scots wha hae" and bearing the subscription "Charleston, S.C., October 17, 1860." The author was identified as "a girl . . . who has a good margin yet within her teens." Although LSM's daughters both would qualify, and the ease and finish of the song could suggest an adult adviser, Hannah and Louisa were recovering from typhoid fever at this time, and the McCord family is not recorded to have visited Charleston in October 1860. Nor is it likely that Louisa Smythe would remember the facts of authorship so differently from the newspaper account. (The Charleston *Mercury* of March 14, 1861, placed "Gaudeamus Igitur" at the head of its printing of the new Confederate Constitution, but in one of the traditional variants of the Latin text.)

4. *PSE*, "Woman and Her Needs," p. 128; Louisa McCord Smythe to William Porcher Miles, Feb. 26, 1880 (printed in *PSE*, pp. 483–84).

LSM's "Memoir of Langdon Cheves" and, in almost all cases, her surviving letters are holographs. Since LSM's intention is thus available without intermediary of publisher or printer, these holographs are transcribed with very little modification. Unless indicated otherwise, each letter printed was written and signed by LSM and is the recipient's copy. Place and date are printed at the upper right above the text of each letter, in LSM's customary order: place, month, day, year (and, if given, day of the week). Placement of salutation, closing, and signature has been regularized. Recipient and address, when given, have been moved to the source line. Omitted are postmarks and annotations made by postal officials, repositories, collectors, and editors. When an em dash follows a period, question mark, or exclamation point, the dash is deleted; otherwise, punctuation is preserved, though this may clash with modern conventions. Punctuation supplied by the editor because deemed necessary for understanding is enclosed within square brackets, as are expansions of contractions (except the ampersand, which is silently expanded throughout). LSM customarily makes paragraph indentations; but when these are absent, though preceded by a line of script falling well short of the right margin, they are supplied. Slips of the pen corrected by LSM are not noted; slips of the pen not corrected by LSM, if these may confuse the reader, are followed by the correct word enclosed within curled brackets (e.g., {see}). Canceled letters, words, and phrases are retained (marked by a single line struck through), for such canceled passages often are evidence of LSM's train of thought or state of mind. Cancellations, corrections, and additional words, when these are interlineated in the original, are in the printed text brought within the line in their proper place as indicated by their position or by LSM's caret or asterisk. Superscript letters have been lowered to the line. Periods are added to "Mr," "Mrs," "Messrs," and "Dr," "Esq" and "Esqr," and "etc" when LSM omits them (her practice varies). Words underlined in the original are printed in italics, words with double underlining in small capitals.

Genealogical Tables

CHEVES

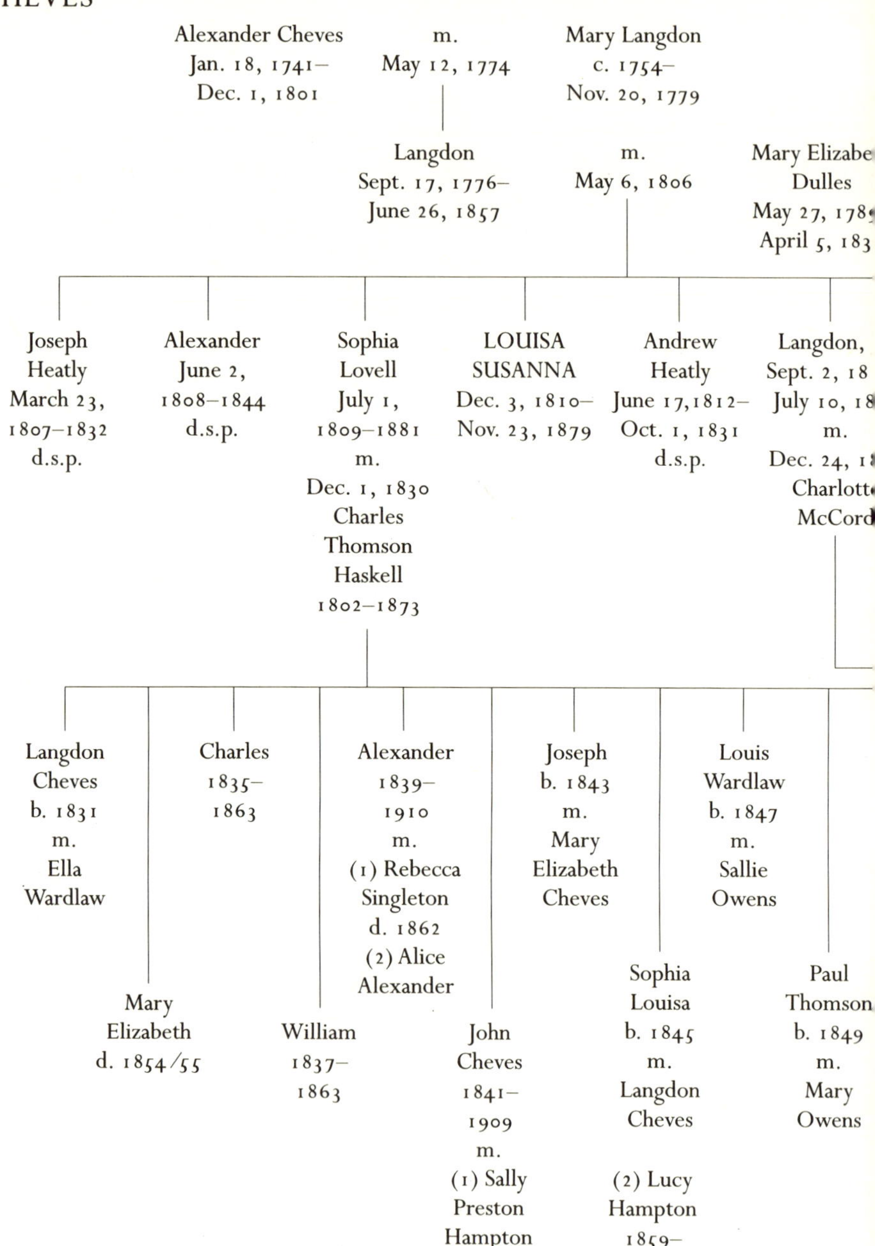
Alexander Cheves
Jan. 18, 1741–
Dec. 1, 1801
m.
May 12, 1774
Mary Langdon
c. 1754–
Nov. 20, 1779
Langdon
Sept. 17, 1776–
June 26, 1857
m.
May 6, 1806
Mary Elizabe
Dulles
May 27, 178
April 5, 183
Joseph
Heatly
March 23,
1807–1832
d.s.p.
Alexander
June 2,
1808–1844
d.s.p.
Sophia
Lovell
July 1,
1809–1881
m.
Dec. 1, 1830
Charles
Thomson
Haskell
1802–1873
LOUISA
SUSANNA
Dec. 3, 1810–
Nov. 23, 1879
Andrew
Heatly
June 17,1812–
Oct. 1, 1831
d.s.p.
Langdon,
Sept. 2, 18
July 10, 18
m.
Dec. 24, 1
Charlott
McCord
Langdon
Cheves
b. 1831
m.
Ella
Wardlaw
Mary
Elizabeth
d. 1854/55
Charles
1835–
1863
William
1837–
1863
Alexander
1839–
1910
m.
(1) Rebecca
Singleton
d. 1862
(2) Alice
Alexander
John
Cheves
1841–
1909
m.
(1) Sally
Preston
Hampton
1844–1888
(2) Lucy
Hampton
1859–
1932
Joseph
b. 1843
m.
Mary
Elizabeth
Cheves
Sophia
Louisa
b. 1845
m.
Langdon
Cheves
Louis
Wardlaw
b. 1847
m.
Sallie
Owens
Paul
Thomson
b. 1849
m.
Mary
Owens

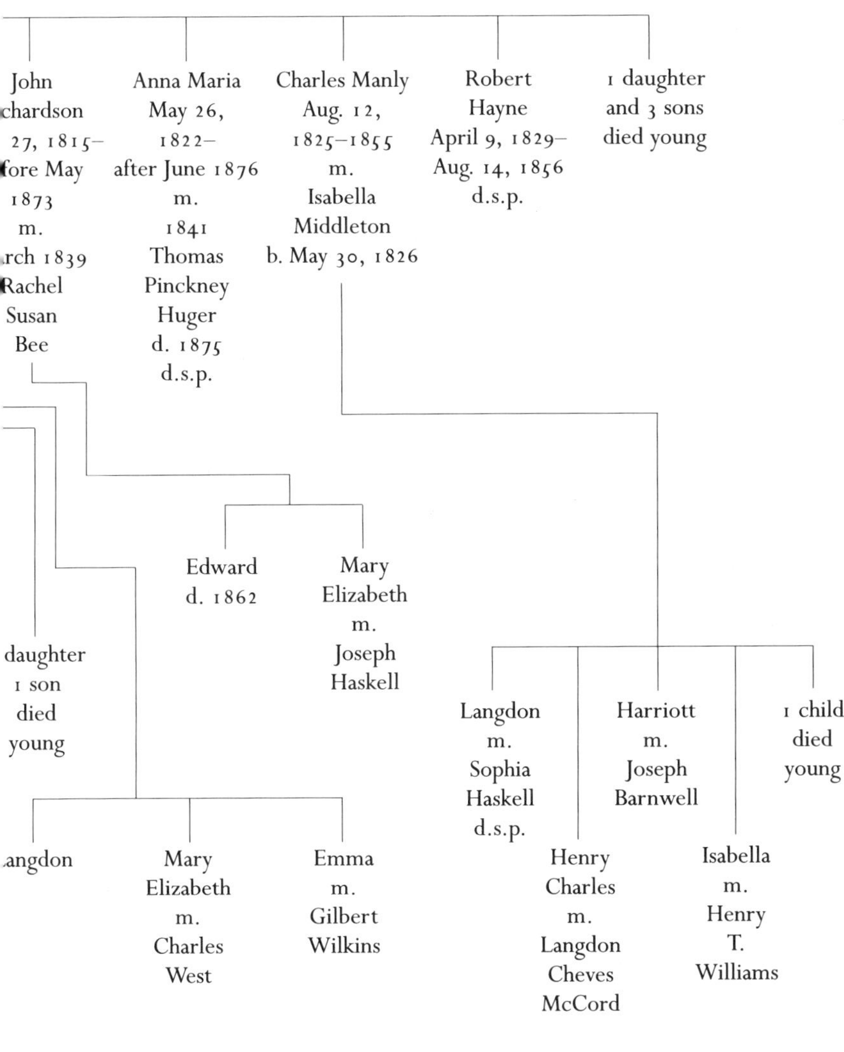
John
chardson
27, 1815–
fore May
1873
m.
rch 1839
Rachel
Susan
Bee
Anna Maria
May 26,
1822–
after June 1876
m.
1841
Thomas
Pinckney
Huger
d. 1875
d.s.p.
Charles Manly
Aug. 12,
1825–1855
m.
Isabella
Middleton
b. May 30, 1826
Robert
Hayne
April 9, 1829–
Aug. 14, 1856
d.s.p.
1 daughter
and 3 sons
died young
Edward
d. 1862
Mary
Elizabeth
m.
Joseph
Haskell
daughter
1 son
died
young
angdon
Mary
Elizabeth
m.
Charles
West
Emma
m.
Gilbert
Wilkins
Langdon
m.
Sophia
Haskell
d.s.p.
Henry
Charles
m.
Langdon
Cheves
McCord
Harriott
m.
Joseph
Barnwell
Isabella
m.
Henry
T.
Williams
1 child
died
young

HEATLY-DULLES

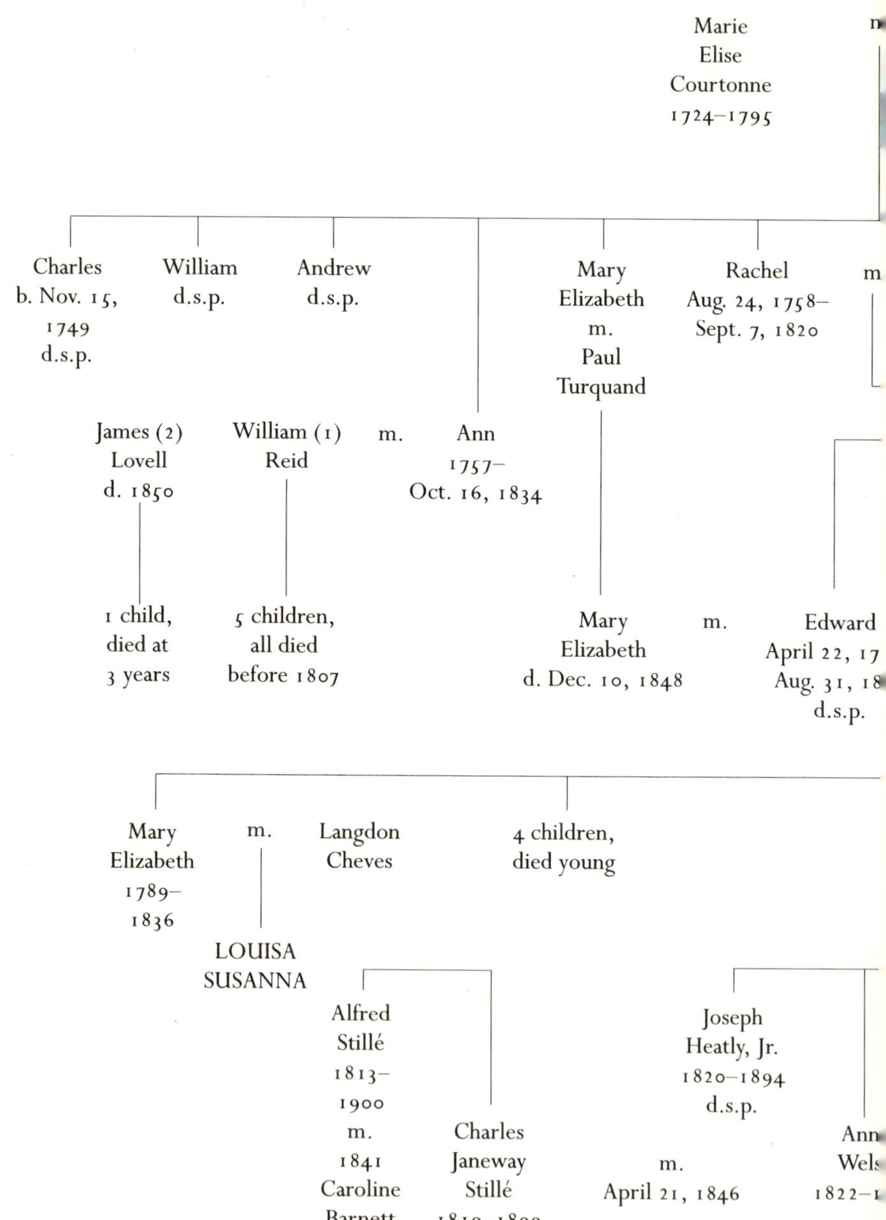

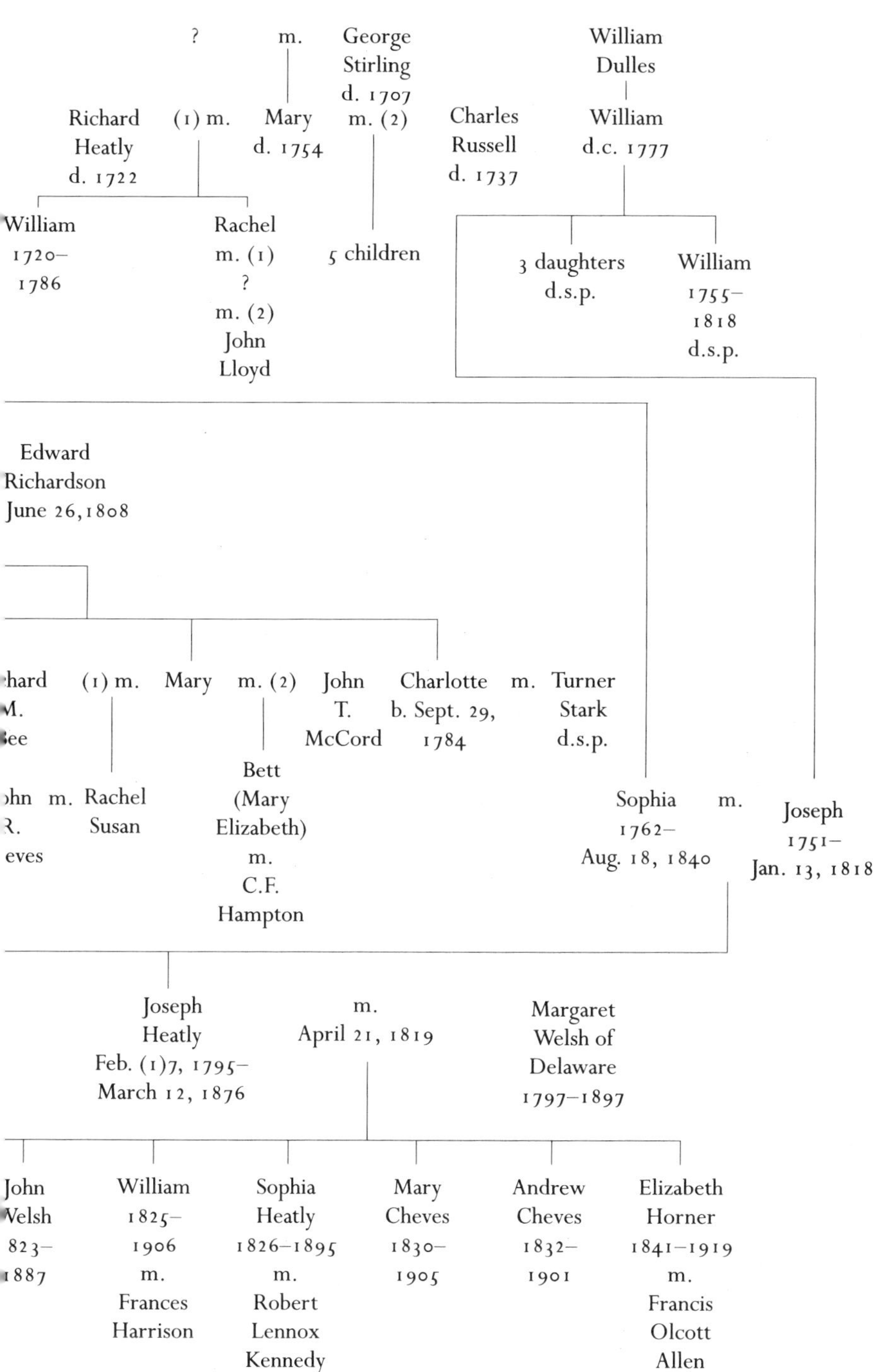
? m. George Stirling d. 1707
William Dulles
Richard Heatly d. 1722
(1) m.
Mary d. 1754
m. (2)
Charles Russell d. 1737
William d.c. 1777
William 1720–1786
Rachel m. (1) ? m. (2) John Lloyd
5 children
3 daughters d.s.p.
William 1755–1818 d.s.p.
Edward Richardson June 26, 1808
hard M. ee
(1) m.
Mary
m. (2)
John T. McCord
Charlotte b. Sept. 29, 1784
m.
Turner Stark d.s.p.
hn R. eves
m.
Rachel Susan
Bett (Mary Elizabeth) m. C.F. Hampton
Sophia 1762– Aug. 18, 1840
m.
Joseph 1751– Jan. 13, 1818
Joseph Heatly Feb. (1)7, 1795– March 12, 1876
m. April 21, 1819
Margaret Welsh of Delaware 1797–1897
John Welsh 823– 1887
William 1825– 1906 m. Frances Harrison
Sophia Heatly 1826–1895 m. Robert Lennox Kennedy
Mary Cheves 1830– 1905
Andrew Cheves 1832– 1901
Elizabeth Horner 1841–1919 m. Francis Olcott Allen

McCORD

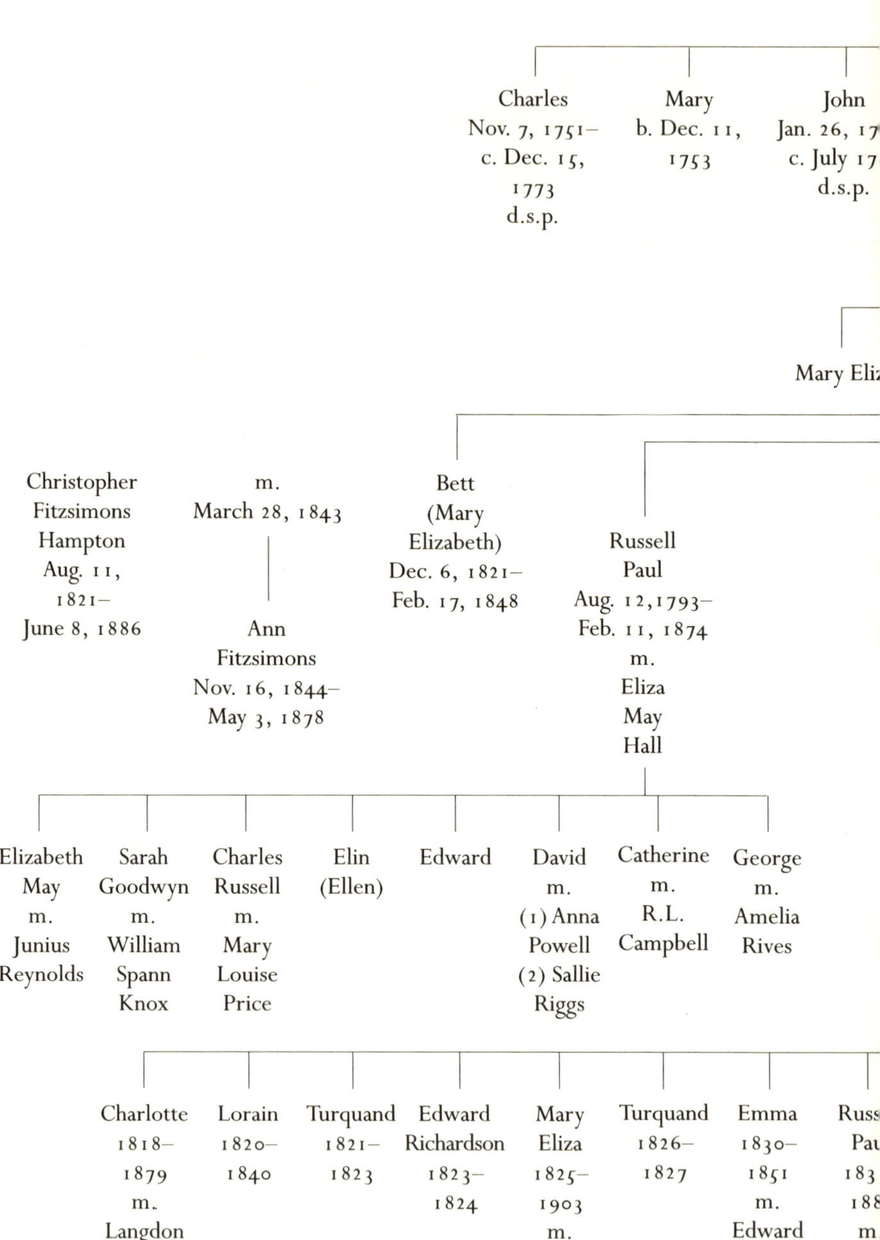

Charles
Nov. 7, 1751–
c. Dec. 15,
1773
d.s.p.
Mary
b. Dec. 11,
1753
John
Jan. 26, 17
c. July 17
d.s.p.
Mary Eli
Christopher
Fitzsimons
Hampton
Aug. 11,
1821–
June 8, 1886
m.
March 28, 1843
Ann
Fitzsimons
Nov. 16, 1844–
May 3, 1878
Bett
(Mary
Elizabeth)
Dec. 6, 1821–
Feb. 17, 1848
Russell
Paul
Aug. 12,1793–
Feb. 11, 1874
m.
Eliza
May
Hall
Elizabeth
May
m.
Junius
Reynolds
Sarah
Goodwyn
m.
William
Spann
Knox
Charles
Russell
m.
Mary
Louise
Price
Elin
(Ellen)
Edward
David
m.
(1) Anna
Powell
(2) Sallie
Riggs
Catherine
m.
R.L.
Campbell
George
m.
Amelia
Rives
Charlotte
1818–
1879
m.
Langdon
Cheves, Jr.
Lorain
1820–
1840
Turquand
1821–
1823
Edward
Richardson
1823–
1824
Mary
Eliza
1825–
1903
m.
A.J.
Magrath
d.s.p.
Turquand
1826–
1827
Emma
1830–
1851
m.
Edward
Parker
Russ
Pau
183
188
m
An
Eli
Fergu

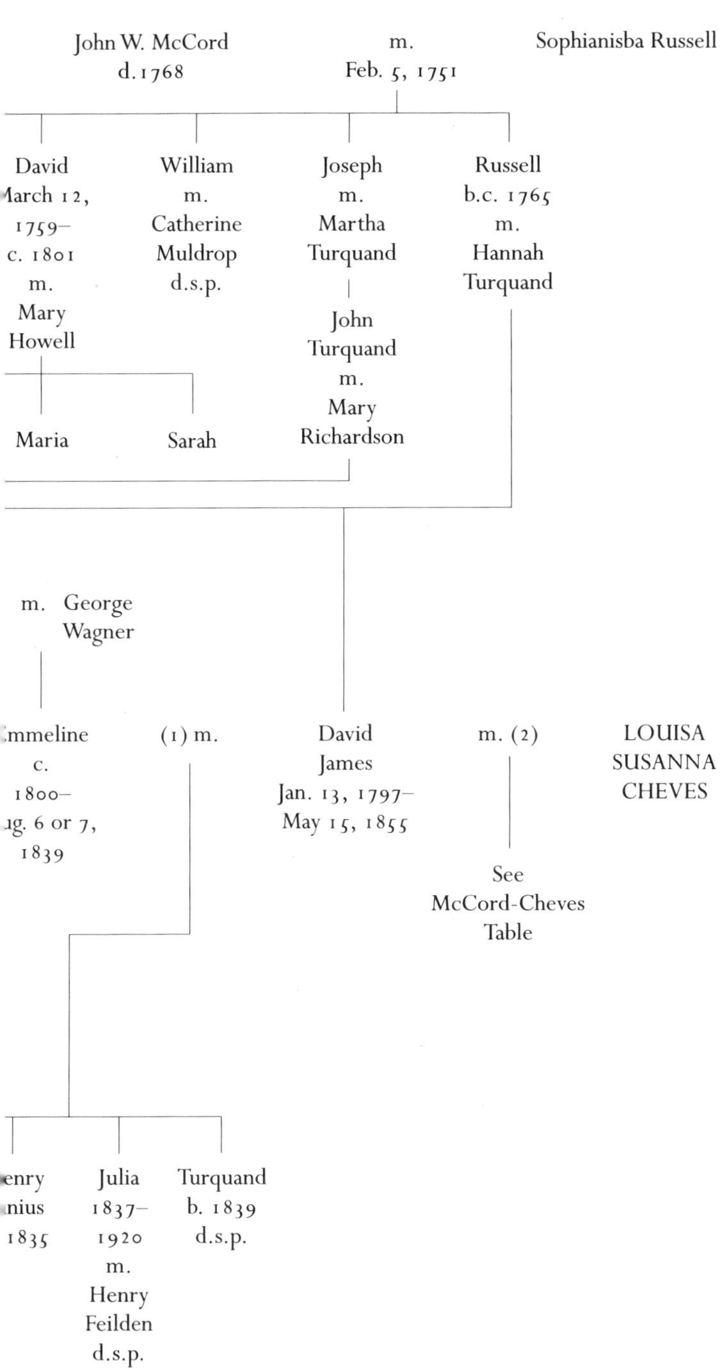
John W. McCord
d. 1768
m.
Feb. 5, 1751
Sophianisba Russell
David
March 12,
1759–
c. 1801
m.
Mary
Howell
William
m.
Catherine
Muldrop
d.s.p.
Joseph
m.
Martha
Turquand
John
Turquand
m.
Mary
Richardson
Russell
b.c. 1765
m.
Hannah
Turquand
Maria
Sarah
m. George
Wagner
mmeline
c.
1800–
ug. 6 or 7,
1839
(1) m.
David
James
Jan. 13, 1797–
May 15, 1855
m. (2)
LOUISA
SUSANNA
CHEVES
See
McCord-Cheves
Table
enry
nius
1835
Julia
1837–
1920
m.
Henry
Feilden
d.s.p.
Turquand
b. 1839
d.s.p.

McCORD-CHEVES

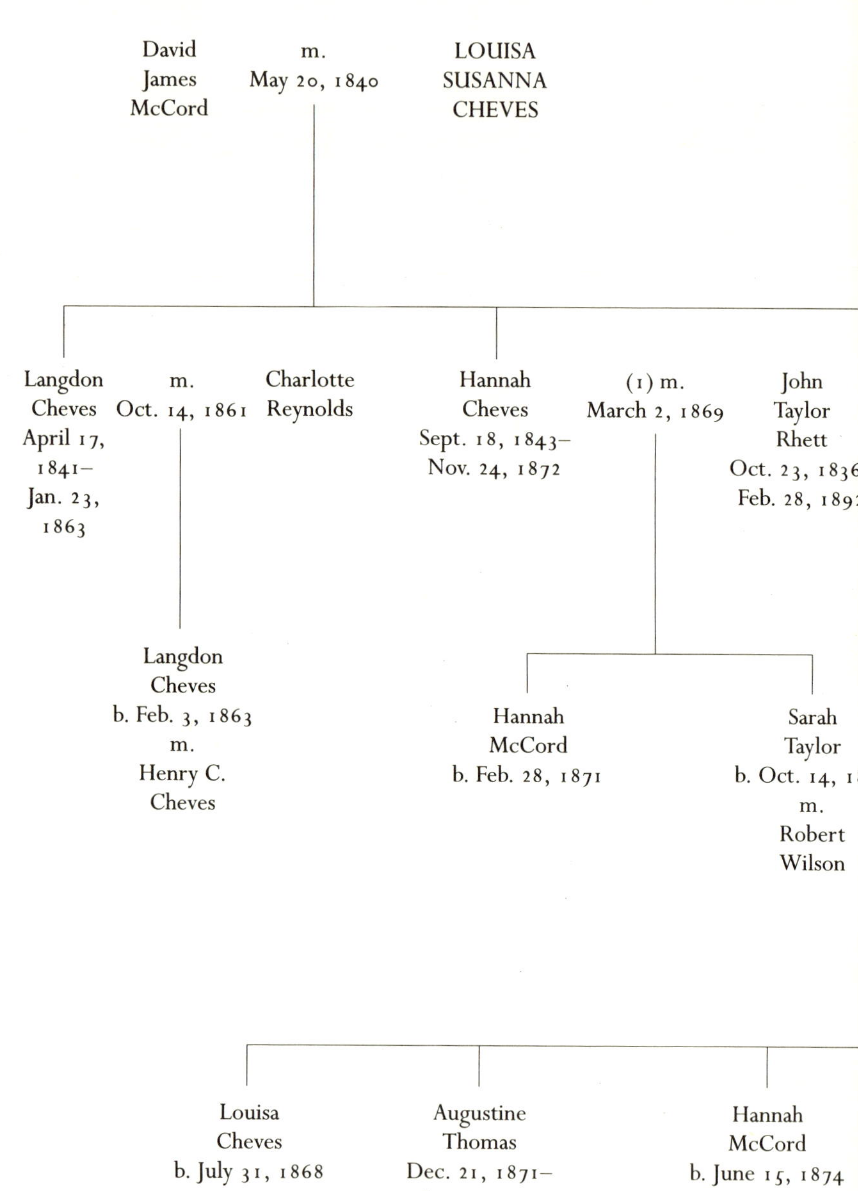

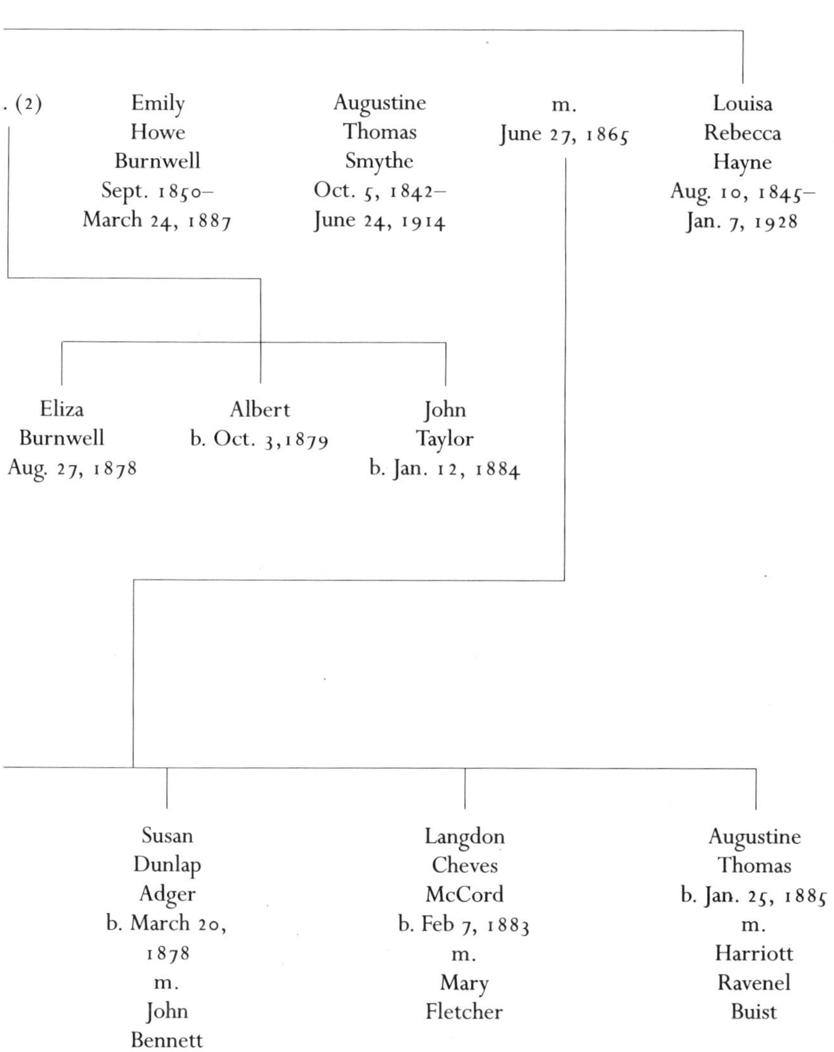
. (2)
Emily Howe Burnwell Sept. 1850– March 24, 1887
Augustine Thomas Smythe Oct. 5, 1842– June 24, 1914
m. June 27, 1865
Louisa Rebecca Hayne Aug. 10, 1845– Jan. 7, 1928
Eliza Burnwell Aug. 27, 1878
Albert b. Oct. 3,1879
John Taylor b. Jan. 12, 1884
Susan Dunlap Adger b. March 20, 1878 m. John Bennett
Langdon Cheves McCord b. Feb 7, 1883 m. Mary Fletcher
Augustine Thomas b. Jan. 25, 1885 m. Harriott Ravenel Buist

Part I

POEMS

1.

My Dreams

Clarior e tenebris[1]

'Tis to create, and in creating live
A being more intense, that we endow
With form our fancy, gaining as we give
The life we image, e'en as I do now.

Childe Harold—Canto 3d.[2]

DEDICATION

To My Father

Oft in my bosom the self-flattering thought
Has roused itself—"I, too, may be a poet."
And again, o'ercome by my own weakness,
Have I shrunk before the blighting consciousness,
The damning fear, that I am built as one

My Dreams (Philadelphia: Carey and Hart, 1848). According to family tradition, David James McCord had *My Dreams* printed for his wife "as a surprise, thinking to please her. The surprise was not a success; she did not deem the verses worthy; and tried to suppress the whole

1. "Brighter from the shadows." Motto of the Irish earldom of Milltown (cr. 1763), the phrase may be adapted from Lucretius *De rerum natura* 3.1–2, describing Epicurus as "e tenebris tantis tam clarum extollere lumen / qui primus potuisti" ("[you] that first were able to raise up so clear a light out of such great shadows"); also Cicero *Pro rege Deiotaro* 11.30.

2. Lord Byron, *Childe Harold's Pilgrimage* 3.46–49 (cf. Byron, "The Dream," ll. 18–22). The stanza concludes:

> What am I? Nothing; but not so art thou,
> Soul of my thought! with whom I traverse earth,
> Invisible but gazing, as I glow
> Mix'd with thy spirit, blended with thy birth,
> And feeling still with thee in my crush'd feeling's dearth.

Amidst the crowd: an atom in the sunbeam;[3]
Nothing more than all the triflers round me.
And yet there is a hope, it will not die;
If I would crush it, still it struggles here,
And in my heart it whispers, "Thou hast caught,
Perchance, one gleam of light from that sunbeam,
Which others may not see." I long to know
If there is in my soul one ray, one gleam,
Of true poetic fervour. I have seen
Thee, with a kind indulgence, read my lines,
Penned with a trembling hand, a tearful eye,
And I have drunk thy hope-inspiring praise,
And hugged myself therein. But out, alas!
On my ill-founded hopes! Too partial judge,
Thou can'st not say if 'twere the man's,
Or but the parent's, heart which felt and throbbed

edition" (Bennett, "Cheves Family of South Carolina," pp. 79–95, 130–52; 91 [adducing as source Louisa McCord Smythe, Susan Bennett's mother]). This story does not accord with evidence elsewhere. Writing to William Porcher Miles after her mother's death (see *PSE,* app. 3), Louisa Smythe said of *My Dreams* only that LSM "often told me that she never liked it to be seen on account of the mistakes made in the printing—and because much of it she did not *now* think worth printing" (editor's italics). In January 1848 David James McCord received at Lang Syne a parcel of twenty copies of *My Dreams* and proceeded to remind the book's distributors that copies were to be sent to those on a list submitted the previous summer, in particular to LSM's former teacher Charles Picot—scarcely likely if his wife had expressed displeasure upon the book's publication (David James McCord to "Gentlemen," Lang Syne, Jan. 23, 1848, Gratz Collection, PHS). In March, McCord reported to William Porcher Miles that "Mrs. McCord thanks you very much for your candid and friendly opinion and criticisms on her Poems. She says she values them more because you have been candid enough to blame, where you thought it deserved, and that she is satisfied that you are right, and hopes that your advice will be of service to her. She would be glad to have your further counsel" (David James McCord to William Porcher Miles, March 17, 1848, William Porcher Miles Papers, SHC). On May 2 LSM herself wrote to Miles that "you alone among my friends, have had the kindness to hint to me some of the many defects of the little volume which I was bold enough to offer for criticism." In the spring of 1848, then, *My Dreams* was circulated among her friends and Miles was invited by LSM to express his opinion. Finally, the form of *My Dreams* tells against Susan Bennett's account. The dedication to Langdon Cheves, a quotation from the last poem in the collection placed in the volume's proem, and above all the careful arrangement of the poems, signify that LSM, rather than her husband acting in secret, had prepared *My Dreams* for publication.

3. Geoffrey Chaucer, *Canterbury Tales,* "The Wife of Bath's Prologue and Tale," ll. 866–68: "limitours and othere holy freres, / That serchen every lond and every streem, / As thikke as motes in the sonne-beem."

Its answers back to *my* heart's throbbing struggles.
Wise in all other points, thou might'st forget
Thy wisdom in the follies of thy child.
Doubting and trembling still, I cast my lines,
Then, here, before the world; and it must judge
'Twixt me, and my own struggling thoughts, which rise,
Now in Hope's wild commotion, and now sink
Back, back, upon myself and nothingness.

CONTENTS

4. "His Life was like, etc." in 1848 ed.; thus also at head of poem; apparently an abbreviation made to fit width of column.

PROEM

Dreams

Of what? For what? Dreams, fancies, airy nothings! to be caught at, as the child follows his flying bubbles, because their bright colors please him, because they amuse and make happy an hour which might be gaped away in discontented uneasiness. And all that drives away discontent is good and useful. Murmuring Discontent, the mother of many a vice, is in itself a sin against high Heaven. 'Tis good, 'tis right, 'tis virtuous, to enjoy; and God smiles when man can forget his ills, and love the sun that warms him. I can sometimes fancy that the kind Heaven which watches over us loves to distract our cares, as the fond mother amuses her sick child by the bright toys she scatters in its way; and I love to cherish the thought, and bow with reverential gratitude, to the parental kindness which would amuse and soothe away ills, of which its wisdom alone can know the cause and end.

Scoff not then at my dreams. What is life but a dream? one long dream, broken, if you will, by fitful, feverish starts, when something whispers the sleeper, "Fool, thou art Fancy's plaything." He doubts for an instant, but the vision pleases more than the reality; he woos its return and, after a turn and a sigh, soothes himself again, to Fancy's gentle lullaby. The wisdom which can but hear the folly of her words, is only too wise a nursling; as the infant who scoffs at the fairy tale which delights and enchains the attention of its companions, but boasts its precocious genius, at the expense of an enjoyment which no knowledge can repay. 'Tis sweet to be deceived; 'tis sweet to deceive ourselves, to fancy a Heaven, tho' we must at last wake to Earth; 'tis sweet to lull ourselves to sleep by Fancy's whispered hushings. 'Tis sweet to dream. Sleeping or waking, 'tis sweet to forget the world and ourselves, in airy visions which are not, which cannot be; which even as we dream, we know them false. But we love them, tho' they die with the gleam which gave them birth, as the rainbow fades with the sunbeam, which called into life its evanescent hues. There is a pain in seeing them fade:

But let us choose
The brighter hues.
What though their colours fade?
When frowns the past,
To Lethe cast
Its every darker shade.[5]

The World of Dreams[6]

There is a world of visions and of dreams,
Where the unshackled spirit seems to roam
Free from the dross of Earth. From judgment loosed,
Imagination plays her boldest pranks;
Now laughs, now weeps, and mocks us with her freaks.
She beckons us, and on we follow still,
Successful scale high Heaven's conquered heights,
Glory in the worlds subdued, which hardly gained,
Again she drags us down, and scenes of wo
And darkness close around us. Demons scowl;
Spirits of mischief, mocking, gather near,

5. LSM, "Oh! Would That I Could Dream On Still," ll. 17–22, reading: "Then let us choose / The rainbow hues."

6. Cf. George Crabbe, "The World of Dreams," in *The Complete Poetical Works,* ed. Norma Dalrymple-Champneys and Arthur Pollard, 3 vols. (Oxford, 1988), 3:247–55.

Mopping and mowing,[7] o'er our fallen might,
E'en as men mock misfortune's agony,
And envy scoffs o'er power's broken wand.
'Tis thus Imagination, queen of dreams,
Makes us her playthings.
                                        On yon bed of straw
See the world's conqueror lie—at least in dreams.
The Macedonian hero[8] ne'er surpassed
The feats of arms his conquering hand performs,
And Caesar's laurels crown his monarch brow.
Day's faintest dawn must wake him to his toil;
His labour-harden'd hand must guide the plough.
    And look, where hunger's victim shivering lies:
E'en here, will hovering Fancy sometimes smile:
His last breath was a groan of agony.
From whence the smile which brightens now his features?
His dreams unlock the miser's iron-bound chests,
Bid gentle pity take a human form;
Now kindness' hand his gnawing want supplies,
And plenty decks his long ungarnished board.
    But now, behold! E'en fancy frowns on wo;
And, while the tempting viands he would reach,
Like Tantalus, he finds them shun his grasp,
And that deep moan speaks once more misery's reign.
    Pass on. Asmodeus-like,[9] we'll wander round,
Watch o'er each dreamer, while her varied tricks
Mad fancy plays, and in strange motley robed
Of joy and wo, shows us with wizard glass
A world of ever-changing shadows, strown
So like the fickle flittings of our own,
We dream it still the same; tho' oft she bids
Us soar, in thought, above reality,

7. *King Lear* 4.1.57–61: "Five fiends have been in poor Tom at once; . . . Flibbertigibbet, of mopping and mowing"; Byron, *The Island* 4.155–56: "There, with a little tinge of phantasy, / Fantastic faces mop'd and mow'd on high."

8. Alexander the Great (356–323 B.C.).

9. In *Le Diable boiteux* (1707) of Alain René Le Sage (1668–1747), the demon Asmodeus entertains Don Cleofas Zambullo, who has released him from the bottle in which a magician had imprisoned him, by removing the roofs from houses in Paris to expose the life within. William Combe (1741–1823) wrote a continuation, *The Devil upon Two Sticks in England* (1790).

Showing us scenes of bliss too bright for hope,
Then veils them in despair.
The infant mind
She fills with dreams of manhood's riper years,
And brings decrepit age to smiling scenes
Of thoughtless childhood back.
The dying man,
By lingering sickness wasted, sees once more
Health smile upon him, and life beckon on
To varied scenes which formed his yesterday,
And promise a tomorrow. Or, perhaps,
Imagination still a fairer picture shows,
Wanders through scenes from which our waking thoughts
Must shrink reluctant back. With fearless step
She dares to tread *thy* realms, *Eternity!*
And, gathering tales of bliss, and heavenly joy,
Brings to the sick man's breast forgotten hope.
Then sometimes in her play she lays a load
Of double grief upon the sufferer,
And makes him dream Hell's torments are let loose.
He groans in flames, and gasps in agony,
While muttering phantoms mock his fainting breath.
Off, fiends! Kind Heaven, dispel the direful vision!
Mark, how the slumberer wakes. His haggard eye
Turns slowly round, dreading, yet seeking still
The phantom fiends, whose fearful shrieks
Still echo in his ear. His shortening breaths
Leave him nor strength, nor power, to know how false
Their shadowy shapes. He sinks, while his weak gasps,
By terror hastened, strangle his painful sighs,
And with one struggling gurgle, one wild stare,
His frightful dream is done. If onward roams
The fancy-beckoned spirit, 'tis in scenes
Detached from yon cold clod, whose stiffening form
Sinks fast to loathed corruption. Let it rot.
It is humanity. The end of life,
The end of dreams.
Turn, and again behold
A spectre-haunted pillow. The murderer sees
His bloody victims frown; now numbers o'er
His tales of sin, and, half-exulting, acts

Again the heartless scenes. Anon, he starts,
Cold sweat-drops damp his brow, for vengeance frowns,
And fancy's hell surrounds him: muttered prayers,
And mingling curses, speak his anxious thought,
Which half would soothe, half dares, offended Heaven.
    And see where softer, brighter, visions woo,
To scenes so differing from these hellish views
We scarce can deem the painter's hand the same.
See, where the goddess of this dreamy world,
Strows rainbow hues, and Heaven-beaming light.
The lover dreams ecstatic joys, and bliss,
Too bright, too bright, for earth. His waking eye
Must see the Houri[10] of his visions fade.
And though the dream may cast its sunny light,
Thro' waking speculations fancy weaves,
Too soon she tires of smiling, and the views
So brightly sketched, fade as Experience turns
Her leaden eye, and coldly points Reality.
As fades the flower 'neath Sol's too vivid ray,
As shrinks the dew-drop from his parching heat,
As timorous day to darkness trembling cedes,
So fade these glimpses of Elysian realms.
As Dagon-worshippers bewept their God,[11]
His broken idols' shattered wrecks he mourns.
    And yonder pallid brow, which gently droops—
As 't were a lily withering on its stem—[12]
As by a moonbeam lit, across it flits
A look of calm, to its worn sadness strange,
As dewdrop 'neath the noon of summer's sun;
So softly mild, we dare not call it joy;
And yet so stilly beautiful, we look,
And wonder what could bring its quiet there.

10. "A nymph of the Muslim Paradise" (*OED*). Byron, *Childe Harold's Pilgrimage* 1.607, 610–11: "Match me those Houries; . . . / There your wise Prophet's paradise we find, / His black-eyed maids of Heaven, angelically kind."

11. 1 Sam. 5:2–4; John Milton, *Paradise Lost* 1.457–61.

12. Vergil *Aeneid* 9.434–37 = Dryden's translation, 9.581–84 (of the dying Euryalus): "His snowy Neck reclines upon his Breast, / Like a fair Flow'r by the keen Share oppress'd: / Like a white Poppy sinking on the Plain, / Whose heavy head is overcharg'd with Rain." LSM is fond of the image: "Zephyr and the Flower" and "The Garden of Experience"; "The Village Churchyard," ll. 59–64.

See, from the grave no spectre-terrors spring,
But forms, as 't were of angels come to earth:
The heavenly pictures of those things she loved,
And, loving, lost—and, losing, wept—until
That brow is faded, spirit-like, and wan,
E'en like to those whom now once more she dares
To see, and love, and fancy still her own.
Hark! to the clanking fetters! Yon dark cell
Scarce gives the prisoner room, to lab'ring turn
His wearied limbs, benumbed with loathèd rest.
Through his murk dungeon's darkness scarce can pierce
Day's brightest sunlit ray, with glimmering light.
Behold his chains burst with Herculean strength:
Once more the sun in all his brilliance shines,
And festive scenes reign through th' extended hall.
E'en in his den of sorrow he may dream,
And bask in mercy's smile. The morrow comes:
What tho' it bring th' unmitigated doom,
The word of death, the sentence, "Blood for blood"?[13]
Tonight, fond sleep, the Lethe of our woes,
Lulls him to peace and calm forgetfulness.
The hollow grating of his dungeon bolt
Must murder hope, and wake him to himself,
And, with the new-born day, despair must rise;
Still of his *now,* the quiet calm is blessed.
Fancy, thou nurse alike of joy and wo,
Strange mocker, whom we love, e'en while thou frown'st;
Who, through each scene of life, or weep'st, or smil'st,
To paint each scene with colours all thine own—
How vision-led we tread this world of sleep!
Here, rudderless, we're tossed on fancy's wave,
And in one moment's little course oft find
A world of happiness or misery.
Strange picture of a life, whose tedious course
But lengthens out our dream. Unfetter'd roams
The wandering spirit? No. 'Tis bound, fast bound
In adamantine fetters: soaring oft
Above these clayey realms, how quickly dragged
Back to its prison-home! We live, we dream,

13. Cf. Gen. 9:6.

And then we die. What more? Ask'st thou what more?
Sleep, wave thy downy pinions—let me *dream,*
I dare not *think,* what more.

Peace! Be Still!

In the summer breeze's lowest sigh,
    In the gentlest tone of the murmuring rill,
Softly the words come floating by,
    "Be still! hush! peace! be still!"

When, hushed beneath the sky of even,
    Tired Nature lulls herself to sleep,
And only stars, like eyes of Heaven,
    Look down, to watch the mourner weep;

Methinks that with their beam there falls
    A tone the throbbing heart to fill;
Gently, it to the sufferer calls,
    "Be still! hush! peace! be still!"

And when May's freshest flowers are springing,
    And balmiest airs their sweets distil,
The softest Zephyrs aye are singing,
    "Be still! hush! peace! be still!"

It seems as 'twere kind Nature wooing
    Her child to slumber on her breast,
And, all its wearying cares subduing,
    Hushing the tired thing to rest.

'Tis the fond mother's lullaby,
    Bidding the wayward one repose,
Soothing its sobbing bosom's sigh,
    An opiate for its restless woes.

Again I dream myself a child:
    My aching brow on Earth reclining,

Fancy, once more, a Mother's mild
    Indulgent eye is o'er me shining.

And thus there is a kind of joy
    To nestle there my wearied head,
Dreaming 'tis but a broken toy
    O'er which my scalding tears are shed.

Once more I hear the soothing tones
    Which lulled me to my childhood's sleep;
Once more are mine but painless moans;
    Once more 'tis almost joy to weep.

For once more comes that magic sound,
    Which used to bid my bosom thrill;
Once more I hear it whispering round,
    "Be still! hush! peace! be still!"

My Mother! In my infant home
    'Twas thou who mad'st these accents dear;
Now but from Heaven such tones may come,
    For now, my Mother, *Thou* art there.

And hark! with storm-subduing power,
    The mandate of high heaven's will,
Raised 'midst the Ocean's angry roar,
    The conquering words are, "Peace! be still!"

The waters know their Maker's call;
    The raging tempest owns his sway;
The mountain billows trembling fall;
    In stifled roars, the winds obey.

"Hush! Peace! be still!" Oh! God of Heaven,
    My heart still let this mandate fill;
Care, passion, sorrow, thou hast given:
    Whisper them, "Peace! be still!"

The Wandering Tear

There was a youth once woo'd a Lady,
 But she spurned him away; Heigho!
And he mourned, until to die he was ready,
 But she heeded him not—Heigho!

And he knelt, and he prayed for Love's warm smile,
 But she turned her away—Heigho!
And that youth—why did he not die, the while?
 He was sad enough. Heigho!

Again he sued, not for love, but pity,
 And he looked so sad, heigho!
Though she did not love, she was not haughty,
 And she dropped a tear, heigho!

And tell me, you who to love have learned,
 Was it strange that he smiled?—Heigho!
He watched that tear, and forgot he was spurned,
 And fancied she sighed—heigho!

That tear, that tear—'twas a gem to him,
 And he sought to grasp it falling;
But it fell in a gently murmuring stream,
And, like the sunshine of a dream,
 'Twas gone, and past recalling.

And that youth, full many a tear he shed
 In the streamlet past him sweeping;
For he deemed that there was in that treasure fled
A charm, perchance, that might have plead
 His cause with that lady weeping.

So dear it was to him, he deemed
 So far above compare,
That gold, and gems, and jewels seemed
But glittering nothings; he esteemed
 All lightly by that tear.

And what can he bring to that lady fair?
What offering can he cast
At her feet to sue acceptance there?
Gems and toys he brings most rare,
And the richest, are still the last.

But that lady's love he cannot buy;
And she turns from his gifts away;
For she feels that in her bosom lie
Treasures too pure for gold to buy,
That such gifts can ne'er repay.

And far he sought, and near he sought
For something her heart to move;
And what was there in the world, he thought,
So pure, so simple, with joy so fraught,
As that tear, though it spoke not of love?

For though love was not there, there was pity, and that
Is a balm to the lover's torn heart;
For if, worn with anguish, lamenting his fate,
He finds pity weeping, the chances are great
That love in his sorrows takes part.

But while he long, 'midst jewels rare,
Its unmatched value sought,
Where then had it fled, that priceless tear,
That glittering gem, to him so dear,
So valued, though unbought?

Of the murmuring stream, where first it fell,
It joined the plaintive tone;
And as it swept along, 'twould tell
Its sorrowing tale, and oft would dwell
On its grief, that 'twas alone.

For, though with mingled waters flowing
It passed from scene to scene,
Oh! say, while kindness e'en bestowing,
'Midst crowds, is the wanderer not showing
To his home that he still doth lean?

And sad was the note of that exiled tear,
On the mimic billows tossed
Of the streamlet, as, wandering here and there,
It murmured, "Oh! give me back what I hold dear;
Guide me to the home I have lost."

Now swifter flow th' increasing waves;
The wandering drop is driven
On, till a turbid river laves
A widened shore, but still it craves
The home it lost—its heaven.

And now, it hoarsely roaring cries
Amidst the cataract's foam;
And wildly o'er the precipice,
'Midst riot dashing, still it sighs,
And still demands its home.

Now, wearied of its furious course,
'Midst ocean's billows lost,
The waters round it murmur hoarse,
As (holding of past storms discourse)
Their might and power they boast.

And still that tear, in plaintive tone,
The murmuring concourse joins,
While ocean vaunts its victories gone:
To its triumphant voice, a moan,
In mingling, rejoins.

But lo! with sullen threatening roar,
The angry billows rise;
And now, with devastating power,
They furious lash the frightened shore,
Now dare the startled skies.

Lost 'midst the whirl of water, where
Hath fled the wanderer now?
Swept by the dashing spray afar,
Wishing but rest, that lowly tear,
It seeks a home as low.

But now, whilst on the shore it lies,
Fast sinking 'neath the earth,
By sunbeams raised, to Heaven it flies,
Bosomed in clouds that seek the skies,
And claim celestial birth.

But not such is the home for which still it would long,
Where its hopes and its fears have birth;
Though bright are the scenes that it wanders among,
Oh! not to such scenes do its wishes belong:
They all centre and lean upon earth.

It was born for earth's sorrow; how then can it dare
To hope or to share Heaven's peace?
Bright Heaven was never the home of the tear;
It ne'er can be aught but a wanderer there,
And an outcast, e'en mingling in bliss.

Back, back, to the earth the forlorn one is driven,
To share in its sorrows and care;
And welcome to grief is the outcast from Heaven;
To its anguish, at least, that one solace is given:
The comfort of wo, is a tear.

Back, back to the earth, as a refuge, it flies;
In a dewdrop from Heaven it falls;
On a flowret's bosom the wanderer lies,
And the youth, as that glittering jewel he spies,
At once the lost tear-drop recalls.

And quick, with his dew-ladened blossom, he goes
To the fair one, and, humbly pleading,
He tells her how Heaven weeps over our woes,
And shows how the flowret its blushing head bows,
As though in his cause interceding.

And he bids her take back that pure tear-drop again,
Which once she bestowed on his woes;
He tells her how long he has sought it in vain,
He tells her how now he has found it with pain,
And he offers the tear-sprinkled rose.

And the lady bent over that flower as he knelt,
And she spoke not a word, but she sighed;
And he asked her, if nothing her hard heart could melt?
If no shadow of love in her bosom had dwelt?
To his question, the flowret replied.

For, as slowly she raised from that flowret her eye,
No more was his passion reproved;
Two sister-drops now on its moist bosom lie;
As he gazes, he hears them breathed on by a sigh,
And he knows that, at last, *he is loved.*

The Voice of Years[14]

It floated by, on the passing breeze,
The voice of years:
It breathed o'er ocean, it wandered through earth,
It spoke of the time when worlds had birth,
When the spirit of God moved over the sea,
When earth was only a thing—to be.
And it sighed, as it passed on that passing breeze,
The voice of years.

From ocean it came on a murmuring wave,
The voice of years:
And it spoke of the time ere the birth of light;
When earth was hushed, 'neath the ocean's might,
And the waters rolled, and the dashing roar

14. "The Voice of Years" was the poem from *My Dreams* especially favored by anthologies: Read, *Female Poets of America,* pp. 207–16, reprinting also "The World of Dreams" and "Forget Thee!"; Duyckinck, *Cyclopaedia of American Literature* 2:252; J. W. Davidson, *Living Writers of the South,* pp. 352–54, who chose it "as illustrative of both tone and art"; Wauchope, *Writers of South Carolina,* pp. 270–72. Fraser, pp. 24–26, singles it out for full quotation. "This is earnest, natural, and direct; nothing feeble or even flowery—nothing Corinthian, but all Doric" (Davidson). Collation demonstrates that the texts in these anthologies have no independent value: the few departures from the 1848 text—"when words had birth" (l. 4); "to take from the spoiler" (l. 54)—are errors imported by Duyckinck and Davidson respectively, then repeated by those coming after, who (including Fraser) seem not to have consulted the 1848 edition directly. Davidson also, in many cases, converts "which" into "that."

Of the angered surge owned not yet the power
Which whispers in that murmuring wave
The voice of years.

From earth it came, from her inmost deep,
The voice of years:
It murmured forth with the bubbling stream;
It came like the sound of a long-past dream—
And it spoke of the hour ere Time had birth,
When living thing moved not yet on earth;
And, solemnly sad, it rose from the deep,
The voice of years.

From heaven it came, on a beam of light,
The voice of years:
And it spoke of a God who reigned alone,
Who waked the stars, who lit the Sun.
As it glanced o'er mountain, and river, and wood,
It spoke of the good and the wonderful God;
And it whispered to praise that God of Light,
The voice of years.

It howled in the storm as it threatening passed,
The voice of years:
And it spoke of ruin, and fiercest might,
Of angry fiends, and of things of night;
But raging as o'er the Earth it strode,
I knelt and I prayed to the merciful God,
And methought it less angrily howled as it passed,
The voice of years.

And it came from yon moss-grown ruin gray,
The voice of years:
And it spoke of myself, and the years which were gone,
Of hopes which were blighted, and joys which were flown,
Of the wreck of so much that was bright and was fair;
And it made me sad, and I wept to hear,
As it came from yon moss-grown ruin gray,
The voice of years.

And it rose from the grave, with the song of death,
The voice of years:
And I shuddered to hear the tale it told,
Of blighted youth, and hearts grown cold,
And anguish and sorrow which crept to the grave
To hide from the spoiler the wound which he gave.
And sadly it rose from that home of death,
The voice of years.

But again it passed on the passing breeze,
The voice of years:
And it spoke of a God, who watched us here,
Who heard the sigh, and who saw the tear;
And it spoke of mercy, and not of wo;
There was love and hope in its whispering low;
And I listened to catch, on that passing breeze,
The voice of years.

And it spoke of a pain which might not last,
That voice of years:
And it taught me to think, that the God who gave
The breath of life, could wake from the grave;
And it taught me to see that this beautiful earth
Was not only made to give sorrow birth;
And it whispered, that mercy must reign at last,
That voice of years.

And strangely methought, as it floated by,
That voice of years
Seemed fraught with a tone from some higher sphere:
It whispered around me, that God was near;
He spoke from the sunbeam; He spoke from the wave;
He spoke from the ruin; He spoke from the grave;
'Twas the voice of God, as it floated by,
That voice of years.

I Dreamed of a World

I dreamed of a world where the flowers never faded,
And rainbows for ever encircled its skies,

And its sunshine by night's gloomy veil was ne'er shaded,
And the race who dwelt in it was one that ne'er dies.

And are there worlds which do not change?
Are there worlds where love may cling?
Still to one, unforced to range,
All its fond affections bring?

Are there worlds where those we love
Need not pine away, and die?
Where the heart which will not rove
May, loving, live eternally?

Are there worlds where hearts may beat,
And not time their throbs to pain?
Where they fondly answering meet,
Fearing not to part again?

Are there worlds where passion brings
Not one poison on his breath?
Where no breeze envenomed flings,
Round our steps, the fear of death?

Oh! tell me the world which I dreamed of was true,
And, love, come and seek for its pleasure with me;
Oh! tell me the world which I dreamed of was true,
And, dearest, I'll flee to its bosom with thee.

But tell me of no happiest lot,
Where thou might'st fail to share my bliss;
The brightest world, where thou art not,
I'd leave, to weep and die in this.

To know, that thou wert lone and sad,
Were worse than tears or pain of mine;
And, struggling vainly to be glad,
I'd find a misery in thine.

If there's no world where love for ever
May bind our hearts in constant bliss,

Our pangs, at least, no power may sever
And we may love, and die, in this.

Then tell me, thou canst still love on,
And still I'll linger here with thee,
Nor seek its pain or death to shun:
For, dearest, they are shared with thee.

Then away with the bright world I dreamed of, for there
'Twas sadly and vainly to find thee I strove;
Leave me only this world of the sorrow and tear,
And here I will cling to, and die with, thee, love.

Who Dares to Say They Died?

Who dares to say they died?
The Great who sunk to rest.
What though his might stern death hath tried!
Who dares to say that these have died?
Their memories on the past
Rise with a heightened power:
No halo of an hour,
But glory's sunbeam, from the grave,
Clinging to what he seeks to save
From dark oblivion and the night
Which comes, with sacrilegious blight,
To doom their names to death.
They rise untarnished from the tomb,
And e'en the grave must lose its gloom,
Stifle its pestilential breath,
To bid them stand forth purely bright.
O'er names like these, how sinks its might!
'Neath its dread power they cannot lie,
For glory will not let them die.

Who dares to say they died?
The good, whose deeds still last,
As moonbeams through the darkness guide
The wanderer, when the day has died,
To light us o'er the waste;

Which round us, wide extending
As desert wild, is blending
Creations wrought by Terror's breath,
The phantoms strange of Hell and Death,
With every new-born hour whose light
Shines sweetly on th' expecting sight,
        To wake our thoughts to hope.
As darkness mingles with its beams,
And vice, with feebler powers, seems
        Victoriously to cope,
These rise to smile, and bid us know
That virtue lingers still below,
While misery half forgets to sigh,
Dreaming that such could never die.

Who dares to say they died?
        Those whom to love we've learned.
They're gone—but yet our hearts have tried
Vainly to think the loved ones died,
        And, throbbing still, have turned
To long-accustomed feeling,
Which will not seek for healing,
But loves to cling, e'en in the grave,
To the same forms to whom it gave
Its fond affections, all unchecked.
What, though all shattered, it be wrecked
        By Disappointment's blast?
The shadows of the loved are here!
See! from the grave their forms appear,
        The visions of the past;
It springs to meet them as they rise;
E'en Death forgets his power, and flies,
Nor longer seeks to turn aside
That love which will not think they died.

The Home of Hope

In olden times, when Hope was young,
    She planted a garden fair;

Bright flowers she scattered all along
    Its paths; no thorns were there.

And when 'twas decked with all that's fair,
    She called on men to come;
"Come then," she said, "dwell with me here,
    And make this spot your home.

"Here care and sorrow ne'er shall tread,
    Ne'er in my paths shall stray;
And here no tears shall e'er be shed—
    I'll drive them all away."

Men heard, and, thronging to the spot,
    Smiled as Hope called them in;
And happy did they deem their lot,
    So bright a spot to win.

And wand'ring there, with Hope they smiled,
    Forgot what sorrow meant,
And many a weary hour beguiled,
    Which else with grief were spent.

Hope loved mankind—was glad to see
    How well her plan succeeded;
And all so happy seemed to be,
    She now no evil dreaded.

But ah! in one unhappy hour,
    Hope left her charge, and slept,
And while she slept, an evil power
    Into her garden crept.

Fear came, and, opening wide the gate,
    Let Care and Suffering in;
And Grief and Sorrow were not late
    To follow in their train.

And then Regret, by Memory led,
    To join the concourse came,

And Pain, and Agony, and Dread,
Stepped in, a place to claim.

And e'en Despair put in his foot,
But linger'd at the gate,
As if to watch the others' lot,
And on their motions wait.

And then alas! poor Mankind wept,
To see that garden spoiled;
For labouring on, while Hope still slept,
To ruin it they toiled.

And not one flower they left uncrushed,
And not one leaf unblighted;
For all lay withering in the dust,
Where Grief and Sorrow lighted.

Hope, wakened by the cries of men,
To aid them now had flown,
But, looking round, scarce knew again
The garden for her own.

For all its beauties now were fled;
It was no more Hope's home,
When every evil man could dread,
Dared boldly there to roam.

When Fear went scattering thorns around;
And where one bud still bloomed,
And Hope would save it—Memory frowned;
Fear muttered, "It is doomed."

Hope struggled vainly to drive off
Th' intruders—begg'd they'd leave her—
But all in vain: a frown, a scoff,
Was all that they would give her.

And then she thought she'd brave them there,
And laughed as if to slight

Their power; but on her fell Despair
Looked—and she fled in fright.

She fled, she thought not how, nor where;
She knew not what she did;
She only sought to shun Despair,
And onward, trembling, fled.

Meanwhile, her garden unattended,
No single flower would ope;
Man, seeing all his joys thus ended,
Soon fled in search of Hope.

And, seeking long the world around,
At last one happy day
The frightened fugitive he found,
Where, trembling, hid she lay;

And pleased to meet with one she knew,
"Oh! help me now," she said:
"Let me but stay and dwell with you;
Grant me for once your aid."

While Man, as glad, his part soon chose,
Received her to his breast;
She, in his bosom nestling close,
There seemed content to rest.

And since Hope has no other home,
And seeks not to depart;
Though Sorrow, Fear, and Suffering come,
Her home is still *Man's heart*.

The Voice of the Star

I looked upon the Heaven; it seemed
To menace earth, e'en while it moaned;
Its threatening clouds with terrors teemed,
And in their big wombs tempests groaned.

The storm, the howling winds were there;
　　The rattling thunder's sullen roar;
With the sharp, vivid lightning's glare,
　　And of heaven's floods the ceaseless store.

And one dark, threatening cloud hung there,
　　Like suffering, lowering o'er man's life;
For ever dark, for ever near,
　　Seeming with every evil rife.

To watch its gloomy darkness lower,
　　A still, mysterious pleasure gave;
'Twas grand, 'twas awful in its power,
　　But silent, as th' all conquering grave.

As in a dreamy thoughtfulness
　　I looked upon its gloomy might,
The darkness, suddenly, was less;
　　'Twas broken by a ray of light.

Th' o'erhanging shroud was torn in two,
　　And o'er its conquered gloom there shone
A star, like Hope, to suffering true,
　　Which shines on; though it shine, alone.

It shone in victory, calm and bright
　　Its lustre, steady, constant, clear—
I loved to look upon its light;
　　To me—I scarce knew why—'twas dear.

Perhaps that midst the starry host,
　　That one, in youth I learned to love;
'Twas that one, which it pleased me most
　　To watch in its bright course above.

That one, I watch, and call it mine,
　　And fancy that a mystic tie
Its brilliance with my life did twine;
　　That in its rays my fate must lie.

And now, when brightly clear it shone,
As though to break misfortune's spell,
I fancied still that 'twas mine own,
And dreamed that it my fate could tell.

I looked upon its clear, bright face;
"Oh! genius of my life," I cried,
"'Tis thou, my fate through life can'st trace:
Tell it; in thee, I would confide.

"Thou knowest what of good or ill
Hangs o'er the years which form my life;
To read their course, give me the skill,
Whether in joy, or wo, or strife."

I scarce had finished, ere a voice,
Distinct and soft, fell on my ear;
"Mortal," it said, "hadst thou thy choice,
Thou'dst weep when I should grant thy prayer.

"Seek not to rend the future's veil;
Live while thou liv'st, and wait thy doom;
Take what thou hast, of good or ill,
Nor seek to pierce the future's gloom.

"Each moment, which with pleasure's filled,
Hail as a gift kind heaven has sent;
When sorrows upon sorrows build,
Submissive bow, and *be content*.

"Tomorrow carries in her lap
Evils which thou may'st have to mourn:
Seek not to read the future's map;
Wait till tomorrow's griefs are born.

"Today, today, hath ills enough—
Then, mortal, seek to pierce no farther;
And if thy present road be rough,
Hope waits to point thee to another.

"Listen to her soft whispered tale:
She only speaks of what is *bright;*
And couldst thou read the future well,
Thou'dst learn, her flattering tale to slight.

"Then, mortal, think not of tomorrow,
But listen to *Hope's* voice alone;
Hearken to her, if thou'rt in sorrow,
And if in Joy—*today*'s thine own."

His Life Was like an April Day

His life was like an April day,
Of mingled smiles and tears,
Which sun and cloud, with varying ray,
Chequered with joys and cares.

Like sunshine shower, tho' tear and smile
Might mingle in his eye,
Young Hope would still each pain beguile,
And check each rising sigh.

The cares of youth, oh! what are they?
Forgotten, soon as born;
The cares of age bear hope away,
And peace is from us torn.

A misery which glisteneth not
As dew within the eye,
It is a misery unfraught
With plaintive moan or sigh.

It is a misery still but cold,
Which grasps and forms the heart
To Sorrow's hard and roughened mould,
Making our life an art:

An art, which bids us sigh or smile
To please the world, not truth;

Unknown the feelings free from guile,
Which smiled and wept in youth.

The still and quiet calm of age,
The calm of worn-out life,
Shows but the wreck of fear and rage,
Of agony and strife.

'Tis calm, because each feeling crushed
Can neither hope nor fear;
Each thing we love, may sink to dust,
And scarcely claim a tear.

'Tis only youth, whose April day
Of mingled smiles and tears,
May change with every varying ray,
Of varying hopes and fears.

She Dreams

She dreams. Oh! say not 'tis of love:
That eye, so brightly beaming,
Knows nought of passion's ardent gaze;
Unkindled aye by sensual rays,
Pure as yon ether vault above,
It knows not passion, knows not love.

She dreams. But say not love's unknown:
That eye, so softly drooping,
Has surely seen his shadow near,
And, half unconscious, lingers there,
Where once his fluttering wings have flown,
Watching for love, tho' still unknown.

She dreams. 'Tis not, and yet, 'tis love
In that soft eye is nestling:
He is not there, nor yet away;
He cannot fly, yet dares not stay;
But, lingering, cheats her thoughts to rove;
She knows not that she dreams of love.

Spirit Watchers

Watch ye, ye beings not of earth,
Watch ye, o'er things of mortal birth?
Watch ye o'er the weary way,
On which earth-born pilgrims stray?
Watch ye o'er the wanderer's tear?
        Watch ye o'er his trembling step?
When he sorrows can ye hear?
        Spirits, can ye see him weep?
Watch ye for him, spirits?—Say,
Watch ye o'er the wanderer's way?

STAR SPIRIT

Rest thee, weary one; we're watching;
        Heaven commissioned, stars are burning.
Thou, thy anxious slumbers snatching,
        Broken oft, to heaven still turning,
There, midst beams of glory, readest
Comfort thou in sorrow needest;
There, thy tearful eye may see,
Weary one, we watch for thee.

OCEAN SPIRIT

Spirit of the foamy billow,
        From my ocean-bed, I rise.
Hear me, on thy restless pillow
        Answering to yon starlit skies.
Hear me now, in murmuring numbers,
Tempt thee on, to tranquil slumbers.
Hear me bid thee sleep and rest thee;
What tho' sorrows have distrest thee:
Hist! the music of the sea
Is, "Weary one, we watch for thee."

RIVER SPIRIT

The ripple of the dancing stream
Woos thee, too, to tranquil dream.
As the bursting of each bubble,
        On the river's sparkling face,
Let it pass, each shadowy trouble,
        Nor its gloomy course retrace.
Weary mourner, cease to weep;
Tired, care-worn, sink to sleep;
Let thy anxious sorrows be;
Weary one, we watch for thee.

SUNBEAM SPIRIT

Glancing from yon sparkling river,
        Hear me echo back its tone;
Heaven's mandate I deliver;
        Troubled spirit, cease thy moan.
Pain has found his home on earth,
But joy, too, has there his birth;
Mortal, rear its struggling being,
Or the young thing will be fleeing.
Nurse not wo; too surely found,
He will touch thee in his round;
And yet not wholly his, for Heaven
Mingled joy and grief has given;
Misery is not its decree;
It bids us, tired one, watch for thee.

WIND SPIRIT

            Whistling in the storm,
                Sighing in the gale,
            With a viewless form
                Now rushing through the vale,
Now on mountain tops, crushing mightiest trees,
Now whispering gently to thee, on the softest breeze,

Hear me, from the zephyr stooping,
As it sighs thro' yonder tree;
Raise that eye, so sadly drooping,
Wake thy heart again to hoping.
From each rustling leaf I speak:
Wake to joy, tired mourner, wake;
We are watching, still, for thee.

SPIRIT OF THE LEAVES

Waked by the winds, we turn to see
Misery, mortal, on thy brow.
Pain and wo not new to thee,
Sorrow hugs thee, sad one, now.
Mortal, wherefore dost thou weep?
Hush thee, mourner, hush and sleep,
While our soothing song shall be,
"Weary one, we watch for thee."

DREAM SPIRIT

Hide thee from this world of care;
Mortal, sleep.
On thy lash tho' hangs the tear,
Cease to weep.
Lulled in tranquil slumbers lie;
We are here.
Angels['] forms are flitting by,
Ever near.
Dream. We'll whisper thee of things
Brighter than the world e'er brings.
Sleep, and we will wake for thee
Visions soft as dreams may be.
Weary wanderer, rest, and we
Will be watching still for thee.
Guardian angels round thee hover;
Mortal, rest.
With their spirit-wings they cover
Thy torn breast.

Rest, weary one, for thou art free
From harm, whilst these still watch for thee.
    God is near thee;
        Mortal, sleep.
    He can hear thee,
        Sad one, weep.
He is watching for thee too,
For He pities mortal wo.
When yon pallid moonbeams reach thee,
    Through the night they seek to quell,
'Tis a sign He sends to teach thee,
    That He watches for thee still.
When the rainbow's Iris hue
Wakes upon thy tearful view,
'Tis a symbol that He's near thee;
When thou prayest, that He can hear thee.
When the evening star is glistening,
    Lonely in her early watch,
'Tis to show, that He is listening,
    Still thy broken sighs to catch.
And when before day's waking ray,
The hosts of heaven fade fast away,
If the morning-star, still beaming,
    Lingers when the rest are gone,
'Tis that, with its kindly gleaming,
    It would teach, thou'rt not alone.
Rest thee, then, whate'er thy cares;
God is near, He sees thy tears.
Rest, whate'er thy sorrows be;
He watches, weary one, for thee.

Poor Nannie[15]

Late was the hour, and dark the night;
    Sharply and chill the cold winds blew;

15. "Nannie" is a form of "Anna"—so used, for example, by LSM of her sister (LSM to Anna Cheves Huger, Jan. 25, 1856).

And gathering clouds bedimmed the light
Which some faint stars still struggling threw.

And still as each a cloud o'ercasts,
And murkier grows the gloomy night,
Howling their rage upon the wastes,
December's blasts are in their might.

Nature in terror seems to moan;
The tardy labourer seeks his home,
And shudders, as he hastens on,
That some through such a night must roam.

And now upon the blast there seems
To rise a soft, a plaintive tone.
He stops, and listening turns, but deems
'Twas but the wind, and hastens on.

Again upon his ear it falls,
Again its soft tone makes him start;
It seems a woman's voice that calls
For pity from the gentle heart.

He turns, resolved to face the blast,
That in its fury threatens death;
He shrinks not from the dreary waste:
A woman's dying near his path!

And as he turns, the thrilling tones
Again sweep by upon the air.
He pauses, though a woman moans!
'Tis not the tempest bids him fear:

No; he has courage which would meet
The warring elements in arms;
Nor would the sturdy woodman's feet
Turn back from any mortal harms.

But he has heard a whispered tale
Of evil Spirits in the gloom;

Which says that, when they weep and wail
Through midnight storms, 'tis o'er a tomb:

An empty tomb, which, ere the morn,
They seek to fill with human corse;
And weep, that wanderers forlorn
May yield them to their hellish force:

Then, wandering through the dreary waste,
They meet their dreary unwept doom,
And hear, borne on the wintry blast,
The dirge which fiends howl o'er their tomb.

'Tis this he dreads; and, as the sad
And plaintive sound once more he hears,
He turns away his hurried tread,
And e'en to listen now he fears.

And hastening on, in whistling winds
He fancies still the ghostly wail;
Trembling, at last, his cottage finds,
And shuddering tells the fearful tale.

And was it then some demon foul
Which sought to mock the wanderer's ear?
Or yet, some evil damnèd soul,
Thirsting his dying groans to hear?

Oh no! that sound was what it seemed,
A feeble woman's plaintive moan.
Nor evil demon, sprite, nor fiend,
But a poor mortal's dying groan.

For on that bare and trackless field,
There lay a being, fair, but frail;
Whose bosom once with pride had swelled
At what her tears did now bewail.

Alas! her fatal beauty led
To shame, and houseless misery;

And now, the earth her dying bed,
She mourned her hapless destiny.

And, as far o'er the gloom she sees
A twinkling taper's feeble light,
"Alas!" she sighs, "what happy days
My folly, in their bloom, could blight!

"Where burns that feeble taper's blaze,
I, with my aged father, dwelt;
And happy was I with his praise,
The greatest pleasure that I felt.

"When, with a parent's joy, he'd gaze
Upon the daughter of his love,
And then his trembling hands would raise,
To call a blessing from above;

"And then would press me to his heart,
Call me his own, his dearest one,
And then tears to his eyes would start,
As he'd pray God for me alone.

"But then came one, whose flattering tongue,
To win me from my father, strove.
Alas! I listened, and e'er long
He made me fly a father's love.

"And when I wept my home to leave,
And fear and doubt were on my brow,
He whispered that I must not grieve—
Said I should be *his* Nannie, now.

"I trusted. And could I forget
The love my father bore his child?
I only was his all, and yet
I fled, by treachery beguiled.

"I fled, and left him here alone,
His gray hairs sinking to the grave;

I fled, and left him here to mourn
 That daughter, whom his love forgave.

"Yes; for they tell me, when he should
 Have called down curses on my head,
Low in the dust, to heaven he bowed,
 And still for his poor Nannie prayed.

"And now I hear that he is sick,
 That age and wo his life-blood numb;
That grief his worn-out heart must break,
 And sorrow drive him to the tomb.

"And vainly have I sought the way,
 To soothe one pang, to dry one tear;
That I might kneel to him and say,
 'Father, your wandering Nannie's here.'"

She hushed, and the loud raging storm
 Howled louder as it swept along,
And seemed to mock the fragile form,
 Whose fate upon its fury hung.

Far roars the blast, the forests groan;
 Ruin all nature doth survey,
And seems to claim it as its own;
 All nature bows, and owns its sway.

* * * * *

But hushed at last, the storm is done;
 Calmly the wrecks of nature lie;
And brightly now, the rising sun
 Smiles from the clear, unclouded sky.

But where is she, who late bewailed
 The cruel wind's relentless rage?
Was it her sad complaints prevailed,
 That Ruin ceased his war to wage?

And did she reach her father's home?
    And may she close his dying eye?
And may she, though with sorrow dumb,
    Show him his Nannie, ere he die?

The old man lay upon his bed;
    Alone he wept his daughter's fate;
Near him he hears a stranger's tread;
    He turns—her corpse is at his feet.

Calmly he looks; one word, one sigh
    Escape not from his agèd lips;
He looks on that dull, clouded eye,
    And from its lids the cold frost wipes.

He seeks to dry the frozen tears
    Which glisten on those pallid cheeks;
His weak hand drops; and all his cares
    Death's touch, at once, now kindly checks.

And low in one cold grave they lie,
    To dust by stranger hands conveyed;
No stone to draw the pitying eye
    Is o'er their earthy mansion laid.

And winter's blast, and summer's sun,
    Have passed upon this silent spot,
And gloomy autumn hastens on,
    And none have come to mourn their lot.

Yet there is one who should have wept
    His ruined Nannie's hapless doom,
That one who like a serpent crept,
    And stole her from her father's home.

*   *   *   *   *

And now by the receding light
    Of the bright sun that sinks to rest,
Behold a stranger gaily dight,
    To yon lone cottage rides in haste.

And when he sees its ruined walls,
    The still grave, now the only home
Of those whose semblance memory calls,
    The living image, from the tomb;

And when he hears the mournful tale,
    Which those can tell who laid them there,
Sighs bid at length his bosom swell,
    And in his eye glistens a tear.

Dashing his hand across his brow,
    Plunging his rowels in his steed,
He hurries on, and seeks to throw
    Off memory with his courser's speed.

But still, as hastening on he'd hide
    The woful scene of misery,
He fancies Nannie by his side,
    Th' upbraider of his treachery.

And, borne upon the gentle breeze,
    A murmuring sigh sounds in his ear,
And a low whispering voice, which says,
    "What, has poor Nannie not one tear?"

Ah! few the sighs her misery
    From that light, thoughtless heart can draw,
And seldom on her memory
    He deigns a backward glance to throw.

In the gay world he drowns the wo
    Which for one moment swelled his breast;
Grown cold as is the frozen snow,
    His heart grief seldom can molest.

And now he haunts its dazzling glare,
    And laughs, and there his smiles are many;
But few the thoughts he gives that tear,
    Which once he shed for his poor Nannie.

The Dream of Life[16]

A struggle, pang, a gasp, and 'tis commenced,
A bubble which we grasp at, and which bursts;
A flower we seize, but to retain a thorn;
A star which, brightly glimmering, is too cold
To warm us with the ray which wakes our hope;
A winter's sunbeam glancing o'er the ice,
To mock us with its cheating show of warmth;
A tantalizing joy we only grasp
To find its falsity; a hope which fades;
A dreary desert waste, of anxious thought,
Resting itself on its own weariness,
And gasping for relief, beyond the ken
E'en of its own ungoverned fancy's flights;
And thus our dream progresses. And then comes,
Amidst the gaping ennui which remains,
To point us back towards its troubled course
(As though it were a thing we should regret),
One other struggle, pang, one other gasp,
And thus it ends. And this our world,
The theatre of all our fleeting fancies,
What is it now? Go ask yon grinning skull,
And, in its silence, find thine answer given.
'Tis nothing, fool! for now thy dream is done,
And life has past away between those gasps
Which marked its entrance and its exit made,
And thou hast lived, for what? vain fool! canst tell?
Was't glory tempted thee? or love? or fame?
Pleasure or riches? learning's hidden depths?
What Will o' the Wisp has dragged thee on so far,
To leave thee here? Ha! ha! turn once again
To thy mute monitor. Like thee, he laboured.
Now, within the dust which clings around
Yon fleshless skull, find all which he may own
Of this—like thine—his world. Thy lesson learned,
To know that life is emptiness, the world

16. "The Dream of Life" is a meditation, suitably composed in blank verse, upon texts by Shakespeare. See *Macbeth* 5.5.19–28; *The Tempest* 4.1.148–58; *Hamlet* 5.1.178–89; *As You Like It* 2.7.139–66.

A cradle but for nothingness and Death,
Then go; and, like the crowd who've struggled on
In the same track thou treadest, struggle thou
In meteor chase,[17] until thy respite comes,
And thou perforce shalt sink to rest, and cease,
Like them, to dream.

Zephyr and the Flower

Laden with dew, it bowed its head,
    While on its leaves the moisture thrown
Like tear-drops o'er its face was spread,
    As tho' it wept for pleasures gone.

It seemed to mourn the sister flowers
    Which, withering now, were round it laid—
And which, weighed down by summer showers,
    Waited not winter's frosts—to fade.

But Zephyr mourns—his fav'rite weeps;
    And sighing, as he passing flies,
He gently to her bosom creeps
    Awhile, with sympathising sighs.

And, fanning dry each glistening tear,
    He lifts the mourning blossom's head,
Who once more smiles, as tho' all fear
    And trace of sorrow now were fled.

'Tis thus that sympathy may soothe
    The many ills she cannot cure.

17. Robert Burns, *The Vision,* ll. 235–38: "I saw thy pulse's maddening play / Wild-send thee Pleasure's devious way, / Misled by Fancy's meteor-ray, / By Passion driven." Cf. also LSM, "The Poet's Home," ll. 13–15.

When kindness seeks our path to smooth,
We learn to smilingly endure.[18]

The greatest agony of wo
Is—that it is a *lonely thing,*
Whose frighted weakness can but know
The solitude its sufferings bring.

But 'tis when Grief is borne alone,
And—despot in its misery—
Allows no brother near the throne,
We feel its deep intensity.[19]

The Blood-Stained Rose

Qui que tu sois, voici ton maître,
Il l'est, le fut, ou le doit être.[20]

The fair white rose can beauties boast,
But when we see the lovely blush
Which decks her sister, who can most
Admire the pallid blossom's hue?
Or who his heartfelt praise can hush,
Nor feel how much that praise is due?

And yet, they say, this blushing flower,
Pale as her sister is, once grew;
And how 'twas changed, and by what power,
I soon will make you know full well,

18. Samuel Johnson, *The Vanity of Human Wishes,* ll. 365–68:

These Goods for Man the Laws of Heav'n ordain;
These Goods he grants, who grants the Pow'r to gain;
With these celestial Wisdom calms the Mind,
And makes the Happiness she does not find.

19. Alexander Pope, *Epistle to Dr. Arbuthnot,* ll. 197–98: "Shou'd such a man, too fond to rule alone, / Bear, like the Turk, no brother near the throne."

20. Voltaire, *Poésies mêlées,* no. 43. The epigram is said to have been designed to be inscribed upon a statue of Cupid owned by Voltaire's friend Jean René de Longeuil, marquis de Maisons. It is quoted in the first chapter of Honoré de Balzac's *Père Goriot* (1834–35).

If to a tedious tale, though true,
You'll deign to listen while I tell.

In days when fairies danced their round,
And divers elfin sports did play;
When every beauteous spot they found,
By tiny steps was often traced,
And made to sound with laughter gay—
In those blest days my story's placed.

"Once on a time," there was a group
Of these light, joyous beings chanced
From airy course their flight to stoop,
And on a flowery spot descended,
Where long with lightsome step they danced
Till daylight with night's gloom was blended.

But fairies dare not to prolong
Their dance, and games, when daylight's near;
The moon may listen to their song,
Peep o'er the meadows while they play,
But the sun's dazzling light they fear,
And vanish with his dawning ray.

Thus the gay group of whom I sing
Scarce saw the first faint light of day,
Ere, breaking up their joyous ring,
Each whispered that the dance was done;
"And now," they cried, "away, away,
We vanish with the rising sun."

But one, who feared that change of place
Might never find a spot so fair,
Proposed that from the sun's bright face
They each should hide till evening came,
And, with the fading daylight's glare,
Renew their sports, the spot the same.

Each pleased with the proposal seemed,
And all they asked was, where to hide?

For e'en the bravest of them deemed,
'Twould be unsafe to face Sol's ray.
But soon this difficulty died;
They sought not long where they should stay;

For soon a refuge near they found,
And each, into some opening blossom
Crept, for the flowers grew thick around;
There safe from danger hid they lay,
And, quiet in some flowret's bosom,
They slept away the garish day.

The fairies knew that thorns oft grew,
And guarded round the sweetest flower;
But ah! another danger too,
Of which they never thought, was there,
A danger, which, until that hour,
They ne'er before had learned to fear.

And while they guarded 'gainst each thorn,
Blunted each point which could distress them,
They dreamed not that their bosoms torn
Might soon be, by another power,
Who lay in ambush to oppress them,
And only waited for his hour.

That hour soon came; for as the sun
Was sinking in his ocean bed,
Thinking the day was almost done,
And almost past was danger's hour,
Each fairy raised his little head,
And 'gan to peep above his flower.

Then was it that the tyrant Love,
Who, patient, long his chance had watched;
And on a bending bough above
Their heads had kept his guard all day,
And all his plans for victory hatched,
While hidden close his victims lay—

And, when they dared to peep above
  Their flowery walls, and look around,
Ah! then it was, the tyrant Love
    Aimed his sharp arrows at each heart;
  And, ere they knew from whence the wound,
    They felt the piercing weapon's smart.

Each writhed with suffering, as he felt
  The point pierce deep into his heart;
And, when Love lit amongst them, knelt
    To crave compassion from the God.
  Love smiled, and, as they feared his dart,
    Threw it far off from where he stood.

"Fear not," he said, "you've felt my might,
  'Tis all I aimed at; fear no more:
To who submits, my wound is light,
    But hard to him who would resist;
  Bend therefore low, and own my power,
    And to oppose it now desist."

Love smiled so sweet and talked so fair,
  And had so late his strength, too, shown,
The fairy-group, well pleased to hear
    That he no farther harm would do,
  Scarce heard him finish, ere they'd flown
    To bow and pay all homage due.

One only stood—silent, apart—
  Swelling with anger and disdain,
A lady fair, whose flinty heart,
    By many a fairy suitor sought,
  Had still made all their suings vain;
    For sweet words ne'er that heart had caught.

"Shall I, too, bow," she said, "to Love?
  Shall I, too, own the tyrant's might?
Forbid it, all ye powers above!
    The fairy race their birth may shame,
  Submitting; but the wound's not light
    Which shall force *me* to blot my fame.

"No power shall see me bow my head,
Or crouch beneath a tyrant's rod;
With servile voice I ne'er have prayed,
And bow not with yon coward troup;
I dare thy power, audacious God;
'Tis not today I'll learn to stoop."

'Twas thus the beauteous fairy spoke,
While on the pale white rose she stood;
That rose from which she shelter took
To shun the sultry heat of day;
From that she looked down on the crowd,
Scornful to see them homage pay.

Love saw her, heard her scornful speech,
And smiling said, "Ah! lady fair,
You think my arrows cannot reach,
While on yon rose you're perched aloft;
But, beauty, of my power beware:
My pride is to make hard hearts soft."

He then the sharpest arrow chose,
That e'er was in Love's quiver found,
Nor, on the fairy of the rose,
His threatened vengeance long delayed;
The arrow flew—a bleeding wound
Deep in her inmost heart was made.

Paler than e'en the rose's hue
Became that beauteous fairy's face.
The arrow to its aim so true,
The deeper for resistance found,
E'en to the heart's core forced a place,
Rankling, with barbèd point, the wound.

Unlike those slighter ones, which did
But skin-deep pierce the easier hearts,
This, deep within the bosom hid,
Must vainly seek a speedy cure;
For common means, and common arts,
But aid the sufferer to endure.

Love saw that he his point had gained,
As the rebellious fairy sank;
And, through her wound, the heart's blood drained
O'er the white rose, was scattered round;
While the pale leaves its colour drank,
'Till, stained, they were more beauteous found.

'Twas all he asked, his only end
Was that his strength should be allowèd;
And now that he his point had gained,
He left as symbol of his power,
To make his might by all avowed,
The once white rose, the blood-stained flower.

Then, maidens, when the red rose blooms,
Remember what may be your fate,
And bow to Love, before he dooms
You, like the fairy of the flower.
Learn here—ere yet it be too late—
That none on earth can dare his power.

The Poet's Dream

'Tis a beam, which through morning clouds still glanceth bright,
Driving night from her throne, waking nature to light;
'Tis yon meteor which flasheth athwart the broad sky,
Which, born midst the darkness, midst darkness must die.

'Tis the moonbeam which glanceth so bright o'er the wave
To seek, in the bosom which bore it—its grave;
'Tis the roar of the sea, with its angry waves dashing;
'Tis the voice of the storm; 'tis the lightning's flashing.

'Tis the whisper of Zephyr; the stars' brightest beaming;
'Tis the murmur of leaves; 'tis the form of our dreaming;
'Tis the wordless idea; 'tis the soul of a passion;
An embryo thought, which must die in creation.

It struggles—but vainly it struggles for birth,
For it was not—it is not—ne'er can be of earth;
'Tis the vision, the loveliest, the frailest, the fairest;
The thought which is brightest, and freest, and dearest.

Invisible wing, through the universe sweeping,
In joy and in sorrow, its light pinions steeping;
'Tis nothing; 'tis all things; 'tis thought's wildest swarm;
'Tis the Dream of the Poet—the form without form.

The Poet's Home

Oh! where is the land where his spirit would dwell,
    And his shackled thought be free?
Where his pent-up sighs may freely swell
The bosom, which dares not now to tell
    How it longs in that land to be!

Is it East? Is it West? that poet home—
    In air? or earth? or sea?
Or must his wearied spirit roam
To some far-distant world, to come
    Where it feels that it dares be free?

Wake! wake ye! ye visions wild; and say,
    Ye rulers of his will,
Where is that world from whence ye stray,
Which, beckoning on with meteor-ray,
    Half showing, ye conceal?[21]

Oh! where is that home?—ye point it afar,
    And I gaze—but a gilded cloud,
As it floats on the gently wafting air,
Is all that my eye can fix on there:
    A shadow of light and good.

Alas! for his hope and the home which he sought!
    A cloud, glanced on by a beam!

21. Cf. LSM, "The Dream of Life," ll. 38–39, and note.

And that world of the poet's wandering thought;
And the fair, and the bright with which 'tis fraught,
    Are the visions of a dream!

His brain with the teemings of Fancy is rife;
    And, lit by her flickering gleam,
His tears and his smiles, and his inward strife,
His sorrows, his joys, his hope, and his life
    Pass like yon cloud with its beam.

But though fickle and light, as a gossamer wing,
    By the breeze wafted idly along,
Oh! still to the joys of that dream will he cling,
Still grasp at the shadows which fancy can bring,
    Still live in the breath of his song—

And blest in his dream, which can drive off life's scenes,
    With which he oft wearied has striven;
For, though but supported on Fancy, he leans;
By a meteor propped, scattered sunbeams he gleans;
    And on gilded clouds soars towards heaven.

The First Beam of Light

Whence came it? that beam which first over our earth
Burst so startlingly forth, calling beauty to birth?
Whence came it? the bright and all-hallowing ray,
O'er a world sunk in darkness, to wake it to day?
Whence came it? that glance o'er the universe sending
A new birth, whence light and love, joy and hope blending,
May live in today, and hope on for tomorrow,
Till earth almost forgets that, in darkness and sorrow,
From the womb of Old Chaos she struggled in night,
Knowing nought of the unheard-of vision of light?[22]
Whence came it? the ray which, a new life bestowing,
Showed a universe, young in its loveliness, glowing?
    The earth was cold and hard, and beauty slept;

22. John Milton, *Paradise Lost* 1.542–43: "A shout . . . / Frighted the reign of Chaos and old Night."

And th' o'erhanging clouds, e'en when they wept,
Wept only tears of ice.
The ocean heaved in darkness; and its wave
Murmured in sorrow, and its low voice gave
But moans and whispered sighs.
And 'twas not night, for night has stars and beams
Of broken brightness; and its darkness seems
The remnant of a lingering light, which sinks,
But will not die; and, struggling still, which links
E'en night, with hope. But it was darkness: still,
Cold, leaden darkness, not of earth, but hell.
A thing all horror, and a sealed-up tomb,
Where unborn life, wrapped in a changeless gloom,
But waked to agony, then sank away,
Cheered by no hope—or baptized by no ray
Of heavenly light. Oh! was not this the hell
Which priests, to fright us, tell
A holy God has made?
Where, o'er the sinner's head
Eternal vengeance breaking,
His heart with anguish racking,
The frighted thing may learn,
When too late to repent,
A God with hate can burn,
And goodness not relent?
If this were hell—bigot, its terrors faded
When Love looked down. A world, with horrors shaded,
But caught his glance, and struggled to be bright;
He smiled, and lo! creation basked in light.
The voice Omnipotent was heard,
The powerful and all-conquering word:
"Let there be light," it said, and forth there sprung
A beam celestial; which o'er nature flung
The light of heaven,
The ray, which given
To suffering man, he looked above
And knew his God, the God of love.
His smile o'er prostrate nature gleaming,
She basked within its cheerful beaming,
Nor satisfied but to receive,
Cast back as much as she could give.

And every smile from heaven that fell,
Reflected back to heaven, would tell
How love may pay a love bestowed,
And man can emulate his God.

He from that smile of Heaven then caught
        The ray which lights the blind;
And thence his darkened mind was taught
        To love, and to be kind.

'Twas thence he learned, that this was day,
        And this the light of Peace;
That this could chase e'en hell away,
        And turn e'en pain to bliss.

To love, and be beloved again,
        The lesson learned from heaven:
To him who hears it not, in vain
        That beam of light was given.

Though brightness shines around, he turns—
        His heart in darkness lives;
Heaven stoops to bless him—and he spurns
        The dearest boon it gives.

My Dead

'Tis still. No footfall's sound I hear,
But yet, there's something lingering near.
'Tis dark. No object meets the eye,
But still, a shadow passes by:
                Ye're here—my dead!

In the midnight gloom, I see ye near,
In the hush of night your voices hear,
And I weep not then—but I gaze, and deem
These airy forms are the things they seem:
                My dead! my dead!

And hands are cold which are locked in mine;
And stiff those arms which embraced I twine;
And dim the eyes which for me are bright,
As ye move around me, with footsteps light,
My dead! my dead!

And no mortal breath nor voice is heard;
Yet my heart beats high, and my thoughts are stirred;
And ye commune of things which I may not know,
And mysteries dark yourselves are now,
My dead! my dead!

But it softens my heart to know you near,
And I love to think that my words you hear;
And I turn to you when with sorrow worn,
And remember that you have lived, and borne
Like me, my dead!

When mortal suffering meets my eye,
If I'd coldly pass my brother by,
I remember that you have suffered and wept,
And kindness into my heart has crept,
For ye, my dead!

When angry passions rise and swell,
And demon powers my bosom fill,
I remember that you from passion are free,
And drive them off, as I think on ye,
My dead! my dead!

Then watch with me still, in the midnight gloom;
Oh! wake ye, my dead, from your silent tomb;
In the hush of night, still let me hear
Your voices, strange to mortal ear—
Watch with me, my dead!

And be with me still as I pass thro' life,
And counsel me still, in sorrow, or strife;
And if grief or joy should beat too high,
Then whisper, that soon like you I die—
Live with me, my dead!

And if heavily weighs of anguish the load,
Still teach me to bow to the mandates of *God;*
To humbly pray a balm for the wo;
Submit to a will that I may not know—
Pray with me, my dead!

And when life must pass, and the hand of Death
Grasps the spasm'd throat while it gasps for breath,
Then whisper that soon the end must be,
And tell me, that ye have died like me;
Be with me, my dead!

Ye're Born to Die

On summer's eve, an opening bud
Cast its fragrance through the wood;
Sweetly blooming seemed the flower,
Born to ope in beauty's bower.
But tho' in forest wild it sprung,
Where wide the oaks their branches flung,
Where the forest giants stood,
Where man's step a stranger trod,
Where all was rough, and wild, and drear,
The timid thing (like Beauty's tear,
Which will not, may not, be refused,
But brighter glistens, harshlier used,
Until the rudest hearts will cower—
They scarce know why—to Beauty's power)
Seemed to deem that roughest thing
Its tribute at her feet must fling;
To feel that, e'en where mightiest spring
The branches of the forest-king,
'Twas not for her to stoop—e'en there
She still might reign, for she was fair.
But through the forest, hark! a sigh;
'Tis mourning Zephyr passing by.
"Sprung from earth, in dust to lie,
Why so fair? Thou'rt born to die."

A butterfly, which on the breeze,
   Borne in random course along,
Had stooped, the budding thing to kiss,
   And, o'er its nascent beauties hung,
Droops its wing: its life is o'er;
Perishing with yon fair flower,
Together sinking on Earth's breast,
One note may hush them to their rest:
Hist! 'tis in the passing sigh,
"Fragile things—ye're born to die."

Proudly, see (its massy form
   Rearing o'er their humble tomb,
As tho' unheeding of the storm
   Which, roaring, threats a sudden doom)
The Oak its unscathed branches spread;
   And tho' some splintered wrecks be strown,
   With withering leaves commingled thrown,
They seem but tokens o'er the dead,
   Which Memory casts to mark the place,
   And show us—what 'tis dear to trace—
   Where those we love have sunk away;
   And dust to dust, and clay to clay,
   To us are but as things unborn,
   Save that they've taught us how to mourn,
   And rise as spectres from their sleep,
   Midst fairest scenes to bid us weep.

   Proudly o'er their relics bending,
   While the storm is vainly spending
   All its rage, he seems to dare,
   Scarce heed the war, that's raging there.

         See the lightning's flash!
         Hark! the o'erwhelming crash!
The roar of thunder, through the forest sounding,
Loudly it calls (earth's trembling caves resounding):
         "Die! die! Thou thing of earth,
         Whate'er thy strength, thy birth
               Has marked thy doom.
Die. Thou wert born—thou liv'st but for the tomb."

'Tis ruin all. Tree, flower, and insect lie,
One formless wreck; for all were born to die.

Heed it not,
The wooing tone
Of the Siren Pleasure singing;
Know thy lot—
Man has but one—
Life to Death is ever bringing
Victims for the tomb:
Fairest things that bloom,
Only to fade away,
Only to smile today,
That, tomorrow, Death may be
Glutted, but as yesterday.

See, the eyeless spectre! What doth he glare withal?
Hark! a tongueless voice! Whence comes the fearful call?

"Ye're mine! Strength, beauty, youth, shrink not. Ye're mine!
Truer than love's, these fleshless arms entwine
In close embrace. And vainly would ye shun,
Poor fools! your lot. 'Tis here. Earth has but one.

"That moment ye woke to life's struggling sigh,
That moment declared, ye were born but to die;
And the pang which first called you from torpor to breath,
Was the stamp and the seal of your mortgage to Death."

The Fire-fly

Starlight gilds the gloomy hour,
Startled darkness shrinks away;
Heavenly beams, with radiant power,
Imitate the light of day.

Whence the fluttering, weakly gleam
Glancing through the placid night?

The fire-fly apes the sky's bright beam!
Soars heavenward with its tiny light,

As though it hoped to yonder star
Its dwarfish brightness it might rear,
And, glimmering feebly from afar,
Would seem the heavenly light to dare.

Fool, thing!—as, spurning thus the earth,
To which, alone, its ray is bright,
It seemed to scorn its humble birth—
Speaking thus, I checked its flight:

"Flitting in thy transient light,
From thy grassy bed arising,
Thinkest thou, because thou'rt bright,
The world is only worth despising?[23]

"With yon studded sky, dost deem
Thy broken light can bear comparing?
Alas! how weak thine efforts seem,
The fire-fly, heaven's effulgence daring!

"Thou, but for a summer's eve,
With inconstant light art gleaming;
Dares thy littleness to grieve,
That yon stars more bright are beaming?

"Sink, then, to thy native earth;
Nor, with rival splendour vying,
But expose thy lowly birth,
As each effort fades in dying."

Lo! the fluttering insect, pausing,
Turns to earth its humble course;
And, its glittering pinions closing,
Thus began to hold discourse:

23. *Twelfth Night* 2.3.114–15: "Dost thou think because thou art virtuous, there shall be no more cakes and ale?"

"Mortal, who so wisely teachest
 How to check Ambition's flight,
Aim'st thou but at what thou reachest?
 Seek'st thou no forbidden height?

"Hast thou never, boldly soaring,
 Dared to track some higher sphere?
Brighter realms than Earth's exploring,
 Sighed to fall and find thee here?

"What though thou, like me, must find—
 Born to Earth, doomed to regretting—
Vainly that the restless mind
 Seeks to soar, its birth forgetting?[24]

"Visions bright to Earth exiled,
 Of fantastic hopes repented,
Let us to home be reconciled;
 Learn at least to be contented."[25]

Shrinking, then, the humbled thing—
 All its higher visions fled—
Folding its ambitious wing,
 Hid it in its earthy bed.

Poor insect, who so boldly chidest
 At my hopes, which soar too high,
As thy starlit wing thou hidest,
 Must *they* veil their light and die?

No! Thus far thy lesson learning,
 Of fantastic hopes repented,
To my earthy home returning,
 I will seek to be contented;

I will learn like thee to lay me
 Where Heaven points my resting-place;

24. William Wordsworth, "Ode: Intimations of Immortality," st. 5, l. 1: "Our birth is but a sleep and a forgetting."

25. Context suggests that this line should read: "Learn at last to be contented."

But *one* hope—will that betray me?—
Lingers still, bright thoughts to trace.

Higher views than earth's inspiring,
Tremblingly its pencil gilds;
Crouched to earth, it learns aspiring;
Humbly daring, now it builds.

Fancy, now, no more is proud;
Trembling Reason scarce dares sway me:
Doubts o'er every path are strewed;
Still I trust 'twill not betray me.

Bent to earth, bowed down by fear,
Our highest hopes are only given,
When, humbled, shrinking, still we dare,
Crouched in dust, to dream of heaven.

The Sunbeam Sprite

It wandered through air, and it wandered o'er earth,
Till, wearied, the tired thing sighed for its home,
And longed for the sunbeam, the place of its birth:
That found, oh! never again would it roam.

But the longer it sought, still the less was its hope,
And bewildered and sad was that Sunbeamy Sprite;
For midst earth's brightest things, there was nothing to cope
With its own lovèd home, with its sunbeam bright.

And he gazed at the glorious orb of day,
And he fluttered his wearied wings in vain;
For alas! it was shining so far away!
Oh! where could he hope e'er to rest again?

As his saddened eye he cast worriedly round,
It lit on a snow-capped mountain top;
So dazzlingly it glistened, he thought he had found
A warm, bright, resting-place, where he might stop.

But alas! when his tired wings had reached
The far-off place, which so brightly shone,
There was ice and snow all around him stretched,
And cold, freezing cold, reigned there alone.

And the ice, with its rainbow hues, here, there
He touched, as he saw it round him lie.
'Twas so cold, that he shrank away with a tear,
And wished that a Sunbeam Sprite could die.

Then he laid him down, as it were his home,
For despair had seized him. His hope was, now,
That some strange numbness like death might come,
And wrap him, in torpor, from pain and wo.

But lo! afar off shining,
Beams the still river's breast.
Upon it, lies reclining,
As 'twere a bed of rest,
As bright a beam, as heaven could send,
With things of earth to live and blend.

My home! my home! cried the joyous sprite,
As the glistening stream caught his dazzled eye;
Oh! yonder's my home, so loved and so bright,
And he clapped his tiny hands for joy.

And away he flew, for fresh strength was given,
By the new hope, sprung in his wearied breast,
And his eye was still fixed on the beam, which heaven,
He fancied, had sent to give him rest.

And he playfully fluttered his wings, and stopped,
One instant, balanced above the waves;
Then, closing them quickly, down he dropped—
Poor sprite! 'tis not there, the rest he craves.

For, if it might be that a sprite could die,
This hour were the last to that wretched thing:
As useless and wet his pinions lie,
The wave whirls him round—he has nowhere to cling.

Plaything of the flood, and resistless, he lay;
For to struggle he had nor the heart, nor the strength,
Till, at last, he was thrown by the rough dashing spray
On the river's bank, extended at length.

And he raised him there, in doleful plight,
As down his cheek streamed many a tear,
And a sorry sight was that sunbeam sprite,
As, dripping and wet, he stood shivering there.

A beauteous blossom, near him blowing,
Seemed, in its opening bosom, glowing
With heat from heaven, so kindly sent.
Thought the sprite, as thither his steps he bent,
I'll bask me there, in the sunny ray,
And drive this shivering fit away.

And slowly and toilsomely, he dragged him along,
And his draggled wings swept in the dust, as he past;
And 'twas but with much toilsome effort among
Its fragrant leaves that he rested, at last.

But there he was, and there for awhile
He fancied his present toil was done,
And, basking beneath the sun's warm smile,
Deemed, at last, that his resting-place was won.

But the God of his worship is passing away:
Sol sinks 'neath the ocean, and fast fades the day;
And the flowret's bosom grows chill as the tomb,
And the night-dews weep over its withering bloom.

And the tired wanderer shuddering sees
The curtain of night fast descending around,
While mournfully past him is sighing the breeze,
As tho' sorrowing over the woes he has found.

Dark, sombre night! 'Twas strange to him,
Who ever had lived in the sun's bright ray,
And who never of darkness in fancy could dream,
For a sunbeam sprite knows nought but of day.

And he gazed around at the darkening view,
    And deemed that some horrible wonder was near;
And shuddered, as darker and darker it grew!
    Who can guess, how the poor thing was trembling with fear?

        A ray of hope is round him gleaming:
        See how brightly near him beaming
        Cynthia's eye attracts his gaze!
        Could he not warm him in its rays?

Doubtful, and trembling, the heart-sickened thing
Crept from the flower; its bruisèd wing
It dragged along—for it could not fly,
Till it basked in the light of that beaming eye.

Did he find what he sought?
    Was there warmth? was there rest?
'Twas colder than ever, the poor thing thought,
    As he wrung his hands; and, sore distrest,
He flung him down on the chilly earth,
Cursing the hour which gave him birth.

And he cursed the earth, and he cursed the sky,
    E'en his own loved beam, where he was nursed;
It was shining so far away on high,
    'Twas nought to him; and its light he cursed,
Which could shine for others, and leave him here,
The victim of suffering, cold, and fear.

And, as he looked round on the thickening night,
How he shook with horror, that anguished sprite,
As he wondered if he were a devil now,
To dwell with darkness, despair, and wo;
And thought it was hell which he had found,
And trembled at his own curses' sound.
Oh! despair seized the heart of that wo-worn sprite,
As he gazed at the ever-darkening night.

*   *   *   *

Gently as the moon's first beaming
Casts its softly trembling ray,
Is there light? or is he dreaming?
Is't but his crazed fancy's day?
There's surely something lingering near,
To talk of hope, and dry his tear.
Unlike the light on the mountain height,
Unlike the cheating river's shining,
Unlike the eye, which could bid him die,
Without e'en a look which spoke repining;
There was a light so gently beaming,
So softly bright, yet so enduring,
That once again the poor Sprite, dreaming,
Could fancy of his pain the curing.

Mary, 'twas from thine eye the light,
Which spoke of that, his wished-for cure:[26]
His heart, it dared not throb with delight,
But oh! it dared to hope once more.

And he drew him nearer, nearer, nearer,
As it shone on still with no fitful gleam;
And now that glance seemed even dearer
Than the light which fell from his own sunbeam.

For the joys which come, e'er sorrows are known,
Smile, but to be quickly forgotten again;
But the hope which brings comfort, such joys being flown,
Is dearer and dearer, the greater our pain.

And he basked him well in the sunny ray
Of that eye, which beamed so kindly o'er him;
And you could not have tempted him now away,
Tho' 'twere to his sunbeam to restore him.

For as he nearer crept, and nearer,
He paused, where her heart, so kindly beating,

26. "Mary" is perhaps to be identified with LSM's cousin, Mary Cheves Dulles; see LSM to Mary Cheves Dulles, June 18 [1851], and note there.

Told him, that 'twas a home far dearer
Than the beam he had been so long regretting.

For *that,* while good around it throwing,
Is all unconscious of the blessing,
While the tender heart, with kindness glowing,
Beats for each pang it is redressing.

And when it melts to others' sorrows,
Or soothes the mourning sufferer's pain,
We love it, that our griefs it borrows,
And, for our tears, gives tears again.

And the tired wanderer nestled near
To that kindly heart, and was happy and calm;
For he felt that, e'en in this world so drear,
There's a comfort for sorrow, for misery a balm.

Fallen Angels

They wander through our world,
From higher regions hurled,
Angel forms, from Heaven thrust,
Grovelling in our earthly dust:
Weep, weep their fallen might.

Seraphic host,
Their glory lost,
Tinged with earth,
Forgot their birth:
Weep, weep their fallen might.

But they bear in their looks still a beam from on high;
Tho' exiled, the exiles they are of the sky;
And their smile is the smile of the home of their birth;
Tho' fallen and sullied, they're angels on earth:

Fond Hope, who so smilingly points us the way
To that sky, whence herself has been driven;

And Mercy, who whispers that man has a stay,
And tells him *her* birthplace was Heaven;

While Charity lingers to ask for a brother—
What ourselves are still seeking—relief;
And Love whispers softly, the joy of another
Is a sunbeam to light our own grief.

And Affection, the gentlest, the kindest of all,
Lingers still, though her sisters be gone;
Oh! scarce, if she might, would she rise from her fall,
And leave man to weep here, alone.

She clings to the outcast: when bent to the dust,
If her tearful eye rises to Heaven,
She prays not for that refuge from whence she was thrust,
But, that comfort to *him* may be given.

She hopes not to rise, for she doth not repent,
But clings to the sufferer here;
O'er his care-furrowed brow is she watchfully bent,
As she answers each pang with a tear.

While others are pointing a happier land,
Nor can learn to content them with this,
She kisses his pale brow—she presses his hand—
He forgets he's an outcast from bliss.

The First Star of Evening

The first star of evening, how it tremblingly shines,
As its faint ray is cast o'er the sky,
While the bright sun to gloom and to darkness declines,
As his fading light sinks but to die.

And why do we turn to yon star's trembling ray,
Which fears even day's *dying* glare?
And why does the eye to yon sinking sun stray,
And why is his fading light dear?

It is, that man's sad heart is tutor'd to wo,
    Tho' oft dazzled by joy's brilliant ray;
To the sun in his glory we worshipping bow,
    But *love* him when sinking away.

The star, while its lustre shines brightest, may please,
    Like the rapture which joy can impart;
But the weeping eye turns to its trembling rays,
    And they vibrate a chord in the heart.

Oh! I love that pale star, that tremblingly shines,
    And its faint ray is cast o'er the sky;
Oh! I love that bright sun who to darkness declines,
    As his fading light sinks but to die.

Combat of the Powers of Good and Evil

Fierce! terrible! a combat wild and fearful!
A mystery of power; dark in its might;
And indistinct, and vast, and horrible.
                    'Twas in the howling blast;
'Twas in the thunder's roar; 'twas in the deep,
Which echoed back Heaven's rage, in sullen voice.
The cataract's bounding torrent spoke of it;
The whirlwind's crushing might spoke of it;
The crashing forest's ruin spoke of it;
The earthquake's trembling horrors spoke of it;
It hissed within the fierce volcano's flames,
And angered Nature's voice echoed it.
And in the silent gloom of horrid night
Fiends spoke of it, and demons howled it forth.
A combat fierce, and horrible, and strange;
The Evil Spirit with the power of Good.
    Sad triumph! for behold the demon's might
Victorious raging. Hark! his voice, alone,
Laughs o'er the waste of prostrate Nature's wreck,
And darkness—not of night; thick, viewless darkness,
Full of horrible imaginings—and things
Which only sport them in that fearful gloom,

When frighted Reason shrinks, and coward Fear
Wakes demon forms, and calls its devils round us,
To crush and stun our trembling, dizzied minds;
Methought 'twas done, and Evil reigned supreme.
                                        A ray of light!
It struggled forth; a faintly beaming star
Shone through the gloom. A voice was there; it said,
"Hope! mortal, hope."
'Twas gone. The demon raged again supreme.
No more in darkness, but a scorching light;
A sun which warmed no more, but seared and blighted
The withering earth, which shrivelled 'neath his rays,
Until, itself, was as a globe of fire,
To parch the every living thing it bore;
While panting nature gasped as 'twere for life.
The rivers, too, were by the thirsty earth
Drunk up; and streams and fountains were not.
The heavens refused their aid; the brazen sky
Seemed one vast mirror of reflected heat.
Evil had conquered, and the universe
Was blighted at his tread.
                                        One dew-drop fell:
From heaven it came; so cool, so fresh, so pure,
Methought it seemed a tear, sent by that power
Which could not conquer, but which watched us still.
Again, that voice I heard, which whispering said,
"Hope, mortal, hope."
        'Twas cold and chill: The sun had lost his heat;
His pallid ray but faintly waked the thought
Of genial warmth, and only shone to light,
With sickly beam, the fearful desolation,
Which o'er earth now held its dismal reign.
'Twas ice, and howling winds, and endless snows;
And shivering misery, and frozen tears;
And life, which was not life, but turned to stone,
With agony of suffering; and thought was still;
And mind itself lay stunned; chilled by the view
Of statued agony, of "Life in Death."[27]

27. *Venus and Adonis,* ll. 413–14: Love "is a life in death, / That laughs and weeps, and all but with a breath"; *2 Henry VI,* 3.2.151: "For, seeing him, I see my life in death." Also "The

'Twas Evil now uncombated. Methought
The power of Good no longer struggled—
Hark!
The voice again. And from the frozen earth
There budded gently forth one timid blossom:
Drooping it rose, and half-retiring stood,
But it was there, the shrinking flower which comes
To whisper of the wished-for bloom of spring.
The snow-drop reared its head; and softly then
Murmured that voice; and its soft murmuring was,
"Hope, mortal, hope."
What fearful tumult comes to drown its tones?
Sprung from the womb of earth, in direst earthquake,
Rose the fiend of War, while nature trembled;
Shrieking terrors, pallid fears wait on him;
Strange horrors dog his steps; and thirsty Death
Laps thickened gore from out his bloody tracks;
While Famine stalks, with loathly Pestilence,
Triumphant in his rear.
It was a field
Of carnage. Far and wide, 'twas death and slaughter;
Man with man, passion with passion warred;
It seemed a hell, where devils were let loose;
No world of human charity and love.
And mingling with the clashing arms were cries
And groans of misery—and no one heeded them.
The cannon's roar was answered by the shriek
Which mangled corpses breathed in agony,
And no one heard it. Or, perchance, 'twas heard,
And scoffed at. Were these men, or fiends? I gazed
In horrid wonderment. Then, midst the din,
A fiendish howl of fearful laughter rose:
Hell's demons triumphant that all good was crushed;
One scene of sin on sin, and wo on wo.
I wept and hoped no more.
"Hope, mortal, hope!"
The voice was in my ear, distinct in words,
No longer only murmured on the breeze;

Order for the Burial of the Dead," *Book of Common Prayer,* p. 338: "In the midst of life we are in death."

Its plaintive tones were spoke by mortal lips.
I turned—and kneeling near me bent a form,
It seemed of heaven, but yet it was of earth.
'Twas gentle woman's voice which whispered, "Hope."
She wiped the cold sweat from the clammy brow,
And raised the sinking head, and tried to soothe
The anguish of yon crushed and broken thing,
Which could so lately call itself a man.
And, as his fainting breath gasped forth a sigh,
Then hushed itself in death, she bent her down,
Kissed the loved lips, then turned her to her babe,
And, wrapping in her arms th' unconscious thing,
Pointed to heaven and sighed, "Hope, mortal, hope."
And then, with smile of patient sufferance, bent
Her trembling steps to trace the troubled path
Of life's tumultuous course. And then methought,
As unsustained she tracked her timid way,
An angel form was near her, guiding still
Her tearful looks for ever tow'rd the sky,
And whispering that a home of peace was there.
And ever, as it propped her tottering steps,
To cheer that lone one, cast upon the world,
Its constant lesson was, "Hope, mortal, hope."
        I gazed upon that angel-form, and knew
It was the *power of Good,* which conquered there.
'Twas he who waked the star, who dropped the tear;
'Twas he, who called the snow-drop from its bed;
'Twas he, who gave the timid mortal strength
To hope, and hope, and hope in misery.

The Star Which Followed Me

In childhood, as beneath yon starry sky
My tiny steps would track their devious way,
Still as in winding flight, or fast or slow,
Their varied course would turn, yon star shone down
Direct upon me still. Backward or forward,
Round and round, methought it followed still.
And well I loved it, for I deemed it shone

Only for me, and that it watched to bless me.
And in my youthful fancy it would wake
Dreams of far greater, brighter, happier things
Than the world held for others; and it seemed
To talk of happiness and hope, and all,
And more than, fancy's wildest, fairest views,
And all for me! Oh! how I loved that star!
And as I watched, and dreamed of all it promised,
Meseemed itself, perchance, might yet be mine;
And I would stretch my longing arms, and call,
And almost wonder that it would not come,
When thus I summoned it. I loved it with
A fancy, wandering, bright as its own rays!
Ay, almost with a wild devotion, worshipped
That star which ever watched and followed me!
And now, where is it?
                                        Lo! in yonder sky,
Brightly it still shines on—but not for me!
My childhood's dream is vanished, and I've learned
'Twas but to fancy's eye it followed me,
And that afar off, in unmeasured space,
It dwells, unconscious of my dreams, myself;
A world within itself, and no bright thing
To guide *me,* grovelling worm! upon my way.
        And now, proud science, that thy lesson's learned,
And childhood's errors have forgot themselves,
Perchance, I may be wiser; but alas!
I've lost, for ever lost, the star which followed me.

The Daughters of Hope

Bright Hope, when first she came to earth,
        To smile o'er mankind's cloudy life,
Two beauteous daughters, at a birth,
        Brought to this scene of wo and strife.

And both she saw so brightly fair,
        So gentle, amiable, and mild,
These two, she said, shall ease man's care—
        By them his woes shall be beguiled.

Fancy shall woo off sorrow's tear,
And gild the eye with smiles of joy;
While Happiness shall follow near,
To hinder even Fear's alloy.

Nor did these beauteous nymphs belie
The words which their fond mother spoke,
For ever where they could descry
Fell Sorrow's bonds, his chain they broke.

And eyes that met them bathed in tears,
Scarce saw them ere to smile they learned;
And hearts which withered with life's cares,
To joy and health were soon returned.

But one day, as their course they bent,
To dry the tear, to hush the moan,
To heal the wound which Suffering sent,
Fancy found Happiness was gone.

And all in vain, alone, she tried
To do what both were wont to do;
Men saw her, smiled—but then they sighed,
That Happiness was not there, too.

"And where is Happiness?" they said,
"And why is Happiness away?"
And then some whispered she was dead;
Some, that to Heaven she winged her way.

Still Fancy smiled. "Come, follow me,
We'll find," she said, "the truant soon."
Men listened, as her smile they'd see,
And followed, where she led them on.

But soon she found she'd not the power
To give them all they from her asked;
Tho' from her sister's flight, each hour
Her every faculty she tasked.

Away then to Hope's home she flew,
    Complained that she was now alone:
"If thou," she said, "to man art true,
    Aid me—for Happiness is gone."

Hope started. "No, it is not so!
    Fancy," she said, "it cannot be;
In search of Happiness I'll go,
    And cannot fail aided by thee.

"We'll find her, wheresoe'er she's hid,
    Bring her once more to man's relief;
Once more, by us the truant led
    Shall come to war with Fear and Grief."

They started, and to find her strove;
    Nor tired, for Hope sought for her child,
And Fancy ne'er could cease to love
    That sister, who so brightly smiled.

They search, but still they cannot find,
    While man, despairing, says she's dead;
At least, that she has ceased to mind
    His cares, and to high Heaven is fled.

But Hope and Fancy promise still,
    Still bid us seek for Happiness,
Till, e'en while tears of sorrow fill
    And cloud the eye—we dream of bliss.

The Falling Star

And the rivers, who, all the world must know,
Were in love with the stars ever since they could flow.

—Bulwer[28]

The river that loved yon star so bright,
    How soft was its plaintive tone,

28. Edward George Earle Lytton Bulwer-Lytton, "The Assurance," ll. 14–15, in *Corn-Flowers,* bk. 2.

As gazing it drank in the far-off light,
And joyed in those beams alone.

And how could it woo, away so far?
It worshipped that distant one.
But a river! Oh! how could it reach a star?
It hoped not, but murmured on.

And aye, as it wended its constant way,
It gazed on each beam that fell,
Till mirrored the star in its bosom lay,
And its bliss was, to watch it still.

And the star, did it always unheeding shine
Of that river's silent prayer?
Or perchance did its rays more brightly incline
To stamp its own image there?

*　　*　　*　　*　　*

Silent was their love;
Each seemed doomed to live alone.
But from its seat above
That star, one night, was gone.

A brilliant meteor falling,
Thro' the sky, 'twas seen to glide.
To that river's silent calling,
It, as silently, replied.

And we are not farther led,
In their hidden loves t' explore;
That star contented fled
From its home of light and power.

Nor, perchance, would pity bid
To bewail its fallen state;

In that river's bosom hid,
May the star not love its fate?

*   *   *   *   *

Gently murmurs on the river:
In its murmuring tone is peace;
Of that peace, the kindly giver
Leaves in heaven its vacant place.

But in the lowly home 't has sought,
There's quiet love, tho' splendour flies.
Perchance, it deems not dearly bought
That home, where it forgotten lies.

The Comet

Hast thou no resting-place, thou wandering thing?
Art thou an emblem of the soul, which roams
Eternally, and seeks a home and rest?
What art thou, that thou flashest o'er us thus
In course eccentric?[29] Lo! as some wanderer
Thou passest, a lone stranger through the sky,
And every star peeps forth, as if to watch
Thy meteor course, and, as thou passest, pales
Its timid ray, and seems to whispering say,
"We know thee not, strange thing, thou'rt not of us."
And, in calm brightness, the pale moon looks down,
And thou, as 'twere a troubled spirit, shrink'st
From her soft light, while with her gentle smile
She seems to say, "Wanderer, thou'rt not of us."
And the earth answers her, from rustling leaves,
And wave, and murmuring stream, "Thou'rt not of us."
'Tis echoed through the universe. And thou,
Outcast from Heaven and Earth, whence art thou?—Say,

29. Perhaps a reference to the Great Comet of 1843, the brightness of which, and its tail nearly two hundred million miles long, caused a sensation. Also, Halley's comet appeared to the earth in 1835–36; and in 1846 Biela's comet, as, observed by astronomers, it passed the sun, broke in two.

Is thy wild light some evil thing which spreads,
As has been deemed, sickness and desolation?
And dost thou bear with thee the curse of worlds,
Grim Famine, hungry War, thy satellites?
Or art thou but some wandering discontent?
Some thought, which may not find a resting-place,
Fixed to one constant round of endless change,
For ever wandering, and for ever doomed
To wander on alone; teaching itself
To suffer; gnawing itself, and bringing home
Its direst misery? a misery
Of loneliness unshared, which nought can know
And nought can pity? And (for thou art alone)
Men curse thee; and they point as 'twere a scourge,
Precursor of strange ills; and trembling watch
Thy beaming course, which should be beautiful
But that they deem some new strange ill must follow.
Hast thou a thought to know thyself accursed,
And feel that all things hate thee? An' thou hast,
E'en in thy lofty state, I pity thee,
Bright, lonely one: methinks to find a home
Thou'dst hide thy rays, and sink to loneliness,
And shrink into the bosom of some cloud,
Or drop into the ocean's billowy bed,
That all no more might shrink from thee, and say,
"Strange thing, whence art thou?—thou art not of us."
        Lo! thou art gone, perchance to seek for rest;
And the sky, which but now cast back thy beam,
Has lost thee, and with open smile it seems
As 'twould rejoice to find itself again
Free from thy fearful light. I pity thee,
That all things shun thee thus. E'en tho' thou wert
As foul as thought can paint, or fancy dream,
Some demon spirit, bent on ill and wo,
Still I must pity thee: for thou'rt *alone,*
And *loneliness,* methinks—is *misery.*

The Garden of Experience

Methought a garden round me lay
    With flowers of brightest hue;

Each blossom, decked in colours gay,
Seemed vain its beauties to display,
And turned them to the view.

The rose, the tulip, woodbine too,
Their brightest hues displayed;
The daisy, and the violet blue,
Bespread the ground, as if to woo
Light pleasure's airy tread.

A queen-like lily near me shed
Its fragrance, fresh and pure;
And, as it bowed its snowy head,
To grasp its beauties I was led:
I touched—they were no more.

And, withering on its stem, it drooped;
As, weeping its decay,
We've seen fresh youth, by sickness stooped
Towards the grave, which yawning oped
Its jaws, to ask its prey.

And quickly then I turned to cull
The rose's brighter bloom;
But it too drooped; and withering, dull,
Those beauties which I sought to cull
Seemed fit but for the tomb.

Another and another yet
Midst these bright flowers I sought;
But still, while sweets I tried to get,
They, withering, left me to regret
That aye my search was nought.

At length my fruitless toils I ceased,
And stood in wonder lost.
"And what," I cried, "all which is best,
My slightest touch seems to divest
Of all its beauty's boast."

But, as I spoke, a figure sad
And mournful, near me stood;
In sombre robes of sorrow clad,
She seemed to mourn each blossom dead,
And weep each withering bud.

"'Tis not thy touch," she sighed, "but mine,
Which blights their opening bloom;
And vainly o'er their fate I pine,
And vainly weep as they decline:
To crush them, is my doom.

"And aye where flowers brightest blow,
Where fragrant sweets most dwell,
As if the gathering hand to woo,
There most my power I'm doomed to show;
There's none these sweets may cull.

"For, ever as the grasping hand,
To gather them would try,
'Tis mine their ruin to command,
'Tis mine to wave the fatal wand,
Whose touch must bid them die.

"This beauteous garden charms the eye,
As smiles the world to youth;
But every promise brings its sigh;
The fresh heart aches to see it die,
And trembles at the truth.

"The brightest hues which now delight,
Must wither ere they're yours;
Experience ever stands to blight
All that is loveliest to the sight,
To crush the sweetest flowers.

"Experience maketh wise, 'tis true;
But ah! in tears man earns
The lesson, which but makes him rue
What Wisdom laughs at, as untrue—
He weeps at what he learns."

Love, Wisdom, and Folly

When Love first 'gan the world to range,
  A country wild to him and new,
There's surely none will deem it strange
  That, when from heaven's blest heights he flew,
He should seek out some friend, or brother,
  Some one, to whom to look for aid.
The Baby God, who from his mother
  Had just broke loose, was still afraid
These unknown realms to wander through,
Where, mixed with pleasures, dangers grew.

And long within himself he thought
  Who best could aid and guide him there;
And, as sometimes discourses fraught
  With praise of Wisdom, on his ear
Had fallen while yet he was in heaven,
  He thought he'd look for her, and find
If really to her power 'twas given
  To govern, sway, and rule mankind:
"And if," he said, "so great her might,
Who 'gainst our powers combined can fight?"

This once resolved, young Love soon went
  To seek out Wisdom's lonely home.
He found her, deep in study bent,
  O'er an old, rusty, time-worn tome,
While Solitude was standing near,
  To keep intruders far away,
And Thought, and Contemplation, there
  Kept watch alike, both night and day.
Young Love was awe-struck at the group,
His pride forgot, and learned to stoop.

And bending low, to Wisdom he
  Addressed himself, to ask her aid;
While Contemplation frowned to see
  That Wisdom stopped, her task delayed,
And, while the smooth-tongued boy talked on,
  Seemed pleased with all he had to say;

Till he, more bold and easy grown,
        While Wisdom smiled, now 'gan to play,
Blotted her papers and her books,
And mocked grim Solitude's strange looks;

Asked Wisdom, how she e'er could bear
        To live in gloomy scenes apart
From all mankind, in places drear,
        For ever lab'ring o'er her art;
Said he had heard much of her might,
        The power which she by art had learned,
And thought it would be only right,
        If to man's good this knowledge turned,
That at the same time Wisdom's name
Should rise to glory and to fame.

And then he sketched his journey's plan,
        Told how the world he would subdue,
And laughed to think how helpless man
        Would struggle, when his darts he threw:
And then he said, if Wisdom would
        But put herself beneath his sway,
Their power could never be withstood,
        The world they'd govern in their way;
"So come," he said, "be ruled by me;
None will resist, you soon will see."

Proud Wisdom started when she heard
        Love talk as though he thought to rule;
She scarce believed the saucy word
        Could mean that Love would Wisdom school.
"I listened, Love, as long," said she,
        "As Reason seemed to guide your speech;
But now you talk of ruling me,
        A point, be sure you ne'er will reach;
For, when you'd Wisdom seek to school,
You show too plainly who's the fool."

Love, e'en in Heaven, would ne'er a word
        Of harshness patiently endure,

And now, when Wisdom's speech he heard,
He vowed her pride he soon would cure.
"You call me fool," he said; "'tis well,
Light Folly's home I now will seek:
And when with her Love deigns to dwell,
Two fools we'll be—but Wisdom weak,
Perhaps less proud than she is now,
Will e'en to Love and Folly bow."

Full then of anger and disdain,
Love to his threatening words was true;
Wisdom's excuse he did not deign
To stop and hear, but off he flew;
Leaving poor Wisdom rather sorry,
That she so hastily had spoken,
Somewhat repenting of the hurry
By which all terms with Love were broken;
For all his threats she little cared,
But that he'd ne'er come back she feared.

The flattering boy had pleased her so,
So much she grieved, now he was gone,
That were he back, she did not know
But pride and power she might lay down,
To keep the little wanderer near,
Submitting to his tyrant sway;
And then (who would believe 't?) a tear
She shed, that Love had flown away;
While Contemplation stood aghast,
At all which in her sight had past.

Meanwhile, Love had not wandered far,
E'er smiling Folly crossed his path.
"Ah ha!" quoth Love, "by Jove, I swear,
She greater charms than Wisdom hath.
Why, she is smiling, fair, and gay;
More good-natured than Wisdom looks,
Who scarce would for one moment stay
From pondering o'er her musty books.
With Folly then I'll choose to stray;
Come, beauteous Folly, let's away."

Folly, who had not Wisdom's fear
    Of being by Love's power ruled,
Gave herself little thought or care
    As to how much she should be schooled.
Content to roam the world with Love,
    Quite willing in his paths to tread,
She never dreamt to disapprove,
    But followed on, where'er he led.
She asked not, cared not, where he'd rove,
Content, that she was led by Love.

Together so well pleased they were,
    That seldom, now, they go apart:
Where Love is, Folly's surely near;
    She has the head where he the heart.
And, if it e'er is Wisdom's lot
    To meet this well-contented pair,
Love shows, that he hath ne'er forgot
    The vengeance which he once did swear;
While Wisdom, grown more humble now,
Will e'en to Love and Folly bow.

For, spite of reason, she will still
    To please the little God aspire.
And, though he frowns, and treats her ill,
    She tries to pacify his ire.
But all her efforts still prove vain:
    For still the God, to show his spleen,
In heads which once owned Wisdom's reign
    Makes Folly undisputed queen;
And, spite of all poor Wisdom's art,
She rules the head, where he the heart.

'Tis but Thee, Love, Only Thee[30]

Where the sunbeam glanceth brightest,
    There, my love, I think on thee.

30. Reprinted, together with "Spirit of the Storm," in May, *American Female Poets,* pp. 420–22.

Where the summer breeze is lightest,
        Still of thee, and only thee.
Where the gently murmuring stream
Lulls to soft and placid dream,
Who for ever lingers near me?
Who but thee, love? only thee!

And if fear, or dark misgiving,
        Hover round with evening's gloom,
Fancy's tissues darkly weaving,
        Tracing sorrows yet to come;
Still, one shadow lingering near,
Even scenes like these are dear.
Who the angel hovering near me?
Who but thee, love? only thee!

Thus in hope, and thus in sorrow,
        Fancy paints thy shadow near,
Thou, the brightener of each morrow,
        Thou, the soother of each care.
And the sun which gives me light,
And the star which gilds my night,
And the lingering hope to cheer me,
'Tis but thee, love! only thee!

Birth of the Evergreen

Gay Hope, in a frolicksome humour one day,
From her suitors' fond glances kept hiding away,
And now in the fresh grass, and now in a flower,
She managed to tease them, for many an hour.

At last in a thick bush so closely she hid,
That defeated and vexed they at length 'gan to chide,
And called on the loiterer, and prayed her to hear;
But she laughed at their trouble, and mocked at their prayer.

So pleasant the green bush wherein she had crept,
That wearied with sporting the frolic thing slept;

While her followers, impatient, at last in dismay
'Gan to mourn, as they deemed she had quite fled away.

Great Jove, who on business of state was engaged,
        Disturbed by this tumult, confusion, and row,
Asked not for its cause but, perplexed and enraged,
        Issued orders to stop all that Babel below.

For his lightning bolts quickly one messenger flew,
        And one brought a cloud, from whence they might dart them;
But one glance, ere the murderous weapons they threw,
        They cast down on men, ere so sadly they hurt them.

They saw the bright angel who downward had traced
        Her course from that sky where no longer she'd stop;
For she found herself up there too sadly misplaced:
        They're happy in heaven, and cannot need Hope.

They saw that she frolicked with fond man below
        But to make him more true (while her fair form embracing),
When once more on his bosom she'd smilingly throw
        Herself, the bright vision, which ever he's chasing.

They thought it a pity, so harshly to deal
        With the weak things, who had quite enough to torment them;
Decided that mild means would do quite as well,
        And so cast back the lightnings to Vulcan, who sent them.

But still, as great Jupiter's orders had bound them
        The clattering tongues of us pigmies to quiet,
They sought other means, and full quickly they found them,
        To hush and confound all the turmoil and riot.

They took that dark cloud which its thunder had lost,
        With crystal drops hung, and just ready to fall;
They filled it with snow, and with ice, and with frost,
        And they aimed it direct o'er our riotous ball.

And they called the North Wind, and they bade him to blow,
        'Till earth and her children, in icicles blended,

Perforce would be stilled; ere again they might thaw,
Great Jove would, perhaps, all his business have ended.

Hoarse blew the loud blast—and right angry he was;
From his afternoon nap they had wakened him roughly;
And sure such disturbance is quite enough cause
To make an old gentleman act rather gruffly.

And the snow fell in flakes, and the hail pelted bravely,
And the frost did its duty as well as the rest.
Poor man was soon brought to comport himself gravely,
And Earth's noise Heaven's councils now no more distrest.

Hushed were its voices; all was chilled;
Flowers were blighted, buds were nipped;
Streamlets, which so brightly rilled,
Where the bird its nectar sipped
Ere he carolled forth his lay,
Still might glitter in the ray
Of the all unfrozen Sun;
But it was with such false shining
As but wakes the vain repining
(When its troubled course is done)
Of the heart that trusts the seeming
Of a world which all seems bliss;
Catches at its cheating beaming,
And but grasps a thing of ice.
Withered was each greenest bough;
Flowrets drooped at winter's breath;
Every leaf had changed its hue,
Frighted at th' approach of death.

Past was summer's glory,
Earth one ruined waste,
Like some bygone story,
All its beauties past.

But lo! still *one* bush, which, now greener than ever,
Contrasted with all that was withering round,
Smiled on, by the bank of the cold, frozen river;
Why so green were its unblighted branches still found?

'Twas that midst them a charm lay the frosts to disarm,
And the blast shrunk away from its beauties uninjured;
For Hope there, unconscious of all the alarm,
Slept, close in the hiding-place where she had lingered.

There Hope was still sleeping,
While nature was weeping;
She slept, and she dreamed, and she smiled in her dream.
And the blast which was sweeping
By, touched her not sleeping;
For she dreamed as she slept, and she smiled in her dream.

And man who was shrinking,
In agony sinking,
As his eye turned towards its unwithering green,
Deemed that him it was linking
To Hope, tho' still shrinking,
And smiled as he murmured, "'Tis green, *ever green*."

The Soul of a Sound

As the wind sweepeth by, o'er yon harp-strings which now
Lay in idleness mute (while no power was bringing
To life its soft tones), hark! how startlingly grow,
And burst through the air, in wild melody springing,
Those notes which the power that could wake them but waited,
Darting forth to the touch, which, in wooing, created.

Waked by fairy fingers,
Their voices are unbound;
Some gentle spirit lingers
In every trembling sound.

Oh! say not that they breathe, unknowing,
Their own soft tone.
Oh! say not, while these notes are flowing,
Themselves alone
Are all unconscious of the pleasure,
Waked by the wild and airy measure.

Oh! say not thus, but rather find
A spirit in each wildest note,
Which, borne upon the passing wind,
Dies with the tones which o'er us float.

A light thing which e'en summer flies
May dare to mock as all ideal;
Yet ere the earthborn trembler dies,
Its little life has bade us feel.

Hark! its sweet sound floats through the air,
Wild, but how tremulously soft;
Now sinks, as though 'twere taught to fear
Its own sweet tones; now bursts aloft.

And now, a dying cadence thrills,
In whispered notes, the listening ear;
And now, again, a fresh note fills,
Then floats away upon the air.

And sinking, trembling as it goes,
Fainter the airy sound is thrown
Around us, and a dying close
Whispered we hear, and now 'tis gone:

Gone—like the fading light of day,
Which trembles o'er the Ocean's face;
Gone—like life's joys which pass away,
And fading die, and leave no trace;

Save one—one thought that memory
Summons to mourn their sweetness fled,
Whispering the heart, that misery
Builds on the tomb of pleasures dead.

Her Hope Is in the Grave

Sure, Nature made that eye for smiles—
Whence comes the tear that clouds it?

Instead of all Love's witching wiles,
    'Tis sadness ever shrouds it.

Sure, Nature meant that heart for bliss—
    Whence comes the labouring sorrow,
Which paints with grief the pallid face,
    And casts almost a furrow
Upon her brow, the track of Care,
Which marks his withering progress there?

'Tis that life's morning hour
Has seen its brightest flower
    Wither and pass away.
'Tis that the daylight's beam
Of youth, with sickly gleam,
    Fades with its new-born ray.

Ah! life has cast its poison there,
    Embittered all it gave;
For Memory, lingering everywhere,
    Points to one new-made grave:
One grave, where Sorrow ever sits,
    Where Joy has hid his head,
Nor Hope with rainbow visions flits—
    For there, her hope is laid.
Life only mocks her woes by seeming
    Some other joys to leave;
For how can she of joy be dreaming?
    Her Hope is in the grave.

We cannot always anguish feel,
    And deepest wounds that tear
The tortured breast at last may heal;
    But still they leave a scar.
The grass upon yon grave may grow,
    Her smile once more return,
And pleasure's beam again may throw
    Its ray, where all's forlorn.
But, though that eye may brightly beam,
    That heart more lightly beat,

They have not, howsoe'er they seem,
Youth's brightness, nor its heat.

For Grief has held despotic reign,
Nor, monarch once, will leave
His vacant throne unclaimed by pain:
Her hope is in the grave.

Its shadow, mingling with the glow
Of sunniest scenes, will cleave
To every fairest dream, and show
Her first hope in the grave.

Though nature's storm may pass away,
Unclouded shine the sun,
The heart has ne'er that second ray,
Bright as the one that's gone.

Then, tho' from out the wreck that lies
In shattered fragments round,
She still may hope to cull some joys,
Some comfort may be found,
She may not, must not, hope for one
So bright a joy to save,
As the first, too dearly loved and gone,
The hope that's in the grave.

Forget Thee!

Forget thee!—no, never. How can I forget,
When the sun in yon heaven thine impress has set?
For bright as his beam is the glance of thine eye,
And soft is thy smile as the blue, cloudless sky.

In the starlight of even, I still think thee near,
And thy voice in the whispers of zephyr I hear.
The thought of thee wakes in the stillness of night,
And lingers around me in Luna's soft light.

In ocean it murmurs, and sleeps on the wave,
Casting back to the sun the bright light that he gave,
Or reflects on its bosom the bright beaming star,
Whose wandering rays come to woo from afar.

It dwells in each flower, it sighs in each breeze,
For beauty and sweetness are mingled in these;
While all nature speaks of thee, then vain would it be
To seek to drive from me the memory of thee.

Forget thee!—no, never. While earth has a spot
Where beauty is dwelling, thou art not forgot;
For in all that is bright, or is soft, or is fair,
Thy memory lingers—thy spirit is there.

To a Fly

Away, away, thou buzzing thing!
    What art thou to thus torment me
With thy bustling, idle wing?
    What strange vanity has lent thee
Such an overweening dream
Of thyself, that thou should'st deem
Me (so far above thee born)
One whom thou may'st buzz and turn
And fret and murmur round, as 'twere
Some equal that thou fanciest here?
A thing but born like thee to play
    And dance away an idle hour?
Away, thou restless plague, away!
    Nor tempt me to display my power.
Know I was born for nobler things,
And have no time to lose on thee.
See life her radiant visions brings
To greet my sight, and I am free
To choose the dazzling scenes among,
Or fame, or love, or riches, flung
E'en at my feet; or may I stray

In learning's mystic paths, and see
Deep science's mysteries. Then away,
Trifler, I've nought to do with thee.
Youth smiles upon me; life is new,
Hope is beckoning, Joy in view;
What have I to do with thee?
Thou thing of nothing!—What with me?

*   *   *   *   *

Life is passing. Have I found
        Those bright things it promised? Where
Lingers now the magic ground
        To my cheated sight so near?
Yonder—in the distance gleaming
        Far away—far away—
Brightest things are round it beaming,
        Far away—far away.

Buzzing thing, I spurned thee harshly:
        True, thou triflest life away;
But, perchance, 'twas all too rashly
        I condemned thy frolic play.
Glorious visions bade me spurn thee
        As a thing too mean to slight;
Half I from these visions turn me,
        Now to mark thy airy flight.

*   *   *   *

Passing, passing—life is passing;
        Where's the halo of its youth?
Where the shadows I've been tracing?
        Fade they at the glance of truth?
Glimmering yonder—far away,
        Farther yet—farther yet—
Scarce we catch their fading ray,
        Farther yet—farther yet.

Buzzing trifler, can it be
        That, like thine, my hour is past;

Fretting round, that I, like thee,
End with nothing found, at last?
Only thou, perchance more wise,
Contented sought'st no higher bourne;
I proudly could thy course despise,
And aimed at more, and failed, and mourn.

* * * * *

No more passing, now 'tis done:
Life is past, life is past,
All its fading visions gone,
Past—all now are past.

Hither turn thee, buzzing thing,
On thy careless, fluttering wing;
Kindly I can greet thee now,
For I've learned, too well, to know
My life, like thine, an endless chase,
Where all we find is change of place:
New scenes to drive the old away,
Mine passed in labour, thine in play.
No more I spurn thee, thoughtless one,
For nought remains; tho' both are gone,
One only lesson learned, I find
That lesson which makes harshness kind,
And humbles pride, and teaches man
More justly his own rights to scan;
Nor deem that he is made to spurn
Or, with contemptuous glance, to turn
E'en from a buzzing thing like thee.
That lesson is humility:
The truest, last, and wisest thing
Which life in varying search can bring;
A lesson built upon the wrecks
Of shattered hopes—pride crushed to earth.
E'en where our fancied Wisdom breaks
Her useless wand, the true has birth.[31]

31. "The Village Churchyard," l. 251 ("The fairy wand of pleasure, broken lies"); Shakespeare, *The Tempest* 5.1.54–57

My Dream Child

It came on a beam from yon heaven-lit star,
 And I knew not but darkly the things which it spoke;
But, tho' strange were its tones as they fell on my ear,
 My heart beat with fear, lest its spell should be broke.

It came on a rain-drop, as pure as the tear
 Which trembles and glistens in Innocence' eye;
And its whispers were strange as some far-distant sphere,
 And I loved it: my heart knew, words cannot say, why.

It came in the silence, when quiet was flung
 O'er earth, nor winds whispered, nor murmured the stream.
In the stillness it lingering over me hung,
 And my heart throbbed to clasp it, the child of my dream.

And wild were the thoughts that it waked in my soul,
 And wild were the feelings it roused in my breast;
My being was wrapped in its presence, and full
 Of things and of thoughts which must die unexpressed.

And I knew them not;
 They were strangers there;
Not of thoughts forgot,
 Nor of things, tho' fair,
That ever my mortal eye had loved;
They were wanderers from far realms that roved;
They were nor of earth, nor of air, nor of sea;
They were things which *are* not, which may not be;
Thoughts of a dream, which come and go;
Thoughts we may feel, but may not show;
Thoughts which are born for ourselves alone;
Thoughts we must mourn when they are gone.

Bright as beam of heavenly birth,
 Pure as rain-drop from on high
Ere it meets the soil of earth,
 Comes it from yon ether sky:

The child of my dream—thought's untamed creation,
Which bends o'er its parent in silent compassion,
To wake some wild fancy that soothes life away,
And makes me forget the tired thing called *today.*

Spirit of the Storm

Wild spirit of the storm, who rid'st the blast,
And in the growling thunder speak'st thy rage,
Would I could soar with thee!
Untamed, unfettered, roaming through the vast
Expanse of universe from age to age,
'Tis thine, thine! to be free!
'Tis mine, to lie, and grovel in the dust,
And wonder at thy might,
And, in admiring amazement lost,
To tremble at the terrors of thy fearful night.

But no! with thee my spirit longs to rise;
It doth not tremble. Genius of the storm!
Thou art but tameless, wild,
As I would be, could I enfranchise
My chained being—cast off the grovelling worm.
Nature's untamed storm-child,
With thee the whirlwind in its might I'd ride,
Revel in the howling blast,
Play with the forked lightnings, and deride
The timorous world, by thee with weary fears harassed.

Borne on the hurricane's extended wing,
And in the whirlwind sweeping over earth—
Then, in the billowy deep,
To wake the voice of Discord, mastering
The ocean's stillness, to riot giving birth
In those still caves where sleep
In silent majesty is wont to reign,
Would I could roam with thee!
The throbbing wish bounds in my every vein:
Wild spirit of the storm! like thee, I would be free.

Pretty Fanny

Reared in shades and sweet seclusion,
    Far from worldly noise and strife,
Fanny, free from man's intrusion,
    Passed her tranquil, happy life.

Friends, 'tis true, she had not many;
    But a Grandame good and wise
Ruled the thoughts of pretty Fanny,
    More than learned, in her eyes.

Not the Delphic priestess ever,
    Pythoness, or Sibyl, grave,
To her votaries could deliver
    Such wise saws as Grannie gave.

To dispute them, pretty Fanny
    Would have thought the strangest thing!
Who could know so well as Grannie?
    Who could such wise reasons bring?

Thus life passed its happy morning
    Like the dawn of summer's day;
Innocence each spot adorning
    With her dew-drop's purest ray.

But the quiet waking over,
    Fanny sighs, she knows not why;
Grannie's wisdom to discover,
    Still her docile heart doth try.

Spurns not at the dullest lesson,
    Which her childish ear hath schooled;
Owns, by prudence and discretion
    Maidens should be always ruled.

Ne'er disputes—for Grandame says—
    That man's a heartless, false deceiver;
Believes, from him a maiden's ways
    'Tis Heaven's best mercy to deliver;

Owns that wives have much to suffer;
That such fate 'tis wise to dread;
Thinks a husband or a lover
Is a thing to shun indeed;

Deems the wisest thing for Fanny
Is to fly his flattering tongue;
But sometimes wonders what her Grannie
Thought of men, when *she* was young.

'Tis very strange, but not less certain,
Once she was a wedded wife—
Fanny sighed, and dropped the curtain
O'er *that* blot in Grannie's life.

But, in sighing, still she ponders
How that false deceiver, man,
With his tongue could do such wonders,
More than Grannie's wisdom can.

While she lingered thus o'er cases
For philosophy too deep,
Lost in theoretic mazes,
Fanny's prudence fell asleep.

And one day, when, o'er her bending,
Softly woo'd a lovesick youth,
All these thoughts their shadows blending,
For herself she sought the truth.

"Perchance"—the gentle sceptic dreaming
Whispered to her timid heart—
"Perchance 'tis but to Grannie's seeming
That men act so sad a part;

"Surely there is nought so fearful
In the gentle voice I hear;
I'll look—tho' I'll be very careful—
See if there's *really* much to fear."

Fanny, boldly thus resolving,
    Tow'rds the youth her eyes doth bend;
Perhaps she hoped, by thus revolving
    Their magic orbs, to chase the fiend.

Alas! the fate of sceptics ever,
    Waited on poor Fanny's doubt.
Dare but one pris'ner to deliver,
    He's sure to let another out.

The eye that, with love's radiance beaming,
    Caught the glance of pretty Fanny,
Oped such worlds to her wild dreaming,
    That quite forgot was poor old Grannie.

Men were false, she never doubted;
    But *he* whispered, they were true.
'Twas strange how much that whisper routed,
    What resistance it o'erthrew.

Men were fickle, harsh, unkind:
    What a world of faults disgraced them!
But *he* smiled, and Fanny's mind
    Deemed that Grannie had misplaced them.

Thus from doubt to doubt she threaded—
    Grannie's lessons all forgot—
Fanny soon was what she dreaded,
    And a wedded life her lot.

Would ye follow pretty Fanny?
    Learn the end of her career?
Perchance you'll find some withered Grannie,
    Lecturing in a maiden's ear.

While the blooming lass, ne'er doubting,
    All her lessons sage receives;
Till one glance their phalanx routing,
    Like her Grannie, she believes.

The Bright Sun

The bright sun! the bright sun!
He smiles, though our tears flow.
The bright sun! the bright sun!
He smiles upon our wo.
Upon the earth,
In wo or mirth,
Alike he smiles unceasing;
And care may sleep,
Or bid us weep,
Without his smiles decreasing.
The bright sun! the bright sun!
He smiles, tho' our tears flow.
The bright sun! the bright sun!
He smiles upon our wo.

Oh! is it that he mocks
Alike man's griefs and cares,
And high in glory stalks,
Unconscious of our tears?
Or doth he smile
But to beguile
Our suffering and our sorrow?
Sent by the God
Who marks his road
To bid us hope—tomorrow?
The bright sun! the bright sun!
He smiles, tho' our tears flow.
But kindly smiles the bright sun:
'Tis to beguile our wo.

The Mirage

As phantom shapes on sea or sand,
Waked by the mirage fairy hand,
Light and gay,
Bid Fancy play,

While the weary wanderer smiling
Hails their lovely forms beguiling:

As they vanish at his tread,
Castle, hill, and valley, fled;
        Vale and mountain,
        Stream and fountain,
Leave the desert and the sea
One trackless waste, one boundless way:

Thus our dreams, asleep or waking,
Brightest forms and visions taking,
        Not from earth
        They hold their birth,
And at mortal touch they die;
We may gaze—approach—they fly,

Flitting through th' abstracted mind,
When earth, with all the cares that bind
        Our grovelling way
        To things of clay,
Leaves us happy, leaves us free
To fancy all that may not be.

Seem they not of heavenly birth?
Sky-born things, come down to earth?
        Lightning's gleam?
        Stars which beam?
Stooping from their high career,
To light and bless, and cheer us here?

So pure, 'twere vain to try to grasp:
We may dream, but dare not clasp.
        Fade they must;
        Mortal dust
May not touch them: mirage fair,
They have vanished into air.

The Village Churchyard[32]

Unwalled, thrown open
To the public gaze, the vulgar tread,
Yon ruined churchyard lies. Forgotten now,
The tales of wo these little mounds once told;
Forgotten—yet Imagination's eye
Discovers still the sorrows they revealed,
And, peeping 'neath the grassy turf, may read
Where mouldering bones lie shrinking from the day,
Hiding themselves beneath fresh budding flowers:
E'en as tired hearts will wrap themselves from light,
Concealing, in the dark recess of thought,
Their worn-out strength, their fearful rottenness,
And deck with smiles an ever-varying brow,
Which wraps their veiled sorrows; as yon turf,
In its green bosom, holds embraced a corpse,
Seeming the fresher and the gayer for
The rotten thing which, mouldering, crumbles there.
See, here and there, some mossy stone declares,
One raised above the common herd there sleeps.
'Tis here, perhaps, the venerable sire,
The patriarch of the village, lowly lies
Unconscious of the tears his loss calls forth.
By him unheeded rise the plaints of wo;
No longer now he hears the voice of grief;
No longer now his ready hand is raised
To hush its clamourings. Here he sleeps, and here
Want wails a father, misery weeps a friend.
A little farther—here to dust returned—
Behold the statesman lies. Ambition's slave,
By fame and glory's glittering bait drawn on,
He sought new honours, rose above the sphere
Of this his little world. The village left,
His humble birth despised, he seeks, he gains
All that the world can give—but, all being gained,
He, sighing, feels the want of something more.
Earth's glittering toys are shattered in his grasp;

32. Cf. Thomas Gray, "Elegy Written in a Country Churchyard"; Oliver Goldsmith, *The Deserted Village;* George Crabbe, *The Village.*

Her gilded baubles show their nothingness;
Deluded, grieved, he throws the world away,
And comes to lay his bones with kindred dust.
Life's visionary joys, her little cares
All passed alike, oblivion now has seized.
But see yon grave, with summer flowers decked,
The emblems of its tenant. Bright they bloom,
Today how frailly fair, tomorrow—gone!
'Twas thus with her whose grave they now adorn.
The village beauty she, so gentle, fair,
That all must love: so good, no rival mourned
Her far excelling charms. Beloved, admired,
She knew her beauty's power; and, although
A little pride might sometimes swell her breast
When all adored, 'twas Nature bade it rise,
And quick 'twas checked by wiser thoughts.
None ever called her proud; none called her vain.
But there's one common doom for all of earth,
And, with the vilest, fairest flowers must die.
The Autumn leaves fall thickest, but in Spring
The blighting mildew, or the chilling blast,
May nip them in the bud, and bid them fade.
Thus passed she, like the bud whose tender bloom,
By some untoward blast—a lingering sigh
Of Winter, ere he sinks into his grave—
Too early stricken, droops its head and dies,
Ere yet its blighted bloom had learned to know
Why it was born to deck this changing world.
Its lesson all unlearned, it shrank away
From the rude touch which on life's threshold met
Its tender bloom: perchance, but happier in
Its early fate. It might have lived to ope;
Then to be crushed by some unthinking hand;
Or in its blooming beauties gathered but
To be the scorn and mockery, e'en of those
Who plucked it from its stem, and cast it forth
To wither 'neath the stern decree, which dooms,
To ignominy and shame, the trembling thing,
Whose weakness may not let it dare a world
Too harsh, too cold, for aught which has not strength
To meet the torrent, and the whirlwind crash,

The wild commotion of an o'erwrought mind;
Or, ceding to its maddening influence, stand
To boldly face the chilling, icy blast
That hisses o'er it shame and obloquy.
She died. And round her tomb we fancy still
That voice, whose thrilling sound so sweetly tuned
Its modulated tones to gentlest thoughts.
Its soft tones speak of death; yet, if we weep,
We dare not weep for her, but for ourselves,
Ourselves, who linger here to watch the fading
Of fairest things, which, frailest, e'en are dearest.
That very weakness which we tremble for
Wakes hourly some new fear, and fear wakes hope,
Until our thought and being all seem wrapped
To shield the fragile thing from every breath
Which sways it, tottering on its pedestal.
It falls; and, gazing o'er its shattered wrecks,
We scarce can deem that centre of our mind,
That object round which all our feelings cling,
That idol of our heart, has passed away,
And we are lingering here. We touch ourselves,
As though misdoubting life, and wondering if
Ourselves are breathing, thinking, sentient things,
Or but the phantasms of some wild thought,
Strange, hideous nothings, which must pass away
And leave the purer air: some
Dread spectre which thus mocks us with ourselves.
We touch, and start to feel that we are still
Sensible, palpable, and full of being,
While IT lies there, a thing, but not of life.
        But whose is this? the low, the lonely grave?
No kindly hand has scattered flowerets here;
No weeping mourner here bewails the loss
Of father, brother, friend. No kindred tear
Bedews his turf; no sympathizing eye
Has marked the spot where the lone wanderer lies.
A stranger, poor, deserted, and alone,
Life had no friendly hand to ease its load,
And death no comfort to allay its pang.
The wandering, friendless, houseless stranger, here
At last has found the resting-place he sought;

At length he now no longer stands alone;
No longer now his heaving bosom pants,
And seeks in every fellow-man a friend.
Neglected, and alone, he breathed his last.
In agony he moaned; no answering sigh
Responsive rose. One tear, one struggling groan,
One gasping sigh, and the world fades before him:
Its last wild hope, his heart hath throbbed away;
No more its noisy beatings cheat his ear,
And bid him catch some passing footstep's tread,
E'en in that sound which speaks his solitude.
No more the gurgling of his spasm'd throat,
In the dead stillness echoed loudly back
Upon his listening ear, bids him arouse
His dying powers, and, turning, think to find
Some kindly lingerer o'er his dying couch.
'Tis done; and (as his tired heart) for him
The world and all its turmoil, now, is still.
How silent is the grave! Forgotten here
Life's agitating dream, in quiet lie
Mingling their dust, "th' oppressor, and th' oppressed."[33]
The poor, the rich, the humble, and the proud,
Alike each has his little spot of earth,
And none, the most ambitious, wishes more.
Here ends our every hope, our every fear;
Here avarice forgets to hoard, and here
Ambition's dreams must end. Here poverty
No longer pines. Here misery's sighs are hushed.
Here all may rest, in quiet undisturbed.
The dead may rest, but here the living mourn,
As o'er the earthy tenements they bend
Of those they love. Lo! where a mother stands,
In speechless, lost, bewildered agony.
Her one, her only hope, her cherished boy,
Untimely snatched by Death's relentless hand,
She seeks to weep, but tears refuse to flow;
Her bursting heart weeps blood. She seeks to pray,

33. Alexander Pope, *Windsor-Forest,* ll. 317–18: Henry VI and Edward IV (both buried in St. George's Chapel at Windsor) "the Grave unites; where ev'n the Great find Rest, / And blended lie th' Oppressor and th' Oppresst."

But on her faltering tongue the accents die;
Her wandering thoughts no longer seek her God;
Her head and heart, alike, are filled—they burst—
With the one, sole, and all-engrossing thought:
Her one—her only stay—her hope, is gone!
    A little farther, here a father stands,
Bowed less with age than grief. A single tear,
Drawn from the bosom's agony, flows down
His manly cheek; unchecked, unbidden flows;
He knows nor feels it not; his heaving breast
Seems rising 'gainst its load, as 't could repel
The grief which weighs upon it. Snatch'd in youth's prime,
He mourns, to him the loveliest, and the best:
His age's comfort, and his brightest hope
In life's decline; the last connecting link
Which bound to earth his wishes and his hopes.
All now lie buried in the grave of her,
The last of all who lived to call him father.
But hark! what shriek is that which sudden breaks
Upon the silence of this still retreat,
And, echoing through the chambers of the dead,
Thrills on each heart, and hushes every moan?
Each listener, startled from his own despair,
Feels there's an agony which can exceed
The gnawing grief, which bids his heartstrings crack;
Each for one moment quite forgets his wo,
And shuddering asks, from whence the fearful sound?
Behold! 'tis here. The lovely maniac darts
Across my path. And hark! another shriek
Of wild despair, rings through the vaulted heaven!
And then a long, loud, hollow laugh, which seems
To mock the startled echoes, which repeat,
From hill to hill, the dismal cry of wo.
Now, at the foot of yonder grave she falls,
And pleads the quick return of him she loves;
And chides, and wonders that he stays so long;
Then murmuring asks, whither and why he's gone?
Poor mourner, cease; thy useless wailings hush;
And if thou canst, if feeble reason yet
A glimmering ray can lend, look round and learn
That thine is but the fate of all who tread

This world of wo. Thine's but a varied shade
Of human misery, that all on earth must share.
"Who breathes must suffer, and who thinks must mourn."[34]
The sting Death (which [is] at our birth received)
Poisons and irritates our struggling life,
Until, at last, the venom does its part,
And we, too weak to struggle longer—die.
Here, bent beneath affliction's iron hand,
The widowed mother bows. See meagre Want,
And hungry Poverty, and all the woes
That sorrowing flesh can feel, their victim claim.
The mother sees, and shuddering at the train
Of threatened ills, her helpless infant clasps.
"Poor baby! what hath life in store for thee?"
She murmuring asks. "Ah! what for thee the world?
Thou see'st not, know'st not yet, the scowling train,
Who watch thee for their prey. See Poverty,
Who leads the band, while close behind her, look,
Lean Hunger pines. Then follows cruel Scorn,
Who smiling lifts her scorpion lash, and laughs
And points at Shame; pale Shame, who shrinking shuns
The passing glance, and cowers at every look.
Then see cold Pity comes, her pittance drops,
And passes on, forgetting the kind word,
The look of sympathy, which eases wo,
And soothes the wounded heart—the bread she gives
Is bitter, and the noble heart rejects it.
Close on her steps, heartless Neglect draws near;
And, led by her, behold the fiend—Despair;
Despair, who, darkening e'en this gloomy view,
Drives off the wretch's only comfort—Hope."
The mother stops in speechless agony,
And thick the tears fall on her thoughtless babe,
Who smiles unconscious of its parent's wo.
Smile on, poor babe! smile on, while yet thou may'st;
Too soon, alas! thou, too, must learn to know
That life's a bitter cup. We taste—and taste,
And try to think it sweet; and then, although

34. Matthew Prior, *Solomon* 3.240–41: "Who breathes, must suffer; and who thinks, must mourn; / And he alone is blessed, who ne'er was born."

We loathe the sickening draught, again we taste,
And still, as muddier grow the dregs, taste on,
And fancy coming sweets we never find.
        The happiest life, what is it but a dream?
A ceaseless search for pleasures never found:
Bright fairy shapes, which glitter and attract
As we approach them, vanish into air,
And leave us gazing round in stupid vacancy,
Until another dazzling shadow comes
Across our path, and we resume the chase?
'Tis not until the chilling hand of death
Is laid upon the sleeper that he wakes:
At that cold touch, we start and look around
On all for which we've toil'd. Alas! how changed![35]
Our hoarded gold, shines now but glittering dust;
Ambition's wreaths are withered in our grasp;
The fairy wand of pleasure, broken lies;
All which we saw, in Hope's bright, flattering glass,
Is now reflected back, by dull reality;
We see its nothingness, and turn away,
Sighing to think how long we've been deceived.
        But may I not—here by the charnel'd dead—
Learn, yet in life, one lesson which regret
Need never follow? There is a wisdom
Sleeps among these graves. Woes stalk around us,
Spectre-like they rise; but there's an angel form
Which follows them—though tearful, lovely too.
'Tis by the grave, 'tis in the house of wo,
We find her lingering. Man to man she binds
In the strong brotherhood of sorrow. Never
Midst joy and laughter, doth man know his heart.
It wakes to consciousness but in that grief

35. Alexander Pope, *Eloisa to Abelard,* ll. 99–100: "Alas, how chang'd! what sudden horrors rise! / A naked Lover bound and bleeding lies!" Also, John Milton, *Paradise Lost* 1.84–87: "But O how fallen! how changed / From him, who in the happy realms of light / Clothed with transcendent brightness didst outshine / Myriads though bright"; Byron, *Childe Harold's Pilgrimage* 2.711: "In all save form alone, how chang'd!" These in turn are derived from Vergil *Aeneid* 2.274–76: "quantum mutatus ab illo / Hectore qui redit exuvias indutus Achilli / vel Danaum Phrygios iaculatus puppibus ignis!" ("How changed from that Hector who returned, clothed in the spoils of Achilles, or having flung Phrygian fires into the ships of the Danaans!").

Which tells him, *men are brothers.* Man learns then
To worship the great majesty of man.
'Tis sorrow raises thee above the brute;
'Tis sorrow wakes the heart, the mind, the soul,
And rouses up the Deity within thee;
'Tis sorrow which inspires the poet's song,
Which breathes its life in fire-tongued eloquence,
And stamps its burning words upon the heart;
'Tis sorrow makes thee *man.* And, onward still,
'Tis Sorrow bids thee soar above the world,
Forget the petty cares of flesh, and live
In the great *soul of being. God,* I bow
To *her,* thine handmaiden. From soul to soul,
She leads me on to *thee,* thou *first great soul,*
*Creation's all—Infinite Being—*God!

Oh! Would That I Could Dream On Still

Oh! would that I could dream on still
  Of brighter things than these!
But motley hues our dreams must fill
  From life's reflected rays.

And life is but a Harlequin,
  In various colours dressed,
Where virtue mingles in with sin,
  Where joys with sorrows rest;

Where tears and smiles divide the eye,
  Nor fear or hope comes single;
Where laughter's echoed by a sigh,
  Where cares with pleasures mingle.

And now 'tis sad, and now 'tis bright,
  Now sunshine, and now gloom;
The smiles of day touch close on night,
  The cradle on the tomb.

Then let us choose
The rainbow hues.
What though their colours fade?
When frowns the past,
To Lethe cast
Its every darker shade.

Sweet, sweet are the blossoms; their beauties let's seize,
Nor mourn that the morrow must see their decay;
Bright, bright is the sun; let us bask in his rays,
Nor weep that his brightness is passing away.

The flow'rets, 'tis true, will too soon cease to bloom,
But why not enjoy all their sweets ere they're past?
The bright sun, alas! will too soon sink to gloom,
But are his smiles less bright, so long as they last?

Oh! better, far better, to gather the flowers,
And, while their sweets last, to make them all our own.
Oh! better, far better, in sunshiny hours,
To bask in the rays of the comforting sun.

What tho' soon, too soon, must be withered the flowers?
What tho' the bright sun doth already decline?
Oh! still while they last, let us yet make them ours;
And, when they are gone, 'twill be time to repine.

2.

Poems from the Southern Literary Gazette

Look Not Back

A tear and a smile for the scenes long gone by,
    Fond memory calls as I look o'er the past,
But in vain the faint smile seeks to brighten the eye,
    For the tear comes and drowns its young sunshine as fast.

Oh! memory, why would'st thou bid them contend?
    'Tis vainly the poor smile thy mandate must hear;
It but struggles to live, ere its bright course must end,
    For the eye that looks back, is the home of the tear.

Then, man, look not back when thy course is begun;
    When thy plough's in the furrow, withdraw not thy hand;
But bravely push on, till that course, fully run,
    Proclaims that the goal, by the victor is gained.

Look not back; for the soldier, who flinches, has lost
    His place in the battle, and trampled must lie;

Southern Literary Gazette, n.s., 1 (Feb. 21, 1852): 94 ("Look Not Back"), (March 6, 1852): 112 ("Constancy"), 2 (Nov. 13, 1852): 226 ("Guardian Angels"). Each poem is signed "L. S. M."

While the brave heart, who dares to stand firm at his post,
Shouts victory, whether he conquer or die.

The proud soul that shrinks not, can never be crushed,
Nor surrenders before the hard buffets of life;
His body, the armour, he leaves in the dust,
But the spirit unconquered, sinks not in the strife.

Aim then at the future; strive on in your might!
Child of Earth, like the Eaglet, gaze still at the sun.
Look not back! look not back! With your soul in the fight,
Keep your eye on the goal, till life's duty is done.

Constancy

"Why should I prate of Constancy
While Nature's law is change?
Or why confined to sameness be,
While Fancy bids me range?

"Creation's universal voice
Th' ideal thing mocks away;
And every morrow's dawn destroys
The tissue of today.

"The flitting clouds a form scarce know
Ere varying they are seen,
In newer shapes their masses throw,
Forget what they have been.

"The waters of yon flowing stream,
When mingled with the sea,
Scattering midst ocean's waves, ne'er deem
That here their home should be.

"The Zephyr breezes sweetly woo;
But roaming unconfined,
Oh! who can call the Zephyr true?
Or who his homage bind?

"And this our Earth, as fickle quite,
Now flowers, now thorns displays,
And sunshine mingling in with night
Now shuns, now gilds our days.

"If earth, air, sky, and waters teem
But with incessant change,
What foolish fancy then would deem
That I'm forbid to range?

"No, no, I'll laugh at Constancy,
And with the Zephyr woo;
Changing and fickle I will be,
And, as the Zephyr, true."

Thus sang a youth whose shallow mind
Creation's surface swept,
Nor (like the insect on the rind)
The fruit's ripe flavour reaped.

Then, whispering clear, a voice replied,
"Not thus man's soul shall read;
'Tis thus that folly doth deride
Deep truths from folly hid.

"Earth's changes here, like sighs and tears,
Light o'er the surface skim;
But deeper moral still she bears
God's holy truths to hymn.

"In constant, never varying rule,
Each atom finds its course;
Majestic order through the whole,
Majestic laws enforce.

"And man best works his Maker's law,
When earnest thoughts declare,
And earnest word and action show,
God's truth is everywhere."

Guardian Angels

Echoing from yon rose-tree's branches,
Laughter pealing long and gay,
Merriest tones mirth heavenward launches—
There my children are at play.

Honey-suckle tendrils twining,
Grasping catch their wavy hair;
While their mirthful eyes peep shining
As though stars were glimmering there,

In and out, 'midst flowers gleaming
Glistening now, and now withdrawn,
As 't were heaven-sent sun-rays beaming
Light from angel-watchers down.

And are not these angels?—watching
Every step and look?
Beam these eyes not near us, snatching
Young ideas from thoughts unspoke?

Yes; untaught they learn to know them;
From my heart each thought they win.
Can I dare that heart to show them
Torn with passion, smirched with sin?

No, my babies! Echoing round me,
When I hear your voices thus,
Heavenly links I feel have bound me,
Which I may not, dare not, loose.

Ye my guardian angels linger,
Bidding me each thought review;
And I feel that Heaven's finger
Points me to the right through you.

3.

Woman's Progress

And is this progress? Are these noisy tongues—
In fierce contention raised and angry war—
Fit boast for womanhood? Yon shrewish things,
In wordy boisterous debate—are these
Perfected woman's exponents to show
Her model virtues to a later age?
And shall our daughters cast their woman robes,
A useless cumbrance, aside, to seize
Some freer imitation of the man,
Whose lordly strut and dashing stride attract
Their envious love for notoriety?
Shall they, with flashing eye and clanging tongue,
Mount in the rostrum, lecture in the streets,
And, in the arena of election strife,
Claim with shrill voice, and rude dishevelled locks,
"Your votes! your votes!" ye loud-mouthed populace!
Nay. Should that peach-like cheek but feel the breath
Of yonder foul-mouthed crowd, methinks its bloom
Should wither in the contact. God hath made
A woman-nature holier than the man's—
Purer of impulse, and of gentler mould—

SLM 19 (Nov. 1853): 700–701. The poem is signed "L. S. M."

Let her not stain it in the angry strife
Which these, our modern female Reverends,
Learnèd M.D.'s, and lecturing damsels, seek
To feed their hungry vanity, and bring
Unnoticed charms before the gaping crowd.
'Tis surely not for this that God hath given
That soothing voice, so sweetly taught to whisper
Pity, and hope, and sympathy, and love,
And every holier thought, whose gospel tongue
Can preach its comfort to grief's riven heart!
Here, in the crowd, 'tis harsh and dissonant;
Its softer notes must struggle to a scream
Of impotently shrill, unmeaning effort.
'Tis surely not for this that God hath given
The soft light hand, whose velvet touch can soothe
The achings often both of head and heart.
Here, it would illy stand her in the strife;
And doubled fist, and tiny foot advanced
In attitude of combat, were a mock—
And oh! alas! how foul a mimicry!—
Of man's contemptuous life. 'Tis not for this,
Sweet Sisters! not for this! that God hath given
That purer soul, whose impulse (like the flower
Instinct with life that ever seeks the sun
And in his rays doth live) turns to the truth
And loves, and hopes, and doth expand itself
Only to nobler instincts! Stronger to hope,
Loftier to bear than man's; yet meeker too
To patiently endure—this soul, methinks,
To strife of grosser passions God formed not.
The fallen woman is the viler man,
Even as her fall is greater. From the height
Of her own nature's lofty pedestal,
She flings herself with grovelling pride, as though
The nightingale should cease its chaunt, and turn
The aspiring wing, which nature taught to rise,
Earthward again, stooping its course to spar
And jangle with some harsh, unnatural note,
In emulation of yon dunghill cock.
Sweet Sister! stoop not thou to be a man!
Man has his place as woman hers; and she,

As made to comfort, minister, and help,
Moulded for gentler duties, ill fulfils
His jarring destinies. Her mission is
To labour and to pray; to help, to heal,
To soothe, to bear; patient, with smiles, to suffer;
And with self-abnegation nobly lose
Her private interest in the dearer weal
Of those she loves and lives for. Call not this
(The all-fulfilling of her destiny,
She the world's soothing mother), call it not,
With scorn and mocking sneer, a drudgery.
The ribald tongue profanes Heaven's holiest things,
But holy still they are. The lowliest tasks
Are sanctified in nobly acting them.
Christ washed the apostles' feet, nor thus cast shame
Upon the God-like in him. Woman lives
Man's constant prophet. If her life be true
And based upon the instincts of her being,
She is a living sermon of that truth,
Which ever through her gentle actions speaks,
That life is given to labour and to love.
Through this rough world her angel ministry,
Like sweetest water bubbling through the sands
Of arid desert, cheers the weary heart,
And leads the restless soul which cursed its fate
To pause, to think, and learn to love that God
Who, midst the parching waste of suffering,
Has dropped this comfort like a boon from Heaven
To bid him drink and live.
                                        Sweet Sisters! thus
God wills that we should be; and who profanes
This, the last formed, so the most perfect, work
Of His creative will—this woman nature—
Who seeks to drag it down, to smirch and blot
Its purer being with the tainting blight
Of passion's license, doth profane the hope
Of God's creation; doth blot out the light;
Sully the purest beam of reasoning life,
And cast man's nature back upon the beast
To strive and grovel in the lowest lusts
Of passion's vile excess. As God is love,
So reasoning nature lives in him through love;

And Woman in the trueness of her being
Is still the never-ceasing minister
Of love which wearies not, which toils and bears,
And, sorrowing for the loved ones, doth forget
Her own life's anguish, soothing others' woes.
Then let our holy task be still to cleanse,
But not to change, our natures. Let us strive
To be *more* woman—never to be man.
These reverend Misses, doctors in mob caps,
And petticoated lecturers, are things
Which make us loathe, like strange unnatural births,
Nature's disordered works. Yon chirping thing
That with cracked voice, and mincing manners, prates
Of rights and duties, lecturing to the crowd,
And in strange nondescript of dress arrays
Unfettered limbs that modesty should hide;
Thus raising, as it were, rebellion's flag
Against her being's nature—call it not,
Sweet Sisters, call not that unsexèd thing
By the pure name of Woman. Let us strive
With silent effort in the Woman's cause,
Perfecting, in its destinies, our sex,
And cast aside this foul attempt which clings
To degradation as it were our pride.
Oh! let us be the woman of God's make;
No Mrs. Bloomer, Abby Kelly thing
Aping man's vices, while our weaker frame
Knows not his harsher virtues.[1] Let us be
Strong—but as Woman; resolute in right—
All woman—perfect woman—no false ape—
No monster birth—no female Caliban,
Mocking our nature with unnatural shades
Of strange and foul resemblance.[2] Gentle, pure,

1. Amelia Jenks Bloomer (1818–94), woman's rights advocate; founder and editor of the journal *Lily* (1849–55); promoted the item of apparel now named for her, on which see *PSE,* "Woman and Her Needs," p. 142n. Abigail Kelley Foster (1810–87), born in Pelham, Mass.; abolitionist and woman's rights advocate.

2. *Othello* 1.3.401–2: "Hell and night / Must bring this monstrous birth to the world's light"; *Hamlet* 1.5.27–28: "Murder most foul, as in the best it is, / But this most foul, strange and unnatural." The use of "resemblance" is Miltonic: *Paradise Lost* 4.363–64, 6.114–15, 9.538.

Kind, loving Woman never can degrade
Her own God-given nature. Only then
When she distorts it to unnatural ends
Doth she degrade her being. Man may rail,
Or mock, or pity her; with tyrant strength
May trample on her weakness, or may sneer
As though his being were of higher mould;
But not for this is she degraded; rather
Ennobled, in the gently bearing it.
There is no degradation which springs not
From our own inmost being. Noble things
Are never trampled into meanness. Low
May be their uses, but vile purposes
Soil not the diamond's hue. Our inmost worth,
At our own heart's tribunal, rights itself,
And e'en midst persecution calmly rests
On its proud consciousness. A noble thing
Is Woman's undistorted nature. Let
No taunt, nor jeer, sweet Sisters, shame us from it.
Woman, true Woman, is of larger worth
Than rank or power can fashion. Far above
All that the loud reformer ever dreamed,
Her virtues are no wordy theories,
But sky-born instincts touching on our earth
Still in full flower from Heaven.

4.

Later Poems

What Used to Be

Happiness that ne'er was fading,
Dreams that darkness ne'er was shading,
Flowers that were not born to wither:
These are things I used to see!
Fancy, aye the future wooing,
Hope, her heavenward course pursuing,
Pluming each unruffled feather:
These are things that used to be!

Of the three poems designated in this edition by the title "Later Poems," the first two were published in Sargent, *Harper's Cyclopaedia of British and American Poetry,* pp. 675–76; they were presumably selected from those sent to Sargent by Louisa Smythe, "some little fugitive pieces cut from newspapers which seem to me better than some of those in the book [*My Dreams*]" (see *PSE,* app. 3). Sargent's selection, which also includes excerpts from *Caius Gracchus* ("To My Son," 2.4.16–28, 56–60, 3.1.76–83, 5.4.68–74), carries the following headnote (derived from William Porcher Miles' sketch, *PSE,* pp. 485–88): "Mrs. Louisa S. McCord / American / Mrs. McCord (1810–1879) was the daughter of Langdon Cheves, a distinguished lawyer and statesman, who as member of Congress helped Clay and Calhoun to carry the declaration of war in 1812. She inherited much of her father's intellectual vigor, and wrote ably on politics and political economy, translating Bastiat's well-known work. She married a prominent lawyer, the well-known author of *McCord's Reports.* Her first essay in poetry was a little volume entitled *My Dreams,* published in 1848. This was followed in 1851 by *Caius Gracchus,* a tragedy in five acts, abounding in striking passages, full of noble thought

But alas! their transient being
To the future's night was fleeing;
And, when brightest, they were fading,
        Those bright things I used to see!
Life no more such pleasures giving,
Memory, with our present striving,
All her stock of joys unlading,
        Points us to what used to be.

But doth not this past deceive us,
Cheating thus, with joys that leave us,
Souls which have a higher duty
        Than those things I used to see?
These were toys for youthful folly;
Life has duties high and holy—
Robed in Truth's, not Fancy's, beauty
        Like those things that used to be—

Duties holy, duties binding,
Where the soul, its errors finding,
Reason's light from Truth deriving,
        Learns, those things it used to see
Were but beacon-lights, to guide us
Where life's battle-fields betide us;
Where, in nobler efforts striving,
        We forget what used to be.

---

aptly expressed. Though not written for the stage, it has many flashes of dramatic power. Born to affluence, literature was to her, however, a pastime rather than a pursuit. A devoted daughter of the State of her birth, proud of its history, and sensitive to its honor, she generously gave her aid to the South in its struggle for independence, sincerely believing she was on the side of right. Her only son, Cheves McCord, fell gallantly in battle. To the mother's heart it was a fatal blow. She was a large contributor, both in money and personal effort, to the hospitals and other institutions, and she lived to be cheered by the dawn of brighter prospects for South Carolina."

The third poem is an untitled holographic draft, probably to be dated to 1876, found among other notes related to LSM's "Memoir of Langdon Cheves," in the Langdon Cheves I Papers, SCHS. Its verse and meter (heroic couplets, concluding with a triplet and alexandrine), otherwise not to be observed in LSM's poetry, together with the diction, suggest that it was an attempt to imitate the panegyrical style of the seventeenth and eighteenth centuries, and of John Dryden in particular, and may have been intended as an introductory poem (compare the dedicatory poems in *My Dreams* and *Caius Gracchus*) to the prose work on her father, fuller than the extant "Memoir," which LSM seems to have been contemplating.

Thy Will Be Done

Thy will be done! Almighty God,
Our weakness knows no other prayer
        But this: "God's will be done!"
We cannot shape our future good;
To mark thy mercy's bounds we fear:
        Father! thy will be done!

Still to our weakness clinging fast,
With naught to point or guide our way,
        We cry, "God's will be done!"
And 'mid the storm of life, the blast
Of warring tempest, still we say,
        "Father! thy will be done!"

And this the surest charm to lull
The tempest in its raging might,
        Great God! thy will be done!
Should universal nature fall
To wreck and ruin, 'mid its Night,
        Father! thy will be done!

We know that Thou canst guide us best;
And if we live, or if we die,
        Thy will, oh God! be done!
Our weakness seeks on thee to rest;
It loves to cling to thee and cry,
        "Father! thy will be done!"

[On Langdon Cheves]

Look at the statesman, husband, Father, friend[.]
Alike in each his varying virtues blend[.]
Nought on the Earth can tempt him fr[o]m his way[;]
Glory unheeded leads him not astray.
Duty but points, no other path he views[:]
Onward the track of Honour he pursues[.]
Not gold he seeks nor fame. But truth's own star[,]

Changing with no fantastic beam afar,
He sees near, guiding always with firm light[,]
Ever unwavering, ever calmly bright.
Vain fancy tempts him not to turn aside—
Eternal duty, honour, truth abide[;]
Strongly he follows on, and knows no path beside—

Part II

DRAMA

5.

Caius Gracchus
A Tragedy in Five Acts

The seeming truth which cunning times put on
To entrap the wisest.

Merchant of Venice[1]

To My Son

Too young thou art to read a Mother's heart;
Too young to guess that quenchless fount of love
Which ever gushes forth in joy and woe,
Limitless, always. If careworn and sad,
By want or sickness bowed almost to earth—
Or yet if triumphing in life's success,
Flattered, beloved, admired—the Mother finds
(Be she true woman with a woman's heart)
No moment when that heart can idly rest
From the long love which ever fetters it
In bondage to her child. My boy, thine eye
Some day perchance may fall upon these lines;

Caius Gracchus: A Tragedy in Five Acts (New York: H. Kernot, 1851). LSM's source for the outline of the plot, and for much of its detail, is *Gaius Gracchus* by the Greek biographer Plutarch (c. A.D. 46–after 120). In the notes below to the play, all dates are B.C. Gracchus' *praenomen* is more accurately spelled "Gaius" (abbreviation "C."), and thus it is given in the notes when referring to the historical Gracchus; when to LSM's character, "Caius" is retained.

1. *Merchant of Venice* 3.2.97–101: "Thus ornament is but the guiled shore / To a most dangerous sea: the beauteous scarf / Veiling an Indian beauty; in a word, / The seeming truth which cunning times put on / To entrap the wisest."

And, catching here the shadow of my love,
Thy soul may guess its fullness, and may feel,
Through every struggle in this changing life,
That, like a guardian angel hovering round,
To comfort, check—to pity, or to blame—
To chide, to hope, to pray—it watching stands,
But never to condemn. A Mother's heart
Might throb itself away in patient woe—
Might break to end its pang—but never, never
Could deem her child a thing of vice or shame.
God bless thee, boy! and make thee stainless, pure,
Upright and true, e'en as my thought doth paint thee.

DRAMATIS PERSONAE[2]

CAIUS GRACCHUS.

OPIMIUS, LUCULLUS, } *Roman Senators.*

POMPONIUS, LICINIUS, } *Friends of Gracchus.*

FULVIUS, *Factious Citizen.*

SEPTIMULEIUS, *Citizen.*

LIVIUS DRUSUS, *Tribune.*

PHILOCRATES, *Slave of Gracchus.*

CORNELIA, *Mother of the Gracchi.*

LICINIA, *Wife of Caius Gracchus.*

Senators, Citizens, Tribune, Child, etc.

SCENE: *Rome; Carthage.*[3]

2. Designated "Characters," and preceding "To My Son," in 1851 ed.
3. "The Scene is at Rome. First Scene of Fourth Act, in Carthage" (1851 ed.).

ACT I.

SCENE I. *A Street of Rome.*

POMPONIUS[4] *and Citizens.*

Pomp. Orestes stays to keep his quaestor with him.[5]
First Cit. And will he bear it, think you?
Pomp. Will who bear it?
First Cit. Why, Caius Gracchus.
Pomp. Truly, I think not.
He's not the man I deem him, if he bear
Outrage so foul and grossly palpable.
No longer mince these senators their doings,
But boldly now (enough that Gracchus did them)
His noblest acts they read in backward sense.
With juggler's slight the cheated eye to trick,
They show black, white; white, black; and merit trip
From virtue into fault.
Second Cit. We've heard the talk
How, when the Senate could not manage it,
He from the cities for our troops procured
Their needed clothing; and how fumed the Senate
Because, forsooth, 'twould make the people love him.
Pomp. Yes, but ye have not heard how, few days since,
Micipsa sent ambassadors to say
That, through regard to Caius Gracchus, he
To our Sardinian troops would furnish corn—
And wot ye, how the Senate sent their thanks?[6]
First Cit. Well, what said they?
Pomp. They said—but mark me well;
Note what paternal love they guard us with—

4. Marcus Pomponius (Rufus?) and Licinius are recorded as the *hetairoi* (comrades) of Gaius Gracchus (Plutarch *Gaius Gracchus* 16.4–17.1). Velleius Paterculus (2.6.6) adds that Pomponius was an *eques* (knight) and compares him in his death to Horatius Cocles, who "kept the bridge" against King Porsenna. See also Valerius Maximus 4.7.2.

5. Lucius Aurelius Orestes as consul in 126 went to Sardinia to suppress an insurrection there and remained as proconsul until 122, when he came back to Rome to celebrate a triumph. Gaius Gracchus was a member of his staff as quaestor but in 124 returned to Rome without his commander's permission.

6. Micipsa (misspelled "Micipia" in 1851 ed.) was, from 148 to 118, king of Numidia, in northern Africa, south and west of Carthage.

They said they would not take one grain of the corn;
Our troops might starve, ere they should live from aid
That through the means of Caius Gracchus came.
First Cit. Fie! Fie! you joke with us! Did they say that?
Pomp. Ay, and the ambassadors, with loud insult thrust
Forth from the Senate-house, were bid begone,
To tell Micipsa that his proffered aid
Rome needed not; that we were rich in corn;
That Caius Gracchus had no other end,
Only his name to wind to Rome, by sending
These hired flatterers of his proud ambition.
Such words, and other oft, as rough repeated,
They were bid take with them, and pushed away
From our proud Senate-halls. And now our troops
May starve, forsooth, or steal, or eat their bucklers.
Ye know, ye Roman citizens, how full
Our granaries are! What though we die like rats,
And through our sewers if dead corpses sweep
Foully putrescent? Our patricians bear
Musk to their noses, scented vinegar,
Snuffing of spices; swear these corpses have
A stench plebeian, most unfit and vexing
To their patrician, nice olfactories!
We die! What then? The Senate is content,
So we live not through Caius Gracchus' means!
First Cit. These are our rich!
Pomp. Ay; and the sequel now
We find of this, his crime unpardonable,
That Caius still must in Sardinia drag
A longer life of exile.
Third Cit. Of our Senate
This then is the decree?
Pomp. Ay; doff your caps!
Be humbly thankful; bow to it, my brothers;
This the decree of our patrician fathers! *Clamors and hissing.*

Enter OPIMIUS *and* LUCULLUS.[7]

7. Lucius Opimius as praetor in 125 suppressed the revolt of Fregellae; as consul in 121, his colleague being absent in Gaul, he was instructed by a senatorial *consultum ultimum* (final decree) to deal with Gaius Gracchus and his followers, killing or condemning to death by trial some three thousand citizens; restored and dedicated the temple of Concord; found

Opim. What noisy riot's here? What have ye, thus
Gathering in crowds, to plot and murmur at?
First Cit. We would have Gracchus back.
Opim. Have Gracchus back!
Gracchus is at his post; what would ye more?
He's honored in his office, and remains
Selected to it, by the Consul's will.
Third Cit. Ay; long enough you've honored him. We'd like
To see him back, and hear his own account
Of matters in Sardinia.
Opim. Wranglers ever!
Thus are ye always, restless, discontent,
And gaping with large mouths, at what, ye know not.
Leave Gracchus to his duties, and the Senate
Will give to the country's servants honor due.
Off to your work! The days are turning long,
That ye find time in the streets to linger thus,
So many hours of your nothings talking.
First Cit. We talk of Caius Gracchus.
Opim. Insolent!
Who heeds of what ye talk! Off! off! I say.
Are ye not satisfied your share to leave
To your own tribunes, of the government?
You'd all be lords, forsooth, and make your laws
The hungry appetite to suit of each
New, squalling brat, who comes into the world
To help eat out our city dry, and then
Put finger in his eye, and pule and whine,
To catch his neighbor's dinner. Off! begone!
Away to your work; and meddle not, nor make;
For ye might chance to break, where ye would mend.
First Cit. [*Aside.*] Thus they out-talk us. We had best away,

---

guilty in 109 of corruption and accepting bribes when supervising the partition of Numidia after the death of Micipsa, he went into exile. The identity of LSM's Lucullus is not certain. A Lucius Licinius Lucullus was praetor by 154, consul in 151; another Lucius Licinius Lucullus, praetor in 104; a Publius Licinius Lucullus, tribune of the plebs in 110. None is plausible; it is likely that LSM created a necessary confidant to Opimius, borrowing for her fictional character the name of the most famous Lucullus, general and aesthete of the first century B.C., whose biography was written by Plutarch. No Lucullus appears as a character in Marie-Joseph Chénier's *Caius Gracchus* (1792), Vincenzo Monti's *Caio Gracco* (1800), or James Sheridan Knowles' *Caius Gracchus* (1815, 1823).

But let us give one cheer before we go.
[*Aloud.*] Huzza for Caius Gracchus!
Citizens. Huzza! huzza!
Exeunt Citizens, with Pomponius.
Luc. Do you note that?
Opim. Ay, damn him! Note it well!
He'll be the incubus will ride us yet;
And faith, he'll spare no spurring when he mounts.
His flashing eye has that within it speaks
A daring spirit, near which, did he live,
Tiberius now would seem to us mild and humble.[8]
His voice has tones which strike into the heart.
I late was in Sardinia, and I heard
When he addressed the troops. There was a thrill
Upon each noted wording of his tongue
That made me shiver. Terror was upon me,
And why I knew not. While I hated him,
And could have plunged a dagger to his heart,
Tears crept into mine eyes, and I must weep
When he upbraided them their want of duty.
I felt as if myself had sinned, and been
The recreant soldier whom his tongue disdained.
And when he spurred them to a nobler course,
My bounding heart burst forth its loud huzza;
Spite of myself, it worshipped Caius Gracchus.
And yet I hate him. If his burning words
Can stamp them so, upon a heart like mine,
Which nature, circumstance, and every tie
Point him its bitter, great antagonist,
What wonder if the people hail him home,

8. Tiberius Sempronius Gracchus, elder (by nine years) brother of Gaius, as tribune of the plebs in 133 proposed agrarian legislation intended to reform the use of Roman public land, now in the hands of the wealthy, by redistributing it among poorer citizens. Despite the support of many aristocrats, the Senate was able to oppose the legislation; thereupon Tiberius took his laws directly to the people's assemblies, an act legal but against custom, where the laws were passed and a commission, of which Tiberius and his brother were members, set up to carry out the laws' provisions. When Tiberius announced his intention to run for the office of tribune the following year, he and some of his supporters were surprised on the Capitol by a mob of senators and their clients, led by the Pontifex Maximus, Scipio Nasica, and murdered. Scipio Nasica and his victim Tiberius Gracchus were first cousins, their mothers being sisters.

Not with applause, but wild and frantic transport!
Luc. He must not come; for the ripe city waits,
Like willing damsel, wanton at his wish,
To fall into his arms.
Opim. He must not come,
If art or fraud can hinder. I have feared him
Since first (how well I note the day) he stood,
Forgetting all the sham of modesty
That he had nursed to cheat our foresight off,
And in the rostra boldly dared to stand
In loud defence of Vettius.[9] How he threw
From his bared shoulder the discarded gown!
And stamped, and strutted, in fierce passion casting
His fluent words in eloquent appeal
Forth to the trancèd people, who screamed out,
Maddened almost for joy, their raptured triumph,
In hailing their plebeian orator.
I hate the villain, from my heart's deep core,
And I would scant at nothing which could cast
The people from their love and worship of him.
Pshaw! here comes trooping back the noisy crowd;
I have no stomach for their prate today—
Let us pass on. *Exeunt.*

SCENE II. *The same.*

Enter Citizens, with POMPONIUS *and* FULVIUS.[10]

First Cit. Huzza for Caius Gracchus! Coming back!
Huzza! Huzza!
Second Cit. Huzza for Fulvius too!
Come, three times three! Huzza! huzza! huzza!
Third Cit. But tell me first, what mean you? that he'll come
Spite of the Senate's orders?
Ful. Bah! unlearn,
If ye are Romans, that poor starling note,

9. This speech is mentioned by Plutarch (*Gaius Gracchus* 1.3); Gaius Gracchus enjoyed a very high reputation as an orator, as such praised by Cicero, although disliking Gracchus' politics (e.g., *Brutus* 125–26). Nothing is known of Vettius or the charge against him.

10. Marcus Fulvius Flaccus, a supporter of Tiberius Gracchus, was elected a member of Tiberius' agrarian commission (which survived its founder) in 130, consul in 125, and tribune of the plebs in 122; his two sons were killed with him in 121.

Ever the same of "*orders*," "*Senate's orders*"!
Are ye not men to feel when ye are trampled?
Are ye not men to turn, if ye be struck?
Or will ye bide the *Senate's orders* still,
And fight, and work, and pine, and starve, and die,
By senatorial, august decree!

Third Cit. But still it is unheard of that a quaestor,
Abandoning his post, should suddenly,
Thus unattended, leave his general.
It is a knotty question, and I'll ask
Our tribune Livius Drusus, who comes yonder,
What is the law of right, in such a case.[11]

Pomp. Ask Livius Drusus! He's but half a tribune;
For with his conscience while the Senate tampers,
He dallies with their gold, and fingers it
Until truth finds no color in his eyes,
But only yellow gilded. Let him pass.

Second Cit. Nay, let him speak; he is our tribune still,
And slander may mis-speak him.

Enter DRUSUS.

You have heard
Some talk perhaps of Gracchus' coming home,
And that he's looked for presently. We're puzzled
To know what we should think of the affair.

Dru. Think of it, as all quiet citizens
Should think of mutiny against the laws
Of our paternal Senate. Think of it
As of a bad example, to be shunned,
And meet him with your frowns.

Ful. Ah! who is this?
My once-time friend! Why Livius Drusus, you,
When last I quitted Rome ('tis, let me see,
Some three, four years ago) were then, me-seems,
A noble-minded Roman, who cringed not
Flattering the mighty rich. 'Tis true, this gown

11. Marcus Livius Drusus, tribune of the plebs in 122, opposed Gaius Gracchus and his adherents; consul in 112; celebrated a triumph after his proconsulship in Macedonia (110); censor in 109. LSM's harsh view of his character is not shared by her source, Plutarch (*Gaius Gracchus* 8.4–10.2).

Was of a coarser texture; Livius showed
Less exquisite in dress. I'm from the camp,
And have forgot how city manners change;
This butterfly, fresh from the chrysalis,
Must read my lesson to me. When he crawled
In caterpillar form, I can remember
That Caius Gracchus was to him a God,
To whom he could not low enough demean
And bow himself to the earth; but now his wings,
Belike, being spread, he'd soar a higher flight.
I crave your pardon, Drusus; you would take
Your place in the Senate; or, at least, have lands
And monies to re-gild those gaudy wings.
True! true! all this must be; and then, of course,
When, in the palm of every Senator
Who meets you bowing, glittering silver lies,
And with his "Good-day, Drusus," he doth slip
The bait into your sleeve, how can it be
That Gracchus should be other than a scoundrel!
Faugh! Let us go! His cant doth sicken me!
Paternal Senate, says he? Ha! ha! ha!
Paternal humbug! Curse it! Let me pass.

Exit with Pomponius.

Dru. Hear, citizens! This is your Gracchus' friend!
Note how he taunts your tribune, and judge then
What to expect from him who taught the lesson.
This forwardness it is for you to check.
When Gracchus comes, be shy of him, and cold;
With distant look as of inquiry stand,
Staring as though his features were forgot,
And you would try to think if you had seen
The stamp of them before; then shake your heads
And turn away indifferent. Hark ye farther,
Let's have no palming with him. Mark ye well?

Second Cit. Ay, ay; let us alone. We'll make him know
How to respect our honorable Senate.

Dru. Well then, remember. *Exit Drusus.*

First Cit. That's our tribune, is it?
And you will mind him! Curse you for a fool
And scurvy knave! This Drusus is not worth
One little finger of our Caius Gracchus,

And yet you stand there, staring while he talks
As though his words were oracles.

Second Cit. Be still;
Let me alone and mind your own affairs.
See how your Gracchus will work out of this! *Exeunt.*

SCENE III. *Room in* CORNELIA'*s house.*

CORNELIA[12] *and* LICINIA.[13]

Cor. Nay, stay within doors, daughter; 'tis the place
Most meet and fitting woman. In a crowd
Showing like this the angry feelings, jarring
And froth of human passion, if you track
In loneliness your unprotected way,
You chance to meet rough words and harsh misuse.

Lic. But only some few yards! Pray let me go!
I'll wrap my mantle well, so none shall know me.

Cor. And should you chance to meet your husband thus,
What would you gain? With that wild crowd around you,
You would not dare to greet him to his home:
A quiet comeliness there is, becomes
A woman's greeting; and believe me, dear,
However daring bold himself may be,
Man never loves, within a woman's eye,
To see the mimic of his conduct glassed.
'Tis meek endurance, quiet fortitude,
That make her life and beauty. We may rear
Heroes, whose dauntless will shall shake the world,
Or like a moral Atlas, bear its burden,

12. Cornelia was the daughter of Publius Cornelius Scipio Africanus, the conqueror of Hannibal. Her maternal grandfather, Lucius Aemilius Paullus, was one of the consuls commanding the Roman army at the battle of Cannae in 216, in which he was killed (see *PSE*, "Separate Secession," p. 215). Her husband, Tiberius Sempronius Gracchus, was twice consul (177 and 163), celebrated two triumphs, and was censor (169). Her learning and cultivation were renowned; her letters, of which some disputed fragments survive, were commended by Cicero (*Brutus* 211) and Quintilian (1.1.6).

13. Licinia was the daughter of Publius Licinius Crassus Dives Mucianus, who replaced Tiberius Gracchus on the agrarian commission; succeeded Scipio Nasica as Pontifex Maximus in 132; was consul in 131; proconsul of Asia in 130, he was captured by rebels against Rome and put to death. Forbidden, like the wife of Fulvius, to go into mourning for her dead husband, Licinia was also deprived of her dowry (Plutarch *Gaius Gracchus* 17.5). There seems to have been one daughter of the marriage; no son is known.

A universe of care, upon their shoulders.
But in our bosoms if too fierce the flame
That feeds such spirit-struggles, we must check,
Or drive it back, at least, to seeming quiet.
If hard the effort, it is woman's task.
Her passions, if not smothered, must be hid,
Till, in their faintly-beating pulse, herself
Will scarcely know her blood the same which bounds
Through manlier veins unchecked.

Lic. But mother, you
Methinks are hardly glad to know he's coming.
Your cheek has found no flush of expectation,
Your eye no glance of triumph. There you sit
And argue calmly with me, while I'm mad
To strain him to my heart.

Cor. Your love, my child,
Is wild with youth. Mine, sobered with life's age,
By thought and sorrow tamed to curb itself,
Is therefore not less true, and might perchance
Die for the loved one, full as soon as yours.

Lic. But tell me, mother, when you heard it said
Your son was coming home, why did a tear
Start to your eye? And while my poor heart beat
And fluttered with the wildness of its hope,
Why did you simply wipe that tear away,
Nor ever even say, "I'm glad to know it"?
Surely you love him, mother!

Cor. Surely, yes.
But see, the loved one here!

Enter GRACCHUS.[14]

14. Gaius Sempronius Gracchus adopted, and expanded, the policy of his brother Tiberius, whom he also desired to avenge. As tribune of the plebs in 123, and again in 122, he secured the passage of a large body of legislation which, among other things, assured wheat to the Roman plebs at a subsidized price, founded colonies to relieve overpopulation in Italy (including one at the site of Carthage, destroyed in 146, the founding of which Gracchus supervised in person), and transferred the courts trying senatorial extortion from the senators to the equestrian order. But his legislation extending Roman citizenship to Rome's Latin allies and Latin status to other Italians was opposed by Livius Drusus and others, who sought to detach the plebs from Gracchus by surpassing Gracchus' own laws in the plebs' favor, and by taking advantage of the plebs' reluctance that their own privileges should be extended.

Grac. Ah! my sweet bird,
Who watchest for thy mate, now tune thy song
To welcome home the wanderer. Mother, here
I bring you home the heart whose thought hath been
Ever for you, this dear one, and for Rome.
Cor. Welcome to Rome, my boy.
Lic. But thou art strange!
Why truly, mother, thou didst promise right
That I had lost my love. This is not he!
This bearded soldier, seamed and browned in the wars!
Grac. What, saucy one! Would'st thou disown thy lord?
Nay, I am used to keep a stricter rule,
And will allow no mutiny in the camp.
So rebel, come, that I may punish thee
With this, and this—and thus with kisses plague thee!
Lic. Nay; get thee gone. I must perforce admit,
By these rough ways, thou'rt still the feather-head
Who left me here, some many years agone.
I thought thou hadst grown wiser.
Grac. How's this, mother?
You have not been half strict enough, I fear,
In the training of this sauce-box. But, your pardon,
I am a fool; for I stand trifling here,
While your grave look has some big import in it.
What is it, mother? Speak. I too have learned
To wrap me much in deeper thoughts of late.
Lic. Nay, Gracchus—prithee, love! nay, not that look!
Thou mak'st me thus already weep to think
That thou art come again to this stern Rome.
Grac. What, have you not grown older? Still the same
My little pet must pout its rosy lip,
And sulk at business, when it rivals love!
Smooth down thy ruffled feathers, pretty one;
For surely not my wish, but need, doth force
My thought aside so soon, to wander from thee.
Mother, your anxious look should find its words.
Cor. Unwillingly, with harshness thus to break

Gracchus and his ally Fulvius, when they were not reelected to the tribunate for 121, were faced with the dismantling of much of their work; riots broke out (on whose responsibility, is not clear); and Gracchus, along with Fulvius and many others of their supporters, was killed.

Upon our happy meeting; but I fear
Each moment lost is so much life-blood drawn,
Weakening your cause, to make it hang its head
As evil-conscienced, or as sick at heart.
Rome's all afire; and your best lovers now
Half-turned against you, pondering, shake their heads
As doubtful of your course.

Grac. What! would they wish
To see me drag out life the Senate's drudge?
To rot away my soul, like worthless carcass
In the highway cast, for daws and crows to pick at!
Toil down my spirit to old age's weakness!
All for the profit of the proud usurpers,
Who from between our teeth the hard-earned bread
Snatch wantonly, to make them luxuries
At which the starving people stare, and wonder
What are their uses and their purposes!

Cor. Be cool! be cool! and heed that you do not,
In blaming one extreme, to the other rush.
But for the present, think first of yourself,
And purge yourself from rashness. Claim your right,
Making appeal to the censors of your cause.[15]
Where you are slandered, charge the slander back,
And cleanse the name that envy seeks to blot.

Grac. Mother, you're right. I loiter here too long.
Farewell, Licinia, I'll be quickly back.
Send your best wishes with me and cheer up. *Exeunt.*

SCENE IV. *Street of Rome.*

SEPTIMULEIUS[16] *and several Citizens.*

Sept. Now is the time for Gracchus' friends to rise;
And I may count, I'm sure, as one of them.

15. Two censors were elected at Rome to conduct the census, or enrollment, of the citizen population every five years; they also had responsibility for public morals, leasing public lands and buildings, and examining the rolls of senators and knights, any one of whom the censors could eject for offenses falling under their jurisdiction; they served for eighteen months. Gracchus appeared before the censors of 125–24, Gnaeus Servilius Caepio and Lucius Cassius Longinus Ravilla.

16. Septimuleius (misspelled "Septimulieus" in 1851 ed.) is mentioned by Plutarch as an enterprising friend of Opimius: having stolen the head of Gracchus from those who had killed him—Opimius had promised an equal weight in gold for it—Septimuleius enlarged

He knows what he's about, and he has forced
The censors to a hearing. He's an eye
Into the marrow of a thing that looks
As deep as any man's—

First Cit. And you, who watch
Ever the veering wind, make up your mind
That now into his sails it fairly blows,
And trim accordingly. I hope indeed
Your judgment may, for his sake, be a true one.

Sept. 'Tis time we should of the event hear news.
Ah! here it comes! Licinius and Pomponius;
They'll tell us all about it.

Enter LICINIUS *and* POMPONIUS

Good-day! Good-day!
My hearty greetings do attend ye both.
Good luck to you, and all of Gracchus' friends!

Pomp. You love him well.

Sept. Ay; and I hope not low
He counts in his esteem my humble service.
Now pray ye, let us hear how goes the trial!

Pomp. Fully the censors have acquitted him.
How could they less, when truths showered on them so?
He showed how he his duty had surpassed,
And served for years, more than the law obliged;
How he had gone forth rich, and come back poor,
While others piled their wealth of hoarded gains,
Stolen treasures, griped from conquered provinces
And towns 'neath taxes groaning. When they dared
Implied conspiracy to charge him with,
His flashing indignation struck all dumb
The cowardly accusers, flinching, who
Did eat the words which scarce had passed their lips;
Their strangled statements shuffling, turning o'er,
Backward their import, to excuse it, working.

Sept. Of what conspiracy could they accuse him?

Pomp. Of favoring commotions 'mong the allies,

---

his reward by scooping the brain out of the skull and replacing it with molten lead (*Gaius Gracchus* 17.3–4).

And waking up revolt throughout the states
Of conquered Italy.

Licinius. Ah! there peeps out
The stumbling block, that lies in Caius' path.
But we'll pass on. Good-day to you, citizens.
Will you walk with us, Septimuleius?

Sept. No,
I have much pressing business on my hands.
Wish you good-day, and much prosperity,
To you and all of Gracchus' friends. Their merits,
Weighed truly, are enough for them. Farewell. *Exit with Citizens.*

Pomp. Fair words and soft, but, like the babbling brook,
Not over deep, methinks.

Licinius. He is of those
Who follow with the stream, and guides his course
By the full current's veering; a light thing,
Whose talk is worth the noting, as it shows
Only—true weathercock—the changing wind.
But not so Fulvius, whom just now we named;
He in his character, I fear, is fixed,
And that none of the wisest; while so far
He has besotted the great mind of Gracchus
To think too kindly of him, that it thus
Doth much out-calculate his true desert.
'Tis oft a lofty spirit shows in this
The weakness of its temper, taking up,
Through love of one of a far meaner soul,
Some high conception, which doth catch the stamp
And likeness of its own excelling virtues.
Of noble natures 'tis the practised fault,
Thus to mislead their judgments to the thinking
Those whom they love as noble as themselves.
And thus his soul in keeping Caius gives
To Fulvius, who by noisy blustering drags—
And by his plottings and dissentious riot—
Unkind suspicion on the name of Gracchus.

Pomp. But you're too hard on Fulvius. There's no proof
That he has tampered with the states, nor been
The cause of this disturbance.

Licinius. No—no proof;
But there's suspicion rank; and his demeanor,

With loud and quarrelsome debate, doth give
Much strength to rumor. Were't not for the love
That Gracchus bears him, there had been a search
Of close inspection, when great Scipio died,
And all men whispered "poison."[17] Many then
On Fulvius cast suspicion's clouded eye;
But he was Gracchus' friend. This was the claim
That made his evil sacred. The great love
That from the city's heart flowed out on Gracchus
Hushed up the loud-mouthed vengeance. But there was,
In this heart-homage even, a dark taint
Upon the name of Gracchus, which was joined
With that of Fulvius, while men whispered low—
Casting uneasy glances, as though thought,
Fearing to speak, yet could not hush itself—
Longed to find words, yet doubting trembled still
To think those words o'erheard. While no man dared
To boldly name a guilt, yet all seemed stunned,
As wildered by some dark imagining.
O'er Gracchus fell the shadow of a shame,
Whilst he, for love of Fulvius, dared not stand
To boldly face inquiry, and cast off
The sickly taint of that day's damnèd work.

Pomp. Would it had never been! For Drusus now,
The Senate's tool and their most vigilant spy,
Makes this the point, whence all his venom casts
Its evil spite on Gracchus. 'Tis a lever,
Which, though it lies all rusted by disuse,
From its forgotten corner now he drags,
To work his mischief. Still I have a kindness
That clings to Fulvius. Had you heard him lash
This very Drusus, when he wagged his tongue
In evil words to raise the citizens

17. Publius Cornelius Scipio Aemilianus, twice consul (in 147 and 134), elected censor in 142, the destroyer of Carthage in the Third Punic War (149–46), was by birth the grandson of Lucius Aemilius Paullus who died at Cannae, and thus Cornelia's first cousin; he was adopted by the childless son of Cornelia's father, Scipio Africanus; he married (the marriage was unhappy and childless) Sempronia, Cornelia's daughter and the sister of Tiberius and Gaius Gracchus. Gaius Gracchus served under him at the siege and capture of Numantia in Spain (134–33). Despite these connections, however, Scipio Aemilianus was opposed to the policies of his brothers-in-law. His sudden death in 129 was attended with rumors of murder.

'Gainst the return of Gracchus, you'd have felt,
With all his noisy faults, he has a heart,
And that belongs to Gracchus.
Licinius. I yet doubt it. [[*Exeunt.*]]

ACT II.

SCENE I. *Street of Rome.*

SEPTIMULEIUS *and crowd of Citizens.*

Sept. I knew it! bless the Gods! We're almost now
Upon the ladder's top. The people's voice
Will hoist up Gracchus! Then, good luck, his friends!
First Cit. Spite of the Senate they will make him tribune.
Sept. Ay; to be sure they will! and he will make
A glorious tribune too! Pray ye, remember
I've always been his friend. No shuffler, I,
To catch the passing time. I've ever kept
My service in his cause, and I know, too,
He notes my merits kindly.

Enter FULVIUS.

Ful. Huzza, boys!
The votes are counted. Gracchus is our tribune!
Huzza for Caius Gracchus!
Citizens. Huzza! huzza!
Sept. I told you so! I'm one of his best friends!
Huzza for Caius Gracchus!
First Cit. Now we've got
A tribune who, as cunningly as need be,
May pose the law against your Livius Drusus.
Ful. Ay, let our lordly rulers champ the bit
And fret their hearts out; 'tis not like that Gracchus
Will abdicate the tribuneship to please them.
He's fairly mounted and he'll ride them down.
'Twill do me good to see the proud patrician
Bending beneath the spur, plunging and foaming,
Like high-bred courser vaulting from the will
Of who would ride him; forced again to crouch,
Groaning in mingled rage and agony,

Till whip and spur at last have done their work,
And the proud blood is tamed to bow its neck,
Offering its head to meet the ready rein
Which leads him to his task.

First Cit. Bravely we did
Our duty, did we not, in the election?

Ful. Bravely you did, and well. Before your might,
Like a scared thing, the startled Senate shrank.

Second Cit. Now let's away to drink our tribune's health.

First Cit. No, no. You know that Gracchus said we should
Be orderly, and that the people showed—
These were his words—"most nobly when they spoke
With calm decision and with majesty
The nation's voice; and that each citizen
Should as a fraction of the breathing whole
Maintain in him his country's dignity."
So let us all go home, and have no noise.

Ful. Pooh! pooh! 'Twas for the Senate Gracchus spoke.

Second Cit. He said the people, though.

Ful. Well, I know that.
But, simpleton, his words were meant to move
The Senate's ears, not yours. 'Twas but a flourish.

First Cit. And yet, I thought the words were from his heart;
And more than that, I found a judgment in them.
We citizens are too much given, in truth,
To drunkenness and riot.

Ful. Bah! good sheep!
Would you too turn philosopher? Be off!
And if you like, get drunk. Why should he curb
(Gracchus is far too wise a man for that)
Of their poor pleasures, the vexed citizens?

Third Cit. Come; Fulvius ought to know; he's Gracchus' friend,
And has a heart too, for the people's cause.
He knows the right, I'm sure, better than we. *Exeunt.*

SCENE II. *House of* CORNELIA.

LICINIA, CORNELIA, *and* LICINIUS.

Lic. Come, tell us all about it. Pray, Licinius,
Be not so chary of your words. My mother,
Though she says little, loves as well as I

To hear you talk of Gracchus. 'Twas, they say,
The greatest crowd that ever was in Rome;
And we know well, that all the Senate's power
Was listed to oppose him.

Licinius. Lady, yes.
But 'gainst their combined force, backed as it was
By most obsequious bribery and corruption,
The stream of life came pouring into Rome,
As though, the being of the state in danger,
Its life-blood all came rushing to the heart
To keep existence in. And boldly did
The general pulse beat forth new-given life.
'Twas a new Rome, as through its crowded ways
The swaying populace, bent on its course,
And o'er the Campus Martius sweeping, showed,
In its flood-tide, a human ocean rising,
The murmuring of whose restless waves spoke out
Oppression's death. Your husband, noble lady,
And your proud son, Cornelia, through its midst
Passed stately on; the people's voices claiming
Not as a favor done him, but a due
Owed to themselves and Rome. And boldly they
To the call responded. From their bending rafters
The house-tops even, straining 'neath the weight
Of gathered thousands, echoed back the name
As spoke the people's voice, "Gracchus for Tribune."

Cor. Then it was nobly done! No need was there
To cringing beg a flattered people's voice.

Licinius. No; rather even then, when he did ask
Their voices from them, firmest he rebuked.
But gently 'twas, with nobleness, as would
The follies of his child a parent check.
And still, meseemed, at each rebuke, they thronged
More loving close around him.

Cor. Gods! I thank ye,
For that his spirit lags not in the race
Of its youth's glorious promise. Here he comes.
We'll go and greet our tribune to his home. *Exeunt.*

SCENE III. *Street of Rome.*

OPIMIUS, LUCULLUS, *another Senator, and* LIVIUS DRUSUS.

Luc. We're beaten to our trenches, and we fight
Now for existence.
Sen. We must back a step.
Luc. Give back and we are lost. Our enemy
Will scarce with one step only let us pause;
But back, and back, and back, will hustle us,
Till his position he at will may choose.
Opim. He's like to choose it, act howe'er we may;
And yet with you I say, we must not back;
'Tis certain ruin. You must help us, Drusus.
Dru. Nay, I have tried my best. The people's will
Outdoes your plottings. I'm almost ashamed
That with them I too am not striving.
Opim. Pshaw!
Where's your ambition which would crush down Gracchus
And make yourself (what you to aspire have right
At least as full as he) Rome's one great man!
Have you so soon renounced the noble task,
That you already shirk its burden off?
And more, do you forget the benefit
That, in this duty's exercise, accrues
To your own person and your properties?
Your fortune will be made, e'en with the blow
That drives away these hungry blood-suckers.
Monies and lands a grateful Senate gives
To who thus nobly props his country's cause.
Dru. In truth the Senate doth with liberal hand
Dispense its favors; and, although the mob
Doth cavil at the freedom of the gifts
Its generosity dispenses to me,
My conscience clears me; and I must confess
Too hungry grasping is this eager mob;
An humbler deportment it should bear;
And, while I love the people, I must side
Thus far with noble Senators. I'll do
What in me lies, to crush the spirit out
From this proud faction. Honesty doth point
As well as interest to the quelling it.

Opim. Most certainly; and common sense doth prove
There's honesty in interest. Shall I starve
Or live a beggar because chance hath put
What should be mine in food and property
Into another's hand? Most surely not;
For thus defrauding self and wife and children,
Is it not greater sin, than if I drain
The stranger's surplus off? I much misdoubt
This ever-prosing honesty that leaves
On homely pulse its advocate to starve,
To rear in rags his children up, while thrusting
By way of comfort down their hungry throats
Old saws and adages, importing still
That honesty is the best policy.
'Tis a fine lesson for who'll act it out;
Though, truth to say, I've found it ever was
A glorious virtue to grow lean upon,
And apt excuse for lazy ne'er-do-wells
To trap their misery in— *Noise without.*
What tumult's this?

Sen. It is the crowd whom Fulvius feeds with drink
And tops them to the height of all their whims.
I have a hope to see this Fulvius prove
The doubtful spoke, where Gracchus' wheel shall crack;
A rotten prop at heart, which must give way
When most the pressure of the time shall need it.
Hark! How they join his name with that of Gracchus,
Twin-brothers in their hearts.

Noise approaches, with cries of "Gracchus," "Fulvius," etc.

Dru. They come this way;
'Twere best I should pass on. 'Tis fault to them
That I too much frequent the company
Of honorable Senators. I'll go.
Though pure my purposes, most prudent 'twere
I should not meet them here. *Exit Drusus.*

Opim. Ay; go thy ways
To salve thy conscience for the job on hand,
And into love with meanness cheat thy thought.
Bah! It is rank, and his offence's foulness
Doth cast its filth upon ourselves who use it.

Would we were rid of the necessity!
The rotten thing doth haunt me with its stench.
But what means this?

Enter Citizens, riotously and drunken.

How now! What would ye here?
And whence this loud uncivil conduct? Come ye
By Gracchus sent, to edify the town
With beastly scenes of drunken merriment?

First Cit. [*drunk*] Please your honorable senatorships, we would—

Opim. Ye would—vile things! What care we what ye would!
Ye refuse of the city, foul excrescence
Upon a sickly growth! Is it for ye
We are so bandied by this Gracchus? Off!
If ye will play the beast, go shut ye up
In your own houses, tumble as ye will;
Get drunk and beat your wives; be hogs at home,
Ye drudges, it is all that ye are fit for!
But if your sovereign majesties would spare
Such exhibitions in the public streets,
Meseems to hide them were some point of wisdom.

Second Cit. Will't please your lordships hear us?

Opim. Hear ye! No.
But rid the soilèd streets of your foul tread,
And for the purer air you'd leave, we'll thank you.

Third Cit. Would you the right of citizens deny us?

Opim. Ye citizens, in troth!—Be off, vile spawn!
Ye refuse scum of a licentious city!
Your breaths do load the air. Be off! I say.

First Cit. We'd better go. They have small patience with us.
And truth to say, our addled brains are fit
But poorly for encounter with their wits. *Exeunt.*

SCENE IV. *Another part of Rome.*

Enter GRACCHUS, FULVIUS, *and* LICINIUS.

Grac. But you are too unruly. You have schooled
The citizens to riot. When they should
By hardy temperance, steady perseverance,
Push on to their great end, you rouse them idly
To drinking and excess. Those powers of mind

Which to a resolute effort should be turned
You make them drown in license and debauch.
Ful. Why, one would think, you had not yet unlearned
Your school-boy lesson; that you truly deemed
The popular majesty an enthroned thought,
And not a joke to gull the dirty crowd
And coax the votes from its high mightiness.
Grac. You word it well; an enthroned thought it is!
The might of mind, whose myriad streamlets meet,
One gathered flood of condensed light to form.
Each dirty rivulet its ripple brings,
Which, in the sweeping current mingling, drops
Its dust and dross. Its purer part goes on,
And on, and on—until at last the whole,
By the great alchemy of reason, flows
Pure as it must be, from its origin.
Thought sprang from God; and all bestained with earth,
Struggling and creeping still, at last the truth
Is forced upon the day. The world's great mind,
Though stumbling oft in error, must at last
Work out its vexèd problem, and perfection,
Wrought from reflected deity in man,
Burst sun-like from the mist of error forth.
Ful. Strange pantheon this our mottled world, in sooth,
Of embryo deities? At a cheap rate
You make your Gods, and their divinityships
Do trick themselves as easily in wisdom
Picked up, 'twould seem, in filth and public gutters.
Yon drunken blackguard, rolling in the dust,
And yonder snub-nosed, wide-mouthed, gaping crowd,
With their shag-heads, and vacant staring eyes,
Are these the exponents of your godlike thought?
Grac. These, even these, are men; and I could weep
To see their nobler natures thus debased.
It is the sin of those who, better knowing,
Do dam the stream, instead of cutting out
A clearer course to give its current way.
If yours the better mind, its effort turn
To raise, not crush them lower in their mire.
Ful. I must be off, or you till midnight preach,
And their divinityships, the citizens

Whom you today address, will take it ill,
If you are hoarse, and thence not eloquent.
Farewell! may all the Gods shower blessings on you. *Exit Fulvius.*

Licinius. You waste your teaching on a heart like that.

Grac. The heart is good. The head, in truth, sometimes,
For want of thought to steady it, doth wander
On bootless errands. 'Twill correct itself.

Licinius. The heart is sapless, rotten at the core;
And the head weakened by its selfishness.
From head and heart alike, great thoughts are born;
The truly noble cannot sever them.
I'd shun the man who at his nature scoffs
And, trampling on his own divinity,
Feels not the *consciousness* of human greatness.
Forgive me, that, but dealing in few words,
In honest sooth I'd warn you: shun this Fulvius.

Grac. He is my friend. I'll hear no ill of him.

Licinius. Gracchus, it cannot be, a mind like yours
Should fail to fathom such a shallow thing
As this same Fulvius. Pray you—

Grac. Pray you, cease,
Nor stun me with unwelcome counsellings.

Licinius. But one word, only!

Grac. What! You'd quarrel, would you?
Who underrates my friend, doth carp at me.

Licinius. Would it were only at yourself I carped,
For then you'd listen patiently; but here—
Well, well; I've done. Your frown speaks stinted patience,
And anger listens to no argument. *Exeunt.*

SCENE V. *House of* CORNELIA.

CORNELIA *and* LICINIA.

Lic. Mother, I'm sick with fear, and mad to see
Your brow so calm, while every heart-throb bursts
My breast with expectation. There are plots
And underhanded councillings; glances dark
And sidelong whispers, of I know not what.
I fear me much, there's something wrong of late.
Caius seems wrapt and moody in his thought;

And, when I question him, he answers short
With matters of no moment; how he hears
This neighbor's bitch has puppied; or belike
This other's cow has sickened in her horn;
And how the corn hath musted in the ear,
And harvest should be coming. These are not
The thoughts which wrench his anxious heart in twain,
And rob me of its larger moiety.

Cor. Poor child! You have not hardness for the time,
And run to meet your sorrows—hugging them
Like cherished visitors. I know not what
The unquiet face of Rome doth indicate.
We can but watch the struggle.

Lic. Mother, no;
We can do more; much more. Remember, mother,
How you have lost one son. You've often wept
And told the story to me of his fate.
Oh mother! save this last one! Keep him close
As jewel on your heart. Watch over him
Like unweaned infant nestling at your breast!

Cor. Daughter, we can but wait until we find
What darkens in the cloud which overhangs us.
We know not if ambition stocks it full
Big with black mischief, or if nobler worth
But works its virtuous ends through shaded ways.

Lic. We know there's risk in it. This is enough.
Then, mother, stop your son! Oh! hold him back!
By all the throes that brought him into being,
By all the hopes and fears that watched his growth,
By all the pangs that even now I know
Must rend your mother-heart to think of him,
Oh! save him to that heart! Save him to me!

Cor. Daughter, to guide his course is not for me;
Complete he stands, and in full manhood strong.
No more my task his pliant youth to mould;
Himself the drama of his life must make.
But of his course, believe me, dear, could I,
By the deep aspirations of my heart,
Its unsketched outlines fix—the struggle come
'Twixt life and honor—I would bid him die.

What though the effort burst my mother-heart!
When virtue's weighed 'gainst vice, good men must die
To throw their lives in the balance.

Lic. Mother! mother!
You fright me with this passion! Not for nothing
Did Etna late her baleful fires cast
Ominous of evil. Trembling Sicily,
To her foundations shaken, saw huge flames
Burst from the bosom even of the sea;
While the big waters swallowed up her coast
In hungry menace of some coming ill,
And subterranean mutterings spoke of woes
Unmeasured and unknown! They come, and dark
Their scowling shadows fright me.

Cor. But why thus
Trick out imagined ills in giant form,
And ghastly robe with terrors! Thus we act
Like foolish children, whispering goblin tales
Until on end their bristled hair stands up;
And, in the unnatural sound of their cramped breaths,
They fancy whispering spirits at their backs,
Strange steps in the loud beating of their hearts,
And in their garments rustling some wild blast
Of unimagined horror! Come, my girl,
Cheer up, and be to Caius, if you can,
A friend who loves his life less truly far
Than his unsmerchèd honor.

Lic. I will try;
But mother, 'tis a lesson sad to con,
And young am I to learn it.

Enter GRACCHUS.

Gracchus! Ah!
My heart's best life!

Grac. What! weeping, sweet one? fie!
Your eyes are full of tears; you have not wrung
The baby yet from out their stainèd lids.

Lic. Treat me then as a woman, and I'll try
To hush the baby in me. Tell me what
Works in your mind to make you almost shun me?
And why I see you ever with such look

Of grave abstraction? Why you whispering start
When suddenly I meet you with your friends,
As though my presence jarred you? And that Fulvius
Who haunts your company, I love him not;
What have you still to do, whispering with Fulvius?

Grac. Pooh! pooh! a jealousy you have of Fulvius;
Some grudge of the young bride, yet unforgiven.
He made me frolic once too late of night,
When you, the pretty tyrant of my house,
A new-made wife (some se'nnight old) sat watching
And deemed my duty cold. Forgive him, love!
We'll lecture him to greater gravity.

Lic. It is not *that* which frets me, and you know it.
There's mischief in the wind. What is it, Gracchus?

Grac. A mischief, say you? Ah! belike the storm
Has scattered mother Tyra's brood of chicks.
Poor soul, I passed her at her post this morning,
Cluck, clucking on, as she herself had been
The very hen that hatched them.

Lic. Gracchus! Gracchus!
You'll break my heart, and yet I needs must laugh
To hear your folly.

Grac. Laugh then, sweet; 'tis best.
That rainbow face is pretty. Is't not, mother?
Forgive me, though, I am in haste; pray, mother,
The gown you fitted for me yesterday;
I must be off again. *Exeunt.*

SCENE VI. *Public Square.*

Crowd of noisy Citizens.

First Cit. He must come presently. Would I could meet him
With clearer conscience. On last night's misdeeds
My aching head an ugly sermon preaches.
Of Fulvius I scarce know what we should think.
They say he's Gracchus' friend, but certainly
Their lessons oft run counter.

Second Cit. Truly, he helps
To make sad fools of us. Here Gracchus comes.

First Cit. I wish yon drunken crowd would hush its riot.

Enter GRACCHUS.

Great cheering and much drunken noise among Citizens.

Grac. Be still and hear me. You who've drugged your brains
Until their surfeit doth of mind and thought
Exclude the entrance quite: get home, sleep off
This self-taught idiocy. Be men again
Before ye come to prate of governing
A people's councils. Your own vices lash,
Lay bare your consciences—starve them to reason,
And then you may be heard. Your voices now
Are but the idiot's babbling, madman's yell!
Ay, cower—shrink away; ye are no things
To keep men company. Yourselves have cast
In wantonness your noble birthrights from ye!

Many citizens steal away.

Friends, brothers, Roman citizens, I come[18]
As ye have willed it, that I may explain
And speak to you concerning your own rights.
Man has, in every station, rights his due.
Our slaves look to their masters for support.
The very claims we hold upon their labor
Make us a rule to tender them again
What comforts we can furnish to their lot.
If placed by circumstance, necessity,
Beneath our rule, protection thence we owe:
And he evading basely these, degrades
Himself below the thus defrauded slave.
You, Romans, have a sterner government;
For our rich nobles, who do make themselves
Perforce the country's purse-holders, forget
To leave some portion of your gains for you
Whose toil and heart-ache won them. Are ye poor?
Why do your starving infants beg in vain
A hard, dry crust? Why are their shivering limbs
Wrapt but in rags, as they cower tearful round
The dying embers of your empty hearths?
Are there no vacant lands, the people's due?
Where are the rich fields that your fathers conquered?

18. This speech invokes the precedent, by echoing the first lines, of Antony's speech over the corpse of Julius Caesar (*Julius Caesar* 3.2.75–109).

And where the exuberant harvests that yourselves
Have made Rome's property? What justice gave them
New riches to the rich? The proud patrician
Who toiled not, bled not, in the gaining them;
Who sat at home by the fire and warmed himself
By talking over battles that *you* fought;
He waited for no law to make them his;
But by the strong hand of oppression seizes
The bread which should have fed your hungry babes.
Is there no corn in the market? You will find
A large abundance. There have lately been
New importations from the provinces.
Why do you starve, then? Why do you not buy?
You smile as though the bare idea were strange.
You cannot buy. You have no monies. Rich,
Usurious, speculates the plunderer
On your starvation. Beggars which you are
His robberies make you, and he taunts you then,
Mocking your poverty by this display,
Showing how rich the country is in grain,
While he, from hunger-clenchèd fingers, screws
To pay for a mere handful, your last doit!
With poverty your chilling bed-fellow,
And hugged by hunger, while ye thus are driven
To wrap ye in your rags and wait for death,
Who are those laborers, well-dressed, happy, sleek,
Tilling the fields which, citizens, are yours?
From the depopulated country fly
The shepherd and the husbandman, to make
Room for the rich man's slave. Beasts have their dens,
They hide them in their caves, and there may rest;
But you, who in the cause of Italy
Your heart's-blood spill, ye Roman citizens—
To you she gives no home! She leaves you nought
Save only God's light and the air you breathe!
The poor man has no home; he claims no shed
'Neath which his huddling brats may gather them.
From place to place the forlorn things he drags
And with their mother lays them on the earth
There, where the soldier sleeps. What mockery, then,
To call on such, ye generals of Rome,

And bid them fight for their domestic Gods,
Their homes and sepulchres! *Their* sepulchres!
Their fathers' bones are scattered to the winds,
And the patrician ploughs them through his fields,
Nor heeds plebeian graves! And yet they fight;
Plebeians fight and die. The Roman blood
Boils up in the combat and the victory's won,
For what? That these proud rich may sit and revel
In some new luxury, some dear-bought pleasure,
While you, ye so-called masters of the world,
In your possession hold no foot of ground!
To your assistance you have summoned me;
And, where the anxious thought you dared not word,
Your walls speak to me. Public monuments
In blotted and scrawled sentences implore
Succor to Rome. Dare ye then help yourselves?
On you I call, to make your effort too.
What can my single power? The slough is deep;
We must, if we would pass, unite our strength;
With shoulder to the wheel, and a great heart
Of resolute effort, we must bring the force
Of a whole people's thought, a nation's might.
And, when a nation acts, if 'twould not end
Its struggling cause in anarchy and license,
With calm endurance every citizen
Should feel the weight of the whole cause is his.
Rise to your task! Upon your souls let in
The light of reason. From the agglomerate crowd
Spring forth to life as individual men,
Conquering the world within yourselves, ere grasping
To rule the external. Be self-conscious, bold,
But never violent; though firm, yet curbing
Your passion's fierceness to due energy.
Your cause is just, and in its justice strong.
Make it not weak by tumult, angry riot,
Obstreperous threat, and vulgar, wordy menace.
Let reason, based on conscious truth, be backed
By resolution firm, and stubborn will,
With all its nerves strong knitted to endure.
If these the temper of your striving souls,
Then let us on. The trial lies before us.

But much I fear that ye will flinch the struggle.
There was a noble heart which throbbed to free
This trampled people to its natural rights;
And how were its bold efforts seconded?
Ye called on him for succor, as ye now
Call for my feebler help. Ye called, implored,
Entreated him—and then, and then—your blushes
May speak the tragedy, whose damning stain
Doth stamp upon your annals its dark blot!
What need I name that name, whose syllables
Each, in its separate wording, should call forth
A newer vengeance on the coward hearts
That shrank in danger from him! Ye know well
I speak to you of Tiberius. He who strove
With you, and for you, in the noble cause
Of his true heart's devotion. Are ye, Romans,
The sons of those who starting flew to arms
When, from a wanton insult to their tribune,
They by a foreign war wiped off the stain
Thus cast upon the country's majesty?[19]
They thought the doom of death fit punishment,
When, failing in respect, Veturius stood
Heedless, nor making way before their tribune
Who in the Forum passed him.[20] But *ye* saw,
In your most awful consecrated temple—
The holy capitol of Rome—the blood
Of your own sacred magistrate defile
Its violated walls; ye saw, nor shuddered;
Or, if ye shuddered at the sacrilege,
Ye stood and let his bloody corse be dragged
Like refuse carrion, through your city's streets.
Ye saw him, like a dead dog, tost in the waves
Of Tiber, which reluctant shrank, as fearing
To sanction crimes so horrible. 'Tis said
The naiads of the river rose that night,

19. The tribune, one Genucius, should perhaps be assigned to the year 241, when Rome went to war with Falerii; but Plutarch's reference is otherwise unattested (*Gaius Gracchus* 3.3).

20. Plutarch *Gaius Gracchus* 3.3. This Gaius Veturius, together with the date and details of the incident, is otherwise unknown.

And terrible forebodings mourning shrieked
Of misery to Rome, for such a deed.
Ye Gods avert the omen, and accept,
Ye angered deities, the sacrifice,
Which here I vow to make you, of my life,
In the great cause for which my brother bled:
The cause of Rome, of liberty, and man!

First Cit. Let us go home.
Second Cit. Shall we not cheer him?
First Cit. No.
Let us go home and con his lessons well;
Tears and obedience are his homage due;
Cheers are too boisterous. *Exeunt.*

ACT III

SCENE I. *House of* CORNELIA.

CORNELIA *and* GRACCHUS.

Grac. Wolves breed not lambs, nor can the lioness
Rear fawns among her litter. You but chide
The spirit, mother, which is born from you.[21]

Cor. Curb it, my son; and watch against ambition!
Half demon and half god, she oft misleads
With a bold face of virtue. I know well
The breath of discontent is loud in Rome;
And a hoarse murmuring vengeance smoulders there
Against the tyrannous rule which, iron shod,
Doth trample out man's life. The crisis comes;
But oh! beware, my son, how you shall force it!

Grac. Nay, let it come, that dreaded day of doom,
When, by the audit of his cruel wrongs
Heaped by the rich oppressor on the crowd
Of struggling victims, he must stand condemned
To vomit forth the ill-got gains which gorge
His luxury to repletion. Let it come!

21. *Coriolanus* 3.2.125–30 (Volumnia to her son Coriolanus): "let / Thy mother rather feel thy pride than fear / Thy dangerous stoutness, for I mock at death / With as big heart as thou. Do as thou list. / Thy valiantness was mine, thou suck'st it from me, / But owe thy pride thyself."

The world can sleep no longer. Reason wakes
To know man's rights, and forward progress points.

Cor. By reason led, and peaceful wisdom nursed,
All progress is for good. But the deep curse
Of bleeding nations follows in the track
Of mad ambition, which doth cheat itself
To find a glory in its lust of rule;
Which, piling private ill on public wrong,
Beneath the garb of patriotism hides
Its large-mawed cravings; and would thoughtless plunge
To every change, however riot waits,
With feud intestine, by mad uproar driven,
And red-eyed murder, to reproach the deed.
Death in its direst forms doth wait on such.

Grac. Man lives to die, and there's no better way
To let the shackled spirit find its freedom
Than in a glorious combat 'gainst oppression.
I would not grudge the breath lost in the struggle.

Cor. Nor I, when duty calls. I am content,
May but my son prove worthy of the crisis:
Not shrinking from the trial, nor yet leaping
Beyond the marked outline of licensed right;
Curbing his passions to his duty's rule;
Giving his country all—life, fortune, fame—
And only clutching back, with miser's care,
His all untainted honor. But take heed!
The world doth set itself on stilts, to wear
The countenance of some higher, better thing.
'Tis well to seek this wisely; but with haste
Grasping too high, like child beyond its reach
It trips in the aspiring, and thus falls
To lowlier condition. Rashness drags
Remorse and darkest evil in her train.
Pause, ere the cry of suffering pleads to Heaven
Against this fearful mockery of right:
This license wild, which smothers liberty
While feigning to embrace it.

Grac. Thought fantastic
Doth drapery evil thus with unsketched ills.
No heart-sick maid, nor dream-struck boy am I
To scare myself with these. There's that in man

Doth long to rise by nature. Ever he
Crouching in lethargy, doth wrong himself.
Cor. Most true and more. I reverence human mind;
And with a mingled love and pride I kneel
To nature's inborn majesty in man.
But as I reverence, therefore would I lend
My feeble aid, this mighty power to lead
To its true aim and end. Most often 'tis
When crowds do wander wide of right, and fall
To foul misuse of highest purposes,
The madness of their leaders drags them on.
I would not check aspiring, justly poised;
But rather bid you "On!"—where light is clear
And your track plainly marked. I scorn the slang
Of "greedy populace," and "dirty crowd,"
Nor slander thus the nature which I bear.
Men in the aggregate not therefore cease
Still to be men; and where untaught they fall,
It is a noble duty, to awake
The heart of truth, that slumbers in them still.
It is a glorious right to rouse the soul,
The reasoning heart that in a nation sleeps!
And Wisdom is a laggard at her task
When, but in closet speculations toiling,
She doth forget to share her thought abroad
And make mankind her heir.[22]
Grac. [*Looking towards the street.*] Ah! Fulvius comes.
Cor. Your evil ghost doth haunt you in the form
Of this same factious citizen, who errs
From no bold error which outstrips the right
(And thus misleads oft by exaggerate good),
But, selfish to the core, he counts the worth
E'en of his madness.
Grac. Mother, you are harsh.
But I've no time to battle in his cause.

22. The preceding passage (3.1.1–83) was chosen to represent *Caius Gracchus* in Duyckinck, *Cyclopaedia of American Literature* 2:252–53; the same excerpt was repeated in Forrest, *Women of the South Distinguished in Literature,* pp. 482–84; and J. W. Davidson, *Living Writers of the South,* pp. 354–57.

Forgive my haste. I've business which must make
My best excuse for lack of courtesy. *Exeunt.*

SCENE II. *House of* Opimius.

Opimius *and* Drusus.

Opim. Enough, I say, of this vile, canting folly!
From its endurance out beyond the verge
You push my fretted patience. Leap at once!
Into it, man! Speak out: what is your price?
We'll pay you what you will, so you will rid us
Of this bold demagogue. Speak, hungry leech!
Come, we are private. Something chokes you. Gulp it.
Your honesty I'll not betray, nor tell
The secret to your compeers, by what star
You trace your windings. But one thing you see—
I know you; so leave off your shuffling; speak,
And speak out boldly. What's your will? your price?
Dru. But you, too quick, at nothing fire up.
I tried to think, if it were best for Rome—
Opim. Pshaw! pshaw! man! Let Rome be. We'll talk of her
When you'll have settled all your own affairs.
What think you of the fine Sardinian fields,
Or Agathyrnum[23] garden? Lycia has
Groves too, luxuriant, where her saffron grows.
Come, courage, man! plunge to the crumb o' the loaf,
Nor stand like hungry mouse, nibbling his crust
The while he eyes some well-stocked larder's store
Where longing dares not enter. What's your will?
Dru. Nay, if your generous liberality
My honest zeal sees fit to compensate,
With thanks I'll take the rich Sardinian field
And Agathyrnum garden.
Opim. What—*both,* man?
Thy maw is large—the swallowing chokes thee not.
But we've no time to chaffer. Mind our bargain!
Gracchus to Carthage—or the fields of Drusus
Must seek some other tenant.

23. Town on the north coast of Sicily, between Tyndaris and Calacte.

Enter LUCULLUS.

Ha! Lucullus,
Well met. Our wise good friend—our honest Drusus—
This worthy benefactor of his country,
Agrees with us, that for the destined plan
Of colonizing Carthage, there is none
So fit as Caius Gracchus, and doth promise
To so bestir himself that he will make
The post fall to his lot. Good man! he sees
(Moved by considerations of much weight)
How hangs the city's weal upon our plans. [*To Drusus*]
Good-day, my worthy friend; I see you're off. *Exit Drusus.*

Luc. It would have saved us many an aching head
Of wearing thought, and anxious watchfulness,
If we a nest had sooner found to lodge him.
To think is fearful, over all the laws
With which his influence has already checked
And bounded in the Senate's shackled power.
In every thing he does, the people praise him;
And, truth to say, were it not Caius Gracchus,
My thought would fix him honest. He so strongly
Doth dwell upon the majesty of Rome,
Whate'er the under-current of his feeling,
It shows most fairly. Where he even finds
His bitterest foes, within the Senate's heart,
He to a noble line of duty works them.
It was a wise and moderate decree
That he, for instance, argued them to pass
About the corn that our propraetor Fabius
Sent us from Spain.[24] Most needed too it was,
As antidote to angered feelings roused
By Fabius' tyranny throughout the province.
I wish the thought had come from any man
Sooner than Caius Gracchus. 'Tis a stamp
Of new-coined honor to him—a fresh feather
To deck his plumèd cap. But what's the good

24. In 123 Gracchus persuaded the Senate to pass a decree ordering that the grain which the governor of Spain, Quintus Fabius Maximus, had compelled the Spanish cities to send to Rome should be sold, and the money returned to the cities (Plutarch *Gaius Gracchus* 6.2). Fabius was Opimius' colleague in the consulship of 121.

From this short banishment we can expect?
Opim. Drusus is schooled and ready (curse the fate
That needs me tamper with so foul a thing!)
To make the most of his absence. He'll propose
Some petted laws, the people's love to coax.
Or rather (for they have no thought to love)
To catch the popular voice which drowns itself
With its own echoes often. Thus we'll soothe
And, flattering, choke with their own wish the crowd,
The turbulent throat of its loud worship hushing
That ever follows Gracchus; and the idol
Thus undermining from his pedestal,
The fickle homage of the people bring
To this our man of wax—nice-moulded thing—
That we must prop on Gracchus' vacant stool.
Luc. He has a law, they say, that strikes us home
Closer than any yet, and in the Forum
He will propose it presently.
Opim. I've heard
Much talk of it; and we I fear must stand
To witness one more triumph. May it be
At least his last. [[*Exeunt.*]]

SCENE III. *Street of Rome near Forum.*

Enter POMPONIUS *and* LICINIUS.

Pomp. On! We've no time to lose. I fear already
We've lost the argument. In all due form
Before I left was every right discharged.
By the presiding tribune prayer was said,
The business noted, and the herald read
The law which was proposed. A noble one!
Associate with the Senate it would give us
Three hundred knights to share the authority
Of our judicial courts. Quick, let us in. [[*Exeunt.*]]

SCENE IV. *Forum.*

Assembled People, LICINIUS, LUCULLUS, POMPONIUS, *etc.*
GRACCHUS *is addressing the Assembly.*

Grac. You've heard the law proposed. You've heard my colleague[25]
Declaim against it in no measured terms.
Branded you've heard it by our noble consul[26]
As most licentious, revolutionary.
Citizens, to you I turn. *Turns his face towards the Forum.*
Opim. [*Aside to Lucullus.*] Do you mark that?
Luc. 'Tis clap-trap cunning, which will take the people.
Grac. To you I speak, the country's pulse and life;
Ye are Rome's masters—her true governors
At once, and truest servants. 'Neath those shreds
The ragged emblems of your poverty,
And parti-colored badges of your rank,
Beats the great heart of Rome. This law is made
Not for convenience to the cradled rich,
Who, wrapped luxurious in the dainty folds
Of purple robes, and on their downy cushions
By sweetest music lulled, now frighted start
At the harsh tones I utter; it is made
For your necessities, ye struggling poor;
Judge *ye* then, of its merits: If it be,
As says our consul, revolutionary,
I do deny that it can be licentious.
Your courts of law I would not make less strict,
Nor from the doom inherited by vice
One hair's weight would I take. I would but give ye
Judges who in their duty read their law.
I would, at least in part, snatch frighted Justice
From bold Corruption's lucre-stainèd hand.
Who[m] have ye now for judges? Who[m] but those

25. Livius Drusus.

26. Gaius Fannius, consul in 122, in charge of Rome while his colleague Gnaeus Domitius Ahenobarbus was commanding Roman forces in southern Gaul. With the support of Gracchus, Fannius had been elected over Opimius (who had to wait until the following year) but had turned against his ally after entering office. When a great concourse of Italians was expected to flood into Rome in aid of Gracchus' legislation (including, presumably, the law extending Roman citizenship), Fannius pronounced an edict barring from the city during the voting period all who were not Romans; see below, 4.3.4–11.

The enthroned rich? Of all our natural rights
The bitterest foes! The Senate is your judge:
At once aggressor proud, and vengeful tyrant.
Where then is your appeal? Your refuge, where?
Romans, the fathers of this Senate were
Rome's noblest citizens; the country's prop,
And every way her boast. They won them rights,
From which, with all their vices, still their sons
Ought not to be cast down. Leave them the dues
Their Fathers' virtues won. Revere in them
The noble legacy of by-gone deeds;
But rouse ye 'neath oppression! See ye not
How with slow step and guarded look she comes;
Oft pausing; watching opportunities;
Doubtful advancing; seizing timidly
Some right disputed; till, now bolder grown,
With fearless stride, and open face of guilt,
She grasps at what she wills, nor feigns to hide
Her bold aggressions beneath justice' sham;
Corruption seizes with her myrmidons,
And every avenue to justice blocks.
    I have proposed, that with our Senators
An equal number of associate knights
Should now be added in authority
To judge all causes. Why the loud outcry
Indignant raised against me? 'Tis that thus
Our Senate feels the people has some voice,
Dictating its own councils; that the law,
Half wrested from that class which has no heart,
Nor with you, nor yet for you, may be spoken
Thus, through another court. Decide ye now;
To you, from that high Senate, I appeal:
Ye poor—ye suffering—ye sorrow-taught—
Ye crowd of trampled men, with souls as high,
And blood as red, as those who trample ye!
Because ye are plebeians, nor can boast
The blood of twenty fathers, have ye less
The rights of Romans and of citizens?
Plebeians have done noble acts in Rome,
And stamped in lines of blood some glorious deeds
Upon our country's annals. Have ye heard,

Or has the Senate bade ye blot it out
From Roman memories? Have ye forgot
That once, twice, thrice, Rome saw her battles turned,
Appeased her angry Gods, and victory snatched
From enemies already triumphing?
Three generations to the Decii owed
Their rescued safety.[27] Curius, from our coasts
Who drove the Epyran Pyrrhus—and, to tempt him,
When, from his earthen pot and frugal meal
Of garden vegetables, he was offered
The gold and luxuries of conquered Samnites,
Turned smiling from them, telling them to learn
That but an added lustre was the stamp
Of poverty, to who by virtue governed—
Was not *his,* too, this scorned plebeian blood?[28]
I will not shame you, by recounting farther
The noble deeds that every child should know;
Your hearts will count them for me. But one more,
And that my noble brother, I will name.
I thank my mother that she gave me not
For father, an Egyptian Ptolemy;
But, from the offers of a kingdom turning,
Gave heart and hand to a plebeian Roman,
And son and brother to a Gracchus made me.[29]
Are there of us, Plebeians, those whose gains,
By honest hoarding, prosperous adventure,
Among the richer class give them a place,
And who would spurn the poor, to rank themselves
By flattering adulation of the great?
Oh! learn ye that there is no higher place
Than that from which the self-ennobled turns

27. Three Roman consuls named Publius Decius Mus—father, son, and grandson—became types of unselfish dedication to the Republic, having each died in battle (340, 295, and 279) to secure Roman victory.

28. Manius Curius Dentatus, consul four times, censor in 272, conqueror of Samnites, Sabines, Senones, Lucani, and King Pyrrhus of Epirus (in 275), was the hero of many stories illustrating his humble birth and incorruptibility.

29. Gracchus (or LSM) alters chronology for the point of the argument: Cornelia received a proposal of marriage from a King Ptolemy of Egypt (probably Ptolemy VIII Physcon) after the death of her husband, Gaius' father (Plutarch *Tiberius Gracchus* 1.4).

A helping hand to lend to who would rise,
Like him, from abjectness.
Are there would sell,
For dirty gold and for patrician hire,
The city's rights? Shame them, if such there be,
Ye nobler hearts, in your coarse woven gowns;
E'en midst their ill-got luxuries, and their robes
Of showier texture, shame them with the sight
Of poverty, which is too proud to take
The price of virtue!
Romans, I leave you now
To answer for yourselves, and by your voices
Decide your fate. Speak out: Freemen, or Slaves?
Ay, more, ay, worse than slaves: outcasts and beggared,
The crouching suppliants to a lawless rule.
One word to you, ye noble Senators;
Though ye misdoubt me, as a friend I speak,
Of Rome and of no party. Conscript fathers,
I plead to you, with filial duty bending,
As son to a harsh parent. Let us end
This so unnatural struggle. Be but just,
We ask no more. This quarrel once removed,
Our rights acknowledged, and our privileges
Laid open fairly, to the strengthening 'tis
At once of you and us. Some ill-got gains,
Some power unjustly grasped, once given o'er,
Proud in your aristocracy ye stand,
And to Rome sacred. Strong in property,
Strong in construction of our laws ye stand,
Strong in the people's love, and in opinion;
Strong in the association of great deeds;
Strong in the immortal memory of the past.
Rome's history is yours, and is your fathers'!
The people love you for the names that grace
The glorious annals of our brightest years.
Oh! cast not from you all the homage due,
Which now a nation stands prepared to pay!
I've done, and leave the question to the vote
Of you, our here assembled centuries.

Presiding Magistrate. [*Rising.*] According to your judgments, speak, Quirites.

The people commence separating into centuries preparatory to giving their votes. [[*Exeunt.*]]

SCENE V. *House of* CORNELIA.

CORNELIA *and* LICINIA.

Cor. Well, who comes now, Licinia, that your eye
So often plays the truant to your work?
Lic. 'Tis Fulvius with Licinius; I will beckon,
That they may tell us how the day has turned.
Cor. Do so. 'Tis like enough they have the news.

Enter FULVIUS and LICINIUS.

Ful. Hurrah! Let's have a bout! But pray ye pardon;
I had forgot myself, most gentle ladies.
And yet I wot, your best wine were poor pay
To greet such news as mine.
Cor. Well, give the news,
And you shall have the wine; right good, forsooth;
A true old bottle of the finest stamp. *Servants bring wine, etc.*
How goes the day?
Ful. A glorious victory!
The law is carried, and three hundred knights
Hold judgment now, as with the Senate equal.
A glass for that; my news is thirsty, ladies,
And I must wash my throat, ere I go further.
Lic. Nay, give the rest; and you shall have full time
To drink your wine at leisure. Say, what next?
Ful. What next? Why next, the glorious people voted
That Caius should, from the equestrian class,
Himself make the selection, to fill up
This most important post. What think you, lady?
A kiss of thanks from those same rosy lips
Would scarce be more than, by their great deserts,
The greasy rascals have a right to claim
Their honest guerdon. But again I see,
Lady, I'm trespassing. You blush reproof
Stronger than words can speak it. Pray forgive.
Cor. You're too rough, Fulvius. In your news I know not
If good or evil lurks.
Ful. Good! *Glorious,* call it!

Gracchus, supreme in power, may govern Rome.
What shall we make of him? We need but choose.
Consul? Dictator? Say, what shall it be?
Cor. Nothing but Caius Gracchus and the friend
Of Rome, and of no party.
Ful. You are humble!
Cor. Humble? My pride ne'er found a higher flight!
To see my son the greatest man in Rome
And wish him virtue to maintain his place!
Call you this humble? 'Twere a grievous fall,
To have him barter, for a foolish rank,
The glorious title of his country's friend!
But here he comes.

Enter GRACCHUS.

Lic. Ah! Gracchus, my heart's throne!
Grac. My pretty bird, and my home's blessing, thou!
Mother, you've got the news. Fulvius, I know,
Lags never, in the telling of what's strange.
Licinius. And yet he has not told them what's more strange
Perhaps than all the rest. They have not heard
How you from the Comitium[30] turned away
And from the Senate-house, to which their looks
Our orators in reverence always fix,
And to plebeian Rome dared word your speech;
While frowning muttered the incensed patricians
Their unheard words of anger. 'Twas an act
Which must have weight, all simple though it seemed,
Through all Rome's history. The turning point
Betwixt patrician crushing tyranny,
And true plebeian freedom.
Cor. May it prove
But freedom, and not license!
Grac. Nay, good mother,
What means your ominous word, chilling our hope?
Cor. I tremble at the spirit you have raised,
And anxious watch its full development.

30. A broad rectangle of ground, in front of the Curia Hostilia (the Senate House) and between it and the Roman Forum; for what Gracchus' innovation in oratorical posture implied, see Plutarch *Gaius Gracchus* 5.3.

Perchance a thing of light, Minerva armed,
Sprung from the teeming brow of deity;
Perchance a demon foul to blast our eyes,
With fiendish horrors, and mad revelling,
Frighting off hope, to wither up our hearts.

Grac. But mother, thus you'd fright off effort too,
And weaken thought with gazing on itself.
No victory is gained but meeting risk;
And no abuse, however wild the rage
To which may run unlicensed tyranny,
But should be better than the stagnant pool
Of abject brutishness, and cringing fear,
Misery unstruggling, and imbècile woe,
To which, 'neath the dominion, Rome drives fast,
Of lawless aristocracy's abuse.
The madness into nature may be tamed;
The spring, too strong at first, be tempered right,
The exigencies of its need to suit;
But crouching idiocy, that, 'neath the stripes
Of unchecked power, doth drivel out its last
Of crushed humanity, can only rise,
As doth the monster, beastlike from its lair,
To fury roused at last, but not to reason.

Cor. You argue well. And yet in purposes
Well reasoned even, oft to evil leads
Too rash precipitance. As half-spent torch,
From a child's hand, the mighty forest fires,
Thus human passions, easily aroused,
Storm forth their angry blaze. The frighted thing
That waked the crashing storm, bewildered shrinks
From fierce destruction, in its raging might,
Which, hissing, roars alternate; and doth gaze,
In terror stupified, at its own work.
You drop the spark, but can you rule the flame
Of unchained passion's might?

Grac. I know not, mother.
But 'tis a thing to try.

Cor. Step coolly, then;
With well directed foot of prudent caution.
Haste trips us in the race.

Grac. My foot is in,
And I have boldly met the threatened risk.
Ful. Ay, more than boldly; nobly! Rome must make
New words to praise you.
Grac. Pray you, praise me not.
I'd rather see my mother's clouded brow
In complacent approval smooth itself,
Than catch the flattery of crowds like you.
When the whole soul of energy is bent
To work some object that it needs must win,
Or find itself undone, no will it has
Of words to catch the windy flattery;
But, in its conscious effort wrapped, it finds,
So greedy for success, no thought nor taste
To greet a smaller praise.
I had forgot
To tell you, mother, what annoys me much.
It seems, determined by some adverse luck,
I must be off to Carthage.
Cor. Ha! indeed!
Thus evil chance doth work; and yet, perhaps,
'Tis better thus. We'll talk of it again. [[*Exeunt.*]]

ACT IV.

SCENE I. *Carthage.*

Workmen occupied in building.

First Work. This Caius has a resolute heart, methinks,
Or from the start he would have given up.
With my good will, I'd not have struck one stroke
After the breaking of our standard staff.
It was an evil omen.
Second Work. And—far worse—
When by the winds our solemn sacrifice
Beyond the marks laid for the city's bounds
Was scattered borne; and when the howling wolves
With deafening clamor came, and carried off
The very marks themselves. It was a daring,

Most manifest of outraged Heaven's will
To persevere against such fearful omens.

First Work. And yet we have succeeded. It would seem
Some other way the Gods their warning meant.

Third Work. For Gracchus' self, some say, it was intended.

First Work. And that is what I fear. I love so well
His noble heart—almost, to ease him of it,
On my own shoulders I'd take all the risk.

Second Work. Hush! do not be so foolhardy, to dare
The judgment of the Gods! I shudder thus
To hear you speak. Do you not see, there's that
Doth mark out Gracchus as one made for sorrow?
He is of those who bear upon their brow
The stamp of some sad doom.

First Work. And yet methinks
A noble brow it is.

Second Work. Ay, oftenest thus
The noblest do the Gods mark out to bear
The sorrows of the world.

Third Work. Stop! Here he comes.

Enter GRACCHUS *and Messenger.*

Grac. An information, say you, against Fulvius?

Mes. Yes, sundry charges—and, in truth, no light ones.
'Tis likely to go hard with him, for Drusus
Gains ground in every way, and bears his power
In its full strength against him: while Opimius
Pampers at wish the now o'ergorgèd crowd,
Till, with indulgence cloyed, the multitude,
Drunk with the surfeit of its palled desires,
Doth, as the boon of so much license, promise
The consulship in guerdon.

Grac. Ha! Opimius!
This doth need looking after. We will sail
With the first favouring wind. My duties here
Have prospered so, that they my present eye
No longer need. An hour or two, and then,
Some few directions to my workmen given,
I will be with you. *Exeunt.*

SCENE II. *Street of Rome.*

SEPTIMULEIUS *and Citizens.*

Sept. I do not like at all the looks of things.
This information against Fulvius bodes
No good to Gracchus. It is certain, too,
That from the tribuneship he'll be turned out.
First Cit. The people may find means to hinder that.
Sept. They can't! They can't! Opimius is a man
Will have his way. He's a great man; and I
Begin to think, an undue noise we've made
And pother for this Gracchus.
First Cit. Ha! I thought
You were no timeserver; his best of friends!
Sept. Timeserver! surely not. But if a man
Is thick with faults, I've got an eye to see them.
First Cit. And his bad luck doth make each fault a twin,
To who rates merit only by its gains.
Sept. Pshaw! you're a crabbèd fellow! I care not
For further talk with you. But mark my words,
Gracchus has seen his last of the tribuneship. [[*Exeunt.*]]

SCENE III. *Another part of Rome.*

Enter GRACCHUS *and* LICINIUS.

Grac. Scarce have I set my foot in Rome, returned
From an accomplished business, which they hoped
Would keep me for a lifetime from her walls,
Than boldly shows their game. When was the time
That ever Roman consul dared to issue
Such proclamation as the Senate now
Has coaxed from Fannius?[31] Citizens of Rome
Not born within her limits, must forthwith
The city's precincts leave! Chased like mad dogs!
Deprived at once of citizenship, forsooth!
Because the Senate cannot buy their votes.

Enter DRUSUS *and another Tribune.*

31. See above, 3.4.3–4 and note.

Dru. Gracchus, good-day. Would I could hail you still
Colleague, and brother tribune. With regret
We lose your valued service.

Grac. [*turning from Drusus, speaks to Licinius*] Bah! 'tis foul!
Would you believe it: these two worthy tribunes,
These noble, true, and honorable men,
Who, for the disappointment I have met,
Now speak their sorrows—would you think that these,
These very two, with simpering look, and lip
Of flattering condolence, were the men
Who at the election counted up the votes,
And thus procured by fraudulent return
That I, a tribune fair elected, stand
Here officeless? Faugh! Let's away! This meanness
That crawls and licks the dust, it sickens me.
I'd sooner meet Opimius, or such villain,
Who, what he does, does boldly. There's a show
Almost of honor in his dashing crime.
But this mean, crouching shame, that blushless seeks
Its smerchèd visage with the soilèd cloak
Of honesty to wrap! Faugh! 'tis the taint
Of carrion—dead game. True hound will shun it.
They are not worth the running down. Let's off.

Dru. This 'tis to serve one's country! Taunted thus,
My conscience stands me true.

Grac. Conscience, quoth he!
Where picked he up the word? Conscience! ha! ha!
I had a parrot once, could talk and prate
And chatter words in its sharp querulous tone,
As though it knew their sense. Conscience, forsooth!

Dru. To rail abusive is the loser's wont.
Upon the gainer's side the laugh doth rest.

Grac. Call you it gaining, winning as you do?
Truly you've gained what you can never lose:
A stamp of vice, a never changing shame
That haunts you to your grave. Did you but know it,
You've gained a loss, which makes you as a stench
In every true man's nostrils! Come, Licinius.

Exeunt Gracchus and Licinius.

Dru. I would arrest him in the people's name
For disrespect to their tribunes, but that—that—

Trib. But that we are ashamed. Drusus, he speaks

Such bitter truths as we deserve to hear.
Would I had never joined the dirty game!
His words cling to me as a nauseous soil,
And my whole soul, meseems, doth stink of it!
We've played our honor and our souls of men
Against the Senate's monies and their lands;
And, as he tells us, we have gained a loss
That damns us in the filth of our own acts.

Dru. Why, man! what means this puling face of grief?
Doff it; or you'll betray to peering eyes
The mysteries of our nice diplomacy.

Trib. Time has been—ere I let the Senate's gold
Filthy my itching fingers—I could stand,
Bare my clean bosom to the crowd, and feel
Lighthearted by inspection.

Dru. Pshaw! Cheer up,
And don't give way to whimsies such as this.
It was to serve the country that we labored,
And slightly doubtful means are often fit
To work an end of certain benefit. *Exeunt.*

SCENE IV. *Street of Rome.*

FULVIUS *and* GRACCHUS.

Ful. Pluto and the infernal Gods! Give up?
What, man! Back out before this rascal consul?
This proud Opimius? Why, ere this I thought
His lawless rule, and grinding usurpation,
Had purged your halting conscience of its doubts.

Grac. Fulvius, my soul hath fire enough, nor needs
Your flashing speech, of flint to tinder words,
To rouse it into action. Of my breast
The tight-drawn cord, vibrating with the touch,
Like high-tuned instrument rings back your words
In tones of passion, till almost it bursts.
What unskilled tuner are you, thus to screw
And tighten up a string already wound
Above its pitch of tone?

Ful. But what's the matter,
That we must tamely stand, to bide this insult?
What's this Opimius? Is he god, or ghost,
Or fiend, or devil, that we shrink, and shrink,

And cower before him thus? A consul he
Of yesterday's election! Hardly more—
And yet already he hath lessoned us
To due humility, 'twould seem: for ever
"*Give way*" 's the word! Give way! give way! forsooth!
And in the Furies' name, I would know, why?
I'll not give way. No! Let him fight it out,
I'll meet him where he dares. For you, how meekly
You stand to see your labor's fruit laid waste!
Your life's work thrown aside! These he prepares
All to undo. Your laws he will repeal.
The colonizing Carthage, which himself
So lately thought—and the assembled Senate—
Then all important, now he will annul.
The faintest trace which of your name is left
Upon the country's acts, he'll foul, and blot,
And from the city's memory trample out.
Why such unheard of course? Hardly in power,
The rein he strains of his authority
Almost to bursting. Cramped and fettered laws
Are dragged and fretted to find out some term,
That to your injury may be worded thus;
The import of their execution ever
Being still the same and one, to lash at Gracchus.

Grac. Curse on his heart, 'tis true! Find but the means—
I tell you, find the means!—nor ever ring
The changes thus of his accursèd wrongs
On my impatient ear! Find but the means:
This doublehearted traitor I will meet,
Nor shrink the struggle, be it to the death!

Ful. Come with me to my house; you'll meet some friends
Who wait to talk upon this matter there. *Exeunt.*

SCENE V. CORNELIA'*s House.*

GRACCHUS *and* CORNELIA.

Cor. All wrong! all wrong! What mean, thronging our streets,
These hired bands? No Roman faces these!
Strangers who skulk at noon-day, 'neath the garb
And roughness feigned of country reapers hiding

Some ill intent. I like it not; it smacks
Of evil purpose.

Grac. Nay; to be trampled on!
Forever driven to the wall by fraud
From these our task-masters, yet be reproached
When in their own base coin we pay them home
Some trifling arrears! Curse them, I'll strike,
And with their own unholy weapons maim them!

Cor. This is a mistimed anger, and I grieve
That you to beard Opimius have resolved.
His aim is your imprudence; and you thus,
By this hotheaded Fulvius spurred, now cast
Your every point into his ready hand.
'Tis the calm right that you should seek to win,
Nor cheat your heart, while nursing its revenge,
To think that duty works it. Call you this,
This rampant hate, and angry violence,
Which drives a thoughtless people to the verge
Of lawless anarchy, which grasps at fraud
To work its selfish ways, and makes success,
Not right, its rule of action—call you this,
Because you link with it some real wrong
Inflicted on a thoughtless populace—
Call you this patriotism? Search your heart
And read its motives clearer.

Grac. You much wrong me,
And travesty my truest feelings, mother,
In most unworthy garb.

Cor. Would it were so!
Most willingly I'd take the wrong myself,
To know your object pure. But you have let
Your passion much mislead you. You have been
So erring in your selfish thought, to lose
The higher point of action. May you find
Occasion fitting to retrace your steps!
The time's unripe, and you would force it on,
Not by a gentle teaching to the truth,
But gag it to your own ideas of right,
And force mankind to gulp your system down.
Oh! check this energy, whose mistimed warmth
Has in the crowd a storm of passion roused

Of inauspicious aspect. Con again
The lessons you yourself had taught, ere letting
Our moneyed landholders' oppressive frauds
Opposing frauds within your bosom wake,
Driving the noblest feelings to that verge
Where virtue becomes rashness, and ambition
Outtracks the path of right. If yet 'tis time,
Unspeak your spell. The angry turmoil sooth[e]
Of differing tempers, which now clashing rage
Like the wild waves of some tumultuous sea,
Each lashing each to anger.

Grac. Can it be
That I in passion thus have drowned the right?
There is a half contrition in my heart
That speaks your judgment true. Your calmer thought
Doth damp the fierceness of my anger's hate;
And, with cooled passion, my big faults do rise
To taunt me with their folly. I will try;
Trust me, I'll do my best; and now farewell.
Licinia need not know all that is passing.
She has, you know, not half your courage, mother;
Let her be quiet; if the storm must burst,
She'll learn it time enough. [[*Exeunt.*]]

SCENE VI. *Capitol.*

OPIMIUS, *Lictors, friends of Opimius, Senators, etc.*
GRACCHUS, FULVIUS, *and friends of Gracchus.*
OPIMIUS *standing by the altar, robed in white, and crowned with cypress.*

Opim. Thou, Jupiter Capitoline, to whom
Acceptable thus far our offerings seem,
Watch over us and Rome!
Lictors, remove,
And let these entrails by the aruspices[32]
Be in accordance with all form examined.

Lict. [*Passing with the entrails strikes against Fulvius and exclaims.*]

32. "Auruspices" in 1851 ed. The (h)aruspices were diviners imported from Etruria, who predicted events by inspecting the entrails of sacrificed animals.

Stand off, ye crew of traitors, and make way,
That honest men may pass.

Ful. Traitor to me! *Strikes him.*
Take that to mend your manners, ribald tongue!

First Cit. And that!

Citizens rush with daggers upon the Lictor, who falls.

Second Cit. And that!

Grac. [*Rushing forward.*] Fulvius, you ruin all!
What means this mistimed brawl, unmannerly?

Ful. I've been insulted, and have not the temper
To suck up harsh words, fattening on abuse,
And nurse its quiet with the promised dream
Of what some "by-and-by" may bring to pass.
I've been insulted; and, if corpses speak,
Quintus Antyllius there may calculate
What strength my passion casts into a blow.

Grac. Too much, alas! and not, I fear, to end
With this, of a poor lictor the one death;
For many, noble are the heads whose doom
Is in that one impatient blow entailed.

Opim. [*Advancing.*] Tremble, ye Roman people! Citizens,
No more I bid you now be bold—but rather,
In the amazement of my terror, warn ye
Before offended Deity to crouch.
Ye have full cause for fear! Our sacrifice
Profaned by blood in passion shed, unholy—
Accursèd on our heads our prayers cast back,
Heap vengeance from the gods: for murder soils
With bloody sacrilege our holiest rites.
Here at the altar of our angered god,
Let us now seek to humbly expiate
This impious deed. *Turns and kneels at the altar.*
Great Jove! hear us and pity!
Promiscuous let thy thunders strike us not.
In wisdom judge thou, and in justice doom!

Corpse of Antyllius is brought forward on a bier.

The innocent victim which to thee we bring,
Receive in expiation of this deed
Ill-omened and unrighteous. Of our hearts

See every spouting wound interpreter,
In blood speak forth our will to right the insult
Of thy profanèd temple; from its walls
Polluted, to wash out the bloody stain,
And make revenge co-equal with the crime.

Rises and turns towards attendants.

Now through the Forum, by our weeping Senate
All in its bleeding livery escorted,
The consecrated victim bear, and rouse
The frightened people to revenge their god.

Exit OPIMIUS *with attendants, bearing the body and followed by Senators, making loud acclamations of grief and indignation.*

Ful. A fig for all their weeping! What have they
To whine and wail, like over-pampered child,
Because a noisy lictor meets his death?

Grac. They weep for joy that in that same dead corse
A weapon you have given, which they will wield
With deadly import. Curse your reckless passion!
That in a moment's space has done more harm
Than years of sober council can unmake.

Ful. Pshaw! You'll turn orator, and make a speech
In honor of this beggar's funeral!
With care and watching your mind wearied out
Doth, thus enfeebled, turn to start at shadows.

Grac. Would it were so! But from this hasty deed
Doth spring a progeny of thick-coming ills,
That but to gaze at chills me. Come, Licinius,
And you, Pomponius, I would speak with you.

Exit with Licinius and Pomponius.

Ful. It is a noble heart, though somewhat slow
To meet the exigencies of the time.

First Cit. I would we had not killed this lictor, though.
Slowness sometimes is virtue. It were well
If we had been less sudden.

Ful. Well, I wish
As prompt an arm there was for every one
Of these our Senators who weeping stand
Around a paltry lictor's bier to wail.
Who would believe that this same capitol,
Which now so loudly they proclaim profaned,

Shows yet upon its walls the scattered stains
Tiberius Gracchus' blood had sprinkled there?
Him they cast forth, the refuse of their hate
(Rome's tribune by her Senate done to death);
No funerals were granted to our prayers:
He was the people's friend—what needed he
Of sanctifying forms and ceremonies?
But now, behold! in this unrighteous farce,
About a hireling's corse Rome's nobles stand,
In feignèd penitence to bow their heads;
And, in their weeping expiation, seek
To magnify a fault, whose heightened crime
Upon the people's head their hate would pile.

Enter Messenger.

Mes. Sent by your friends, I come to tell you, Fulvius,
That, with pretence to save the commonwealth,
Opimius, sanctioned by the Senate, issues,
To the patricians and the knights, an order
That they shall all, well armed and well escorted,
Attend him in the morning; and 'tis said
A price is set on your and Gracchus' head.
Ful. Hear you this, citizens? Who stands by me?
Citizens. I—I—and I—and I—and all of us!
Ful. I thank you all. Come with me, and we'll hold
All things in readiness to meet the morning.
Huzza for Rome! but down with our proud Senate!
We will pronounce them traitors to the people,
And set a price upon their heads. Let's vote it.
Who will say "ay"?
Citizens. Ay, ay.
Ful. It is pronounced.
We do decree these reverend Senators
Shall lose their heads whenever we can catch them;
And that their weight in gold shall be the prize
Of every man who can pick up so much
By pillaging the overflowing hoards
Of these our sacred rats: time-worshipped scourges,
Deities to whom, not hoping good we've prayed,
But rather for the ill we sought to shun.
Huzza then for the people! For the Senate,

Down with them! Hang the Senate!
Citizens. Huzza! Huzza!
Down with the Senate. *Exeunt, riotously.*

SCENE VII. *Street near the Statue of the Father of Gracchus.*

Enter GRACCHUS, POMPONIUS, *and* LICINIUS. *Citizens passing and following.*

Grac. All then seems vain. Our every scheme is nought.
Each, as it nears us, in the light of hope
All radiant glitters, as, in early beam
Of morning's sun, the dew besprinkled web.
But stretch the eager hand to seize it—lo!
Our lightest touch its nothingness but proves;
And, with the broken fragment of its thread
All shattered in our grasp, forlorn we stand,
Orphaned of hope, and our own fancy's fool!
Oh! had I steeled my heart against ambition,
And in its unity but held the hope
That worked me first to action—seeking to bring
The people to that perfectness which nature
Makes their inherent right—I had not been
Thus in the web of mine own faults entangled!
My soilèd hands, ungrateful to the Gods,
In impure sacrifice have lost their strength.
The workman is not equal to his task.
Pomp. Rather the task is one impracticable,
From nature doomed to failure. For who talks
Of the crowd's fickleness, talks nothing new.
How oft tomorrow finds, where now they fawn,
Their bitter mockery, or their loudest hate!
And today's idol is the cast off thing
Which yesterday they trampled under foot!
Blame not the weakness of your hand, but rather
The rotten stuff you work on.
Grac. Yet, I feel
There dwells in them a self-redeeming power.
They must by nature's instinct have the sense
That I have sought to rouse. But I, unskilful,
Play not upon their hearts. Some loftier mind
Must wake the spirit that to me is dead:

Rousing the human soul that in them sleeps,
To its high note of harmony and truth.

As they pass the statue of his father, GRACCHUS *pausing stands for some time earnestly gazing at it.*

Pomp. Let us pass on.
Licinius. He heeds us not. He's wrapped
In contemplation of some distant thought
That finds no home with us.
Pomp. 'Twere best to leave him.
We but upon his privacy intrude.
He seems as he, by gazing, hoped to drag
A spirit from his father's statue forth,
And would hold converse with him. Let us on,
And leave him to himself.
Licinius. Nay. Rather we
Should closely watch him; for in times like these
He needs his every friend. We intrude not;
He heeds us not, nor longer knows our presence.
Following the heaving sigh, see that slow tear!
In mute communion spring they from his bosom,
All anguished with the throes of some big thought
That seeks to force its being into life,
Then struggles back into his panting breast,
Which hugs the living torture to itself.
Pomp. It is a fearful struggle—but he wakes.
Grac. Let us go home. My mother watches for me;
While my young wife, novice in sorrow, wraps
Close to her beating heart my baby boy,
And wonders why its father stays so long.
Exit with Pomponius and Licinius.
First Cit. Would I could right him, were it with my life!
At least let's follow and keep watch for him.
Second Cit. Yes—we will cheer him up; huzza about him,
As does the crowd round Fulvius.
First Cit. And get drunk,
Go mad as they do? No, no. In the face
Of Gracchus look, and learn there to be sober.
Third Cit. Truly it is a face that doth draw tears!
I never thought so great a man, and wise,
Could need the pity of poor folks like us.

But now to look at him, 'twould seem indeed
That his tried heart doth throb and ache, all one
As 'twere my own poor son's! [[*Exeunt.*]]

ACT V.

SCENE I. *Street near* GRACCHUS' *house.*

Enter CORNELIA *and* LICINIA, *with Child.*

Lic. I will watch here. He needs must pass this way,
And I will see him.
Child. Mother, are you cold?
Lic. No, child.
Child. What ails your hand to shake so, then?
Cor. Come hither, little one. Your mother's sad;
Her head aches; she's not over well today.
Let her be quiet. She'll be better soon.
Child. If she's not well, why does she stand in the street,
And gazing round to see who passes by?
Cor. Hush! hush! you should be with your nurse at home,
Instead of coming to ask idle questions
Thus at street corners.
Child. Nay then, what have you,
And what has mother either, got to do
Thus at street corners? I have heard you say
Often, that women should not run the street.
Lic. Peace, malapert! Your nurse is watching for you.
Run to her and she'll take you home.
Child. I will not.
Lic. You will not? What!
Child. I am not naughty, mother!
I only wish you'd let me stay with you.
You look so sad and grave, as father did
This morning when he kissed me.
Lic. Chatterbox!
You were asleep until your father went;
And 'twas in dressing you, I left him time
To give me thus the slip.
Child. I did not sleep;
I only held my eyes close shut, because—

Lic. Because? Say on.
Child. Because you talked so sad
It made me cry to hear you, and you know
Father laughs at me when I cry, and says
I'll never make a soldicr. So I kept
My eyes close shut, and then he could not see
And thought I was asleep. It was no harm;
Don't look so sorry, mother; was it wrong?
I did not think there had been harm in it.
Cor. Poor baby! get thee home. 'Tis a sad thing
To tutor thee thus early to thy griefs.
Go home! go home!
Child. Do let me stay. I'm good.
Cor. No, no; go home, and we'll come presently;
And look you on my table, you will find
A pretty toy, with the new whip you wished for
To drive your wooden horse. Run home now; quick!
Or you'll not find them there.
Child. [*Kissing her.*] Dear Grandmama!
Mama, do kiss me too. I'd rather stay;
But I'll be good, and you'll come quicker home,
And then I'll show you how my horse will trot.
Perhaps he'll canter too, with his new whip. *Exit Child with Nurse.*
Lic. Sorrow! thou earnest teacher! to whom life
Is but a school wherein man's heart is curbed
To do thee homage—lay thy heavy hand,
Gently as sorrow may, on that young head.
Let the deep anguish of my burdened heart
Work out the task at once, for him and me!
And for myself, I only pray that I
May be so tough of heart, it shall not break
Until my double duty is performed.
Cor. Hush! Here are steps.
Lic. 'Tis Caius comes. I knew
He could not else, but he must pass this way.
Cor. It is not Caius. Here are rapid steps,
And noisy words, and clashing arms, with sounds
Of boisterous brawling, and of drunken mirth. *Noise without.*
Lic. Mother, I am afraid! Where shall we go?
Cor. Be still and stand aside. They will not hurt you.
I see now: it is Fulvius with his friends.

Oh Rome! how art thou sunk, when such as these
May claim the name of patriots!

Enter FULVIUS *and noisy crowd of Citizens, armed.*

Cit. Which way now?
Ful. On to the Aventine hill! Seize it, and make
These proud patricians learn to know their masters!
Citizens. On to the Aventine hill! Death and revenge!
Hurra! down with the Senate! Hurra! on!
Death to the proud patricians! Death and sorrow,
Hunger and cold, as they have brought on us!
Starvation seize them! Let them rot in gutters
And gasp their lives out, sprawling on the ground
As they have bade us do. On! on! to crush them! *Exeunt with Fulvius.*
Lic. 'Tis fearful, mother! Surely these are not
The men who call themselves the friends of Gracchus!
Cor. I would they did not. 'Tis the festered limb
That makes his cause to halt, and there's no surgeon
So skilful he can lop the gangrene off.
I fear me, the whole body dies of it.
Lic. I would I were a man, with a man's soul,
And not the coward nature modelled me!
Cor. What would you, fair face, if you were a man?
Lic. I know not what I would, but I would try
To stand by Caius as another self.
I would have cast myself before that crowd,
Instead of shrinking from its noisy riot;
And would have frowned on them, as Caius might,
Borrowing the solemn thunder of his voice,
And, with his quiet majesty of mien,
Bid them go home, and hush their savage tumult.
I am a coward—ay—a very hare
For panting fearfulness, and yet, methinks,
I could for Gracchus cast my life away,
E'en as a worthless straw! I heard last night,
When he believed me sleeping, sighs burst forth,
With groans of bitter anguish, as his heart
Would burst itself in the uttering. On his brow
I laid my soothing hand. Big sweat-drops there
Stood, as when, labor-worn, the workman tired
Doth resting pant, from overstrainèd toil.

I rose and pressed my lips to his, which burned
With a hot fever; quivering, too, they seemed
All tremulous, as nerved with agony.
Clinging, I hoped to cool them with my breath;
But tear-drops then came coursing from his eyes
Slowly, as thunder-drops before the storm;
And then, from head to foot a shivering came!
Oh mother! It was fearful thus to see
The strong man in his agony!

Cor. My child,
E'en in my breaking heart, which overcharged
With its own miseries bursts, I feel there's room
Still left to pity thee. But helpless all,
While pity grasps the burden, until reason
Doth totter 'neath the load, yet fails she still
To ease thee of one fraction of its weight.
Let us go home. You can do no good here.

Lic. No, I must stay. Gracchus went out unarmed,
As though on simple business to the Forum,
And I have brought him this. [*Shows a dagger.*]

Cor. 'Tis a small help.
But here he comes.

Lic. Dear heaven! I give you thanks
For this one comfort, in so many sorrows!

Enter GRACCHUS *and friends.*

Grac. Mother! Licinia! What do you here?

Lic. We watch for you. I pray you, Caius, come,
Come with me home! You shake your head; well, then—
Come with me anywhere! In other worlds
We'll make a home elsewhere.[33] Nay, smile not thus,
As though in mockery of my simple suit!
What's Rome to you that you should die for her,
And leave your wife and boy?[34] Come, dearest—do!
Come, drown ambition, drinking deep of love!

Grac. Licinia, would you save your husband thus?

33. *Coriolanus* 3.3.133–35: "Despising / For you the city, thus I turn my back. / There is a world elsewhere!" The speaker is Coriolanus.

34. *Hamlet* 2.2.553–54: "What's Hecuba to him, or he to her, / That he should weep for her?"

If I have erred ambitiously—at least,
Not by a foul desertion bid me swell
My much repented fault. Should I a traitor—
Recreant—turn cowardly, to shun my friends,
Would you, love, longer own my tarnished name,
Or rather weep for Gracchus as one dead,
With horror shrinking from the counterfeit,
Whose shame could blight his honor! E'en yourself,
With all your gentle cowardice, would shun
And blush to name the father of your boy.
Entreat me not, then, with an early shame
To blot his fair young brow; but rather let
A father's blessing guard his orphaned pillow.
Bear him my parting kiss, and now, *farewell.*

Lic. [*Falling on her knees catches his robe.*]
No, no! Come home with me! I'd love you still,
Though you of the world's shame were made the butt;
I'd love you in my heart's world, and forget
Men's flouts and hisses, as the howling cry
Of savage beasts that roam in unseen wilds.
Men's voices hurt us not; we'll let them pass,
And think that they are spirits, gibbering ghosts,
That wander in some stranger world to ours.
The wind doth blow and hiss us every day,
And howls and whistles in its mocking rage,
And yet we heed it not. The forest trees
Do constant whisper 'mong their summer leaves,
And yet we never fret to learn their secrets!
Men's talk, as innocent, would hurt us not,
Would we but doom them exiles from our world
And live in our own hearts!

Grac. Dearest, you'd spurn—
None sooner than yourself—this foolish dream,
Did once your better reason find its sway.

Lic. Speak to him, mother! Bid him stay with us.
What is the world to him? Its thought wounds not.
He would not bleed because it frowned! Speak, mother!

Cor. Alas! I cannot in your cause, my child.
Our life is for the world. Man doth forget
His every highest purpose, scorning it;
And from the level of his high intent

Doth thus degrade himself.
Lic. Oh! I am mad!
I cannot reason; I but pray: "Come home."
You do not leave me now as formerly,
Tribune or lawgiver, from the rostra speaking;
Nor yet a glorious war doth summon you,
Where, should death be your lot, at least I'd see
Your corse brought home for noble funerals.
Meek victim of an angered foe, you go—
Oh Gods! for what? I had forgot—take this. *Gives the dagger.*
Grac. As a last gift I take it. But I go
Unarmed, as he should do whose mind is fixed
To suffer violence, rather than commit it.
Lic. You go before the murderers of Tiberius
To throw your life away! And I must soon
A weeping suppliant to the river stand
To beg the corpse of Gracchus! Mother, kneel!
Do you not love your son? Does your heart beat?
He is your all on earth! Kneel with me, mother;
Draws Cornelia to her knees.
Pray to him here, as though he were some god!
He will not dare refuse you! 'Twere a shame
To see him spurn his mother! I am mad;
I cannot pray. Pray *you* as though great Jove
Were looking down upon us! Mother, pray!
Grac. Mother, have pity! Rise. Remember, now,
Your oft-spoke lesson. Death is nothing, standing
Close elbowed by dishonour. Kneel not to me.
Cor. I do not kneel to you. Hear me, ye Gods!
My supplications are to you for this
My last, best hope in life; my *only one!*
I pray ye now to give him strength to bear
This heavy trial; parting, worse than death,
From the heart-stricken loved ones! Go, my son.
I have no word to stop you. If your life
Without dishonour can be saved, remember
You owe it to your wife, and to your boy.
Farewell! The gods protect you!
Grac. Noble mother!
Forgive me that I have so often spurned
Your wiser councils. Now the ghosts of them,

While your reproach is mute, look mournful back
To show me all my folly, and my sin.
Farewell! *Disengages himself gently from Licinia, who falls fainting into Cornelia's arms.*
And for this poor heart-broken thing,
Receive her, mother, as the legacy
Of all the love I bear you. *Exit, with friends.*

Cor. He is gone!
What mean my niggard eyes that they do leave
Their fount for sorrow dry! Let madness come!
Or drivelling idiocy, that droops its life
In moping corners! It were peaceful rest! *Pauses thoughtfully.*
But this is weakness. Thus Heaven wills it not.
My laggard spirit faints before its time;
My task is not yet done. Up! up! and work!
Life yet has duties, and my comfort is
Yet to fulfil them. Daughter! Daughter! wake!
We must go seek our boy, who waits us still,
To show us how his wooden horse can trot!
Oh! what a motley is this struggling world! [[*Exeunt.*]]

SCENE II. *Aventine Hill.*

GRACCHUS *and* FULVIUS.
Crowds of Citizens in the distance.

Ful. I'll bear no further cringing.

Grac. I ask none.
But rather that you'd meet a noble risk
To save our friends by what perchance may prove
Our proper immolation. Come with me
To plead before the Senate.

Ful. I am tired.
You have my son; do with him what you list.
He's soft enough to coax and wheedle for you!
His mother's readiness of tears he has,
And blushing face, and gently cringing voice.
No gift have I of words, nor will I crouch
The Senate from its crabbèd whim to move.
I come here armed for fight.

Grac. And will, I fear,

Make sooner than not meet the war you seek.

Enter Messenger.

What news? Your eager look seems full of speech.
Mes. The Senate mock your offers, and have seized
Young Fulvius prisoner. Criminals, they say,
Before they plead for mercy, should surrender.
Ful. They say we plead for mercy! Hear you that?
Mes. Opimius, eager for hostilities,
Advances with a corps of infantry,
Backed by a company of Cretan archers.
Ful. Hurra! I will prepare for them. Ho! friends,
Come up! we've work on hand. *Exit.*
Grac. And I, alas!
Have nearly done that share which falls to me. [[*Exeunt.*]]

SCENE III. *Streets of Rome.*

Confusion of fighting. Citizens and troops passing to and fro. Then enter two Citizens, wounded.

First Cit. I pray you bind my arm. Nay, not so tight!
Your whole of fear was cast into that jerk.
Be easy; of too little moment are we
For them to follow us. Beneath their thoughts
Are we to feed or kill. As we may starve
Until our bodies trip them in the streets,
So may we live, if from their dignity
We of our lubbard carcass keep the sight,
Nor shock them with the thought that we are men
Who breathe Heaven's air like them.
Second Cit. Well, I'll take heed
To keep me from their track. That rascal Fulvius
Will scarce again tempt me to meet them.
First Cit. Hang him!
It was most foul to run and leave us there,
All weltering too, in wounds and broken bones!
And then of men to see the difference!
How Gracchus stood, and with his cry of "*Peace!*"
Did check Opimius (who strewed corpses round),
And cried, "*Shame on you, Consul! Spare your people!*"
And would not leave the ground, though all unarmed,

Until he was dragged off, and crying still:
"Consul, you break the pith of your own strength!
The people is the sinew of the country.
In mercy spare your slaughter!"

Second Cit. Here are troops!
Help us, great Jupiter! Troops! troops! Let's run. *Exeunt.*

SCENE IV. *Temple of Diana.*

GRACCHUS, LICINIUS, PHILOCRATES.
Enter POMPONIUS.

Pomp. Fulvius, unsaved by his ignoble flight,
Is seized and slain. Our victors lap up gore
Like thirsty hound, and livid death now sits
The close familiar of our firesides.
Mothers, who but just now sent forth their sons
With life all blooming, hug a bloody corpse;
While widows weep, bewildered children stare
On stiffening limbs which but this morning's sun
Might see them frolic with. One slaughter-house,
Rome suicidal dies 'neath her own blows.
The dastard crowd, all frightened, crouching shrink
From the red death that tracks them, and, in hopes
To win impunity, now crack their throats
With loud huzzas, and adulation forced
Of these their task-masters. With bended brows,
Heads leaning towards each other, then they name
What price your head doth in the Senate bear;
While their slow fingers, as an itching seized them,
Do round their weapons' handles rub themselves.
I would not trust their love.

Grac. Slight cause have they
Longer to couple love and Gracchus' name.
Oh! I have sinned most heavily to drag them
Like sheep thus to the slaughter. There's an instinct
That makes man bold in right, but coward stamps him
Defending wrong. This holy weapon I
Struck from the people's grasp, and blunted it
With bold injustice. By aggression roused,
I answered with aggression. Wrong met wrong.
Blood followed; and, upon its smoking tracks,

How with fierce joy the Senate raised its cry,
Hallooing to the vengeance, while, unnerved,
All paralyzed of strength, the people's arm
Fell lifeless in its effort! Vice met vice.
When moral virtue fled, Reason abashed
Shrank timid from her post, and Justice threw
The tangled reins of the State to open license.
Might reared her haughty head, and frowned down Right.

Enter CORNELIA *hastily.*

Cor. My son, seek surer refuge. In this shrine
But slender trust is left.
Grac. You, mother—here!
Follow not thus this shattered wreck, but think
Your son is dead already.
Cor. Slander not
The uninjured shapings of your body's strength,
Nor shame your mother, calling thus her son
Some weak and shattered thing.
Grac. 'Tis not indeed
The body fails me, but my heart is sick.
I'm wearied in the struggle and would die!
Death frights the happy; but the sorrow-worn
Springs to its rest, all hopeful as the school-boy
Rejoicing in his promised holiday.
Cor. Man has no right to name his hour of rest.
Up and be doing! 'Tis our being's law,
Till heaven shall give release. Life's duties swarm;
Each moment, with its task, marks lethargy
The heaviest sin of man. Up! up! and work!
How should we dare to make a whim our guide,
When obligations crowd us with their claims?
Fulfil the uncanceled bonds! Let reckoned dues
Prove life by right is idle, then might man,
Manumised at will, his fettered being shift.
But you, high duty's bondsman, would defraud—
Shunning its task—the world of what you owe!
Grac. I've striven till my heart with hoping faints.
All wearied shrink I from the thought of life,
Whose fear doth fright me like the hideous dream
Of some strange midnight horror.

Cor. Rouse! For shame!
Wake up your flagging energies; be bold
To probe beneath these flutterings; you will find
Your courage sound beneath them. For the right,
Man even in despair should ever strive.
The very effort, howsoever vain,
Is always something gained. To the great work
It warms the blood of the world, which wrestles on
Still against failure, like the strong man struggling,
Until the end of truth at last is reached.
We are the thews and sinews of the world,
And in our efforts there is nothing lost;
All work to good or ill. Go with these friends;
For life and duty strive; nor be the coward
Who, shrinking, dreads on his own heart to look,
And dies, to shun responsibility.
My son, I know, can never thus be brought
By fear to shirk his manhood.
Grac. Mother, I go.
May heaven so bless you, as your son shall strive
To prove the honor and the love he bears you,
By working out the noble thoughts you teach.
Cor. Then once again farewell! These bursting tears
Now come to show the woman's heart, whose boldness,
Your sickly resolution to upbraid,
Usurped the man. Oh! were they tears of blood,
Feebly they'd speak my anguish. *Exit Cornelia.*
Grac. Come, Pomponius,
Lead on. I'll follow you. Philocrates,
You've ever been a true friend to your master;
Take with my thanks this trifling boon as token
Of gratitude and love. Be to my son [*Offers a ring*]
What you have been to me.
Philo. Have I offended,
That, sharing with you thus far all your fortunes,
I now should from your danger be thrust off?
I will not leave you.
Grac. True heart! Then, come on. *Exeunt.*

SCENE V. *Bridge near Rome.*

Enter GRACCHUS, POMPONIUS, LICINIUS, PHILOCRATES.

Pomp. We've reached our point. You, Gracchus, hasten on.
Philocrates, 'twere best to follow him.
Methinks, Licinius, you and I, at bay,
With the vantage of this bridge, should hold awhile
Some scores of our pursuing enemy.
Our farewells, Gracchus, have no time for words.

Grac. True deeds live not in words. 'Twould pain me more
To leave you to the death you rush to seek,
But that I feel, though striving still to keep it,
My life is forfeit to this day's disasters.

Philo. The enemy is on us. Master, fly!

Grac. Come then, good friend; and you brave hearts, farewell.

Exit Gracchus with Philocrates.

Licinius. Now at their highest let us stake our lives;
A bloody ransom for the life of Gracchus.

Enter OPIMIUS *with troops.*

Opim. Off, traitors! Clear the way!

Pomp. Stand back! we carry
Deaths for some score of you.

Opim. Out, villains! Back!
Charge them, my men! This mockery of fight
Doth shame your manhood. What, ye coward rabble!
Shrink ye before two men? Get on, ye scum!
You rate your lives too high! They are not worth
Such doubt and higgling for. On! There you go!
Cut down the rascals. *They fight; several are slain. Opimius strikes at and wounds Licinius.*
Ha! You got it then.

Licinius. A scratch! I'd stand my ground with fifty such.
Come on; we're only warming to the fight.

They fight again and Licinius falls.

I've done my last, Pomponius. Make the most
Of your unaided strength. Each moment brings
Perhaps a life to Gracchus. *Dies.*

Pomp. Noble friend,
I have no time to weep. Your merits speak
Full as the hundred mouths whose gashes pour

Your flooding lifeblood out. *Soldiers attack him again.*
No breathing time!
They fight. Several of the enemy fall, and at last Pomponius.

Opim. You're done with now.
Pomp. Curses on this weak arm
That could not stay you longer. *Dies.*
Opim. Fellows, on!
We've lost here too much time. Its weight in gold,
Remember, is the price of Gracchus' head.
Soldiers rush over the bridge, trampling on bodies, and exeunt.

SCENE VI. *Public Road.*

Several Citizens.

First Cit. May the Gods guard him. 'Tis a hard run chase.
Second Cit. And he'll be beaten in it. Here he comes.

Enter GRACCHUS *and* PHILOCRATES.

First Cit. How the sweat stands in big drops on his brow!
He's quite outworn with running.
Third Cit. Here, on horseback
Comes Septimuleius, who so often boasts
The warmness of his friendship. He'll be like
To lend the beast to save his periled life.

Enter SEPTIMULEIUS *and another Citizen on horseback.*

Grac. Prythee, your horse, my friend. I have no strength
To course it farther thus.
Sept. I've hurt my foot;
I cannot run, and would not dare stand here
To let Opimius see me give you aid.
Make your best speed; I can do nothing for you.
Grac. [*To other Citizen*] And you, are you too, friend, hurt in the foot?
Cit. No; but you'd best pass on. I cannot lend
Nor care to risk my horse.
Philo. Come, master, on!
They have no help for us. Their hearts are dead
For very fright within them, and are numbed
To the forgetfulness of friendship. Fear

Doth from the coward's choked up bosom chase
All feeling else. The enemy is here.

Exeunt Gracchus and Philocrates.

First Cit. You might have lent your horse, if for the sake
Only of bygone kindness.

Sept. Hold your tongue,
Or I for treason 'gainst the state impeach you.
Huzza! I say, for Rome and for Opimius!

Enter OPIMIUS, *etc.*

Opim. Which way went Gracchus? *Septimuleius points.*
Thanks, good fellow! Come,
There's gold, you know, for him who wins this game.

Exit Opimius, followed by Septimuleius, etc.

First Cit. That fellow owes to Gracchus his son's life;
And more than that, saving his family
From beggary and ruin. Gracchus lent him
Four thousand sesterces to aid him once
When troubles thronged him, and I know right well
These never were repaid.

Second Cit. Let's follow on
To watch what's doing. *Exeunt.*

SCENE VII. *Grove of the Furies.*

Enter hastily GRACCHUS *and* PHILOCRATES.

Grac. Here must I stop. Exhaustion seizes me.
Ye Goddesses, grim tenants of this grove,
Sprung up in vengeance from the angry blood
Of Coelus, shed by his exasperate son,
Receive me, a self-offered sacrifice
To ward your vengeance from unhappy Rome.
Let my spilt blood, that soon will sprinkle round,
Upon your dark-leaved cedars' roots, its life,
Smooth down those jealousies, and heal dissensions
Whose earthquake troubles in their tremblings rock
The fated city to its threatened fall.
Methinks ye heed my prayer. I see ye now.
Your blood-shot eyes gaze on me with a look
Inexorable and yet half in pity.
Your serpent hair towards me hissing seems

As 'twould th' expiatory victim seize!
Officiating priest, my brow I bind
With cedar wreaths, for my own sacrifice,
And wait the blow that to your vengeance gives me.
Philocrates, there yet is time. Escape.

Philo. Never.

Enter OPIMIUS *with troops,* LUCULLUS, SEPTIMULEIUS, *etc.*

Opim. There stands the traitor. Down with him!
Ye pause, ye rabble crew, as though ye saw
Some god to wonder at.

Soldier. Methinks it is.
I would not dare to touch him for my life.

Second Sol. Nor I. The thought would haunt me to my grave.

They throw down their arms, and Lucullus rushes to strike Gracchus.

Luc. Then take thy death from me. *Philocrates throws himself in the way, receives the blow, and at the same time strikes Lucullus. Both fall.*
Base slave! Stand off!
He's killed me. Oh! to die by a slave's hand!

Grac. [*looking at Philocrates*] And thou art gone, my last true friend, before me. *Septimuleius creeps behind Gracchus and stabs him.*
'Tis done! I thank ye, Gods! *Dies.*

Sept. The gold is mine!
Consul, the gold is mine!

Opim. Villain! it is. [[*Exeunt.*]]

Part III

BIOGRAPHICAL WRITINGS

6.

Langdon Cheves
Review of "Reminiscences of Public Men"

> Whoso is out of hope to attain to another's virtue, will seek to come at even hand by depressing another's fortune.
>
> —Bacon[1]

Number three of *The XIX Century,* published in August 1869, has very recently, and for the first time, chanced to meet our eye, in a short article bearing the title of "Reminiscences of Public Men: Langdon Cheves."[2]

Clarum et venerabile nomen![3] so pure as hitherto to have escaped smirching; so high that the most rabid of political snarlers dared not touch it. Midst the

XIX Century 2 (April 1870): 885–88.

1. Francis Bacon, "Of Envy," in *The Essayes or Counsels, Civill and Morall,* ed. Michael Kiernan (Cambridge, Mass., 1985), p. 27.

2. Benjamin F. Perry, "Reminiscences of Public Men: Langdon Cheves," *XIX Century* 1 (Aug. 1869): 222–25. The sketch of Cheves was part of a series, later gathered together in Perry's *Reminiscences of Public Men* (1882); reprinted in Meats and Arnold, *Writings of Perry* 2:83–87. Page numbers added in the text below are, first, the number from the publication in the *XIX Century,* then that of *Writings,* separated by a virgule; e.g., [222/83]. Benjamin Franklin Perry (1805–86), South Carolinian lawyer and politician; as editor of the Greenville *Mountaineer,* opposed nullification (1829–33); member of the South Carolina House of Representatives almost continuously from 1836 to 1860; opposed secession but held office in South Carolina under the Confederacy; appointed by Andrew Johnson provisional governor of South Carolina (June 1865), served for five months; opposed Radical Reconstruction; retired from public life in 1877.

3. "Illustrious and venerable name." Lucan *De bello civili* (*The Civil War*) 9.202. These words, which are inscribed on Langdon Cheves' monument in Magnolia Cemetery in Charleston and on his bust by Preston Powers, are part of Cato the Younger's eulogy on Pompey the Great, Julius Caesar's adversary in civil war, who was murdered when he sought refuge in Egypt (48 B.C.). Biographies of Cato, Pompey, and Caesar were written by Plutarch.

general wreck of all that is highest and purest in our unhappy land, must even the memory of the noble dead be spattered from the sinks of surrounding degradation!

Judge Cheves, we are here told, "was, intellectually, one of the greatest men America has ever produced, and a purer statesman never lived" [222/83]. Such has been the unanimous affirmation of his countrymen, while the beauty of his private character has been equally undisputed. Would that the "Reminiscences" had here stopped! When the grand old man, crowned with the wisdom of gathered years, rose to check or to guide—standing in the imposing dignity, at once of person and of character, almost like a demi-god among his fellows—we pity the low-seeing eye and the lower judging mind which could draw of him such a picture as the author of the "Reminiscences" has seen fit to give us. This awkward attempt to damn with faint praise,[4] to bring down this representative of Nature's model men to the likeness of some jovial boon companion, can only fall back upon him whose imagination drew it. Alas! for the times that have swept from life those worthy and able to undertake the scattering of insinuated aspersions; times which have left, from the near watchers over the sunset of that noble life, not one survivor—save only a woman; times which made the writer of such aspersions forget that, although it was only a woman, still there did live that one, who, having clung with a daughter's love, and watched with a woman's sensitive intellect, the fading away of light so pure, might have furnished material (however limited) more worthy of his subject, when speaking of the last days of Carolina's so stainless son, than the drippings which he has caught from some sewer of hearsay.

It is utterly false that Langdon Cheves at any period of his life "became self-indulgent and inert" [225/87]; false that he ever "withdrew from society and the world,"[5] other than as, in the calm philosophy of declining years, he withdrew from political struggles, when not even a head as strong, and a heart as pure as his, could arrest the rapidly approaching ruin of his country, which his prescient mind feared, and largely foresaw. He was seventy-four at the Nashville Convention, where his great speech shook that Union which was fast becoming the deadly oppressor of his native South, and where the penetrating words of the "old man eloquent"[6] recalled the days when it was

4. Alexander Pope, *Epistle to Dr. Arbuthnot,* l. 201.

5. Perry, "Cheves," p. 225/87, reading: "He seemed to withdraw from society and the world."

6. John Milton, "Sonnet X: To the Lady Margaret Ley," ll. 6–8: "that dishonest victory / At Chaeronea, fatal to liberty, / Kill'd with report that old man eloquent." LSM thus compares her father to the Athenian orator Isocrates (436–338 B.C.), who had long advocated Greek unity against outside threats and as a remedy to constant warfare among the Greek

said of him by one, no mean judge in such matters,[7] that Mr. Cheves was the first speaker he had ever heard who realized his idea of a Demosthenes or a Cicero. He had well passed the allotted threescore years and ten of man's life. Was it here that he showed himself "self-indulgent and inert"? Only when nearing his fourscore years did he, to a great extent, though even then far from entirely, give up to his son the management of his affairs, and retire to a residence near Columbia; where, daily visited by his daughter's family, he gave a hospitable welcome to those friends who came to visit him, "worshippers to the shrine of a saint," as a friend once remarked to the present writer. Only in his eightieth year, stricken by family sorrow and the weight of age, disabled by a partial stroke of paralysis, did he break down sufficiently to cause his removal to his daughter's home in the City of Columbia, whither he went, not for self-indulgence, but to die, under the watchful care of his eldest then surviving son, and the daughter with whom he had selected to reside. Visited and lovingly tended by others of his family and friends, these two alone were, by circumstances, permitted to watch over him unremittingly to the end. That son, worthy of his sire, found, during his country's noble struggle for her lost liberties, a patriot's grave.[8] That daughter alone remains to bear witness to the stainless purity of a life against which even insinuation has hitherto stood silent.

It is not true that Langdon Cheves "acted with the Union party in opposing nullification."[9] With the Union party he neither fraternized nor sympa-

---

cities. Thebes, Athens, and their allies were defeated by Philip of Macedon at Chaeronea in Boeotia in 338 B.C. LSM had applied the same citation to her father in "Separate Secession" (*PSE*, p. 212), which stated and supported her father's views in the secession crisis of 1850–51; the citation also appears in Isaac Hayne's eulogy of Cheves, transcribed from the Charleston *Mercury* by LSM (Langdon Cheves I Papers, SCHS).

7. Remark made by Washington Irving, when speaking to William C. Preston of one of Mr. Cheves' great congressional speeches. [LSM] The speech is perhaps that delivered by Cheves, as chairman of the House Ways and Means Committee, on Dec. 4, 1812, in favor of the remission of forfeitures on bonds given according to the Non-Importation Act; Irving praises very highly the speech, and the speaker, in a letter (dated Dec. 8, 1812) to James Renwick (although without reference to Demosthenes and Cicero); see Irving, *Letters* 1:346. William Campbell Preston (1794–1860), born in Philadelphia; resident of Columbia from 1822, when he became a law partner of David James McCord; elected U.S. senator as a nullifier in 1833, as a Whig in 1837; resigned in 1842; president of South Carolina College (1846–51). While a student at the University of Edinburgh, Preston was a companion of Irving's on many walking tours.

8. Langdon Cheves, Jr., was killed (July 10, 1863) at the siege of Battery Wagner on Morris Island at the southern entrance to Charleston Harbor, where he was supervising the building of fortifications.

9. Perry, "Cheves," p. 224/86, reading: "In the days of nullification, disunionist as he was, he acted with the Union party in opposing nullification."

thized. Where two stand in opposition, we surely do not act with A, simply because we fail to act with B. Langdon Cheves acted with neither party, deeming both fatally mistaken. A thorough upholder of States' Rights, and a strong secessionist, he opposed nullification only as an impracticability: not that it was too aggressive, but that it was weak and inefficient, a remedy which covered over only, hiding, but not healing, the gnawing ulcer of our wrongs. Disunion, for which he craved the common action of the South, he already looked upon as an inevitable necessity to prevent our ruin—the only haven of the Southern States from injustice and oppression, and their sole hope of salvation from such a fate as, in our recent troubles, has fallen upon us.

The anecdotical parts of the article in question scarcely deserve notice. Many are entirely mistaken; nearly all bear more or less a false tinge. Mr. Cheves never was "a hired day laborer to plow whilst a boy" [224/85–86], although he certainly did plow, and not for amusement, while under the care of relatives. His father was not "a noted Scotch Tory and Indian trader" [223/84]. A sturdily honest Scotchman and British subject, it is possible (though the idea was entirely a novel one to Mr. Cheves' family when for the first time mentioned to them after his death) that his father may, in the early struggles of 1776, have retained some attachment to the land and government of his birth. We cannot speak certainly on this point. He had but recently come to America when the revolutionary struggle began, and was living on the then outposts of civilization. Langdon Cheves was born September 1776, in a log fort, in Abbeville, whither his mother, formerly a Miss Langdon, of Virginia, had fled for protection from Indian attacks. Possibly the father may have looked back regretfully to his recent home, but very certainly "honest Sandy Cheves"[10] never was "a noted Scotch Tory."[11] After keeping a country store, he did move to Charleston, and there established a store; but Langdon Cheves was not a clerk in it. On the contrary, he was at a very early age independent of his father (whose second marriage was not a fortunate one), and the already struggling man-boy found a place as a clerk elsewhere.[12] During this clerkship, and when, at sixteen years of age, trans-

10. Such we have been informed was the epithet he bore among those who knew him. [LSM]

11. Alexander Cheves, indeed, demonstrated his Loyalist sympathies by joining a Loyalist militia, leaving South Carolina with the departing British, and making a claim for damages to a commission hearing such claims from Loyalists after the end of the Revolutionary War. See chap. 8 below, "Memoir of Langdon Cheves."

12. Among the vandal-like acts perpetrated in Columbia by General Sherman and his savage followers in February 1865, was the destruction of all written papers falling into their hands. Individual memories often fail us. The name of that firm is lost to the present writer.

acting as head clerk the business of a considerable firm, he studied law, not as the charity student of Judge Marshall, "whose stentorian voice attracted him," etc., etc.,[13] but in the solitary struggle of the strong proud mind, which conquers its own way and works out its own great life, by its own strong will. His education he thus fought for and gained (while continuing to perform all the duties of his position), not through schooling and teachers, but alone, and unhelped except by those best of teachers, the craving hunger to know, and the strong determination to do. At a later period he became a student under Judge Marshall, for a sufficient length of time to enable him to graduate at the Charleston bar. Thus Langdon Cheves was indeed self-reliant; and through life was self-reliant, as all truly great men must of necessity be. But surely "self-willed" [224/85] is an extraordinary term to connect with the towering intellect of a great ruling mind. We talk of self-willed children, and picture at once a baby fighting for its rattle. Self-willed men and women are more or less weak-minded, obstinate people, opposing sage advisers. Youth, inexperience, something there must be indicative of inferiority, in the self-willed individual refusing wise advice. The great man's consciousness of intellect and sense of power is not self-will. The author of "Reminiscences" has surely misremembered the epithet used by an educated gentleman and attached friend,[14] in speaking of one who has been truly termed "the last giant mind" of his proudly intellectual State.

Neither was Mr. Cheves "sensitive as a woman to the criticisms and censures of the world,"[15] but rather only sensitive to his own firm sense of right. Nor was he "terribly annoyed" [224/85] by complaints or charges against him while managing the Bank of the United States. On the contrary, his children, seeing him in the quiet intercourse of home, would learn with wonder from strangers that any one could think unkindly of the calm and indulgent home-father. A man great always; great in everything; and, like all greatness, calm in endurance, strong in action, firm in all.

[LSM] The firm was the general store of James Jaffray, an immigrant from Glasgow and a fellow member with Alexander Cheves of the St. Andrew's Society; Langdon Cheves worked there for seven years (to October 1795).

13. *Vide* "Reminiscences" for this small piece of romance. [LSM] Perry, "Cheves," p. 223/84, reading: "passing the court house one day he was attracted by the clear, stentorian voice of Chancellor Marshal, who was arguing a case in court." Cheves read law in the office of William Marshall, later a judge of the Court of Equity, from early 1796 to October 1797.

14. Daniel Elliott Huger (1779–1854), South Carolinian lawyer and politician, was the successor of Langdon Cheves as circuit judge of the South Carolina Court of Appeals (1819–30); opposed nullification; member of the South Carolina (1838–42) and U.S. (1843–45) Senate; delegate to the States' Rights Convention of 1852.

15. Perry, "Cheves," p. 224/85. *Writings* omits "and censures."

"He has"—as was very recently remarked to us in a letter from a friend and lawyer of note in our State—"an enduring monument in the hearts of our people. His great character and massive intellect placed him first, and among the first in every position. He was so at the bar, on the bench, at the head of finance, and in the council of the country, at a time when we had a council, and there were giants in the land. In my judgment this remarkable man had no superior." "When I think of Langdon Cheves and of 'the today,' my heart is filled with pride and bitterness."

We do not doubt that the mass of misstatement, which we have under review, may be the result of careless error, rather than deliberate misrepresentation; but we cannot, therefore, hold the writer guiltless. He who teaches falsely does not commit an innocent mistake. In the history of the world there is no more dangerous moral element than active ignorance.[16] Our prostrate land writhes even now under the crushing weight of its monster power. And the ignorant fanatic who first declared a negro the white man's equal, is none the less guilty of the blood of millions, nor less the murderer of nations, because he talked of—he knew not what. Our dead are precious to us, and whoso carelessly profanes them must not be surprised that we repulse his carelessness, whether or not maliciously intended.

As we shield some perfect statue from the stains which the creeping exhalations of a poisonous miasma seek to leave upon it, and the marble still glitters in its natural purity, so stands unblemished the memory of the great dead (mournfully sad, but pure as fresh cut Parian stone)[17] by the ruins of that country for which through life he ever strove. *Clarum et venerabile nomen.*

16. *PSE,* "Negro and White Slavery—Wherein Do They Differ?" p. 200: "There is nothing more frightful than active ignorance." Ibid., "Negro-mania," p. 224: "There is nothing more mischievous than active ignorance."

17. Paros, second largest island of the Cyclades group in the Aegean Sea, was famous in antiquity for its marble.

7.

The Burning of Columbia

My name is Louisa S. McCord. I formerly lived in Columbia, South Carolina, owning the house in which I lived; I was living in Columbia in the early part of the year 1865, and was in the city at the time of its occupation by the United States forces. My house was in the lower part of the city, just opposite the South Carolina College grounds. I have read carefully the testimony offered for the defence in these cases. General Howard makes a mistake in saying in his deposition in these cases that his headquarters in Columbia were at the house of one of the professors of the University; his

Mixed Commission on British and American Claims Established under Article XII of the Treaty of Washington, *British and American Claims. Appendix: Testimony* (Washington, D.C., 1873), vol. 23, "George Symmers *vs.* the United States and Frederick Ward *vs.* the United States, cases no. 228 and 294, depositions in rebutting for claimants," bk. 2, pp. 26–29; also excerpted in *Report of Her Majesty's Agent of the Proceedings and Awards of the Mixed Commission on British and American Claims*. . . (London, 1874), pp. 471–72, 491. Two fragments of a second account by LSM, preserved in James Parsons Carroll, *Report of the Committee Appointed to Collect Testimony in Relation to the Destruction of Columbia, S.C., on the 17th of February, 1865* (Columbia, S.C., 1893), pp. 10, 17, are appended. For the circumstances of the composition of "The Burning of Columbia," see Note on the Texts. LSM's sister-in-law, Rachel Cheves, had been warned by a member of Sherman's staff against leaving Savannah, captured in December 1864, for Columbia and was present in the McCord house during the Federal occupation; her letter to James L. Reynolds [April? 1866] encloses a draft of a statement, requested by Reynolds and John LeConte, describing her experiences of Sherman's troops in Savannah and Columbia. This, together with other letters recounting her visit to Columbia, is extant in the Rachel S. Cheves Papers, Duke.

headquarters were at my house.[1] My family consisted at the time of four ladies; I was and am a widow.

The generals generally state that they knew of no pillaging. General Howard came to my house in broad day (about 2 or 3 o'clock p.m.),[2] when it was actually under pillage of a very thorough kind. One of his officers entered by my front door (which was unbolted in answer to his ring by some of the pillagers, with whom I was surrounded), and must have seen my house then crowded with them. General Howard, on horseback on my front pavement, must also have seen what was going on. I informed him also that I had but a few minutes before been throttled, and my watch was torn from me by a soldier in uniform, while others passed in and out with everything that could be taken in the way of plate, etc., while literally crowding on; the man who seized me was one in sergeant's uniform.[3]

1. Oliver Otis Howard (1830–1909), brigadier general commanding the Army of the Tennessee, was put in charge of Columbia by William T. Sherman after the city had been surrendered to Federal forces in the morning of Feb. 17, 1865; Columbia was burned that night. Howard was appointed chief commissioner of the Freedmen's Bureau in May 1865; he was a founder (1867), and later president (1869–73), of Howard University; retired from military service in 1894; among other works, his *Autobiography,* 2 vols. (1907).

2. Of Feb. 17.

3. "[The servants] brought us word that the Mayor of the city, Dr. [Thomas Jefferson] Goodwyn, had gone to surrender the city to Gen[eral] Sherman, but we still couldn't believe it. But we soon began to hear a distinct roar, a far off confusion which seemed to come nearer as we listened with our hearts in our mouths. Without any warning our back gate was burst violently open and in rushed pell mell, crowding, pushing, almost falling over each other, such a crowd of men as I never saw before or since. They seemed scarcely human in their fierce excitement—the excitement of greed and rapine. In one instant the large yard was full of them. . . . One horrible-looking man wore a coonskin cap with the tail hanging down behind, and the awful way in which that tail swung and jumped as he rushed about will always come to me as I think of that day. In less time than I have taken to write it, they had completed the ruin of all we had outside, and we saw a group of men headed by the coonskin cap coming toward the house. The doors were all locked, and we saw them looking at a large log lying in the yard, evidently suggesting its use as a battering ram—with that, fearing that violence would only excite to more violence, my mother told us girls to bolt the door after her as she went out, and that she would go down stairs and let the men in. Aunt Rache insisted on going with her; so the two went down and let in a perfect stream of thieves and robbers who, as before in the yard, simply spread themselves all over the house in one instant. There was a terrible system and skill about it all—the only confusion was caused by their anxiety to get ahead of each other, and the speed with which they dashed from side to side was wonderful. Again they smashed, tore, and pocketted every thing they could get at, Mamma and Aunt Rache only following them about trying to keep some sort of check on them, and above all to keep them from going up stairs, for the warnings and stories we had heard led us to expect no mercy from them. At last they turned toward the

General Howard "did not see anybody setting fires."[4] If setting fires signifies an attempt to set fire, although not successful, General Howard has forgotten at least one incident of the night of the fire. The roof of my house having caught fire, I took my family down stairs to my sitting room (then occupied by General Howard and suite), stating that we would remain there either until the fire was extinguished or until it became so bad as to drive us into the streets. As we sat there, I was facing an open door giving laterally upon the entrance, and I saw a flake of burning cotton thrown into the entry from the front. It was thrown, not wafted or blown by the wind, but with the movement of a steady throw; it must have been matted by pressure of the hand or otherwise, and then lit; cotton which has been burning any length of time would be smouldering and black; there was no wind coming in by the door through which this cotton entered; the person throwing it must have been absolutely at the door, if not within it; it was a ground floor door, protected by a piazza and a very high and heavy hedge at least eighteen feet high. General Howard entering or coming forward from the back as the cotton fell, and not at the moment perceiving us, said, with some severity to his men, "This must stop; this was no accident, and it has happened several times before"; then looking up he saw my eye fixed upon him, and immediately he came toward me with the remark, "It is a singular thing that your

---

staircase, at the foot of which the two mothers were standing. The coonskin put his foot on the step, but Mamma slipped ahead of him and told him he couldn't go up. He tried to push past her, when she remembered the Masonic signal of distress, and made it, with the result that he struck her hand down, crying out, 'None of that!' He spied then what she thought safely hidden, a little leather thong to which was attached my brother's watch which had been her father's, and was last used by Willy Haskell and sent back to her, after his death at Gettysburg. This wretch caught her by the throat and jerked the watch out of her dress with such force that he broke the leather. Either he or one of the others—it must have been another one—had all of our knives gathered in sheaves in his hands, and shook them in her face. Poor Aunt Rache retreated, and no wonder. She rushed back up stairs to us—we heard her and let her in—and she almost fell into the room, white and faint, calling, 'Oh, girls, they are killing your mother.' It was a tragic moment, but the comic is always close at hand, and I remember the desperate convulsive laugh that went round when she suggested that we must jump out of the window and slip down a big tree close to the house and so get away from the inferno down stairs. What might have happened I don't know, but just as the man was pushing past my mother, the door bell rang. She said the men stopped instantly, which she noticed; so when it rang again she said just on the chance, 'There are some of your officers, and you had better not let them find you here.' In one minute they were gone! Just like a flight of vultures. Sure enough it was an officer—Gen[eral] O. O. Howard, second in command I believe to Sherman, who had been asked by friends in Savannah to make his headquarters at our house as a protection." Smythe, pp. 61–62.

4. In the original, "page 5 of his Deposition in these cases" is added in parentheses.

men in leaving the town set fire to some cotton at the depot, which has been flying about ever since." I may say here, by the way, that, to the best of my recollection, there was no remarkable wind until the fire raised it.[5]

On the morning of the 18th February, 1865, a lady hearing that her house was intended to be burned that night, and after considerable waiting not being able to see General Howard, so urged me to report her case that I finally consented to do so. General Howard's answer was in a low, somewhat confidential voice, spoken while within three or four feet of General Sherman, who was also in the room when I entered. He said, "The fact is, Mrs. McCord, our men got beyond us last night. We had to use severity; we shot some of them; some seventy of them were shot; but there will be nothing of the kind tonight. Rest assured there will be no fires tonight." And there were none.

Apropos of the discipline of the troops, I saw and heard from an enclosed piazza General Howard when a second time called from his sleep, my house having again caught fire. The fire light caused him to be plainly seen as he stood in my yard giving some orders to a sentinel; and in answer to some words spoken by the latter I heard him with raised voice and considerable severity say, "Now and until the fire is over." The sentinel again spoke, too low for me to hear, and again General Howard: "Till daylight then, and take care what you are about, sir." As he turned back into the house, the sentinel began a shuffling-down step to the tune and words, quite audibly sung, "We won't be back till morning, till daylight doth appear."[6]

It may be worth while mentioning, also, as indicating the pre-knowledge of the soldiers of the coming horrors of that night, that while the pillaging of my yards and buildings was beginning in the morning or early afternoon (owing to the seizure of my watch my idea of time through that day is very inaccurate), a slip of paper was secretly brought to me by a frightened servant girl; she said that a soldier had dropped it on the step and told her to bring it to me. It was a few words written in pencil and addressed to the "Ladies of Columbia," advising them to leave, if possible, for some place of safety; that a "terrible fate" awaited them, and adding that he wrote this because he had kind friends among us. This was signed by one giving his name and rank as second lieutenant in company and regiment, both of which he named. I believe this to have been sincerely and kindly intended; but it

5. A heading printed in italics, "Further of setting fire," precedes the next paragraph in the original, presumably an editorial addition.

6. "For He's a Jolly Good Fellow," st. 2: "We won't go home until morning, / We won't go home until morning, / We won't go home until morning, / Till daylight doth appear."

could do us no good, and might do the writer a great deal of harm. I doubted for one moment, and then destroyed the soiled scrap.

[FRAGMENTS]

1

One of my maids brought me a paper, left, she told me, by a Yankee soldier; it was an ill-spelled but kindly warning of the horrors to come, written upon a torn sheet of my dead son's note book, which, with private papers of every kind, now strewed my yard. It was signed by a Lieutenant—of what company and regiment, I did not take note. The writer said he had relatives and friends in the South, and that he felt for us; that his heart bled to think of what was threatening. "Ladies," he wrote, "I pity you. Leave this town—go anywheres to be safer than here." This was written in the morning; the fires were in the evening and night.

2[7]

I showed him the paper, which he glanced at, and then, in a somewhat subdued voice, but standing so near General Sherman that I think it impossible that the latter could help hearing him, he said: "You may rest satisfied, Mrs. McCord, that there will be nothing of the kind happening tonight. The truth is, our men last night got beyond our control; many of them were shot—many of them were killed; there will be no repetition of these things tonight. I assure you, there will be nothing of the kind; tonight will be perfectly quiet." And it *was* quiet—peaceful as the grave, the ghost of its predecessor.

7. This fragment is introduced in Carroll's *Report* (p. 17) thus: "On the following day, the 18th of February, . . . Mrs. L. S. McCord, at the request of a friend, having undertaken to present a paper to General Howard, sought an interview with that officer, second in command of the invading army, and found General Sherman with him. Her narrative of a part of the interview is as follows."

8.

Memoir of Langdon Cheves and Fragments

Langdon Cheves was the son of a Scotchman, Alexander Cheves, from Aberdeen, or its vicinity, who came to America some where about 1770, and married (1774) Mary Langdon, daughter of Dr. Langdon, a physician resi-

Langdon Cheves I Papers, SCHS. The "Memoir" (the title is supplied for this edition) was written at the request of LSM's nephew Langdon Cheves III; see her letters to him, May 4 and May 20, 1876. Besides the "Memoir," extant in draft and fair copy (both in LSM's hand), there are several fragmentary pieces in LSM's hand, placed in no order, which seem to be preliminary materials to a longer treatment of her father. The fair copy of the "Memoir" is printed here; it has been collated with the preliminary draft, and substantial variants are recorded in the notes. The "Memoir" is followed by such of the fragments as extend for more than a few unconnected words and represent LSM's own composition. (There are, for example, not printed here, eight pages of LSM's holograph transcribing extracts from the eulogies of Cheves by Isaac Hayne, Robert Barnwell Rhett, William Porcher Miles, James Louis Petigru—"all above from Ch[arlesto]n Mercury—June 30th, 1857"—and others.) The fragments are presented, as far as possible, in approximately chronological order of events described. Since many of these fragments were written hastily by LSM on scraps of paper, parts are difficult to decipher: illegible words are noted as such, and uncertain readings are followed by a question mark and enclosed within square brackets. Appended to the "Memoir and Fragments" is LSM's epitaph on Langdon Cheves, inscribed on the four sides of the obelisk (raised in 1876) which serves as focal point of the Cheves family plot in Magnolia Cemetery, Charleston; see her letters to Langdon Cheves III, July 11 [1876] and to Preston Powers [May 29, 1878]. See also "[On Langdon Cheves]," in chap. 4 above, "Later Poems." LSM's account of her father is usefully compared with Huff, *Langdon Cheves of South Carolina.*

dent in Abbeville, but by birth and former residence a Virginian.[1] Abbeville being then a border district, exposed to the attacks and depredations of Indians, the young wife was, shortly before the birth of her child[,] forced to seek security in a Log Fort, or Block House (Bull-town Fort) in which Langdon Cheves was born 17th September 1776. His Aunt was murdered and scalped by Indians the night of his birth. His Mother dying Nov[ember] 1779, shortly after her only child had attained the age of three years, he was thus early launched, but ill-protected for its risks, upon the Ocean of Life's struggle.[2] His earliest recollection lasting him—though as a vague and indistinct shadow—to the end of his own career, was his mother's death. The almost infant was then placed with some relatives of his Father;[3] and the father marrying again, and not fortunately, the child continued under their care, until ten years of age; His father in the mean time moving to Charleston, where he kept a store and waggon yard for up-Country produce, and country trade.[4]

The boy, in the family with whom he was left, learned the simple and

1. Thomas Langdon (c. 1737–81), farmer and physician; came from Woodstock in the Shenandoah Valley (c. 1761–66) to Long Canes in the South Carolina backcountry with his second wife Mary and their two daughters; joined the Revolutionary cause in 1775.

2. Longfellow, *Tales of a Wayside Inn,* pt. 3, "The Theologian's Tale: Elizabeth," 4.1–4: "Ships that pass in the night, and speak each other in passing, / Only a signal shown and a distant voice in the darkness; / So on the ocean of life we pass and speak one another, / Only a look and a voice, then darkness again and a silence."

3. Canceled in draft: "(cousins)." The relatives were Alexander Cheves' brother Thomas (died 1785) and his wife Margaret Agnew Cheves.

4. LSM omits the Loyalist experience of Alexander Cheves, which, in chap. 6 above, "Langdon Cheves: Review of 'Reminiscences of Public Men,'" she had denied explicitly against the statement of Benjamin F. Perry that her grandfather had been "a noted Scotch Tory." In September 1775, unlike his brother Thomas and neighbor Thomas Langdon who signed the Association pledging support of the Revolutionary cause against the royal governor, Alexander Cheves temporized. However, after the British captured Charleston in May 1780 and established control over the state, Alexander Cheves enrolled in the local Loyalist militia under Major John Hamilton, who before the war had been, like Cheves, a backcountry trader. After Revolutionary victories at King's Mountain and Cowpens and the arrival of Nathaniel Greene in the Carolinas in April 1781, with other Loyalists Alexander Cheves was compelled to flee to British-held territory on the coast, first transferring title of his property to his son Langdon, then in the care of the boy's uncle, Thomas Cheves. Alexander Cheves followed his commander Hamilton to Nova Scotia (September 1782), thence to England, where on Sept. 20, 1784, he appeared before a commission set up to hear Loyalist claims for recompense of property lost in the war. The commission, dismissing him as a trimmer, refused his claim. Alexander Cheves returned to South Carolina to collect his son, bringing with him a second wife, Susannah Craig Cheves, whom he had married (March 22, 1785) in Old Meldrum, a town about eighteen miles north of Aberdeen. He settled in Charleston.

laborious habits of the scattered population with which he was cast. Few, if any, but the young of the little community could have been native to the soil; and the majority were, of necessity, under the circumstances, agricultural. Of these the Scotch emigrant was always among the first. With such—the best population of the district[5]—did the young ideas of Langdon Cheves, first find development. His infant reading was picked up, at an old-field school to which he was, (as occasion suited), sent; armed on the passage thither, with a stick in one hand to fight the snakes; and in the other a bunch of penny-royal to brush off the ticks. And thus, the undeveloped statesman worked his small way, to the small beginnings of literature. I have said that he was sent as occasion suited; for by no means were the childish hands always permitted to remit the more serious duty of the plough. In an agricultural emigrant settlement, even little hands had their share to take, and he worked his task, as seasons required it, and according to his strength, as, and with, country farmers, then the most respectable class of the community. Already his strength was counted, to make his bread. Up to the time of his leaving Abbeville district, at ten years of age, he had often ploughed, as I have heard him say, (although willingly) certainly not for amusement.

At ten years old, he was sent to his father in Charleston, and there received two years schooling; this being all the education he ever received, except through his own effort in the intervals of other and serious work. Of this very limited school-life I only recall two incidents. The first, (rather an experience than an incident) was a habit of his school master, whose tongue was broad scotch, but who objected strongly to the boys up-country drawl, (probably learned with his A.B.C. lispings, from Andrew Weed his old-field teacher,) and took occasion to ferule him sharply on the hand, whenever the drawl met his ear. The injustice and incongruity of such a process, rather than any suffered pain, lingered upon the young disciple's mind, who, by-the-way, never received a touch in punishment for any other cause, and who, enduring, still meditated upon it; probably thus, early working through those tangled steps from injustice to justice, which puzzle so many whose easier course has not forced them, by hard thinking, to seek the light. Thus

5. Canceled in draft: "of which Mr. Petigru speaks as 'the simple and primitive people.'" James Louis Petigru (1789–1863), lawyer; born in Abbeville District, S.C.; graduate of South Carolina College (1809); attorney general of South Carolina (1822–30); opposed nullification; supported Compromise of 1850; firm Unionist, stood against secession (1860). Of the eulogies of which LSM transcribed extracts (see introductory note above), Petigru's, which she cites in this canceled passage, receives far the lengthiest treatment; the relevant part of LSM's transcription reads, "The first ten years of his life were passed among this primitive people when he learned to think more seriously of the duties of life than of life itself."

his young mind found the first steps upon the way, to that strong love of Justice, and power of judicial reasoning which never failed him in after years. In any wise, the drawl was thoroughly conquered. His enunciation, and modulation of voice, were in manhood, remarkably pure; yet free from anything approaching affectation. Strange as it may seem to you, I never had the good fortune to hear him speak in public; but he was, to my mind, the best reader I have ever met. Was it perchance the harsh, and unjust pedagogue, who, unknown to himself, was thus the first teacher in rhetoric, of the great Statesman, who afterward swayed a nation by his words; and elicited the remark from a distinguished writer, who had listened in both continents to the most noted Orators of the age, that this was the first who made him understand the eloquence of a Demosthenes, or a Cicero.[6]

The other school experience was an Arithmetical struggle with a big boy, much his senior, double his inches, and the school-bully, who threatened to thrash him, if he dared to conquer him in the mental trial of strength. The trial was however made. The big bully was conquered, and your Grandfather, did not, you may believe me, get the promised thrashing.[7]

Following these beginnings, my knowledge of his early life is very scattered. There was displeasure—no overt dispute[8]—between the boy (still child in years) and his Father. The stepmother must naturally have cared little for a child so long a stranger to her. At any rate she was in no wise congenial to that proud spirit, which could not but seek to free itself from an uncongenial element. His mind turned to the recollection (faint as it was) of his own mother; and her substitute was not a pleasant contrast, to her, whom he always remembered with a feeling (undefined as her short life had left it,) of affection and pride. None-the-less, was he however careful, not to do an injustice to her whom he had no cause to love. Early estranged from his father's house, he never interfered with her rights, real or supposed, and at the death of his father, renounced in her favour any share of property that became his due. Continuing, as he seemed born to be, dependant only upon his own strength.

At twelve years old, having received his small allowance of education, it

6. The "distinguished writer" was Washington Irving, as reported to LSM by William Campbell Preston. See chap. 6 above, "Langdon Cheves: Review of 'Reminiscences of Public Men,'" n. 7.

7. Here you already see the appropriateness of the Shevas, Chevas, Cheves motto—*Virtute non vis.* [LSM] This footnote, from LSM's draft, does not appear in the fair copy. The form of the motto, identical with that given by LSM in a letter to Langdon Cheves III of April 6 [1876], is incorrect Latin, which properly should read: *virtute non vi* ("by virtue, not by force").

8. "~~I do not think any~~ no overt dispute" in draft.

was, by his Father, deemed desirable to place him at some trade. By persuasion, entreaty, or possibly more determined resistance, he succeeded in getting himself placed in a mercantile establishment, of which I do not retain the name.[9] Here he continued to struggle on through his youthful trials; the strength of character so often referred to, bearing him forward to posts of trust beyond his years. He once told me à propos of a cure for chill and fever, of his being on one occasion sent as super-cargo, on a river boat. A usual manner at that time of carrying on trade with the planters, and circulating supplies, was for the merchants to send all articles purchased by planters on Flat-boats,[10] to be landed as due. The super-cargo's duty being to effect their safe delivery. In such a boat and in such capacity, he was sent. A most responsible position for one of his age. The Captain was a Spaniard, speaking little English, and was, if I rightly remember[,] both Captain and crew; none else but the super-cargo being on board. The night of the passage was dark with deluging rain. The boy was a frequent sufferer from the scourge of the country (chill and fever) which he had brought from his Abbeville home. A fierce chill, the most violent he had ever experienced[,] came upon him. He lay upon the bare deck of the Flat-boat. The Spaniard, not unkind, could however, only find broken words to tell him that he would probably die, and lent him a heavy Rug for Bedding. The Rain effectually soaking rug as well as clothing, thus he lay the night through. This ought by common reasoning to have killed him, but strangely, it rather seemed to cure him. He had no more chills. I presume it is from such an expedition as this, (only executed in happier weather,) and his being seen about a plantation in some authority, during delivery of goods, that has originated the mistaken statement of his being at one time employed as an Overseer. He never was so employed, but continued in mercantile service, (I believe in the same firm into which he entered at 12 years old) until he finally quited it for the law. In the mean time he had risen at the age of 16, to be head clerk in what was then a considerable establishment. And here, for the first time, there came to him such help as cheers the solitary struggler,—solitary, even in the rush of life,—who knows no birthright but strong honour, integrity, and a dauntless mind.

His employer needed in his business transactions, to borrow money. The sum wanted was of sufficient amount to create difficulty in the obtaining of

9. The general store of James Jaffray. See chap. 6 above, "Langdon Cheves: Review of 'Reminiscences of Public Men.'"

10. Canceled in draft: "(steam boats and Railroads being of course as yet both equally unknown)."

it. The employers efforts failing, a merchant (John Potter) who had marked the young clerk, with appreciative notice, and now perceived the difficulty, handed to him the money, saying "Young man I lend this money, not to your employer, but to yourself, and hold you alone, responsible for its repayment."[11]

The 16 year-old man accepted the loan. He had neither "co-laterals" nor other security to give. He needed none. His friend saw in him the integrity which would have shrunk from asking for a loan of unsafe repayment, and the judgment which enabled him to know whether or not, it would be safe; and his friend was not mistaken.[12]

At about 18 years of age he began seriously to think of the study of the law; devouring at the same time the contents of every volume that fell in his way. A favourite book was Shakespear, and from this through life he frequently quoted. I remember a small edition of Shakespear, purchased by him at this time. One or more volumes of this, were by turns his pocket companions when at a later period "riding the circuit" as was then the custom for practising Lawyers. Although possessing great command of language, he had not I think a facile word-memory, and when wanting a quotation, he would frequently, with his habit of extreme exactness, refer to a volume in his hand; the small Shakespear often doing duty in this way. I have heard him laughingly tell, how on one occasion, when he had thus, book in hand, quoted the lines

> The quality of mercy is not strained;
> It droppeth as the gentle rain from Heaven
> Upon the place beneath; It is twice blessed;
> It blesseth him that gives, and him that takes.[13]

an old countryman came to him when he ceased to speak, to tell him how he could not help "crying" while he listened to him reading those Bible verses. A moment after, his old friend Judge DeSaussure coming up, asked him to give him the volume for his "little son," (the late Henry DeSaussure) who had

11. John Potter remained a firm supporter of Cheves. In 1818–19, as a leader of Charleston stockholders in the Bank of the United States, he actively promoted Cheves to be its president.

12. The following paragraph in the draft begins with this canceled passage: "At about 18 years of age he began seriously to think of the study of the law, devouring at the same time every book he could lay hands upon. Novels did not then flood the world as they do now, and in a his desultory course of reading [as often?] fell into his hands much more solid matter [much matter?]."

13. *Merchant of Venice* 4.1.180–83.

been listening to his speech with great interest; and his Father wished him to remember it.[14]

But I have wandered from my track. My narrative was only at the point when the fierce struggle for education was still going on. He bought books; he borrowed books. His stolen learning belonged also to stolen hours. Midnight, and hours after, night after night, would find him watching. He took Latin lessons; *dancing* lessons; read law books; and still the young store-clerk neglected nothing of his duties. At length he resigned his position and went to study law in the office of William (afterwards Judge) Marshall. Then it was, that the few friends whom the young aspirant could count, shook their heads and exclaimed "What a pity that a young man, cut out for a merchant, should thus throw himself away!"

He remained some 18 or 20 months in the office of Mr. Marshall; and during this time, he did not, as I have heard him say, spend twenty shillings. His cash supplies ceased, of course, on his leaving his clerkship; and he never asked for, or borrowed money, even from his Father. So soon as his age permitted he obtained admission to the practice of the law. His Father making him on this occasion the present of a handsome black coat.

And now the new Arena was opened to him. But how often do we all find, that

> Our very wishes give us not our wish,
> And by success we're tutored to despair.[15]

As the hero of some fairy tale who, having cut his way through tangled forests, and obstacles infinite, finds when arriving at the hoped for goal, some unlooked for, and apparently impassable barrier frowning dark upon him, and blocking further progress; So, for a moment may have stood our youthful candidate for the life-honours so well his due. But unlike the hero of the tale, no fairy wand, nor magic ~~wand~~ sword was there to aid him.

The aristocratick element of Charleston was then very tenacious of its position. The practice of the Law had been rather its exclusive privilege, and almost like the barrier of "Caste" in Asiatic India, was the line of separation.

14. Henry William DeSaussure (1763–1839), studied law in Philadelphia before returning to South Carolina; member several times of the lower house of the General Assembly (1790–1808); appointed director of the U.S. Mint (1795); intendant of Charleston (1797–98); judge of the chancery court (1808–37). His son was Henry Alexander DeSaussure.

15. Edward Young, *Night Thoughts* 1.273–76: "Not Happiness itself makes good her name; / Our very Wishes give us not our wish; / How distant oft the Thing we doat on most, / From that for which we doat, Felicity?"; 2.383–84: "The more our Joy, the more we know it Vain; / And by Success are tutor'd to Despair."

But Langdon Cheves was no craven in the struggle he had sought.[16] His strong will, and purity of purpose, were to him sword and buckler in the fight.[17] I have heard him in later days say, that to the toiler in such a struggle, want of bread, or want of caste seemed to him a needful incentive. He had no relations of influence,—never a patron,—and, in his new surroundings, few friends. Among the latter, I have heard him often speak of the learned Dr. Buist, who had been specially invited from the "Old Country" to the position of pastor of the Scotch Church in Charleston.[18] A kind and genial man he was; ready to extend the right hand of fellowship, where he saw it deserved; and now greeted in friendly intercourse, this scion from his own congregation. I have heard my Father say, that, not unfrequently invited by Dr. Buist to meet his friends, among whom were found many of the first gentlemen of the city, it was with some anxiety, that he would sometimes pause over an engagement, to first carefully examine and brush the sleeves of his coat, wondering whether the thread-bare tendency of the cuffs and elbows was sufficient to attract attention.

Entered then, thus far upon his law life, he waited, as beginners are forced to do, for clients. Time passed, but clients came not. Elder practitioners naturally monopolized the business, which passed his door. This, the common fate of the young Lawyer is only the usual experience. But to him it was something more. It was at once, "Want of bread (at least independent bread) and want of Caste." Still there was no backing down,—no soliciting,—no undue seeking for the needed encouragement. Patient strength and determination were yet to bring it to him. The first case which fell into his hands, was turned over to him by a somewhat careless acqua[i]ntance, who, wishing to leave the city for a few days, and unwilling to be detained by a case of little importance, likely to be called up during his absence, asked him to take it in hand. It was a small beginning on which to vent the pent up energy of patient waiting; but it was gladly accepted; and the young lawyer prepared for what (insignificant as it seemed to others) was to him a marked epoch in life.

He was—you will not be surprised ~~that~~ that I say so—sensitively diffident. True merit, even with the consciousness of power and courage to exercise it, combines nevertheless, a strong element of diffidence. Not that it

16. "'The man's the man, for a' that'" canceled in draft. Cf. Robert Burns, "Song: For A' That and A' That," l. 12.

17. Cf. *2 Henry IV* 1.2, *ad init.*, where Sir John Falstaff enters thus accoutred.

18. George Buist (1770–1808), Presbyterian clergyman; born in Fifeshire, Scotland; educated at Edinburgh; emigrated to Charleston in 1793; principal of the College of Charleston from 1805; a volume of his sermons appeared in 1809. Langdon Cheves was paid his first legal fee by Buist, for researching the title to a slave.

mistrusts itself, for mental power cannot exist without consciousness; but apt to over-rate others, measuring by its own standard, it dreads the being misunderstood. I have already intimated that the coolly confident elder brethren of the young lawyer, firmly established in their position almost by right of prescription, could scarcely estimate the force of a careless word or look which would tell with chilling power upon the acute feelings of one sensible of his right to stand beside them, and yet so quietly, so coolly, so unconsciously ignored, that it needed an indomitable power of resistance to uphold self-assertion. Still that power was there. Not in words was it spoken; not in thought evolved; And yet it was there, the result of the impulse of character scarcely yet known even to himself in its strength,—it came in the quiet summons, not spoken, not heard—but felt;[19] "Make room[;] I am of the first."[20] Diffident then, he stood before the court to speak his first word in public.

John Julius Pringle, a fine sample of the time-honoured old Charleston gentleman, was then in his seat as Attorney General.[21] A slight hesitation on the part of the debutant,—with a momentary feeling of sinking,—was interrupted by an inaudible remark of the court, followed by the somewhat cavalier, and by no means encouraging, loudly spoken response from the Attorney General; "Oh, I suppose the young man does not intend to make a speech about it." And "the young man" roused as it were, in a new strength,—with flushing brow and the calm dignity which the feeling of unkindness, if not injustice, raised within him,—the doubting voice which he himself, a moment before, almost shrank from hearing, now put forth in its fullness,—turning to the bench, said, "No may it please your honour, I do not intend to make a speech about it; but only such defense as my duty to my client requires." The ice was broken; the barrier o'erleaped.[22]

Very soon he counted among his warm personal friends, John Julius Pringle, whose immediate successor in the post of Attorney General, he

19. *Cymbeline* 4.2.306–7: "The dream's here still: even when I wake it is / Without me, as within me: not imagin'd, felt."

20. The above passage, from "I have already intimated . . .," is the lengthiest of the afterthoughts written on the back of pages of the draft and inserted by caret into the text.

21. John Julius Pringle (1753–1843), Charlestonian lawyer; member of the lower house of the General Assembly (1785–88); member of the state convention ratifying the U.S. Constitution (1788) and of the state constitutional convention (1790); attorney general of South Carolina (1792–1808); president of the board of trustees of the College of Charleston (1811–15).

22. *Macbeth* 1.4.48–50: "The Prince of Cumberland!—That is a step / On which I must fall down, or else o'erleap, / For in my way it lies."

afterwards became. I have more than once heard him say that he was sure Mr. Pringle no more meant unkindness, than he intended to excite the unexpected impulse which so effectually aided his young opponent. It was only the carelessness of habit which forgot to "feel what others feel,"[23] and ~~understood~~ showing him nothing of it, from his own experience. Let me add here (in the spirit of a proud gratitude with which my Father often referred to those bygone times) that the same men who thus unthinkingly would have closed the door of entrance against him, were fully and heartily ready to receive him, when once the power and the right to enter were proved.

To such beginnings however, I think was due a feeling of sympathy towards the young, with a disposition to encourage,—never to brow-beat,—which Mr. Cheves showed in every after position of life. I never knew the friends of these earlier days; but from those of a later period, those (now also passed away,) familiar with his manner as a Judge, I have been told, that he was always gentle and encouraging to the young, with an almost Father-like kindness, wherever he was met with truth and candour.

[FRAGMENTS]

Memoir of Langdon Cheves—taken fr[o]m Family Friend pub[lished] by S. A. Godman. (in Columbia somewhere about 185~~0 or 2~~) fr[o]m 1850 to 54— [*illegible word*] Grundy fr[o]m war mess,[24] correct missprints—and say that by an oversight navy speechs ("Father of the American navy") have been left out—[25]

security to give—he needed none. The merchant saw in him the integrity which would have shrunk from asking for a loan which could not be repaid, and the judgment [. . .]

23. *King Lear* 3.4.34–36: "Expose thyself to feel what wretches feel, / That thou mayst shake the superflux to them, / And show the Heavens more just."

24. Felix Grundy (1777–1840), as congressman from Tennessee member of the "war mess" (other members were Langdon Cheves, William Lowndes, Henry Clay, and John C. Calhoun) in support of the War of 1812; U.S. senator (from 1829; reelected 1833); attorney general to President Martin Van Buren (1838–39), before resigning to resume his place in the Senate.

25. This paragraph of notes appears at the end of extracts transcribed by LSM from eulogies of her father (see introductory note above). As part of preparations for what became the War of 1812, Cheves, as chairman of the Select Committee on Naval Affairs, made energetic efforts (such as a naval establishment bill introduced on Dec. 17, 1811) to arm the American republic at sea.

At about [*space left blank*] years of age the idea first began to develop itself of studying law—with encouragement of this kind—personal pecuniary help he never from any one sought ~~not~~ nor received (not even fr[o]m his own father) but worked on in his ~~business, still~~ position, ~~reading~~ [. . .]

Curling and powdering hair as was then the required form ~~in log-cabin garrets~~ with a 3 by 4 inch looking-glass in log-cabin garrets—only lodging houses the judicial corps could find.
and sometimes pause over an engagement to brush the sleeves of his coat and wonder whether the threadbare tendency of the elbows was sufficient to attract attention.

Mr. Lowndes[26] would have been President—"No he was [. . ."]

Threat of duel—newspaper correspondence—Keating Lewis Simons.[27] The editor could not betray his correspondents, but invited them to meet each other in his sanctum. Even in his old age the tear would ~~twinkle~~ tremble in my Father's eye, when he would ~~repeat~~ tell how the friends rushed into each other's arms, and argument was forgotten.
Stuffed a soft saddle for Nick—Mr. name? Harrison Phil[adelphi]a

Three years in Bank [*?*]

Stage coach in interior of Pennsylvania— (Perfect Ovation ~~Tables made me~~ Tables recalled the Sleepy Hollow suppers—)[28] Little Frenchman as a crowd gathered round trying to peep in—"I always treats dese peoples wiz contempts"—my Father quietly seated in a shaded corner, pleased to be sheltered by the little Frenchman, and his children so ignorant of etc.

Many years later
[*page torn*] Springs—"Ah! Of the old Stock" ~~I suppose~~? "The old [. . ."]

26. William Lowndes (1782–1822), lawyer and politician; born in Colleton County, S.C.; went with Langdon Cheves to Congress (1810), served as chairman of the House Ways and Means Committee, and resigned for reasons of health in spring 1822; died the following October; nominated for president of the United States by the South Carolina legislature (1821). Cheves named a son (1824–26) for Lowndes.

27. Keating Lewis Simons (1775–1819) was at his death in command of the Twenty-ninth Regiment of the South Carolina militia.

28. In "The Legend of Sleepy Hollow," the final story in his *Sketch Book of Geoffrey Crayon, Gent.* (1819–20), Washington Irving dwells with exuberance upon the luxurious viands and board of the fortunate inhabitants in the vicinity of Sleepy Hollow, in particular upon "the ample charms of a genuine country Dutch tea table, in the sumptuous time of autumn," at the supper enjoyed by Ichabod Crane immediately before his ride to meet the Headless Horseman (Washington Irving, *History, Tales, and Sketches* [New York, 1983], pp. 1058–88; 1076).

immense practice and left to R. Y. H[ayne][29]

Have sent from Abbeville 5 sheets letter paper. If commence again = 6.

Arrived at the time of his life when the struggle to rise was over. His public life was one ~~long triumph~~ continued triumph of strength, will, and unconquerable probity. I only saw him (child as I was) with a childs eye, and did not know that the great ~~min~~ intellect and the great mind of the man was being curbed in to a childs intellect. He must have known, but did he realize—does the greatest mind ever realize the vast stretch of its power[?]

Recklessness of reputation, no effort to preserve etc.

Was he still Speaker when resigning fr[o]m Congress?

In establishment of U.S. Bank—His casting vote as Speaker prevented its establishment—after he left was established. "Ah Mr. Cheves, you voted against the Bank."

He never offered himself for election to any position except that of Captain of Militia—and accordingly in Jan[uar]y 1800 we find his name as Capt[ain] Langdon Cheves on a Committee for the commemoration of the death of Gen[era]l Washington.[30]

Here you want a stronger hand than mine:—A child during the [1st?] years of my Fathers public life;—I need a history myself to learn it—That history never has, and never will be written.

Mr. Cheves Dec[ember] 1810 Mr. Cheves to fill vacancy in Congress and re-elected Nov[ember] 1811

To Congress Dec[ember] 1810—~~winter~~
To Bank February 1819 ~~early winter~~
~~First knew~~
~~As a boy he~~ [*canceled word illegible*]
~~His Father a Scotsman~~
~~Beauties of Poesy~~[31]
~~Jeffers or Jeffries~~

29. Robert Young Hayne (1791–1839), law student and close friend of Langdon Cheves, who turned over to him his prosperous law practice; attorney general of South Carolina (1818–22); U.S. senator (1822–32); prominent nullifier; argued states' rights against Daniel Webster (1830); governor of South Carolina (1832–34). LSM's youngest brother was named for Hayne; her second daughter, Louisa Rebecca Hayne McCord, was named both for LSM and for Hayne's second wife, whom he had married in 1820, Rebecca Alston Hayne.

30. In 1798 Charlestonians protested after the French, angry with the Jay Treaty, insulted the American minister, Charles Cotesworth Pinckney of Charleston. Among other forms of protest, a militia unit called the Charleston Federalist Company was established, of which Cheves was treasurer and obtained the rank of captain. George Washington died on Dec. 14, 1799.

31. Oliver Goldsmith, comp., *The Beauties of English Poesy* (London, 1767).

Tying bundles
Nashville and speech
Myself and Sister to Springs[32]

His Scotch blood and probably early education—Read Scotch beautifully—Burns was a treat—

~~Dr. Buist's Church—Dr. Buist pastor—black the seams etc.~~

begged by friends to permit his name to be advanced as candidate for the Presidency, he firmly refused—Nothing they said would induce him to seek such a position—

Never spared himself—In settling his Rice plantation he met the hardships which (age?) many a young man would etc.—slept on the floor—Mattress—Rats running over him.

He often said that he had never failed in any business he ever undertook.

Never offered himself for ~~any position~~ election to any position except that of Captain of Militia. Entirely without ear for time—looking at the man behind him to catch the first step and then went on well (time)— Delighted in the happiness of young people—Have seen him before his days of sorrow came upon him[,] standing beating time to the joyous dancing of our young friends[,] too happy for the langour of fashion, and showing how he enjoyed etc.

My grand aunt[33]—very proud of him, very fond of him—wished to leave all her property to himself and certain members of it—as my father spent much and although never heard in debt, accumulated little, until late in life, when he stinted himself, but never anyone else to help his children[,] would have been willing to receive the kindness of the old Aunt, who as I have heard him say was more of a Mother to him than any one[34] else has ever ~~been~~ known, but he would not draw up the papers unless, other heirs were present, knowing its contents—(lost thereby)—

Growing up—Early youth without softening ~~ties~~ social ties—most affectionate remembrance by the kind and somewhat primitive people with whom etc.—But neither etc.—his Father separated from [*canceled word illegible*] him by a second, decidedly non-happy marriage [*two illegible words*] was intensely affectionate, although not demonstrative—

them—Let them alone, if only they do not shake the table or my chair—We took him at his word—and sometimes to the extent (as gazing at forbid-

32. Langdon Cheves escorted LSM and her sister Anna, with their brother Alexander, to the springs of Virginia in the summer of 1839; see LSM to Langdon Cheves, Jr., Oct. 7, 1839.

33. Ann Heatly Reid Lovell.

34. Inserted above line: "his [*one or two illegible words*] Mother [then?]."

den fruit) of[,] with the heedless almost cruelty of childhood, unheeding our Mother's anxiously entreating look[,] to just take care not to shake the table, we would come so near it—so near it in our licensed folly, that I am sure [her?] self-reproach often gave her [pain?] by [just?] showing the [*illegible word*]—as the heedless fool looking over a precipice[.]

My brother Langdon and multiplication table—

Myself on his knees—no disguises from his family—would discuss freely all subjects with his friends—What would I not now give to recall such conversations? Unfortunately[,] ~~from my extreme~~ owing to my extreme childhood, nothing remains of them—Only as I think of them there lingers about a feeling amounting almost to adoration[.] ~~I felt that~~ There was that in his manner and voice which impressed me, though I understood nothing. I felt that true words of wisdom were being spoken though I understood them not.

Never spoke harshly to me—

Never hoarding money—but ~~always~~ always avoiding debt—

Langdon learning multiplication tables—gentle to all children—

R. Y. Hayne—nullification etc.

Merchant of Savannah—"Singular man"[—]extreme modesty—But when certain of his ground[,] firm and immovable. When not acquainted with facts never hesitating to disclaim all knowledge on the subjects in discussion—"You know better than I."—

I seated upon his knee—with any company[,] often business's, he never [repulsed?] me—I quiet as a mouse to be sure[.]

~~my childish Idol~~

My Idol through childhood and womanhood—

Never [petting?] in words—

Keep a stiff upper lip—

Tell the truth and shame the devil[35]—

He whom the dread of want ensnares with baseness [acts?] with meanness [*illegible word*][36]

Tell the truth and shame the devil.

have reached the point of separation—the struggle done—every thing doubtful conquered—now follows the exercised power—always duty

35. *1 Henry IV* 3.1.55, 58: "Tell truth, and shame the devil."

36. Richard Steele, *Spectator,* no. 114: "Usury, Stock-Jobbing, Extortion, and Oppression, have their Seed in the Dread of Want; and Vanity, Riot, and Prodigality, from the Shame of it: but both these Excesses are infinitely below the Pursuit of a reasonable Creature."

his first thought—Private and public—Impossible to separate the man's private character fr[o]m public acts and my childish mind was unable to grasp [that?] in [*illegible word*] strength my Father never boasted—and Congressional reports were scant and ill-done—while others were intimates with Editors—He ~~would~~ acted from the higher ambition—"To do"—never to be spoken of—

To some of his friends in the excitement of nullification which he opposed as a mistaken attempt to ~~strengthen~~ [*illegible word*] but in fact weakening our cause.—a cordial union of the south in favor of secession was supported—R. Y. Hayne in parting "My most revered friend, I am not bold enough to follow you." You strike out far ahead of our temporizing.

Father driving through [McCords?] swamp—to my Aunt's—came following with nurse and other children—Water everywhere and all landmarks covered. Mother clinging to his arm, endeavoured to draw his ~~hand~~ reign hand round to what appeared a clear road through the forest and which was as it afterwards proved doubtless the River (He had no eye for locality and caused her mistrust of his judgement)—There was no possibility of pausing—no time for consultation. One sign[,] one idea had struck him—one sign was faintly apparent to him—none other noticed it—His whole anxiety concentrated and feared to allow his mind to be turned off by persuasion or argument. As she seized his arm He only said to her—"Wife[,] trust me" and turned the horses heads towards what she believed to be certain death—The great sheet of water covered [with?] [*illegible word*] ~~had~~ offered only one ~~cour route whi~~ road which gave ~~him~~ the chance of life—My Mother saw the ~~open road straight~~ way open and clear before her—Turn here, here to the right, and she seized his arm drawing him back fr[o]m the certain death. "Wife[,] trust me and do not touch my arm." He turned to the left into ~~what appeared~~ the much denser part of the forrest.

Here and there at ~~long~~ considerable distances, small flakes of cotton hanging to trees under which loaded wagons of loose cotton (fr[o]m fields) had past weeks before—

Always considerate and indulgent ~~to the young~~ in his judgment of all,—most kind and encouraging to youth—only one class he would turn his back upon—those who were foolish enough to fancy they could flatter him. He would patiently instruct or persuade those who seemed to doubt his opinions but [disgusted?] with the [*two illegible words*] to the extent of [*illegible word*] and I think often, [*two illegible words*] too floridly expressed.

passions of the strongest—though the subdued passion within made his manner at times painfully undemonstrative,—Firm determination to govern himself, when no hope in argument seemed to turn him into an Iron Man—[*three canceled words illegible*] ~~me, but so quietly~~ It seems to me I understood him better than all others—In sudden shocks of grief,—heart-breaking anguish—he was ~~always~~ coldly calm. Rather I would say ~~pas~~ (permit the anomalous expression) *passionately* calm. If that calm was broken, it seemed for a moment to be by unreasonable passion—but it was only an [*canceled word illegible*] unconscious screen[,] as it were, of the boiling passion of grief within him.

I have seen a mean man pretending to be a gentleman maintain a false pretense. He merely turned and looked at him. He did not I believe intend to be impressive—He only looked (first having previously explained) calmly at him. The eye of the other fell—quietly fell before the full unthreatning gaze—

The acute mind of Petigru[,] more than any other, looked into his character, expressing it in strong but simple and plain words, which in their simple character seemed to open to you the being—nature of the man.

I have never known or read of any man equal for completeness of character[.] (This is the verdict I think not of a natural prejudice in his favor~~)~~ but of my well-sifted reason[.]) The very perfection was its limit in usefulness. Had he been more able to give up one inch of the line fr[o]m perfect execution, he might have been able to execute more?—He never could to the smallest extent consent (as by old proverb) to "fight the Devil with his own fire." Where the purer weapon failed him—he paused. Even the interests of his nearest and dearest, could never blot out or render dimn the line of truth—Of his own personal interests their never was a question. Never even could he suppress the right. It is I fear an anomaly to speak of the perfect purity of a man engaged in public life and where he could not force to the right,—He would withdraw but never change the right to suit circumstance. Never mislead by ambition or interest. "Wife[,] what have I lived for?"—Never a symptom of giving up to expediency—Never act wrongly because right is unattainable. Wait if the glimmer of truth may prevail, when the cloud of wrong is too heavy. His only limit.

Came to live near me—moved to my house to die—For greater quiet which he seemed to long for and [*canceled word illegible*] to avoid confusion of many faces[,] I caused to be built in my garden a house of four rooms where he staid with a faithful white attendant until his death—His Sandhill establishment was subject to rude incursion and too far for me to be with him as much as he and myself desired.

He was long in dying—after weeks of forgetfulness, as I leant upon the back of his wheeled chair—He looked me in the face—"Are you not my daughter[?]"—My silent answer was a kiss upon his upturned brow—and he continued[, "]I thought you were my daughter.["]

[Epitaph]

Langdon Cheves
was born on the
17th of Sept. 1776
and died on the
26th June 1857

Husband and Father
Kind and Affectionate
True friend
Indulgent Master
Just and generous to all
With duty ever his great
word of action

So strong so pure
So wise
His Country needed
but death
had called him

Massiveness of intellect
Wisdom of Judgment
Indomitable will
Unflagging energy
of execution
And purity of purpose
Without blot
combined to make the
Patriot Statesman
and the model man.

Part IV

LETTERS AND DOCUMENTS

9.

Letters and Documents, March 20, 1836–December 4, 1860

To Sophia Cheves Haskell

Dear Sophy St. Matthews March 20th, 1836

What has become of y[ou]r last letter I don't know; I was looking for it to see if there was any thing in it to answer but it is poked away in some of my sundry hiding places and they are all at present in a state of pretty considerable confusion;—for I have for all the last week done nothing in the world but play nurse, or rather not play, it is too serious as {a} business being sole directress having all the responsability on my shoulders.

Mother has been very sick, or I should say *ill.* ~~since~~ Sunday she was taken very sick in consequence of excessive constipation which no ~~sickness~~ medecine could conquer; all that she took only produced violent pains and Monday the Dr. who was here almost all day seemed to fear very much inflamation of the bowels. Tuesday and Wednesday she was better;—Thursday f[ro]m the administering of a dose of ~~medecine~~ oil returned to the condition very nearly of Monday;—Since that the Dr. has only tried the mildest medecines and she has been getting better and seems today better than she has been since she was first taken sick—the immediate cause of her sickness remains still uncorrected, but the doctor thinks her nevertheless improveing and thinks that at present there is no cause for uneasiness and that she is doing well although her case is an obstinate one.

We have heard of Langdon's arrival ~~in~~ at Picolata and she {see} by the papers that Elmore's corps to which ~~be~~ he belongs has been sent on to Volusia (where that is I dont know) and that is all I know of him.[1] John arrived here f[ro]m Charleston the even[in]g before the last—full of doctoring. Landed f[ro]m the Steam-boat at Fort Motte and surprised the folks there; he was grown so tall that they took him for Mr. Cheves of Baltimore and never thought of their old acquaintance John.[2]

I have seen very little of the family (the Haskells) lately; the weather was bad for some time and lately Mother's sickness has kept me steadily at home, I do not like to go out for any time. They heard Mother was sick and called here yesterday. They are all well except Eugenia, who is not sick but only reasonably indisposed.——They speak of going to town to-morrow week.——Anna is preparing to go to Philadelphia to Mr. Picot's, early in April with Aunt and Uncle Dulles; we received by the last mail a letter f[ro]m Father giving her leave to do so:[3]—however it has become a little doubtful whether she can go then; they (Aunt and Uncle D.) had intended to go on in the stage, but find it impracticable according to the plan they had proposed, and are now unsettled in their travelling plans:—In case of their going in a private carriage or any ~~thing~~ other way which would make numbers burthensome of course she will stay at home. I beleive I have nothing else to say; it is eleven o-clock and I must be up before 6 to meet the Dr. who is going to Orangeburgh but promised to call and see Mother first;—so being very sleepy—Bon soir. Should Mother go on and get quite well immediately I will not promise to write by the next mail, but should she not do so I shall certainly write; so recollect as no letter is explained to mean "all's well",—you must not complain should there be none. Love to Mr. Haskell and the little ones.——

Your affectionate Sister
Louisa Cheves——

1. The Second Seminole War had begun in 1835. On Feb. 11, 1836, the Richland Volunteer Rifle Company, commanded by Benjamin Thomas Elmore (1787–1841), departed from Columbia to join the force under Gen. Abraham Eustis, which arrived at St. Augustine, Fla., about Feb. 15. Picolata, a town on the east bank of the St. Johns River, due west of St. Augustine, was a supply depot, base of operations, and hospital; at Volusia, a landing on the river about four miles south of Lake George, Eustis' force, having left St. Augustine on March 15, endured a difficult crossing on March 22–26.

2. LSM's brother Alexander (b. 1808), gone to study law in Baltimore in 1827, had remained to practice there. Her brother John (b. 1815) was studying medicine in Charleston.

3. Emigré with his wife from France, Charles Picot was proprietor of a school in Philadelphia, where LSM had studied French.

Addressed: Mrs. Charles T. Haskell / Churchill Post-office / Abbeville District / So. Ca.
Source: Langdon Cheves III Papers, SCHS.

To Sophia Cheves Haskell

Dear Sophy St. Matthews March 28th, 1836 Monday

I wrote you by the last mail that Mother was sick, she has since been and is still very ill. Dr. Goodwyn sent John to Columbia on Friday in search of a Dr.;[4] John returned Saturday even[in]g with Dr. De Leon of that place; he is said to be a very good physician, and is staying with us; he was very anxious to return almost immediately, but has finally promised to remain until her disease comes to a crisis.[5] He says that Dr. Goodwyn's treatment was very judicious, and very much what he would have done himself; they are both in almost constant attendance and one or the other of them up almost constantly for the last three nights. Her sickness is caused by excessive constipation unreleived now for 16 days and the danger is of inflamation—Dr. De Leon thinks that there must be a crisis soon, Dr. Goodwyn that it may be delayed for 10 days or a fortnight—both while they concur in saying, as every body must know[,] that there is danger still say and I beleive sincerely that there is strong reason for hope. She has not much fever and her strength although failing her a good deal is still considerable. I shall of course write again by the next opportunity, but must finish now—every thing falls on my hands. I have been for two hours (f[ro]m incessant interruptions) scrawling this. I have not been undressed ~~or~~ and in bed but 3 times in this last fortnight and for the last 3 days have had both the doctors scolding at me for not

4. "Dr. Goodwyn" is either of two brothers, both practicing medicine in St. Matthews Parish at this time: Robert Howell Goodwyn (1795–1861), born in Richland County, studied medicine at the Medical College of New York (1817–19), before returning to South Carolina; in 1837 he moved to Columbia, abandoning medicine for a career in banking. Thomas Jefferson Goodwyn (1800–1877) studied medicine in New York and Philadelphia, then set up practice and operated a plantation near Fort Motte; moved to Columbia about 1854; retired to Fort Motte after the war. Both brothers were members of the South Carolina Senate and had active political careers. Thomas Jefferson Goodwyn as mayor of Columbia surrendered the city to the Federal army under Sherman. "Colonel Goodwyn, the mayor of the town, fraternized with the Yankee generals freely. *Then,* when they burnt his house over his head, a change came over the spirit of his dream." *Chesnut,* p. 769, echoing Byron, "The Dream," l. 167: "A change came o'er the spirit of my dream."

5. Mordecai Hendricks De Leon (1791–1848), Columbia physician; regent of the State Hospital for the Insane (1841–48); close friend of Thomas Cooper, for whom he named his third son.

doing so but am nevertheless well. Goodbye[.] Love to Mr. H[askell] and the children. The Haskells are all well, all very kind in offering every assistance, but cannot do much.

Your affectionate Sister
Louisa Cheves

Father has just arrived; well

Addressed: Mrs. Charles T. Haskell / Church-hill post-office / Abbeville district / So. Ca. *Source:* Langdon Cheves III Papers, SCHS.

To Sophia Cheves Haskell

Dear Sophy St. Matthews April 8th [1836]

It was all over sooner than I expected; I wrote to you Monday, poor Mother's troubles finished the next day; she died Tuesday afternoon; quietly, satisfied, quite conscious of her state, and talking to us all, until about ¾ of an hour before her last breath; she spoke of you all often wished she could have seen you but seemed to try to let that and every thing else trouble her as little as possible. She was buried in our little burying ground on Wednesday afternoon; it could not be delayed longer owing to the nature of her Malady;——She died without inflamation which made her sufferings, although great[,] less than they might have been. I feel as I wander about the house and have to take her place in a thousand things as if I were doing wrong all the time;—Anna has to be prepared to start for the North in a few days and I have to turn over every work trunk and closet, it absolutely makes me sick to meddle with all her little arrangements, her patterns, clothes cut out for the children etc.

Father seems to feel it very much; so did Anna for the first day or two; the children as usual care for nothing;—poor little things I am almost inclined to punish them, to make them look dull. I must stop. John is starting in half an hour, ~~sudde~~ unexpectedly for Columbia to see about the means of getting Anna and Grandmother to Charleston on their way to the North. God bless you all.

Your affectionate Sister
Louisa Cheves.

Addressed: Mrs. Charles T. Haskell / Church-hill post-office / Abbeville District / So. Ca. *Source:* Langdon Cheves III Papers, SCHS.

To Langdon Cheves, Jr.

Dear Lang, Portman Shoals Oct[ober] 7, 1839

I do beleive I have not written to you once this summer, and I do beleive I need not make many apologies on the ~~subject~~ occasion, for I do beleive *votre Seignorie* will forgive the sin, sooner than you would the infliction of a page of excuses on the subject.

We have been at home just one week; and I have surmounted a summer at the Springs, which thank Heaven *est finie* and I am again released f[ro]m playing belle which, nolens volens, seems some how or other to be my destiny when I go into company. Next time I go to matronise Miss Anna in the gay world, I vow it shall be in a cap, or some such distinguishing mark of old age; folks shall not think that my venerable self, stepping close on nine and twenty, has any ambition to pass as young Lady, any more. I'll pin a piece of paper with, "*aged twenty-nine*," on my shoulder, and if that don't scare off the young seventeen-year olders who come to flirt with me, the dear knows what will. I am tired to death with rivalling Nan in their good graces. But I am talking of by gone ills which really seem now like the confused bustle of a dream;—we have been going thro' such very different scenes of late that the contrast seems unreal. On our way home we met Gen[eral Robert Young] Hayne ill at Ashville; Father of course delayed his journey;—we staid to see him die, and then brought on his widow and two sons here. Poor Mrs Hayne,—the shock has been a fearfully sad one to her. She is in dreadful spirits and not very good health, so I am obliged to be pretty constantly in attendance on her;—and I confess the 24 hours I spent over Gen: Hayne's death-bed with my subsequent attention to my poor friend, have not at all contributed to raise the bustle of the Springs in my estimation; perhaps I might have judged their fooleries more indulgently a few weeks ago, tho' at best, *vraiment,* they don't suit my fancy.——Talking of the Haynes, puts me in mind of my baby (what used to be, that's to say) Hayney. He managed to break his arm some time ago[;] how, I know not; I never received Charley's letter informing me of the accident, only his subsequent notices of its recovery. I suppose the youngster would be almost willing to break his other arm now that the first one is well, as it resulted in his being sent to Philadelphia and getting a month's petting f[ro]m Grandmother. I received a letter f[ro]m Charlotte a few days since, it distresses me to hear of her being sick so often.[6] I wish she could manage to get well and keep so. I presume the cares and anxieties of the summer, have affected her health injuriously, and hope

6. Charlotte McCord, eldest daughter of David James McCord, married Langdon Cheves, Jr., on Dec. 24, 1839. Her mother had died in early August.

therefore that with their passing away and the return of cool weather, she will be better. I was very glad to hear that her Father's health was improveing, I had heard a few days before a report of its being very bad. She tells me you won't grow fat;—however as you have got thro' the summer without melting away altogether, I begin to have some hopes of you.——I hear you are living close in your office still. At least so was reported to me by Mr. Beaufort Watts whom I had the felicity to light upon at Greenville;[7]—He called to see me and bounced in with a most exhilirating "how do you do Miss Cheves?" which ought in Charity to have made me answer with as good-natured a "quite well I thank you," but I was thinking of some thing for Mrs. Hayne at the moment and I was bothered, and my wits, if they were any where had gone a gadding out of my own head, and so I stared at him with that vacant look which says so distinctly "who in the name of wonder can *you* be?" until the poor man had to go thro' the very awkward ceremony of introducing himself. I'm scrawling in a tremendous fashion; I don't think you can make it all out; but I beleive I am, or ought to be in a great hurry, so I can't help it. We leave here the 20th of this month probably, which will take us to Columbia about the 25th. I do not know if we will stop any time;—We go down with Mrs. Hayne and it will depend some what upon her wishes. She leaves her sons in Columbia and f[ro]m there Father purposes taking her to Charleston leaving Anna and myself at St. Mathews.

I beleive I may as well say good-night, for there's the clock striking twelve, and there's the cat mewing at the entry door; for all the world, *jist* like a ghost. Give my love to Charlotte.

Your affectionate Sister
Louisa Cheves.

Addressed: Langdon Cheves Junior Esqr. / Columbia / So. Ca. *Source:* Cheves Family Papers, SCL.

7. Beaufort Taylor Watts (d. c. 1869), secretary of legation in Colombia and Russia; secretary to many governors of South Carolina. "Gentleman to the tips of his fingers. Chivalry incarnate" (*Chesnut*, pp. 52–53, recounting his career).

To Louise Penelope Davis Preston

St. Matthews (Sand-hills)
Dear Mrs. Preston[8] Nov[ember] 3d, 1845

Mr. McCord on his return from Columbia (yesterday even[in]g) tells me that there is a hope that we may see Mr. Preston and yourself here soon. Pray come. We are still at our Summer place but will move to Lang Syne tomorrow or the next day—and will be delighted to see you as soon as you can come down. Mr. McCord will be obliged to be in Columbia, for a few days, by the 1st Dec[ember] being sued by the Pope, before Chief Justice Fitch, for the payment of a leg of beef which he bought of——three years ago, and having paid for at the time, refuses to submit to the Pope's impositions, with whom, as a good Protestant, he has never had any transactions, until summoned by him to pay tribute, the other night after he left your house. So, such great characters coming in the way of his staying at home on the 1st Dec[ember] he joins with me, in begging you to pay us a visit before that time. Do come, and remember to drop a line to me, to say when our carriage shall meet you at the Pump, unless you come, as Mr. McCord says you had better do, in your own carriage.

And now let me exculpate myself for what I fear, with all your Christian charity, you must consider as a great act of neglect, if not a heavy sin. Mr. McCord tells me that you wrote to me some time during the summer and asked him if I had rec[eive]d your letter. I hope that my not answering it, has made you already come to the true conclusion, which is that I never rec[eive]d it. I have not heard a word ~~from~~ of you, except from public report of your husbands whereabouts since I last saw you. I had intended writing to you after my recovery from the birth of my last *trouble-house,* but did not know where you were, nor where to direct to you.[9]——We were much shocked at the exagerated Newspaper reports of Mr. Preston's illness, and then not knowing when you might be coming home, or how long detained I still could not write.[10]——

8. Daughter of Columbia physician and planter in Fairfield District James Davis (1774–1838) and Catherine Ross Davis, Louise Penelope Davis Preston (1807–53) was married in 1831 to William Campbell Preston. Her health, like her husband's, was frail; see LSM to Mary Cheves Dulles, June 18 [1851], June 21 [18]52.

9. LSM's daughter Louisa Rebecca Hayne McCord was born on Aug. 10, 1845.

10. William Campbell Preston was elected president of South Carolina College on Nov. 28, 1845 (entering office on Jan. 5, 1846), although "his health was now impaired, and he was not in a proper condition to meet the labors, the turmoils, and the strife of his ancient profession [the practice of law]. . . . His feeble health interfered much with the discharge of his duties [as president], but no one exhibited a more becoming zeal, or a livelier sense of his high responsibility." LaBorde, *History of the South Carolina College,* p. 295.

Mr. McCord is hurrying me for my letter to take to the mail, so hoping to have a chance of talking to you very soon face to face, I must end now.

Do not be afraid to {of} coming too soon after our move down—I shall be settled in half-an-hour after we get home as the house is all cleaned and ready to receive us. So come soon and stay as long as you can.

With my respectful regards to Mr. Preston and your Mother, believe me ever

Sincerely and affectionately y[ou]rs
Louisa S. McCord

Addressed: Mrs. William C. Preston / Columbia. *Source:* Preston Family Papers, VHS.

To William Porcher Miles

Dear Sir[11] Lang Syne May 2d, 1848

As you alone among my friends, have had the kindness to hint to me some of the many defects of the little volume which I was bold enough to offer for criticism,[12] although I fear you treated me much too gently, I now venture, emboldened by your friendly comments, to take the very great liberty of begging for your opinion of the accompanying manuscript.[13] I am conscious that I am asking what I have no right to do, and intruding upon some leisure

11. William Porcher Miles (1822–99), professor of mathematics at the College of Charleston; member of the U.S. House of Representatives (1857–60); as mayor of Charleston, received the funeral cortege of Langdon Cheves; represented Charleston to the Confederate Congress, where he served as chairman of the Committee on Military Affairs. Miles was a cousin of David James McCord, McCord's mother and Miles' maternal grandmother being daughters of Rev. Paul Turquand, son of a Huguenot refugee.

12. *My Dreams* (Philadelphia: Carey and Hart, 1848); see chap. 1 above. "I received a few days since through Mr. [Joseph A.] Winthrop of Charleston a parcel containing 20 volumes of Mrs. McCord's Poems. They are printed very handsomely and the Book altogether well got up. . . . I hope you remembered to give a copy to Mr. Charles Picot, the old instructor of Mrs. McCord,—and to such other persons as I named in my letter of last summer." David James McCord to "Gentlemen," Lang Syne, Jan. 23, 1848, Gratz Collection, PHS.

13. "Mrs. McCord thanks you very much for your candid and friendly opinion and criticisms on her Poems. She says she values them more because you have been candid enough to blame, where you thought it deserved, and that she is satisfied that you are right, and hopes that your advice will be of service to her. She would be glad to have your further counsel." David James McCord to William Porcher Miles, March 17, 1848, William Porcher Miles Papers, SHC. Also in this letter McCord regrets that Miles had intended to visit Lang Syne just during a planned trip to Savannah, but must go: "My wife had written for some time since to her father promising the visit and to entertain us he has built a room to his house."

hour which you could employ much more profitably and pleasantly,—but still I venture to ask the favour.

It is to me more than an amusement,—it is an absolute comfort, an almost necessity, to put my fancies upon paper, and I have a strong desire to find out whether or not they are worth the putting down. I have no unprejudiced friend near me to whose judgment I can appeal. May I, as the greatest possible favour, beg you to pull to pieces, to be as ill-natured as you can, with the productions which I trouble you with? If they are *abominable trash,* I will really thank you sincerely if you will tell me so, without any sugaring. I do not wish to extract compliments from you;—I would not give a pin for them. I am begging for what would be of real use to me;—for a true and honest opinion, from a person, capable as you are, of giving one. The more fault-finding, the greater will be my debt of gratitude. My wish is, if possible, without making a fool of myself, to dis-cover whether I can do something, or nothing,—and I take the liberty of throwing myself for this once upon your charity, promising never to repeat the infliction, and hoping that you will without disguising or softening in any way, give me your opinion. I assure you that were you to tell me I had sent you the most nonsensical stuff that ever was penned, I should thank you for your sincerity and endeavour to profit by your judgment.

If I impose too troublesome a task upon you, pray refuse without hesitation my request. If you find it convenient to oblige me, let me beg you to do so *entirely at your leisure.* I merely take this opportunity of sending to you as I happen to have a servant going to town on other business.

I regretted much that your indisposition prevented us from seeing you when in town. Hoping that you have long before this entirely recovered and with kind regards to your Mother and Sister, beleive me dear Sir

with much respect
Your's etc.
Louisa S. McCord.

Source: William Porcher Miles Papers, SHC.

To William Porcher Miles

Dear Sir, Pendleton June 12th, 1848

Having left home on the 29th, I failed to receive before my departure, your's of 28th ~~inst~~ ulto which has followed me hither. I am most sincerely obliged to you for your kind criticisms, and so far from thinking them harsh or in any degree "*hypercritical,*" am only most agreeably surprised that you have found in my manuscripts so much to approve of. Although I feel that you have said all the good you can of them, and noted their faults most gently, I still am confident that after the appeal I made to your *charity,* you would not willingly mislead me, and I am much gratified to find, that you think there is in my productions, the proof of *some power.* Although I have been pushed back in every possible way, and have myself endeavoured for many a long year to crush my own propensities, there has been a struggling consciousness of something which has goaded me on to my recent experiments, and one word of sincere and well-judged approbation, though it were mixed with a bushel of fault-finding, would be enough to cheer me on. I only fear your judgment as being too indulgent;—if you had struck harder, I would feel more certain of my footing. My misfortune is, that I am most wofully ignorant, and not knowing even *where* to look for the information that I want, find it now, rather late in the day, to begin my groping in the dark. It is however a comfort even to try,—and try I will. An effortless life, is, to a restless mind, a weary fate to be doomed to; and as no other door is open to me, I may as well push on at this. Should I fail, the very effort will have given an object to many an otherwise dissatisfied hour, and although I shall have gazed at the sun in vain, it will at least have been a comfort to dream that I could reach him. (Don't say "bottled sunbeams,"—please,—though I believe my simile deserves it.)[14]——Of the faults you have pointed out, some I was before conscious of and deemed irremediable;—others, if I had the manuscript at hand, I would set about trying to doctor at once. C. Gracchus at least. The other[15] I do not hope to be able to do any thing with; it was written some dozen years ago, and the spirit of it has passed away from me. I am most annoyed at the idea of my halting lines and defective measure, but must try and hunt up the culprits for correction. You show me some historical blunders which I have fallen into. Livius Drusus for instance I might just as well have made a young man, as an old one, but was really ignorant enough not to know anything about him. I must stand up though for the Gracchi. They are among my *bona fide* heroes. Plutarch from whom I have pilfered largely, gives them I think a high position;—and does not Niebuhr (I ask, for truly I am lamentably difficient in information and have forgotten what little I have known about it) consider them as having nobly

14. In bk. 3, chap. 5 of *Gulliver's Travels,* Gulliver describes a scientist at the Grand Academy of Lagado, who "had been Eight Years upon a Project for extracting Sun-Beams out of Cucumbers, which were to be put into Vials hermetically sealed, and let out to warm the Air in raw inclement Summers." Jonathan Swift, *Prose Writings,* ed. Herbert Davis (Oxford, 1965), 11:179.

15. Not identified.

acted in a good cause?[16] I confess to being a thorough upholder of the people's rights and in present scenes, although I cannot quite go with Louis Blanc and M. Albert,[17] much less can I sympathise with fallen dynasties, however much I may deem beggar-kings an object of pity.[18]——As to my productions being *closet dramas,* what else can a Woman write? The *world of action* must to her be almost entirely a closed book. I am extremely obliged to you for your kind offer to give me the *benefit* (for truly it is a *real benefit*) of your advice, and if I shall in future be able to do any thing, will venture again to appeal to your judgment for assistance. As regards my M.S.S. I am here, too far away, for you to get them sent to me. Pray let them occupy an empty corner of some drawer, until I get home again, and perhaps next winter I may be able to ~~g~~ do something with them. I shall keep your letter as a commentary upon their defects, and will try to dragg, coax, or push them, into perhaps a somewhat better shape.

Allow me to reiterate my sincere thanks for the trouble you have taken in compliance with my request. Pray remember me most kindly to your

16. The account of the Gracchi in the *Römische Geschichte* (1811–32) of the German historian Barthold Georg Niebuhr (1776–1831) is an encomium going beyond even what LSM claims of it. Theirs was a "noble cause," and "the moral part of the account [by Plutarch] is beautiful." "No one can be more spotless in his sentiments than Tib[erius] Gracchus was." His brother Gaius, who excelled him "in point of talent," is a tragic figure, eloquent, "honest and pure like Tiberius; but passionate, superior to him in power, and more conscious of what he wanted." Those punishing the friends of Tiberius after his murder employ tactics "worthy of the Inquisition, or of an Alba." The murderers of Gaius and his party, exclaims Niebuhr with horrified indignation, "called themselves *boni homines, boni cives!*" Indeed, the Gracchi appeal (then and now) to those "who are sincere and open, who seek and love the beautiful and sublime, who delight in eminent men, and see in them the glory of their age and nation." "All the Gracchi are distinguished for their mildness, their unaffected and sincere love of the oppressed. . . . To dwell on such characters as these is the more delightful, as they are seldom met with in Roman history; in our own days they seem to be quite extinct." Barthold George Niebuhr, *Lectures on the History of Rome, from the Earliest Times to the Fall of the Western Empire,* ed. Leonhard Schmitz, trans. Julius Charles Hare et al., 3 vols., 3d ed. (London, 1853), 2:283, 276, 281, 296, 298, 291, 311, 308, 285. LSM was troubled by Niebuhr's hostile opinion of political economy; see *PSE,* "Slavery and Political Economy," pp. 436–37.

17. Socialist politician and author of *L'Organisation du travail* (1840), Jean-Joseph-Charles-Louis Blanc (1811–82) as a member of the Provisional Government in France (1848) secured a guarantee of employment to workers, until forced into exile in England (1848–70). Albert-Alexandre Martin, called Albert l'Ouvrier (1815–95), French revolutionary politician; member of the Provisional Government, then of the National Assembly (1848); imprisoned (1848–59) for his part in uprisings of May and June 1848.

18. King Louis Philippe of France had abdicated on Feb. 24, 1848, and gone into exile in England.

Mother, Aunt and Sister. Tell your Aunt that I am such a shabby letter-writer, and was so busy physicking little negroes and packing up etc. before leaving home that I did not find time to thank her for her kind note and acceptable etc.[']s sent up by my servant Betsy; but in spite of my neglect did not feel the less kindly her attentions.

Mr. McCord joins in kind remembrance to all. We will be very glad to see any of you if you can be tempted to visit these regions.

Believe me dear Sir

very truly and respectfully your's
Louisa S. McCord—

Source: William Porcher Miles Papers, SHC.

To William Gilmore Simms

[1851?]

You are so polite as to ask for the data for a notice of myself. I am flattered by the compliment, but know nothing about myself, except that I am my father's daughter, born Dec[ember], 1810, married May, 1840, and am not dead yet.

Source: Printed in Simms, *Letters* 1:cxxiii.[19]

To Mary Cheves Dulles

Dear Mary[20] [Columbia] June 18th [1851]

For the last week, I have been intending to write to you, but have been really seriously sick from the consequences of the worst sick headache I ever

19. No date, place, or present location of the letter is given. The notice mentioned may have been requested with regard to LSM's *Caius Gracchus,* reviewed (by Simms?) in *SQR,* n.s., 4 (July 1851): 62–68. William Gilmore Simms (1806–70), born in Charleston; editor of the *Southern Quarterly Review* (1849–54); novelist, poet, man of letters.

20. "Cousin Mary was a sweet, gentle, fair headed creature to whom we children had long been devoted cherubs. She was very benevolent, very religious, and had all sorts of rather visionary ideas of improving the negroes, which in my father's life time used to delight his very soul. He would give her full sway, and help her where he could, but I can see his eyes dancing with amusement, when as on one occasion she found that a hymn which she had carefully taught the negro children, in which occurred the line 'Saviour Master, Saviour King,' had been converted into 'Serve your Master, Save your skin.' She was in a terrible state of mind about it, especially when he insisted on her letting it stay just that way, as it was such an excellent moral, though he would have hesitated to teach it himself and was somewhat surprised at her, etc. etc." Smythe, pp. 38–39. Mary Dulles may be the "Mary" whose kindness is celebrated in LSM's poem "The Sunbeam Sprite," chap. 1 above.

had in my life. I have been sea-sick for a week and feel this morning is {as} if I were just out of the black-hole in the Wilmington boat. After this introduction you will scarcely expect anything very enlivening from my present effort. Indeed I do not think I would have had courage to attempt a letter today, but as Cheves has started the sheet, I will attempt at least a long P.S.—always be it understood you are to criticize neither style, spelling, nor anything else.[21]——I was very glad yesterday to receive y[ou]rs enclosed in your Father's to Mr. McCord and pleased to hear that all continue well:—We are having a downright spell of cold weather here; regular fall; which looks very odd at this season of the year. I do not know what effect it will take upon our crops. Mr. McC. was at Lang Syne yesterday, but was prevented by rain from looking much about. He reports cotton as doing well, but corn having a most threateningly doleful appearance. I was so sick all day yesterday that I hardly listened to his report of things, but I do not think he knows anything particular of ~~his~~ your Fathers place, as the weather ~~was~~ has been first too hot and ~~now~~ yesterday too rainy for any communications therewith.——

But these are most uninteresting topics for a city-lady so let me see if Columbia furnishes no news.——Our friends the Prestons are on a ten days visit to Sullivan's Island; not well when they left here. Mr. Hoxie florishing in his store and polite as usual.[22] I have bought sundry yards of long-cloth, levy-calicoes and so forth from him since coming up. Mr. Olmutz has taken his departure whither I am not sure;—all about the N[orthern] States I believe.[23] Oscar Lieber has gone west on some geological expedition, and

21. Cheves McCord's letter reads:

"Dear Cousin Mary Columbia June 17th, 1851

I wish that you were here to get some of the nice figs which come up ~~e~~ from Lang Syne, for Papa brings them up every week or ten days.

It has been very cold all day ~~for the mid season~~ and we have had fire the whole of the afternoon.

Have you forgotten to subscribe to the little news paper which Mamma asked you to do[?] When you do subscribe to it please direct it to Fort Motte in the winter and to Columbia in the summer.

I expect to pay a visit to Lang Syne the next time Papa goes down ~~there~~. I was to have gone this morning but the rain (which we have had all day) prevented my going.

Are you going to Naragansett again this summer[?]

This is a very short letter but it is my bed time and besides I have no more to say

Your affectionate Cousin
Langdon Cheves McCord."

22. Norton A. Hoxie, born in New York, merchant in Columbia, is listed as twenty-seven years old in the 1850 census.

23. Possibly a reference to Francis Kinloch Huger (1773–1855), who, when a medical student touring Europe in 1794, conspired to free the Revolutionary War hero Lafayette

hopes to get a position in some institution in Mississippi.[24]——The Herbemonts were well when I saw them, though Mrs. H. sends me word that she has been complaining of late, since I have been laid up with this awful headache of mine.[25] Mr. H. has taken off his wig Mr. McC. tells me, shows his bald head and is quite improved by the change. Aleck came to see me two days ago, but I was so sick I hardly spoke to him. And now, I do not know whether I am going to betray a confidence or exactly how I ought to act. Some ten days since, he (Aleck) came to ask my advice as to whether or not he had better take a trip to Philadelphia. As he was perfectly candid and did not for an instant pretend to disguise that his only object in going there, was to visit Miss Mary Dulles, I thought I ought to answer as straight as if I ~~was~~ were saying my catechism and so I did, giving the "*pour et contre*" of the question as well as I could and leaving him to sum up probabilities for himself. He went away saying that he would think about it and looked pretty droopy and melancholy when I saw him two days after. As I have heard nothing further of the affair, and the gentleman is still here, I presume he thought what I said sufficiently dis-courageing to dissuade him from the attempt. Now if I have done wrong in so doing, you must give some kind of a hook or a crook, some sort of an intelligible signal in writing to me which I may be able to decipher, to indicate that I have led the gentleman to

---

from the Austrian fortress of Olmütz; Lafayette was recaptured, and Huger jailed for six months. Huger was the father of Thomas Pinckney Huger, husband of LSM's sister Anna.

24. Oscar Montgomery Lieber (b. 1830) was a son of Francis and Matilda Lieber, friends of LSM and David James McCord; he was now accompanying Michael Tuomey, author of *Report on the Geology of South Carolina* (1848), and at this time head of the Alabama State Geological Survey. "Dr. Lieber was at that time a warm friend to the South and even a Slaveholder himself, but some years after [in 1857] he was given a professorship at Columbia College, New York. He moved on there with his wife and [son] Norman, then a young man—an older brother Oscar Lieber preferred to live in South Carolina. With time and surroundings and I fear different interests, Dr. Lieber's principles changed—having sold all his negroes and pocketed the money he gradually developed into an abolitionist and when war and trouble came Dr. Lieber ranged himself on the side of our enemies—it was a shock and disappointment to his old friends and a terrible blow to his son Oscar. I shall never forget the day the students of the college took the bust of Dr. Lieber and with the solemnity of a public execution threw it out of the window. . . . Oscar fought with the Confederates. . . . He never complained or mentioned his people after what he felt their disgrace, but in the delirium before his death he talked constantly of his mother." Smythe, p. 9. Oscar Lieber was mortally wounded at the battle of Williamsburg, May 5, 1862.

25. Alexander Herbemont (1790–1863), lawyer, son of Nicholas Herbemont (d. 1838) who taught French at South Carolina College (1807–17), was appointed U.S. consul to Genoa in 1854; his wife, Martha Davis Bay Herbemont, "an old, old friend," contributed a pair of precious white silk gloves to Louisa Smythe's wedding in 1865 (Smythe, p. 75); the Herbemonts' son Alexander ("Aleck" and "Mr. A. H.") was a suitor to Mary Dulles.

too prompt a decision. It would not take many words *I think* to start him to Philadelphia. I thought (I had a kind of presentiment) that the question was to be brought to me and tried hard to pump you before ~~I~~ you went away from us. If I could look just into your face now for 2 minutes, I would know whether I had done wrong or right. Letters are not so easy to decipher.

Thank you for the trouble you have taken about my shoes etc. Please send me word ~~now,~~ if and how far my cash has *not held out*. I see Cheves is enquiring about his newspaper;—but do not mind him. Mr. McCord tells me there is some difficulty I think, about postage of a newspaper when sent, not from the office. Don't trouble yourself about it therefore if there is any such impediment. If you send Hayne's slippers I will try and have them delivered and at least in the mean time I will let him know of Mrs. Randolph's kindness, when I know where ~~it~~ he is, for I have not heard from him since he left us, and do not know if he is still up the country, or has gone down.——As for Miss Hager, I presumed on not hearing from you, that I was to give up all hope of her. The young girl you speak of would not do, and I have already risked the engagement of an Englishman, who is to come to us next winter; So the teacher question is settled I hope for a year at least.[26] My little girls are quite well and whenever they hear your name mentioned want to know when you are coming back. How comes on the *Deutsch?* Do you study with Miss Hager, or has the fancy for it passed away? Do Anna and Sophie keep up their lessons?

Give my love to them, your Mother, and all the household. I am sorry we are not destined to meet this summer. I should like much to see old Naragansett again, but it will not do?

Goodbye—Shall I say any thing to my young friend A.H.?

Ever, dear Mary

Yours affectionately
Louisa S. McCord

Source: Dulles-Cheves-McCord-Lovell Papers, SCHS.

To Mary Cheves Dulles

Dear Mary Red Sweet Springs Sept[ember] 5th [1851]

I am much obliged for your letter of 26th rec[eive]d yesterday. I am glad to hear that you are all well; but is it not too bad that you did not come back

26. See LSM to Mary Dulles, Nov. 14 [1851], and note.

to us?[27] Cheves had a regular cry about it, and neither he nor the girls would give up the idea of seeing you, until after some days delay, we rec[eive]d Anna and Mr. Stillé's letter, deciding the question.[28] Tell Anna I never expected so much grief in my family, simply from receiving a letter from *her.*——I think your plan of coming South next winter a very good one;—but I have heard nothing of Anna Huger's going North. Does she intend it? If she does not, it still need not prevent your coming;—you will have opportunities enough, besides Mr. Hoxie, to come on with, and as you were so much benefitted last winter, you had better try it again, and make yourself quite fat and rosey.——Mr. McCord left me more than two weeks since, homeward bound; but went on very slowly, stopping by the way, and I have not yet had time to hear of his arrival at home. The only intelligence I have rec[eive]d from home was an overseers letter to Mr. McCord, (supposing him here) to let us know that the storm of the 24th ult. had played the mischief with our crop, blowing over every thing, and doing damage (the letter was written the day after the storm) as yet uncalculable. I presume your Father will have heard more of it though, and I trust it has not hurt him so much.——

I am glad to hear that you are all well, and comfortably gathered at home. Give my best love to your Mother and Sophie, and also kind love and remembrance to your household, Mrs. Horner etc.——I wish you were with us here; though I must say that for my individual part, I am very stupid, and weary to death of this homeless, aimless kind of existence. It will take all the courage I possess, to enable me to carry through my own resolutions and to stay here until the middle of October;—I used to say 20th, but I have cut off ~~ten~~ five days. Cheves is improveing though and the girls well. We

27. "I saw for a short time yesterday a very peculiar person—Miss Dulles of Philadelphia, she is related to the Cheves. Miss Coles introduced her to me in the morning she went with us to church in the afternoon and before night was so intimate as to relate me all her tender experiences. Alick Herbemont, my old acquaintance being the hero of the story—she was a good specimen of a foolish, talkative girl, without discretion, or one interesting quality. She left this morning for the White Sulphur, I dont care to see much of her there." Jane Caroline North, "Journal of an Excursion to the Virginia Springs," entry of Aug. 11, 1851, in O'Brien, *An Evening When Alone,* pp. 163–64.

28. Anna Welsh Dulles, LSM's first cousin and Mary Dulles' oldest sister, had been married (in 1846) to Charles Janeway Stillé (1819–99), biographer of John Dickinson, professor of English at the University of Pennsylvania, and provost. His brother Alfred Stillé (1815–1900) was a physician in Philadelphia, concluding his career as professor of medicine at the University of Pennsylvania; he and his wife were in Paris at the time of LSM's visit in 1858–59. "Under Dr. Stillé's care my mother took courage to go to some rather doubtful places, and as I had either to go too or be left behind by myself, I was taken too, and so had a glimpse of the Jardin Mabille and also a masked ball at the Opera house." Smythe, p. 26.

have (not me, but the company) been tolerably gay here since I saw you; but ~~there~~ it is very quiet now, and there will be a final breaking up before long. I suspect I will have this place almost to myself. The grand finale of the Season is to be a fancy ball which the fashionables of the "old Sweet" are devising for Monday next. I don't know much about it, for my part, as neither I nor my daughters intend to exhibit, but the young Ladies are mighty busy with pink and blue cambric, the only fancy articles furnished by their stores here. Miss Howell is here at present;[29] as also, Langdon and his family. They will all leave though, in less than a week hence. Charlotte rec[eive]d today a letter from Rachel, saying that Hayne was staying with them at present on Wassaw,[30] and that he had been quite sick in Charleston. I have heard nothing farther, but hope and suppose that his sickness was nothing serious.

You ask what to do with Cheves' papers. If convenient send them on here please, as they will serve to occupy him. By-the-way, I never thought of the postage though. It is any thing material? You must please charge it to me. I want you too, if your Father should at any time in the next *3 or 4 months* be sending on bundles or boxes to his plantation, to let me *run into debt* to you for a few trifles, very triffling, and yet of vast importance to the children. We cannot buy at the South such hoops as the children play with all over the streets with you. If you happened to have a chance of putting them into any thing that they would do no harm to, I would thank you much to put in three. Also four little china dolls, such as you made presents to them last winter, and any triffling toys that would do for Christmas. I am writing a long time ahead, but I do not know how soon the chance might occur, and I just happened to think of it now as the young ones are wishing for hoops.——Do write to me again; I am very stupid here, and it is quite an incident to receive a letter. Tell Anna I did not answer her letter because it was a naughty letter, but give my best love to her nevertheless. Goodbye again, and love again to all.

Your's affectionately,
Louisa S. McCord——

Source: Dulles-Cheves-McCord-Lovell Papers, SCHS.

29. Grace Howell (d. 1863), whom LSM mentions also in letters of April 9 and July 17, 1852, was a daughter of Jesse Malachi Howell (d. 1835) and Martha Howell (d. 1851); she was traveling with her brother Jesse Malachi Howell (d. 1882) and a cousin, probably Thomas Taylor (1824–1903); she appears in the diary of Jane Caroline North. The Howells were a prominent Columbia family.

30. Wassaw Island in Wassaw Sound, southeast of Savannah.

To Mary Cheves Dulles

Dear Mary Columbia Nov[ember] 14 [1851]

Would not Anna's return home be a good chance for you to come on,—unless you have a better one determined upon already?

I suppose Anna will come back before Christmas and perhaps she would come up to Lang Syne with you. When I say *you,* I mean you and Sophie both. I should be very glad to see Sophie, and where *one* of you can go *both* can. I may be a little full this winter but you can have your same little room, with changes to the down-stairs one if you like it, when I have no visiters requiring to be treated with more respect than yourselves. I have got a tutor, and *for the present,* a tutor's wife, who will make my spare room less abundant than usual,[31] but the little room is entirely at your service and the children, as well as myself, will be delighted to see both Sophie and yourself if you can come on. I wrote some time since to you to the same effect; I suppose my letter reached you.——By-the-way talking of past letters, I find that Mr. McCord has been guilty of communicating to you something of a slander. In a letter he wrote to you, ~~I~~ he spoke of a certain young gentleman, a friend of ours, as being dissipated or something of the kind. Now in justice to said young gentleman I must correct the mistake. I beleive (indeed Mr. McC. told me to say to you that he beleives) he was misinformed. Mr. A. H. is a young lawyer without business (as all young lawyers are) and having plenty of spare time upon his hands, *idles* a little, but I believe there is no farther charge to be brought against him. In the excitement of party-spirit and electioneering scenes, which Columbia was full of when Mr. McC. wrote, every body on every side is ready to slander the man who votes against him.[32] Mr. McC. was told what he repeated to you, but now says that he beleives it was a false accusation. The young gentleman is certainly not very studious and may lounge about a little, but it is a pity to injure him by any more serious charge which I do not think he deserves. He was enquiring after you a few days since, whether you were expected etc. So did poor Mr. Hoxie but I did not ask him to bring you on again. When he saw me buying mourning for

31. "As our winters were spent in the country we got a tutor—Mr. Williams, a former officer in the British Army who had had African fever and in our opinion had never recovered entirely as to his brains. He was a violent tempered creature who would not hesitate to pull a chair from under a stupid scholar by way of a gentle hint to wake up. He had a gentle sweet little wife with him, and besides that he was a kindhearted soul himself—a great sportsman too, and many a mile we used to trudge after him bird hunting." Smythe, pp. 11–12. LSM refers below to this couple as "Billy" and "Mrs. Billy."

32. See *PSE,* "Separate Secession," and notes there.

poor Emma Parker, he looked quite uneasy and wanted to know how Mr. Dulles' family was.

I suppose you may have heard of Em Parker's death.[33] It was a melancholy end for such a young thing. Goodby. Love to all—

Affectionately
L. S. McCord—

I will be at Lang Syne by 15th December if not sooner

Source: Dulles-Cheves-McCord-Lovell Papers, SCHS.

To Mary Cheves Dulles

Dear Mary [Lang Syne Winter 1851–52]

Mr. McCord is just answering your Father's letter rec[eive]d yesterday even[ing] and so in a great hurry I will scribble off a line in acknowledgement of yours inclosed in it.——I am truly sorry to hear that your health is such as to make you want change of climate; but although sorry for the cause I shall be sincerely glad to see you, if you can make your way hither. I wish you could come on with your cousin Mrs. Holmes;[34] it would be a very good opportunity. Has Heatly given up all idea of coming South this winter? Cannot he or William bring you? I should be very glad to see either of them.

Mr. McCord will be in Columbia next week and promises me that if he meets with any of the merchants of that place going on and likely to come back in time to suit you he will give a letter to your Father. But do not wait for such an opportunity if you can find another, as it is very possible he may not find a suitable one.

When you get to Charleston (if you get there as I hope you will) there will be no difficulty in your getting up here. The conductors on our road are the civillest people in the world, and we know them almost all personally; So if you would get Mr. Holmes or any other gentleman accompanying you to introduce you to the conductor of the Columbia train at the Charleston depot, telling them who you are, and to whom you are coming, I will answer for your being well taken care of. If however you should feel a little *desolate all by yourself,* I *could send a servant to meet you in Charleston* if you would name

33. LSM's stepdaughter Emma McCord, married to Edward Parker, died in Clarkesville, Ga., on Nov. 2, 1851.

34. "Mrs. Holmes" and her husband (mentioned below) are perhaps Elizabeth S. Toomer Holmes and Francis Simmons Holmes (1815–82). Holmes taught geology and palaeontology at the College of Charleston. They may be the same as the Holmes couple mentioned by Jane Caroline North as traveling in Virginia in the summer of 1851 (O'Brien, *An Evening When Alone,* pp. 158, 162).

the day and place where she would find you. Don't be at all uneasy though, if you have not time to let me know and should thus come up alone. I have travelled about a good deal on these roads (the passengers etc. are much more civil than in your Northern cars) and I never met with the slightest difficulty and always found the conductors, when I was put under their care, the best escorts I could have. I hope you will not let little difficulties frighten you from the undertaking; for I should be glad to see you in any case and still more so, if the change would be serviceable to your health.

My whooping cough patients (the white portion) are getting better though still coughing, of course;—I presume that will continue more or less for the winter. I have been quite sick from fatigue and a violent cold which gave me a pretty severe attack of neuralgia, but am quite well again.

I am glad to hear that Hayne left his friends so sorry for his departure. He is a good for nothing fellow sometimes, and yet a very good fellow too. I do not expect to see him this winter; he is to settle down in the Rice swamps with Langdon. When you see Mrs. Randolph do give my love to her; I shall always feel grateful for her kindness to Hayne.[35]

Give my best love to your Mother, Sophie, Anna and kind remembrance to all. Please come on as soon as you can, the winter is slipping away fast. My little ones will all be very glad to see you, as they consider you not as a *young lady,* but as a *big little girl.* I wish Sophie and Lilly could come with you.[36]

Goodbye and believe me ever

Your's affectionately
Louisa S. McCord—

Source: Dulles-Cheves-McCord-Lovell Papers, SCHS.

To Mary Cheves Dulles

[Lang Syne April 9, 1852][37]

Five cents reward.

Lost, strayed, or stolen;—a young Lady of some 5 feet 5 inches in height; fair complexioned etc. Pretends to be very fond of country retirement, but

35. "Mrs. Randolph" (whose kindness LSM had mentioned also in her letter of June 17, 1851) is perhaps Lucinda Anne Patterson Randolph, second wife of the Virginian Thomas Mann Randolph, Jr. (1791–1851); Jane Caroline North met her at Warm Springs in Virginia on Aug. 7, 1851 (ibid., p. 161).

36. "Lilly" was the family nickname of Mary Dulles' youngest sister, Elizabeth Horner Dulles.

37. This letter is appended to the following letter by David James McCord:

"Dear Mary Langsyne April 9, 1852

When I was in Columbia I gave Old Jack a paper of corn seed and some Lima Beans

is suspected of a decidedly greater partially {partiality} for the town. Is supposed to be harbored somewhere about the College Campus in Columbia. The above reward will be given to anyone who will deliver this unfortunate stray-article to her affectionate and sorrowing friends.

Won't Dr. Lieber have the goodness to set up the above advertisement in the vicinity of the College Campus? Maybe some of the idle desciples of the institution may have time to hunt up the runaway.

Look here gall, in earnest, what are you after? This is a pretty way of coming to see me,—aint it? If you don't look out I won't send to the road for you at all, but leave you, in spite, to spend the day with old Mr. Effler. If you don't come home soon, I won't expect you at all.

I am glad to hear from your letter to Cheves that you are enjoying yourself and have hardly the conscience to hurry you back to our stupidity, but will be very glad to see you when you are ready to come. You are a shabby critter.

Tell Mrs. Lieber I will be very glad to see ~~you~~ her if she will come back with you.[38] Not much chance for strawberries this spring though. I shall be glad nevertheless to see her and any or all of the gentlemen, Norman inclusive.——Please to say the same to Grace Howell if you see her. I should be glad to see her here at any time, except about 25th of this month,

to plant, and a few days since I discovered them among my goods and chattels here. I suppose he put them down in the house among my things and they were sent back. If you pass that way pray ask if that is not the fact, and whether he has planted any or not, and if he has not I will thank you if you will give him a quarter of a dollar and tell him to buy some seed at Fisher and Heinitz's, formerly Toland and Curtis and to plant them right off. I will repay you when you return. I am not sure, but that I wrote a note to the same effect to Dr. Lieber. No, by the by, that was to send some seeds down by you.

Is all the time cold or the wind blowing enough to kill hogs. Your little mocking-bird, however[,] seems to be doing well and some times [raises?] his lowly song.

Give our kind regards to all the household

Very truly yours.
D. J. McCord

Green peas to-day!
about a tea-cup full."

"About a tea-cup full" is added in LSM's hand.

38. "Mrs. Lieber . . . was a great friend of our youth. She took a fancy to teach me German and every morning I used to go over to her house to get a lesson either from her or Dr. Lieber. He . . . had a great dislike to bare feet and if I went to him bare footed as I frequently did, I was pretty sure to get a tumbler of cold water dashed on my feet as a little hint not to come that way again. My mother believed in bare feet; so I was very apt to be sent right back to Dr. Lieber still bare footed but carrying as a peace offering an immense bouquet of roses, for [he] was passionately fond of flowers." Smythe, p. 9. Matilda Oppenheimer Lieber (b. c. 1807) was married to Francis Lieber in 1829.

when *possibly,* I may have to go to Columbia for a few days. Very doubtful if I do but possible.——Kind love to the Prestons and Mrs. Herbemont and would be glad to see any of them who are moveable——

With kind remembrance to Mrs. Lieber and the family, and hoping to see you sometime again in this world

I am dear Miss runaway
Yours affectionately
Louisa S. McCord——

I am sorry to hear of your cousins' ill-health. Will their coming South make any difference in your Father's movements? If you would like to meet them you must let me know about where they are etc. so as to get them to meet you here.

I will certainly expect Mrs. Lieber with you, and that soon. Goodbye. Children want to write to you, but no time to wait. Say you ought to come home.

Addressed: Fort Motte S.C. / April 9th / Miss M. C. Dulles / Care of Professor Lieber / So. Ca. College / Columbia So. Ca. *Source:* Dulles-Cheves-McCord-Lovell Papers, SCHS.

To Mary Cheves Dulles

Dear Mary Columbia June 21st [18]52

I rec[eive]d last evening your's of 15th and 16th. I hope you got comfortably over the agonies of the tooth-drawing and that the ether proved a kind friend to you. I am very much obliged to you for your attention to my shopping concerns. At your liesure send the box, but I am in no hurry for it. Mr. McCord made a very hurried trip and although obliged by the irregularities of cars etc. to lose some time by the way his stoppages were always at the most disagreeable places, Wilmington etc. He got home last night, and says he wants to slip a few lines under my envelope, but is just now fast asleep and I think it is doubtful whether he will rouse himself enough to execute his intentions. He has had a fatiguing and very disagreeable journey and seems pretty well tired out. He was sorry that circumstances prevented him from seeing you all in Phil[adelphi]a.

To return to my shopping. I fear I have troubled you in y[ou]r search for birdeye by naming a price. I thought I said, certainly I meant to say if you can get it, give any price that you think reasonable;—12,15,18, anything that is right. I did not mean to limit you, but only to give an idea of what I wanted. But do not trouble yourself too much; the weather is too warm now for much running about and perhaps any time before next winter, you may happen to see what I want. If not never mind. If you have money enough left for the purchase ~~of the birdeye~~ just keep it please, and if you chance to see, get it at your liesure. I am glad that you have had my old silk dyed. I shall feel quite magnificent with my *two* black silks, if I can ever get them made, and with the "*darts*" (is that the word?) in the right place—You ask if I want any thing else—If the cash holds out, I should be glad to have any trimmings necessary for the dresses and particularly the worsted braid to put round the skirt as I saw you do in Phil[adelphi]a. I cannot get it here. I was looking for some for my old silk, which hangs in fringe for want of it, and could not find any. Also please get me, always supposing the means are in your hands[,] a pair or two of sleeve bands, such as you gave me. They are so comfortable that I would not know now, how to do without them.

We are all pretty well here now. Cheves went down on Saturday in Mr. McC's absence to enquire about plantation concerns. He rode about the fields and brings me up quite a business-like report of things. Of course he could hear nothing of your Father's place and I can give no information of that farther than probable conclusions may be drawn ~~by~~ f[ro]m the effect of the seasons upon ours. His (Cheves') report is that our corn crop promises finely. The cotton has been injured by the ~~cold~~ unseasonably cool and wet seasons and the lice have done some damage; but still the promise is tolerably fair, if future seasons prove propitious. They have had too much rain. Here again, we are burnt up and wishing for rain. At this moment it is thundering round us, but I verily beleive the clouds are floating of[f] towards Lang Syne, where they are anything but wanted.

Anna wrote me word that it was *really* Mr. T. P. Huger who had taken the railroad place we spoke of. I was quite surprised at it. He gets a magnificent salary; $3000. Mighty comfortable certainly. I would have been engineer for that, myself.[39] I heard from Hayne some ten days since—He had intended going up the country but stopped at Wassaw Island to be with John who was[,] at the time Hayne wrote, suffering much and confined to his room with a severe and serious inflammation of the eye. Hayne said he would stay with him until he should be better.

What few folks ~~you~~ we know, or you are interested in here, are as usual. Mr. and Mrs. W. Preston have left town, to get some way up the country; both looking badly.[40] Liebers talk of going north. Dr. L. wants his wife and

39. The Northeastern Railroad, of which Thomas Pinckney Huger was engineer and, later, president, was chartered in 1851 to run from Charleston to Florence, S.C., there to connect with lines to Wilmington and Manchester, N.C. The line was opened in November 1856.

40. William Campbell Preston had resigned the presidency of South Carolina College on Nov. 26, 1851, for reasons of health; Louise Penelope Davis Preston died in 1853 at the age of forty-six.

Norman to go next week. I do not think they will go so soon. She is very uneasy at not hearing from her nephew Mr. L~~o~~umnitz (I don't know how to spell his name) who went to Mexico and they have not heard from him for nearly three months.——The Howells I have not seen lately. Their Sister Mrs. Trezevant has been quite sick ~~lately~~.[41] Herbemonts are *à l'ordinaire* all three,—Mme. looking not very strong and frequently complaining; the gentlemen as usual.——I am happy to hear of the good health and spirits of Birdie and hope he will continue to prosper. Where does he live? and who cleans the cage?——

Han and Louise are much pleased with the promised white sun-bonnet and myself quite grateful at the being releived from the task of manufacturing something of the kind, which I was just thinking of as a sad necessity. They have ~~many~~ written some letters, as they call them, which I enclose for your benefit.[42] I see they tell you of the death of poor Nora's child which I brought up here to nurse, but could not help it.

Please give my love to all. I wish I was going with you to Naragansett. I hope your grandmother will soon be well enough to releive you from anxiety on her account.

Goodby——

Your affectionate Cousin
Louisa S. McCord

Addressed: Miss M. C. Dulles / Philadelphia. *Source:* Dulles-Cheves-McCord-Lovell Papers, SCHS.

41. Epps Goodwyn Howell Trezevant, sister of Grace, Jesse Malachi, and Harriet Howell, was the wife of Daniel Heyward Trezevant (1796–1873), a Columbia physician.

42. The letters follow:

"My dear cousin Mary I think that you hav forgotten the violets. but they were dead. Noras babey is dead. it died Saterday week ~~evening~~ send my lowe to Lilly. papa went away and saw Mr Robinson and said that Jemmy gose to school and Annie is a big girl. tell Lilly that I will wrte to her.

Your afectionate cousin
Hannah C. McCord"

"My dear cousin Mary

bubber went down to Lang syne Saturday. Nora's baby died last Saturday week. Papa has been away he has come back yesterday. Mamma has bought us sone tin combs to hold our hair back. We have green corn.

your affectionate cousin
Louisa R. McCord"

To Mary Cheves Dulles

Dear Mary Columbia July 17th, 1852

The trunk is come and I have unpacked the letter paper and so here goes for some sort of an answer to your packet of epistles which lies staring me reproachfully in the face. First of all and à propos of the trunk, I am much obliged to you for the execution of my various commissions. The silk is very handsome; so much so that I will certainly have to leave home some time or other to get a chance to wear it out. And the dyed one will make a very nice one for second best. Much obliged to your Mother also for the purchase of the collar. The diaper looks a little slight certainly, but I think will wash thicker and at any rate will do very well, and is very comfortably cheap. The girls are much pleased with their bonnets and I with my sleeves which give me a new idea and a new pattern. Except for a lucky gift of the kind to me now and then I get sadly behind hand in my fashions and am often tempted to turn quaker just because their fashions I beleive never change. Han and Louise are vastly delighted with the book you sent which Han has already read aloud to Louise all through, they say. Cheves also thanks you for his and I for the Lamp Shade. I sent your jar to Mrs. Herbemont. Have not seen her since sent word she was much obliged. Your sundries for Miss Howells I will send soon. It is now raining and has been for two days. Do not trouble yourself about the remaining cash you have of mine. Just keep it please and if you find it convenient any time I will get you to spend it for me. The thread gloves by-the-way that you got for me are very nice. I should like very much to have a supply of them next winter; if you happen to remember them any time, any of you are coming on; and also by any opportunity something of the same kind for Han and Louise. I can get none such here. This paper too on which I am writing is very nice; Mr. McC. and Cheves are already taking it from me largely and I suspect I will be glad for some more by the next winter. It is better (or at least I like it better) than the gilt-edge.

Billy is gone!! I paid him fifty dollars to clear himself off. Now he is gone I can afford to try and be a little sorry for him; but such a conceited fool,—such a combination of ignorance and arrogance I never had the luck to meet. I was awfully sick of him and would rather keep a school for twenty children than board him for a year. I am of course considerably bothered with the young ones; but any thing is better than *Billy!* I school them all the morning and of course in the afternoon am too stupid and tired to do any thing for myself. So I am just school-mistress, until some other régime is established. Mr. McCord offers to read a little hist[or]y and geography with them, but I do not count much upon his help. He does not like trouble much. In truth too, he has not himself been well lately. He cannot get well from a pretty sharp attack he had about a fortnight since and looks pretty good for nothing. I suppose he will get over it after a while, but it will take some pretty considerable grumbling first. Cheves looks tolerably good-for-nothingish too; he had pretty sharp fever for a few days; but is over it and I will get him along I beleive. Thank goodness *Billy* is gone! It would make me crazy I beleive if I had his sour face and sour temper to add to these sundry other disagreeables which have fallen upon us.

Han and Louise were much pleased with your letter which I had to read to them as they cannot yet quite manage it themselves. I have no doubt they will trouble you again soon with a farther correspondence. I heard from Anna Huger ~~not lon~~ a day or two since. She has just gone to Charleston and perhaps may travel northward this summer. She tells me that brother John who has been suffering much from an inflamation in one of his eyes (which even has threatened the loss of it, I hear), has gone to the North and Hayne in his company. I would write to Hayney if I knew where to catch them but have no idea. If you hear of them any where please let me know; for they will not write unless I can catch them with 2 or 3 letters first. I presume the Liebers will have left you before this. I hope Norman has got well through his eye operation. If still in Phil[adelphi]a please remember me to them kindly. Is Mr. Lomnitz gone? heart-sound? *dites vrai.* Did you have a sentimental parting? And does he never, never mean to come back again?———

I suppose Mrs. Lieber told your Father that she left his Milton in company with my note. His "Claret and Olives," I have not succeeded in getting brought f[ro]m Lang Syne and I fear now he will not see it till next winter. I hope your grandmother's health is doing better. Does Anna Stillé go with you to Naragansett? Do give her my best love and also all sorts of remembrance to Mr. Stillé and your brothers. Tell Lily the girls want to see her very much and Louise tells me every-day that Uncle Dulles has promised perhaps to bring her on next winter. Love to your Mother and Sophie and believe me dear Mary

Your's always affectionately
Louisa S. McCord

You ask after Grace Howell. The girls spent Saturday before last with her and were much delighted. She enquired kindly after you. I have not seen her since. Herbemonts as usual—Dont think anybody goes to Virginia—

Source: Dulles-Cheves-McCord-Lovell Papers, SCHS.

To Mary Cheves Dulles

Dear Mary Columbia August 25th, 1852

As Mr. McCord says that he is going to write to Mr. Stillé, I will slip in a few lines for you; as from my experience of Peacedale post offices, I think my missive would be more apt to reach you under his envelope than wandering about in ~~their~~ its littleness and by itself.[43]

I am glad to hear that you are all enjoying yourselves so well at Naragansett. What would I not give for a walk on the beach (or beech? how do you spell it? neither looks right,) with my brats tumbling along before me[?][44] I am almost sick of this horrid little place Columbia. I hope that Mr. McC. will get his fill of it some day. For surely I cannot see where the society he dreams of is.[45] For myself, I do not care a fig for the society, but I long

43. The town of Peace Dale lies near the western coast of the mouth of Narragansett Bay, Rhode Island.

44. "Naragansett was a beautiful place without doubt, as in addition to its glorious beach it had lovely cultivated farms almost to the water's edge and glorious high rocks and bluffs over which we used to scramble, and gather delicate sea-weed to press, and search among the rocks for the beautiful clear little pools of water filled with brilliantly colored anemones and *such*." Smythe, p. 22. "We have seen, known, and admired some of the best specimens of [Narragansett's] present inhabitants, and have heard them acknowledge their general degeneracy. . . . The reason is apparent. It had been the most thorough slave country in New England; the inhabitants had kept up the habits and education of English gentlemen; they cultivated their lands, and made most of the stone walls now existing; and these old walls may be, now, distinguished for their decided superiority, in neatness and durability, over those since made. They lived in large and commodious mansions, many of which remain to this day, with their old aristocratic air, quite superior to the little 'slice-of-blocks', which the manufacturer now hurries up around the factory. They were hospitable and fond of society, simple in their manners, and elevated in their sentiments, surrounded by slaves, with abundance of horses and the provisions of life; they were a noble people, and well may their sons love to dwell upon their memory. . . . The revolution, and consequent abolition of slavery, have rendered desert many sweet spots of that country, which were once the gardens and happy residences of the most polished and elegant people." David James McCord, "How the South Is Affected by Her Slave Institutions," pp. 353–54.

45. "Oh, the delights of my father's stories! He loved to give dinner parties, not stylish dinner parties with many wines and all sorts of fancy things like present day dinners, but with good cooking, good friends, and best of all, good talk. We children used to slip in, and I was very apt to take my place half under the table cloth at his feet, where I could listen and laugh to my heart's content. I can see him sitting with a quiet smile on his face watching the table in a roar and every now and then cutting his eye down to see the children giggling at his feet. He was elderly and grey headed then, not the handsome 'Davy' of his youth, but still handsome and irresistible. I wish it were possible to convey to you the charm of his quiet, witty voice and keen bright eyes, noticing all of your little ways and doings—snubbing us violently with a glance when we needed it, and watching with such intense enjoyment anything in us that seemed to come up to his ideas. It was so delightful to have him call

for a climate where a family can keep healthy and grow strong; and (perhaps I am wrong) but I do not think that is here. Certainly it does not seem to agree with Cheves. I have been very much worried about him for some weeks past. He has been looking badly and his pulse varying from a hundred to a hundred and twenty all the time. I don't know what to make of him and I am afraid to send for a doctor who don't know much, to experiment on his case. It is evidently a return of the old trouble he used to have when I kept him at home before, but much lighter. I have not sent for a doctor (I am afraid of those we have here) but have fought along as well as I can ~~w~~ by my old prescriptions of Geddings etc. and he is getting better.[46] Today he looks quite smart again and I hope is going to get over it without any thing worse. If so I shall still think myself fortunate. I believe I *do* get too uneasy about him sometimes; but I have had such a deal of trouble with him, how can I help it? He is just looking in at my window and looks *so much better* today that I hope he will not trouble me any more though.

Mr. McC. too has been grumbling and groaning all the summer. He certainly does not look well, but I cannot see what is the matter with him. I verily believe he is just sick, for want of company and a little excitement of some kind or another. He will have it that this is a charming place; but apparently it is charming for me to stay in, and for him to go away. I believe if we had the money, he would consent now to pack up bag and baggage and be off somewhere. He has never tried it so *solidly* before.

The girls talk of writing letters to you, but are too lazy. They are both a little thinned by the summer. Louise particularly is getting long necked and complains constantly of feeling "so bad". She is changing very much. You will hardly know her next winter if she keeps on as she is doing now.——

Tell Mrs. Lieber that Oscar has gone off rail-roading again. He left very suddenly with the party under young Barnes, whom he was trying to get with. He dined with me the day before he left, but had not then received his summons. I don't think there is any body else in town that you know, except the gentlemen Herbemonts. Mme. has been quite sick and has gone on a visit to Sullivan's Island. Mass Aleck has, *entre nous,* been playing the mischief

---

us to his room to be read to and the reading was sure to be something so original, so different from anything we heard from anybody else—so delightfully funny!" Smythe, pp. 9–10.

46. Eli Geddings (1799–1878) founded a private medical school in Charleston (1828); taught at the Medical School of the University of Maryland (1831–37); having returned to Charleston, professor of surgery at the Medical College of South Carolina (1837–58); surgeon in the Confederate army. He was called in to treat LSM's son: "As a baby he had had hip disease and had for two years suffered fearfully. . . . Dr. Geddings cured him and I have often in after life heard him say that it was one of the few cases he had ever known to get well." Smythe, p. 21.

lately, *on dit*. I know nothing about it and don't want to talk about it. I only mention it to you that you may be satisfied that your decision was probably a wise one. Every body else has gone out of town. Even old Mrs. Green has vacated[,] for the time, her mansion.[47] There is no living being in the College Campus, but one solitary young LaBorde and a nig or two.[48] I was going to turn over, but I see this is my last page, so goodbye, it is not worth beginning another. Love to all.

Y[our]s ever
Louisa S. McCord—

Alas! the bird!

Source: Dulles-Cheves-McCord-Lovell Papers, SCHS.

To Mary Cheves Dulles

Dear Mary Columbia Oct[ober] 9th, 1852

I will not write you a letter, but one line to thank you for the little box sent by Mrs. Lieber. The girls would have answered your kind epistle to them, but I have been too busy to rule paper etc. for the poor little things who have been rather neglected by me, owing to my having my hands full with Mr. McCord who has been seriously sick ever since I wrote to you. I do not know what ~~is~~ has been the matter with him. He has been bothered and plagued by numbers of things and people of late and all sorts of disagreeable affairs (I don't mean anything of our own at home) and in truth I believe it just broke him down. He is doing better now; indeed has improved very much in the last 36 hours and I believe is going to get pretty well again. He is a regular spoiled one though and wants a deal of nursing.

If Hayney comes to Philadelphia, do give my love to him. Tell him he

47. Lucy Pride Jones Green (1790–1864), daughter of Cadwallader Jones and Mary Pride Jones, was married in October 1804 to Allen Jones Green (1783–1832) of Rose Hill plantation on the Catawba River; lived in Columbia after her husband's death. LSM calls her "old Mrs. Green" perhaps to distinguish her from Sarah Briggs Green (1811–74), wife of Columbia physician and druggist Frederick William Green, whose house (destroyed during the burning of Columbia in February 1865) stood on Gervais Street, across from Trinity Episcopal Church; Sarah Green's garden was famous.

48. Maximilian LaBorde (1804–73) held various appointments, in logic, literature, and metaphysics, at South Carolina College; he was married twice, first to Sophia Parsons Carroll (1806–41), then to her sister Elizabeth. LSM refers to one of the LaBorde children: John Baptiste (1830–56), James Carroll (1834–98), or Oscar Whitfield (1838–65). "The 1st August 1862 I left Mrs. McMahon's for Flat Rock, North Carolina. . . . The LaBordes and the McCord girls came part of the way with me." *Chesnut*, p. 422.

ought to have written to me. I have not known his direction all the Summer. I guess he is glad to escape the persecution of my epistles.

I think I may as well stop; my head is splitting with pain. I have slept very irregularly for the last fortnight, and to cap the climax of unrest, last night when every thing else got quiet, one of my carriage horses began to kick in the stable. Ben goes off every night and there was nobody to quiet it, and so it kicked away to its heart's content and I lay awake to listen to it, and this morning I feel pretty much as if I had got all the kicks on my head instead of only in my ears.

Please any time, if not too troublesome, get me some gloves a size larger for the girls. Those sent are very pretty but rather tight. 2 pair each will do, and 2 or 3 pair more for *me* will last for six months. I am a terrible glove-consumer.

Goodbye—Love to all—Write to me soon.

Your's affectionately
Louisa S. McCord—

Oh! Mrs. Stowe! One word of that abominable woman's abominable book,—I have read it lately and am quite shocked at *you,* my dear Cousin, Miss Mary C. Dulles, for thinking it as if I remember right, you said you did, a strong exposition against slavery. It is one mass of fanatical bitterness and foul misrepresentation wrapped in the garb of Christian Charity. She quotes the Scriptures only to curse by them. Why! have not you been at the South enough to know, that ~~men~~ our gentlemen dont keep mulatto wives, nor whip negroes to death ~~and~~ nor commit all the various other enormities that she describes? She does not know what a gentleman or a lady is, at least according to our Southern notions[,] ~~no~~ any more than I do a Laplander. Just look at her real benevolent gentleman (as she means him to be) her Mr. St. Clare, or her sensible woman Mrs. Shelby and ~~too~~ two more distressing fools and hypocrites I never met with. The woman (Mrs. Stowe I mean) has certainly never been in any Southern State further than across the Kentucky line at most, and there in very doubtful society. All her Southern ladies and gentleman talk coarse Yankee. But I must stop. The thought of Mrs. Stowe doubles my infliction of horses heels. Read the book over again my dear child and you will wonder that you ever took it for anything but what it is, i.e. as malicious and gross an abolitionist production (though I confess a cunning one) as ever dis-graced the press. Encore adieu—

Yours always
L. S. Mc———

Addressed: Miss M. C. Dulles / Philadelphia. *Source:* Dulles-Cheves-McCord-Lovell Papers, SCHS.

To Mary Cheves Dulles

Dear Mary Columbia Nov[ember] 11 [1852]

Tomorrow we hope to get back to Lang Syne; though it is drizzling a little now and alas! one cannot travel in the rain. However we hope to go and as I expect to be in a shocking bustle for a week at least with the utter incapacity for finding pen, paper or anything else, I scribble a line before going.[49]——You do not seem to have made up your minds (you and Sophie) about coming on to me. I was in hopes you would come on with your Father. Why not do so yet, if he has not started and left you? You know I do not mind such a chit as you at all, at all, I will just shove you into the chimney corner if you should be in my way—And Sophie is such a sensible young Lady, that I will shove her in the other corner if necessary without any fear of offense: taking it for granted that she will understand the necessities of things. You know my house and know the room I have. *Your* little room; The down-stairs chamber which I intend for Anna, and the large room[,] the Library that was[,] out next the one that Mrs. Billy had last year, which I intend fixing for a chamber and which would suit you and Sophie nicely if you would not be *afraid* of going out of doors. It is large enough for a family and if your mother had come I intended it for her if she fancied it. I lived in that house for a long time and preferred it much to my present arrangement, but it did not suit my children. If you liked that I think you could be made very comfortable there, but if not,—your old quarters and as much of the girls room as you choose to use would be at your service while Anna is with me—in her absence you could take her room if you chose. As my invitation to her is of a years standing and as she has not been to see me for five years I think, and as she is older than any of you, I meant to give her the disposal of my best room, such as it is; unless indeed Mr. and Mrs. Preston should come and then I suppose[,] as he cannot walk upstairs, I would have to rout her too and as I began by proposing to put you and Sophie in the chimney corners, I suppose she would have to take the middle; a kind of back-log position. I have a heap of business to do this evening and must be done my scrawl. Thank you for executing my commissions. Your kindness in dressing the dolls will be a mighty comfort to me. I mean to bother you a little bit more—Will you get me some material for making sleeve-bands[?] The

49. "We have been busy removing our Library from the out-house to a room I had built this summer adjoining the dining room—There I am now comfortably ensconced before a good fire the cost of which I need not consider. After all this is a very lonely life, though perhaps less felt than in Columbia. . . . Mrs. McCord, as usual, is busy with the children, with any who may be sick, and with setting every thing right for the winter." David James McCord to Francis Lieber, Lang Syne, Nov. 18, 1852, Francis Lieber Papers, Huntington.

ready made ones are too tight and Mrs. Lieber says she saw Anna with it bought by the yard. I should like to have two yards of it. Also something for making sunbonnets such as those you sent my girls. Something corded you remember. I want some decent sunbonnets much for myself. Your kindness will perhaps make you think of making one for me; but do not do so. My tremendous chuckle head would defy your talent; so do not think of making, but just be so kind as to get me the material. Is my money gone yet? Please keep your account close against me and let me know always what and when I owe you. I hope you are all well and will still half expect to see you with your Father;[50]—

Give my love to all.——Mr. McC. is getting very much better. I begin to think he will get well when he gets to the plantation.

Goodby etc.

Your affectionate Cousin
Louisa S. McCord

Source: Dulles-Cheves-McCord-Lovell Papers, SCHS.

To Henry Charles Carey

Lang Syne Fort Motte, So[uth] C[arolin]a
Jan[uar]y 18th, 1854

Dear Sir

I was pained to see from your kind letter to Mr. McCord, that you considered my article for the "Southern Quarterly" as having been written consequent upon the reception of the copy of the "Slave Trade" etc., which you were so polite as to send me last summer.[51] The truth is, that having purchased a copy of the work some time before receiving the one sent by you, my article was written before the arrival of the latter,—upon seeing which,

50. "Mr. Dulles and Mary arrived here yesterday. Mr. Dulles says I must tell you that he saw your barrel of potatoes on the wharf in Charleston. . . . Mary sends her love to Mrs. Lieber and to Dr. Lieber too, and she will write to Mrs. Lieber soon." David James McCord to Francis Lieber, Lang Syne, Dec. 19, 1852, ibid.

51. See *PSE,* "Carey on the Slave Trade," reviewing Henry C. Carey, *The Slave Trade, Domestic and Foreign: Why It Exists, and How It May Be Extinguished* (Philadelphia, 1853; rpt. New York, 1967). Henry Charles Carey (1793–1879), publisher and political economist, born in Philadelphia; author also of *Essay on the Rate of Wages* (1835), *Principles of Political Economy,* 3 vols. (1837–40), and *The Principles of Social Science,* 3 vols. (1858–59), among other works. Carey's praise of the abolitionist duchess of Sutherland, which is mentioned below, is reproved at *PSE,* pp. 414–17, and the duchess herself in ibid., "A Letter to the Duchess of Sutherland from a Lady of South Carolina."

for fear of apparent dis-courtesy, I was much inclined to suppress what I had written; but, in sober earnest, your book is, in my opinion, (I am sure not intentionally on your part) of so mis-chievous a tendency upon a subject of vital importance to us of the South, that I felt it even a duty to dispute its accuracy. It is,—excuse my saying so,—of a class of works which do us more harm than the most violent abolitionist attacks; assuming the ground of a wrong where wrong does not exist, and with laboured argument upon false grounds, forcing to fearfully practical conclusions. This too upon a subject which we have studied deeply and believe that we understand well; while every line which you write, shows that our system is to you an unstudied one, which you condemn from theory, not insight.——You believe the negro to be an oppressed race, while we believe him to be a protected one. You assume the ground that we are committing a constant injustice towards him, while we are convinced that we are his only safeguard from extermination, at least in this country. We believe ~~that~~ and living as we do, surrounded by, governing, and fostering this people,—we have a right to believe, that we know more of negro-nature, and certainly more of our own treatment of them and of their condition among us, than can the Duchess of Sutherland who understands as little of negroes as of cotton-planting; and yet you have praised her mis-chievous interference in a subject of which she is as profoundly ignorant, as, in all probability she is of Greek and Hebrew.

When you remember that this subject is one with which, nationally, as well as individually, our every interest,—life, fortune, and fame,—is inseperably linked, you will scarcely be surprised that we should be sensitive upon the subject, and intreat our friends to open their eyes before they determine whether or not it is indeed midnight with us.——My blow was aimed at a mis-chievous theory, and, permit me to assure you, without any feeling of personal disrespect.

You refer me to Bastiat's "*Harmonies*". I have read them attentively before this, as well as the correspondence in the "Journal des Economistes." I regret that Bastiat should have agreed with you, to at least a considerable extent, (his premature death prevented his fully developping how far) in what I cannot but believe a mistaken and I fear a harmful theory.[52] It is a subject which I have been studying lately, with much interest, and the more I look into it, the further I am, I must say, from agreeing with you. I shall continue however

52. The French economist Claude-Frédéric Bastiat, whom LSM admired—she translated his *Sophismes économiques* as *Sophisms of the Protective Policy* (New York and Charleston, 1848) and reviewed his work in *PSE,* "Justice and Fraternity" and "The Right to Labor"—died in Rome on Dec. 24, 1850, at the age of forty-nine.

my endeavours to enlighten myself upon the subject, and am much obliged to you for the little volume forwarded to me.

Believe me, Dear Sir, in spite of these widely differing opinions

Very respectfully etc. etc.
Louisa S. McCord—

Addressed: Henry C. Carey Esq. / Philadelphia. *Source:* Edward Carey Gardiner Collection, Henry C. Carey Section, PHS.

To Martha Davis Bay Herbemont

[Columbia] Oct[ober] 16th [1854]
Monday morning

Dear Mrs. Herbemont,

As Mr. McCord has gone out, and I know will come home in a fuss, just to scribble a few lines and grumble at me if I cannot be in as great a hurry as himself, I having accidentally caught sight of his half finished sheet, and remembering the old saw about the cat away and the mouse at play, have boldly determined to take my share of the paper now that the chance is before me. He can finish as well at the end. We are delighted to hear how comfortably you are getting on, and hope that every thing will continue to prosper with you. I feel almost jealous of all your sight-seeing etc., while we are broiling and growling away our time here. We have had a perfectly *infernal* summer. You must excuse the epithet,—for no other can give a half idea of the terrible heat to which we have been subjected. I presume Mr. McCord has informed you of the storm which summed up our amount of suffering, swept away numbers of rice-crops (my Fathers and brothers all gone) and scared the Sullivan's Island folks out of their senses. The inhabitants of the Moultrie house, among whom were my brother Langdon and family with Anna and Mr. Huger took refuge in the Fort. The Moultrie house stood safe, but Mr. Bull's house near it, was entirely swept away and many others in the same way without leaving a vestige of where they had been, but not a single life lost.[53]———Your servants are all doing well, and Kate

53. "The hot weather, with short exceptions has continued the whole summer—yesterday 86 [degrees]. Columbia very healthy, but Charleston awfully afflicted with yellow fever—no body has gone there for months. But Savannah has been a death hole. . . . Then the storm nearly destroyed Sullivans Island, has ruined most of the rice crops and upon the whole we have never had before such a summer of disasters and distress. Judge Cheves and his sons will not make one Dollar but have many expenses to repair. The family has lost more than $100,000. Langdon and Charlotte are here staying with the Judge till frost." David James McCord to Alexander Herbemont, Oct. 15, 1854, Dulles-Cheves-McCord-Lovell Papers, SCHS. On Sept. 7–9, 1854, a fierce hurricane struck the Georgia and Carolina coasts, causing extensive flooding and damage. The Moultrie House was a large resort hotel

rushes round on every intimation of news from you to get it. I have not se[. . .]ce[54] Mr. Herbemont's last letter, and have just sent to let her know a[bout?] it. The *buckra* [. . .] I believe are just what they used to be. The college inhabitants are [finally?] in their nests for the winter; the Pelhams and Reynolds just moving into their new houses, and Dr. Gibbes still vowing vengeance, I hear, against Thornwell.[55] I suppose Mr. McCord mentions the death of Tom Stark.[56] He died horribly, (raving mad), I am told. Poor Mrs. Stark was up at her sister's here for a week or two after his death, looking wretchedly, shutting herself up in her room and so forth. I was sorry for her but really thought some kind of illumination or rejoicing would have been more suited to the circumstances. I am told that she has bought William Goodwyn's Sand-hill house and is to reside there in future.

I am just over a great deal of trouble with my Cheves. I let him go to visit his Aunt in Abbeville where he was taken sick, and on going to him, which I immediately did, I found him alarmingly ill. After a fortnight though I got him home again, and although he is still looking badly, he is improving and I think will do well with cool weather; if indeed we are ever again destined to enjoy that luxury for a week at a time. We have had two or three promises of a change, but it gets as hot as ever again. Today is charming if it will only last us. And I have made up my mind to the necessity of spending our winter here. Cheves and Hannah have commenced their schooling and must now, if Cheves' health allows[,] keep at it. It is quite tantalizing to see your empty

---

on Sullivan's Island, opened in 1850. Fort Moultrie, on the southeast corner of Sullivan's Island, guards the entrance to Charleston Harbor. The Charleston *Courier* of Sept. 11, 1854, carries a description of the destruction of the "Owens house," currently occupied by William Izard Bull (1813–94), planter, member of the South Carolina House of Representatives (1836–47) and Senate (1848–64).

54. This and following defects are caused by tears in the original letter.

55. Charles P. Pelham, professor of Roman literature (1846–57), of history and political economy (1857–58). James Lawrence Reynolds (1814–77), professor of moral philosophy and sacred literature and criticism, whose daughter Charlotte was married to LSM's son Cheves in 1861. Robert Wilson Gibbes (1809–66), Columbia physician; protégé of Thomas Cooper, in late 1820s and in 1834–35 taught chemistry and mineralogy at South Carolina College; contributor to the *Southern Quarterly Review;* surgeon general of South Carolina during the war; admirer of Lucy Holcombe Pickens. At this time Gibbes was a trustee of South Carolina College; he was still feuding with James Henley Thornwell in 1862 (*Chesnut,* p. 429).

56. "Tom Stark is dead—and the place bought by Baker and given to y[ou]ng Trezevant who married his daughter." David James McCord to Alexander Herbemont, Oct. 15, 1854, Dulles-Cheves-McCord-Lovell Papers, SCHS. Thomas Taylor Stark died on Aug. 28, 1854. James David Trezevant (1822–92), son of Daniel Heyward Trezevant, married on Nov. 23, 1851, Ann Elizabeth Baker of Sandy Run, S.C.

house instead of having you as good neighbours in it. Mr. McCord gets desperately cross for want of somebody to bestow his idle evenings upon, and goes up to bed at eight o'clock sometimes, growling desperately at the state of society and mankind (at least Columbia mankind) generally. Poor little Mrs. Brown (I believe you hardly know her;—the little widow you remember at the corner) has come back looking wretchedly. If looks tell truth, she can scarcely, I should say, survive a twelve month. I believe I have stolen as much of Mr. McCord's paper as I have a right to, considering his prior right of possession and so must end. Remember me very kindly to Mr. Herbemont and Aleck. I hope we shall hear as good accounts of you all when you reach Genoa. Have *you* started to grow fat yet? You know you promised to put yourself in such florishing condition as should weigh me down in the scale when you get back at the end of two years; for mind, you are not to get so delighted with your grandee sights and associations as to play truant any longer than two years. Goodbye and with best wishes to you all, believe me

Yours affectionately
Louisa S. McCord

Addressed: Mr. Alex[ande]r Herbemont / Consul of the U. States / Genoa / via New York and Havre. *Source:* Dulles-Cheves-McCord-Lovell Papers, SCHS. See also Anderson, *Two Scholarly Friends,* pp. 297–98.

To Mary Cheves Dulles

Dear Mary [Columbia December 1855]

My little ones have been writing, and with their usual thoughtlessness I presume only of nonsense.[57] I suppose you will have heard from some other source, of our new and recent affliction in the sudden death of my poor

57. LSM's letter is appended to the following letter by her daughter Louisa:

"Dear cousin Mary

I hope you are quite well, you must be sure to come and see us soon. Give my love to Lilly and tell her that I will write to her when I have time. I wrote another letter to you before but mamma forgot to send it. We have got four nice little pet pigeons, we only had three before but a little one came here yesterday and so we took it, my pigeon flys all about but it allways comes home again, the two oldest ones will eat out of our hands but the other two are not tame enough. Machy is alive yet and just as playful as ever. I saw Mr. [James Wood] Davidson the other day. Week before last we went to the commencement and we had so much fun, Jenny Thornwell, Patty Thornwell, Charlotte Rinals, and Hannah and brother and I all went together and we got a seat where we could ~~hear~~ see every thing but could not hear a word but all of us said that we did not want to hear except brother who said that he would go down stairs where he could hear for we were up in the gallery and come for us when it was time to go away, and he brought us

young brother Charles. It was a sad shock to us all and a fearful blow to my dear old Father.[58]———

I have not seen y[ou]r Father, who is I hear at St. Matthews. I would have gone to Lang Syne about this time but for the recent calamity which we have suffered and which made me unwilling to leave my Father.

I only write a few words to send my kind love and remembrance to you all.———Believe me dear Mary always

Your affectionate Cousin
Louisa S. McCord.

Source: Dulles-Cheves-McCord-Lovell Papers, SCHS.

To Langdon Cheves, Jr.

My Dear Brother Columbia January 16th, 1856

I only write a line to tell you that Father was moved in to my house the day before yesterday. He has never assented to the idea of change, but seems constantly to think himself on a journey and in a boarding house; refers now to the Sandhills as his home and frequently asks when we will get back. He seems anxious indeed to get back, says he was comfortable there etc. It is very painful and makes me feel like a jailer, but perhaps he may get better

---

some papers with the names of the students who were going to speak printed upon it. After a while when the speaking began, an old fat jewess and a young jewess and an old jew came and sat down on our seat that was full enough already and mushed me up between them but at last I got up and sat on the banisters that are fixed just like a seat and it was so comfortable that every one of us got up and sat there and lost our seats for it too, after a while I made a funny old man out of my paper and gave it to Jenny and she dropped it by accident right on the nose of a student and then we all had so much fun laughing at her. Mrs. Lieber is teaching me German and I like it very much. But this is the longest letter I ever wrote in my life and besides I have no more to tell you so goodbye

Yours affectionately
Louisa R. McCord

P.S. You must write to me soon and tell Lilly to too[.]"

58. "My dear old Father, who till he was seventy nine, seemed to possess a power of mind and body, to last for a century[,] within the last two years, but more especially this last[,] has been failing very very fast. My brother Charley's death was a dreadful shock to him; it was so sudden and unexpected; in the midst of every thing that earth can give, he was snatched from all, after a few days sickness, when no one, not even the physician, was anticipating danger. . . . Charley had a whole family of babies[,] five under eight years old[;] the youngest died a few hours before him." Sophia Cheves Haskell to Eleuthera Du Pont, Nov. 11, 1856, Langdon Cheves III Papers, SCHS.

accustomed to the change. He is altogether much as when you left him. If there is any change either for the better or worse I will let you know.——— I hear by a letter from Mr. Huger to Anna that you left Charleston as you expected with Charlotte. I hope that she and baby are well, and that you left the girls happy at their school.

I enclose an acc[oun]t sent to Father for foreign reviews. I suppose you had better pay it and if you see fit stop them.———Father of course makes no use of them and I take them myself———Anna is still here but leaves I believe in a few days———Hoping that you are none the worse of your journeyings in such uncomfortable weather and with love to Charlotte and Baby, believe me my dear Brother, always

Most affectionately Your Sister
Louisa S. McCord

Source: Langdon Cheves I Papers, SCHS.

To Langdon Cheves, Jr.

Columbia Jan[uar]y 20 [1856]

My own Brother, it seems as though our troubles cannot end. Pinckney Huger has written to you and perhaps you have heard otherwise of poor Hayney's illness. We only know here what Mr. Huger tells us. My poor boy! There seems no hope for him. Oh! that he had been with us!———

I write this only to let you know of Father. This dreadful intelligence we must not tell him, at least now. If he must know it, it had best be, only when every shadow of hope is done.———I rec[eive]d yesterday yours of 17th and have written to you some days since to say that Father is here. I have seen no change in him, until yesterday afternoon, and this morning. His mind seems much more clear. He knows where he is, and without enquiring how he came, continues to express a wish to return to the Sandhills. I do not think he is at all in a state yet for you to be able to consult him on any business, although on things generally round him, his mind seems today perfectly balanced. Considering the heavy shock which is to come, I could wish it were not so—

If you hear anything of dear Hayney, good or ill, you will I know send it to me at once. He is to me as my eldest child. I will write to you regularly with any change in Father's health. Take care of *yourself* my dear Brother, in the midst of all this trouble and sorrow—Try and keep well and strong.

Your affectionate sister
Louisa S. McCord

Source: Langdon Cheves I Papers, SCHS.

To Langdon Cheves, Jr.

My Dear Brother Columbia Jan[uar]y 23d [1856] Wednesday

As yet we have heard nothing from you upon the sad subject of our anxiety. You have of course heard nothing more than we already know and we must yet remain in suspense.——Father has improved much in a few days past. I look almost with dread at his slow progress forward and shudder to think of the new blow that awaits him.——In proportion as he improves he insists upon a return to the Sandhills; though as he has not yet insisted upon an *immediate* return, as yet the question has not been brought forward. It is strange to me that while he is evidently unconscious as to when and how he came here, he has never asked the least explanation of it from me, or so far as I know, from his servants.——He often speaks of *you* and expresses a frequent wish to see you; seems indeed to think that you are under an engagement to see him very soon. I think he has forgotten your having been here lately. When I tell him that you ~~were here to see him~~ paid him a visit but a very short time since, he assents to it, but does not seem to understand it. You told me that you wished to know when he should be better, that you might have to communicate with him on business. It is impossible for me to say whether he would be capable of business;—but today I should think that he may be so, so far at least as to comprehend and be able to consent to, or disapprove of, any plan suggested for his consideration. He has spoken several times today of his affairs, seeming to wish to be informed of them, and expressing the idea which he always does lately that he is very scarce of means. I do not know what to answer, for fear I may do wrong; and so say nothing, except that I am sure that all is doing well and that his means are abundant. Had I better tell him that as he was too sick to communicate with you, when you came to see him, that you determined to call upon Messrs. Fraser and Co. for necessary funds?[59] I believe it might be best to do so, and that by degrees he will put it out of his mind.——I will write to you every few days and let you know how he is, at least until there seems to be something decided in his state of health. It appears to me that he is now mending and I think will continue to do better. I scarcely know how to wish that he may do so. If he gets better, he must hear about poor Hayney.——Let me

59. Located at North Central Wharf in Charleston, the factor and shipping firm of John Fraser and Company was founded by John Fraser (c. 1777–1854), an immigrant from Scotland who set up business about 1803. By 1853 branches had been opened in New York and Liverpool. The company was very prosperous, able to process 20,000 bales of cotton in a morning, by 1860 operating five sailing ships, and playing an important role in Confederate trade with Europe during the war.

know at once if you hear from Europe, no matter what it is. I *cannot* hope, and yet I am eagerly anxious to hear. Dear Langdon believe me always

Your affectionate Sister
Louisa S. McCord

Love to Charlotte and your little boy

Source: Langdon Cheves I Papers, SCHS.

To Langdon Cheves, Jr.

My dear Brother — Columbia Jan[uar]y 25th, 1856

I wrote you two days since that Father was doing much better. Yesterday he was again worse (in wandering of mind, and *excitement*) than I have ever seen him. The Doctor has been with him for hours, and has made him consent *temporarily,* to stay where he is. But it will not last. He is resolute (and will I am certain recur to it,) to go as soon as possible, and he fixed upon the Sandhills because when he speaks of it people have to tell him that it belongs to him. I do not think it will be possible to keep him here, unless he could get the impression that this house belongs to him. Would it not be possible to make him go through the form of a purchase? I think if you could come up it could be managed. He might appear to buy this and sell the other. So long as he has the impression of owning that place, so long as he thinks this is not, and that is, his home, these attacks will constantly bring on the same results. Yesterday he was much excited and with an unusual persistance of determination, while wandering in his mind worse than I have ever seen him and with much more excitement. I do not know what to do, I am giving up every moment of my time, neglecting business, children and every thing else, but without success. I do not know what to do. I know my dear Brother that it is difficult, very difficult for you to leave home and yet I fear I can do nothing without some assistance from you. Father seems stronger, better; but in proportion as he is stronger and better it is more difficult to controul him, and in truth my dear brother with his mind in its present condition, he *needs controul.* I think if you could come up and speak to him decidedly which you could do, even though his mind is wandering (which I believe it *always* is, more or less) you might be able to do something. He would submit to your advice, (being under some restraint with ~~him~~ you, as with a stranger) in cases where I could do nothing with him. I think with judicious persuasion, the influence of the doctor, and you at hand to appear to make payments and manage money matters, that such an apparent transfer might be made of this place, as would incline him to believe us when we might say "it is yours," and he would at least submit to what everybody would tell him; as he did at the Sandhills even though not in his own mind conscious of the truth of the fact. Could such a state of affairs be brought about I think he would stay in one place just as soon as another for he is now entirely without any ideas of localities, though clinging most tenaciously to those of property. Could not some arrangement of the kind be made, and the Sandhill establishment broken up? I think it could if you could be here for a few days, perhaps for a single day—I think I now understand the state of his mind much better than I did before he came to my house and I think there is no possible way of controuling him without giving up in this one point. He must own property, he must be told "this is yours," wherever he stays; and in the midst of all his confusion of mind it is useless to tell him so now. Some form, some apparent transfer must be gone through, before he will submit to be so told. He now gets angry ~~if I say so~~ or at least displeased if I say so, and seems the more resolute to go away. I am almost *certain,* that a feigned purchase, if you could only be here to act as his agent and appear to arrange matters for him, might be effected and then I think the difficulty would be at an end.——I am sorry to trouble you my dear brother. Like myself you have heart and hands[,] both, fuller than you know how to bear with. But I know not what to do. I think you could help Father now as no one else can do, because you can assume a kind of authority as manager of his business. I do assume a great deal in other points, but the moment business of any kind is spoken of, Father immediately speaks of you and says it will be arranged when he sees you, which he seems to expect to do almost daily. He seems to have forgotten your last visit. When you come up again, *speak to him sick or well, about business.* It will do good. If he cannot transact business, we can at least deceive him into the belief that he is doing so. This *must* be done my dear Brother, for his own sake as well as ours. If he leaves me here, as he *will* do under present circumstances, it will be a wretchedness and a shame to us all. People will not understand that we have done our best and it will seem that the old man who has been what he has, and who has made us all, is turned out to pine and to suffer. Besides he *will* suffer. I find ~~tha~~ since he has been here that June has recurred to his old habits, and although[,] under my eye, I can trust him, ~~I~~ it would be madness to do so were he alone.[60]——

As yet I hear nothing from my poor Hayney. Do you think there can be

60. "I see I never told you about the beginnings of Marianne. Her father was a very valuable servant of my grandfather's, named June. He was a mulatto, wonderfully clever, but a hard drinker and very bad-tempered. His wife was a favorite maid and houseservant, who died of consumption leaving two delicate little children to be rather ill treated by their father. . . . Marianne was four years old when I was born [1845]. . . . As she grew older she became my mother's personal attendant and remained faithful to her through all the vicissitudes of war, freedom, and everything else." Smythe, p. 8. This Marianne is likely the same as the "Mary-Anne" mentioned in LSM's letter of Feb. 8 [1874].

hope? I send twice every day to the office in hopes of hearing something, but it is the same blank suspense continually, continually.——If you have rec[eive]d the letter young Heyward is said to have written you, let me see it my dear brother, no matter what it is.[61] Let it be the worst, it cannot kill my hope for I have no hope to kill. But I want to know about my poor boy. He belonged to me so young and so long, I cannot but feel that it is my child.

Dear Langdon, believe me

Your affectionate Sister
Louisa S. McCord

Source: Langdon Cheves I Papers, SCHS.

To Anna Cheves Huger

Dear Nan Columbia Jan[uar]y 25th, 1856

I received yours yesterday. Do not bother about Father's gown; get it only at your liesure. In his present frame of mind I should be almost afraid to produce it before him. It will be very well to have it in readiness and if you have got it and do get it, well; but I could not venture to show him anything of the kind today.——Yesterday he was worse as to wandering of mind than I have ever seen him; painfully restless and with great excitement. I will never be able to keep him here unless I can get Langdon to come up and get him, as perhaps he can, to consent to purchase this house. We could go through the form of a sale, make him believe he owned it, and he would be quiet, as he was (even though unconvinced) at the Sandhills when told "it is yours."——I had a dreadful day yesterday with him, more painful than anything I have ever had to go through with him; and June thinks he was more excited than he has ever been. Today he is better. The Doctor sat with him some hours and he has consented very reluctantly to stay *temporarily* where he is. He thinks himself on somebody's plantation in Pocataligo and is continually regretting having brought me and my family here.

61. Joseph Manigault Heyward (1830–62), son of Charles Heyward, a planter on the Combahee River, and Emma Barnwell Heyward; died of exposure in Virginia. "I remember how Joe Heyward astonished people in Washington, when he said he had never known anybody but planters." Mary Chesnut also records that, ordered by General P. G. T. Beauregard to deal with an incompetent horseman on his staff, who had already disgraced his commander by drunkenness at a reception for a visiting Bonaparte prince, Heyward "seized the A.D.C.'s horse by the bit and roughly backed the horse down in a ditch. Called to some soldiers: 'Come here and carry off this fellow.' Then Captain Heyward rode back. No word was said, and Captain Heyward was too well-bred to be ruffled by any such trifle. His face betrayed no emotion." *Chesnut,* pp. 137, 788.

No news yet from dear Hayney. Dr. Powell tried to make me believe this morning that there is hope for him.[62] I fear he is only trying to keep me from going quite crazy under my trouble, for I could not help showing him that I was half so. He did however, whether truthfully or not, hold out hope. He says that an *active* hemorrhage for *ten days* would be impossible; that anyone would die under it, and that if surviving that time the hemorrhage must have been checked. God knows whether he tells the truth or is deceiving me! Did you send y[ou]r letter to the poor boy? Would it not be well to do so, even with the risk of his not receiving it[?] It is six weeks since any of us have written, and if the poor fellow should be better and weak and sick it would distress him not to hear from home. Send your letter, dear Nannie, it cannot do any harm and if he should be alive he must not think we have forgotten him. Always seated as I am at Father's elbow I cannot write.

Father in health and strength (all except this wandering of mind which is I fear a fixed thing) is better.

I need not say let me know so soon as you hear anything from my poor boy. Has Langdon heard nothing? I send to the office continually, but continually, continually, is the same blank suspense. Remember me to Mr. Huger, I hope he is well—

Your affectionate Sister
Louisa S. McCord

Source: Langdon Cheves I Papers, SCHS.

To Langdon Cheves, Jr.

My dear Brother Columbia Jan[uar]y 28, 1856

Since my last letter to you Father has been better. That is, decidedly better in general health and strength and at times in mind. There is a constant disposition to confusion and wandering from which he is never (and I presume never will be) completely clear. The most painful part of it all is, that he is almost always dissatisfied and unhappy. He still talks of expecting you and was complaining yesterday (while speaking kindly of you, still with some bitterness of complaint) that he knew nothing of his business and could not

62. LSM's physician in Columbia, John W. Powell was married to Lucy Elizabeth Blanding in 1846. He was thirty-five years old in 1860, according to the U.S. Census, Richland District, possessing $14,000 in real estate, and personalty, including slaves, worth $40,000. Of his six children living in 1860, one, three years old, was named Louisa M. Powell. In 1858 he accompanied the McCord family on their tour to Europe, until called back by illness in his family. During the war he served as surgeon to the First Regiment, South Carolina Volunteers.

see you. I told him you had spent some days with him but a fortnight since and only did not speak of business because he was too sick to permit of it. He first said it was impossible; then assented, but evidently remained unconvinced and may complain in the same way tomorrow.

For myself I have given up my whole lower story to him except one small back room, have shut the door on every acquaintance and done every thing I can imagine to satisfy him; but it will not do and I sometimes think that he has a jealousy of the part I act in retaining him here.——At the same time a most painful feature of his case has within a few days come to my knowledge making it doubly imperative that he should reside constantly and permanently with one of his children and yet the same cause acts to make him desire to ~~leave me~~ return to the Sandhills. I cannot write more plainly on this subject, and *must see* you. It is painful, but some authority must be brought to bear which I cannot exert. I despair under the circumstances of any assistance from Dr. Geddings. Indeed ~~he~~ Father says that Powell understands his maladies much better than Geddings can do. Some ~~influ~~ *family* influence and *gentleman* influence must be here exercised. *I* cannot speak to him, but *you* could. Any son could; and I have none to appeal to but yourself. Brother John for reasons that you know, could not exercise[,] I fear, a beneficial influence, and our poor Hayney I dare not think of now. Father has reluctantly, on the Doctor's insisting upon it, consented to remain here until this cold spell is over; but he eagerly watches for a change with the avowed wish and decidedly declared intention of getting away. And he will do it, ~~without~~ unless something can be done to satisfy him that a move is out of the question. I repeat my dear Brother, I *must see some gentleman of the family.* If you absolutely cannot come within some moderate period of time, write me word to that effect (only three words will do) and I will be obliged to beg Pinckney Huger to come up. *You* however I would much rather see and unless I hear from you, I will take it for granted that I am to see you before long. I shall not write again soon, unless there is some change of affairs. *Remember,* you *will write if you cannot come,* say within a fortnight or thereabout, and if I do not hear from you I will tell Father that I expect you. You will understand me better when you see me and you will excuse me my dear Brother, even if you may now perchance think me unreasonable. With love as usual, I am dear Langdon

Y[ou]r affectionate Sister
Louisa S. McCord

Source: Langdon Cheves I Papers, SCHS.

To Langdon Cheves, Jr.

My Dear Brother Columbia Feb[ruar]y 1st, 1856

In my last letter to you I told you that I would probably not write again soon. I am *sure* that letter will bring you here, but still I think it safest to write again. My situation is so intensely painful that I cannot help troubling you. I *cannot* detain Father here; and the motives are stronger than you know and stronger than I can tell you (until I see you) why he should remain. He determined to go tomorrow, and will listen to no obstacle or argument. The Doctor sees him daily but cannot get such influence as I think will prevent his going off some morning before the Doctor comes. It needed a concocted falsehood about the horses and the roads to stop him this morning. In this way he is put off from day to day, but is getting out of patience at being trifled with. I believe that nothing but a firm remonstrance and expostulation with him can do good. Circumstances of which we knew nothing when I saw you, which have come to my knowledge only within a week, and ~~to~~ at which I hinted in my last letter to you[,] have entirely changed the view which must be taken of the case, and made it doubly difficult to deal with. As it is, I have, I believe[,] persuaded him to give up the idea of going until he sees *you,* which he is very anxious to do, and which I have endeavoured to give him the impression he cannot do if he leaves here. I have told him that I expected you in the course of ten days; and as I could not get on without a lie, I have been obliged to say that I have rec[eive]d a letter from you, promising that you will certainly be here before the 15th of this month. I must trust you my dear brother to make my word good. With the prospect of your coming I can get on for a fortnight, perhaps. But in proportion as Father gets better, it is more difficult to deal with him. He is certainly now a great deal better, much stronger, and at times his mind seems (of course without its strength) free from confusion. I believe however it is never entirely so; for, while speaking most connectedly, some remark will make me perceive that he does not know where he is. Unfortunately as he gets better, the power of will, strengthens more than the power of mind; and hence a great portion of my difficulty. This scrambling on, and detaining him from day to day, by coaxing and deceit, will serve no longer. He will be obliged to consent to remain; to make up his mind that this is his home; to abandon all idea of leaving it; so that in his moments of *better reason* he may be governed by this decision. *Then* it is the time of difficulty. With such attacks as you saw him under, there is no difficulty; but when better, the firm will is uncontroulable.

I have this instant rec[eive]d y[ou]r kind letter of 28th and 29th. John has written to me, giving the information about poor Hayne. I have but little hope, but look anxiously for further intelligence.——For yourself, my dear Brother, *do* NOT *come up if y[ou]r cough continues.* Not unless or until it is *perfectly well.* I entreat and insist that *you must not come* until perfectly PERFECTLY well. If you are not so, it is reason enough not to come. I must tell Father that you are not well; I must tell him about poor Hayne; I must tell him all. He MUST stay. I will speak to him of every thing. We must not spare his feelings now, to run the risk of greater agony. For God's sake do *not* come. *Be perfectly well* before you even think of it. I have been thoughtless and selfish to press you as I have done, and to forget that cough, which I noticed when you were here. Forgive me my dear Brother, and show me that you forgive me by not coming until you can do so with entire safety. I am perfectly well, and tough, and can stand a great deal; and Powell is very kind and knows all my difficulties and will help me all he can.——I will hold out to Father the promise that I have assumed for you, that you will come by the 15th; ~~but~~ It will keep him quiet that long, ~~But~~ and something in the mean time may bring a change. But you must not keep the promise for me unless you are perfectly well, and able to come without the slightest risk. If you are not by that time perfectly well, a line from you or even from Charlotte putting off for a week or two longer, will help very much. Only hold out the prospect of a visit. I can manage it. Do not come then until you are quite well and the weather good. Shut up perpetually with big fires here, I even forgot the weather when I wrote to you.——Have I said enough my Brother? *Do not come* until you do so with perfect safety. You are almost all that we have left. You must take great care of yourself. I am so well now, I can do almost anything. I will only *say* to Father that you come the 15th.——There is no harm in the lie.——Goodbye Dear Langdon. Take care of y[ou]rself.

Y[ou]rs always affectionately,
Louisa S. McCord

Source: Langdon Cheves I Papers, SCHS.

To Langdon Cheves, Jr.

Dear Langdon — Columbia Feb[ruar]y 3d, 1856

I write now at Father's particular desire to beg you, from him, not to come up until *you are perfectly well, and the weather shall be settled and pleasant.*

The truth is, my dear Brother, after finishing my letter to you of the ~~night~~ day before yesterday I came back to Father and found him so determined to go to the Sandhills that he would listen to no argument or obstacle suggested; and in answer to my promise that you would come, he would only say that he knew better, you would never come etc. I was then obliged to tell him decidedly that you had been sick and suffered much from a cough, taken on your last visit to him from exposure to inclement weather. This has, as I anticipated, made him very uneasy, and he now insists upon my writing to stop you until your health and the weather shall combine to make a visit entirely safe and proper on your part. He will stay now until he sees you, I feel quite certain; and I entreat most earnestly that you do not hurry or expose yourself in any way. It is a painful weapon to be obliged to wield, but sorrow conquers where nothing else can. Father's anxieties now being excited on your account, he will be patient, perhaps even for weeks. It is he himself who now says that even if you are well you must not expose yourself until the weather becomes pleasant and settled; and he says this, under promise to remain here until he sees you. Do not hurry yourself therefore my dear Brother, come only when it is quite right and quite safe. I hope you are getting your cough quite well and taking good care of yourself. We have wretched weather again; cloudy and threatening snow. You have no business about in such weather. I shall never forgive myself if my letters will have caused you to come up under such circumstances. Do not come; pray do not come, until it is right.

I see the Arabia has arrived.[63] Will it bring us any intelligence? I trust that it may, although I dread it.

Take care of yourself my dear Brother.——Give my love to Charlotte and y[ou]r children. Father is improving now daily; and I will promise at all risks to keep him here ~~at all risks~~ until it is quite safe for you to come up. Goodbye Dear Langdon

Your affectionate Sister
Louisa S. McCord

Source: Langdon Cheves I Papers, SCHS.

To Langdon Cheves, Jr.

Dear Lang Columbia Feb[ruar]y 18th, 1856

I have just now received yours of 16th. It is as you say too soon to build up hope of exemption from measles, but I trust you may escape its spread. I thank you for writing. Every little thing that can help to soothe Father is of

63. The *Arabia,* and the *Pacific* mentioned in the next letter, were transatlantic steamers; their arrivals in New York were regularly announced in newspapers there, for they brought European news.

some use.——We have been doing much as when you were here. Father's bodily health seems quite good and his strength gradually and constantly I think increasing. His state of mind just what it was; constantly confused, constantly restless, constantly changing; fixed only in the one point of unfixedness and determination to move. I can bear it better however since seeing you and getting y[ou]r advice. There is something so dreadful to me in this state of affairs, that until you stood by me and saw it with me I felt all the time as if in a horrible dream. Now I hope to keep firmness to go on steadily.

The "Pacific" I see has arrived. I think her mails must bring us some intelligence.[64]

You will write I am sure again before very long. Give my love to Charlotte and Baby. Anna who came here on Saturday to spend a few days, says she saw y[ou]r girls Friday even[in]g, and that they seem quite well and happy.

Always dear Lang, believe me

Your affectionate Sister
Louisa S. McCord

Source: Langdon Cheves I Papers, SCHS.

To Langdon Cheves, Jr.

My dear Brother Columbia Feb[ruar]y 29th, 1856

As you are so near to Brother John, I presume you have received the intelligence which he has sent me. Lest you should not, I give the extract which he sends from Mr. Heyward's letter. Date Jan[uar]y 22d—

64. The *Pacific,* of the Collins Line, had departed from Liverpool for New York on Jan. 23, 1856, with 45 passengers and a crew of 114. Having left Liverpool on Jan. 26, the Cunarder *Persia* (Captain C. H. M. Judkins), a paddle steamship with a capacity of 250 first-class passengers, arrived in New York on Feb. 9, concluding her maiden voyage. On Feb. 2 she had "encountered heavy ice in lat. 46 lon. 46, which detained her thirty-six hours, and injured her starboard wheel" (New York *Daily Tribune,* Feb. 11, 1856; "entirely disabling the starboard wheel," according to the New York *Times* of the same date), and there was now surprise that the *Pacific* had not arrived before her. Ships were sent immediately in search, but no trace of the *Pacific* was ever found. LSM sailed on the *Persia* both to and from Europe (1858–59). "We sailed for home, on the *Persia* again, and Coco [a pet squirrel] went too, though everyone prophesied that Capt. Judkins would never let him come on board. If we had tried to hide him we would never have succeeded, but Mamma made me carry him right up to the Captain who only grinned and said something about coals to Newcastle." Smythe, p. 36. On Sept. 29, 1858, Henry Adams sailed for Europe on the *Persia,* "the newest, largest, and fastest steamship afloat," and later recalled the educational value of a storm encountered the third day out (*The Education of Henry Adams,* ed. Ernest Samuels [Boston, 1974], p. 71).

"Since I wrote to you Hayne has been doing very well, regaining a great deal of strength and is now able to sit up some five or six hours a day, and I am in hopes that in the course of a month or two when the weather becomes warmer, will be able to go out, and perhaps return to America. He appears to be perfectly aware of his situation; and his spirits are very good."—— Perhaps I ought to be satisfied that this is good news; but some how or other I do not feel it so. There is something in the wording of it, which makes me feel it rather as a reprieve than a permanent hope.——

Father is not so well as when I last wrote to you. I fear more and more that he must have (or at least appear to have) his house to himself. Since my last (to which as yet I have received no answer) I made an offer on my own account for the adjoining lot to me; but failed; it cannot be purchased; is mortgaged I believe and unsaleable. I have determined to steal a portion of my own lot and have engaged a workman to run a fence across the lower portion of it and build me after such separation shall be made (so as to prevent Father's noticing the building) two servants houses which are now becoming peremptorily necessary. I would have preferred doing this on some other land, but could do no better and found it necessary to act before you would be able to come up, even should you think of coming before long, which you will scarcely do. I find to my dismay that Father's woman is in such health as requires accomodation out of the house, (she ~~has h~~ is now occupying my down stairs chamber to be near him) as she is *enceinte,* needs rest etc. she says, and will need nursing etc. in 2 or 3 months. This, and the necessity of furnishing out rooms which I have not at present, has obliged me to act, as ~~there~~ the building process is slow here, and I have no time to loose. The expense of what I have ordered will amount to about (a little over) $300. I have further told Father that I have a lot in Columbia and am ready to move any day. Sometimes this soothes him and I therefore think that I may have to build a house of a few rooms to appear at least to move to it. I dislike spending money on my own lot which cannot be afterwards sold, ~~to any advan~~ and would be so much dead loss, but I really see nothing better to be done. You must advise me whether to go further than the servants houses which I have ordered. A house of a few rooms would cost perhaps some $1500, making in all not over $2000 at most. Father is very unhappy today, thinks he is ruined, that I am cheating him, you are cheating him and every thing is wrong. I hope you are doing well with your measles, and that your family is well. Ever my dear Brother

Y[ou]r affectionate Sister
Louisa S. McCord

Source: Langdon Cheves I Papers, SCHS.

To Langdon Cheves, Jr.

My Dear Brother Columbia March 1st, 1856

It distresses me to have to trouble you so often; but it cannot be helped. Father is at this time in a more excited condition than I have ever seen him. He takes positions in which it is impossible not to oppose him and, as you know, all opposition irritates. For instance, his besetting idea is now that *he is ruined.* If I assent or dissent the consequence is a storm of indignation in either case. I send for the Doctor[;] it does little or no good. The Doctor has combined he supposes with me to deceive him. June he accuses of officious impertinence and intermeddling. In short all have combined against him and he is most unhappy. I try to stay away from him as you advise; but he sends for me constantly and constantly the same scene follows. If I tell him he is not ruined, he says I do not know what I am talking off and that he is tired of being dictated to and does not want to be advised. If I assent either by word or silence that he *is* ruined, he then insists upon my accounting to him for all the missing funds and accuses me of having managed things for my own benefit and made him a beggar. I tell you all this, not to complain and not that I expect much help (for I know it cannot be given) but only that you may not think me unreasonable in annoying you so often with my letters.——At present I write to you by his particular and urgent order, that you may answer immediately and let him know the state of his affairs. This he urges you to do by the most solemn and even pitiable appeals. What you can say my dear Brother, I do not know, but perhaps it would be well for you to write something, more or less accurate as you please.——Excuse me if I suggest; but suppose for instance you make a rough statement of ______ thousand p[ai]d for old acc[oun]ts; ______ thousand plantation expenses; ______ thousand remaining in factor's hands. Close accuracy would be a matter of small moment. He wishes to know too whether *this house* is paid for. If you see fit you can set down $2000 which he has stumbled upon lately as its value. He insists that he is in debt for it to somebody he does not know who; that the debt will accumulate and ruin him and all his family and he wishes to know that it is settled. Sometimes he seems to think I must stay with him and then again tells me he can never consent to my living in the same house with him. I sometimes think it will be best actually to take the $2000 and put up buildings on a part of my lot as I suggested to you in my letter of yesterday, where I can take refuge and send my children as may be found needful. I *must* have a hiding place for them, if this state of affairs is to continue long. For weeks, for months it may be resisted, but to go on and on and on with not a corner of the house sometimes where I can sit with them quietly as a mother with her children, with nothing to soothe and everything to excite them, must affect their young minds dangerously and is enough to turn them all into maniacs. My own head reels under it.——My idea is to put up a house with about four rooms where my children could be sent (calling it their homes) or where I could myself go whenever it should be thought best that the house should seem clear of them; or where in fact we could stay in case of necessity. Father would then be convinced that this house is his own, while I could manage and do with every thing precisely as I do now staying here except when necessary to leave temporarily. I think it likely that we would thus do better. If you say so, I will engage workmen at once. If I could even tell him that I am building a house, that I had some place independant of him, I think he would be less suspicious of me. He thinks I am here with a kind of vulture wish to devour his substance and complete the ruin which he believes that I have been largely inculpated in bringing upon him.

Will you write? Do, please! It is useless to bother you to write to Father; only in answering me, slip in something in the shape of an account, stating roughly if you think fit, as I suggest above; and if you think right you may if you choose give me credit for the $2000, and I believe I will build something at once. I told you yesterday that I have already engaged some servants houses to be built with all speed. My yard is too much crowded to be safe for warmer weather, and only two days since I had to turn 3 servants out of their bedroom, to turn the little apartment into a wine room. Besides Cilla must have accomodation.

Believe me my dear Brother it distresses me to trouble you about all this; but I cannot act without your authority, and although it may be all useless, it seems to me the best chance for getting on. Besides, Father is at once violently peremptory and pleadingly urgent in his desire to know from you, as soon as possible, whether he has the means of subsistance.——

I hope you have had no measles beyond the first case. It would indeed be sad for you to be troubled now with such a disease among your people. Indeed my dear Brother in the midst of all my own difficulties and troubles I do not forget how much you have to bear and to do, and it is with shrinking and pain that I feel myself obliged to write to you on these annoying subjects. Is your own health quite good now? Take care of it, for all our sakes. With love to Charlotte and Baby, believe me my dear Brother, always

earnestly and affectionately y[ou]rs
Louisa S. McCord

Source: Langdon Cheves I Papers, SCHS.

To Langdon Cheves, Jr.

[Columbia] March 5th [1856] Tuesday night[65]

I send the above[66] my dear Brother, as an excuse for what I fear you will consider my persecution of you. It is an attempt of our dear old Father to write something; I believe a letter to you. He is very anxious to hear from you and evidently much irritated with *me* because he does not do so. He seems to think it is *my fault.* I offered to write for him but he would not allow me to do so, and says[,] when he found he could not write, that he will send down June with a message. Indeed he wished to send him today, and with difficulty has been prevented. He is much irritated, much displeased, and is altogether in a far more painful condition than when you saw him. Could you not my dear brother, write or even cause Charlotte to write, if it be but 2 lines, say every week? It would I think assist in soothing Father. My position is here so intensely distressing that you must excuse me if I press upon you more urgently than you think right. I know you have troubles, I know you have cares; perhaps even, you are not well yourself, perhaps I am goading you beyond endurance; but God help me what can I do? Do write, my own dear Brother; write, just a few lines and if you think no harm of it, remember my suggestion in my last letter. Father is alternately moody and violent on the subject of his affairs; now urgently pleading that you will send him a statement of them, and again angrily insisting upon it. I tried to deceive him, to make him believe that I had heard from you, and gave at a guess the amount which I supposed might be in the factors hands as if stated by you; but he asked to see your letter, and when I had to say I had mislaid it, you may imagine what he thinks of me. Can you not make a rough guess or calculation of the state of things? A thousand or two here or there, would make little difference. All that is needed is the appearance of giving an account, for he has little or no idea of numbers. He told me yesterday that he had *150 thousand dollars* in his factors hands, and then talked of it as only *15 hundred.* Just give a statement of some balance and it will be right. I am sure I need not say any more. You will write. I only fear that I cannot keep him quiet until you will have time to receive and answer this; and that he will send June down; which I wish very much to avoid, ~~and~~ as June is his only efficient attendant, and I should fear his getting into trouble if he is sent off alone, after all the excitement and worry he is going through. You will write I am sure and immediately.

As regards the question of building some small house to call mine, and

65. March 5, 1856, was a Wednesday.

66. Two lines of a tiny scrawl, wavering across the head of the first page of this letter; scarcely recognizable as handwriting; see illus. in *PSE.*

pretend at least to live in, and to hide out of the way in if needful, I more and more fear that it is indispensable. Indeed if Father lives for many months as he is (getting indeed as he has done constantly worse) I see no possibility of doing without it; He will become frantic if he believes that I am fixed on him here with no other home; and I have determined if I can possibly get any thing done *immediately,* to undertake it on my own responsibility. The only question is whether the carpenter can get lumber etc. which it seems is difficult to obtain, in time for my purposes. I have spoken to a carpenter and find that I can probably get what is needful for $1500 or not much more, including the servants houses already ~~building~~ ordered, and I believe in the act of framing. This is much less than I thought would be required, and if you think yourself not authorized to meet the expense on Father's acc[oun]t I will not push you further. I would not my dear Brother make you do anything that would embarrass you or that you think doubtfully right, only as I happen to be scant of funds, if you think it wrong to advance to me, say so; that I may borrow in time for the payment of this sum. I am sure if you think it wrong to ~~do~~ advance it, it *is* wrong. You know much more of business than I do and if you tell me that you ought not to give it, I shall not misunderstand you, and have no doubt that you will do what is right. Please however whether you give it or not, *pretend* to have paid $2000 for this house. Father will never be satisfied, I think, until he has been told that this sum is paid. I told him that it was paid, but he says he wants *you* to tell him so. He is constantly confused about localities, thinks he is constantly moving etc., but still always refers to his $2000 house, and his uneasiness about the non-payment of the debt which he insists is owing without any fixed idea as to whom owing. If *you* tell him it is done, I think he will perhaps be satisfied on that point.

I hope you have had no more measles and that things are well with you. I have received but one letter from you since you were here. I say this not complainingly but only pleadingly. I am sure you will write to me soon.—— I trust that your little boy has escaped the measles. Anna writes me that your girls both look remarkably well. I wish my poor little things were with them; but they are nearly two years younger than yours; too young to send from home. With love as usual, I am my dear Brother always

Y[ou]r affectionate Sister
Louisa S. McCord

Perhaps before getting this you will have written in answer to my last. If so; so much the better, and this may go for nothing.

Dear Lang — Wednesday morning

I have opened my letter to tell you that Father seems much weaker this morning, having taken a little walk out and had to be brought home—lifted in a chair. He will probably now[,] as always when weak, be quieter for a while; but even now asks anxiously if I have heard from you and seems very uneasy at not doing so. He cannot calculate that you have not had time to answer since my letter of last Saturday and is very unhappy at not hearing from you. I will do the best I can in every thing. Always my dear Brother

Y[ou]rs affectionately
Louisa S. McCord

Source: Langdon Cheves I Papers, SCHS.

To Langdon Cheves, Jr.

Dear Langdon Columbia March 7th [1856]

Again I am disappointed, no letter today. Father is much troubled at not hearing, though he is much better today; sufficiently well to put the blame where it is deserved, on *you* instead of *me;* and he frets much less when he has not me to be displeased with. Still he is very uneasy and tells me I must write to you *every day* until I get an answer. I am sorry to worry you so much, I am sure I shall hear tomorrow or the next day at furthest; and if you have written you must only not be worried by my numerous epistles. I write partly because I *must* to satisfy Father, and partly because when he gets as he has been lately, I become almost crazy myself and do not know what to do. He is quite calm today and almost satisfied. He has discovered my fenced off lot which I told him was a new purchase and he seems pleased and begins to believe that I really have renounced claims upon this establishment. I think he will be much happier when he sees ~~mo~~ something of a house getting up on *my* lot and will feel that *this* is *his.* I am actually in treaty with a carpenter for a house with two rooms and two little closet rooms and a piazza to look as if it was a sizeable house. I will never live in it, (~~but~~ it is altogether too small,) but it will do to go to if needed, and to hide my children when he is as he has lately been; and I am convinced will do much good. I hope you will not disapprove of my course; I am sure you would have advised it if here. But as I said in my last, do what you think right; you know better than I do what is fit; and if you think Father ought not to pay the expense of building out-buildings for me (which this really is, ~~do~~ although only for his service) do not force a point, I will borrow. Only let me know what you think right; and above all in the species of account which you will have to render to soothe Father (any sort of a summing up to look like an account) do not forget to put down $2000 for this house in which he is now living as if paid. If you do not think it right to spend it or the larger part of it on what I am doing, it will go for Father's general expenses.

I hope my dear Brother, you are getting on well. I really am anxious myself to know how you are and whether the measles are troubling you. I think I will hear tomorrow.

With love to Charlotte and Baby, believe me always

Y[ou]r affectionate Sister
Louisa S. McCord

Source: Langdon Cheves I Papers, SCHS.

To Langdon Cheves, Jr.

Dear Langdon Columbia March 12th [1856]

Yours of 7th, postmarked 11th, has this moment been rec[eive]d. It is exactly what was wanted and Father is *perfectly* satisfied, if he will only stay so. He will for some time, until he forgets again, and then I will ~~keep~~ produce y[ou]r letter (I must keep it awhile) to refer to, but have written a memorandum on the back explaining the circumstances under which it is rendered. We are doing now as well and as comfortably as circumstances can allow.——I wrote to you yesterday giving you the amount which I think will be necessary for the objects which I have now in view for Father. When it suits you to set me in the way of drawing money on these demands, I am beginning to need it. My Carpenter is I understand getting in his materials and wishes to present accounts as ~~he does so~~ they become due. He has indeed already begun to do so.——I have written to Anna begging her or Mr. Huger to get a suitable carriage made, if there is none to purchase. The one in which Father rides is really dangerous.

I think I said to you that $2000 at present, with $500 quarterly from 1st April prox. (i.e. next month) will probably be not too much, but I think enough for all purposes.

Father bids me thank you for y[ou]r letter. He says he is very much obliged to you and really seems so relieved that it would well pay you for the trouble of writing if you could see him.

I am truly sorry to hear that you have not been able to keep off the measles. It will be a sad trouble to you at this season. You are so good a doctor that you will think it very impertinent of me to make suggestions; but as I had upwards of 80 cases of it to manage two years since, I had at least some experience in the disease, and believe I profited much by a rule that no negro left his room until he had been *ten days* perfectly well, paying also extreme attention to diet[,] and did not go to work for 4 or 5 days longer. From upwards of 80 cases, I lost only 2 feeble children. I know y[ou]r climate is a worse one than ours for the disease, but still you may get well through it I trust.——I hope Charlotte may succeed in keeping y[ou]r baby from it. He is so young perhaps you may keep him from coming in contact with it.

Give her my love and best wishes for getting through this trouble. With the same for yourself my dear Brother, and thanks for y[ou]r kindness in writing, I am always

Your affectionate Sister
Louisa S. McCord

For the money I need you can either order a remittance here, or give me a note on Fraser etc., as you prefer.

Source: Langdon Cheves I Papers, SCHS.

To Langdon Cheves, Jr.

Dear Langdon Columbia March ~~18~~19th, 1856

As it is a week today since my last letter to you I write to report progress. We have got on much better lately. Though Father has been much confused in mind, he has been generally speaking less irritable and therefore more comfortable. I have succeeded in so strongly impressing upon him that this house is his, that he no longer wishes to leave it, only when he fancies himself in Savannah or elsewhere, insists upon returning to Columbia.——I have fairly begun the buildings which I told you would be needful and am glad I have done so; as I am daily more and more convinced of their necessity and indeed the impossibility (unless things change much) of doing without them. I constantly tell Father that I have my establishment independant of him, and he is as constantly soothed by my doing so. Though I hope to get on without an absolute and entire turn out on my part. For it would be an immense expense and indeed I have not ground room for kitchen, carriage house etc. etc. I do not however imagine that anything to such extent will be needful. What I have undertaken will, I think, be completed in two months, or but very little more. I pay something extra for speed.——By the way, I am at my last extremity for funds. I pay lumber accounts, bricks etc., as fast as they are got (such was my agreement with the workman) and thus have spent every thing of my own on hand. Can you give me immediately authority to draw, or cause Fraser and Co. to make me a remittance? I am truly sorry to trouble you. I know you are very busy, but I am wretchedly stupid about money affairs, and as you think it right to give what I need, suppose it will be as convenient to you, to do it now as later. To save you trouble, general instructions to Fraser and Co. as suggested in my last, would probably prevent my ever having to trouble you further about money at least, and would save me much annoyance. Should the sum I ask for quarterly prove too much, it would be always easy for me to set that right.——I asked you to let me have $2000 to pay for my buildings and a carriage which Father needs very much, and $500 quarterly commencing from 1st April. Father has in bank here $750, but that I cannot meddle with. He likes to squander a good deal to his own servants and trifles and of course must not be prevented, but is so pinchingly economical for some things that I am obliged to get all clothing etc. for him ~~withou~~ (in which he was in coming here even to a beggarly extent deficient) without his knowing anything about it. You have, I know, not sent me funds yet, only because you did not think about it;—or possibly you have written to Fraser and Co. to credit me to the extent needed, and only have not told me of it. If I do not hear from you within a week, I will take the last for granted and will venture to apply to Mr. Trenholm for what I want.[67] I am sorry to trouble you but really at this moment I cannot command more than $100 without borrowing. In ten days I shall have again some few hundred dollars of dividends, but nothing sufficient to meet present demands upon me. If you would rather I should not write to Mr. Trenholm, you must write and tell me so.——

I hope you are getting on well with the measles, though I know it must be a terrible stumbling-block to you at this season. At least I trust you do not loose your people by it. Has Charlotte succeeded in keeping y[ou]r baby from it? If she has time to write, I shall be very glad to hear from her how the health of all gets on. Give my love to her and the little man, and believe me my dear Brother always

Y[ou]rs most affectionately
Louisa S. McCord

Source: Langdon Cheves I Papers, SCHS.

To Langdon Cheves, Jr.

Dear Langdon — Columbia March 27th, 1856

I thank you for yours of 24th rec[eive]d last night. I am ashamed at having had to trouble you as much as I have done; for I know you have had distress enough without my goading. I am sure however that things here will do

67. George Alfred Trenholm (1806–76), Charleston merchant; from July 1864, Confederate secretary of the treasury. At this time he was senior partner and principal owner of John Fraser and Company, which he had joined as a clerk in 1835.

better now. I am at least satisfied that I have now ordered and have the means of doing every thing I think best for Father; and however things turn out, it is a comfort to have neglected nothing. Father has been much better lately; that is to say much better satisfied. In his paroxysms of wandering, (for he varies very much) he has been much less irritable; rather frets now than becomes angry, and never shows the slightest indication lately, of any wish to leave here. On the contrary when he fancies himself to have left, is always anxious to return, and pleased when he can be convinced that he has returned to "the house with the garden" as he usually designates this. However things now turn, I do not see that you can do anything more for me and I will fight along as I can. I will write from time to time to let you know how things are doing and will try not to trouble you any more. I am quite sure that you are willing and ready to do all you can; but there is no use loading upon you, if it can be helped.

I am truly pained to hear how much you are troubled with the measles; and the cold blustering wind we have today if it extends to ~~the~~ your river, will do you I fear no good. It is at least a comfort to you and Charlotte that you have kept the baby free of it.——I delivered y[ou]r message to Mrs. Lieber and she tells me she has determined to leave here, on a visit to you, next Monday. I think she has written to that effect.——

With love as usual, believe me, my dear Brother always

most affectionately y[ou]rs
Louisa S. McCord

Source: Langdon Cheves I Papers, SCHS.

To Langdon Cheves, Jr.

Dear Langdon Columbia April 12th, 1856

I write only, as I promised to do occasionally, to let you know how Father is. When Mrs. Lieber left here I thought him in a very critical condition, and had almost written to let you know of it, only hesitating because you had so much else to trouble you. But he is over that again. There seems in him still a wonderful strength of constitution which strangely surmounts every thing. He is now much as when you saw him last, only moving with more difficulty; not f[ro]m any increased weakness I think, but rather from some failure in the power of moving his limbs. His mind [is], much as it then was, catching first at one thing then at another, always with a strange and distressing perversity of wrong ideas but with less irritability than a few weeks since.

This is a sad letter which John has received from Heyward. It is no more than I had made up my mind to long since, only I did hope that my poor boy would at least get home to us to die. I think he would wish it. Perhaps still he may come; but this long silence of late frightens me. The stormy season is over now, and letters written in the last two months ought to have reached us. These are useless speculations though and I ought not to worry you with them.

I trust you are getting on favorably with your measles and planting. I hope to hear of you through Mrs. Lieber when she comes up, and after that I must beg Charlotte to write a line occasionally. I know she will do it to help Father when you are too busy.

With love as usual, my dear Brother, believe me

Your affectionate Sister
Louisa S. McCord

Source: Langdon Cheves I Papers, SCHS.

To Langdon Cheves, Jr.

Dear Langdon Columbia April 13th, 1856

Although I wrote to you yesterday, I must, to satisfy Father, do so again today; merely to make a statement to you upon which he insists. I did not mention yesterday, because I hoped then to avoid bothering you with it, that one particular fancy by which Father is constantly beset, is a determination to free June, Cilla, and any child or children they may have. This is a constant, daily, sometimes hourly, subject of discussion with them, and I am called in to promise etc., which I have been obliged to do over and over 50 times, in the most solemn manner, to the servants themselves as well as to Father. I hoped this would satisfy him, but he now insists upon calling in a lawyer to draw up papers etc., and has even named that drunken creature Treadwell whose name he has got from the servants.[68] Of course if he insists

68. "We have just elected our 4 representatives for the state legislature, and the one who has received the largest vote is a Mr. Treadwell, who in consequence of drunkenness has been once in the asylum and often in the gutter—I speak literally—who has committed all sorts of outrages and immoralities openly and shamelessly." Francis Lieber to Dorothea Dix, Oct. 14, 1852, Francis Lieber Papers, Huntington. LSM's and Lieber's Treadwell is apparently James D. Tradewell, graduated (although involved in a near-dueling escapade in 1828) from South Carolina College in 1830, admitted to the bar in Columbia in 1832, and "dreadfully drunk" in Mary Chesnut (p. 356).

upon seeing a lawyer, I must have DeSaussure;[69] but I am anxious to prevent the unpleasant discussion and exposure consequent upon anything of the kind, and have promised him to write to you, and you must give your promise, as I have given mine, that if surviving him the required arrangement shall be made. At present June belongs to me by deed of gift, given some 10 or 12 years since, and Cilla, as you know, is willed to me.[70] They will be perfectly worthless after all that has passed and I would ask nothing better for my own comfort than to let them go if they choose it. This, Father cannot however be made to understand, and he insists that you are to *promise compensation to me from the estate and ~~to~~ assistance to me in insuring to these servants their promised freedom.* All I wish you to do is to say that you make this promise which will be only so far binding, that in case of my death before Father, you will remember that the promise to the negroes is a *bona fide* one, if they choose to leave the State at his death. This promise I have been obliged seriously to make them, in order, if possible, to prevent their tampering with and exciting Father, which I sometimes (perhaps unjustly) fear they do. The compensation part may be forgotten, except to satisfy *him,* for they will really be worthless after all this. I am not even certain that they will be willing to release *me* from the ownership; but Father will not listen to such a suggestion, and I think it best not to carry the discussion of the subject with them, further than it is forced on by Father himself. All I want you to do then is to say that you will see his wishes attended to.

This is all that I now have to trouble you with. Father is, as usual, wandering extremely, but fortunately now entirely satisfied about his house. The building of the little establishment which I am getting on with rapidly, has already done much good. He watches its progress, and seems now thoroughly satisfied, not only that *this* is *his,* but that it is my intention some day to leave it; and in proportion as he is convinced that I really intend to go

69. William Ford DeSaussure (1792–1870), prosperous Columbia attorney, judge, politician, U.S. senator (1852–53), and delegate to the secession convention in December 1860. "The Governor has appointed Wm. F. DeSaussure (little Billy) to succeed [Robert Barnwell Rhett]. He is a dapper fellow that I dare say no one ever dreamed of for Senator before. He will hardly be a candidate for election in Dec[ember]. Yet why not? He would fairly represent the hollow, pretentious, and shuffling spirit which now characterizes So[uth] C[arolin]a." Bleser, *Secret and Sacred: The Diaries of James Henry Hammond,* p. 253 (entry of May 12, 1852).

70. "I give to my daughter Louisa, my house servant Priscilla, also, my house and the land whereon it stands in the Sand-Hills near Columbia, with my Library, Carriage and Horses, and the Household and Kitchen furniture, to hold to my said daughter, her heirs, executors, administrators and assigns, to enure and be settled to the same uses and limitations as the property heretofore settled on my said daughter Louisa, at the time of her marriage." Langdon Cheves, "Last Will and Testament," Nov. 6, 1854, printed copy, Langdon Cheves I Papers, SCHS.

away, he becomes anxious that I should remain. He wants me, but cannot bear that he should be *obliged* to keep me; and thus the sight of a house in which he thinks I can live, keeps things right. His greatest annoyance now, besides the June and Cilla emancipation question, is a habit of imagining that there are two of sundry persons habitually about him, and particularly myself. I have a double, whom as I cannot give a name for, he constantly calls the "nameless one" and "the lonely one", and whom he thinks I have displaced in his house and in the Lang Syne property. Indeed it is with this "lonely and nameless one", rather than with myself, that he desires the arrangement about June and Cilla to be made. He considers them to belong to her and not to me, and because he cannot see her, wishes you to be a surety for the promises made. He is constantly annoyed with the fear that I am doing her some injustice and says he is sure I must have some dispute with her; otherwise he would see us together or at least I could tell him where she is. In all this you can do nothing except to say that you will see his wishes concerning the negroes in question fulfilled. It will be better if you can write it, but if you do not do so in a few days, I must only do my best to make Father believe that you have done so.

He sends you many messages about coming up etc. which can only be painful to give and receive, and so I leave them. I know you could not come now, unless under urgent necessity, and I do not think any such now exists.

Give my love to Charlotte and kind remembrance to Mrs. Lieber if she be still with you, though I think she was to leave about this time. I am anxious to hear how you have got on with y[ou]r plantation troubles.

I am, dear Brother,

Y[ou]r affectionate Sister
Louisa S. McCord

Source: Langdon Cheves I Papers, SCHS.

To Langdon Cheves, Jr.

My dear Brother Columbia April 21st, 1856

I have just rec[eive]d two letters, one from poor Hayne and the other from his kind good friend Heyward. Hayney's is of 25th March and Heyward's of 20th with a P.S. of 26th. Poor Hayne's gives no information. It is patient, uncomplaining, and trying to give hopes to comfort us, which plainly he does not himself feel. Heyward's in answer to one from me to him is most kind but gives no hope. He says;

"Poor Hayne's state of health is very little improved if at all from the first.

It is now three months, his cough has been incessant, which has reduced him to a mere nothing. He has never been able to walk but once or twice during all that time. With my own hands do I take him out of bed every day and seat him in his chair where he remains some five or six hours which time he spends reading and receiving a few visits from his friends." He then mentions the consultation of Physicians and its hopeless result. They recommended nothing but cod-liver oil and that after a month's trial had to be given up as not agreeing with him. He now "only takes something to soothe his cough that he may sleep at night." Again he says; "He never speaks of his situation, but at the same time I am sure he is quite aware of it. He has entrusted everything to my charge, which I strive to the best of my ability to fulfil, both for him and for you all, that which I hope is most satisfactory. I begged Dr. [John Richardson] Cheves to give me any advice and instructions that he may think proper. I should then feel much relieved."———

Good, kind Mr. Heyward! In answer to my expressions of gratitude he says "I can assure you that I feel that I am doing nothing but my duty towards him." And this after three months kind watching; and God bless him! I believe he will watch on. Oh! if I could only go to my poor boy!———

Dear Langdon, did you remember to write about money that may be wanted? And had you not better write to Heyward? You know you hold Father's place now, and silence may look like neglect and indifference. Write to Heyward, dear Langdon, or if you cannot write, tell me what to write for you.———Mrs. Lieber tells me that John is really going she believes, and immediately. Is he so? Still even if he does, you ought to write (Do you not think so?) or at least authorize me to say for you something; what ought to be said.

I regret to hear from Mrs. Lieber of y[ou]r continued suffering from measles and to such an extent among your people. I hope you are nearly through with it. She could not tell me.

Father is much as when I last wrote. I managed to get over the necessity of a Lawyer which he insists upon, by calling in our Doctor, who listened and promised every thing needed; and while ~~promising~~ assuring the negroes that the promise should be fulfilled still told them very decidedly that the subject must be dropped. I am convinced now that they have been tormenting ~~him~~ Father about it (at least the woman has) for a long time.

Dear Langdon, don't forget about poor Hayne and money that may be needed. His expenses may be very great and it will not do to let Mr. Heyward pay them. Heyward has been consulting Physicians, hiring nurses and so on for him. He named as the doctors consulted Dr. Trotman and Dr. Punta "an eminent man and physician to the court." Of course all this must lead to expense. Perhaps though my dear Brother you have already attended to what is needful. If I can write or do anything, please tell me. I would do it so gladly.

With love as usual, dear Langdon believe me always and most truly

Y[ou]r affectionate Sister
Louisa S. McCord

Source: Langdon Cheves I Papers, SCHS.

To Langdon Cheves, Jr.

Dear Langdon Columbia April 25th, 1856

I know you have much to occupy your care and attention. Entreat Charlotte (I am sure she cannot refuse) to write to me about once a fortnight any information she can get about crops and things in general. Accuracy is of no great importance and it is very difficult for me to get on without some assistance of the kind.

Father is lately again very irritable, and insists upon seeing you constantly and blames me that he does not. A letter now and then would I am sure prevent or at least lessen this. I have been obliged to distress him by telling him about measles and all y[ou]r difficulties and troubles except about poor Hayne, but all will not do. He thinks himself in Charleston and Savannah and all about and must see you. A letter now and then with any information however inexact would be of infinite assistance to him and to me. Surely Charlotte will write to me for Father's sake. I put in a line to beg her to do so; For Father's sake and also for y[ou]r own; for when he becomes so anxious he constantly insists upon my writing to you (he must hear f[ro]m you he must see you) and I am sure hearing occasionally would soothe him.——— I wrote you of letters received from poor Hayne. I have given up all hope of ever seeing him, but I wish John and Rachel were gone. They might be in time to see him and that would be some comfort to him; and that *he* should be comforted is all that I think of; not for myself[71]———

71. "Our poor Hayne . . . received his death blow in Florence. He was attacked with a dreadful haemorrage of the lungs, which threatened him with immediate death on the 10th of Dec[ember] last; but he partially recovered, and lingered on till the 14th of August last. My Langdon was with him, sent by his Uncle Langdon who was not able to leave, on account of my Father's health and other circumstances. My other brother John with his family went to Europe, but did not arrive in time. We had been kept in the dark as to poor Hayne's state by the loss of important letters in the Pacific, that was lost; which told us his case was hopeless; the next only said he was better, and able to sit up, and ride out if the weather became milder; and he wrote quite cheerfully himself; so that we began to think he would come back to us." Sophia Cheves Haskell to Eleuthera Du Pont, Nov. 11, 1856, Langdon Cheves III Papers, SCHS. The "other circumstances" alluded to were that LSM, on account

You will give the enclosed to Charlotte if you have no objection but read it first and beg her to write me a few lines——

Dear Brother, always

Your affectionate Sister
Louisa S. McCord

Source: Langdon Cheves I Papers, SCHS.

To Langdon Cheves, Jr.

Dear Langdon [Columbia] May 5th [1856]

If I were to send you all poor dear Father's messages I would do nothing but write, for he sends them hourly; but he has so often and earnestly petitioned for this one that I must beg some answer. Any answer will do[,] you know; and you can change if needful with circumstances. He wishes to know when he is likely to see you. He thinks he has a hundred important communications to make and a period for an interview must be fixed. I have told him that you expect to come up in six or eight weeks; but he says I don't know what I am talking about and wishes to know from *y[ou]rself.* It is not easy (perhaps from want of tact in me) to make him believe that I have received a letter or a message which I have not got. I can change but not quite invent. Do therefore[,] if not writing yourself, beg Charlotte to say that *you intend to see him in 4, or 6, or 8 weeks* (just as you please[;] only fix a time) and when the time comes, if you cannot come, only write to put off a little longer, and so on to soothe him. He has got worse than ever about houses, and localities; and wants to see you about all sorts of imaginary purchases and residences which he supposes himself to have made. Of course in all this you can do nothing; but naming a time when you expect to see him will confirm my words and help to quiet him. A message by Charlotte will do, and will trouble you less than to write.

I hope John and Rachel have started for Europe.[72]

Dear Langdon I trust I am not troubling you much——

Y[ou]r affectionate Sister
Louisa S. McCord

Addressed: Langdon Cheves, Jr. Esq. *Source:* Langdon Cheves I Papers, SCHS.

---

of her threatened eyesight and that of her son, was compelled to resign to her brother Langdon the care of their father, while she and her family departed to spend the summer in the North.

72. John Richardson Cheves was still in New York at least until July 13, 1856.

To Langdon Cheves, Jr.

Dear Langdon — Columbia May 17th, 1856

In writing to Charlotte (today is a week) I mentioned (begging her to tell you) that Father seemed very weak etc. He is much better again and seems wonderfully to recover from these periods of prostration. He is now tolerably well again, though much troubled in mind, unhappy and restless. His total inability to rise from his chair or to walk even a few steps is a great privation to him. I had a large chair made for him with wheels, which pleased him only for a few days and I have as yet been unable to get a carriage for him in which he can ride. I hope to have one soon as it is now more than 2 months since Mr. Huger ordered one for me and Father seems to wish for it very much.——I have promised him that you will come up to see him some time next month (say the 20th). Of course there is no business to see him about; but he thinks there is, and speaks every day of his wish to see you and counting the time to your coming. I shall keep to the 20th June unless you wish me to say some other time. I presume you are now very soon leaving your plantation. You or Charlotte must please let me know where you are for I *must* hear from you sometimes. Charlotte's letters have helped me very much.

I hope you are all quite well. Believe me dear Langdon

Your affectionate Sister
Louisa S. McCord

Source: Langdon Cheves I Papers, SCHS.

To James Henley Thornwell

Dear Sir — [Columbia? July 1856]

I take the liberty of sending you the half of an article nearly finished when interrupted by my failure of sight.[73] I hope little by little, as I get better to finish the copying of the remainder

My eyes forbid me many words. I will therefore only say that I do not expect this article to suit you but send it lest publishing elsewhere without doing so might look like a discourteous attack. I hope you will not for one instant hesitate to reject it as I *expect you to do,* but return it as soon as you

73. See *PSE,* "Slavery and Political Economy," responding to [George Frederick Holmes], "Slavery and Freedom," *SQR,* n. s., 1 (April 1856): 62–95. James Henley Thornwell (1812–62), Presbyterian clergyman; professor and (1851–55) president at South Carolina College; professor (from 1855) at Presbyterian Theological Seminary in Columbia; editor of the *Southern Quarterly Review* (1856–57).

please. Some trifling erasures will suit it for De Bow's review which will I know be glad to have it.

Should it by possibility suit your judgment which I pray you to remember, *I do not expect,* I can send you the remainder probably in a few weeks, in full time for your Nov[ember] number. My indisposition has prevented my having it some weeks since—

I am dear Sir, with the truest respect and most sincerely

Yours etc.
Louisa S. McCord

Source: James Henley Thornwell Papers, SCL.

To Langdon Cheves, Jr.

Dear Brother Columbia Dec[ember] 18th [1856]

I wrote to you yesterday about June—I find there are obstacles preventing his remaining in the Guard House, as I wrote you that he would, and I send him down by this even[in]g's cars to Charleston, to be placed in the Work House in care of Messrs. Capers and Heyward to whom I have written desiring them to *keep him for ten days subject to your order,* and at the end of that time, (failing to receive instructions from you) to sell him to *leave the State* and in such manner as to prevent his return.[74]———

This is a painful business to me, but my life ~~and~~ or that of my children may depend upon proper action and I cannot hesitate.

Always, dear Langdon

Your affectionate Sister
Louisa S. McCord

Should it be desired that June's wife (who I think he cares nothing about) and child should go with him, only write me at once, and I will send them down.

Source: Langdon Cheves I Papers, SCHS.

To Langdon Cheves, Jr.

Dear Brother Columbia Dec[ember] 20th, 1856

You have doubtless before this rec[eive]d my two letters concerning June. I beg you to do in ~~it wh~~ the business what you think best. I have no wish to receive one cent for him;—Only I must never see him again. His wife and

74. Capers and Heyward was an auction house and commission merchant firm located on the south side of Adger's Wharf, Charleston; owned by Thomas Farr Capers and Thomas Savage Heyward.

child are with me and subject to your orders, should you deem it desirable to send them with him. It is absolutely necessary for me to go to my pla~~ce~~ntation early next week. Should you wish therefore to give any immediate order concerning the woman *write to Mr. Boyd*.[75] I have not spoken to her to know whether she has any wish on the subject. She is behaving quietly.— I wrote you that I directed Capers and Heyward to hold June subject to y[ou]r order for ten days. This gives you time to direct any thing or to prolong the time indefinitely as you may desire. I want to put the thing off my mind; it makes me sick.——I will not write about it again unless in answer to anything from you.——

Father is perfectly quiet and composed. Boyd shaves him, drives him, assists in dressing him and not the slightest objection is made. This confirms my previous suspicion that for some reason June kept up the excitement of his mind in order to have his own way with him. Perhaps I am wrong, but unless accounted for in some such way, the change is singularly sudden.——Father is evidently and constantly failing gradually. This cold weather would be against him, but *four* large fires constantly kept up in his house keep it comfortable even for him.——

I must go to my plantation on Tuesday if possible, and if possible remain there for 2 or 3 weeks. Father is doing so well with Boyd that I will leave him more willingly than I could ~~have done under any~~ have done under any other circumstances.

I will need more money. What I draw f[ro]m Frazer and Co. is by no means sufficient. I have to draw more largely than I can afford on my own factor, but I will not bother you with this now. I will write again if I do not see you by some time in January. I know of no immediate necessity for y[ou]r coming up, only if you should come before I leave Lang Syne I would come to meet you. But there is really no need for you to come——

Affect[ionate]ly L. S. McCord—

Source: Langdon Cheves I Papers, SCHS.

75. "When we landed in New York [Oct. 26, 1859] . . . a letter [came] from Uncle Dulles begging [LSM] to come to Philadelphia to see after a Mr. [Boyd], formerly a nurse employed during the last year of my grandfather's life. . . . He was a plain man, but cultivated and educated in the most remarkable manner, entirely from reading. There was nothing the man would not read, or could not talk about—well and modestly, and all in his sweet Scotch dialect. Often Mamma would insist on his sitting with us and would draw him out to talk, while, of course, he had the run of the Library. . . . He had been struck on the head by a violent patient [in an asylum in California]—was blind, paralysed, and gradually losing his mind. His one idea seemed to be to get back to Columbia and to us, and he had actually got as far as Philadelphia—but would evidently go no farther. . . . Mamma soothed and talked to him, promising him she would hurry home and arrange his room, and move him just as soon as it was possible. But it never was possible." Smythe, p. 37.

To Langdon Cheves, Jr.

Dear Langdon Lang Syne Fort Motte January 7th, 1857

Your's of 23d Ult. was forwarded to me here. I cannot regret my dismissal of June. It pains me to think of on *his* account, but I had no alternative. He had become really dangerous for me and mine. My man Ben is still much the worse of the treatment rec[eive]d f[ro]m him and indeed will I presume always be the worse for it.——As regards Father, there is nothing to regret. I enclose you two letters from Boyd which will shew you that he is doing better than he did with June.——I will return to Columbia in a week. I ~~will~~ have got a new Overseer who seems to "take hold" well and I must hope to get on tolerably. The last year has been a most disastrous one to me in every way.

I hope y[ou]r thrashing machine and all else is doing well with you. With love to all y[ou]r family I am dear Brother, always

and most affectionately y[ou]rs
Louisa S. McCord

Source: Langdon Cheves I Papers, SCHS.

To Langdon Cheves, Jr.

Dear Brother Columbia Jan[uar]y 29th, 1857

I wrote you some 2 weeks since a long letter which I fear has by irregular mails, failed to reach you. I cannot write over as my eyes suffered f[ro]m doing too much. I only repeat the principal point which is that I need money—I said that the past year (Doctor etc. paid) leaves me *minus* some 700 dollars. Each day some new expense occurs. Yesterday I bought a chair (absolutely needful) 40 dollars—Today shingles and carpenters employed to stop very great leak in Sandhill house etc. etc. Something perpetually——I am sorry to trouble you now but I really need money—Of ~~13000~~ $1300, set aside to pay for mules and bacon, I am now more than $700 deficient and am expecting my accounts daily without means of paying them. I never ~~go into~~ run up accounts and pay for Father, as myself, immediately on purchase—Won't you please give me an order on Fraser and Co. for $700 at least. If you make it more, I will keep as close an account as possible and credit with it. But $2000 a year is entirely insuficient for Father's expenses at present. You know Boyd was not with him when I made my estimate last year. Now it is boarding 2 instead of one in ~~the~~ a very expensive manner and at enormous prices. It will take (if I mistake not) $3000, besides Boyd's salary payable July next. I receive now only $500 quarterly. *What I ask for now is needed to pay up extra expenses of the past year. I am already going further in advance for extra expenses of this year.* I am sorry to trouble you but really need money. My arrangements are regularly made for the year, but I counted on this payment to enable me to meet present calls——

Father continues well as usual. There is a gradual decay (greater continually) of remaining faculties; but in bodily health no apparent deterioration, except in so far as greater helplessness may be so called. He still rides out in suitable weather. Has in no way suffered from the late cold; indeed, owing to constant large fires all through his house, has not felt it, and has a regular and even more than usually large appetite. He is perfectly calm of late and complains of nothing.[76]——

I hope you all keep well and that you are getting over y[ou]r plantation difficulties which I have heard of with much regret. With love to y[ou]r household, I am dear Brother always, though I have to plague you sometimes,

Y[ou]r anxiously affectionate Sister
Louisa S. McCord

Source: Langdon Cheves I Papers, SCHS.

To Langdon Cheves, Jr.

Columbia Feb[ruar]y 5th, 1857

My dear good Brother, you are one of the best people in the world, but you cannot write letters. I am really getting embarassed for want of funds, and have determined to write to Fraser and Co. I give below a copy of my letter. I know you have had, and perhaps still have, a deal of trouble, and I do not blame you at all for not writing about my little wants; only I can't do without money and I hope you will not be displeased with what I have done.——Father keeps quite well; only as he becomes more and more helpless, needs constantly more and more attention and appliances for comfort. He is with his full weight and size, helpless almost as an infant. Love to you and yours—

Dear Brother, always

Your affectionate Sister
Louisa S. McCord

76. "I was with Mrs. McCord yesterday. . . . [She] is still suffering but in a mitigated degree from her eyes. Judge Cheves is better[,] that is[,] he has sunken from his condition of worrying unreliability into one of infantile imbecility[,] a phase of dotage less oppressive and distressing." William Campbell Preston to Francis Lieber, March 6, 1857, Francis Lieber Papers, Huntington.

Copy

Messrs. J[oh]n Fraser and Co—

Gentlemen, Columbia Feb[ruar]y 5th, 1857

I have written to my Brother for funds needed for my Father, but in the multiplicity of business at present accumulated upon him, he has failed to answer me, and as I begin to be a little inconvenienced, I take the liberty of applying at once to you—I think there can be no doubt that my Brother will fully approve of my drawing upon you for what I need—I find myself in arrears for the past year and beginning of this, nearly $1000, and for this sum wish to draw upon you as soon as permissable. If you see no reason against receiving my order, I will draw upon you about this day week, (say Thursday 12th Inst.) for One Thousand Dollars ($1000). The delay will give you time to let my Brother know of my intention (I myself write to him this morning) and should he not object, I think I may take his silence for consent—

For the future I must beg you to have an understanding with him that I may draw upon you to a larger amount than hitherto; the sum which I fixed last year having proved entirely inadequate. I think it would be best to leave it discretionary with me to draw as I need. But it will be equally satisfactory to me to draw quarterly $750, besides the salary of my Father's attendant which is $600 due in July next—

Hoping to be excused for the liberty I take in thus applying to you, I am gentlemen

With great etc. and very truly y[ou]rs etc.
Louisa S. McCord

Source: Langdon Cheves I Papers, SCHS.

Receipt of Payment

$450 Columbia June 2~~6~~5, 1857

Rec[eive]d paym[en]t from L. Cheves Jr. four hundred and fifty dollars by draft of this date charged to acc[ount] of Hon. L. Cheves—being in full for money advanced for the use of said Hon. L. Cheves[.]

Louisa S. McCord[77]

Source: Langdon Cheves I Papers, SCHS.

77. Signature alone in LSM's hand; the rest in the hand of Langdon Cheves, Jr.

To Langdon Cheves, Jr.

Fort Motte S[outh] C[arolina]
My dear Brother Lang Syne Dec[ember] 26th, 1857

Y[ou]rs of 19th was forwarded to me hither. I am glad to hear of y[ou]r safe return. As regards John (cook) I wrote to Anna because I understood last spring that she would probably be glad to have him for a cook and I supposed such might be his best destination. He is a good fellow, perfectly orderly and anxious to do right, but has a great dread of being put to field work, for which indeed he is entirely unfit. He wishes to remain in Columbia and I would gladly permit him to do so, only in case of my prolonged absence they might need assistance where there would be no one to attend to them—

I can of course do nothing until my return home and then must give his employer I suppose a week's warning at least and a little while for his *own* preparation. It would probably be February before I could send him off. If you wish me to send him as you say, you must therefore write to me in the course of the next month giving me *the address of Ravenel and Co.* as ~~they~~ John etc. would not know where to go when they got to Charleston.[78] John who is an excellent fellow has very little knowledge what to do, so soon as he gets out of the kitchen, and would need very particular directions.——You tell me also to send papers of importance. What kind of papers do you mean? I know of none except a bundle which I gave you and which you told me to take care of till called for. I cannot look over these as my eyes continue almost useless, but will send the packet if you wish. If you mean acc[oun]ts still due I know of none but Dr. Powell's, and Bowers' which last was sent to me some time since, but to which, being away from home, I paid no attention.[79]

If you wish John sent down please tell me about what funds I shall furnish him with; whether only to Charleston or through; and how much, if through.

There is another subject I would call to y[ou]r attention before a settlement of the affairs of the estate. One of the last things which Father seemed anxious about before his health failed, was that attention should be paid to the erection of three tomb-stones or monuments of some kind, over his

78. Ravenel and Company, commission merchants and factors, was located at 16 East Bay Street, Charleston, throughout the 1850s. William Ravenel was senior partner, others of his family being associated in the business with him.

79. In the *Columbia City Directory* of 1859, George S. Bowers, owner of a furniture store at 218 Richardson Street, advertises "funerals served at short notice." His bill for burial expenses, dated June 26, 1857, is extant in the Langdon Cheves I Papers, SCHS.

Mother's grave in Abbeville and our Mother's and Aunt Lovell's on this place. He delayed it, either because he intended something ~~handsome~~ more handsome than I think desirable, or because as I believe, he thought the expense greater than it really is. There is I know no legal obligation to the erection of these, but Father was very anxious that it should be done and indeed had told me to attend to it; when new troubles caused the state of health which prevented further action. I know that Anna is as anxious as myself that this matter should be attended to, and of course Sophia will not object to it. $500 (about) will cover the expense of all three. I think it ought to be immediately attended to, and if you will furnish the means from the estate I will have the two here attended to at once. Doubtless Sophia will see to that in Abbeville.

I shall return to Columbia early in January (5th or 6th) and hope to hear from you there and then, if not sooner.

Give my love to Charlotte and the children—and believe me always, my dear Brother

Y[ou]r affectionate Sister
Louisa S. McCord

Source: Langdon Cheves I Papers, SCHS.

To Langdon Cheves, Jr.

Dear Brother Columbia Feb[ruar]y 5th, 1858

I thank you much for y[ou]r kind letter rec[eive]d yesterday; which I must answer as laconically as possible as my vision continues painfully perplexed, I hope temporarily, but—

There are several large boxes of papers which I had forgotten locked up in my store-room. I regret that I can do nothing to assist in over-look[in]g but will send if I can. I think Pinckney, perhaps y[ou]rself, will be in Charleston this month—If you will write me *when* and *how to meet him* I can probably get Cheves to take them down—He is indisposed just now, but I hope not to last.

I regret to learn that there is any doubt as to construction of Father's will in disposition of negroes which in justice ought to go to all the heirs alike. If any testimony as to evident intention of the testator can be of use I am ready to give mine that the residuary clause was considered as nothing. The last time I read over Father's will to him, he remarked of that clause to the effect that it could cover nothing but his clothing and trifling personal effects—The proceeds of crops up to 1860 were intended to equalize his daughters with sons to whom he considered he had given the larger share. He never contemplated the calamity which has left a larger residue and there could be no equity in a decision which[,] after all had been carefully equalized[,] would throw so large an advantage on one side certainly in opposition to thc whole intention of the Testator when the will was drawn—If it is a case for witnesses, summon me—I am quite willing to appear anywhere and do what is right in spite of blind eyes and straw flats pulled over them.——

Pinckney will see to getting the slabs ~~of~~ for which I applied. I thank you both for attention to my application.

I hope you will get the railing—Has anything been done about Father's bust and intended monument? I *must* go to Europe next summer. I only want advice as to best time of going etc.—probably in June. If I could do anything while there to order the desired work I would be very glad—I could easily get letters f[ro]m Preston here, which would make Powers exert himself to do well what is required if put in his hands[80]—If I can do anything let me know. It will do me good to have some objects before me. I *must* go and for a year at least——

I think I have done, dear Brother—*Do not forget to write* if you wish papers sent to Charleston. I can send *Cheves* or a *careful servant*. Only say *when and where*.

Love to all—

Y[ou]r affectionate Sister
Louisa S. McCord

I send receipts (enclosed) of Dr. Powell and Bowers—

Source: Langdon Cheves I Papers, SCHS.

To Langdon Cheves, Jr.

Dear Brother — Columbia March 23d, 1858

In the letter you wrote me some two months since, you spoke of North Eastern Rail-Road Bonds and $15,000 in cash which as *residue* you would soon be ready to "turn over" to my sisters and self—I wish you would let

80. Hiram Powers (1805–73), sculptor; born in Woodstock, Vt.; studied in Cincinnati before moving to Washington, D.C., in 1834, among his works there being busts of Andrew Jackson, John Marshall, John C. Calhoun, Martin Van Buren, and William Campbell Preston; in October 1836 met John Smith Preston, who offered patronage with which Powers established a studio in Florence in 1837, its fame decorated by visits from the grand duke and grand duchess of Tuscany and from travelers like Nicholas I of Russia; the *Greek Slave* (1843) was his greatest public success; his son Preston Powers was named for William Campbell Preston, to whom LSM suggests here that she may apply for letters to the sculptor.

me know *when* this is likely to be. I have (hoping against hope for the restoration of my sight) determined as a last effort to try a year in Europe. My expenses will be enormous for my means, and I have also liabilities to meet before going which necessitate the drawing in of some of my vested funds. I can only fix the extent of this by knowing what I may expect from you.

I am sorry to trouble you as you dislike writing so much; but I am very ignorant of business and having nobody to help me, stumble along very blunderingly. And of course I want to know all I can to fix my affairs as well as I can (stupidly it must be at best) before I can leave home.———

As regards Estate papers, I still hope to see you before I go~~, but should I be dis~~. I hope you may find time to come up here; but should I be disappointed shall I leave *all* papers with my servants where you can get them?———

Please answer me dear Brother soon. I am vastly bothered in my lonely and helpless condition, and do all sorts of blundering things that I suffer by. And as to Lawyers' help! If I only look at the tip end of the nose of one, he makes me pay fifty Dollars.———

With kind love to y[ou]r family one and all, I am always

Y[ou]r affectionate Sister
Louisa S. McCord

If Anna is with you still, do tell her I will write in a day or two—I can only manage a few lines at a time. If she receives a *big* letter f[ro]m me to Pinckney, she will be so good as to take care of it. It is only ~~a copy of~~ my Will.

Source: Langdon Cheves I Papers, SCHS.

To Langdon Cheves, Jr.

My dear Brother — Columbia April 3d, 1858

I have this moment rec[eive]d y[ou]r letter. John's course distresses and surprises me. The property given by Father to his daughters (particularly Anna and myself (Sophia rec[eive]d something in Texas lands)[)] was so *very much less* than that given to his Sons that I could never have anticipated opposition from any of them in the execution of an intention so plainly expressed as his is, however the *law* may possibly throw it aside. In my own case, my shattered health and injured property resulting from devotion to Heim,[81] when none other (but y[ou]rself) could or would assist, I never expected to be paid for; but it seems hard that this should be the end of it. I did not

81. "Home" in German.

expect it of John. Were I a pious Christian, I would say "God forgive him!" As it is I can but *try* to forgive him myself——I trust at least that in the disputing the will there is no disrespect to Father's memory. I will try to say no more and to think as little of it as possible.——

I must beg you to write to me once more dear Brother and speedily. First as regards the papers—You tell me to send to Ravenel and Co. Is such the direction? Simply "*Messrs. Ravenel and Co.*"? Are there not other Ravenels and ought I not to designate these more clearly for fear of mistake? Please answer *immediately* dear Brother. I am anxious to do what is right—will have all boxed up and only wait y[ou]r answer to send them off. I would send them tomorrow, but fear doing wrong without definite directions as to address.

I must also beg you to tell me from whom shall I receive the R.R. Bonds and the funds of which you have ordered distribution? Will anybody write to me? or must I write to somebody?

I do not think now that I can go to Europe until July *if at all.* My very limited income would not nearly suffice to meet my necessarily enormous expense in such an expedition. I had counted principally upon the yearly income which I knew Father had left me until 1861. I thought I could spend *that,* and still take my share with the other heirs. Under present circumstances it is very doubtful what I ought to do—As it is a life and death struggle with me, I ~~must sti~~ may still try to go. But even should I determine to do so, I must take time to consider how and to what extent I must gather funds for the purpose. I must try and see you or Pinckney before I can see my way—It is a sad thing to be as helpless as I am. But I will not bother you, for I know you are plagued enough—

Only dear Brother answer me the two questions. *How shall I direct the papers?* and *from whom shall I receive R.R. Bonds and the $5000?* The latter, I particularly need, to meet engagements already contracted—Answer me now, dear Brother, only two lines will do—

Your always affectionate Sister
Louisa S. McCord

The Sandhill house here, which *was given me by Father during his life,* and which was killing me with its drunken vicinage, I have *sold* or rather *thrown away* and it *cannot be recalled.*[82] If I am to be broke up for it. They must come after me; that is all—

Source: Langdon Cheves I Papers, SCHS.

82. The Sandhill house was specifically bequeathed to LSM in her father's will.

To Langdon Cheves, Jr.

Dear Brother Columbia April 4, 1858

I wrote to you yesterday, but must do so again. I am very unhappy about John's intention. On what ground opposition to the Will should be made, I cannot imagine. Surely the death of on[e] Legatee cannot invalidate the paper as regards others. I am as fairly a Legatee in that will (though to a less extent) as was poor Hayney—And yet it is not the loss of property (although ill-fitted to bear it) which so much distresses me; but rather the bitter scandal of such a dispute. In God's name, why can we not take the will as it is worded up to 1860 and then let the whole be divided as of right, among the heirs[?] The negroes ought not to go as residue. You know I have already protested against that; and perhaps it is the possibility of that which has irritated John. I have just written to John to propose such a compromise i.e. That my sisters and self should receive the proceeds given to us (*and no more*) up to 1860 inclusive, and the estate then be divided as of right among the heirs. I feel sure that both Mr. Haskell and Huger would acquiesce in this. At least let it be proposed. Let it be tried! Dear Brother let it be tried!——I would give up every thing sooner than have a disgraceful squabble over what our dear Father has left; but I suggest only this much because it could not fairly be asked of Mr. Haskell and Huger to do more—

Do write to me. I have a right to know on what ground John, if continuing bases his opposition to the Will. *What plea does he bring to invalidate it? When is the case to be brought forward? Who is his Lawyer?* and *who the Lawyer in defense?*——

I have written to Messrs. Ravenel and Co. asking their address. So soon as I hear if the letter is rec[eive]d I will forward the papers. If it be not received it will prove the address wrong and I must wait to hear f[ro]m you—

Dear Brother always

Most affectionately
Y[ou]r Sister
Louisa S. McCord

I have this instant rec[eive]d notice of R.R. Bonds f[ro]m Messrs. Ravenel and Co. and presume will soon receive similar notice of funds—As I now know their address, I will have the papers boxed tomorrow and send on Tuesday——

Source: Langdon Cheves I Papers, SCHS.

To Langdon Cheves, Jr.

Dear Brother Columbia April 23d, 1858

You have been so kind in writing to me lately. I should have thanked you sooner for y[ou]r last, but have been quite sick lately and am only just getting about as usual, again.

Please throw into the fire the note I enclosed for John. If I have given no offense and done no harm, I am very glad, and so let it end. I will say nothing and do nothing more in the case. As I can do nothing to help you, I will at least do nothing to trouble you and so am done. Only (perhaps you will laugh at my warning) beware of Mr. H[askell]—I have had business connections with him off and on, for Seven and Twenty years, and I think I know him. If the valuation of what has been rec[eive]d by him and myself is ever required, you will be surprised to find how ~~small it~~ much smaller it will be than you probably suppose. It is *really* smaller than you would think (for both he and myself have striven hard and with great economy and probably with good management) but I fear that it can be made to appear *legally* smaller that it *justly* is; and you may depend upon it, his conscience will bate no tittle of what is "*in the bond*".[83] Excuse my saying this much. If we ever meet, and you think it worth while, I can explain in detail ~~what~~ more than I ~~cannot~~ can write. And so, (turn up what may), farewell to the subject, once and forever, until I am called out by somebody else.——

I regret to hear by an "*On dit,*" that y[ou]r little boy has been seriously sick. I trust it may not be true, and that he and all y[ou]r family are thriving. Will any of you be in Charleston soon? I must go down for business in May or very early June, and would be glad to meet you.——Thanks for y[ou]r suggestion of getting Lieber's help in engaging passages. It was too late for me however, as I had a day or two before written to Heatly Dulles to do it for me. He will do it kindly and I dare say very well, though Lieber would doubtless know more about it. I have written for Heatly to take my passage in Cunard Steamer of 7th July.——

83. *Merchant of Venice* 4.1.253–58: "*Portia.* Have by some surgeon Shylock on your charge, / To stop his wounds, lest he do bleed to death. / *Shylock.* Is it so nominated in the bond? / *Portia.* It is not so express'd, but what of that? / 'Twere good you do so much for charity. / *Shylock.* I cannot find it, 'tis not in the bond." Also *Coriolanus* 2.2.139–41: "Sir, the people / Must have their voices; neither will they bate / One jot of ceremony"; John Milton, "Sonnet XXII: To Mr. Cyriak Skinner upon His Blindness," ll. 6–8: "Yet I argue not / Against heav'n's hand or will, nor bate a jot / Of heart or hope."

Give my love to all y[ou]r family and with hopes that all are doing well, and the little man thriving in spite of ill reports, I am dear Brother,

Always and most truly

Your affectionate Sister
Louisa S. McCord

Source: Langdon Cheves I Papers, SCHS.

Deposition before the Equity Court of Appeals, Charleston District

The Answer of Louisa S. McCord, who is impleaded with Charles T. Haskell and others, to the bill of complaint of Langdon Cheves, Executor of the Honorable Langdon Cheves, deceased.[84]

This defendant not excepting to the frame or form of the said Bill, for answer thereunto, says: That it is true that her father, the Honorable Langdon Cheves, advanced all his children, except his youngest son, with portions corresponding to the amount of his estate, and this defendant in fact says, that he provided at an early period for his daughters, and if his means had been so restricted as to prevent him from providing suitably for all his children, he would have abridged the portions of his sons, rather than leave his daughters without a competency, for it was a cherished opinion with him, that the want of fortune was not so great a hardship to young men as to the weaker sex. But his circumstances improved with years, and after providing for his daughters, he was able to gratify his generous mind by giving to each of his sons a settled plantation. But the plantation which he gave to his son John was far less valuable than those which he afterwards gave to his sons Langdon and Charles; and as this defendant has been informed, he made a subsequent addition to said portion in land and money. That the Testator designed to divide his estate among his children equitably, but he did not mean an arithmetical equality, nor intend to have his estate scattered and sold for their satisfaction as creditors. That he did not intend, as

84. Robert Hayne Cheves having died before his father, who was however by that time incompetent to write a new will, and Hayne being at his death unmarried, childless, and leaving no will of his own, the question arose how the legacies made to Hayne in his father's will—a plantation on the Ogeechee River in Georgia, together with the plantation's property and slaves, and a sum in cash—should be distributed. Charles Haskell, acting for his wife, argued that Hayne Cheves' legacies ought to be understood as residuary property, which property, according to Langdon Cheves' will (dated Nov. 6, 1854), was to be divided among his three daughters. But Langdon Cheves, Jr., his father's executor, held that Hayne's legacies should be regarded as intestate property, hence to be distributed equally among all the heirs under his father's will. See Pease, *James Louis Petigru,* pp. 103–5.

this defendant has good reason to know, that strangers should be called in to value his estate for the purposes of partition, but chose to take that duty into his own hands, and to make such a partition as he thought proper. This defendant admits that he made his will as stated in complainant's bill, in furtherance of the scheme which he had partly executed. That his youngest son was then abroad traveling for pleasure and improvement, without any experience of ill health, and the Testator retained the portion intended for him. That he made his will as stated in the bill, and created a trust for the benefit of his daughters out of the portion ultimately intended for his youngest son. And when he had done this, he conceived that he had done ample justice by his daughters, and made an equitable distribution among his children. That after making his will his mind decayed. That his son, Charles Cheves, died, an event which deeply affected him; and then, his son, Robert Hayne, was struck in a foreign country with symptoms of a rapid consumption, and never returned home. This defendant admits that her father was an inmate of her house when the intelligence was received that Robert Hayne's health was dangerously affected, and that she did not communicate it to him, but intentionally kept the same from his knowledge. That she did this under medical advice, and because in his then state of health he was incapable of any exertion which the case might call for. That the said Robert Hayne lingered about eight months, and then died in Italy, and his father survived him nearly a year, and died leaving his will in full force. This defendant does not doubt that he would have altered his will if he had been of ability to do so, and she knows that he did not at any time suppose that the fortune of his youngest son, if added to the portion of his daughters, would tend to promote equality or be an equitable distribution. This defendant hopes that those views which confine the residue bequeathed to the daughters, to matters not before mentioned by Testator, will prevail as being in consonance with the law, as they are in fact with his intentions, and that the reversionary and residuary interest of her said brother, will be distributed among the heirs of the Testator as in case of intestacy. Such distribution being, she believes, nothing more than justice to her brothers. All which matters and things this defendant is ready and willing to aver, maintain, and prove, as this Honorable Court shall direct, and prays to be hence dismissed with her reasonable costs.

Petigru and King,[85]
Def[en]d[an]t[']s Sol[i]c[ito]rs

85. James Louis Petigru's partner Henry Campbell King (d. 1862) was the son of Charleston lawyer Mitchell King and husband of Petigru's daughter, novelist Susan DuPont Petigru King.

State of South Carolina,
Charleston District.

Personally appeared before me, Mrs. Louisa S. McCord, who being duly sworn, deposes that the matters and things in the foregoing answer contained, so far as they depend on her own knowledge, are just and true; and so far as they are derived from the information of others, she believes them to be so.

Louisa S. McCord

Sworn to before me, this twenty-first day of May, A.D. 1858.

Henry C. King, Magistrate.

Filed 21st May, 1858.

Source: Printed copy, Langdon Cheves I Papers, SCHS.

To Langdon Cheves, Jr.

Dear Brother, Columbia May 26th, 1858

I am just returned (last night) from Charleston *via* my plantation. Mr. Petigru called upon me here, and again several times in Charleston. I needed, he informed me, a solicitor and he is to act for me. I have told him all I can to prove, (what I am perfectly certain of,) that Father not only never intended, but would never have knowingly permitted the possibility of such a claim as this residuary Legacy now asked for. I wanted to give my testimony, but Mr. Haskell's Lawyer objects to my doing so. They object, I presume, to my speaking out the truth. I have left with Mr. Petigru my answer to the Bill in Equity filed for you. I have done all that he advised and I suppose all that can be done; but if I can do any thing more to make justice prevail, I must beg you as *a favor to me,* to let me know. The whole affair is very painful to me; but it is nobody's fault but Mr. Haskell's. I can only hope that it will be decided as it should be;—And to relieve myself from the embarrassment of apparently conniving at, and profiting by what I consider an unjust and disgraceful proceedure (whether or not the law sanctions it) I beg as a *personal favor to myself* to be informed if any thing I can do will be useful in bringing about the proper result.——

I must trouble you also dear Brother, with another subject. The apparant neglect of Father's grave has become an object of remark. Friends unconnected with the family, both here and in Charleston, have spoken to me on the subject, and I know that it is talked about. If the lot were enclosed with a railing, and perhaps a temporary slab, these would come under Estate business and would prevent the appearance of neglect which, I confess, pained me very much, on my visiting it lately. I know *you* cannot attend to this; but Pinckney Huger or Mr. Ravenel would I am sure promptly attend to anything of the kind if you will only authorize it. It ought to be done, without delay, dear Brother—please authorize some one to do it. People talk about it more than you think, and the look of neglect is greater than you think. A railing, if nothing else, would be a great relief.——

I wrote to you last Winter to know if I could be of any assistance in procuring the final monument intended. In doing so, I named Powers, simply because my intimacy with Preston procures me the highest interest with him and such introduction as would make him do his best; but if you would wish it in *any other hands,* I would be glad to be useful in the matter; and as I intend stopping at Washington for a few days, I could doubtless get a letter to *any* sculptor whom you might name, and would do my best to effect what might be desirable. If you will permit me to do anything, please write to me and give me any directions. Tell me who (if any one) you would wish me to apply to; and I know I can, before I sail, get a letter, or whatever may be needed. Only please write soon; for I expect to leave Columbia about *June 18th,* and would probably receive nothing coming after that date—I have taken *passages* for 7th July but will need to take time between this and New York in some little preparations.——Forgive my bothering you this time; I will be gone soon now and out of the way of plaguing you for a whole year.

I hope you have left y[ou]r plantation long before this. Anna tells me she believes you stop, at least temporarily in Savannah—

I saw y[ou]r girls in Charleston looking nice and lady-like. Give my love to Charlotte and the little Boy and believe me, dear Brother, always

Your affectionate Sister
Louisa S. McCord

You will, I know, write once before I leave—Remember I leave *here 18th June.*——

Source: Langdon Cheves I Papers, SCHS.

To Langdon Cheves, Jr.

Dear Brother New York July 7th, 1858

I have waited and hoped to hear from you, but must give up hope now. I must be off unless the indisposition ~~(illness~~ of one of my party who has been ill all night, prevents it. It is a little doubtful what the next hour may decide. I have had much difficulty already and am almost ready to give up. If we go, it must be presently. And so, IF I go, Goodbye—I feel very sad that you have not written to me. Perhaps you will write to me to Liverpool. My address is to the care of

Messrs. Stuart and Warry
No. 1 Rumford Place
Liverpool.

I am sadly disappointed at not hearing here. Love to all y[ou]r family. I hope they are well—

Most truly, dear Brother

Your affectionate Sister
Louisa S. McCord

If you write to me (and I think you will dear Brother) answer me about the contents of my last letter. And also dear Brother if the law-case is decided, let me know the result.[86] I trust the decision is, or will be, with justice. But if the contrary, (which it will be if Mr. Haskell's claims are made good), you must help me to set it right, as far as I am personally concerned. I have no right to anything but what Father's will gives me f[ro]m the proceeds, and then one *sixth part* of poor Hayney's rights. If the law gives me more, it is by an unjust decision, and you must let me give up any thing more to *you,* and thus reinstate *you* at least in the rights of which you are defrauded. Do dear Brother, In justice only to me, help me to do this simple act of justice.

Write to me dear Langdon about my former letter. I love you so much it is hardly fair for you to throw me off—

Most affectionately and always
L. S. M——

Source: Langdon Cheves I Papers, SCHS.

To Langdon Cheves, Jr.

Dear Brother Paris Oct[ober] 30th, 1858

Not knowing how to direct to you, I enclose a few lines to Nan which ~~Nan~~ she will have the goodness I am sure to forward for me.——I have

86. "The Chancellor's decree was filed on the 1st inst; and I regret to say is entirely in favor of the case made by Mr. Haskell, so far as it is explicit, and so far as it is not explicit is very obscure." James Louis Petigru to Langdon Cheves, Jr., Charleston, Nov. 13, 1858, Langdon Cheves I Papers, SCHS. The court had found that the real estate bequeathed to Hayne Cheves in his father's will was intestate property, hence descending to all the heirs; but that the personalty bequeathed to him (which included slaves) was residuary property, thus passing to the residuary legatees (i.e., Sophia Cheves Haskell, LSM, and Anna Cheves Huger). Petigru filed an appeal on behalf of Langdon Cheves, Jr.; it was dismissed on Feb. 3, 1859. Documents relevant to the case are found in the Langdon Cheves I Papers, SCHS.

nothing that will interest you, for I travel as usual with all my shyness and want of knowing how to push, about me. Besides you have been in these regions, and already know more about them than I can tell you.——My great object in writing, is to put you in mind that I will need some communication from you on the subject of the plaster casts to be sent for Father's bust. If you hesitate about ordering it, I will take upon myself the responsibility of so doing. I think the family will generally approve, but should it displease, the result of my order can be retained by myself. This can do no harm and it will be optional with all to do as they please. This will be right; will it not dear Brother? Only now, how can I receive the casts? Where and how will you send them? Will you not write to me, my dear Brother about this? I will remain in Paris until early January (two months more) and so will have full time to hear from you, and to receive any instructions if you have any to give. I will try and do exactly as you say, and only act for myself in case *you prefer* me to put it on that footing. You will write to me I know. When you do, please direct as heretofore, care of

Messrs. Stuart and Warry
No. 1 Rumford Place
Liverpool.

Theyse gentlemen forward my letters regularly and I think it safest to get through them—

I have been a month in Paris and have not gone into ecstacies with it yet. On the contrary have a stupid longing all the time for my own chimney corner. I am in *apartemens meublés* and have my two servants with a carriage and driver which I found myself obliged to hire. I spend money (because I don't know how to manage) until it frightens me, make no acquaintances, get very tired etc. etc. My eyes, face light better than they did, but I do not think mean ever to let me use them as I wish and have been accustomed to do——My children are taking some lessons which serve to keep them amused and prevent too much home-sickness. They are as usual. Cheves does not like to talk about his eyes and I do not worry him about them. I do not think there is any change in them, or he would tell me.

Dr. Powell who came over with me returned some weeks since, being recalled by ill health in his family. I intend going to Italy in early January, and not knowing how to do better have already engaged a courier who was highly recommended to me to take care of us when we leave. I suppose he will tell me where and how I had better go first. I have not thought of any plan yet, but I will certainly (so far as such a thing can be certain) go to Florence and probably remain there two, three weeks, or a month. By hearing from you before I leave this, I will know better what to do.——

Anna writes me that you have been to North Carolina. You have I hope had a healthy summer and find your little boy improved by the change. I regretted to hear that he was delicate in the early summer——Do give my love to Charlotte and the girls. Lou would give a great deal to have Mamie and Emma with her. She needs company very much and quite misses her sister whom we left behind.——

Before this reaches America, I trust that a frost will have put an end to the Yellow Fever in Charleston and Savannah, and suppose that you will be about returning to your winter home—Hoping that all may be well with you there and with continued good wishes to you and yours, believe me dear Brother always and most affectionately

Your Sister
Louisa S. McCord

Source: Langdon Cheves I Papers, SCHS.

To Hiram Powers

Dear Sir Naples April 3d, 1859

I had hoped, as I told you, to be in Florence about 12th inst., but find that there is no steamer in which I can take passage until the 12th which will delay my arrival to the evening of 14th. Hoping for no further delay I shall be glad to find you at liesure to receive my visits, and will see you as soon as convenient after I reach your city.[87] I am Dear Sir

Very truly and respectfully yours etc.
Louisa S. McCord

Source: Hiram Powers and Powers Family Papers, Smithsonian.

To Hiram Powers

Dear Sir Civita Vecchia April 13th, 1859

I find myself here arrested in my progress by the great desire of my children to turn aside to Rome for the Holy Week. It will thus be some time

87. "It was at Florence that your Grandmother sat to Hiram Powers for the bust you know so well. She had engaged him to make a bust of her father, and she had had sent out a box of casts, photographs, etc. as material from which he could work, as she hoped to be there to assist by her recollection of her father's face; but things went wrong and the box did not get there in time. She did not like after having pre-engaged the time of such a 'big man' to throw him over, and so kept the engagement by sitting for her own bust. We were not specially pleased with it as a likeness at the time, as we thought it too hard and old; but she grew more like it with years, and now I am inexpressibly thankful for it as the only likeness at all good that we have of her. The hair is just as she always wore it—she never changed it as I can remember." Smythe, p. 30.

before I can resume my way to Florence. I will leave Rome on, (or as soon as possible after) Monday 25th Inst., and will hope to be in Florence in two days after leaving.

I trust you will excuse the apparent whimsicality of my course, which is the result of our ignorance of the ways and times of the stranger land in which we are journeying. Hoping for your forgiveness, I am Dear Sir

Most truly and very respectfully y[ou]rs
Louisa S. McCord

Source: Hiram Powers and Powers Family Papers, Smithsonian.

To Hiram Powers

Dear Sir London July 9th, 1859

I have waited so long in the expectation of hearing from my Brother, and being able to let you know something of the casts which I hoped to have forwarded to you for the execution of my Father's bust. I regret to say that I have received no word from him, and feel now that I must abandon all hope of doing so—I can only account for his silence by the fact that although a most excellent gentleman in most respects, he is an exceedingly unpunctual one, and dilatory always in letter writing. Possibly he may have forwarded the casts to you, and only neglected to write to me on the subject. If so, it is all right. If he has done nothing, I am very sorry for it, and can only apologize to you for having given you so much trouble to so little purpose. I will myself be at home, (no unforeseen accidents preventing), early in the winter and will then, should nothing be done sooner, make it a point to attend to the business, and to write to you immediately on the subject. In the mean time you must at least exhonerate me from all fault in the case, for I have written to my Brother five times on the subject, and now give up, only because I am hopeless of doing any good by continuing. Be assured that you shall hear from me immediately on my return home, and in the mean time should you have heard from my Brother, or have any reason for communicating with me, if you will take the trouble to address a few lines to me to the care of

Messrs. Stuart and Warry
No. 1 Rumford Place
Liverpool

I will probably receive it (with considerable delay) but receive it at last.——

I expected before this to have left England and returned to the continent, (for Germany and Switzerland) but have been detained for the last fortnight by the tedious tho' not dangerous sickness of my son. I hope now to be off in a few days.

Pray present my kind remembrance to Mrs. Powers and your daughters and believe me, dear Sir, with the greatest respect and very truly yours etc.

Louisa S. McCord

Source: Hiram Powers and Powers Family Papers, Smithsonian.

To Langdon Cheves, Jr.

Dear Brother Columbia Nov[ember] 9th, 1859

I am at home at last and *must see you.* If you were any body's brother but my own, I would tell you that you must come *here* to see *me,* it being impossible for me to leave my daughters (still children) alone in my house; and ridiculous to drag a whole family down for the transaction of an hour's business with you; and one hour is all that is necessary. As to paying you a visit it is at present out of the question, every thing here (after so long an absence and still longer incapacity) requiring my presence, at least for 2 or 3 months. Surely you can come up if only for one day. If you cannot, then at least, for pity's sake, write only *one line* to say when I may meet you *in Savannah,* that I may go, at least with the certainty of meeting you, and being able to return at once. If you can do nothing more, put on any scrap of paper the name of any hotel and the date where and when you can meet me. I will come down at once (unless prevented by illness or accident) and never again (I think) ask such a favor of you. There are certain things now which decency requires that I should attend to. I will not trouble you further than simply to require such information and authority as may enable me to act. To do this (as you will not write) I must see you and as soon as possible. *By return mail* therefore, I shall expect an intimation as to what day I may meet you at (say) the Pulaski Hotel (unless you prefer another) and unless you can come up here.

I hope that your family is well. I saw Mary in New York looking well and much improved. I am, dear Brother, in spite of a neglect which I cannot but feel as unkind, always and most affectionately

Your Sister
Louisa S. McCord

Source: Langdon Cheves I Papers, SCHS.

To Hiram Powers

Dear Sir Columbia—South Carolina Dec[ember] 12th, 1859

After a delay which I fear you may ~~have~~ (though mistakenly) have attributed to negligence, and after every effort on my part to obtain from my Brother the cast taken of my Father after death, I am now obliged to send you only Mills's cast.[88] My brother who is a most impracticable man in some affairs, has failed to answer a score of applications which I have made to him, and neither writes, nor sends me the cast. I have caused him to be applied to through others, and still hope for the possibility of success. I have however requested my factors in Charleston to forward to your agent in New York, without further delay, the Mills cast; (This they doubtless have, as they promised me, done by the steamer of Saturday) and should we succeed in obtaining the other it will be sent afterwards. Should it however not be received, I must beg the favor of you to do the best you can for me with the materials which I am able to furnish you. I am deeply pained at the apparent inconsistency of my conduct in this affair, which, I beg you to believe, is entirely owing to an excentricity in my Brother, of which I have had frequent previous experience, though never anything quite so marked as this. You will I am sure forgive my involuntary share in it, and do for me what you can, under the circumstances.

Will you also do me the favor to let me know, as they occur, my pecuniary obligations to you and instruct me how any transfer of funds may be made to you by my agents in Charleston (Messrs. Ravenel and Co.).

In writing to me please address to "Columbia, South Carolina."

I have seen lately our friend W[illia]m Preston who remembers you always kindly and was pleased to hear of you through me.

With my kind regards to Mrs. Powers and your daughters, believe me always, dear Sir

Yours most respectfully and truly,
Louisa S. McCord

Addressed: Hiram Powers, Esq. / Florence. *Source:* Hiram Powers and Powers Family Papers, Smithsonian.

To Hiram Powers

Dear Sir Columbia Jan[uar]y 13th, 1860

I am glad to be able to inform you that at last I have waked up my dilatory Brother to the sending of the plaster cast I have so long tried to get. It was

88. "Dec[ember] 16th [1844]. Engaged all day shopping and preparing for my journey. Spent the evening with Judge Cheves at Mrs. Rob[er]t Y[oung] Hayne, where we saw a well executed cast of her son, and we all united to solicit Judge Cheves to have his taken for his children. 17th. The Judge consented to have his bust taken and at 12 o'clock attended the artist Mr. Mills and the model was taken in the course of half an hour or so, and one bust for each child was ordered and one for Mrs. Hayne." David James McCord, "Journal of a Trip to Texas, 1844" (typescript), Dulles-Cheves-McCord-Lovell Papers, SCHS. Clark Mills (1815–83), sculptor and bronze founder; born in Onondaga County, N.Y.

a few days since, shipped by my agent in Charleston to Theodore Dehon, Esq. New York.[89] This is the cast taken after death, and is (combined with Mills's previously sent) all the guide I have to give you. The Mills cast is an unpleasant likeness defective both in feature and expression. The other (which I have never seen) will I hope aid you in correcting the features. As regards the expression you need not be told that the fire of intellect (extinct in the dead cast) can just as little be looked for in the representations of which Mills was guilty. You will need to seek it in your own genius; and I regret that I can aid you no further than by saying, that our State has produced no man of higher intellect, or greater purity, firmness and at the same time kindness of character, than my Father. You can devine what the face of such a man should say.——I have heard nothing from my Brother since seeing you and have therefore no further suggestions from him than the few lines which I left with you from a letter of his. Will you kindly remember that I have begged you to let me have for myself a life-size copy of the colossal bust made for the monument?

I hope your kindness will forgive all that may perhaps have been annoying to you in the unavoidable delays I have met with in this business; and I trust that yourself and family are happy and in good health.

A line directed to me care of *Messrs. Ravenel and Co., Charleston, South Carolina,* is, I believe the surest mode of communication with me. You will oblige me also by drawing as it may suit your convenience upon the same gentlemen for funds to meet expenses incurred in the execution of all which I have asked of you, I alone being responsible in the matter. I have forgotten who is y[ou]r Banker in Florence——

With most kind regards to your wife and daughters, I am dear Sir

with great respect
Yours very truly
Louisa S. McCord

Addressed: Hiram Powers Esq. / Florence. *Source:* Hiram Powers and Powers Family Papers, Smithsonian.

To Langdon Cheves, Jr.

Dear Brother Columbia Jan[uar]y 18th, 1860

This moment I have rec[eive]d y[ou]rs of 15th. I thought I never was going to forgive you and behold, already I can't help it.——Ravenel wrote me

89. Theodore Dehon was the banking partner of Sidney Brooks, Hiram Powers' close friend and adviser since 1843.

that the cast was sent, and I have just written to inform Powers. It is all I can do—If you will give instructions of any kind he (Powers) will be glad to receive them from you; as to you, (when I spoke to him a year since,) I referred him.

As regards the estate you must do what you think best. I have heard nothing from Mr. Haskell on the subject. As regards negroes I cannot consent to receive any more, for I am almost out of my senses with those that I have, and with my now permanently established defective vision, am entirely unfit for learning anything about planting concerns. Those that I have now, I must keep, only till Cheves is ready (which with *his* drawbacks of vision etc. will not be for years) to take them. To embarrass myself with more would be wretchedness to them and death to me.

I hope the land will go "below what you consider its value" and that you will thus want the negroes. You will find me making no difficulty or opposition to anything you think right. I am sure I will meet with justice in whatever arrangement may be made, and if you will consider y[ou]rself as authorized to act for me in the matter, you may consent to, or refuse anything in my name (except giving me negroes to take care of) according to your own judgement.——I must see somebody and get advice as to disposal of funds etc.—(I did ~~had~~ not know that you intended to sell this year) but perhaps there will be no immediate payments. *Can* you let me know if I must put myself in a flurry about it?——I feel that in the whole affair the law has done you an injustice, and if I cannot set it right, at least I shall put no impediments in your way.——I want dreadfully to see you. The Dulles family (4 in number) are staying with me and will not leave until some time in February; but I must leave them if it will do any good. I think I had better go down by 1st or 2nd February if boats etc. will take me. Can you not write a few lines only to tell me what day to come down, what boat to take (when and how) and tell me how you can get me over the river to your house[?] Do dear brother. If you will write only the few lines needful, I will come on any day you think most suitable. ~~If I come,~~ In going to you I am *entirely alone,* and so will want you to give me these few lines of information. I am as much alone here as regards all assistance in business affairs as if I were on a plank in the middle of the Atlantic, and as much bewildered with papers as a child of ten years old.[90] Write me only a few lines and I will come down any day you will name and try and settle every thing so as not to bother you to write

90. Edward Young, *The Revenge* (1721), 4.1.251–54: "Why did I leave my tender father's wing, / And venture into love? That maid that loves, / Goes out to sea upon a shatter'd plank, / And puts her trust in miracles for safety." The speaker is Leonora, the tragedy's heroine. LSM cites 4.1.13–14 of *The Revenge* in *PSE,* "Negro and White Slavery," p. 201.

again for a year at least to come. I shall hope for y[ou]r answer by return mail and will act upon it immediately. If I do not hear from you of course I cannot come, as I would not even know how to get to y[ou]r house or anything else.

Hoping therefore two lines by return mail and with love as usual to y[ou]r family, I am dear Brother always

Your affectionate Sister
Louisa S. McCord

Source: Langdon Cheves I Papers, SCHS.

To Langdon Cheves, Jr.

Dear Brother Columbia Jan[uar]y 23d, 1860

Your's of 18th just rec[eive]d. Also one from Pinckney of 17th ~~and~~ he then knowing nothing of the proposed sale being deferred. As I presume John's objections will be speedily overcome, I still suppose it best that I should see you, in order to understand and give my assent to any desirable arrangements, ~~in order~~ that no difficulty of communication with me, should put any obstacle in your way whenever action may be determined upon.——I have just written to Pinckney that I shall hope to meet him and you both, by taking the steamer f[ro]m Charleston to Savannah on *Thursday night 2d Feb[ruar]y.* If any later time will suit better, let me know, and I will go down at any time you will appoint. Only, he or you must please write a line to say how and where I can meet you. My visit must of course be an exceedingly hurried one, as I am obliged to go down alone.

Will I meet you in Savannah or at your house? If in Savannah, where? If at your house, how shall I get over to you?

I hope and believe that you will write, or that Pinckney will write for you, to tell me what to do. At any rate if you do not write to stop me, you must expect me to come plunging on per steamer of Thursday night, which will, I presume, take me to Savannah early Friday morning; and there (if in the mean time I do not hear f[ro]m you) I will stumble on according to circumstances the best I can.

In the mean time, dear Brother I am, as always

Very affectionately and truly y[ou]rs
Louisa S. McCord—

Love as usual to y[ou]r household—

Source: Langdon Cheves I Papers, SCHS.

To Hiram Powers

Dear Mr. Powers Columbia Feb[ruar]y 9th, 1860

I am just returned from a visit to my Brother, who has at last given me his views on the subject of my Father's monument. He has been much harrassed by painful business and you must excuse his non-attention hitherto. It has been owing entirely to overwork and a bad habit of dilatoriness in writing. His opinions are, much more than mine, likely to be suggestive to you, and I accordingly take the liberty of sending to you as he wrote it what was given merely as a memorandum for myself in writing to you. I think it is best so.[91]——I should only differ from my Brother as to my Father's eye

91. This memorandum by Langdon Cheves, Jr., survives, both in his fair copy, received by LSM and enclosed with her letter to Powers, and in Cheves' draft, found in the Langdon Cheves I Papers, SCHS. The text of the draft follows; the fair copy's departures are noted within square and angle brackets:

"The general contour of the Mills bust I think is better than usual with those taken the same way. The set of the head [up]on the neck is very good. The lips, naturally rather thin and firmly compressed <rather thin and compressed>, are exaggerated in the last <latter> particular, probably by the instinctive <by instinctive> resistance to the entrance of the plaster. The ~~irregular~~ unsymetrical form of the nose, a true and characteristic feature, is also exaggerated by excessive contraction of one wing. These two faults unite in giving an expression of disgust which is not natural; the true character being a rather austere, but quiet and commanding <but quietly commanding> gravity. The relaxed mouth of the post mortem cast is farther from <is, however, much wider of> the truth than Mills's. The eye which was not an expressive feature and the brow are I think fairly represented by Mills. For form and proportion of the hard parts the post mortem ~~was taken in~~ in a way to be perfectly reliable <For the proportions of the head and solid parts, the post mortem was taken in a way to ensure accuracy>; but between the time of taking that and the Mills, some ten years (from 70 to 80) had elapsed, attended by considerable deterioration from age and illness.

I can only add that the height was 5 feet 10 <five feet ten> inches, the trunk rather disproportionately large (corresponding perhaps to a height of six feet), figure erect—weight about 200 lbs. Measurements taken immediately after death gave ~~for breadth of shoulders~~ across the shoulders in a strait line 18 inches[;] ~~circumference of~~ round the trunk at the shoulders 41 1/2 inches[;] perpendicular height from the point of the humerus <shoulder> to [the] top of [the] head 12 inches. [The shoulders were perhaps rather round and sloping than square, but without the least tendency to stoop.]

A rather simple individual once remarked that Judge Cheves was the only man he had ever seen who came up to his idea of a king; and the conceit is not unsuggestive of his quietly commanding and severely benignant air.

As to the style of the work; submitting always to Mr. Powers better judgment; I think the bust should be very considerably over the ~~nat~~ life size—sufficiently so to prevent its having a *little* effect in the open air; and that the [*canceled letters illegible*] shoulders should run after the antique fashion into the solid square block. For the monument I have imagined nothing [very] definite; ~~of~~ only that it should be subordinate to the bust—of <and in> the

not being an expressive feature. Its look was, under excitement, very remarkable and severely penetrating. It is singular too how often the vulgar idea of kingship (to which my brother in one instance alludes) attached to his person. Careless in dress, unostentatious in manner, never seeking to be looked at, nor ever thinking of the effect of his appearance, deficient to a fault in (to speak phrenologically) love of approbation, there was yet about him that calm commanding dignity which the vulgar associates with the idea of royalty, and which the nobler man bows to, even sometimes in spite of himself. I have never seen my Father in company with any man of whatsoever position who did not by a deference of manner seem to acknowledge in him this inherent right to command, however in the general course of life and opinion the two might be in opposition. And this withall accompanied by a character whose benignity, benevolence, and sympathetic tenderness of feeling were to the last fresh as though ~~the~~ life and its asperities had been unknown to him.

Would it be asking too much of you to beg your idea of the suitable size and extent of the monument intended[,] with a suggestion of plan? Indeed for such parts (if any) that you may deem best for us to have executed of our home granite, we would have to request of you details with such directions and drawings as would be necessary for the execution of the work here.

I trust that the casts will in due time reach you safely. I have since my return home in November twice before this, written to you and trust that my letters have been duly received.——You will have the kindness to acknowledge this (will you not?) that I may be satisfied of all being right. Please address me, *to the care of Messrs. Ravenel and Co. Charleston, South Carolina.*

Pray present my kindest regards to your wife and daughters. I trust that they as well as yourself are well and happy. I am dear Sir with pleasant remembrance of our past acquaintance

Very truly and respectfully yours
Louisa S. McCord—

Source: Hiram Powers and Powers Family Papers, Smithsonian.

---

simplest and severest style that would escape the affectation of baldness. It has occurred to me that the use of granite, ~~whether~~ [either] in the whole <in whole> or in part, might ~~be used with good effect~~ contribute to the desired massiveness of effect <the desired solid effect>. If this idea should be acted on, it happens fortunately that[,] in the works established for the construction of the Capitol~~e~~ at Columbia, the utmost facility offers for procuring a native Carolina rock of almost unrivaled ~~quality~~ beauty <of-uncommon beauty> and convenient for transportation[,] and skill and appliances <with appliances and skill> for working it to any pattern ~~of which~~ the material ~~is susceptible~~ admits of.

These suggestions <This suggestion> I mean rather as hints <a hint> to Mr. Powers of what may be done if desired, than as advice or even opinion on a matter ~~in~~ which I would

To Langdon Cheves, Jr.

Dear Brother Columbia Feb[ruar]y 29th, 1860

Being almost as inimical as yourself to letter writing, I have delayed writing until I could get your wine packed. I have this morning sent to the R.R. three large boxes directed to care of R[obert] Habersham and Son.[92]

The contents are, of largest box, *118 bottles "Blandy", 55 "Madiera 1821", 27 "Old Madiera (parcel unknown)"*—of second sized box, *17 bottles "Old Cercial", 34 "Old Murdoch", 45 "Old Grape Juice", 42 "Tinto"*—of third sized box, *141 bottles "Blandy".* I have placed a large label, pinned to a newspaper, *on top* of, and to seperate[,] the different qualities of wines as put in. They are labeled as taken from my store room; but I fear there was error and great carelessness in placing them there. Owing to my ill-health at the time, it was left in part to June, whom I then trusted, unfortunately in that and other more important things, far too much.——In the third sized box particularly (containing, according to label, only Blandy) there is an evident mixture of older looking bottles. I engaged the best packer to put it up, and I hope it will go safe; though I cannot say that I liked his way of doing it.

I was glad to hear from yours of 10th that you were likely to have no impediments from lawyers etc. I hope, with all my heart, that things will go on smooth with you. You must be troubled about *my part* as little as possible—

On returning home I found that the order given by me for a slab for Mother's grave, had *not* been executed, and I [*canceled word illegible*] countermanded my order. If the remains are removed, it will be better to get what is wanted in Charleston. What was ordered by me was for my own little graveyard (with the idea of the probability of its being temporary) and might be quite unsuitable. So there is nothing done now, and every thing may be directed as is thought suitable.——

I suppose you have Mary at home by this time, as Anna wrote me, that she expected to lose her soon.

With kind love to her, Charlotte, and all of you, and hoping that all are quite well, I am, dear Langdon,

Your affectionate Sister
Louisa S. McCord

Source: Langdon Cheves I Papers, SCHS.

~~more willingly rely~~ rather submit to his eminent professional ~~genius~~ ability <on a matter which I am sure will be safest under the untrammelled direction of his eminent professional ability>."

92. The Habershams were an eminent and prosperous mercantile family in Savannah.

To Hiram Powers

Dear Sir, Columbia July 29th, 1860

Your kind letter of April 18th was received so long ago that I have no excuse for not having answered it sooner. Frequent indisposition, and an intensely hot summer will, I hope, go some way to excuse me. I had hoped too, that I might hear from you again, on the subject of the little design for my Father's monument which you promised me. I know however that you are a busy man, and I wait your liesure. My own bust too, you said you would soon ship, and give me notice of.[93] All this has made me delay from day to day, and week to week, thinking I might hear from you; until more time has past than I thought. We grow old so fast without knowing it!

I shall still hope to hear from you soon with the promised design, and also when you send my own bust,—which I shall value, not only as your work, but as a remembrancer of a friendly acquaintance with you, which I hope some day to renew in our own land.——Pray do not imagine that the nation which has given birth to a Powers, is so little appreciative of the Sculptors art as to regard Mills as a sculptor. I don't know how it happens, while every body knows that he is a humbug,—a mere plaster-dauber, too ignorant even to be called an imposter, he yet is called to what ought to be great works.[94] The truth I fear is, that we are a bragging rather than an earnest

93. "Your bust has been in Leghorn this long while waiting for a very first class ship—I do not like to send by any other for on account of the dangerous freight (marble in heavy blocks) many inferior vessels founder at sea. I have waited in the hope of telling you that the bust was shipped, but have not yet received notice of it. It will go to N[ew] York to the care of Theodore Dehon, Esq. who will insure it and forward it to you—unless you send him other instructions." Hiram Powers to LSM, Sept. 16, 1860, Hiram Powers and Powers Family Papers, Smithsonian.

94. "It would be quite as reasonable to expect a successful surgical operation at the hands of an ignorant butcher as a perfect statue from a Clark Mills—a man who, by the aid of southern influence and northern favoritism and ignorance, received the highest honor ever given to any sculptor, ancient or modern[,] by the unanymous vote of Congress, viz., the order for an equestrian statue of Washington. . . . I have never seen this monument, alike disgraceful to our government and to its author, but [Edward Everett] wrote me that, if possible, it was 'more execrable than the equestrian statue of Jackson.'" Hiram Powers to Nettie Van Vliet, Oct. 22, 1866, Hiram Powers and Powers Family Papers, Smithsonian. Mills' *Andrew Jackson,* the first large bronze equestrian statue raised in the United States, was dedicated in Lafayette Square in Washington on Jan. 8, 1853; its success had procured for Mills, in April following, the commission for a like statue of George Washington. This was dedicated on Feb. 22, 1860, the oration in its honor being delivered by the Virginian Thomas Stanley Bocock (1815–91), replacing William Gilmore Simms who had declined the invitation because of ill health.

people; and our wise legislators, in their eager scramble for power and place, deem such subjects I presume scarce worth consideration. They had to spend some hundred thousands of the people's money; it did not take 5 cents from their individual pockets. What cared they for the result? They had to canvass for the next Presidency, or to send comfort to John Brown, or to preach a tirade against Southern slave-holders, and so they snapped their fingers at Art. (Art! Half of them don't know what the word means.) But the business was to be done some how or other. Mills was near, (If it had been the hod-carrier who brings his plaster, it would have done as well.) he, or somebody for him, had the impudence to ask for the *job,* (yes,—*the job!* For I don't believe the question of art was considered half so much as it would have been, had there been question of building a brick wall) and so they gave it to him.———My dear Sir, have you lived so much in your Studio, that you have not learned that in this world, and most particularly I fear, in these United States, "he that asketh receiveth;"[95] and the more impudently he asks the better[?] Verily we are a great nation for go-aheadativeness. But when people go ahead so dreadfully fast, they are like the saucy chick running about with the egg-shell on its head, apt to tumble into dirty places. For my part I despair of any good result from such legislation, and as our rulers are, generally speaking, almost as well fitted to their places as Mr. Mills to his, I look forward to a general "*smash up*" as the only regenerating hope of our country. You perceive I am a thorough disunionist:—and so ends my discourse of which Mr. Mills has been the text.

You have doubtless heard of the death of our old friend Wm. Preston.[96] I found him, on my return, much enfeebled in body and mind. He continued gradually to sink through the winter until his death, which came in good time to prevent his feeling too acutely his worn-out condition.

I shall hope to hear from you again before very long. You must excuse me, my dear Sir, if I again put you in mind that I have forgotten your banker, and am ignorant of how a remittance should be made to you. You will I am sure have the kindness to inform me on this subject whenever you write giving notice of the shipment of my bust. Possibly in these times of Italian commotion there may be a difficulty of communication;—I do not know;—I am happy to believe however that in Florence you enjoy comparative quiet.

95. Matt. 7:8; Luke 11:10.

96. William Campbell Preston died at the home in Columbia of his brother John Smith Preston on May 22, 1860.

With kind regards to your wife and daughters and from my young people, believe me always Dear Sir

With sincere respect
and very truly, yours
Louisa S. McCord

Addressed: Hiram Powers Esq. / Florence.[97] *Source:* Hiram Powers and Powers Family Papers, Smithsonian.

To Langdon Cheves, Jr.

Dear Brother Columbia Dec[ember] 4th, 1860

I see it stated in one of our papers that you are nominated for the Convention;[98] and as these nominations, seem almost equivalent to election, it is probable that you may be coming up here in ten or twelve days. I write to say that I will be glad to see you if you will stop with me; and as the town will I suppose be full, you may find it comfortable to do so. Perhaps you may choose to bring up your family and it will give me much pleasure to see you all. Mary seemed to have half an idea of coming up any how. Can you not bring her?

Yourself then, or yourself and Mary, or yourself and household, will be received with the greatest pleasure by me and mine. Hoping to see you soon, and with much love to Charlotte and the young folks, I am dear brother always

Your's affectionately
Louisa S. McCord

I forgot to say that the alarm of Small Pox of which I wrote to Mary seems to have died out very much—There have been three cases of supposed small-pox (though 2 doctors dispute it) and 7 or 8 of varioloid. If we may credit board of health reports there is no increase of the disease since the first alarm—

Source: Langdon Cheves I Papers, SCHS.

97. "I received your admirable letter of July 29th about 8 weeks ago when I was at the Baths of Lucca on a short visit to my friend Mr. Wm. B. Kinney—formerly our Minister at Turin—and I could not forbear reading it to him. It seemed to agree with his views exactly and he commented on it in high terms." Hiram Powers to LSM, Sept. 16, 1860, Hiram Powers and Powers Family Papers, Smithsonian. William Burnet Kinney (1799–1880), diplomat and journalist, was chargé d'affaires at Turin 1850–53.

98. On Nov. 10, 1860, the legislature of South Carolina called for a convention to consider secession of the state from the Union. The convention met in Columbia on Dec. 17; on Dec. 18 it reconvened in Charleston on account of an alarm of smallpox.

10.

Letters and Documents, December 24, 1860–c. June 1879

To Hiram Powers

Columbia, So. Carolina
Dec[ember] 24th, 1860

Dear Mr. Powers

Your kind letter of 16th Sept[ember] has remained too long unacknowledged. It found me in the wild mountains of North Carolina (where I had taken my young people for a few weeks recreation) nursing two daughters, desperately ill of Typhoid fever. With happier result than was anticipated, both are, after three months struggle against the malady, convalescent.——But now, we are in the midst of a revolution. Our spirited little State has declared its independence. On the 20th Inst. she threw down the gauntlet by an ordinance of secession from the United States government, and now waits the result. A bloodless revolution (an unheard of event in history) can scarcely be expected; and yet some of us hope that such may be. Our example will, we firmly believe[,] be in a few weeks followed by Florida, Georgia, Alabama and Mississippi. Other States we hope will (although not yet so fully compromised to action) soon fall in with us, and a Southern Confederacy be constructed.——You have been so long away from America that you will probably know little of the cause of complaint and sympathize not greatly with the throbbing spirit of our now fully roused country. Besides, we of the Southern U[nited] States, have been constantly so misrepresented,—loud mouthed fanaticism has so cried down our institutions, and pretended philanthropy so covered us with slander and falsehood, that it would be asking too much of a far-off spectator to understand and appreciate our action. I wish I could show you how right we are; but it would require a perfect volume of a letter, to give the history of almost half a century of slowly encroaching injustice. I have no right to trouble you with all this, and can only say that slandered as we have been before the world, we yet have courage to "bide our time", and the day will yet come when the recollection of the honors bestowed on such foul-mouthed railers as a Sumner, or a Mrs. Stowe, will bring a blush to the cheeks of those who have been guilty of them.[1] I must trouble you no more about our politics; though I am sure if this little sheet had room enough for all I want to say, I could make a good South Carolinian of you. I see it in your eye. This much I have said, only to excuse my apparent neglect of your kind letter. My Brother to whom I forwarded the designs enclosed has been, head and heart, occupied in our struggle—Called from a quiet agricultural life, he is a member of the Convention which has just cast the die of action for us. I saw him for an hour lately; the Convention having been summoned to meet in Columbia, whence an alarm of Small-Pox caused its adjournment to Charleston. With the adjournment, he of course left, and had only time to tell me that, thanking you for sending the designs, he will[,] with your permission, perhaps use one of them, with slight modification[,] for a construction of South Carolina granite, which he deems better suited to our time and present action, than marble would be.[2] If this is permitted, he would of course desire to make to

1. "A revolution effected by mere animal excitement is inevitably a failure. Revolutions ought not to be made too easily: they are fierce remedies, for fiercer ills, and, when rashly applied, they become, like the knife of the surgeon in the hands of the quack, instruments, not of healing, but of death." *PSE,* "Separate Secession," p. 216. Charles Sumner (1811–74), U.S. senator from Massachusetts (from 1851) and antislavery advocate, celebrated for his invectives against the South; on May 22, 1856, he was caned in the Senate chamber by Congressman Preston Smith Brooks (1819–57), angered by Sumner's abuse of South Carolina and its senator Andrew Pickens Butler, Brooks' kinsman. On Harriet Beecher Stowe see LSM to Mary Dulles, Oct. 9, 1852, and LSM's review of *Uncle Tom's Cabin* in *PSE,* pp. 245–80. The phrase "bide our time" alludes to George Croly, "The Woe upon Israel," in *Scenes from Scripture, with Other Poems* (London, 1851), ll. 35–40: "Israel, where are now thy wise? / Woe to those who live by lies, / Calling (all their souls deceit) / Evil good, and bitter sweet, / Selling justice, pampering crime, / But revenge shall bide its time!" LSM cites from these lines also in *PSE,* "Separate Secession," p. 213.

2. "You will find enclosed with this two designs for monuments, both of a substantial form. The 1st one can be done here in 2d quality of marble (best always for out doors and almost always used—) and delivered on ship board at Leghorn well encased and in order for 15,000 francs—without the bust—you will perceive by the scale that bust and all, it would be about 15 feet high. The base . . . would have to be made at home—of granite or other stone, all the rest would be done here and in marble. I think I should modify somewhat the proportions of the bust and its arrangement at top—the chest part looks long—I like

Prof[esso]r Fantarchiotti such compensation as is proper for the trouble he has taken and will be glad to do so when we shall communicate with you in the same way.

Will you remember that I have begged you to make me a duplicate (only life size) of my Father's bust? I shall hope that our political disturbances will not interfere with the safe arrival of the busts both of my Father and myself, when you find opportunity to send them. Whatever be the condition of our country, your New-York agent (Mr. Dehon) will doubtless be able to arrange to send them safely to Charleston.[3] I anticipate indeed that we will ere long be better friends with our Northern neighbours than (writhing under the oppression of an unjust government) we have hitherto consented to be.

You perceive that we are in full condition to sympathize with your Italian struggles.[4] In the surging waves of national struggle against oppression nations fraternize in heart. Garibaldi's is truly a splendid character. Can it be

---

the simplicity and severe style of the design which has been furnished to me by Prof[esso]r Fantacchiotti who would undertake to execute the monument as above. I am not an architect and have therefore got him to supply these designs. . . . The other design is on a scale of about 9 feet—bust and all. I have not the estimate of the cost of this, but of course it would be comparatively little." Hiram Powers to LSM, Sept. 16, 1860, Hiram Powers and Powers Family Papers, Smithsonian. Odoardo Fantacchiotti (1809–77)—LSM's misspelling below is owed to Powers' unclear handwriting—was employed briefly by Powers as a finisher before opening his own studio as a sculptor, and also as a forger of Italian Renaissance pieces; Powers passed along to him many commissions.

3. "The next morning [after the departure of the Federal army from Columbia on Feb. 19, 1865] we went home greatly relieved to find the house still standing, but what a scene of desolation it all was. Every out-building had its door burst open—fences were thrown down—the garden trampled, furniture broken, books torn up and thrown about, pictures smashed and cut out of their frames and everything small carried away. As we reduced chaos to order we found of course that many things were still left—the oil paintings for instance that were afterwards burned in Henry Cheves' house and my mother's bust—but the first look was of utter sweeping destruction." Smythe, pp. 69–70.

4. "We are now in great excitement about the state of things so near us. . . . What a splendid character is Garibaldi—a seller of candles in Hoboken only a few years ago! now the center of the world's observation and deservedly so. Europe is almost hoarse shouting his name. It is a glorious thing that humble virtue has such power. It is Samson over again. His shoulders to the proud palace of the tyrant who flies from the crumbling walls of his strength." Hiram Powers to LSM, Sept. 16, 1860, Hiram Powers and Powers Family Papers, Smithsonian. Revolutionary leader Giuseppe Garibaldi (1807–82)—after a variable career in South America, Sardinia, with the republican government in Rome and consequent escape to the United States (1850–51), and return to Italy and farming in 1854—joined in 1859 the forces of King Victor Emmanuel of Sardinia, invaded Sicily in May 1860, and expelled King Francis of the Two Sicilies from his own capital of Naples on Sept 7. The Two Sicilies were annexed to Sardinia, and Victor Emmanuel declared king of Italy on March 17, 1861; Garibaldi retired to his farm until taking up two assaults on Rome (1862 and 1867) and other adventures.

that he is destined to receive only the reward of his own conscious power and rectitude and that after Europe has, as you well remark[,] "become hoarse with shouting his name," he is to be past over and forgotten by those into whose hands he has placed the results of his efforts! His reward has perhaps been great enough in the resounding cry which passing through Europe has been again echoed back from our Western shores giving him a world fame above that of monarchs; but yet it is a sad comment upon worldly justice, if such be the end of the Strong Man.———

Excuse my long letter, but even a Woman has the right to wake up when revolution is afoot, and when our Sons (even boys) throw aside their Greek, Latin and mathematics to practice rifles and study military tactics.

Remember me kindly to Mrs. Powers and your daughters. Tell the fair haired one, that I saw only yesterday a rose bud that she gave my little girl, pressed into a bouquet with one which you gave me, and kept as a memorial of Florence and your household—

Believe me dear Sir

Most truly and respectfully yours
Louisa S. McCord—

Addressed: Hiram Powers Esq. / Florence. *Source:* Hiram Powers and Powers Family Papers, Smithsonian.

To Langdon Cheves, Jr.

Dear Brother Columbia April 20th, 1861

I just missed meeting you and the girls, a few days since, in Charleston. You left, I was told, on Friday and I got in on Saturday just as the white flag was raised on Fort Sumter. I went down to see where the company with which Cheves is, was likely to be located. They are now on the outskirts of Charleston, near the Ashley River bridge, and, as (for the present I suppose) all is quiet, I came back to my girls.———This has been a glorious affair of Fort Sumter, and truly it would seem to have set old Lincoln crazy. Did ever any stupid animal ever so set fire to its own nest! He has given us Virginia already, and how much else will follow?

In the midst of affairs so all absorbing you must excuse my troubling you with a few words of business. My Factor's books show my funds run dry, and I find it needful to consider coming demands. Being most anxious for you to do just as you please, I only need to know whether or not you *desire* to make any payments to me this year. Please do exactly what you wish. There is no inconvenience to me, except to know what to anticipate. It is very probable that the times will make you willing to let alone all payments for this year. Pray do so if it suits you; only dear Brother you will let me know (will you not?) what you wish.———

I hope Charlotte keeps well. With kind love to her and all at home with you, believe me dear brother, always

and most affectionately y[ou]rs
Louisa S. McCord—

Source: Langdon Cheves I Papers, SCHS.

To Langdon Cheves, Jr.

Dear Brother Columbia April 21st [1861]

I hear that you are at the Mills House. My two girls and myself wish to go down for a few days, (or more probably weeks,) according to circumstances, and are very anxious to get into the Mills House where we have many acquaintances. I have written today to Mr. Nickerson to ask for rooms but I am not sure that he knows me.[5] Will you not do me the kindness to try and get him to furnish suitable accomodation (at least the best he can) for me? I trust to you to help me if possible, and I will go with my girls immediately on arrival to the Mills House. I will be in Charleston *Tuesday afternoon 23d Inst.*

Please help me with a good word to ~~the~~ Mr. Nickerson and with love from my girls, believe me dear Brother

Your's affectionately
Louisa S. McCord

Source: Langdon Cheves I Papers, SCHS.

To Augustine Thomas Smythe

My dear young friend Columbia June 25th, 1862

I was much pleased to hear from you after your fighting experience, and thank you for making so prompt a report of yourself. We had all watched anxiously the papers and come to the conclusion that at least you were not

5. Businessman Otis Mills (d. c. 1869) shared with his hotel manager Thomas S. Nickerson (d. 1871) the planning of the Mills House, commended upon its opening in 1853 for its luxury and fashionable exuberance. Nickerson was manager of the Moultrie House at the time of the hurricane of 1854 (see LSM to Martha Herbemont, Oct. 16, 1854); during and after the war he was proprietor of the Nickerson House in Columbia.

hurt. But it is much more satisfactory to get this information from yourself; and your letter was I assure you, very welcome.

I had just sent my daughters off, (half against their will,) on a visit to some friends in Abbeville. I wish to get them for a little while, away from the heat and sickness of Columbia. I knew however that I would never be forgiven, if I failed to send your letter, fresh from the battle-field, and accordingly I forthwith enclosed it to them—In return, I have just received their warm thanks, and their congratulations for you. They say you must certainly have the geranium leaves, and Miss Lou deputises me to pick some of the sweetest from your old friends; which accordingly I have done; with the heartsease also from your own plants. The Rose-geranium leaf and the little myrtle-bloom she sent from Abbeville, as she said she must really send you some of her own picking, and these were all she had there.——You need not make apologies for "shabby notes," but believe that we will be always glad to hear from you, fight or no fight. In truth, you, who are on coast service, are meeting worse than the danger of battle all the time. I dread the effects of our malarious low-country. You must not be afraid of it, and you cannot avoid it; but you can be prudent; and I hope you are so.——Your friends and relatives generally, are I think, in the upper country. I don't expect you to get sick or hurt or anything else of the kind. Try to keep well and all right. But if you *do* get into any such trouble, and if I am right in supposing those nearer and dearer to you, out of your reach, remember that I am upon the old ground, and come to me to be taken care of.

We are going to have the sick in plenty near us here. They are just turning the College buildings into hospitals, and it is calculated that they must hold six or seven hundred. They are now moving in the first arrivals—I have been so busy trying to help in this, that I have hardly left myself time to scrawl this. But I am determined that you[r] kind letter shall not go one day longer unanswered—

Goodbye—Take care of yourself and let us know how you are sometimes. I find these war-times, as the risks thicken, make me think more and more of my soldier friends. My young ladies, as I tell you, send numberless kind words, and I am sure boundless good wishes with them. God bless you! Goodbye once more.

Affectionately your friend
Louisa S. McCord—

Source: Smythe-McCord-Stoney Collection, SCHS.

To Mary Boykin Chesnut

Dear Mrs. Chesnut, Columbia Dec[ember] 8th, 1862

I think your sister should by all means "try for blankets and shoes, etc. etc.," rather than go on making hospital boxes. From the little I have seen and all I have heard, I think we have a hard task before us to keep our soldiers from freezing to death this winter. My son, who is improving, thanks you for your kind inquiries and agrees with me. Heaven only knows what is to become of our ragged, shoeless troops in Virginia this winter. It seems a Herculean task for us to be thinking of such an undertaking; but even little helps, and every *one* relieved is a fraction of the great whole.

Carolina troops are now proverbially the raggedest of the ragged. We must work. I am about trying here to buy up old carpets, old blankets, anything which if I can get we will line with cotton dyed some sober color and cut into blanket size. I do not know if we can do anything, but it is to be tried at least.

Affectionately yours,
Louisa [S.] McCord

Source: Printed in *Chesnut,* p. 787.

To Mary Boykin Chesnut

Dear Mrs. Chesnut, [Columbia before January 23, 1863?]

May I beg you to ask Col[onel] Chesnut what I shall do with a few guns etc. which my son some time since begged me to give where they may be wanted, but which I only succeeded in getting yesterday. There are

2 double bar[rele]d guns in good order
2 flint-locks horsemans pistol "
1 old sabre "
and 3 old muskets needing all sorts of repairs.

Shall I send them to Badcliffs or where? Pray excuse this *Sunday* morning's message, but I only got the articles last evening and wanted to give them up. I was glad to find you so well when I called the day before yesterday—as you had gone out. Hoping that you may keep well and have no more chills, I am yours very truly

Louisa S. McCord

Source: Recipient's transcription, Williams-Chesnut-Manning Families Manuscripts (letter book), SCL.

To Mary Boykin Chesnut

[Columbia between January 23
[Dear Mrs. Chesnut] and February 3, 1863]

Forgive me, my dear friend, if only in a few words I can answer your kind letter.

The light of my life is gone, my hope fled, and my pride laid low. God pity my poor girls. I can scarcely rouse myself to take care of them. My helpless daughters! And his poor young wife, who daily expects her confinement.

I cannot write more, but only to thank yourself and Colonel Chesnut for your efforts to help my darling.

It is all over now, and it is right perhaps that the country will never know how much it has lost in my glorious boy.

Affectionately your friend
Louisa S. McCord

Addressed: Mrs. M. B. Chesnut.[6] *Source:* Printed in *Chesnut,* pp. 787–88.

To Augustine Thomas Smythe

My dear young Friend Columbia April 28th, 1863

Since the terrible calamity which has stricken down the hope and the joy of my house, I hardly know how to write. The "vacant chair,"[7] and desolate hearth are too constantly before me, to let me think of much else. Still I must send a few words to thank you for your remembrance of us in our sorrow. My heart, springs forward to every touch or sign of affection from those who have known and loved *him.* Many letters I have received, but yours is the first word that comes to me from any of those whom I have known principally as his college companions. If it wakes afresh the sources of my grief,—believe me, there is still a mournful pleasure in feeling that the link is not quite broken. It brings sadly before me (and yet I love to remember them) the bright young faces of a year or two back. How changed now could the remnants of that little circle be collected![8] We have gone through a life-

6. "I think I shed the bitterest tears that ever came into my eyes—for him, cut off so soon—and for his mother!! . . . I meant to copy Mrs. McCord's letter, but the cry of a soul like her in agony—I could not do it." *Chesnut,* p. 429.

7. Longfellow, "Resignation," st. 1: "There is no flock, however watched and tended, / But one dead lamb is there! / There is no fireside, howso'er defended, / But has one vacant chair!"

8. See chap. 1 above, *My Dreams,* "The Village Churchyard," l. 248, and note.

time of struggle and of sorrow in the interval. May God grant to all (to those who like my own One have gone from us, as to those who remain) that this terrible war may have worked out its purifying blessings; and that in the sudden wrench which has thus cast so many forth from boyhood to manhood's fiercest struggles, the saddening influence may have left its ennobling result. My all is gone; but I cannot cease to watch with loving interest those (his friends) who have yet to work through the struggle in which he has fallen. God bless you! I can write and think of nothing but as connected with him. It is as well to stop. This is enough to say (and you will believe me) that thinking of you with affectionate kindness I shall always be pleased to hear from, or to see you.

My Daughters remember you always with kind regard. They have not been well; but I hope are improving. This War is a fearful trial to all who think; and its shock falls sharply upon the young.

Again I pray may God bless and guide you.

Always and most truly
Your friend
Louisa S. McCord

Source: Smythe-McCord-Stoney Collection, SCHS; also printed in *FOLS,* p. 17.

To Sophia Cheves Haskell

My dear Sister, Columbia July 16th, 1863

Until your letter, (received last evening,) I had heard nothing of our latest sorrow. *Our* sorrow I say, for I claim to halve it with you. Willy and Aleck, since my great agony, have seemed half to belong to me. They could not fill the place of my own lost darling,—but they were so kind and so linked with him in my thoughts, that I took them into my heart as some thing left of him. Do not think me selfish that I thus put my sorrow side by side with yours for the loss of one of these. I rather think to give you such sad comfort as we find in the recollection of what was loveable in our lost ones; and Willy was not only brave, but very kind, and gentle, and good. It is a great comfort to think, (as I said of Charley) that nothing can be more painless, than a prompt death on the battle field.[9] Not death, indeed, should it be

9. William Haskell raised a company for Brig. Gen. Maxcy Gregg's First Regiment, South Carolina Volunteers, and on Sept. 2, 1861, was appointed its captain. In January 1863 he was made commander of the regiment's battalion of sharpshooters; on July 2, 1863, he was killed in the battle of Gettysburg, as he led his sharpshooters against Federal skirmishers. On July 10 his brother Charles, a captain of artillery, was killed, together with their uncle Langdon Cheves, Jr., at Battery Wagner on Morris Island.

called;—for death is the struggle, the doubt, the anguish of parting, while the weakened mind dreads the transit which in its strength it could face calmly. Here, in its full strength, it finds an easy passage from *life to life.* Death has no time to startle even with the shadow of its terrors. To us alone (lingerers by the wayside) is left the sorrow and the loss.

Falling as he has done, so far away from us, there will perhaps no relic of dear Willy come home to you; and you will, I think, like to know that I have in my possession the sword which he carried through 12 battles. It was brought to me by one Col. McCready (sent by Willy) only a few weeks since, for me to take care of.[10] I wrote him word that nobody should touch it till he came for it himself. But to you and his Father it now[,] of right, belongs. Should it chance that a watch be sent to you, do not think it a mistake. I lent him the last one used by Cheves, begging him to wear it in the fight and bring it home to me.[11]——I would come and see you but would do you harm. I need to be alone a great deal, and cannot always command myself as I should. With any change I would likely be ill and a burden to you. My girls seem to feel as if their brother was lost a second time. Poor children, these shocks are very trying to them. This fearful war brings to our daughters a sadder fate than to their slaughtered brothers.——Once more dear Sister you know my sympathies are with you all. Would to God, I had anything else to give—

Truly yours
and most affectionately
Louisa S. McCord

Source: Langdon Cheves III Papers, SCHS.

To Augustine Thomas Smythe

My dear young friend Columbia August 26th, 1863

I thank you for your letter, and feel the kindness which does not forget us, in the midst of your present perils. I have often thought of you;—for the

10. Lawyer and historian Edward McCrady, Jr. (1833–1903), was promoted lieutenant colonel on June 27, 1862; severely wounded at Second Manassas on Aug. 30, 1862; injured by a falling tree Jan. 27, 1863; although thus incapacitated for fighting, until December 1863 McCrady continued in various capacities to serve his unit, Gregg's First Regiment, South Carolina Volunteers, in which William Haskell also served. Among McCrady's works, *A Review of the Resolutions of the Press Conference* (1870) and *The History of South Carolina,* 4 vols. (1897–1902).

11. "The night before Willy went back Mamma gave him the watch my brother had worn. It was one of her Father's. Willy objected to taking it for fear that in case of his death it might be lost. I remember her arguing with him—begging him not to talk so as he had

greater the troubles we go through, (and I have had, as you probably know, very heavy ones to meet, even since I last saw you,) the more, it seems to me, do we cling to what is left behind; and when our nearest and dearest are torn from us, we turn to those whom our minds associate with them.——You mention that all your Father's family has left, or is leaving Charleston. If they are out of your reach, I hope you will keep in mind that in case of your being sick or wounded, you will always find a room and a welcome with me. My vocation is to help soldiers, and when the soldier is a friend, I am only the more ready for my duty. Come to me therefore (if need be) to be nursed; though I trust that God may protect and keep you from the need.

My Daughters send their kind remembrances and best wishes to you. They call themselves well; though in truth the only bright one of my household is Baby, who grows fat and laughs as if there was no such thing as war. The rest of us think only of making sand bags for the forts, listening for the guns which we hear from Charleston, watching for the last war-news, and I go to the hospital;—and thus the dreary days go on[12]—

Goodbye. Again and again, may God bless and take care of you—

Always most truly
Your friend
Louisa S. McCord—

Source: Smythe-Stoney-Adger Papers, SCHS.

---

always been the 'lucky' one of the family—having been shot through his clothes and even his hat without ever receiving a scratch. I can see the look with which he said that by all the laws of chance, if we believed in chance, the next turn would be his. But to please her he took the watch, promising that if possible it should be sent back to her in case of his death. And it came back to her not very long after, from the bloody field of Gettysburg." Smythe, p. 54.

12. "With all this hardship my mother was very careful and particular—she did not believe in young girls at the hospital; so we never went there, but stayed at home to be ready for any calls that would come from her as they frequently did come—either for some little addition to her supply or for a book, or a sheet of paper, or bandages, or as I remember once in a great hurry for the flannel jelly bag to be filled with water and hung so as to drip on a terrible wound threatened with gangrene. She sat by and held the poor fellows' hands in their sufferings. She kept up their courage by promising before the chloroform was given that *she* would not allow *too* much of the limb taken off. She was there again when the chloroform passed off and the poor boys would wake crying for their wives or mothers. She wrote their letters, read to them, comforted the dying and helped to bury them. I have known her drive all over the town to find a minister of some particular denomination for some poor dying creature who could not be quite comforted by the chaplain. I saw her once for hour after hour walking and driving with the hand of a poor feeble half-demented man dying of homesickness (Nostalgia they called it) clasping her skirt like a baby while she pursued the authorities to get him a furlough. . . . After all this she would come home and

To Mary Boykin Chesnut

Dear Mrs. Chesnut Columbia Oct[ober] 18th, 1863

I should have sooner thanked you for your kind notes, the one enclosing $100 for the Hospital uses—the other introducing your old neighbour Mrs. Milly Trimblin.[13]

For the latter I could do but little. As the poor old woman (beset with the very natural idea that it was needful and right to get her Son furloughed from the hospital) began to find imaginary maladies in the Son, of which the suggestion could in truth only do harm: for our harsh Doctors have little sympathy with Mothers yearnings[—]All I could do for her was to try and make her quiet.

Since her departure—I have spoken to the Son and his wife—and will do what I can for them; though I fear *furlough* is out of the question.

Hospitals are hard places, in which Women may be comforters but Doctors too often are tyrants.[14]

---

the first thing would be to slip up the back steps to her room, [where] Marianne would be waiting to receive her quickly dropped clothing which would be taken in the piazza and carefully searched for the dreadful 'grey backs' as the soldiers called them, which even the best and the cleanest might bring from camp. My mother knit day and night, walking, driving, under all circumstances. When troubles and sorrows came thick and fast and sleep came no longer to comfort her, I used to wake at night and listen to the click, click of her needles, and shudder at the groans and sobs that accompanied them when she supposed no one heard her." Smythe, pp. 49–50.

13. "Today H[arriet] Lang [was] told that poor sandhill Milly Trimlin was dead, that as a *witch* she had been denied Christian burial. Three times she was buried in consecrated ground at different churchyards and three times dug up by a superstitious horde and put out of their holy ground. . . . About this time last year Mrs. McCord was doing all she could to soothe her maternal bosom, wrung by anxieties in regard to a wounded son." *Chesnut,* p. 830.

14. "As soon as my brother was able to travel, she brought him back [from Virginia] and we were sent for [from Abbeville]. . . . The hospital was then in charge of Dr. [W. C.] Horlbeck who had the reputation of being a splendid Doctor, but a hard rough man. One afternoon Mamma and the other two girls were out and I was in charge of the invalid—Dr. Horlbeck came in and after examining the wound in my brother's head told his servant Tom to bring a basin of water as he wanted to cut that bullet out. I took courage to beg him to wait until Mamma came home, but he paid little attention to me—only telling me to go and wait outside the door while Tom held the basin. So the bullet was out but—the head bandaged and the Doctor left, saying that it would heal in a day or two and he would then be fit for service. . . . When the others came in they were told—Mamma was troubled and indignant but there was no help. The wound healed in a few days and my brother presented himself before the examining board as ready for service. Mamma entreated him to ask for ten days more, but he refused, saying that Dr. Horlbeck had performed the operation and knew his condition and had told him to go—he *could* not ask for delay—so he went—went for the last time." Smythe, pp. 52–53.

I see another battle at Manassas is reported.[15] We are yet to learn its results——At the last—my all was at stake—

Affectionately Yours
Louisa S. McCord

Source: Recipient's transcription, Williams-Chesnut-Manning Families Manuscripts (letter book), SCL.

To Sophia Cheves Haskell

My dear Sister Columbia Oct[ober] 9th, 1864

Mrs. Singleton will doubtless forward by this same mail the distressing dispatches which she has received.[16] God help us! we *must* bear; but it is hard!——I still trust that the very remarkable recuperative powers which Aleck has hitherto shown when wounded, may aid him through this, so much worse than his preceding wounds. (John as Mrs. Singleton will no doubt inform you is well again from a very slight injury.)[17]——So long as Dr. Gibson says that there is some hope and the last dispatch *does* say so, I cannot but have faith in the strength of Aleck's constitution which has so wonderfully stood preceding shocks.[18] I hope that you may have seen through the paper that your boys are wounded and that you may come down by

15. On Oct. 15, 1863, the Army of Northern Virginia under Robert E. Lee and the Army of the Potomac under George Meade met in a series of skirmishes at places along Bull Run, among them Manassas. On Oct. 17, amid further skirmishing, Lee began to withdraw his forces toward the Rappahannock.

16. Mary Lewis Carter Singleton (1817–87), wife of planter John Coles Singleton who had died in 1852; her daughter Rebecca, wife of LSM's nephew Alexander Haskell, died on June 26, 1862, having given birth to a daughter six days before.

17. Alexander Haskell had been wounded in the right shoulder at Fredericksburg (Dec. 13, 1862), in the ankle at Chancellorsville (May 1–4, 1863), and (having been promoted lieutenant colonel in April and colonel in May 1864) at Cold Harbor (June 1–3, 1864), being struck by seven rifle bullets, one shattering a lens of his field glasses, one carrying off a ring from his sword, one entering his body, one his horse, and three being lodged in his clothing. On Oct. 7, 1864, during skirmishes on the Darbytown Road east of Richmond, Alexander's brother John, who had returned to active service with a jacket tailored to take account of his amputated arm, was grazed in the head by a Minié ball; but Alexander was not so lucky. "The ball entered my left eye and came out behind the left ear. . . . 'We have killed the General.' As I fell heavily to the ground, I said to myself, with a sort of grim mental smile, 'Only a Colonel, Gentlemen, only a Colonel!" Daly, *Alexander Cheves Haskell,* pp. 150–51.

18. Surgeon in Richmond and professor of surgery at Hampden-Sydney College before the war, Charles Bell Gibson (1816–65) was briefly surgeon general of Virginia, then head of the Officers' Hospital.

tomorrow's car. If so, you will not receive this. Should you however be still at home I shall hope very soon to see you down. If in my crippled condition I can do anything, let me know, and believe me with earnest sympathy

Affectionately your Sister
Louisa S. McCord

Should you leave home and Sophie not ready to leave with you let her come down with Hannah and stay till your return.——

Source: Langdon Cheves III Papers, SCHS.

To Mary Boykin Chesnut

Dear Mrs. Chesnut— [Columbia November 1864]

At the hospital today I spoke to a Frenchman who, indeed, seemed to have not much the matter with him.

He says he is in our service because martial law compels it—but that he cared nothing about the cause and would as soon fight for the North as the South. And only wants to get away.

His manner altogether struck me as fiercely discontented and—except that he can speak little or no English—calculated to do harm.

I do not know whether I am wrong in supposing that I ought to communicate his unlucky state of mind to somebody in authority. Should I speak to Mr. Chesnut or anybody else? If this (perhaps) trifling thing is of sufficient importance to require Mr. Chesnut to be troubled with it, shall I step round to your lodgings at any time this evening to make my report?

Hoping that you may feel better

Yours very truly
Louisa S. McCord

Source: Printed in *Chesnut,* pp. 675–76.

To Thomas Smyth

Dear Sir[19] Columbia August 15th, 1865

Highly flattered, as I am by the compliment paid me in your requesting my opinion of your argument on the currency question, I must, at the risk

19. In *PSE,* "Diversity of the Races," p. 163, LSM had noticed the work of Thomas Smyth (1808–73), pastor of the Second Presbyterian Church of Charleston; in August 1863 Smyth removed his family from their house in Charleston, vulnerable to Federal shelling, to Summerton in Clarendon County, where they remained until the autumn of 1865; on June 27, 1865, his son Augustine married LSM's daughter Louisa.

of appearing ungracious in return, dissent entirely from your views.[20]——There is no form in which we can ask payment of our debt from Yankee rule, which would not be considered by our enemies (such I still cannot but feel them to be,) as a begging of Charity; and moreover it will be a charity as certainly refused as asked. I would therefore quietly keep my poverty, content to save my honest pride, where I cannot my purse.——The *State* is too poor to do anything; and her rising money-makers will never consent to be heavily taxed for their own, their children's, their grandchildren's, even to five generations of life-times, to save those who are already conveniently disposed of, on the list of the ruined. Indeed, crushed and driven, as we are[,] to the wall, by a power which has now no law but its own mandates, it would be suicidal, in whatever is left to call itself "the State", to assume such a debt.——

Excuse me for so entirely differing from you, and believe me with none the less high respect and cordial regard

Very truly yours
Louisa S. McCord—

Addressed: Rev. Dr. Smythe. *Source:* Dulles-Cheves-McCord-Lovell Papers, SCHS.

To Augustine Thomas Smythe

Dear Augustine Lang Syne Fort Motte Feb[ruar]y 19th, 1866

You are a real good boy to think of me and write so often. You have done for me just what I wanted about my business affairs. I will leave both now to Messrs. Campbell and Seabrook.[21] If anything comes of them so much the better. If nothing, I can live without them, and my children must do the same. I hope you are well, and I am sure will enjoy your visit. Nobody must fret about me for a minute; I am getting on first rate. Betsy who is always splendid in an emergency, moves on like a new locomotive, and draggs the heavy freight car (Becca) a little resistingly, but so far successfully after her.

20. "It is difficult for those who are away to understand the utter pecuniary prostration in which the war has left this section of the country. . . . It is as if at a single word and in a single moment the issues of every state and national bank and of the government should prove without value or effect, and the people, instead of currency, should find that they had, as representative of toil and years of labor and hard-earned competency, pieces of waste paper." Charleston *Daily Courier,* July 7, 1865. How to counter this obliteration by the war of most of South Carolina's wealth was much discussed.

21. The law firm of James Butler Campbell (1808–93) and Henry Seabrook, located at 50 Broad Street, Charleston, specialized in recovery of property confiscated by the Federal forces.

She even made Ellison, (who was sent her by Champagne) work, yesterday. Israel moves on good temperedly, and I go for the mail daily myself, in the Merrimac. Poor Witte as yet is nowhere. Her child seems to have got well. She is quite amiable, but does not seem to be quite awake. I doubt if she ever wakes up. What a blessing that Ty Anne is out of the way. I have not seen her since you left.

Tell Lou that Pic is well, and Toto ditto.[22] Also that one bed is done, and the other will probably be done to-day. Old Jack (horse I mean) was claimed for the wagon by Jake who said he had your orders for the claim, and being confirmed in his say by Israel I let Jack go. Now you see, I am doing all right, so please get over the nonsense notion that I need, as yet, to be taken care of. Time enough for that when I make my breakdown. And, à propos, my dear son, do make your determination as to business affairs, (whether city or country business) quite independently of all consideration of me or my *supposed* wishes. Think only of yourself and your wife. I can (believe me), make myself comfortable any way you fix it. If my children are satisfied and prospering, nothing in the world but Yankees and negroes can trouble me much now.

I can live quite as comfortably as I deserve or desire, whether in town or in country, in y[ou]r house or in rented rooms; and I can make the means I have reserved, (short of unexpected disaster) support me anywhere. So, as I can see only one side of the subject, you shall not know what I think about it. I only beg of you not to let yourself be too much swayed by others, who, however prudent and far-sighted, are by the necessities of circumstance, only as one-sidedly wise as myself. You, knowing by experience, something of both sides, can feelingly determine for yourself. And however you shrink from the responsibility, you have to meet it at last, suffering or profiting in your own person. Nobody knows as well as yourself what you wish, or what you are ready to do. Therefore consult only your own and your wife's inter-

22. Pets belonging to Louisa Smythe. Pic(cola Cane) was a terrier bought for her by her cousin John Haskell to replace her pet squirrel brought back from Europe and accidentally killed in Richmond on the journey back to Columbia. "The house [in Columbia] was sold [on Sept. 23, 1865] and everything was being pulled to pieces. . . . Mamma and Hannah went temporarily to Dr. Reynolds; and after seeing the house emptied of what we were able to take away, we turned our backs finally on my old home . . . and took our weary way back [to Lang Syne] on the jolty ambulance. This time we brought back a wagon load of furniture, books, etc., and my little dog Pic. Pic was put on the wagon and taken to the plantation house while we went to the sandhills. The next morning she had disappeared. I was greatly distressed but we couldn't find her, and the next thing we heard of her was that Dr. Reynolds had found her half starved at the gate of our old Columbia home. He took her home and kept her there." Smythe, p. 82.

est and comfort. Make up your mind. Think of other people, (as you should) only afterwards, and as a secondary duty.

All will come right, if you only make the first step in accordance with your own deliberate judgment, unbiased by any attempt to enlarge the circle of your responsibilities. Let alone thinking of me and Han, except when I ask your help, which I will do whenever I need it. I can take care of myself and Han too, if she wants me to, yet awhile. May God bless you in your decisions, and turn all things for the best.

With my respectful regards to your Father, kind love to your Mother, Aunts and Sisters and to my own girls all the love that they know I want to send, I am

truly and affectionately yours,
Louisa S. McCord

Source: Typewritten copy (corrected), Smythe-Stoney-Adger Papers, SCHS.

To Louisa McCord Smythe

Loulie darling September 16th [1866] Sunday

I was going to write to you but Han says she will write so I leave it to her today. I feel a little afraid that you and Augustine are going to take your turns with the prevalent fever; and now more than half wish that I had succeeded in getting to Charleston. But I suppose it is better so; and I know that you are in good hands. I hope we will hear f[ro]m you though that you have escaped it.

Han will answer you doubtless about the seal that Mr. Fielden asks for.[23] I do not think she has it with her. When you get it however or when you answer Mr. Fielden's letter you will remember that it is *not* the McCord arms. If there are any McCord arms, I am ignorant of them. Your Father neither had them nor sought them I think. The seal in question is only of the Turquand arms which he happened to come across when in Europe. I presume these would be of no use for the purpose wanted though of course it will be well to send the impression when Han can get it for you. Heaps of

23. Henry Wemyss Feilden (1838–1921), a former British officer who became an aide-de-camp to Robert E. Lee, married David James McCord's daughter Julia. His later career took him to the Arctic, the Boer War, friendship with Rudyard Kipling, and recruiting duties in Sussex during the First World War. "He ran the blockade of the U.S. Civil War, and wedded his Southern wife in Richmond with a ring hammered out of an English sovereign, 'because there wasn't any gold in Richmond just then.' Mrs. Feilden at seventy-five was in herself fair explanation of all the steps he had taken and forfeited." Rudyard Kipling, *Something of Myself for My Friends Known and Unknown* (New York, 1937), p. 209.

love to Augustine and kind remembrance to all y[ou]r friends. I do hope that ugly fever will not trouble you—

always your affectionate Mother
Louisa S. McCord—

Source: Dulles-Cheves-McCord-Lovell Papers, SCHS.

To Louisa McCord Smythe

Dear Daughter   Abbeville August 22d [1867] Thursday

Thanks for your letter of 17th—tho' I was sorry to hear of Augustine's detention at Lang Syne. I hope all may turn out right, and that he may be paid for all his trouble at last. It has been raining a great deal here for 2 or 3 days. I have not seen anybody to know if it is doing harm[;] cleared up today. I hope in coming up here, the rain stopped with you; for evidently both f[ro]m what you say, and from the papers, the low country had too much a week ago.——I hope Gus is safe at home with you now, and still with cheerful hopes; though I don't know what the nigs are about to need extra hands to pick cotton. But whether the crops are good or bad, try and keep the "old fellow" up to his recent better ways. Make him take care of himself, both in the Quinine line, and the sitting up etc. After he has kept well for six months, he will begin to see the good of behaving sensibly. Write me the truth about the crops and every thing else—Don't try to cheat me into believing things better than they are. It only makes the "let down," harder when it comes.——I notice by newspapers, rows etc. Nothing else can be expected. Six months must do something one way or the other. Oh my! I wish I was near you—No use wishing though. Don't go to fancy anything the matter here. I am well, and all right.

And you are really not thin? Your photograph certainly looks so,—but I believe you, if you say you are not. But do not be afraid of getting too fat. If Gus is wise, he will encourage you—You never were in better health, nor looked better, than when you weighed—I forget what,—but heavier than you have ever done since—Tell Annie and Ellen I am sorry to hear there is need of such violent combined efforts to make you good for anything;—and Mr. Adger's report of the brain malady is certainly alarming.[24] I fear your

24. Louisa Smythe was at this time living with her husband's parents in Charleston; LSM seems to refer to members of their family. "Annie" is perhaps Augustine T. Smythe's sister Sarah Ann (b. 1846) or, less likely (since "Janey" was a nickname used in the family), Jane Anne (b. 1849); or Annie Ransom Briggs Smyth (b. 1838), who with her husband James Adger Smyth, Augustine's brother, was residing at this time with his parents. "Ellen" may be

surroundings are not healthy. There is an old proverb about evil communications etc.[25] In spite of it all though, I am glad to believe that you are all well and happy. I am so glad that Annie has come home to stay. You are good company for each other when the gentlemen desert you. Nothing new here that I know of. Jeanie came to sit an hour or two day before yesterday;—is quite gentle-ised by recent affairs. The extreme respect with which "Cousin Frank" has always treated me, has come so plumb against her recent *brusque* manner to me, that, considering circumstances, one or the other had to change; and so far, it has been all the change with her. She seems very well satisfied with arrangements. Told me she wanted to write a note to you by my first letter, and I have let her know that I would write today. I shall not be very much surprised however if the note gets put off; for although she was certainly sincere in intending it, she must be very much occupied;—a large family,—some trouble about servants,—and F. T. M. of course very devoted.[26] He expects to leave next week too, so it would not do to check his frequent visitations, whether for notes, letters, or etcs. If therefore her note does not come in time, I will not keep this waiting, but enclose by itself. And at any rate if you fancy to write to her on the subject of her engagement, you have the full right to do so on the strength of the double announcement made to me both by gentleman and lady.——The village folks, as represented by my domicile, have come to a sudden "pull up" in their small talk on the subject. They have nothing more to say. It *is* an engagement and nobody denies it. It really is almost distressing; they seem so *flat* about it. I am not a little anxious as well as curious, to find how it will affect Han. The romance of the affectionate friendship, with Jeanie's despotism and Han's submission, must come to a sudden termination; for I *know* it was a great surprise to Han. When she wrote you "to look out for an engagement" she already knew of its existence and wrote to me somewhat in the same way, believing herself bound to secrecy. In a letter

---

Ellen Crawford, whom in January 1844 Thomas Smyth brought from the Charleston Orphan House to be nursemaid to the baby Augustine and who remained as a permanent member of the Smyth household. Augustine Smythe's mother was the eldest daughter of James Adger (1777–1858); the "Mr. Adger" mentioned here is probably one of her four brothers alive at this time.

25. 1 Cor. 15:33: "Evil communications corrupt good manners."

26. Francis Turquand Miles (1827–1903), "Cousin Frank," a younger brother of William Porcher Miles, married Jeanie Wardlaw. He taught at the Medical College of South Carolina after taking his M.D. there in 1849; studied comparative anatomy under Louis Agassiz at Harvard University; served at Fort Sumter for various periods during the war; was wounded at the battle of Secessionville June 16, 1863; after the war, returned to teach anatomy at the Medical College in Charleston; later moved to Baltimore; held chairs of anatomy, diseases of the nervous system, and physiology at the University of Maryland.

written the day before she heard of the affair having come to a crisis, she expressed her utter disbelief of any such possible result.——Have seen nothing of the Haskells since my visit, except a stupid nig just now with a little basket of grapes and nothing to say for it, or himself, or anybody else.——There is a great church excitement (Presbyterian;—church just under my window—) going on at present. Day light prayer and morning and night service. I heard f[ro]m Han 2 days since;—nothing new. So good-bye, and kind love to all of y[ou]r household who will receive it. To Gus and yourself, so much that I don't know how to send it. Always, dear child

Your anxious and affectionate Mother
Louisa S. McCord

Source: Dulles-Cheves-McCord-Lovell Papers, SCHS.

To Augustine Thomas Smythe

My dear Son April 8th, 1868

I have written opposite, order for interest on stock as you worded it, "either for Miss H. C. McCord, or Miss L. R. McCord" etc., though there can I think be none for Han, as her stock was sold in January—I wrote as you said though, supposing it could do no harm; and if, as I presume, it is a mistake, there will only be nothing to pay. If wrong however, send me word to write it over——I am glad you have sold Lou's stock and I hope well. Thanks for sale of Han's scrip and deposite of $80.23—That will, I hope, with what she still has in Mess. I. A. and Co's hands (in my name) carry her through the year.——Thanks for your little messages about Lou. You *are* a smart boy. You don't know how grateful I am for those same little messages and what a comfort they are to me. Bless the child! I know she is as proud and as happy as may be; and I know well that you are taking good care of her.[27]——Glad to hear that you are busy. Will it continue?

I have written to the "Mercury" and to Russell to send my paper and Review, to Columbia—I suppose they will do so.[28] I still hope to be off on

27. Louisa Cheves Smythe, her parents' first child, was born on July 31, 1868.

28. The Charleston *Mercury* ceased publication with the issue of Nov. 16, 1868. John Russell (1812–71), Charleston bookseller and publisher. The "Review" may be the *Southern Review,* ed. Albert Taylor Bledsoe (Baltimore/St. Louis, 1867–79).

Monday, though (as I have written to Lou,) in some doubt. The squally future makes me doubly anxious to leave these regions of darkness.

With much love to all friends as usual—I am dear son

gratefully as well as affectionately
Your Mother
Louisa S. McCord

Addressed: For A. T. S. Esq. *Source:* Smythe-Stoney-Adger Papers, SCHS.

Appeal as President of the South Carolina Monument Association

[1869]

Women of South Carolina, there needs no urgent appeal to your sympathies in a cause so sacred as that which we now undertake. The great tide of adversity which has swept over our unhappy land, has hitherto stifled effort in this direction; but not, therefore, have our hearts ceased to beat for the glorious dead. Scarcely is there one among us whose thought does not, on the first mention of our object, turn at once with loving affection to some grave which this monument is intended to honor.

Mothers, widows, sisters, daughters, whose hearts thus cling to the soldier's grave, let us unite with an earnest loving effort in this holy duty. Let even our lisping little ones be brought to give their mite to its accomplishment, that, thus impressed upon their minds, they may never forget to love and honor the memory of those who battled and fell in our cause. If a lost cause, even therefore the more holy. Even therefore does it become the more incumbent upon us to bring to this great sacrifice of pure purpose and heroic deed, that homage and veneration which the world pays only to success.

With the wish that all who have shared in a common sorrow, may share also in the privilege of raising this testimonial to our lost heroes, the annual subscription for membership is put at the lowest point practicable, that thus it may be within the means of those who, having little to give, have still the right, through tears and suffering, to join us in the fulfillment of this most sacred duty. To all others—men as well as women—old and young—to all who cherish the name of Carolinian and cling with a fond love to whatever is left of {to} us of our 'good old State,' we would say, give to us freely according to your means; give generously; give gratefully to the memory of those who gave their lives for us.

Source: FOLS, p. 15.

To Hiram Powers

Charleston, South Carolina
March 20th, 1870

Dear Mr. Powers,

Remembering your kindness of eleven years back,—subdued by troubles,—and led by that clinging which draws us towards scenes and persons connected with the calmer or brighter spots of past life, I would almost venture to address you as "my friend." More than you said or did when I was with you there was that in your look which made me think that you could appreciate the courage of enduring suffering, and that your sympathies would be with the oppressed. I have been wishing,—almost intending,—daily, for three years to write to you. But the laying bare of bleeding wounds is an agony, and I have shrunk from it. My want of health for some time made me scarcely able to bear it,—and even now I feel myself a coward in the effort.

Besides I have been told, but I will not believe it, that Hiram Powers has warmly expressed his sympathies against the heroic struggles of our recent lost but glorious cause.[29] I *cannot* believe it. As I remember your calm, but penetrating eye, looking as it were, into the thought of your sitter for his likeness; I think that I too caught the idea of *your mental* likeness, and I will not believe that you can now say "well done" to the destroyers of a noble people. But we *are* destroyed, and I fear as a people past from life forever. The true-hearted among our survivors have to look with pride, only upon our sufferings, and upon the graves of our dead. We fought for our rights and our liberties. Our very boys were heroes in endurance, and in death. But now, ground down, and writhing beneath the heel of a brutal conqueror, none can even live, without giving up something of the purity of his feelings by submission to the unblushing and utterly lawless tyranny of a brutal rule; and the wreck of as noble a people as ever trod *God*'s earth, must, I fear, inevitably fall away from its higher characteristics. *God* only knows how much a wearied Soul can bear, and still live on uncontaminated! Alas! too often those whom we thought strong, bend under the load; and the proud

29. LSM's source may have been John Smith Preston, who, after returning from Europe in 1860, had severed relations with Powers in Florence; their friendship had grown strained when another of Powers' friends, William Burnet Kinney, had in a New Jersey newspaper attacked Preston as an advocate of slavery. John Smith Preston (1809–81), South Carolina senator (1848–56), owned prosperous sugar plantations in Louisiana. He and his wife, Caroline Martha Hampton Preston (1807–83), lived in Europe, chiefly in Rome, from 1857 to 1860, when they came home to Columbia and to the imminent Confederacy. Preston was "a great admirer of Mrs. McCord" (*Chesnut*, p. 329); both husband and wife were close friends of LSM, and of Mary Chesnut, in whose diaries they figure prominently.

heart bows, when, failing the power to resist, it ought to break. I thank *God* that I am of those whose age gives hope of a release before the complete moral extinction of my people shall be effected. The open endeavour, the shameless boast of our conquerors is, to displace the high-toned Southerner, by the vilest of Yankee white and brutal negro. Is it unchristian or unphilosophical, that I find a comfort,—at least a small hope, in the fact that the lawlessness of the so-called general government is fast dragging it to its destruction? That already open bribery governs every thing from the president down;—That already actions worthy only of a common swindler are considered no shame, scarcely glossed over, in the highest places. And for our down-trodden state, is it not enough to say that the Bench of its supreme Court is filled by a renegade jew, a low Yankee lawyer, and a Yankee negro?[30] That the congressional member from South Carolina (a wandering Yankee preacher, and even in his own home, an acknowledged imposter) has just been expelled because he was a little too barefaced in the *selling* of U.S. Cadet Commissions, and has come back to be probably returned again by negro votes.[31] Our State, so-called, Legislature——But why go on with details that sicken in the recital? You know what such a rule must bring.

For myself only, and to excuse my hitherto not writing to you, I would say, that the last I heard from you was late in 1860 or early '61. I cannot say which, as the wanton destruction in Columbia (where I was during the Vandal-like performances of Sherman) of all papers etc. deprive[s] me of data. About that time a letter from you informed me that your bust of my Father, Langdon Cheves, was completed and would very shortly be shipped from Genoa—Further I know nothing from you. Then came our struggle for all that was dear to us,—and with it a seclusion from the outer world, preventing any communication. Then followed the sweep of our dearest and noblest; and all whom I then had to depend upon, now lye under the soil they fought to defend. Left a son-less widow, with two daughters, and an infant grand daughter (born after her Father's death from the field of Man-

30. The South Carolina constitution of 1868 established a supreme court replacing the courts of appeal at law and in equity; it was to be composed of one chief justice and two associate justices, elected by the legislature for a term of six years. Its members to whom LSM alludes here are, in order: Franklin J. [Israel] Moses, Sr. (1804–77), chief justice; Amiel J. Willard (1822–1900), emigrated from New York; and Jonathan Jasper Wright (1840–85), born and admitted to the bar in Pennsylvania.

31. Benjamin Franklin Whittemore (1824–94), born in Massachusetts, a minister of the Methodist Episcopal church, resigned as a member of Congress on Feb. 24, 1870, preventing by one day his expulsion for accepting bribes in return for assisting appointments to the military and naval academies; as LSM predicted, he was reelected; but, Congress declining to reseat him, he accepted election instead to the South Carolina Senate (1870–77).

assas) I am now, ruined in property, and a partial dependent upon a son-in-law; (the husband of the little girl I had with me in Europe) a young man struggling for the support of his family. My Brother under whose suggestions I was acting when seeking to procure from you my Father's bust, died from the first shell cast at Morris Island.

I ought to have written to you immediately after our war came to its sad termination;—but I *could not*. Neither have I at any time been able to command the sum necessary to meet the expense of getting the bust, if it be still in existence. Hoping however that at no distant period, I may effect this object, I have tried, but vainly, to dis-cover any thing about it. I was told that your agent, Mr. Theodore Dehon, died during our war;—and I do not know who may now act for you.[32] I write therefore to yourself, that you may at least not deem me forgetful of the proper respect due to you,—as well as to the memory of my Father,—by what may seem to you a strange neglect of the commonest proprieties of life. But truly it has seemed to me often, that I belonged to life no longer, and could you know one half of the troubles I have gone through, I would need to make no apologies to gain your forgiveness.

Can you tell me anything of the Bust? Do you know if it was ever shipped, or anything of its further fate? If it came to America, is it likely that I can do anything to find it? Excuse me if these questions may seem out of place but possibly Mr. Dehon, unable to communicate with us here, may have mentioned the difficulty, and told you what disposition was made of the bust.[33]

And if you will write to me, will you not tell me that you have been slandered, when they said that you could cast an unkind thought or word, upon as noble a cause, and as heroic a people as ever the great *God* in his mysterious wisdom, has permitted to be crushed![34]

32. Theodore Dehon died in June 1861.

33. "You are in error in regard to my letter saying that the bust of your dear father had already been done. I would not have so informed you, for it has not been executed. The war commenced before I could begin it and I found it difficult to pay expenses during the war. I could proceed only with those few commissions which commanded ready money." Hiram Powers to LSM, April 12, 1870, Hiram Powers and Powers Family Papers, Smithsonian.

34. "I am bound not to deceive you[,] for in politics as in religion I must claim to be free and I grant equal liberty to all my fellow men holding them responsible to me only in regard to open and fair dealings in our intercourse. My friendship for all who have been kind to me in the south has not diminished on account of political differences, while at the same time I have never allowed that friendship to bias my acts under the stern necessities (as I have deemed them) of my country. I hardly need to add that throughout the late disastrous war, I have stood firmly against friends and enemies who have striven to break up the United States. Will you accept my warmest sympathies for you personally,—after the above remarks. If

If you will write to me, direct to Mrs. McCord, care of Augustine T. Smythe, Charleston, South Carolina.

If after this tardy explanation, anything in my conduct toward you may still appear remiss, remember how hard it must be to rake up the ashes of the past from the most painful scenes of a life which shows me now everywhere little but graves, and you will excuse, in whatever I may still seem to fall short.

With kindest regards to your wife and daughters if they still remember be {me}, I am, Dear Sir always with the greatest respect and regard

Yours very truly
Louisa S. McCord

Source: Hiram Powers and Powers Family Papers, Smithsonian.

To Davis, Brooks, and Company

Gentlemen:[35] Charleston, S[outh] C[arolina] April 6th, 1870

On information that you are the Agents of Hiram Powers (Sculptor) I take the liberty of making enquiry of you if you can give me any information concerning a case containing a bust (Colossal) of late Hon[orable] Langdon Cheves, which should have been shipped from Genoa very late in 1860, or early 1861. It should have been directed either to Langdon Cheves, Savannah or more probably to Mrs. Louisa McCord, Columbia S[outh] C[arolina]. If you can give any information concerning the same, you will confer a favor by so doing—

The events of the war having deprived me of all papers and memoranda, I am unable to be more definite in stating time of shipping and address. Please answer Mrs. McCord care of Augustine T. Smythe, Charleston, S[outh] C[arolina]

And very much oblige

Yours respectfully,
Louisa S. McCord

Addressed: Messrs. Davis and Brooks / New York. *Source:* Recipient's transcription, Hiram Powers and Powers Family Papers, Smithsonian.

---

you will, then we are still friends." Hiram Powers to LSM, April 12, 1870, Hiram Powers and Powers Family Papers, Smithsonian.

35. "I received the letter yesterday of which the attached is a copy. On the receipt of this will please write me all you know about this bust of Mr. Langdon Cheves. Please write at once." Sidney Brooks to Hiram Powers, New York, April 12, 1870, Hiram Powers and Powers Family Papers, Smithsonian.

To Lyman Copeland Draper

Sir,[36] Charleston June 3d, 1870

In answer to your favor of 23d. ulto lately received, I regret to have to say that I own no copy of the Eulogy in memory of Gen[eral] Sumter delivered by my late husband D. J. McCord.[37] Pamphlets, manuscripts, and every thing of the kind, formerly owned by me, were for the most part destroyed by our brutal invaders at the close of our Southern Struggle for Liberty. Whatever escaped *them,* was wantonly scattered by our ignorant negroes excited to join in their brutal Saturnalia. In our devastated homes little of value remained after the Vandal like progress of Sherman—

Being thus unable to comply with your request to furnish the address in question, I presume the notes asked for as connected with it are of no moment to you.

Regretting my inability in the matter, I am

Respectfully etc.
Louisa S. McCord

Addressed: Lyman C. Draper Esq. / Madison etc. *Source:* Draper Manuscripts, no. 13DD94, State Historical Society of Wisconsin, Madison.

To the Board of Managers of the South Carolina Monument Association

Copy

Ladies Charleston June 17th, 1870

Permit me to tender you my resignation as president of your association. Much as my heart has been with you in our work, I know not now, how to

36. Lyman Copeland Draper (1815–91), born in Hamburg, N.Y.; secretary of the Wisconsin State Historical Society (1854–86); assembled an enormous collection of documents and other historical materials. His inquiry to LSM, like similar inquiries to other South Carolinians, arose from his research into the battle of King's Mountain, S. C. (Oct. 7, 1780), for his book *King's Mountain and Its Heroes* (1881).

37. Thomas Sumter (1734–1832), eponym of Fort Sumter; born near the later site of Charlottesville, Va.; having settled in South Carolina (1765), one of the state's heroes in the War of American Independence; wounded in battle at Blackstock's plantation with enemy forces under Col. Banastre Tarleton (Nov. 22, 1780); member of the U.S. House of Representatives (1789–93, 1797–1801) and Senate (1801–10). David James McCord delivered his eulogy on June 9, 1832, at the Presbyterian church in Columbia. "We have rarely listened with a more excited interest to any speech. The details of the multifarious, important, and dramatic incidents of General Sumter's life were sketched in the most interesting manner; and the traits of his daring, adventurous, and firm character, admirably illustrated." Columbia *Telescope,* June 12, 1832.

continue it. A powerful faction in our State, which seeks for her the degradation of negro equality, is forcing itself fearfully forward; and from such, I neither wish nor could ask help. Their abandonment of principle, throwing a shame hitherto unknown, on the once honored name of South Carolina[,] is too odious for me to be willing to come in contact with it.

I have been asked what need of ineffective opposition ~~to no effect~~? and why can I not work on quietly?

Because I could not ask help from negro-fraternizers. Because to our beloved dead, principles are a nobler monument than marble. Because three generations of honored graves that for me, South Carolina bears upon her breast, would become to me a constantly haunting reproach, could I link hands, even in the performance of a good act, with the murderers of her fair fame. South Carolina is fast becoming to me, but as one great grave of the great past;—One proud memory which must pass away before the sweeping tide of corruption. The deed of 16th June has taken the lead in the cutting away of the dike which might have saved her from destruction.[38]——May *God* grant that some great head and heart shall yet arise to the rescue! But I see them no where.

Accept with my resignation my heartfelt regrets for its necessity.

I am

very respectfully yours
Louisa S. McCord

Addressed: To The Board of Managers of So. Ca. Monument Association. *Source:* Retained copy, Dulles-Cheves-McCord-Lovell Papers, SCHS.

To Augustine Thomas Smythe

My dear Son, Charlottesville Nov[ember] 14th [1871]

I see that the papers announce Charleston as having been freed by frost from the fever. If this is, as I hope[,] true, Lou will soon be with you to prepare for her approaching sickness.[39] I have, in truth, been very uneasy

38. On June 15, 1870, a convention of what came to be called the Union Reform party (among whom were, it was announced, from twenty to thirty black delegates) met in Columbia in preparation for the state elections to be held in October. (On the background of this convention, see *PSE,* "To the Editor of *The XIX Century,*" source note.) The following day, it adopted a platform (reported in the Charleston newspapers of June 17) declaring support of the Fifteenth Amendment as fundamental law and affirming that the changes effected as results of the war should be "regarded as verities having the force and obligation of law" (Charleston *Daily Courier,* June 17, 1870).

39. Augustine Thomas Smythe, Jr., was born on Dec. 21, 1871.

about her; there having been so much to add to the usual nervous excitement naturally attendant upon her condition. There has been no object nearer my heart than to help her, and yet I have been utterly powerless to do any thing; and now I do not know whether I may do the more mischief, trying to do, or not to do. I need scarcely say to *you,* that were I to follow my impulse, my place would be, where it has always been in her suffering or sorrow, with my hand on hers. I know, although she will try not to show it, that the tension of feeling excited by her condition in recent surrounding circumstances must be severe; and in any hitherto period of her life, I would weeks since have written to her, that I would be with her in the time of trial. But truly (and not doubting her affection and your kindness) I fear that my doing so would in the end bring more pain than comfort. I therefore write to you, rather than to her, to advise me what you would wish me to do. Seeing her, after she will have become settled in the return, to what I must call her home, will better enable you to judge if there is anything sufficiently urgent to change the plan which I had thought most prudent—i.e. to stay away. I want you to answer me, as sincerely as I write, and quite independantly of all consideration of my supposed feelings. One honest, kind, and truthful word, is more grateful to me, than all the made up apologies and courtesies ever spoken. I have loved, and I do love you because I think you truer with me than other people are.——You know my difficulties. They are in no wise lessened. In Charleston I can never be quiet, even in appearance, except permitted to remain in such seclusion as I require. I want no civilities from any body; but only to be permitted to come and go, as coldly and as quietly as I please, and having nothing to do with visits. I am so tired, I do not want to argue or dispute to no good purpose, and if I see people, they talk and goad me on to impatience and hard words; and then comes mischief and sorrow to Lou, whom I am trying to help. Now would my presence under these circumstances tend most to irritate or to soothe?——Neither am I sure that Lou is not going to be confined at your Mother's house. I do not know whence I have this indistinct impression.——Again, this KuKlux inquisition despotism—will it not probably stretch its arms through the State?[40] In truth Charleston deserves no exemption from it. Through her, from the egg of Reform was hatched out the ugly abortion styled "Tax payers Convention,"—which, laugh at it as you may, had none the less a telling effect; and the cowardly notice which this meeting saw fit to take of the

40. Activities of the Ku Klux Klan in South Carolina provoked annoyance and anger in the Federal government, until on Oct. 17, 1871, President Ulysses S. Grant suspended habeas corpus in nine upstate counties. Federal forces arrested several hundred persons and tried them in Federal courts, with eighty-two convictions secured through November 1872.

KuKlux, did, I believe, largely help to call down recent reckless attacks.[41] Now, might not the presence of an offensive and discontented individual like myself, even though only an old woman, help to draw disagreeable attention. Do not laugh, as though thinking that I make myself of much importance. Men have quarelled and shot each other, for a dog—for a shadow;—and I have heard it stated, right or wrong, that women have been threatened and watched, in the dragonade district. I might be, under some circumstances[,] a dangerous inmate, and it would be too late to move out of the way when the lash would be raised, not over me personally but over my nearest and dearest.

All these things considered, had I not better stay away? Tell me the truth;—and only don't let Loulou think that I am unkind or unloving. I am more anxious for her than ever,—even because I cannot tell her so.——

Answer me entirely at your liesure. If you say "Come on" I will do so towards middle December, (D.V.)[42] for some weeks only. But it will be a sin and a wrong in you, to say so, if you think that I had better not. Defer answering as long as you please. Twenty-four hours would be enough to fix me either way. I enclose a slip from yesterday's paper showing that the Habeas Corpus is, to use the slang of the day, being "played out" all over these so called U[nited] States.——

Excuse my long letter—I know you don't approve of such. I congratulate you, on escaping better than you deserve, the risks of fever; (Lou writes me that you keep well) and am always

Your affectionate Mother
Louisa S. McCord

I just see by an old Charleston paper lent me, resolutions debated by the Survivor's Association in Columbia against *the KuKlux*!!![43] And these were

41. The Taxpayers' Convention met in Columbia May 9–12, 1871, called, amid clamorous charges of mismanagement and theft of public funds, to investigate the government's accounts. Responding to a motion by Attorney General Daniel Henry Chamberlain, James Chesnut, as chairman of the convention's executive committee, agreed in deploring the "prevailing violences" but blamed them on the climate created by "bad government, corruption in high places," which "set the example of moral decadence and disregard of law." *United States Congressional Serial Set, House Reports,* 42d Cong., 2d sess., ser. 1531, v. 2, pt. 3, n. 22, pt. 3, pp. 494–95. After its deliberations the convention was widely held to have been duped by Republican governor Robert K. Scott and his officials.

42. *Deo volente* (Lat. "God willing").

43. The Charleston *Daily Courier* of Nov. 13, 1871, reported a meeting of the statewide Survivors' Association, held in Columbia the day before. The meeting unanimously adopted a resolution, called "the KKK resolution" by the reporter, that "at no time has this Association given countenance or encouragement to any organizations or combinations for the purpose of violating the established law of the land, or the rights of any persons thereunder, and

So[uth] C[arolin]a generals, soldiers etc. "Knock him again—He has no friends."[44]

Could they not at least say *nothing?* Must they get on their knees to lick the boots of Grant's drunken soldiery! The whole country has stood aghast at Grant's lawless proceedures and now and now those who should be S[outh] C[arolina] gentlemen, would appear to endorse them! They will get their pay in kind if they do not take care, the next time votes are called for.

Source: Smythe-Stoney-Adger Papers, SCHS.

To Louisa McCord Smythe

Dear Daughter Drummondville Feb[ruar]y 8 [1874]

Thanks for your letter of 30th. I was glad to get all your details of the little ones. There is no want of news or matter of interest to me, when you talk of yourselves. Gussy must be a funny little fellow. I am glad that my dear little Loula is looking better again. I suppose you are doing her education very gently. If she grows fast, *raison de plus* for so doing. Sweeping, and digging and playing, and a very little lessons is wisest.——I am sorry Dr. Reynolds is so much afloat.[45] It is very hard;—but I wish they would quit hanging on to the Leitch's.——I fear Lottie is not the better ~~for~~ or rather I should say, I fear she is the worse for their indecision. She does not seem to have been very well lately. I wish Dr. R. would go to Virginia and set up a little boys school, or anything for a decent maintenance, and be satisfied with that if nothing else comes.

I am glad to hear that Mary-Anne etc. have gone to Zimmerman's.[46] They

---

hereby earnestly and solemnly declare their disapproval of all such organizations, if any there be, existing in this State."

44. *The Oxford Dictionary of English Proverbs,* 3d ed. (Oxford, 1970), p. 374, cites Dinah Maria Mulock (1826–87), *Woman's Thoughts* (1850), p. 156, for "the familiar tragio-comic saying: 'Hit him hard; he's got no friends!'" *Punch* 23 (Dec. 18, 1852): 261, has a cartoon with the caption, "'Hit him again! He has no friends.'—Old Saying."

45. "The Radicals in possession of the State turned out all of the old faculty of the South Carolina College, putting in their place Yankees and negroes. By this Dr. Reynolds' family were driven from Columbia and made their home for a short time in Greenville." Smythe, p. 90. On Oct. 7, 1873, Henry Elliott Hayne, secretary of state and black, was installed as a student; the resulting tumult included the resignation and dismissal of the faculty, among them James L. Reynolds, who secured a position at Furman University in Greenville, S.C.

46. "Mary-Anne" is probably LSM's former servant, daughter of Langdon Cheves' servant June (see LSM to Langdon Cheves, Jr., Jan. 25, 1856, and note). Son of planter William Zimmerman (1763?–1815) and Mary Ann Dozier Zimmerman, Daniel Alexander Zimmerman is listed in the 1870 census as sixty years old, married with three children, and resident

will probably be able to make themselves useful enough to secure a tolerably comfortable home, so long as things do not blow up. If it would be useful to them, I should be glad that Gus should help them from me a little, to any amount not exceeding $20 p[e]r annum, and put to my debit. He will be the better judge though, if it would do more harm or good. Too much help might make them slack in their own efforts and Mr. Z. slack in assisting them, as their service might entitle them to be assisted.——

I have already written that the money business (last check) was all right with me at last. I am getting on quietly here. Took a sleigh-drive a few days since to the Falls. The ice from the River was scattered a few weeks since by a wind storm, and the water is of a dirty brown. The surrounding woods were beautifully laden with snow and ice, which would have glittered magnificently if the sun had shone;—but the sun just would not. Today the Sun is brilliant for the first time lately, and I see quite a number of sleighs flying about. It is Sunday though and I cannot venture—being a stranger here. I do not want to get myself talked about as a dissipated old character. I went to church this morning. Unfortunately met with the misfortune of losing my neutral tint spectacles the other day. Hope in a week or so to get a pair (by order of a storekeeper here) from Montreal. Have got a very abominable pair of blue ones now, that hurt almost as much as they help. My bad writing is not all from my faulty eyes—I have got my pen in an abominable condition.

Long ago I got letters from you that I could not answer then wherein you seemed to distress y[ou]rself much about "Aunt Anna." It is useless and wrong for you to do so. She has the misfortune to be very effortless and has been kept entirely in the dark about her own affairs. Pinckney has been always a very bad manager and doubtless there is a pretty bad muddle in their affairs. But Mr. C. Huger will get himself fairly compensated for board etc.[47]—and as Anna's Trustee, he ought to try and manage something for her, if Pinckney continues, as he doubtless will do, incapable. They still have a part of the Ogeechee Plantation and the Altamaha Place. The first I told you, Sophia wrote me that Paul had rented.[48] Does Nan still keep her servant[?] I fear so. She ought to do without her. If she has Cara, it costs ~~her enough~~ to keep her, as much as would maintain herself. In such troubles as we go through, we must all make efforts or suffer. I have

---

of Darlington County; he purchased Lang Syne and Goshen plantations on Dec. 1, 1870 (see *PSE*, pp. 492–93).

47. Probably Cleland Kinloch Huger (d. 1892), Thomas Pinckney Huger's younger brother.

48. Sophia Cheves Haskell's youngest son, Paul Thomson Haskell.

been displeased at the evident efforts of the Hugers to draw us into the net of their own folly. I did not at all like a letter I rec[eive]d some time since from my old friend Miss E. P. Huger.[49] Poor old Soul she has suffered too—but I have enough to do with my own. If Nan and her Husband need help, it should come from his relatives who have helped to squander her property. Only do not let yourself be made unhappy about it. Dear love to all.

Source: Dulles-Cheves-McCord-Lovell Papers, SCHS.

To Augustine Thomas Smythe

Drummondville, Ontario, Canada
March 29th, 1874

My Dear Son

Thanks for y[ou]r letter of 23d rec[eive]d last evening. The enclosure[50] was yet not needed; and yet I am glad it has come. I have a restless feeling (I do not believe in presentiments) that I must go somewhere or do something soon,—and keep most of my funds in nasty green backs ready. It is, I know, only the anxious habit of a mind, used to trouble and going ahead to meet it. But I feel safer with $50 or $100 in my trunk. I wrote you more than a week ago a letter that I hope did not worry you,—but I could not help it. I took into my head (I hope I was all mistaken) that Lou's letters indicated etc. etc. I won't talk about it again. Only let me trust you to tell me honestly and sincerely if anything is wrong with her.

I have been not a little anxious too about Lottie. She is a sacred charge to me, (none can be more so—) and I am very anxious to know if and how I can be of use to her. I do not see that you can help me though. But if anything should occur to you, I think you will say it.——If remaining where I am, (and I will not move unless for causes above suggested) I can scarcely need further funds (still retaining as I wish to do $50 always on hand) until about first ~~May~~ June[.] But do not trouble y[ou]rself to remember. I will write a fortnight before needing it. I am at present abundantly supplied for all contingencies. Forgive me for troubling you so much. An old Lady here of 85 deliberately pitched herself headforemost into a well the other day. If I were not as firm to my principles, as you sometimes want to quarrel with me for being, I would feel some days mightily inclined to follow her example. *A*

49. Elizabeth Pinckney Huger (d. Jan. 4, 1882, aged 78), Thomas Pinckney Huger's eldest sister.

50. Not found; presumably a bank draft or other instrument.

propos of principles or the want of them,—I hear that Semmes(!) has gone over to glorifying the Union, and wanting place![51]——

I will write tomorrow morning (i.e. per same mail as this) to Lottie, so you *need not tell them* of my obnoxious letters—Only remember, it is my right to know if I am *wanted* at any time.——Forgive me and believe me

most affectionately
Y[ou]r Mother
L. S. McC——

Source: Smythe-Stoney-Adger Papers, SCHS.

Last Will and Testament

The State of South Carolina—

In the name of God. Amen!

I, Louisa S. McCord, widow, late a planter of St. Matthews Parish, Orangeburgh District, and State aforesaid, but by the sad results of our War, and our crushed out Liberties, now with no settled home, and much a wanderer—being of sound and disposing mind—do make publish and declare the following as and for my last Will and Testament; hereby revoking all former Wills by me at any time heretofore made.

First — I direct that as soon as possible after my death, all my just debts and liabilities if any such there be, shall be paid by my Executors hereinafter named, out of the first monies that may come into their hands from my estate—together with my testamentary and funeral expenses and a suitable stone to mark my Grave; all which latter expenses, I request may be strictly limited to suit the times of adversity and sorrow, wherein it has pleased Almighty God to cast my lot of life.

Second — I give and bequeath to my only remaining daughter, Louisa

51. Probably Raphael Semmes (1808–77), Confederate naval commander, most famously of CSS *Alabama;* arrested and imprisoned after the war (Dec. 1865–April 1866); lawyer in Mobile. But there are also Raphael's first cousin Thomas Jenkins Semmes (1824–99), lawyer, member of the Confederate Senate; and Thomas' brother, physician Alexander Jenkins Semmes (1828–98), who had served the Confederacy, now professor of physiology at the Medical College in Savannah (1870–76); ordained priest in the Roman Catholic church (1878). The particular incident to which LSM refers has not been identified. Raphael Semmes spoke at the unveiling of a monument to the Confederate dead raised in Magnolia Cemetery, Mobile, on April 27, 1874, on which occasion he spoke of reconciliation while honoring the fallen cause; it is possible that some report of these views preceded their expression; if so, he got no place by them.

McCord Smythe, wife of Augustine T. Smythe of Charleston, all clothing, furniture, and all personal and household effects which I may own at the time of my death; and particularly my bust by Powers.

Third I give and bequeath to my Executors hereinafter named, or to such of them as shall qualify, the sum of Five Thousand ($5,000) Dollars, to be held by them, or the survivor of them, in trust to invest the same, and to use the interest and income arising therefrom, or so much thereof as they shall think necessary or advisable, for the maintenance[,] education[,] and benefit of my grand-daughter Langdon Cheves McCord, only child of my deceased son Langdon Cheves McCord, until she shall attain the age of twenty one years, or shall marry, and when she shall attain the age of twenty one years or shall marry, which ever shall first happen, then in trust to pay over and deliver the said sum of money and the property and securities in which the same may be then invested, to the said Langdon Cheves McCord, freed and discharged from any further or other trusts. But if my said grand daughter shall die before me, or surviving me, shall die before attaining the age of twenty one years, or marrying, then the said Legacy and the property and securities in which the same shall be invested, shall revert to, and become part of my residuary estate, subject to the provisions of this my will in relation to the residue of my estate.

Whatever portion of the interest and income derived from the said fund, shall not be used for the maintenance and education of my said grand daughter, shall be invested by my Executors as part of the principal of said legacy, under and subject to the trusts above declared.

Fourth I give and bequeath to my Executors herinafter named, or to such of them as shall qualify, the sum of Three Thousand ($3,000) Dollars, in trust for my grand daughter Hannah McCord Rhett; and Three thousand ($3,000) Dollars in trust for my grand daughter Sarah Rhett, only children of my deceased daughter Hannah McCord Rhett, to be invested and held by my said Executors or the survivor of them, upon the same trusts and subject to the same conditions and provisions as to interest and principal as are herein expressed in relation to the Legacy given them in trust for my grand daughter, Langdon Cheves McCord. If either of my said grand daughters, Hannah McCord Rhett, or Sarah Rhett shall die before me, or surviving me shall die before attaining the age of twenty one years, or marrying, then the Legacy of Three Thousand ($3,000) Dollars given in trust for the one so dying, shall be held by my Executors, or the survivor of them, in trust for her surviving sister, upon the same trusts, and subject to the same conditions.

And if both of said grand daughters Hannah McCord Rhett and Sarah Rhett shall die before me, or surviving me, shall die before attaining the age of twenty one years, or marrying, then the Legacies so given in trust for them, and the property and securities in which the same shall be invested, shall revert to and become part of my residuary estate, subject to the provisions of this my will in relation to my residuary estate.

Fifth I give and bequeath unto my Executors hereinafter named or to such of them as shall qualify, the sum of Five Thousand ($5,000) Dollars in trust for my grand daughter Louisa Cheves Smythe; and Three Thousand ($3,000) Dollars in trust for my grand son Augustine Thomas Smythe; and Three Thousand ($3,000) Dollars in trust for my grand daughter, Hannah McCord Smythe, children of my daughter Louisa McCord Smythe; to be invested and held by my said Executors or the survivor of them, upon the same trusts and subject to the same conditions and provisions as to interest and principal as are herein expressed in relation to the Legacy given them in trust for my grand daughter Langdon Cheves McCord.

In the event that any or all of my said grand children Louisa Cheves Smythe, Augustine Thomas Smythe, and Hannah McCord Smythe shall die before me, or surviving me shall die before attaining the age of twenty one years or marrying, it is my will that the Legacies so given in trust for the said grand child or grand children so dying and the property and securities in which the same shall be invested shall be paid and delivered to their mother the said Louisa McCord Smythe, through whose liberality and that of her husband in returning to me the larger portion of the limited means given to them at their marriage, I am alone ennabled to make the bequests of this will to her[,] her heirs, executors, administrators and assigns absolutely freed and discharged from any further or other trusts.

If my daughter Louisa McCord Smythe should die before me it is my will that her interest under this my will shall not lapse but shall pass to and be vested in her heirs at law and distributees.

Sixth In case of failure or deficiency of assetts of my estate to pay all the foregoing Legacies in full, it is my will that all the said Legacies shall abate proportionately.

Seventh All the rest and residue of my estate real and personal wheresoever situated, of which I shall die seized and possessed, I give devise and bequeath to be equally divided between all my grand children living at the time of my death share and share alike; the same to be invested and held by my Executors or the survivor of them for the use and benefit of the said grand children respectively, upon the several trusts, and subject to the same conditions and provisions as to principal and interest as are herein before limited and expressed of and concerning the specific legacies and bequests for my said grand children repectively.

Eighth I hereby nominate, constitute and appoint my son in law Augustine T. Smythe and my friend Charles Richardson Miles (who has consented to be named, at my earnest and urgent request) Executors of this my Will and Trustees of the trusts therein declared;[52] giving unto them or such of them as shall qualify, and to the survivor of them full power and authority to sell and dispose of any or all of my estate at public or private sale whenever, as often, and in such manner and upon such terms as they or he shall deem expedient; and to make any change in the investments of my estate and as often as they may think fit; and it is my express will and direction that they shall not be liable for any errors of judgement in the administration of my estate and the performance of their duties as Executors and Trustees, provided they shall have acted in good faith: And it is also my express will and most earnest wish that my said Executors shall charge and retain the usual and regular commissions allowed by law for such services as they shall render.

In testimony whereof, I have to this my will, written on this and the foregoing five pages, fastened together at the top, set my hand and seal this twelfth day of February[,] Eighteen hundred and seventy six.

Louisa S. McCord[53]

Source: Probate Court Records, County of Charleston, South Carolina.

52. Charles Richardson Miles (1829–93), brother of William Porcher and Francis Turquand Miles; Confederate States attorney for South Carolina from 1862; lawyer in Charleston; elected to South Carolina House of Representatives (1878); elected attorney general of South Carolina (1882), and reelected (1886). "Richardson Miles: '[Patrick] Cleburne and [States Rights] Gist are killed [at the battle of Franklin, Nov. 30, 1864].' And (mournfully): 'Can any victory pay for so much death?'" (*Chesnut,* p. 691).

53. To the Last Will and Testament is appended:

"Signed, sealed, published, and declared by the said Testatrix Louisa S. McCord as and for her last will and testament in our presence, who at her request, and in her presence,

To Langdon Cheves III

Dear Langdon[54] Abbeville April 6th [1876]

I seldom make excuses, and so in answer to yours of 13th Ulto, without any preliminary reasons for my delay, I only say that I wish I could, better than I am able to do, help you in your present line of research. It would in truth be to me a labour of love. My feelings towards my Father, have through life been almost those of worship, rather than simply of affection. In answer to your questions—1st Alexander Cheves came from Aberdeen or its neighbourhood. The time I should think to have been between 1760 and 70.

2d—During a day spent in Aberdeen, in a hurried tour through Scotland, walking with my children, we passed a large druggist establishment, bearing the name of (I do not recollect the Christian name)——*Chevas* "Chemist and Druggist to her Majesty the Queen" etc.——I went in, and asking for Mr. Chevas, was told that he was absent. I left my card, with an apology for the intrusion, as induced by similarity of my own name, and was told that there was a Mr. Chevas, bank manager, who would probably be informed on any such subject. I had arranged to leave Aberdeen and did not seriously expect to find,—nor know how to set about finding, the Bank manager, which as I afterwards found, meant what we call *President* of a Bank, and I left the next morning thinking no more on the subject. After a visit to the Orkney Islands etc., in returning we again struck Aberdeen; and needing funds, I found my circular letter referred me to the Branch Bank of England. I went there accordingly with my son, and presenting my circular, found myself the object of close attention from an elderly gentleman, who presently coming forward, asked if I was the Lady whose card had been left etc. On receiving my affirmative answer, he expressed great delight at meeting me,—said that he was the son of a favorite cousin of my grandfathers,—That he had often heard his father speak of his cousin Sandy, after whom he was himself named Alexander. He was very pressing for me to stop and let

---

and in presence of each other, have hereunto subscribed our names as witnesses to the execution thereof.

A. M. Huger
Henry A. M. Smith
Louis DeB. McCrady"

Arthur Middleton Huger (b. 1842), son of Arthur Middleton Huger (d. 1870) and Margaret Campbell King Huger; Henry Augustus Middleton Smith (1853–1924), lawyer, judge, historian of South Carolina; Louis DeBerniere McCrady (b. 1851), younger brother of Edward McCrady, Jr.

54. Langdon Cheves III, son of LSM's brother Charles and Isabella Middleton Cheves, was engaged in genealogical research into the Cheves family. A canceled draft of this letter is extant among LSM's notes to her "Memoir of Langdon Cheves."

him see more of us. Unfortunately I had arranged to leave immediately, and have since much regretted that I did not change my plan. This is all that I know of my Father's Scottish relatives. I promised to write—but our War came,—and sorrow upon sorrow piled until I scarcely felt the whole world worth writing about.

3d—I do not remember to have heard of any relatives of my Father in Scotland as assisted by him. I have heard of persons bearing some similar name whom my Father assisted; though believing while doing so, that they were imposing upon him, and I think they were in this country. But I was too young to remember a circumstance which according to my impression my Father laid little stress upon. Certainly the Gentleman whom I met in Aberdeen was not one needing assistance nor appearing to belong to a family at any time needing it.

4th—The spelling of the name appears to have been various—Chivas, Chevas, Cheves, Shivas are or were, I think[,] all written in an old bible, which Lou still has in Charleston;—delapidated, and I fear some of the names torn out, or injured by the hands it past through, during, or rather after our War, when the negroes were turned loose by Sherman upon my plantation residence with orders to destroy and ruin in any way they liked best. Tell Lou to lend you the old Bible if you would like to see what is left of it.

5th—As to assistance of Judge King in investigations regarding spelling etc., I think you must have misunderstood my Sister.[55] My Father in early youth, adopted, (rather retained) the name, as oftenest spelt by his Father. You will find among many old Scotch names an indifference to varied spelling. Take for instance the name of the author of "Douglas" which was indifferently Hume, Home, and I think Holmes.[56] Many other similar instances you may probably have come across. Judge King was a friend of my Father but I think his junior in years, and still more, if I mistake not, in life. Langdon Cheves had made his mark, while Judge King was still Michal Kingo, a clever young schoolmaster. Later in life however, some 40 years back I think, Judge King when on a visit to Great Britain, looking over books of Heraldry, met the Coat of Arms of the name Chivas, Chevas, Shivas etc., and taking note

55. Mitchell King (1783–1862), born in Crail, Fifeshire, Scotland; Charleston lawyer; recorder of Charleston and judge of the city court (1842–44). Arriving in Charleston (1805) after adventures in London, Prussia, Malta, and a prison in Malaga, King obtained a post at, then charge of, the College of Charleston, a phase of his career, before he began to practice law in 1810, to which LSM makes reference below; in 1857 the College of Charleston conferred an LL.D. upon him.

56. James Home (1722–1808), Scottish clergyman and tragedian; his greatest success was *Douglas* (1756).

of them, wrote enclosing them to my Father. I only now recall the motto they bore, which was Judge King thought (and I agree with him) particularly suited to my Fathers character. *Virtute non Vis.* Ask Lou to lend you these papers. I know she has them. Tell her I think she will find them in her paper-drawer, in thc study. Also if you would care to see it, is a copy of the Langdon arms given by a Virginia family who were trying to prove relationship with the South Carolina Statesman.

I ought to know more of all this; but my Father always kept off questions which appeared to aim at giving material for a written Life. Indeed left practically an orphan at three years of age, he himself was scantily informed upon these subjects, and never stated as fact anything which bore to his own mind even the shadow of a doubt.

As to your further request, something of a memoir, I am now quite unfit. A few scattered anecdotes, and those perhaps, already given to you by others, would be all I could do.

If such would be desirable to you I will try to collect them some day when I am in brighter mood than now;—should such come upon me.

Affectionately yours
Louisa S. McCord

Source: Langdon Cheves I Papers, SCHS.

To Langdon Cheves III

Dear Langdon Abbeville May 4th, 1876

I have here endeavoured to fulfil a part of my promise to try to write a sketch of y[ou]r grandfather's private life "as a man rather than a states man". I am now rather old and forgetful for such an attempt. If this would meet your idea, I will (D.V.) make another step forward another time. What I have written stops abruptly you will perceive. There were but a few lines to finish what I had blotted down, and I thought best to wait for another sheet another time. Tell me honestly if it was something different from this that you wished—or if this I can try for some more another time. Very slowly though, as I may think of something—My hand is tired and I stop this, I fear, rather illegible scrawl—Sophie and her Mother join me in kind love and regards to your household[.]

Affectionately your Aunt
Louisa S. McCord

Source: Langdon Cheves I Papers, SCHS.

To Langdon Cheves III

Dear Langdon Abbeville May 20th [18]76

In spite of stiff finger's which bungle over my paper, even more just now than usual, I think best to send you what I have written. I am very soon on the wing for your "*terra incognita*" Cleveland Springs, where Lou writes me she hopes to try a couple of months rest and change for herself and little ones. They all need it, and I hope her husband will be able to be with her. I will leave this in about ten days, and as a messenger goes to the mail tomorrow I take the opportunity of (for the present) winding up my small efforts in your service. If I can still make the subject interesting to you, I will (D.V.) continue it by-and-bye—Though the character of facts will be, I fear[,] more beyond my reach, and therefore less interesting as less known to me. *Nous verrons* however when the time comes. But I expect you to be candid with me and to say, if perchance you may already be satisfied and ready to call out, "hold! enough!" neither will I put the Macbeth curse upon you, if you do.[57]———

My last communication broke off with the words, "*If I rightly remember*"— This takes up the broken sentence and continues, as you will find[,] "*both captain and crew[")] etc.*

I will not attempt anything more so long as Lou is at Cleveland. I expect to have my grand children much round me,—to say nothing of the noise and confusion of a No[rth]-C[arolin]a-watering-place, which I have hitherto frequented only in its extremest quiet. You know my days of fuss and company are long gone by;—I have therefore avoided hitherto the bustling season, and only now purpose going there, because Lou has determined that it is of comparatively easy access. Thanks for your two letters lately rec[eive]d together. I shall be more than pleased to hear from you again if you feel disposed to write to me

care Judge Brevard[58]
Cleveland Springs
Shelby—No[rth] C[arolin]a

I *think* from some old deeds that your Aunt has, that my Grandmother's grave where I have put the slab, is on the ~~lot~~ tract of land in "Granville county" covered by the deed of 200 acres to Alexander Cheves of which you speak; the River-fork to which you refer bears ~~not~~ now the name of "Little

57. *Macbeth* 5.8.33–34: "Lay on, Macduff; / And damn'd be him that first cries, 'Hold, enough.'"

58. Joseph Francis Brevard (1788–1877). The Brevards were a prominent and numerous North Carolina family.

River." (I know nothing of my Grandfather ever having been in Edgefield.) The grave is in the middle of an old field, under a large tree which has been left as a mark—about five miles f[ro]m here on what was Judge Wardlaw's plantation.[59]

I hope for you Savannah River planters, success in the "Cross Tides" Case.[60] I don't know what to think of the "Hawaiian Treaty." As we have no government now; no public morals, and need money to live—I suppose in spite of Political Economy and Free Trade truths, you will have to wish for *protection*.[61] Goodbye—Love to and from all—

Affectionately y[ou]rs
L. S. McCord

Source: Langdon Cheves I Papers, SCHS.

59. "Judge Wardlaw had an only son and five sons-in-law in the army and I cannot say how many other relatives. With every battle came trouble. . . . Through it all the dear old Judge moved, comforting, upholding, and helping everywhere—'mothering' his seven daughters and all the other helpless women who came under his roof." Smythe, p. 52. David Lewis Wardlaw (1799–1873), whose eminent career as lawyer, judge, politician, signer of the Ordinance of Secession, and president of the South Carolina constitutional convention of 1865 earned him a place in Benjamin F. Perry's *Reminiscences of Public Men,* was a neighbor of Charles and Sophia Haskell near Abbeville.

60. In *South Carolina* v. *Georgia* 93 U.S. 4 (1876), South Carolina filed in the U.S. Supreme Court a bill in equity, seeking an injunction to restrain the state of Georgia and the U.S. secretary of war from building "a crib dam at a point known as the 'Cross Tides', for the purpose, by diverting a sufficient quantity of the water passing through the Back River into the Front River channel, of securing to the city [of Savannah] a depth of fifteen feet at low water." (The common border between South Carolina and Georgia, the Savannah River is divided into two channels, the Front and the Back rivers, at Hutchinson Island to the north of the city.) South Carolina's grievance was that the proposed dam would impede navigation on the Savannah River; its argument appealed (among other texts) to article 1, section 9, clause 6, of the U.S. Constitution. Finding that navigation would not be impeded and that the constitutional provision did not apply, Associate Justice William Strong (1808–95), delivering the Supreme Court's opinion in October 1876, dismissed South Carolina's bill.

61. On Jan. 30, 1875, a reciprocity treaty was signed, to take effect eighteen months later, between the United States and Hawaii. The treaty, opening American markets to Hawaiian exports, provoked opposition from American producers, such as the growers of rice and sugar in the Southern states.

To [James D.?] Chalmers

Sir,[62] [Abbeville May 1876]

I have a letter from Mr. A. T. Smythe saying that he has sent you, as I requested, post office order for $100.00. I presume you have duly rec[eive]d it. Please let me know by bearer. Also whether you have been able to arrange ~~for me~~ for the enclosure of the slab which ~~we~~ you have laid ~~I expect~~ for me—I expect to leave the neighbourhood in a week or ten days and will if possible drive to ~~see the~~ the grave, early this coming week———

Addressed: Mr. Chalmers / Abbeville Village. *Source:* Draft, Langdon Cheves I Papers, SCHS.

To Langdon Cheves III

Dear Langdon Charlotte, No[rth] C[arolin]a July 11th [1876]

I have been intending[,] and intending, to answer your letter of 14th Ulto. But in truth, I have been so utterly demoralized by all that has been going on through our (?) State,—Lou's continued sickness exciting personal anxieties; and then the jollification, and fraternizing, and gush of loyalty and love;—and the burying of hatchets; and dancing in chains;[63]—that, as I could not kneel down and shout "glory! glory!,"—nor find my way to the "love, peace, and charity" frame of mind,—I have been trying to keep very quiet and very stupid, hemning, in good-woman style, pocket handkerchiefs, and so forth. I left Cleveland Spr[ing]s (because it was hot, and because I could better find here the pocket h[an]dk[erchief]s etc. to hemn) nearly two weeks since. But here,—hot, is hotter, and hottest!! People say, unprecedented weather. Here, however, I am trying to stay until Augustine Smythe can get away from the law, and start with Lou etc., for V[irgini]a—whither I shall, with all speed, join them *en route.*

I presume the ladies of your family are all off long before this for Flat Rock; and, I hope, escaping such heat, as (judging from what is experienced here) Charleston, I fear, must have. Are you and Henry[64] such thorough men of business, that you do not intend to indulge yourselves in your usual recreation of a mountain holliday? This is a hot season in which to begin

62. Abbeville newspaper and cemetery records show that a James D. Chalmers married Christiana Ramey on Dec. 11, 1856, and died May 30, 1894, at the age of sixty. James Chalmers, presumably the same man, is listed as thirty-five years old in the 1870 census, Abbeville County.

63. LSM appears to refer to celebrations of the Centennial on July 4, 1876.

64. Langdon Cheves III's brother, Henry Charles Cheves.

with such a change.——I hope Rice crops get on safely, and suppose if Tilden is elected, there will no longer be fear of Hawaiian treaties etc.[65]——I have of course written,—and can write,—nothing of my Father in my present restless state of mind. If I live to get back to Charleston next winter, it will depend, I suppose[,] upon the turn of things, whether I can again gather up my scraps of recollection to write more. I wish you had thought of asking it of me a half dozen years ago. By-the-way, my Fathers monument is I hear at last raised. The blessed S[outh] C[arolina] Centennial blotted it out as much as possible. It is eight months after date of contract. I hope the inscriptions will be satisfactory to you. I would have consulted you about them; but they were all done before I knew you. For in truth, only since our short correspondence, have I known you as Langdon Cheves. My heart warms to the name, and to my nephew, who is, I believe[,] worthy of it.

You ask in your letter whether I can tell anything of the farm in V[irgini]a left to my Father by his grandfather. I cannot. I only remember to have heard, in my childhood[,] that Father made ~~en~~ research for, and I believe found it. That it had been taken possession of, and passed to other claiments whom it would have been difficult to dispossess—my Father probably possessing no papers or titles securing it. I do not know whether it was a farm or a house in the town or village of Woodstock.

As for the lot in Abbeville, on which my Grandmothers grave is now covered and enclosed—Your Aunt Sophia writes me that I have proved to be right in the reasoning which led me to the conclusion that it belonged to Alexander Cheves, and was the home of the young Mother, destined never to know her son. Old Mr. Perrin knows all about it and says that titles and papers were burned with Village C[ourt] House.[66]——The Langdon arms were given to Father, by Mrs. Elwyn (Langdon-Elwyn the family were called) originally Miss Langdon daughter or descendant of Gov[ernor] Lang-

65. Samuel Jones Tilden (1814–86), governor of New York; Democratic candidate for president, won about a quarter of a million votes more than his competitor, Republican Rutherford B. Hayes, but lost on account of contested electoral votes which an electoral commission assigned all to Hayes.

66. The Perrins were a prominent Abbeville family, James Monroe Perrin leading the company of Abbeville Minute Men joined by LSM's nephews William and Alexander Haskell by the time it departed for Charleston in January 1861; James Perrin was killed at Chancellorsville (May 3, 1863). Alexander Haskell later served under Brig. Gen. Abner Perrin, killed at Spotsylvania (May 12, 1864). "Old Mr. Perrin" is Thomas Chiles Perrin (1805–78), lawyer and planter; member of the South Carolina House of Representatives (1842–45) and Senate (1846–47); president of the Greenville and Columbia Railroad Company (1853–66); delegate to the secession convention (1860); Democratic nominee for lieutenant governor (1868).

don of I think Massachusetts but of V[irgini]a stock, and when we knew them hailing from New Orleans.[67]

I hope that Harrie is better of the tendency to "not very well" which was hanging about her when you wrote and that she and others are all comfortable at Flat Rock.[68] To yourself if in Charleston, I must only I suppose wish you such patience under heat as I cannot practice myself, and am

Affectionately y[ou]r Aunt
Louisa S McCord

Source: Langdon Cheves I Papers, SCHS.

To Langdon Cheves III

Dear Langdon [1876]

As your Mother thought probable that the following remarks of Judge Huger repeated to me by Alfred Huger (during a visit paid me a few years before the death of the latter) would be of interest to you, I copy them below.[69] The conversation turning upon the love and admiration entertained by Judge Huger for my Father,—the Judge, he said, had once remarked to him, "In one respect, Cheves differs from any man I ever met. With men of the highest integrity, I have always found truthfulness is a principle, a sentiment,—but with Cheves it is not only a sentiment, it is a passion."—— On another occasion, "Yes Sir;—Not only have I never known him to suppress, but never to permit the suppression of truth."

In a discussion of nullification my Father said to him (Judge Huger), "I

67. Elizabeth Langdon Elwyn, wife of Thomas Elwyn and mother of Philadelphia physician and philanthropist Alfred Langdon Elwyn (1804–84), was daughter of John Langdon (1741–1819), born Portsmouth, N.H., and governor of New Hampshire 1805–9 and 1810–12. John Langdon's mother was a descendant of Governor Thomas Dudley (1576–1653) of Massachusetts Bay Colony, of whom LSM may be thinking when she makes John Langdon governor of Massachusetts. The Langdons being settled in Portsmouth, N.H., since the mid-seventeenth century, it is not clear how LSM ascribes to them "Virginia stock," unless she assumed this from the residence in Virginia of her great-grandfather Thomas Langdon before his emigration to South Carolina.

68. Langdon Cheves III's sister, Harriott Cheves.

69. Alfred Huger (1788–1872), cousin of Judge Daniel Elliott Huger whose remarks he passed to LSM; member of South Carolina Senate (1818–34); opposed nullification; postmaster general of Charleston (1834–67); Unionist; delegate to the South Carolina constitutional convention of 1865.

oppose nullification because it must strengthen the hands of Federal Power, and is thus a Union measure. I object to it as a Union Measure."[70]

I am glad to send you these should they be of interest to you, and am

Affectionately your Aunt
Louisa S. McCord

Source: Langdon Cheves I Papers, SCHS.

To Preston Powers

Dear Sir[71] Charleston, South Carolina April 21st, 1878

Your letter of 27th Feb[ruar]y has hitherto remained unanswered, owing to a long and severe indisposition from which I have suffered.

I fear that I can do little in the way of assistance to your models, (defective as I know them to be;) and even that little, I can effect only after ~~some~~ considerable delay—I would need trust much to the sculptors genius, (if success can be attained at all,) to fill up,—by appreciation of the character of the man,—the dead features in his hands.

Your terms are ~~naturally~~ of necessity more difficult than those for similar works of art, twenty years back; while my means then of opulence, are now restricted, through the overwhelming ruin brought by War. I will however be prepared to meet them:—That is ~~—as you say—~~ the first payment of £50 together with the order as you say. You will do me the favour to tell me how and to whom to make it. Of the remaining £90, I could meet the payment at any time on or after 15th June, ~~a year hence, (June 1879) *possibly sooner*, but I could not certainly, so bind myself.~~ 1879. Should the work be finished before that date, you would run no risk, as I could give you an acknowledgement which would, in case of my death, perfectly secure the payment, at the above date,—or[72] it would be at your option to delay sending, until June, when ~~I would be ready for you~~ my funds would come in.

I shall, so soon as I am able, see to sending on anything possible, to assist

70. A draft of these anecdotes, in LSM's hand, apparently in preparation for writing this letter, is found in the Langdon Cheves I Papers, SCHS.

71. Third son of Hiram Powers, (William) Preston Powers (1843–1931) took charge of his deceased father's studio in September 1874. But feuds with his family compelled him to open his own studio next door to his father's, which was thereupon closed down; in 1880 began a series of lawsuits made against him by his mother—these shattered the family into divisions preserved in their descendants to the present.

72. The words from "you would run no risk" down to and including "at the above date,—or" are enclosed within a balloon open on its left margin; but there is no indication if or whither the passage so marked is to be transferred.

in modelling; and you will then determine if the work can be accomplished.——To do justice to your subject, you would need to put soul into the ~~dead~~ lifeless plaster ~~now in your hands~~ before you. These models were taken, the one in advanced old age,—the other after death; and both by ~~work men without skill~~ unskilled workers. ~~There is no likeness of him at the age~~ Can you put into those features what they must have shown when during our War with England (in 1812,) he swayed our Country's action by his eloquence—and when it was remarked of him by ~~our American Author Writer~~ Washington Irving, that Langdon Cheves was the only Orator he had ever ~~heard~~ listened to, who realized his ideas of a Demosthenes or a Cicero.——When I sat to your Father, ~~it was with~~ I indulged the faint hope, that he might retain from the family likeness, (which was said to be considerable in me, such as Woman may bear to Man) some ~~very~~ far off glimmer of the grand head, of which such models as you have, ~~could~~ can give only the size and rough form.——I ought also to mention, what your models could give no suggestion of,—That his shoulders were broad, and his chest full and well-formed. In every ~~age~~ way, a man of strong and impressive appearance; conveying always the unmistakable stamp of intellectual power. Am I unreasonable in asking you to see all this through my words?

With kind regards to your Mother and Sisters, who flatter, by so long kindly remembering me,

I am, Dear Sir

very truly and respectfully yours
Louisa S McCord

pray address any communication to me always to care of Augustine T. Smythe Esq.

Addressed: Preston Powers / Studio Powers / Florence Italy. *Source:* Draft, Langdon Cheves I Papers, SCHS.

To Preston Powers

Dear Sir [Charleston May 29th, 1878]

I ~~have~~ rec[eive]d, yesterday, ~~recd~~ your letter of 8th Inst. ~~I today~~ and today enclose such likenesses as I can procure of my Father ~~wh but but~~ and which are I regret to say exceedingly faulty. I cannot understand why these photographs taken from paintings seem~~s~~ to distort the face,—The mouths in both being ~~abominable~~ quite crooked—The ~~better likeness of the two~~ roughest looking of the two (taken f[ro]m a ~~pa~~ very inferior painting ~~of~~ by Morse, since of telegraphick ~~fame~~ celebrity, but beginning his career as a portrait painter)[73] ~~conveys (rough as it is) more idea of the expression of face of forehead face though the mouth is fearfully distorted than the smoothly finished one. The profile likeness is essentially correct—The Morse picture~~ conveys (rough as it is) more idea of the expression of ~~face~~ face forehead and eye~~—(the mouth is quite fearfully distorted)~~ than the smoother one. The profile likeness is ~~probably~~ an essentially correct profile outline. None of them can give ~~even the~~ [*two? illegible words*] shadow of the man—~~the greatest~~ who although now almost forgotten in the scramble which follows our noble but disastrous war ~~almost forgotten~~, was the greatest ~~that our State ever gave to the country~~ in self poised character and massive intellect that our State has ~~produced~~ ever given to the country—

To describe his appearance I can only give my own recollection, of impressive and commanding ~~appearance~~—"King-like" ~~as a~~ [*two or three illegible letters canceled*] to use a common ~~rather than correct~~ rather than correct ~~expression~~ comparison [which?] was by the masses frequently applied to him [*line missing from torn page*]—and no personal ambition beforehand. he looked born to command ~~penetrating eye chest thick formed~~—penetrating eye—chest well formed with square and broad shoulders.

To further illustrate character I copy a part of the engraving upon his ~~tomb~~ monument which is usually ~~granted to be~~ considered to correctly designate the man—

viz—"Langdon Cheves"

"so wise,—so pure,—so strong,—his country needed,—but Death had called him."

Again

"Massiveness of intellect,—purity of purpose,—wisdom of judgement,—and indomitable energy of execution,—combined to make the patriot statesman and the model man."[74]

~~Now I can do nothing more and Now I have only further to repeat that I can do nothing more to help you.~~ I think I can say or do nothing more to help you and must now put my trust in your artist skill ~~to help me to a good likeness to the bust which I ask wish for~~—I am ~~however~~ in no ~~w~~haste ~~whatever~~ and ~~should~~ would prefer that you should take your time and suit yourself to your own spirit of inspiration for the working impulse.

Would ~~it be~~ you object as the man is now 21 years in his grave and in such

73. Samuel Finley Breese Morse (1791–1872), whose career as a painter culminated in his establishment of the National Academy of Design, of which he was first president, had a studio in Charleston during the winters from 1818 to 1821.

74. The complete text of LSM's epitaph for her father is appended to chap. 8 above, "Memoir of Langdon Cheves."

a country as ours now is, that is enough to stamp into oblivion every thing worth remembering—~~would~~ would you object to engrave upon the base of the bust the name "*Langdon Cheves*["] and below it "*Clarum et venerabile nomen*"—

[*word missing from torn page*] ~~the statue of Calhoun and~~

Regarding the replacing of the statue of Calhoun I would be most happy to do any thing useful or agreeable to you;[75] but I not only have ~~of later~~ for years shrunk too much from the world to ~~be kn~~ have influence with anybody, but I know little of what is going on—and have not ~~the smallest~~ connection or acquaintance with ~~the~~ any of the town council nor with those moving in the matter. My world is dead and in the past. ~~In fact~~ My ~~own~~ private impression however is that the town council has not the slightest idea of doing anything in the ~~matter~~ business and that ~~the town is too poor~~ whatever may be talked about in that line, the citizens ~~have~~ will save their ~~surplus~~ funds to ~~pay~~ pay the onerous taxes laid upon them,—~~and consuming~~ Our corner of the world does not prosper, and if the Calhoun monument or Calhoun statue shall ever be raised, it ~~will~~ must be without help of mine.

In a day or two the Bill of Exchange on London for £50 will be forwarded to you. The person upon whom I depend for ~~its execution~~ arranging it for me is for a ~~day or two out of~~ short time absent f[ro]m the town.

Source: Draft, Langdon Cheves I Papers, SCHS.

To Preston Powers

Dear Sir Charleston May ~~29~~30th, 1878

I enclose £50, Bill of Exchange (*First* of *Exchange*) on Messrs. Brown, Shipley and Co.—London.

Trusting that this will reach you safely, I ~~still~~ shall nevertheless for greater security forward the *second of Exchange* in about ~~ten days~~ a week.

75. Hiram Powers carved a statue of John C. Calhoun, commissioned in 1842 by Francis W. Pickens, congressman from South Carolina (Powers' bust of Calhoun, modeled in 1835, had been much admired). Shipped in April 1850, the statue went down with the *Elizabeth* (and Margaret Fuller) off Fire Island, N.Y., on July 19. Salvaged, and a lost arm restored, the statue was placed in the Charleston City Hall until, for fear of Federal bombardment during the war, it was sent to Columbia, where it was destroyed in the burning of the city during Sherman's occupation.

My Photographs, such as they are were sent yesterday, and I hope may be of some use to you.

Very truly and Respectfully yours
Louisa S. McCord

Addressed: Preston Powers / Studio Powers / Florence. *Source:* Draft, Langdon Cheves I Papers, SCHS.

To Preston Powers

Dear Sir [Charleston June 1878]

Please find enclosed—Bill of Exchange, Second of Exchange on Messrs. Brown, Shipley and Co—London—Duplicate of First of Exchange forwarded 30th Ult—

One or the other (if not both) will I trust certainly reach you. Hoping my poor photographs will ~~I trust be~~ have been equally fortunate—I am dear Sir with kind regards as always

Truly etc
L. S. McC——

Addressed: Preston Powers / Studio Powers / Firenze. *Source:* Draft, Langdon Cheves I Papers, SCHS.

To Preston Powers

Dear Sir Charleston, South Carolina July 22d, 1878

I have to thank you for your letter of 14th Ulto—

Regretting much that I can do nothing more to assist you in the task you have accepted from me I am pleased that you ~~should be~~ are willing to take time upon the work, and would be sorry in any way to hurry you.—— The words to be ins-cribed are as you have ~~copied~~ ~~written~~ copied them. Viz.

Langdon Cheves
Clarum et venerabile nomen.

I thank you for the suggestion that they be gilded; and accept it, under your judgment, of "not disturbing the harmony of the work."——

I fear that our frequent correspondence, ~~has~~ must have been rather a troublesome necessity to you, in the midst of the absorbing occupations of [*canceled letters illegible*] your Art. Trusting however that it may not have been sufficiently so to interfere with a kind and friendly recollection of me~~, I would beg you, dear Sir, to always believe me yours~~

~~Very truly and respectfully~~
~~Louisa S. McCord~~

~~and with kind remembrance always to y[ou]r Mother and Sisters with kind remembrance always Dear Sir~~

Believe me Dear Sir with ~~kind remembrance~~ [*illegible word*] regards ~~always~~ to y[ou]r Mother and Sisters always

Very truly and respectfully yours
L. S. McCord

Addressed: Preston Powers, *Sculptor / Florence—Italy. Source:* Draft, Langdon Cheves I Papers, SCHS.

Codicil to Last Will and Testament

The State of South Carolina.

I, Louisa S. McCord, do make, publish and declare this as and for a Codicil to my Will bearing date the 12th day of February A.D. 1876, written on the foregoing pages.

Whereas, since the execution of my foregoing will, I have purchased a House and Lot in the City of Charleston, on the West side of Legare Street, adjoining the House and Lot of my Son-in-Law, A. T. Smythe, to the North, I desire that in the administration and settlement of my estate, under my foregoing Will, if I shall continue the owner of said House and Lot at the time of my death, my Son-in-Law, A. T. Smythe, shall have the privilege and option of taking the said house and lot on account of the legacy or legacies in said Will given to any one or more of his children, at the price and sum of $3,500; and upon his said election and option, that the said House and Lot shall be held by my Executors, or such of them as shall qualify, at and for the said sum of $3,500, upon the trusts and subject to the powers and conditions prescribed in my said Will in relation to the said legacies.

I hereby revoke the Seventh Paragraph of my said Will, being the residuary clause thereof: and in lieu and stead of the disposition therein made, I give, devise and bequeath all the rest and residue of my estate whatsoever to be equally divided between such children of my said daughter Louisa McCord Smythe, other than are named in said Will, who have been or may be born after the date of my said Will, and who shall be living at the time of my death; to be invested and held by my Executors, or such of them as shall qualify, or the survivor of them, upon the same trusts and subject to the same conditions and provisions as to interest and principal, and to the same limitations in favor of their mother, Louisa McCord Smythe, as are expressed in relation to the legacies bequeathed to the other children of my said daughter named in the fifth clause of my said Will.

And the foregoing provision as to the House and Lot in Legare Street, purchased by me, shall apply as well to the residuary legacies as to those given in my said Will.[76]

In all other respects I ratify and confirm my said Will.

In Witness whereof, I have hereunto set my Hand and Seal this twenty fifth day of March, in the year of our Lord One Thousand Eight Hundred and Seventy nine.

Louisa S. McCord[77]

Source: Probate Court Records, County of Charleston, South Carolina.

To Charles W. West

Dear Mr. West[78] [Charleston c. June 1879]

Your letter of April 18th (to my Son-in law) with enclosures has been shown to me. I am sorry that you have been set hunting on such a chase after the non-existant. Mr. Powers has already all the material (poor as it is) that

76. "I received a letter from Mr. [John Taylor] Rhett yesterday, perfectly courteous to me, but so full of anger and bitterness that I do not intend either to answer it or show it to you. I do not see why he should have so written to me, about his disappointment that Mrs. McCord did not divide her estate equally between the members of her family[;] but it is very painful to be the recipient of such letters." Charles Richardson Miles to Augustine T. Smythe, Jan. 5, 1880, Dulles-Cheves-McCord-Lovell Papers, SCHS.

77. To the codicil is appended:

"Signed, Sealed, Published and Declared, by the Testatrix, Louisa S. McCord, as and for a Codicil to her last Will and Testament, dated February 12th 1876, in our presence, who, at her request, and in her presence, and in the presence of each other, have hereunto subscribed our names as witnesses to the execution thereof.

James P. Lesesne
Langdon Cheves [III]
W. W. Johnson"

James Petigru Lesesne (1848–92) was the son of Henry Deas Lesesne (1810–86) and Harriette Petigru Lesesne (1813–77), sister of James Louis Petigru; William Wragg Johnson, son of Oscar Emmons Johnson (1826–99) and Gabriella Strobel Johnson.

To the Will and Testament and Codicil as a whole is appended:

"Probate, Will and Codicil in Common form before, William E. Vincent, Esquire, Judge of Probate for Charleston County on the 28th November A.D. 1879.

On 9th December, A.D. 1879 qualified Charles R. Miles, one of the Executors therein named."

78. Charles W. West was husband of LSM's niece Mary ("Mamie"), daughter of Langdon Cheves, Jr.

can possibly be furnished him. Photographs were not of my Father's time. No good painting was ever made of him. As to plaster casts Mr. Powers has the only *post mortem* one ever taken of him—It was taken the night of my Father's death under the superintendance of my brother Langdon who had ~~caused~~ ordered a workman to come f[ro]m Charleston for the purpose—No other cast was then taken. The only one made by Mills was ~~of~~ about 12 years before. Several were taken on the same mould—poor enough I fear—But the two were both sent by my Brother Langdon to Hiram Powers ~~Sr who left when~~ before our war began and I heard f[ro]m the son Preston Powers a year ago, that both were in his possession.——He then thought he could make what I wanted f[ro]m them. If he fails I shall be troubled, but all has been done that can be done. Of course I would not want Mills' cast ~~as there is the exact~~ the duplicate of it ~~with~~ being as you thus understand in the Studio Preston Powers. Also there is ~~one~~ another in this house. I thank you therefore for your kind offers; but there is nothing that you can do for me.

Your letter is so entirely a business one that you say nothing of ~~Mary~~ Mamie and the little fellows. I trust all are well—

With very much love to them and affectionate regards to yourself

[*illegible scrawl*]

Source: Draft, Langdon Cheves I Papers, SCHS.

To Preston Powers

Dear Mr. Powers [Charleston c. June 1879]

I have been surprised at receiving an enclosed note f[ro]m yourself to Mr. C. W. West (Baltimore) making enquiries concerning a *Post mortem* cast of my Father, taken by Clark Mills. ~~There was~~ *no such cast was ever taken*—My father died at my house and under my care in his 82d year. There was a cast taken by a workman ~~before his interment. The only one taken;~~ whose name I never heard on the night of the death and none other was taken. This cast is one of those forwarded to your Father before our war began. The ~~other~~ cast ~~they~~ sent with it was ~~of~~ by Clark Mills taken 12 or 13 years before. ~~I never saw the first. My Brother who fell in our war considered it as likely to give a better guide~~ and Is necessarily from the manner of its taking (i.e. covering the head and neck with plaster) heavy and inanimate. From these ~~perhaps~~ we hoped however the features ~~can be guessed at or approached~~ could be brought out[.]

Mr. Merryman in his note speaks as though you had no guide other than the photographs I sent.[79] He must however have misunderstood you, as these casts were the only ~~ones~~ models referred to in our past correspondence when I first wrote to ask if they still existed, and in your answer of 27th Feb[ruar]y 1878, you ~~remarked~~ wrote "*I have hunted up the casts you refer to and found them in excellent condition*" ~~and again it that of 8th May~~. And again in ~~that~~ y[ou]r letter of 8th May, you write "*I can make a good bust from the casts I have here and shall, I have no doubt, be able to please you*". ~~Certainly~~ You did indeed go on to ask for something more if possible—but the wretched attempt I made, shows how impossible it is to do anything. ~~for~~ Truly I tried my very best. You have every thing ~~I~~ that can possibly be collected—If description in words can help you,—I would tell that he was the grandest looking man I ever saw. Broad-chested, head erect,—eye penetrating,—with a general air of (what he was) born to command. His head was magnificent. I wrote you sundry letters trying to make you see him though my words—but that is I fear impossible—~~But~~ If anything I can write will be useful,—ask me ~~all the questions~~ anything you please—I will never tire of ~~writing~~ answering you if it can be of any use. But believe me, in the way of models nothing more can be done. Photographs were not known in my Fathers time, and even their predecessors, as Daguerrotypes etc. were unsatisfactory and by no means in common use with us. ~~When we~~ Going as I do quite beyond your memory—my Father had been taken away before I visited ~~at~~ your ~~house~~ Fathers family in Florence—you in your *modern* world, can hardly understand how far behind we were.[80]

Trusting that your Mother and Sisters continue in health and that all with you are well and comfortable—I am etc.

Source: Draft, Langdon Cheves I Papers, SCHS.

79. Hiram Powers wrote in 1852 to an Oliver A. Merriman from Manchester, Vt. (who was hoping to save money for study in Italy), refusing the eighteen-year-old sculptor's request that Powers accept him as a pupil. Possibly this is the "Mr. Merryman" to whom LSM refers. See Powers to Merriman, March 17, 1852, Hiram Powers and Powers Family Papers, Smithsonian.

80. The completed bust of Langdon Cheves arrived in Charleston in January 1880. Papers relating to its shipment and payment, exchanged between LSM's executors and the shipping companies, are found in the Dulles-Cheves-McCord-Lovell Papers, SCHS. The bust is reproduced and discussed in Wunder, *Hiram Powers* 2:29–30.

Afterword

I. *"He will find her quite savage"*

"A brilliant anomaly in our literature." That was spoken of *Caius Gracchus* but as easily might be applied to its author. Indeed, the equation was drawn at the time. "I had 'Caius Gracchus' to myself," wrote Jane Caroline North of a visit from Louisa McCord. Mary Chesnut narrowed the application to Cornelia, proverbial mother. A "country cousin" visiting Columbia, apprehensive of missing her train at five o'clock in the morning, roused the household just after midnight, and with difficulty was restored to bed. Later, Louisa McCord was awakened by "two ice-cold hands pass[ing] cautiously over her face and person. It was pitch-dark. Even Mrs. McCord (the 'Mother of the Gracchi') gave a scream in her fright," only to find it was the cousin once again. More serious business was the rescue of Cheves McCord from the field of Second Manassas. His mother was blocked at Richmond; her cousin William Porcher Miles said that the conditions of war compelled her to go no farther.

> "I let him talk," said Mrs. McCord, "for he does it beautifully. That very night I chartered a special train. We ran down to Manassas and I brought back Cheves in triumph. You see he is nearly well, with our home nursing."
>
> "Mother of the Gracchi," we cried.[1]

1. "Mrs. M'Cord's Caius Gracchus," *De Bow,* n. s., 1 (Oct. 1852): 427–29; 428; Jane Caroline North to Mary Charlotte North, Sept. 11 and 12, 1851, Pettigrew Family Papers, SHC; *Chesnut,* pp. 683, 428.

"Every circumstance of birth, life, and character," Sarah Josepha Hale wrote of Cornelia in her enormous compendium, *Woman's Record,* "conspired to give her a glowing and ever-living page in history." That summation was irreproachable. For it rested upon the commonplace, adopted for example by *De Bow's Review,* that thc most famous of Roman mothers was "that glorious woman, Cornelia—the mother, whose great heart knew no other thought than that of Rome." From a scanty biographical tradition Mrs. Hale drew three inferences: that "Cornelia must have been educated in a very superior manner *by her father*"; that "she must have been, from the beginning, a woman of *fixed principles and undaunted courage*"; and that "she must have cultivated literature and the graces of conversation." An admirer of Mrs. McCord is unlikely to have required the guidance of *Woman's Record* in order to detect so manifest, indeed inescapable, a resemblance. Tutor to the McCord children at Lang Syne after graduating from South Carolina College in 1852, James Wood Davidson observed that, having a mind "Roman in its cast, and heroic in its energy, . . . in person Mrs. McCord might personate Cornelia herself." Mary Chesnut mistook the title of the tragedy—mistook, too, the sequence of the Cheves children—but did not mistake the woman, when she introduced into her diaries her friend Louisa McCord, "she who wrote *The Mother of the Gracchi*—the eldest daughter of Langdon Cheves. . . . She has the brain and energy of a man."[2]

In 1851, at the springs of Virginia, where the belle ruled, Jane Caroline North reported to her sister: "Mrs. McCord has just paid me quite a long visit. . . . She was very pleasant—of course very talkative. What a strong masculine person she is! . . . She told me that when 'Mr. [Benjamin Franklin] Perry and others of the submissionists were on one occasion being abused, as all the party are you know, when the person who was speaking mentioned your Uncle Mr. [James Louis] Petigru, he paused, Oh!—Petigru is a fine fellow, a very fine fellow, but—he's queer.' She laughed heartily then and said 'it was all covered with that—he's queer.' Tell Aunt May, I did not give in, but to her question said, 'yes, I was staunch on the same side.'"[3] It was at the springs again, this time in the summer of 1857, that Mrs. McCord received a visit from Francis W. Pickens and his beloved, "the beautiful belle" Lucy Holcombe. Miss Holcombe was not pleased when her hostess—preferring to converse with the former nullifier and congressman, now candi-

2. Hale, *Woman's Record,* p. 33; "Caius Gracchus," *De Bow,* n.s., 4 (Aug. 1851): 224; J. W. Davidson, *Living Writers of the South,* pp. 351, 357; *Chesnut,* p. 304.

3. Jane Caroline North to Mary Charlotte North, Sept. 11 and 12, 1851, Pettigrew Family Papers, SHC. "The acute mind of Petigru[,] more than any other, looked into his character, expressing it in strong but simple and plain words, which in their simple character seemed to open to you the being—nature of the man[.]" Chap. 8 above, "Memoir of Langdon Cheves," p. 261.

date for the United States Senate—paid no attention to her. She attempted a snub: departing, she said that she had come expecting to see another Mrs. McCord, "the editress of a New Orleans newspaper." Louisa McCord, who told the story to Mrs. Chesnut, was unlikely to have been repentant. She knew the type. Not that youthful amusements, or youth itself, displeased her—like her father, she understood well, and did not deplore, the pleasures taken by the young in music and dancing, and it is clear from Jane Caroline North's report that her visitor was amiable and enjoyed her conversation—but in general: "Look at the ballroom belle," said Mrs. McCord. "Why is she a flirt, a coquette, a heartless trifler with hearts? Not because there is harm in the ballroom enjoyment of youth; in the joy-waking music, or the spirit-rousing dance; but because she would be *talked* of, and forgets duty, conscience, and heart, in the love of notoriety."[4]

But whether it was noted by Carey North, or rebuked by Lucy Holcombe, or praised and relied upon by Mary Chesnut, that Louisa McCord was endowed with qualities which her society agreed in naming masculine was a truth universally acknowledged. Her appearance seemed to concur: "she was a magnificent physical specimen of womanhood; tall, commanding, strong, very active," until broken by the war. Her horsemanship was remarked upon; her own horse, a Canadian mustang, could be ridden by nobody else. Applauding her essays as, "upon fair comparison, equal to any that form the higher articles in the very best Reviews," Mrs. Hale's *Woman's Record* observed also that Mrs. McCord "has distinguished herself in what may be styled political literature, a species of writing seldom attempted by woman." In the view of her critics, whether they were amiable or disapproving, "the almost masculine force of her character," as her daughter named it, was complemented by, was indistinguishable from, the force of her intellect. To Mrs. Chesnut, together with "the perseverance and endurance of a woman" Louisa McCord had "the intellect of a man." "A mind of masculine calibre and resource," declared *Women of the South Distinguished in Literature,* was needed in order to combine—as Mrs. McCord did combine—"the essential qualifications of a political writer, philosopher, and poet." An anthology of prose written by American women affirmed that her writings on political economy were "characterized by masculine vigour and an enlarged acquaintance with the subject." James Wood Davidson deemed her to choose "all living, manly subjects; no rose-water or kid-gloves about them. Strength and independence of thought mark all that she has written." "She has a vivid imagination

4. *Chesnut,* p. 369; *PSE,* "Woman and Her Needs," p. 132. Her father "delighted in the happiness of young people—Have seen him before his days of sorrow came upon him[,] standing beating time to the joyous dancing of our young friends[,] too happy for the langour of fashion, and showing how he enjoyed etc." Chap. 8, "Memoir of Langdon Cheves," p. 258.

and warm feeling," Caroline May's *American Female Poets* conceded, "but they are not well disciplined by good taste and correct judgment," the latter virtues perhaps not to be expected from a mind "by nature strong." The *Southern Literary Gazette* judged that *Caius Gracchus* was "characterized by more than common vigour of style, and displays, indeed, a masculine energy of thought and utterance quite *germain* to the theme. The characters are drawn with a bold pen, and yet with such nice tact that delicacy is rarely sacrificed to strength." "Her mental attributes are all masculine," pronounced the *Southern Quarterly Review.* That was well for prose, but for poetry it would not do. Poetry demanded "harmony, symmetry, and exquisite arrangement." Mrs. McCord's *Caius Gracchus* disregarded these; her "metrical abruptness," her "eager and impatient temperament," took little account of "the graces which should always wait upon the Muse." Still, "a tragedy by a Southron, and a lady, is surely no such ordinary event, that we should pass it with indifference."[5]

Where the *Southern Quarterly Review* saw and condemned, the Charleston *Courier* and *De Bow's Review* saw and approved. "The powerful conception of character, the masculine strength of thought, and the rigorous expression, scorning all artificial ornaments, but rising, often, by its own elastic energy into lofty beauty, cannot fail to strike the most careless reader." Mrs. McCord had renounced the popular poetry, shrouded in mists of Romanticism and German philosophy, "superficial and ornate, abounding in brilliant and transient beauties, fanciful imagery and melodious versification," to return to older and finer models, older and finer ambitions. It was the masculine quality of her mind that allowed her to strive better and reach further. "Our female writers, especially, have avoided [the drama]. Some, indeed, have written fine poems cast in a dramatic form, but we know of no genuine tragedy or comedy, glowing with the vigorous exhibition of character and passion, or rich in the faithful delineation of life and manners, which gives the drama its substance and vitality, from the pen of an American woman."[6] Hence *De Bow's Review,* having noticed *Caius Gracchus* briefly in August 1851,

5. Susan Smythe Bennett and John Bennett to Jessie Melville Fraser, April 21, 1919 (typescript), Dulles-Cheves-McCord-Lovell Papers, SCHS; Hale, *Woman's Record,* p. 894; Smythe, p. 76; *Chesnut,* p. 677; Forrest, *Women of the South Distinguished in Literature,* p. 480; Hart, *Female Prose Writers of America,* p. 187; J. W. Davidson, *Living Writers of the South,* p. 352; May, *American Female Poets,* p. 420; *Southern Literary Gazette* 4, no. 9 (June 28, 1851); "Caius Gracchus," *SQR,* n.s., 4 (July 1851): 62–68; 62–63, 68. In contrast, William Gilmore Simms thought it worthwhile to inform readers that LSM's anonymous review of *Uncle Tom's Cabin* (*PSE,* pp. 245–80) was written "by a female hand" ("Critical Notices," *SQR,* n. s., 7 [Jan. 1853]: 233).

6. Charleston *Courier,* April 24, 1851; "Mrs. M'Cord's Caius Gracchus," *De Bow,* n.s., 1 (Oct. 1852): 427.

more than a year later bestowed upon it a full review, reprinted in *The Knickerbocker,*[7] in which the play has become a text upon which to mount a sermon upholding masculine over feminine poetry:

> South Carolina has produced the only American poet whose productions may be said to belong to the elder school; which appeal to the intellect more than the fancy, and are marked by such sinewy strength of thought and expression as to be stamped at once with a character of originality. It is easy to see that Mrs. McCord is familiar with the early standards of those days when there were giants of English literature; her cast of thought and style of utterance show that she has studied them lovingly, and it is equally evident that the more ephemeral beauties of a later school have had little favor with her. She is wholly unlike any of her sisters of the lyre, and writes with a terseness, vigor, earnestness, and masculine energy, which show her to be altogether of a different order. . . . Her acquaintance with the poets of Greece and Rome in their own language has enabled her to impart to [her tragedy] a purely classical tone which no unlearned writer could have given.[8]

Since the age of ten, when she was apprehended by her father as she eavesdropped upon her brothers' lessons in mathematics, Louisa McCord had poached in alien territory. As she said herself, it was "Greek, Latin and mathematics" that boys flung aside in their haste to prepare for war.[9]

Suitably, then, a Roman poet—Lucretius—may be called upon to denote Louisa McCord's essential quality. The obstructions lying in the way of his teacher, the philosopher Epicurus, had acted only to drive him more energetically against them, until the living force of his mind conquered (*vivida vis animi pervicit*) and broke through to probe the secrets of natural philosophy.[10] *Vivida vis animi:* the living force of Mrs. McCord's mind was not blocked, as Epicurus' force was blocked, by the awe of religion or the gods' thunder or the threatening heavens. Not so majestic, the obstacles set against her were yet not trivial; she knew their legacy, "my crush'd feeling's dearth," as Byron named it. These obstacles—not what they were (they may be guessed), but that they were, she said plainly enough in the first lines of her first known published writing:

7. "Caius Gracchus," *Knickerbocker* 41 (Jan. 1853): 69–72.

8. "Mrs. M'Cord's Caius Gracchus," *De Bow,* n.s., 1 (Oct. 1852): 428–29.

9. LSM to Hiram Powers, Dec. 24, 1860. LSM's nephew Alexander Haskell, having been shot in the left eye on Oct. 7, 1864, spent Christmas at his parents' home in Abbeville. "My memory began to return. I picked up Greek and Latin books, and, while they looked strange at first, what I had known soon looked like acquaintances again." Daly, *Alexander Cheves Haskell,* p. 160.

10. *De rerum natura* (*On the Nature of Things*) 1.66–74.

> Oft in my bosom the self-flattering thought
> Has roused itself—"I, too, may be a poet."
> And again, o'ercome by my own weakness,
> Have I shrunk before the blighting consciousness,
> The damning fear, that I am built as one
> Amidst the crowd: an atom in the sunbeam;
> Nothing more than all the triflers round me.
> And yet there is a hope, it will not die; . . .
> Doubting and trembling still, I cast my lines,
> Then, here, before the world; and it must judge
> 'Twixt me, and my own struggling thoughts, which rise,
> Now in Hope's wild commotion, and now sink
> Back, back, upon myself and nothingness.[11]

When she asked advice about a draft of *Caius Gracchus* and some other pieces, there was a like combination of ambition and uncertainty, hesitancy and purpose, echoed from another of her poems. "Although I have been pushed back in every possible way, and have myself endeavoured for many a long year to crush my own propensities, there has been a struggling consciousness of something which has goaded me on to my recent experiments. . . . An effortless life, is, to a restless mind, a weary fate to be doomed to; and as no other door is open to me, I may as well push on at this."

> What though thou, like me, must find—
> Born to Earth, doomed to regretting—
> Vainly that the restless mind
> Seeks to soar, its birth forgetting?[12]

And near the end of her life she recollected, in her father's early strivings, something perhaps of her own:

> He was—you will not be surprised that I say so—sensitively diffident. True merit, even with the consciousness of power and courage to exercise it, combines nevertheless, a strong element of diffidence. Not that it mistrusts itself, for mental power cannot exist without consciousness; but apt to over-rate others, measuring by its own standard, it dreads the being mis-

11. Chap. 1 above, *My Dreams,* "Dedication to My Father," ll. 1–8, 25–29. Compare the remainder of the stanza from Byron chosen for epigraph to *My Dreams:* "What am I? Nothing; but not so art thou, / Soul of my thought! with whom I traverse earth, / Invisible but gazing, as I glow / Mix'd with thy spirit, blended with thy birth, / And feeling still with thee in my crush'd feeling's dearth" (*Childe Harold's Pilgrimage* 3.50–54).

12. LSM to William Porcher Miles, June 12, 1848; "The Fire-fly," ll. 45–48, chap. 1 above.

understood. I have already intimated that the coolly confident elder brethren of the young lawyer, firmly established in their position almost by right of prescription, could scarcely estimate the force of a careless word or look which would tell with chilling power upon the acute feelings of one sensible of his right to stand beside them, and yet so quietly, so coolly, so unconsciously ignored, that it needed an indomitable power of resistance to uphold self-assertion. Still that power was there. Not in words was it spoken; not in thought evolved; And yet it was there, the result of the impulse of character scarcely yet known even to himself in its strength,—it came in the quiet summons, not spoken, not heard—but felt; "Make room[;] I am of the first."[13]

The force of Louisa McCord's writings did not, therefore, come without struggle. But it did come, more urgent from the obstacles heaved aside before it. It came, too, with darkness, and apprehension of disaster. In her first two periodical essays, the preponderance of translation (from French political economists) suggests reluctance to assert her skills too openly; her commentary to the words of others prefers the safety of praise, prudently introduced with reservation:

> We are not ultra-reformists—far from it—and yet we are of those who see, in the present condition of the world, the waking up of a new era. We are of those who believe in—if not the perfectibility of man—at least his great, lasting, and boundless improvement. Thought is roused, mind is awakened, which never again can sleep. Vainly are we told that preceding ages have shown equal civilization and similar improvement. Vainly is our attention directed to the great Nineveh, to Egypt, to Greece and to Rome. These certainly do show—these have shown—progression and retrogression, rise and fall, as the great pulse of humanity has throbbed in its breathing of ages; but never has the world soul been roused, as now, by the expansion of thought, circulating to distant points of our globe, whose very existence was not dreamed of by the wise of ancient days. Never has the great heart of civilization cast, as now, by its every pulsation, its lifeblood to the farthest extremes of a universe, rousing itself from unconscious infancy to the full action of a reasoning being. Great as were the efforts of the ancients—great as were the results of those efforts—they were confined to little corners of a world, which now basks under the full radiance of extended and extending light.[14]

13. Chap. 8 above, "Memoir of Langdon Cheves," pp. 253–54.
14. *PSE*, "Justice and Fraternity," p. 58.

Did such writing need more prudence still? Her essay "Justice and Fraternity" had "one good idea—tho' not a new one—and perhaps not a true one, that a civilized world cannot fall back"; but the rest was "mere stuff—puerile declamation not above common stump oratory."[15] But if Louisa McCord was like Ernest Pontifex, who had taken a notion "from Kingsley's *Alton Locke,* which . . . he had devoured as he had devoured Stanley's *Life of Arnold,* Dickens' novels, and whatever other literary garbage of the day was most likely to do him harm,"[16] nevertheless, again like Ernest Pontifex, she could find her way to better notions, and better utterance. Besides, by the time she came to review *Alton Locke* (in July 1851), "the civilized world seems struggling almost in its death throes." There was little to betray her into stump oratory now.

> The cloudy future stands before us, a terrible uncertainty of horrors, and, like the mystery of some fearful dream, frights us the more from its undefined magnitude:
>
> > Without me and within me; not imagined—felt.
>
> This only sure—the accumulated civilization of eighteen centuries must fall, and one sweep of barbarism cast back the world to the blind struggle, in which physical force is the only might, and the strong arm the only law. It may be said that God, in his wisdom, sees fit to sweep the moral world with something similar to those cataclysms which have operated his great crises in the physical. As one race of beings has followed upon the destruction of another, thus our civilization, religion, existence, must, perhaps, give way to some hidden rule, some mystery of mind, which must sweep us into utter annihilation, ere itself can struggle into being. It may be thus; for thus, only, can we explain to ourselves the fearful progress of the annihilating principle which advances upon us. Destruction hangs over us, like the sword of Damocles, suspended by a single hair; and yet we look at it, and laugh, and play with the fatal point, whose fearful vibrations threaten, with every instant, to bring down upon us our doom.[17]

This passage, concluding Louisa McCord's fourth periodical essay, with its plangency, grimness, and astute use of quotation (from the author whom she quotes most frequently, Shakespeare), has her characteristic persuasiveness, her characteristic vigor. Already by 1851 she was known, even to

15. James Henry Hammond to William Gilmore Simms, July 9, 1849, Simms, *Letters* 1:531, n. 119.

16. Samuel Butler, *The Way of All Flesh,* Everyman's ed. (New York, 1992), p. 218.

17. *PSE,* "Negro and White Slavery—Wherein Do They Differ?" p. 198.

a grudging reviewer, as "a remarkably vigorous writer of prose," with a mind "of great directness—straightforward, earnest, and singularly energetic"; her poetry, notable for "the freedom and energy" of its versification, "afford[ed] frequent passages of remarkable energy and force—bold and enthusiastic bursts of sentiment—and morals and points of reflection which are delivered with epigrammatic terseness, and all the condensation and emphasis of the apothegm." Also in 1851 the professor of the history of intellectual philosophy and Greek literature at the College of Charleston, James Warley Miles, writing to his cousin David James McCord, decried "the thoughtless inanities and flatulent verbiage of our current literature" and upheld in contrast *Caius Gracchus,* "in which vigorous and philosophical thought, just and true sentiment, and enlarged and wholesome views, are presented in nervous diction and attractive garb." And after Mrs. McCord's death, William Porcher Miles called her articles "vigorous and trenchant" and acknowledged her as heir to much of her father's "force and vigor of intellect." Force and vigor, however, had consequences, which could complicate encomium. "She reasons well; her style is excellent," Sarah Hale affirmed, comfortably, in 1855, "and flashes of wit, 'temperately bright' as a woman's should be, please without wounding." But the editor of the *Southern Quarterly Review,* close not only to Louisa McCord but also to some of her quarry, must rue even as he recognized her "very spirited" articles, such as that on a book by "my old friend, Mr. Henry C. Carey": "He will find her quite savage. I could have wished, for *auld lang syne,* that she had found any other victim."[18]

II. "Tones which strike into the heart"

Vigor, living force of mind, energy. Louisa McCord seems to have valued these characteristics, not always by these names. Fréderic Bastiat's "well known power as a writer" she commended, his "striking views" clothed in "his usual terse and concise diction."[19] Not the least fault of Elizabeth Oakes Prince Smith's *Woman and Her Needs* was its confused and vapid style, "halting grammar," inept figures. "If the lady is not a very careless writer," said Mrs. McCord, "she has to complain of a very careless printer": "'I long,' says Mrs.

18. "Caius Gracchus," *SQR,* n.s., 4 (July 1851): 62, 64; James Warley Miles to David James McCord, June 16, 1851, in "Letters of James Warley Miles to David James McCord," *SCHM* 43 (1942): 185–93; 191; William Porcher Miles, "Sketch of Mrs. David J. McCord," in *PSE,* app. 3, p. 485; Hale, *Woman's Record,* p. 894; William Gilmore Simms to Henry Carey Baird, Dec. 17, 1853, in Simms, *Letters* 3:267.

19. *PSE,* "The Right to Labor," p. 98.

Smith, 'to see my own sex side by side with man in every great work, and free to see the light, when his vision is dimmed with the dust of his chariot-wheels in the mighty race in which he is engaged.' And how will she do this, if she throws herself even in the thick of the dust beside him?" Better the plain speaking

> of a certain Mrs. Mehitable Haskell, who, rising to make a speech at the first Worcester Convention, frankly acknowledges that "she does not know what are woman's rights, but for forty, nay, fifty years, she has known what woman's wrongs are, for she has felt them." Now there is something right hearty—something earnest and downright—in the declaration of this good lady. . . . We fancy we can see the good Mrs. Mehitable before us: broad, square-shouldered; somewhat raw-boned; sharp gray eyes; teeth deficient (she would disdain to mend her oratory or her looks by false ones); a bony hand which hath shown service over the washtub, and well calculated, in its mere appearance, to excite admonitory twinges in the flagellatable parts of luckless youth, said hand being used with some vehemence of gesticulation. All her motions angular; all her forms angular.[20]

The vigor preferred by Louisa McCord is evident, too, in her translations from the French. A good example, since it derives from a public occasion demanding some eloquence, is a passage from a speech delivered by Léon Faucher before the French assembly:

> Je ne crains pas, quant à moi, le socialisme qui marche ouvertement à son but, celui qui dit: "Je ne veux pas de la famille, je ne veux pas de la propriété." Celui-là je ne le crains pas; ce que je crains, ce que je redoute, c'est le socialisme indirect, le socialisme inconséquent, bâtard, qui vous mènerait sur la pente et qui vous cacherait l'abîme. À celui-là je dirais volontiers ce qui j'avais l'honneur de dire à un membre du gouvernement provisoire, qui s'écriait dans une conversation: "Le socialisme, c'est la peste," à quoi je faisais cette réponse à mon tour: "Oui, vous avez raison; le socialisme, c'est la peste; mais vous êtes tous malades de la peste."

> I do not fear, or at least fear but little, the socialism which, moving openly to its extreme object, declares boldly, "No family! No property!" Much more to be dreaded is the indirect, bastard, half-way socialism, which constantly tempts downward and downward upon the descent, still hiding the abyss that yawns at its foot. A member of the provisional government recently

20. *PSE*, "Woman and Her Needs," pp. 153n, 128, 149–50, 129–30.

remarked, "Socialism is the plague!" Ay, it is the plague, but who of you is quite free from the infection?[21]

Louisa McCord has pruned and shaped the French original to strengthen its force. The doubling of "celui-là je ne le *crains* pas; ce que je *crains*" is moved ahead to "I do not *fear,* or at least *fear* but little," absorbing (and modifying) "je ne *crains* pas, quant à moi." The dialogue is brought forward by reducing, or cutting entirely, the surrounding material: "à celui-là je dirais volontiers ce qui j'avais l'honneur de dire à un membre du gouvernement provisoire, qui s'écriait dans une conversation" is shrunk into "a member of the provisional government recently remarked"; and "à quoi je faisais cette réponse à mon tour," separating the two halves of the concluding exchange, is omitted. The dialogue itself is distilled. Shorn of verbs, the exclamation "No family! No property!" abbreviates and sharpens the milder French version; and "vous avez raison" is dropped from the final retort, itself converted from statement to the more urgent form of a question. Force is strengthened, too, where translation expands the original. The trisyllabic "infection," replacing "plague" to render the third instance of "la peste," gives the alliterations "*qu*ite *f*ree *f*rom the in*f*e*c*tion." Enlarging "qui vous mènerait sur la pente et qui vous cacherait l'abîme" into "which constantly tempts downward and downward upon the descent, still hiding the abyss that yawns at its foot," the translation uses repetition ("downward and downward"), alliteration (*d*own-war*d,* *d*ownwar*d,* *d*escent), and rhythm. Rhythm echoes sense: "up*on* the de*scent*" and "that *yawns* at its *foot*" are identical (iamb and anapest); "still *hid*ing the a*byss*" matches them but for adding one unstressed syllable; the three cadences, all terminating two unstressed syllables with a final syllable stressed (the de*scent,* the a*byss,* at its *foot*), combine to represent the victim of socialism who, hurried down the slope and wary too late, must inevitably be pitched over the precipice of his credulity. The placid discourse of the French original has been made eloquent.

For Louisa McCord loved eloquence, and loved to explore and revel in its wealth. Of her father's eloquence she was proud, citing more than once Washington Irving who compared Langdon Cheves to Demosthenes and Cicero; and twice, early in defending her father's opposition to separate secession, and late in defending his character from inept anecdote, she quoted from John Milton's "To the Lady Margaret Ley" in praise of the Athenian orator Isocrates, "that old man eloquent," whom "that dishonest victory /

21. *PSE,* "The Right to Labor," p. 89. The passage translated is cited in "Chronique," *Journal des économistes* 21 (Sept. 1848): 219–24; 222.

At Chaeronea, fatal to liberty, / Kill'd with report."[22] But although she celebrated, she had never heard, her father's eloquence upon those occasions of state and policy that had made it famous.[23] Perhaps she never chanced to be at hand; perhaps such occasions were not for women. Louisa McCord must find occasions of her own.[24]

"It abounds with striking passages full of high and noble thoughts, clothed in language well fitted to give them just expression. . . . [Gracchus,] with due poetic license, as the hero of the play, is portrayed in fairest hues as the ideal patriot and citizen. Some of his speeches are very fine and effective." Gaius Gracchus was a great orator; Cicero praised him so; and Louisa McCord cast her hero's spell upon even his enemies.

> His voice has tones which strike into the heart.
> I late was in Sardinia, and I heard
> When he addressed the troops. There was a thrill
> Upon each noted wording of his tongue
> That made me shiver. Terror was upon me,
> And why I knew not. While I hated him,
> And could have plunged a dagger to his heart,
> Tears crept into mine eyes, and I must weep

22. *PSE,* "Separate Secession," p. 212; chap. 6 above, "Langdon Cheves: Review of 'Reminiscences of Public Men,'" p. 236. At Chaeronea the allied Greek cities, heeding at last Isocrates' call for unity against a northern threat, were defeated by Philip of Macedon in 338 B.C.

23. "Strange as it may seem to you, I never had the good fortune to hear him speak in public; but he was, to my mind, the best reader I have ever met." He "read Scotch beautifully—Burns was a treat." Chap. 8 above, "Memoir of Langdon Cheves," pp. 249, 258.

24. As a girl LSM had observed the House of Representatives. "When Aunt Sophia and my mother were fresh from Monsieur Picot's French boarding school in Philadelphia, . . . they were taken to the visitors' gallery in the Hall of Representatives and left there to listen to the speaking. After a while, Hugh Legaré, quite a celebrated and prominent South Carolinian and a great friend and admirer of their father's, came in with some ladies. He was a fine French scholar and liked to show it; so he turned to his party and in very fluent French began to comment on the very 'gauche' young ladies next them, making quite uncomplimentary remarks. They stood it with rising anger, for they recognized Mr. Legaré perfectly, until human nature could bear no more and they in their turn began a very clear and pointed conversation in French, referring several times to their father. Mr. Legaré left the gallery very soon." Smythe, p. 102. Hugh Swinton Legaré (1797–1843), born in Charleston; educated at South Carolina College and in Edinburgh; member of the South Carolina legislature; frequent contributor to the *Southern Review* (1828–32); attorney general of South Carolina (1830–32); chargé d'affaires at Brussels (1832–36); member of the U.S. House of Representatives (1837–39); attorney general under John Tyler (from 1841); ad interim secretary of state (1843); *Writings* published in two volumes (1846).

When he upbraided them their want of duty.
I felt as if myself had sinned, and been
The recreant soldier whom his tongue disdained.
And when he spurred them to a nobler course,
My bounding heart burst forth its loud huzza;
Spite of myself, it worshipped Caius Gracchus.[25]

Eloquence to Mrs. McCord, then, must satisfy two requirements: it must be directed to the passions, such as, here, terror, grief, joy; and it must be moral in purpose and freight, to reprove and to exhort. That it may invoke the passions, it will itself be passionate; it will be energetic, vigorous, spirited, the qualities customarily assigned to her own writing; but this passion must be disciplined, a moral energy. The boasting and bombast favored by advocates of separate secession contrived no more than to raise doubts and resentments, for such a "'blood and ashes' style of oratory suits only the schoolboy, or the vaunting Bobadil." That "energetic writer" Thomas Carlyle was "popular and plausible"; and Louisa McCord's style demonstrates that his eloquence had had much to teach her own. But his eloquence, with its "groans and appeals for suffering humanity," roused passion without purpose, or clear purpose. "Scoffing bitterly," and "working up discontented, and even well-intentioned minds, to a restless feeling of the need of something better," Carlyle bewitched many who, "to save themselves the trouble of thinking (and do not ninety-nine in the hundred shirk this when they can?), . . . range themselves"—Mrs. McCord's metaphor is, significantly, military—"under his banner." "His heart, we believe, is good, his intentions pure; but does he himself know—has he ever put the question to his own heart, and answered it fairly?—where he is leading? . . . To what does all this complaining lead? There is sorrow—ay, and wretchedness and suffering, oppression and injustice, trampled misery and heartless power, enough, too much—in this world of ours; we see this as well as he—but where is *his remedy?*"[26]

Available by example throughout the biographies of Plutarch, and in Demosthenes and Cicero (Plutarch wrote their lives) whom she delighted to array with her father, classical eloquence was Louisa McCord's eloquence. Her orator was the classical orator, not only the *vir bonus dicendi peritus,* "the good man, skilled in speaking"—for Carlyle answered that criterion—but also the leader of his people, wise in their interest, trained in their service, representative himself of them at their best, looking ahead where they can-

25. William Porcher Miles, "Sketch of Mrs. David J. McCord," in *PSE,* app. 3, p. 486; Cicero *Brutus* 125–26; chap. 5 above, *Caius Gracchus* 1.1.92–105.

26. *PSE,* "Separate Secession," p. 210, and "The Right to Labor," pp. 82–83.

not yet perceive. What she could not be, she could perform; and she became Caius Gracchus, whose two formal classical orations, the one evoking "tears and obedience", the other to "rouse ye 'neath oppression," form the pivot of her play.[27]

III. "I, too, may be a poet"

Louisa McCord's political eloquence found its place in tragedy, where Shakespeare had set it before her. But not all eloquence was political; the poet's eloquence she explored in *My Dreams.* Here she might benefit from, and indulge her characteristic pleasure in, the purely aural. To prove Harriet Beecher Stowe's ignorance of Southern "manners, feelings, and even habits of language," she relied upon her ear. "She makes her Southern ladies and gentlemen talk rather vulgar Yankee-English. Her Louisiana negroes all talk 'Kentuck.' She is probably not aware that the negro dialect varies even more than the white, in accordance with the local bringing up of the speaker. No negro, we believe, except a Virginia or Kentucky one, uses 'thar,' for there; 'har,' for hair; 'that ar,' for that; 'hev,' for have, etc. They have a *patois,* much more unintelligible frequently, but not the Kentucky lingo which she puts into their mouths. We doubt if Mrs. Stowe has ever crossed the line of a slave state at all. If she has, it has evidently not been further south than the mere crossing of the Kentucky border."[28] This accuracy of ear—Mrs. Stowe's personal experience of slavery had occurred in 1833 when, a teacher at the Western Female Institute in Cincinnati, she had visited a student across the border in Kentucky—was aspect of a nicety and a care for sound of which *My Dreams* provides continuous evidence. The collection delights in, even boasts of, a variety of meter both among and within poems—not for ingenuity only. In "Ye're Born to Die," for instance, the metrical multiplicity is made to point contrast to the singleness of the poem's import, spoken by "the eyeless spectre" of Death as it reaches out to embrace: "vainly would ye shun, / Poor fools! your lot. 'Tis here. Earth has but one" (ll. 77, 81–82). "The Soul of a Sound" seeks to apprehend sound as it flies, to impart into notes some knowledge of their own meaning:

> Oh! say not that they breathe, unknowing,
> Their own soft tone.
> Oh! say not, while these notes are flowing,
> Themselves alone

27. Chap. 5 above, *Caius Gracchus* 2.6.9 167, 170, 3.4.7–137; 40.
28. *PSE,* "*Uncle Tom's Cabin,*" p. 270.

Are all unconscious of the pleasure,
Waked by the wild and airy measure.

Oh! say not thus, but rather find
A spirit in each wildest note,
Which, borne upon the passing wind,
Dies with the tones which o'er us float. (11–20)

As conscious of sound, so *My Dreams* is conscious of art. From its first lines, of the dedication, "Oft in my bosom the self-flattering thought / Has roused itself—'I, too, may be a poet,'" it announces the aspiration with the doubt, the skill with the uncertainty, of the poet. "The Poet's Dream" evokes forms of that dream, but all proving transient, gone with the thought of them, hence "the form without form": "For it was not—it is not—ne'er can be of earth" (ll. 20, 14). The home of the poet, which is itself also a dream, is likewise transient, because shaped by what cannot stay, light and sound and their color (constant tenants of Louisa McCord's poems):

But though fickle and light, as a gossamer wing,
By the breeze wafted idly along,
Oh! still to the joys of that dream will he cling,
Still grasp at the shadows which fancy can bring,
Still live in the breath of his song—

And blest in his dream, which can drive off life's scenes,
With which he oft wearied has striven;
For, though but supported on Fancy, he leans;
By a meteor propped, scattered sunbeams he gleans;
And on gilded clouds soars towards heaven.
("The Poet's Home," 31–40)

The language of rising, soaring, freeing the spirit from something clinging from below, plunges through the entire collection of *My Dreams* because it is a work of ambition which yet must always prove itself. Hence the various meters, a proclamation of skill. Hence an emulous treatment like "The Dream of Life," recalling the theme of "sound and fury signifying nothing" as modulated in *Macbeth, The Tempest, Hamlet,* and *As You Like It.* Hence the variations upon an argument, a poem like "The Fire-fly" arguing that ambition, absurd, is necessary, and "To a fly" arguing that ambition, necessary, is absurd. Hence the many avenues to and flights from the themes of loneliness, grief, and loss.

Art thou but some wandering discontent?
Some thought, which may not find a resting-place,

Fixed to one constant round of endless change,
For ever wandering, and for ever doomed
To wander on alone; teaching itself
To suffer; gnawing itself, and bringing home
Its direst misery? a misery
Of loneliness unshared, which nought can know
And nought can pity? . . .
Lo! thou art gone, perchance to seek for rest;
And the sky, which but now cast back thy beam,
Has lost thee, and with open smile it seems
As 'twould rejoice to find itself again
Free from thy fearful light.

("The Comet," 23–31, 45–49)

The poet shares the comet's baleful solitude. Solitude is proper for Romantic melancholy, and Romantic melancholy shields, or muffles, the poet of *My Dreams;* quite properly, its longest poem—"The Village Churchyard"—is, after the fashion of Thomas Gray's "Elegy Written in a Country Churchyard," Oliver Goldsmith's *The Deserted Village,* and George Crabbe's *The Village,* a meditation upon death and the dead. But solitude is not only convention; it is the collection's subject and its aspect. Remedies are uncertain, and never human. They are the powers and principalities of the air, sometimes given form as sprites or spirits that occupy sunbeams, stars, ocean, winds, or a river; sometimes personified, as in "Love, Wisdom, and Folly"; sometimes evoked directly as ideas, dreams, desires. These "beings not of earth," Zephyr coming to the flower, seem to bring solace or rest against "the greatest agony of wo . . . that it is a *lonely thing.*"[29] But the remedies are not constant; like "The Star Which Followed Me," now "in unmeasured space, . . . unconscious of my dreams, myself" (ll. 27–28), they can desert their votary; and where they do not fail, they yet are incomplete. Granted that, in "Combat of the Powers of Good and Evil," the "*power of Good*" conquers against the work of Evil, which is "one scene of sin on sin, and wo on wo," nevertheless its conquest is only to give "the timid mortal strength / To hope, and hope, and hope in misery" (ll. 91, 122–23). Experience teaches a lesson no less bleak:

This beauteous garden charms the eye,
As smiles the world to youth;
But every promise brings its sigh;

29. "Spirit Watchers," l. 1, and "Zephyr and the Flower," ll. 21–22, chap. 1 above.

The fresh heart aches to see it die,
And trembles at the truth.

The brightest hues which now delight,
Must wither ere they're yours;
Experience ever stands to blight
All that is loveliest to the sight,
To crush the sweetest flowers.

Experience maketh wise, 'tis true;
But ah! in tears man earns
The lesson, which but makes him rue
What Wisdom laughs at, as untrue—
He weeps at what he learns.

("The Garden of Experience," 56–70)

My Dreams is not without zest, without humor. To grasp pleasures more fiercely because they last so little, that—the *carpe diem* theme—is the theme chosen for "Oh! Would That I Could Dream On Still," a poem which, having something of Herrick's verve, is placed last in *My Dreams,* its importance amplified by being cited in the collection's proem.[30] "Pretty Fanny" recounts the failure of a grandmother to warn a maiden, since "man's a heartless, false deceiver," against marriage; much as she reveres the old woman's wisdom, the maiden

sometimes wonders what her Grannie
Thought of men, when *she* was young.

'Tis very strange, but not less certain,
Once she was a wedded wife—
Fanny sighed, and dropped the curtain
O'er *that* blot in Grannie's life. (39–44)

But this theme, the conflict between loyalty to blood and the new attachments following from marriage, is treated again, and much otherwise, in "Poor Nannie." Among the mourners in "The Village Churchyard,"

a father stands,
Bowed less with age than grief. A single tear,
Drawn from the bosom's agony, flows down
His manly cheek; unchecked, unbidden flows;
He knows nor feels it not; his heaving breast

30. Robert Herrick, "To the Virgins, to Make Much of Time" and "Corinna's Going A-Maying."

Seems rising 'gainst its load, as 't could repel
The grief which weighs upon it. Snatch'd in youth's prime,
He mourns, to him the loveliest, and the best:
His age's comfort, and his brightest hope
In life's decline; the last connecting link
Which bound to earth his wishes and his hopes.
All now lie buried in the grave of her,
The last of all who lived to call him father. (161–73)

Death which here divides, in "Poor Nannie" unites, father and daughter. "Poor Nannie" is a narrative poem, told about four characters. A "tardy labourer," returning home during a December storm, is frightened (he remembers tales of spirits haunting graves) from investigating strange cries heard upon the wasted plain through which he makes his way. The cries, we learn, are those of a young woman: she has deserted her aged father to run off with her suitor and now travels through the icy tempest to see, a last time, the father whom she has heard to be on his deathbed. But the father wakes in the morning after the storm to find his daughter dead by his bed, and dies beside her. The fourth character, the suitor "who like a serpent crept, / And stole her from her father's home," visits the common grave of father and daughter; then, his heart "grown cold as is the frozen snow," he rides away to forget the tear which he shed there for the woman whom he had betrayed. Cast into the form of a ballad, yet "Poor Nannie" is somehow told of the poet, and the daughter of Langdon Cheves, and it is designed so to be told. Who dedicated her book to her father for his "hope-inspiring praise" nourishing her poetry, was Nannie, doomed daughter, who

with my aged father, dwelt;
And happy was I with his praise,
The greatest pleasure that I felt. (74–76)

"Somehow told of the poet"—but how, no clues are vouchsafed. Although a collection entitled *My Dreams,* the poems tend to be impersonal; not many are spoken in the first person, and in many of those the first person is but narrator or interlocutor; narrative and dialogue suit the purpose more. Although speaking much of death and loss, loneliness and equivocal hope, the poems are potent with their own ingenuity and the pleasure taken in skill.[31] They are not about Louisa McCord, but about Louisa McCord writing. They are the work of an apprentice who means to be a journeyman, and may

31. So the epigraph chosen for *My Dreams:* "'Tis to create, and in creating live / A being more intense, that we endow / With form our fancy, gaining as we give / The life we image, e'en as I do now" (Lord Byron, *Childe Harold's Pilgrimage* 3.46–49).

hope to be a master. That is their common ground with *Caius Gracchus* and the essays.

IV. "What argument avails?"

Genres were opportunities. The duty of women might be argued in a review published in a periodical; that was the readiest course; but a poem in blank verse, "Woman's Progress," could find a place there, too. Against the inflated absurdities of *Uncle Tom's Cabin* and its admirers, of a social consciousness run mad and hypocritically selective, argument was not enough, for "what argument avails against broad, flat, impudent assertion?" Better for Mrs. McCord to reply in kind, to compose a novel herself, or an outline of such, with representative dialogue and character sketches, out-Kingsleying Kingsley in order to out-Stowe Stowe.[32] Another genre, the epistle, and in particular Edmund Burke's *Letter to a Noble Lord* (which defended his career against the censures of the eighth duke of Bedford), bequeathed to Mrs. McCord form and model for her address to the chief of Mrs. Stowe's British patrons, the duchess of Sutherland. An ignorant and presumptuous nobility was much of a piece; a pampered aristocrat who, owing his wealth to a multitude of enormous pensions got by truckling and judicial murder, protested against a modest pension granted to a life of public service, might as well preach the rights of the oppressed, having, by the useful arts of chicanery, starvation, exile, and arson, dispossessed whole families and villages because sheep were more profitable than clansmen; a duchess of Sutherland would do for a duke of Bedford, and a nation making war to the benefit of opium traders would do for a sovereign plundering subjects and church.

> In the name of common sense, why should the Duke of Bedford think, that none but of the House of Russel are entitled to the favour of the Crown? Why should he imagine that no King of England has been capable of judging of merit but King Henry the Eighth? Indeed, he will pardon me; he is a little mistaken; all virtue did not end in the first Earl of Bedford. All discernment did not lose it's vision when his Creator closed his eyes. Let him remit his rigour on the disproportion between merit and reward in others, and they will make no enquiry into the origins of his fortune. They will regard with much more satisfaction, as he will contemplate with infinitely more advantage, whatever in his pedigree has been dulcified by the exposure to the influence of heaven in a long flow of generations, from the hard, acidulous,

32. *PSE*, "*Uncle Tom's Cabin*," pp. 266–68.

> metallick tincture of the spring. It is little to be doubted, that several of his forefathers, in that long series, have degenerated into honour and virtue.[33]

> I will not ask you, noble Madam, why America particularly has, of all countries of the earth, chanced first to attract your effort for the improvement of mankind. I will not ask you why slavery, which is in one form or another almost co-extensive and co-existent with society, should appear so peculiarly obnoxious among us. I will not ask why, when the great Empire of China, with its three hundred and fifty millions of souls, is systematically drugged under English legislative enactment, your Grace and the honorable sisterhood have not turned your sympathies towards its perishing millions. I will not ask why, simply because these people are yellow and not black, they should so escape your Grace's sympathies that you calmly, and without remonstrance, see your own government almost force the poison down their throats, condemning millions to a mental and bodily prostration—to a lingering and brutish death, compared to which the ancient punishment of the hemlock bowl were a charity and a mercy. This entire oblivion of the woes and oppressions of other nations presents at first sight a strange contrast to the warm sympathies excited for America. But of this, it surely is not for us to complain. It is, as I interpret it, but a proof of the greater affection which you entertain towards us. As the parent chasteneth his child, as the friend reproveth his friend, your anxieties are naturally most alive where your sympathies are strongest; and great indeed must be the affection which can make you thus turn your whole effort toward us, even to the detriment of the morals of your own beloved England. You leave her groaning under the shame of the Opium trade, until through your generous interference we shall be relieved of our sin and our sorrow.[34]

Weapons from the armory of classical rhetoric (erotema, anaphora, praeteritio, tricolon and tetracolon abundans) and—what Louisa McCord shared, by nature as by apprenticeship, with Edmund Burke—an excellent ear: these are united with the arts of the invective, distilled by the artificial and ironic detachment furnished in the epistle.

Encomium, too, was a genre with its uses, and—being traditionally the kind of writing to demand the most elaborate architecture taught by the grand style—it attracted ambition. A sample of the grand style is displayed in the following pattern, designed to emphasize the articulations of its structure:

33. Edmund Burke, *Letter to a Noble Lord* (1796), in *Writings and Speeches* 9:169.

34. *PSE,* "A Letter to the Duchess of Sutherland from a Lady of South Carolina," pp. 352–53.

If there is any community
whose system of government works better for *all classes* than our own
we are willing to abandon the defence of ours But
if after all honest investigation
it has to be conceded
as in spite of travellers' slanders
is conceded
has been proved by many an able essay and
can easily be proved again
whenever space and time are allowed for the subject
if we say
it be acknowledged that
no where are the higher classes more elevated
no where are the lower more comfortable
no where do both and all work together in their several positions
with less of bitterness or
more of the genial spirit of christian love and
charity
that
no where is there less misery and
less vice exhibited
than under the working of our system
if cases of wrong and oppression
which exist in every system and
must exist
so long as man is not perfect
are
as in all good governments they must be
exceptional cases and not
cases in rule
if all this is as we contend it is
proved and conceded
what matters it
if Mrs. Stowe's theory or
Mr. Horace Mann's or
Mr. Giddings's or
Mrs. Stowe's store-clerk brother's theory
points it out as iniquitous?

This pair of conditional sentences constitutes a form of hypothetical syllogism (if A, then B; but if C, then D); the overwhelming preponderance of the second sentence in length and elaboration pushes the reader into accepting the proposition D, itself made surer by being cast as a rhetorical question. Within the second sentence itself, there is a like preponderance in length and elaboration, but now coming first: the bulk of the conditional clause (subdivided into four parts, the fourth being much the shortest) is ordered by anaphora (if-if-if-if, no where–no where–no where–no where), doublets (conceded-conceded, proved-proved, more-more, less-less, exist-exist, cases-cases), interlocking and chiastic order of the doublets (more-more-less-more-less-less and conceded-conceded-proved-proved-proved-conceded), and pairs of distinguished and likened words (space-time, higher-lower, elevated-comfortable, both-all, bitterness–genial spirit, love-charity, misery-vice, wrong-oppression, exceptional–in rule). After the main clause, only three words long ("what matters it"), comes an indirect question, but seeming (although here if = whether) to parallel the conditional clause; it, too, like the conditional clause, is built in four parts (but here the fourth part is longest). The word "theory" in the first part, absent by ellipsis from the second and third, is repeated in the fourth part, which, with possessive case piled upon possessive case, debouches into the doubled rhythm (stressed-unstressed-stressed) at beginning and end of the predicate, "*points* it *out*" and "-*i*qui*tous*." "Theory" takes the last doublet of the sentence, for, as the passage goes on to argue, "evils, to be felt, must be tangible and not theoretic evils. It is not enough that a master *might* do this, and *might* do that. The question is, what *does* he, in the majority of cases, do? How does the system work? not how *ought* it to work, according to my theory, or your theory, or his theory? Theory has done, and is doing, wild work in our world, of late years."[35] The immense and harmonious sentence is constructed not for the pleasure in the building (although there is something of that) but so that the force of argument be fittingly reproduced in frame of words, sounds, cadences, upon which the reader, or more properly the listener (for, as always with Louisa McCord's prose, what is said is real to the ear rather than to the eye), is borne along. In her longest encomium, of political economy, is to be found a sentence of comparable elaboration;[36] the

35. Ibid., "*Uncle Tom's Cabin,*" pp. 253–54.

36. "If in so doing she could show, as she has shown, as she will yet in her future progress more clearly show, more beautifully develop (for the apostleship of Political Economy has but just begun), if, we say, she can prove that the good of all is irrevocably linked in the good of each; if she can prove (as she does prove) to the purse-proud capitalist that to preserve or increase his wealth his laborer must be fed, his country and his nation must thrive, or all his wealth, like fairy gifts, turns in his hands to dry leaves and trash; if she can prove (as she does prove) to the hungry laborer that his bread is none the dearer, his labor none the less in demand, because the rich man is accumulating his millions—that on the contrary even

grand style is sought throughout; even ill and harassed—she was caring for her dying father, and blindness threatened her and her son—when she encountered an occasion for eloquence, she did not hesitate to accept its challenge.

V. "A Wife, so hung with Virtues"

Impartial and imperial, that was the vizard voice of the reviewer, plural and singular, sexless customarily, now and then masculine, or feminine.[37] There was the elusive "I" of *My Dreams.* The author's own voice disappears entirely from the drama; yet in *Caius Gracchus* Mrs. Chesnut found Mrs. McCord, found the mother of the Gracchi. Cornelia was of excellent, even formidable, family. She was daughter of Scipio Africanus, who had conquered Carthage in the Second Punic War; granddaughter of Aemilius Paullus, who when consul had fallen at Cannae; niece of another Aemilius Paullus, who subjugated the kingdom of Macedon to Rome. Of her twelve children—to whom, surrounded by Greek tutors and rhetors, she devoted her whole care, refusing, after she was widowed, a proposal of marriage from King Ptolemy of Egypt—three survived childhood. Her daughter was married to Scipio Aemilianus, Cornelia's cousin and her nephew by adoption, destroyer of Carthage in the Third Punic War; her elder son Tiberius, as tribune in 133 B.C., was murdered by a mob incited against his proposed reforms; the younger, Gaius, tribune for two years (123–122), the year after was hunted down and killed, with three thousand other citizens, by order of the consul Lucius Opimius. The deaths of her sons, and the ruin of their political cause and hopes, Cornelia survived "with a noble and undaunted

---

the most selfish hoarder hoards for the good of all; if she can prove (as she does prove) that labor and capital are not inimical, but rather, working in unison, assistant handmaids each to the other; if she can prove (as she does prove) the truth of all these, at first sight, apparent paradoxes, and reconcile interests hitherto in unnatural and fraternal war, is she not indeed a prophet of peace, the beautiful development of christian civilization?" Ibid., "Slavery and Political Economy," pp. 437–38.

37. "On what principle then can I be denied the right of disposing of the labor, or the proceeds of the labor of that hour? I may give my life to my country or my friend, and this is acknowledged to be a noble or generous action. I may give it by a sudden and abrupt sacrifice of life, or by a long, patient, and laborious one. The last I do for my wife or children, when passing a life of toil in their service." Ibid., "The Right to Labor," p. 92. "We—even we, the reviewer—must acknowledge ourselves of the feminine gender, of the female sex—woman. . . . We have been obliged to confess ourself woman, because only as woman can we take the defensive in this question." Ibid., "Woman and Her Needs," p. 145.

spirit." Having retired to Misenum on the Bay of Naples, she received friends and visitors amid a circle of learned Greeks and other scholars and corresponded with foreign princes. Her *doctissimus sermo,* her cultivated style, as handed down in her letters (disputed fragments are extant), was admired by Cicero and Quintilian, fastidious critics: "we read the letters of Cornelia, mother of the Gracchi; there it is shown that her sons were nursed not so much at their mother's breast as upon her discourse."[38]

Cornelia was the classical *exemplum,* the precedent and the model, of heroic motherhood. Family tradition assigned to Louisa McCord a variation of a celebrated story told of Cornelia, to whom one day a wealthy lady flourished her jewels. "These are *my* jewels," replied Cornelia, pointing to her sons. "As mistress of a plantation . . . when asked once why she wore no jewelry," Mrs. McCord said that "a woman with two hundred children could hardly afford diamonds." But could Cornelia do more than to suggest an anecdote? The *Southern Quarterly Review* was suspicious of the entire saga of the Gracchi. Monotonous events; vacillating character; Gaius Gracchus no Macbeth, his wife no Lady Macbeth; his objects trivial; the Roman people "capricious, selfish, timid, and unworthy," who needed a Sulla or a Caesar to take them in hand: nothing, in short, of the stuff of tragedy. The historian Barthold Georg Niebuhr was of a different opinion; in his *Römische Geschichte,* very influential and much translated, the Gracchi (but more especially Gaius Gracchus) were exalted as at once heroic and tragic characters, of purest and wisest patriotism, destroyed by brutal and arrogant oligarchs. Such was the Gaius Gracchus of Marie-Joseph Chénier, whose Girondist *Caius Gracchus* was presented in Paris in February 1792; such, too, of Vincenzo Monti, who, after reading Chénier's version, completed his *Caio Gracco* in 1800 during his exile in France, having fled the Cisalpine Republic which, established by French Revolutionary armies in 1797, in 1799 had fallen to Austrian and Russian troops. Only in James Sheridan Knowles' two versions of the story, in 1815 and 1823, was the heroic figure shrunk into a cutout in a sentimental tableau of doting husband, adoring wife, and agonized partings. Louisa McCord returned to the heroic and tragic possibilities of the tale. Not, it is true, to the revolutionary enthusiasms of Chénier and of Monti, for "witness France, where revolutions have become the bloody toy of the multitude;

38. Plutarch *Gaius Gracchus* 19, in the Dryden Translation, 2:383–84; Quintilian 1.1.6; Cicero *Brutus* 211: "Legimus epistulas Corneliae matris Gracchorum; apparet filios non tam in gremio educatos quam in sermone matris." David James McCord, "How the South Is Affected by Her Slave Institutions," p. 358: "At the South, children are never put out to nurse, but are brought up from their birth under the careful and jealous eye of the mother, and, as with the Romans, *non tam in gremio quam in sermone matris.*"

who fight for they know not what; spurning today the idol of yesterday, and calling for revolution as they would for a parade or 'un spectacle.'"[39] But, whatever was the individual treatment of the story, oppression resisted was the story's constant theme; Gaius Gracchus resisting oppression could be variously transcribed. The Gracchi appealed personally to Louisa McCord: "they are among my *bona fide* heroes." They appealed to her as a South Carolinian (so *De Bow*'s reviewer pointed out): "In the agitated state of public feeling which has prevailed in South Carolina for some years past, exist important requisites for the nourishment and development of the poetic faculty in its greatest vigor. The idea of external oppression, exciting personal feeling, and turning the mind to the contemplation of examples of heroic resistance, has, in past times, produced the noblest specimens of eloquence, and plumed the wings of poesy to her most sustained flights." They appealed to her, finally, as a woman, for "woman, as a body, has never sided, and never can side, with the oppressor."[40]

But how should a woman stand against, if she must not side with, oppression? She should look to Cornelia. Louisa McCord could be skeptical of examples from the illustrious and illustrative past—when these were cited by advocates of woman's rights. Queens, regents, peeresses merely proved that chivalric codes (which of course such advocates derided), other "laws and habits of society," and, in the case of Joan of Arc, religious position, all had conferred upon women especial status; all were necessary to protect modern women as well. If fictional creations, like the heroines of Charles Kingsley's *Alton Locke,* were "distressingly vapid," plundering even her beloved Shakespeare worked no better. Portia and her like "are so entirely poetic as to require all Shakspeare's genius to cause them to be tolerated even on the stage"; and "if ladies will borrow arguments from imaginary characters, why not take at once the powerful Minerva springing full-armed from the brow of Jove?"[41] But Rome was different, or Roman women. If Roman

39. Valerius Maximus *Facta et dicta memorabilia* 4.4 *praef.;* Bennett, "Cheves Family of South Carolina," p. 91; "Caius Gracchus," *SQR,* n. s., 4 (July 1851): 63; *PSE,* "Separate Secession," p. 216.

40. LSM to William Porcher Miles, June 12, 1848; "Mrs. M'Cord's Caius Gracchus," *De Bow,* n. s., 1 (Oct. 1852): 428; *PSE,* "A Letter to the Duchess of Sutherland from a Lady of South Carolina," p. 351; also, ibid., "British Philanthropy and American Slavery," p. 319: "However individual exceptions are to be found, woman (as a class) never sides with the oppressor."

41. *PSE,* "Enfranchisement of Woman," p. 117, "Negro and White Slavery," p. 190, and "Woman and Her Needs," p. 143. "Joan of Arc (decidedly the most remarkable of heroines . . .) was a wonderful woman; great as a woman; a phenomenon in her way, certainly, but still a woman phenomenon. Her deeds were unusual for woman, but, nevertheless, done as a woman, and claiming for their sanction, not the rights and habits of manhood, but divine

courage was to be deprecated, the context was polemical: Roman courage could be desperate courage, and South Carolina, unless fooled into the folly of separate secession, had no need of it—although Mrs. McCord's sentiments in December 1860 suggest she had modified her judgment.[42] In Roman women, however, Louisa McCord placed her confidence; they were the guardians, even more, the fellows, of the Penates (the Roman household gods), and "to be a divinity, a genial, household divinity, . . . to *be worshiped* at that holiest altar of the Penates, the home hearth; to be the soul of that home, even as our great Father-God is the soul of creation; to be the breath, the life, the love-law of that home; the mother, the wife, the sister, the daughter—such is woman's holiest sphere, such her largest endowment."[43] Preeminent guardian in Roman story, the mother of the Gracchi was alone cause enough to write a *Caius Gracchus.*[44] Mrs. McCord laid aside her hesitation to speak authoritatively about classical antiquity.[45] Niebuhr, as she told William Porcher Miles, backed her up; and Shakespeare's *Coriolanus,* drawing from Plutarch, presented to her in Volumnia the eloquent and majestic mother who persuades her son, "brought up under the widowhood of his

---

inspiration. She never levelled herself to man, or, so doing, must have sunk to the rank of the coarse *femmes de la Halle* of the French revolution." "Enfranchisement of Woman," p. 117.

42. "We are not strong enough, we of South Carolina alone, to maintain our cause. We can die! ay, and bury our children beneath the ruins of our hearthstones, that our enemies may triumph and our names be forgotten. But it would be desperation, not courage, which would prompt us to this. True courage can bear and forbear, can wait and watch, and strive and endure. It is impatience, not courage—it is coward shrinking, not resolution—which casts itself upon the sword point to terminate its struggles. The ancient Roman was half a barbarian, when he sought death as a cure for life's evils; a higher civilization—a nobler philosophy—teaches us to *bear* and *conquer* them." Ibid., "Separate Secession," p. 213. Cf. LSM to Hiram Powers, Dec. 24, 1860.

43. *PSE,* "Woman and Her Needs," p. 152.

44. Not all agreed. "The wife of Gracchus, in this play, does nothing; nor is Cornelia—the proverbial Cornelia—of more importance to the agency. Both should have been endowed with more character, and been made active auxiliaries of the hero. By the way, Cornelia, the mother—and not Licinia, the wife—should have given the dagger to Gracchus. The act is not consonant with the characteristics of the latter, as the author has portrayed her. For that matter, it is rather more in keeping with the *historical* Cornelia, than with the same personage in the play. As a piece for the closet, these objections are of minor importance. But, could the author have done more for the women of the piece, its claims in stage and closet, alike, would have been wonderfully increased." "Caius Gracchus," *SQR,* n. s., 4 (July 1851): 67–68.

45. "To our reviewer [George Frederick Holmes], much more a classical scholar than a political economist, we are quite ready to do all honor, and, acknowledging our childlike ignorance where he excels, to offer homage to his superiority on a ground where we have often lamented our own deficiencies." *PSE,* "Slavery and Political Economy," p. 430.

mother," to the right course of action. Volumnia, indeed, is Cornelia thrown back into Rome's mythical past; converting Volumnia into Cornelia, then, Louisa McCord but reversed the transfiguration.[46]

Cornelia was a paragon indeed, but what paragon casts no shadow? Some said that she had driven her sons to mad ambition by reminding them repeatedly that she was called the mother-in-law of Scipio Aemilianus, not yet the mother of the Gracchi; others even accused her of conspiring with her daughter to murder Aemilianus, so removing an obstacle to her sons' schemes.[47] But from antiquity the harshest verdict was delivered by the satirist Juvenal. "Free from strife," yes, "Rich, Fair, and Fruitful: of Unblemish'd Life: / Chast as the *Sabines*," and of the noblest blood, too, and yet

> A Wife, so hung with Virtues, such a freight;
> What Mortal Shoulders cou'd support the weight!
> Some Country Girl, scarce to a Curtsey bred,
> Wou'd I much rather than *Cornelia* wed:
> If Supercilious, Haughty, Proud, and Vain,
> She brought her Father's Triumphs, in her Train.[48]

Juvenal's Cornelia was not Cornelia the daughter of Africanus, nor Cornelia the mother of the Gracchi, but Cornelia the wife of—whom? The husband had got lost: Tiberius Sempronius Gracchus had been consul twice, twice had celebrated a triumph over Rome's enemies, and had held the crown of an aristocrat's career, the censorship—but still he had got lost.[49] The widow was proper to the plot; the wife had no place in the elevated and elevating tradition of Cornelia, and no place in Mrs. McCord's *Caius Gracchus*.

In 1850, ill in a hotel in New York, Mary Chesnut, visiting the bookstore downstairs, came upon the first volume of Thackeray's *Vanity Fair*. The illustrations, the very paper, her delight, she remembered precisely; so, too, the response of some persons to whom she declared her admiration: "he was evidently a coarse, dull, sneering writer; . . . he stripped human nature

46. LSM to William Porcher Miles, June 12, 1848; Plutarch *Coriolanus* 1.2, in the Dryden Translation, 1:291. Coriolanus himself is now thought by many scholars to be an entirely fictional creation.

47. Plutarch *Tiberius Gracchus* 8.5; Appian *Bella Civilia* (*Civil Wars*) 1.20.

48. Juvenal *Satire* 6.162–70 = Dryden's translation, 6.234–47.

49. Chap. 5 above, *Caius Gracchus* 3.4.89–93:

> I thank my mother that she gave me not
> For father, an Egyptian Ptolemy;
> But, from the offers of a kingdom turning,
> Gave heart and hand to a plebeian Roman,
> And son and brother to a Gracchus made me.

bare, made it repulsive, etcetcetc." Hence was it, then, that the narrator in *Vanity Fair* was not so willing to allow the elision of Cornelia's marriage? "The best of women (I have heard my grandmother say) are hypocrites. We don't know how much they hide from us: how watchful they are when they seem most artless and confidential: how often those frank smiles which they wear so easily, are traps to cajole or elude or disarm—I don't mean in your mere coquettes, but your domestic models, and paragons of female virtue. Who has not seen a woman hide the dulness of a stupid husband, or coax the fury of a savage one? We accept this amiable slavishness, and praise a woman for it: we call this pretty treachery truth. A good housewife is of necessity a humbug; and Cornelia's husband was hoodwinked, as Potiphar was—only in a different way."[50]

VI. "States of bondage"

"Many a woman of dominant intellect is obliged to submit to the rule of an animal in pantaloons, every way her inferior." Such a woman might return home to find, "troubled and indignant," that in her absence a physician has invaded her house, swept aside her daughter's protests, and, without consulting her, has operated upon her son, removing a bullet from his skull, and declared him fit for military service: "Women may be comforters but Doctors too often are tyrants." Such a woman must stand by, to "gaze and tremble at the lowering darkness of our threatened destiny," while her society and her South were harassed by foreign busybodies and "fanatic visionaries," and governed through "the petty optics of interested politicians, who, burrowing in the blind paths of selfish policy, know not that, in their eager and unprincipled plottings, they may, like the mole under the princely castle, be drawing down over their own heads a ruin too vast for their cramped and grovelling policy to understand." Such a woman, like any woman, with the children who were her care, was a slave. "The positions of women and children are in truth as essentially states of bondage as any other, the differences being in degree, not kind. They are states of subjection to the supremacy of others, and of greater or less deprivation of the rights of self government. This, the true definition of slavery, applies equally to the position of women in the most civilized and enlightened countries."[51]

But this slavery was indispensable—for the slaves:

50. *Chesnut,* p. 546; William Makepeace Thackeray, *Vanity Fair,* ed. Peter Shillingsburg (New York, 1994), p. 175.

51. *PSE,* "Carey on the Slave Trade," p. 406; LSM to Mary Chesnut, Oct. 18, 1863, and note; *PSE,* "Diversity of the Races; Its Bearing upon Negro Slavery," pp. 185–86, and "Slav-

> Society requires from its members, on condition of certain advantages accorded, an abandonment of certain rights. Woman has been required to abandon more than man, because her nature needs more protection. As she requires a larger protection for her weakness, she gives up a larger portion of her natural rights. She pays for what she receives. She needs the arm of man to defend her against man himself. She, therefore, cannot be his equal. In many things his superior, she is still the dependent upon him for that protection which her physical weakness requires. Individual women may sometimes suffer from such a state of things; but society, which consults the good of all, requires it for the good of all; and, however talented may occasionally be the women who thus step out of their woman sphere, it is a defective system of reasoning which has led them to this course. . . .
>
> Equally, and more, with the negro as with the woman: he needs protection, and must pay for it by the abandonment of privileges which otherwise might seem to be his right. The universal rule of nature, by which inferior races have invariably disappeared before the advance of the superior, has, in the case of the negro, been arrested to his advantage; and, instead of extermination, he has, in the Southern United States, met protection. For this protection, he has been required to give up such rights as the superior man claims, under what is usually termed a free government. This protection withdrawn, his fate is as certain as that of the red man, whose ruin has preceded him. Nature, as though tired of the destruction of her feebler offspring, holds out to him this refuge.[52]

Louisa McCord might deem human nature to be caught between reason and passion, God and beast, in itself neither evil nor good but capable of both; it was a view with a long pedigree, celebrated in Pope's *Essay on Man,* and her revered political economy was framed to assist this divided nature to find the truth of things.[53] Nevertheless her opinion of men's nature, in prac-

---

ery and Political Economy," p. 441. "What is slavery? We answer: *involuntary legal subjection* of any individual to another. This condition does *not* imply oppression on the part of the ruler, nor suffering on that of the ruled, or slave." *PSE,* "Carey on the Slave Trade," p. 402. Cf. chap. 5 above, *Caius Gracchus,* "To My Son," ll. 7–11: "the Mother finds / (Be she true woman with a woman's heart) / No moment when that heart can idly rest / From the long love which ever fetters it / In bondage to her child."

52. *PSE,* "Carey on the Slave Trade," pp. 406–7.

53. "An inscrutable Providence has made an imperfect world, and, in the exercise of a wisdom incomprehensible to us, has created man a strange bundle of faults and virtues, passion and reason. Governed alternately by truth and error, he gropes his way midst phantoms of darkness. Sophistry parades before him her twilight theories, strutting in the robes of wisdom. Folly peeps from behind her harlequin mask, while fanaticism stabs with a prayer, and hand in hand with hypocrisy dares call down Heaven's blessing upon deeds of

tice, was less balanced, less paradoxical, darker, grim: strong, proud, pitiless, greedy, insolent, men by themselves dwelt in a violent world that mirrored their being, and "the *voie de fait* [assault and battery] is, after all, the only way of defending disputed rights in this world." A savage husband came readily to her pen as it sketched a novel to match Mrs. Stowe's. The "fiend of War," with his companions Famine, Pestilence, and Death, was male, raging in "a field of carnage," of "death and slaughter," but "'twas gentle woman's voice which whispered 'Hope.'" *Caius Gracchus* exhibited men's deadly world, and woman, "designed, by nature, the conservative power of the world," trapped in it.[54]

We may rear
Heroes, whose dauntless will shall shake the world,
Or like a moral Atlas, bear its burden,
A universe of care, upon their shoulders.
But in our bosoms if too fierce the flame
That feeds such spirit-struggles, we must check,
Or drive it back, at least, to seeming quiet.
If hard the effort, it is woman's task.
Her passions, if not smothered, must be hid,
Till, in their faintly-beating pulse, herself
Will scarcely know her blood the same which bounds
Through manlier veins unchecked. (1.3.18–29)

"She may counsel, she may teach, she may uphold the weary arm of manhood—of the husband, the brother, or the son—and rouse him to the

---

Hell. Knee-deep in error, man works out the truth only by patient investigation and laborious research; and society must find its way to the goal of such perfection as earth permits only by the study of itself. Political Economy is this study." Ibid., "Slavery and Political Economy," p. 463. Cf. Alexander Pope, *An Essay on Man* 2.1–18. She had early, and with approval, cited a more generous view out of Bastiat, who endeavored to demonstrate that human interests are not (despite socialist opinion) antagonistic but can be understood, through political economy, to combine toward the general welfare (*PSE,* "The Right to Labor," pp. 98–99): "Is it certain that *interests are naturally antagonistic?* that an irremediable cause of inequality is thus fatally developed in the natural order of human society? and that *God* has manifestly made a mistake in ordaining that the tendency of man should ever be towards well-being? This is what I propose examining into, taking man as it has pleased God to make him, capable of foresight and experiences, perfectible, loving himself certainly, but with an affection tempered by a sympathetic tendency in his nature, and every where held under restraint by the contact with an analogous sentiment, universally pervading his theatre of action."

54. *PSE,* "Woman and Her Needs," p. 141, and "*Uncle Tom's Cabin,*" pp. 267–68; "Combat of the Powers of Good and Evil," ll. 70–98, chap. 1 above; *PSE,* "Woman and Her Needs," p. 153.

struggle for which nature never designed her; but she may not (without foregoing her nature) rush into the combat of blood, shouting man's war-cry and the victim's death." Yet Cornelia could not, entirely, hold back. Abandoning her source Plutarch, Mrs. McCord sent Cornelia to her son at the last, exhausted, pursued by assassins, in the temple of Diana. Even now Cornelia would suggest, advise, exhort; even to do this much, now, "usurped the man." It made no difference. Her son was killed. "We can but watch the struggle."[55]

Philocrates, the slave of Gracchus, dies in the last moments of the play, interposing his body to receive a blow aimed at his master. But for this (his heroism is recorded by Plutarch), slaves and slavery are not much noticed in *Caius Gracchus.*[56] This might seem odd, Louisa McCord writing so much on this subject and insisting on its continuity and compass.[57] However, as she reminded George Frederick Holmes, who as a classical scholar ought to have known better, "United States negro slavery" was a new thing. Ancient slavery was not racial slavery. Political economy, "almost entirely a European study, . . . in so far as it has noticed slavery, has regarded it as an exploded system, and as preceding an enlightened civilization. This is a limited but, for a European, most natural point of view; such indeed is, or rather was, the slavery of Europe, to which, in default of answering information from us, their observations have been confined. Where slavery lingers in Europe, it is in process of change, showing the beginning of the end. Ours is of an entirely dissimilar stamp, and the European knows as little of the inferior race of men which it has fallen upon our clime and our day to utilize, as he knows of our swamps and our forests." This new slavery, "of an entirely dissimilar stamp," had not yet been properly studied. Even so praiseworthy a

55. *PSE,* "Woman and Her Needs," p. 153; chap. 5 above, *Caius Gracchus* 5.4.89, 2.5.20.

56. The only considerable mention occurs in Gracchus' speech contrasting the stability of the slave's position with the purloined rights of citizens (2.6.24–32):

> Man has, in every station, rights his due.
> Our slaves look to their masters for support.
> The very claims we hold upon their labor
> Make us a rule to tender them again
> What comforts we can furnish to their lot.
> If placed by circumstance, necessity,
> Beneath our rule, protection thence we owe:
> And he evading basely these, degrades
> Himself below the thus defrauded slave.

57. "Equality is no thought nor creation of God. Slavery, under one name or another, will exist as long as man exists; and abolition is a dream whose execution is an impossibility." *PSE,* "Negro-mania," p. 241.

political economist as Adam Smith could offer no guidance, having written "before the day of United States negro slavery, nor could he read in the future its great results." The student must look to those results. "The wonderful development of this western continent, effected only through and by the means of slavery—her immense produce scattered over our globe, carrying food and clothing to the hungry and the destitute; her cotton and her sugar sustaining not only herself but the might of Europe's most powerful nations; her ever increasing expanse of new land, opening an asylum for Europe's starving millions, and staving off menaced revolutions—what are these but the glorious results of American negro slavery?"—results, too, to the benefit "not of [the] master only, not of one country only, but of the world." "The results of United States negro-slave labor are such as no other system of labor yet known upon earth could have accomplished. It has explored regions under whose miasmatic influences the white man sickened and died. It has drained swamps and made habitable the pestiferous marsh. It has conquered the pestilence and opened to a growing world a garden of hitherto unknown comforts and luxuries. It has called the hungry to be fed and the naked to be clothed. It has given a home to the homeless and a new world to progressive and aspiring man."[58]

And it preserved the slave. "You believe," Louisa McCord wrote to Henry Carey, "the negro to be an oppressed race, while we believe him to be a protected one. You assume the ground that we are committing a constant injustice towards him, while we are convinced that we are his only safeguard from extermination, at least in this country." The white race, fierce and predatory, must destroy an inferior race set against it; slavery—for sound economic reasons which even the fiercest and most predatory must acknowledge—stood as the only bulwark: "nothing but the extinction of the negro race in America can eradicate slavery." Could not equality among the races, however recognized or achieved, prohibit the destruction of one race by another? "The negro can never be the white man's equal," and equality itself was "a dream which the necessities of nature refuse to recognize."[59] "'Thus far shalt thou go, and no farther,' hath God said, not to the great ocean only, when he chained it within its bed, but equally to every creature within the limits of its uses and its intelligence. To the white man, he has given *his* place; to the negro, *his.* The white man who abuses his God-given power, is indeed criminal, both to God and to man. Hitchings there are, and disorders numberless, in the great world-system of machinery, which

58. Ibid., "Slavery and Political Economy," pp. 428–29, 431, 452, 456.

59. LSM to Henry C. Carey, Jan. 18, 1854; *PSE*, "Slavery and Political Economy," p. 453, and "Carey on the Slave Trade," p. 406.

Omniscience has not seen fit to make perfect; but what are these, compared to the general crash which would follow, should man, with his tinkering, upset the whole fabric that he may rectify its errors by his puny wisdom?"[60] It was such puny and presumptuous wisdom, wrote Mrs. McCord in her earliest essay (and modulated her theme thereafter), which engendered the follies of socialism and communism, engendered "free-soilers, barn-burners, anti-renters, abolitionists," engendered "that most crushing of all tyrannies, the tyranny of dominant and bigot opinion." Such wisdom had been the destruction of nations, and was the American republic—was even South Carolina "whose principles, we had fondly persuaded ourselves, were among the most conservative in all the country"—immune? "Fearful examples there have been—more fearful there yet may be—marked-out States, who, in their own folly, shall constitute themselves the terrible beacon-marks of man's impious madness, when, combatting Providence, he rails at the workings of its high behests. Our own country is perhaps among those which now stand most prominent in this peril." The lesson was simple. "God directs and man perverts."[61]

VII. *"The stamp and seal of God"*

Recalling her young days in Columbia, "one day we went to church and found," wrote Louisa Smythe, "some young men in our pew at Trinity Church. On our return home we were dilating on the subject and Mamma asked if they were students, whereupon I said, 'Oh, no, they were gentlemen.' And my father was heartless enough to repeat that to a room full of students and I never heard the end of it." The McCord family maintained a pew in Trinity Episcopal Church, a block away and around the corner from their property in Columbia; letters indicate that, probably more than occasionally, David James McCord went to church in Columbia and while in residence at Lang Syne. However, the McCords' daughters, and probably their son, were not baptized; and Mrs. McCord did not attend her husband's funeral at Trinity Church. Indeed, she is not recorded, by herself or by others, to have attended church at all except once, in Drummondville, Quebec, so as not to draw attention to herself as a visitor. In Abbeville she watched "a great church excitement (Presbyterian;—church just under my window—) going on at present. Day light prayer and morning and night service"—she watched from a detachment consistent with an opinion, retained in her family and reported in 1962, that she and her husband were "conform-

60. *PSE*, "*Uncle Tom's Cabin*," pp. 271–72.

61. Ibid., "Justice and Fraternity," pp. 73–74, 77, and "*Uncle Tom's Cabin*," p. 270.

ing deists." Certainly, she "was very particular" that her children should join with her in observing outwardly the religious customs of a Roman Catholic household whom in 1857 they were visiting near Old Sweet Springs in Virginia, and she would spare no effort, during the war, to find clergymen for wounded soldiers dissatisfied with the hospital's chaplains; as certainly, none of this pertained to her own personal religious beliefs. "Were I a pious Christian," she wrote of her brother John, who was inclined to contest the terms of their father's will, "I would say 'God forgive him!' As it is I can but *try* to forgive him myself." The Bible being, with Shakespeare, her favorite source of quotation and allusion, yet the founder of Christianity is mentioned by name only twice in her writings. "Not only learned and good men, but christian preachers, honest teachers of Christ and his doctrines," now reject certain beliefs which, arising from literal interpretation of the Christian scriptures, "none but a madman or half idiot would, with the universal opinion of the civilized world against him, now maintain, that the earth is the centre of the universe, and that the sun revolves round it. Few, among well-informed men, are bigoted enough to contend for the long-established biblical chronology and six days creation." And in her poem "Woman's Progress," if woman's proper tasks may seem lowly, "the lowliest tasks / Are sanctified in nobly acting them. / Christ washed the apostles' feet, nor thus cast shame / Upon the God-like in him." It would be unwise, from the use of "God-like," to place Louisa McCord in the conflict of "homoousion" and "homoiousion," to dub her Arian and not Athanasian; albeit she might notice that an opponent's chaotic argument ranged "from Christianity to free-thinking," for Louisa McCord Christianity was a matter not of belief but of conduct.[62]

That conduct, when affected by abolitionists at home and, even more, in Great Britain, roused her sarcasm and anger. "The malignant bitterness (we had almost said ferocity)" of Mrs. Stowe's poisonous novel worked "under the veil of christian charity." Unlike Sandy Mackaye in *Alton Locke,* "clothed with all true Christian graces," who, having rejected the forms of his native Calvinism, adopted "a higher philosophy and religion . . . than either Cameronian or Athanasian creeds: the philosophy and religion of true Christian charity," the American and the British abolitionists, and their noble patrons,

62. Smythe, p. 17; David James McCord to Alexander Herbemont, Oct. 15, 1854, Dulles-Cheves-McCord-Lovell Papers, SCHS; and to Francis Lieber, Dec. 19, 1852, Francis Lieber Papers, Huntington; Smythe, p. 54: "Hannah and I being country children with no minister at Fort Motte while we were babies were . . . unbaptised"; LSM to Louisa McCord Smythe, Feb. 8, 1874, Aug. 22, 1867; C. G. Davidson, *Last Foray,* pp. 107–8, adducing correspondence with David McCord Wright and Samuel G. Stoney; Smythe, pp. 23, 49; LSM to Langdon Cheves, Jr., April 3, 1858; *PSE,* "Diversity of the Races," p. 165; chap. 3 above, "Woman's Progress," ll. 75–78; *PSE,* "Woman and Her Needs," p. 130.

held such Christian charity up before their true faces of callousness and hypocrisy. Mrs. Stowe's Augustine St. Clare, that "intelligent, humane, christian gentleman," indulges in sentimental abuse of slavery and "yet continues to hold the iniquitous possession and, without the courage of a Pilate to wash his hands clean of the sin, he continues to receive the price of blood, and idly luxuriates in the income of his slave-labour, in as matter-of-course a manner as Queen Victoria does in hers." Pretty words and prettier representations could not disguise "the nauseous froth-scum of sickly philanthropy and new-light Christianity." But did not the bonds uniting all women prop the abolitionist crusade? What a compliment it was, observed Mrs. McCord to the duchess of Sutherland, to be "condescendingly invited to your confidence in terms of christian sisterhood"! True, it might seem strange to be told one's Christian duty by one who, although, "I do not doubt it, actuated by a laudable spirit of philanthropy, and a general wish for the well-being of humanity," knew nothing of the circumstances of the case. True, it might seem stranger still that a South Carolinian woman, although "moved by the additional and closer feeling of interest in those who are near to me, such a feeling . . . as may have existed in olden times between the Highland Chief and his kindred subjects," should be reproved by one who, wife to just such a Highland chief, paid for the opulent levée held for Mrs. Stowe at her great mansion in London out of the revenues got from her husband's estates, from which his clansmen had been starved, evicted, banished, and burned out. Nevertheless, how flattering it remained to be noticed by a great aristocrat who would not permit mere ignorance of what she was talking about to obstruct "the beautiful spirit of christian love which is at the foundation of, and pervades, your whole course of action in this affair"![63]

Political economy, too, had to suffer attacks, of those who from Christian sentiments supposed its precepts to be self-interested, its purposes narrow, and its proponents unfeeling; and, again, such thinking came from ignorance, but now not wanton or self-deluded, but more because political economy had not explained itself properly. Louisa McCord therefore turned to exhortation and encomium. Does political economy not demonstrate that "christian charity is national policy"? Is political economy "not indeed a prophet of peace, the beautiful development of christian civilization? Ever thus she comes before us, the teacher of that most beautiful of christian lessons, 'Help ye one another.'"[64] This Christian civilization stood at the cen-

63. *PSE*, "*Uncle Tom's Cabin*," p. 246, "Negro and White Slavery," pp. 191–92, "*Uncle Tom's Cabin*," pp. 265–66, "British Philanthropy and American Slavery," p. 283, and "A Letter to the Duchess of Sutherland from a Lady of South Carolina," pp. 351, 356–57.

64. Ibid., "Slavery and Political Economy," pp. 453, 438.

ter of Louisa McCord's encomium (but with an important reservation) of Christianity itself, composed for "Diversity of the Races; Its Bearing upon Negro Slavery." There she had revealed a suspect allegiance to the freethinker Josiah Clark Nott and others skeptical of "the old notion of Adamic descent." Yet she had to treat somewhat delicately clergymen, two of them resident in Charleston, who argued that Genesis must refute the theory of the diverse origin of the human species. "We mean no attack upon a religion which only the bitterest enemy of mankind could wish to enfeeble. To the philosopher and the philanthropist, independent of personal belief, christianity is equally sacred. With it modern civilization walks hand in hand; from it proceed all those softening influences which make us feel, spite of the *chefs d'oeuvres* of ancient art, now inimitable, that the world is better and wiser than it has been. It stands, after a trial of eighteen centuries, the purest code of philosophy and morals that the history of man has ever developed."[65] "Code of philosophy and morals," Christianity worked its "softening influences." "None less than ourselves would underrate the beautiful and softening influence of this great christian virtue" charity, and in woman, of course, was that charity most to be found. She was, or should be, "a self-denying, patient model of Christian love and charity," her task to teach "the true lesson of Christian charity and philosophical forbearance." "Her's are the noble weapons of philosophy and Christianity. She may find it difficult to wield them, and, in her human weakness, sometimes murmur at the hardness of that lot by which a mysterious Providence has assigned a task so difficult to her feeble frame; but she cannot, she dare not, call degrading a task which, executed in its perfection, would make her the truest personification of our great Christian law. . . . Her's is the Christian law of love and charity, to which (however passion may tempt) unvarying points the finger of duty." Woman was an instrument, although not the sole instrument, of Christianity softening civilization—and softening, in turn, slavery, a slavery "such as ours, which, softened by christianity and civilization, by the ties of dependence and propinquity, shows us the subjection of race by race in the mildest, most humanizing form in which it is possible for this necessary subjection to exist." It was a "Christian slavery," into which, "shorn of the barbarities with which a slavery established by conquest and maintained by brute force is always accompanied, we have begun to mingle . . . the graces and amenities of the highest Christian civilization."[66]

65. Ibid., "Diversity of the Races," p. 164.

66. Ibid., "Slavery and Political Economy," p. 455, "Enfranchisement of Woman," p. 120, "Woman and Her Needs," pp. 130, 149, "Diversity of the Races," p. 182, and "*Uncle Tom's Cabin*," pp. 279–80.

"Have begun, we say, for the work is but begun." The work was being annoyed, obstructed, perhaps (it must be feared) stopped. Just as "once in the history of the world we have heard the insane cry, 'Crucify him! Crucify him!' and the good and the holy, the just and the pure, blown upon by the popular breath, misrepresented by envy and bigotry, was adjudged vile and iniquitous," so now "zealots of progress," misreading or merely ignoring "the invariable and regulating influence of creation," were, in their "piddling efforts to clear . . . a way in opposition to the Almighty rule of order, produc[ing] those mighty cataclysms in the moral world at which we gaze and shudder. Blind moles! thinking to build their tiny homes, how often have men shaken down over their own heads the magnificent structures of ages!" To remove that blindness was not simple. To be sure, the human mind had before it "that greatest of Bibles, *God's* Holy book of nature"; however much "the hue and cry of 'infidelity'" might frighten, "*facts* must have their way," distorted by "no prejudice, no dogmatic assumption (no foolish fear that *God's* word may be found in opposition to *God's* works!—revelation to fact!)"; and "man's reason is given him to *find* the way which Omniscience points."[67] But Nature and Reason, while they are "truly high authorities,"

> too often, like the cheating oracles of old, . . . render a doubtful response, the erroneous interpretation of which becomes a snare to the feet, and a pit of destruction, to the hasty interpreter of destiny. Long and laborious is the task of him who would read the truth. Like the worshipper at the cave of Trophonius, a life-long sadness, a wearing out of soul and body, in the eager pursuit of the great reality, is the price to be paid for its acquisition. The enthusiast seldom reaches it. Blindly zealous, ignorantly active, in proportion as he has the least certain foundation for his opinions, he defends them with impulsive fervor; stirs, in fanatic haste, the bubbling cauldron of society, little heeding what poisonous scum and froth may thus be floated to the surface; and lauds himself at last, like a Robespierre, . . . even in the chaotic ruin which his madness has effected.[68]

Yet the business must be tried. "Men may seek to dispute and stumble in their search after any truth, but the truth nevertheless exists." When found, it cannot be gainsaid. "The laws of nature and necessity . . . are the laws of God," and "whatever God has made ought to be."

> In constant, never varying rule,
> Each atom finds its course;

67. Ibid., "Charity Which Does Not Begin at Home," pp. 323–24, "Diversity of the Races," pp. 165, 161–63, and "Charity Which Does Not Begin at Home," p. 324.

68. Ibid., "British Philanthropy and American Slavery," pp. 300–301.

Majestic order through the whole,
  Majestic laws enforce.

And man best works his Maker's law,
  When earnest thoughts declare,
And earnest word and action show,
  God's truth is everywhere.

An anthropologist had declared that a "cruel law . . . seems to have doomed to eternal inferiority all the tribes of our species which are unfortunate enough to have a depressed and compressed cranium." "A cruel law!" Louisa McCord exclaimed, "which God has made! and shall *we* better it?" The inferiority of one race to another was a fact, and a fact only. "Inferiority is not a curse. Every creature is suited for its position, and fulfilling that position can certainly not be called cursed. What God has made, dare we to call it cursed?" "Mark me, your Grace," said Mrs. McCord to the duchess of Sutherland, "God creates not with a curse." We human beings must ever attempt to understand, even if our attempt must ever be vain: "The nearer the position of each class can be suited to its capacities, the nearer is the law of nature (that is of God) fulfilled, and the nearer is perfect justice attained. Perfect justice it is scarcely within man's capacities to attain, and all that can be done by the science of morals is to approach nearer and nearer (as does the mathematician in the squaring of the circle) to perfect truth."[69] In Ireland, wrote an English reviewer, it had become necessary not only "to remove redundant numbers, but to replace them by a more energetic, more aspiring, and more improvable race," the Saxon.

> The poor Celt, then, must be unhoused, turned forth upon the world—to work, beg, steal, or die, it matters little; for the powerful and "improvable" Saxon needs his land. He is incapable of self-government; ergo, he must be governed. Or, the governing power being deficient, he must even make himself scarce in just such proportion as will establish the equilibrium between the *minus* and the *plus* quantities. He must emigrate or die, according to circumstances. The world must progress and his place is wanted. There is no longer room for him. Let him vanish! Amen! Is this wrong? We dare not say so. It seems rather a hard necessity than a wrong. The inferior people always have, always must, it would appear, pass away before the wants of the superior, and the necessities of progress. "Begone, ye incompetent!" is surely the

69. Ibid., "Slavery and Political Economy," pp. 424, 452, and "Woman and Her Needs," p. 151; "Constancy," ll. 45–52, chap. 2 above; *PSE,* "Negro-mania," p. 232, "British Philanthropy and American Slavery," p. 291, "A Letter to the Duchess of Sutherland from a Lady of South Carolina," p. 354, and "Slavery and Political Economy," p. 441.

stern law of man's existence. Begone, from your land, from your home—ay, if it be necessary, from your life! The short spasm of a being, or of millions of beings, counts low in these calculations. We shudder at the thought, and yet, we repeat, we dare not call it a wrong. A necessity is never a wrong. A necessity of God's making—is it not a right? From such a dilemma where is the escape? Heaven only knows, and to its high mystery we bow.[70]

Did Louisa McCord, facing with characteristic constancy an intellectual conclusion, reflect that the Cheveses and the McCords, that her revered father and beloved son, were Celts? that they would "count low in these calculations"? Did she consider if the arrogant, perilous certainty which she derided and dreaded in the convictions of her opponents might not taint her own convictions? To *know* necessity, to *know* what was necessary, that—as Herodotus understood well—was to usurp the knowledge of gods; it was pride, *hubris;* and unimaginable sorrow was the punishment saved for Xerxes, Great King of the Persians, for the cause he knew to be noble and the heroic people he knew must conquer. Salamis and Plataea, Second Manassas and Appomattox, taught unexpected lessons from the axiom, composed by Mrs. McCord in prosperity, that "*power* is the stamp and seal of God to indicate His will." "Should universal nature fall," she said in a later poem, "to wreck and ruin, 'mid its Night, / Father! thy will be done!" Sorrow, she had written in *My Dreams,* "from soul to soul . . . leads me on to *thee,* thou *first great soul, / Creation's all—Infinite Being*—GOD!" Sorrow led her, now, to another truth. With the death of her son—and of "as noble a cause, and as heroic a people as ever the great *God* in his mysterious wisdom, has permitted to be crushed"—"the light of my life is gone, my hope fled, and my pride laid low."

Humble? My pride ne'er found a higher flight!
To see my son the greatest man in Rome
And wish him virtue to maintain his place![71]

VIII. "A hungering intellect"

Descried in others, pride provoked anger in Louisa McCord, and her anger was sharpened by the frustration come from recognizing that little could

70. *PSE,* "British Philanthropy and American Slavery," pp. 288–89.

71. Ibid., "Woman and Her Needs," p. 151; "Thy Will Be Done," ll. 16–18, chap. 4 above; "The Village Churchyard," ll. 279–81, chap. 1 above; LSM to Hiram Powers, March 20, 1870, and LSM to Mary Chesnut, between Jan. 23 and Feb. 3, 1863; chap. 5 above, *Caius Gracchus* 3.5.36–38.

correct the smug and deaf ignorance, the bad language and bad thinking, the "cant of charity," which pride generated.[72] Evidence, when found at all, was distorted contemptuously: "Documents here—documents there. White, they are; presto, black. True, they are; presto, false. Pretty jugglery! and worthy of all admiration!" From "Mrs. Stowe, Lucretia Mott, Gerritt Smith, and all the other old women, breeched and unbreeched, who go into hysterics of agony over the evils of a system of which they know absolutely and literally nothing," what need or expectation of evidence? "False assertions cannot be argued against. If a man insists, as a fact in his experience, that the rainbow is black, what argument can be advanced to the contrary? We may talk of decomposed light, refracted rays, etc., etc. It does no good; he still swears that he saw it. You may call him fool and liar if it will comfort you, but that is the mere enjoyment of personal luxury, and in no degree advances your argument."[73]

Perceived in herself, pride was the peril of a restless mind, which impelled her to aspirations—to be a poet, first of all, to imitate Shakespeare, "that great master of the human mind," then to stand forth as defender of her state and the South—making her wonder if humility, "the truest, last, and wisest thing," ought to cause her, like Prospero, to "break my staff" and "drown my book."[74] To this humility she made obeisance, preferring ano-

72. *PSE*, "Carey on the Slave Trade," p. 397. The anger effective in LSM's essays could mark also her family life. "I received your letter this morning and am very sorry on every account that your Aunt Louisa has chosen to act in so harsh a manner towards you. I do not blame you in the least and think you acted perfectly naturally and correctly. You know the whole cause of grievance and I have no wish to break with the Goodwyns or show them any coldness on account of it. I did at the time feel very much provoked and angered at the Colnol's having even repeated such a report but nearly three years have passed, the false report I believe died immediately, and I have never felt disposed to cherish any anger about it and met the two girls when they called on me affectionately and as relations. I know this provoked your Aunt at the time and as she knows I will not enforce her views of the subject wishes to do it herself. I hate family quarrels and the more so now there are so few of us left. . . . I have written to Alic . . . that he is not bound in any way to follow your Aunts opinions or be guided by her angry feelings." Sophia Cheves Haskell to her son Charles Haskell, March 10, 1857, Langdon Cheves III Papers, SCHS. Sophia's husband Charles Thomson Haskell was first cousin of Charlotte Ann Thomson, who in 1821 had been married to Robert Howell Goodwyn. Goodwyn's brother Thomas Jefferson Goodwyn had in 1826 also married into the Thomson family, his wife Elizabeth being a daughter of Charlotte Thomson Goodwyn's sister Mary Eugenia Thomson Darby. Both Goodwyn brothers were physicians (see LSM to Sophia Cheves Haskell, March 28, 1836, and note there).

73. *PSE*, "British Philanthropy and American Slavery," p. 300, and "Carey on the Slave Trade," pp. 394, 386.

74. *PSE*, "*Uncle Tom's Cabin*," p. 250; "To a Fly," ll. 82–88, chap. 1 above; Shakespeare, *The Tempest* 5.1.54–57.

nymity often (albeit almost as often allowing "L.S.M." to abridge it), and reluctant to give any details of her life "except that I am my father's daughter, born Dec[ember], 1810, married May, 1840, and am not dead yet." In this she followed her father, who "always kept off questions which appeared to aim at giving material for a written Life." After a precocious and rapid career in national politics, Langdon Cheves had retired to South Carolina, where he had continued to avoid public office or public notice, unless, as at the Nashville Convention of 1850, he judged the dangers of his state to demand his eloquence. In this, too, his daughter followed him. "I am, Madam," she proclaimed to the duchess of Sutherland, "by birth, parentage, education, marriage, and residence, a South Carolinian."[75] As such, she would remain.

And complain. Columbia, especially in the summer when most fled the heat and the deserted campus, had little to attract her—and even less when, an incapable tutor having been discharged, his duties, added to her own, filled her mornings "and of course in the afternoon [I] am too stupid and tired to do any thing for myself. So I am just school-mistress, until some other régime is established. Mr. McCord offers to read a little hist[or]y and geography with [the children], but I do not count much upon his help. He does not like trouble much." Lang Syne, remembered very fondly by her daughter Louisa in her "Recollections," appears in her own writings rather as a source of uncertain income, a place of seasonal responsibilities and nuisances. "She told us that she would prefer to have $25,000 in good bank stock rather than $100,000 in negroes and plantations," recalled James Burrill Angell, visiting in 1850. "I am glad to hear from your letter to Cheves," she wrote from Lang Syne to her cousin Mary Dulles, "that you are enjoying yourself [in Columbia] and have hardly the conscience to hurry you back to our stupidity, but will be very glad to see you when you are ready to come." Her sister Sophia also knew well plantation life. "We live a very retired life seeing but little company except friends who come to stay with us. Indeed country life in the South is one of great seclusion generally[,] particularly for the ladies, who insensibly fall into almost too domestic habits. We stay at home till it becomes such an effort to go out, that it is hard to make the exertion." At Lang Syne, wrote David James McCord in October 1846, "we are as dull . . . as stupidity can make us"; and, a few months later, "I have

75. LSM to William Gilmore Simms [1851?]; to Langdon Cheves III, April 6 [1876]; *PSE,* "A Letter to the Duchess of Sutherland from a Lady of South Carolina," p. 353; cf. William Porcher Miles, "Sketch of Mrs. David J. McCord," ibid., app. 3, p. 487: "It is not as a poet that the name of Louisa McCord will be most honoured and cherished in her native South Carolina. It is as a devoted daughter of the State, proud of its history, sensitive of its honour, willing to sacrifice all she possessed and all she held most dear in its defence, that her memory will live longest among her people."

scarcely been out of my house since my return home. I am not blessed in neighbours, do not shoot, and therefore do not take exercise enough. . . . My mind is just now as flat, as the country around me." "We see nobody," he reported in the spring of 1848, hindered even from his books by ditches and manure, "and have no news." "This is a very lonely life, though perhaps less felt than in Columbia," he wrote four years later. "I have not seen a newspaper since I left Columbia!" In town, too, said his wife, "Mr. McCord gets desperately cross for want of somebody to bestow his idle evenings upon, and goes up to bed at eight o'clock sometimes, growling desperately at the state of society and mankind (at least Columbia mankind) generally."[76]

But travel could seem little better. "I am very stupid," she wrote from Red Sweet Springs, "and weary to death of this homeless, aimless kind of existence. It will take all the courage I possess, to enable me to carry through my own resolutions and to stay here until the middle of October." To spend a year in Europe, which her physicians had assured her was imperative if her sight was to be saved, alarmed her. Obliged to write to her brother Langdon for business advice (the journey would be expensive), she was yet apologetic. "I am very ignorant of business and having nobody to help me, stumble along very blunderingly. And of course I want to know all I can to fix my affairs as well as I can (stupidly it must be at best) before I can leave home. . . . I am vastly bothered in my lonely and helpless condition, and do all sorts of blundering things that I suffer by." At the dock in New York, she was still havering about whether or not to depart: "I have had much difficulty already and am almost ready to give up." From Paris, "I have nothing that will interest you, for I travel as usual with all my shyness and want of knowing how to push, about me." She was impatient with her own gloom. "I have been a month in Paris and have not gone into ecstacies with it yet. On the contrary have a stupid longing all the time for my own chimney corner." Her friend William Campbell Preston reported that a letter of hers to him was "somewhat of a Smelfungus order," alluding to a character in Laurence Sterne's *Sentimental Journey* who during his travels carped and complained at everything; in the spring of 1859, "Mrs. McCord seems to be continually animated by the *animus revertendi*." Back home, she was still troubled by business difficulties. "I am as much alone here as regards all assistance in business

76. LSM to Mary Dulles, July 17, 1852; *Reminiscences of James Burrill Angell,* p. 60; LSM to Mary Dulles [April 9, 1852]; Sophia Cheves Haskell to Eleuthera Du Pont, March 24, 1857, Langdon Cheves III Papers, SCHS; David James McCord to William Porcher Miles, Oct. 15, 1846, William Porcher Miles Papers, SHC; to Francis Lieber, Dec. 18, 1846, Francis Lieber Papers, Huntington; to William Porcher Miles, March 14, 1848, William Porcher Miles Papers, SHC; to Francis Lieber, Nov. 18, 1852, Francis Lieber Papers, Huntington; LSM to Martha Herbemont, Oct. 16, 1854.

affairs as if I were on a plank in the middle of the Atlantic, and as much bewildered with papers as a child of ten years old."[77]

Just as the lonely aspiration of *My Dreams* and *Caius Gracchus* was burnt away by the communal ardor of defending the South, so worry for a brother, or a cause, or her son's eyesight and her children's delight in their European tour, brought out her strength. "I am perfectly well, and tough, and can stand a great deal," she wrote to Langdon Cheves, Jr. (who had taken a chill), begging him to neglect, until he should be completely recovered, her appeals for help in caring for their father. War swept away business troubles; her plantation was converted to the needs of war; every exertion went to her hospital and her willingness to assume, friends sometimes thought, the entire martial effort in Columbia. "My vocation is to help soldiers." Albeit the traveler might complain of her timidity and clumsiness, her tour in Europe took her to the Orkneys, to the summit of Vesuvius, through Alpine passes by mule; she made her way without disaster in the society of Paris, Rome, and Florence. In Paris the poet was honored. A brother and sister visiting from Boston "gave a little literary evening party for my Mother to which naturally I did not go, but I remember her saying when she came home that France was certainly the place to learn to do graceful and tactful things. When she went into the 'Salon,' . . . one of her books lay open on the table, and to all who arrived she was introduced as the authoress of the book. It rather amused but at the same time pleased her."[78]

"The duties of life are its only legitimate enjoyments to the reasoning, thoughtful mind." It may be doubted if the opinion of the impersonal reviewer was wholly shared by the poet and the tragedian. That reviewer maintained woman's mission to be "even nobler than man's," and woman herself, "in the true fulfilment of that mission, certainly the higher being." That reviewer set forth "the highest model of womanhood—the woman of thought, of mind, of genius, and yet filled with deep-brooding woman-love and woman-nature. She, the earnest striver, wrestling with life's cares, but contemning not its duties, feels so sensibly her noble nature, that she scorns to degrade it by placing it in an unnatural antagonism with man's, and presents in her pure woman-existence, we truly think, the highest model to which humanity is capable of attaining."[79] But the author of *Caius Gracchus,* in a letter

77. LSM to Mary Dulles, Sept. 5 [1851], to Langdon Cheves, Jr., March 23, July 7, Oct. 30, 1858; William Campbell Preston to Francis Lieber, Nov. 14, 1858, March 6, 1859, Francis Lieber Papers, SCL; LSM to Langdon Cheves, Jr., Jan. 18, 1860. *Animus revertendi* means "keenness to return."

78. LSM to Langdon Cheves, Jr., Feb. 1, 1856; to Augustine T. Smythe, Aug. 26, 1863; Smythe, p. 28.

79. *PSE,* "Negro and White Slavery," p. 192, "Enfranchisement of Woman," p. 109, and "Woman and Her Needs," p. 148. Such sentiments she repeated and varied, e.g.: "A true

otherwise of adamantine modesty, answered abruptly to one criticism. "As to my productions being *closet dramas,* what else can a Woman write? The *world of action* must to her be almost entirely a closed book." The author of *Caius Gracchus* knew that a woman "may have a great, a longing, a hungering intellect, equal to man's"—asked, "Is not all intellect suffering?"—and said:

> In the field of literature, how many women have enjoyed all the advantages which men can command, and yet how very few have distinguished themselves; and how far behind are even those few from the great and burning lights of letters! Who ever hopes to see a woman Shakspeare? And yet a greater than Shakspeare may she be. It may be doubtful whether the brilliant intellect which, inspiring noble thoughts, leaves still the great thinker grovelling in the lowest vices and slave of his passions, without the self-command to keep them in sway, is superior to that which, knowing good and evil, grasps almost instinctively at the first. Such, in its uncorrupted nature, is woman's intellect—such her inspiration. While man *writes,* she *does;* while he imagines the hero-soul, she is often performing its task; while he is painting, she is acting.[80]

Beneath assurance, surrender. "Who ever hopes to see a woman Shakspeare?" Not long before, it was the author of *Caius Gracchus* who had hoped.

IX. "I scarcely felt the whole world worth writing about"

Duty, then, remained—exacted, accepted, executed. It was not enough. Somebody must remember.

---

woman, fulfilling a woman's duties (and do not let our masculine readers suppose that we would *confine* these to shirt-making, pudding-mixing, and other such household gear, nor yet even to the adornment of her own fair person), a high-minded, intellectual woman, disdaining not her position, nor, because the world calls it humble, seeking to put aside God's and Nature's law, to her pleasure; an earnest woman, striving, as all earnest minds can strive, to do and to work, even as the Almighty laws of nature teach her that God would have her to do and to work, is, perhaps, the highest personification of Christian self-denial, love, and charity, which the world can see." Ibid., "Enfranchisement of Woman," p. 108. "There is with us of the Southern United States a strong *corps de reserve* of sober, quiet women, who, satisfied to find out duties at home (not for want of thought, but because thought teaches us that therein lies woman's highest task, and the fulfillment of her noblest mission), can nevertheless start up with the true feeling of womanhood in defence of right and property, hearth and home. *Ora et labora*—strive and pray. Such is the lesson of our life, ladies, and it were hard to find a better. With us woman finds her noblest rule, her highest privilege, a privilege which, in the aggregate, her sex has never abused." Ibid., "British Philanthropy and American Slavery," p. 319.

80. LSM to William Porcher Miles, June 12, 1848; *PSE,* "Enfranchisement of Woman," pp. 110, 121–22.

Who dares to say they died?
        The Great who sunk to rest.
What though his might stern death hath tried!
Who dares to say that these have died?
        Their memories on the past
Rise with a heightened power:
No halo of an hour,
But glory's sunbeam, from the grave,
Clinging to what he seeks to save
From dark oblivion and the night
Which comes, with sacrilegious blight,
        To doom their names to death.
They rise untarnished from the tomb,
And e'en the grave must lose its gloom,
        Stifle its pestilential breath,
To bid them stand forth purely bright.
O'er names like these, how sinks its might!
'Neath its dread power they cannot lie,
For glory will not let them die.
("Who Dares to Say They Died?" 1–19)

Yet the father of Cornelia stood as example to warn. Victor over Hannibal and the Carthaginians at Zama, chosen (the choice was obvious) to supervise Roman resistance to King Antiochus III of Syria who, accompanied by the exile Hannibal, had invaded Greece, Scipio Africanus was proof that time conquered victory, gratitude, reputation, even resentment and a disappointed grave. The historian Livy, writing not two hundred years later, was unsure how to adjudicate discrepant accounts of the last years of Africanus, whose brother, titular commander in the war against Antiochus, had been accused, though victorious, of malfeasance and bribe taking. Africanus was associated with the allegations, perhaps prosecuted. After the first charges were stopped by veto of the tribune Tiberius Sempronius Gracchus (some said he received as a reward Africanus' daughter in marriage), further charges were laid a few years later. Gist, accusers, event were alike unclear; insulted, or guilty, Africanus withdrew to the small town of Liternum; when he died, and where, where the funeral, the burial, nobody agreed, there being tombs and commemorative statues in Liternum and in Rome.[81]

Time devouring need not wait for death. Langdon Cheves "lived himself into the oblivion of posterity." The family at least must not forget. Should

81. Livy 38.56, 39.52.

their care be seen to be insufficient, wrote his daughter Louisa, "it will be a wretchedness and a shame to us all. People will not understand that we have done our best and it will seem that the old man who has been what he has, and who has made us all, is turned out to pine and to suffer." Their father was thus both a private ("who has made us all"), and a public ("who has been what he has"), responsibility. Louisa McCord, as it turned out, was burdened with both. The former she had taken upon herself, and must be prepared to accept the consequences—such was the opinion of her brother John, when, by troubled eyesight, her own and her son's, and the consequent necessity to travel north, she was constrained to ask her brother Langdon to relieve her in the summer of 1856. "It was entirely by her persuasion and influence" that their father "was induced to make his residence in Columbia," where he was "separated from all his family but Louisa," medical care was inadequate, and the proper advice "in such delicate matters" was not to be found. "No light matter can exhonerate her from the obligation and . . . any demand by her on other members of the family to take her place can not be considered as an exaction of duty to Father but as a favour asked for herself."[82]

The duty, accepted or usurped, was not to be easy. Her letters to her brother Langdon in 1856, that "most disastrous" year, are a grim record of an abject and unworthy dying. Another death—that of her brother Charles—came at its beginning; a second, of her brother Hayne, attended the first part of its course, and it was harder, being prolonged, and after their mother's death she had for Hayne taken a mother's place. "He is to me as my eldest child," she wrote in January upon receiving word of his collapse in Florence; her physician attempted to persuade her that Hayne's illness might not be mortal, but "I fear he is only trying to keep me from going quite crazy under my trouble, for I could not help showing him that I was half so." In April, "Oh! if I could only go to my poor boy!" But she could not, bound to her father "as if in a horrible dream." It was a dream in which her father was being deformed and distorted into somebody else. "I do not know what to do, I am giving up every moment of my time, neglecting business, children and everything else, but without success. I do not know what to do."[83]

The father of Louisa McCord had been her example, her model, her "Idol through childhood and womanhood"; and she had been most his heir, in appearance (as she said to Hiram Powers) and above all in intellect. That

82. William Campbell Preston to Waddy Thompson, July 17 [1856], William Campbell Preston Papers, SCL; LSM to Langdon Cheves, Jr., Jan. 25, 1856; John Richardson Cheves to Langdon Cheves, Jr., New York, July 13, 1856, Langdon Cheves I Papers, SCHS.

83. LSM to Langdon Cheves, Jr., Jan. 7, 1857, Jan. 20, 1856, to Anna Cheves Huger, Jan. 25, 1856, to Langdon Cheves, Jr., April 21, Feb. 26, Jan. 25, 1856.

inheritance he had announced in bequeathing to her his library; to it she had testified in composing (in "Separate Secession") a manifesto of her father's position in the secession crisis of 1850–51; in sharing his fondness of Shakespeare, whom "through life he frequently quoted"; and in claiming him as friend and sustenance to her aspiration, whose wisdom might fail only through love:

> I have seen
> *Thee,* with a kind indulgence, read my lines,
> Penned with a trembling hand, a tearful eye,
> And I have drunk thy hope-inspiring praise,
> And hugged myself therein. But out, alas!
> On my ill-founded hopes! Too partial judge,
> Thou can'st not say if 'twere the man's,
> Or but the parent's, heart which felt and throbbed
> Its answers back to *my* heart's throbbing struggles.

"My feelings towards my Father, have through life been almost those of worship, rather than simply of affection." She remembered him as he had talked during her childhood, "myself on his knees—no disguises from his family—would discuss freely all subjects with his friends—What would I not now give to recall such conversations? . . . As I think of them there lingers about a feeling amounting almost to adoration." He "never spoke harshly to me"; unlike her society, he had never disapproved or ridiculed—or, what would perhaps have been worse, been unable to understand—her literary and intellectual ambitions; and her "Memoir" of him closes with his "feeling of sympathy towards the young, with a disposition to encourage,—never to brow-beat": "he was always gentle and encouraging to the young, with an almost Fatherlike kindness, wherever he was met with truth and candour."[84]

That kind and confiding man now refused to discuss his business affairs with her, suspected her of joining in a conspiracy to ruin him. Now the grandfather who had welcomed her children at his Sandhills place grew harsh and peremptory such that she was driven to build a separate house "where I can take refuge and send my children as may be found needful. I *must* have a hiding place for them." The loving daughter became now to him a sinister jailer, an alien and unrecognizable presence. "I have a double, whom as I cannot give a name for, he constantly calls the 'nameless one' and 'the lonely one', and whom he thinks I have displaced in his house and in the Lang Syne

84. Chap. 8 above, "Memoir of Langdon Cheves," pp. 259, 251; chap. 1 above, *My Dreams,* "Dedication to My Father," ll. 14–22; LSM to Langdon Cheves III, April 6 [1876]; chap. 8 above, "Memoir of Langdon Cheves," pp. 259, 255.

property. . . . He is constantly annoyed with the fear that I am doing her some injustice and says he is sure I must have some dispute with her; otherwise he would see us together or at least I could tell him where she is." There was no help for this, until decay of mind made her father careless of all things, efficiently manageable by a nurse. "He was long in dying—after weeks of forgetfulness, as I leant upon the back of his wheeled chair—He looked me in the face—'Are you not my daughter[?]'—My silent answer was a kiss upon his upturned brow—and he continued[, ']I thought you were my daughter.[']"[85]

Her father dead, his memory now became her charge. In it others of the family were associated at first, especially her brother Langdon, who as elder surviving son and executor of their father's will might be expected to contribute much; but he was dilatory, seldom wrote letters, could not be relied upon. "I alone being responsible in the matter," the reputation and remembrance of Langdon Cheves were Louisa McCord's business—interrupted by war and what followed—from his death to her own. In this, again, her example was her father. "One of the last things which Father seemed anxious about before his health failed, was that attention should be paid to the erection of three tomb-stones or monuments of some kind, over his Mother's grave in Abbeville and our Mother's and Aunt Lovell's on this place. . . . There is I know no legal obligation to the erection of these, but Father was very anxious that it should be done and indeed had told me to attend to it; when new troubles caused the state of health which prevented further action." These monuments, also, fell to her concern. Although her sister Sophia lived near Abbeville, it was Louisa who placed a slab upon their grandmother's grave there; and after her return from Europe she found that the order which she had made of a slab for Mary Cheves' grave at Lang Syne had not been executed—evidently none of her family had troubled themselves to see to the matter in her absence.[86] But this was a happy omission, for by now was planned in Charleston a more elaborate burial site for the Cheves family, in keeping with the Langdon Cheves whom his daughter had from the outset had it in mind to commemorate: the public man.

In this, in intention though not in effort, her brother Langdon concurred. She was hesitant, therefore, at first, lest she seem to press upon his prerogative. "Has anything been done about Father's bust and intended monument? I *must* go to Europe next summer. I only want advice as to best time of

85. LSM to Langdon Cheves, Jr., March 1, April 13, 1856; chap. 8 above, "Memoir of Langdon Cheves," p. 262.

86. LSM to Hiram Powers, Jan. 13, 1860, to Langdon Cheves, Jr., Dec. 26, 1857, Feb. 29, 1860; to Langdon Cheves III, May 20, 1876.

going etc.—probably in June. If I could do anything while there to order the desired work I would be very glad—I could easily get letters f[ro]m [William Campbell] Preston here, which would make [Hiram] Powers exert himself to do well what is required if put in his hands—If I can do anything let me know. It will do me good to have some objects before me." But nothing had been done. In April 1859, coming to Powers in his studio in Florence, she found that the casts and other materials which Langdon had promised to send before her had not yet been received—had not, as became clear, been sent at all. Perhaps she was not surprised: the spring after their father's death, she had had to call to Langdon's attention that "the apparant neglect of Father's grave has become an object of remark. . . . If the lot were enclosed with a railing, and perhaps a temporary slab, these . . . would prevent the appearance of neglect which, I confess, pained me very much, on my visiting it lately." But Langdon was occupied with other trouble, now to trouble her, for it might injure their father's name—a quarrel over the will. If there must be such, "I trust at least that . . . there is no disrespect to Father's memory." And, in a letter written the next day, "I would give up every thing sooner than have a disgraceful squabble over what our dear Father has left."[87]

Secession and the war put an end to worries of this kind. After that, commemoration itself became suspect, or vain. In 1869 Louisa McCord could believe that monuments to the fallen of Carolina were worth raising, and in March 1870 she wrote to Hiram Powers for news of her father's bust. In June, however, she resigned the former hope; and not until 1875 did she arrange for an obelisk to adorn the Cheves tomb in Magnolia Cemetery; in 1878 she was corresponding with Hiram's son Preston Powers to execute the bust, now no longer the colossal bust of the original plan, meant to stand as the focus of the funerary monument, but a smaller piece substituted for the life-size copy of the colossal bust which she had ordered, for herself, from Hiram Powers. Even this remnant—what could be hoped for it? "We *are* destroyed," she wrote to Powers in 1870, "and I fear as a people past from life forever. The true-hearted among our survivors have to look with pride, only upon our sufferings, and upon the graves of our dead. We fought for our rights and our liberties. Our very boys were heroes in endurance, and in death. But now, ground down, and writhing beneath the heel of a brutal conqueror, none can even live, without giving up something of the purity of his feelings by submission to the unblushing and utterly lawless tyranny of a brutal rule; and the wreck of as noble a people as ever trod

87. LSM to Langdon Cheves, Jr., Feb. 5, May 26, April 3, 4, 1858.

God's earth, must, I fear, inevitably fall away from its higher characteristics." In 1878 she had come to doubt even the poor refuge of sufferings recalled and graves observed. It was the doom of Scipio Africanus. Langdon Cheves was "now almost forgotten in the scramble that follows our noble but disastrous war," although dead only twenty-one years: "in such a country as ours now is, that is enough to stamp into oblivion every thing worth remembering."[88] Memory, which had failed her father in his last days, now was failing her people.

The bust of Langdon Cheves was delivered in Charleston after Louisa McCord was dead. Why had she chosen stone, or stone only, for the frail hope against voracious forgetfulness? Stone did not stay; Powers' statue of Calhoun, sunk, salvaged, sequestered, burnt up, will have taught her that; and Shelley's "shattered visage" and "colossal wreck" warned patrons haughtier and wealthier than she. Moreover, there was Horace's *aere perennius,* and her own ambition and passion for eloquence and language, to tell her that while all things, like stone, must perish, words perish last. "Our War came,—and sorrow upon sorrow piled until I scarcely felt the whole world worth writing about."[89] Why? It was not from failure of her powers. Although declining at first a nephew's request for "something of a memoir" of her father—"I am now quite unfit. A few scattered anecdotes, and those perhaps, already given to you by others, would be all I could do"—soon she took up the charge, and accomplished it in part; for the rest, the fragmentary notes attest to the continuous vivacity of her apprehension, once engaged. In 1867, and in 1873, her eye for detail and capacity for narrative were undiminished, and made by the occasion ardent, when she recollected her experiences during the Federal occupation of Columbia. Did her silence, then, spring from peril, the impropriety of a woman engaging that peril? Amid celebrations of the Centennial, "as I could not kneel down and shout 'glory! glory!,'—nor find my way to the 'love, peace, and charity' frame of

88. LSM to Hiram Powers, March 20, 1870, to Preston Powers [May 29, 1878].

89. LSM to Preston Powers [May 29, 1878]: "Regarding the replacing of the statue of Calhoun [destroyed in the burning of Columbia,] I would be most happy to do any thing useful or agreeable to you; but I not only have for years shrunk too much from the world to have influence with anybody, but I know little of what is going on—and have not connection or acquaintance with any of the town council nor with those moving in the matter. . . . My private impression however is that the town council has not the slightest idea of doing anything in the business. . . . Our corner of the world does not prosper." Percy Bysshe Shelley, "Ozymandias," ll. 4, 13; Horace *Odes* 3.30; LSM to Langdon Cheves III, April 6 [1876]; cf. Phil. 2:27: "For indeed he was sick nigh unto death: but God had mercy on him; and not on him only, but on me also, lest I should have sorrow upon sorrow"; "The Voice of the Star," ll. 59–60, chap. 1 above.

mind,—I have been trying to keep very quiet and very stupid, hemning, in good-woman style, pocket handkerchiefs, and so forth." Or during Federal anger with contumacious South Carolina in 1871,

> might not the presence of an offensive and discontented individual like myself, even though only an old woman, help to draw disagreeable attention[?] Do not laugh, as though thinking that I make myself of much importance. Men have quareled and shot each other, for a dog—for a shadow;—and I have heard it stated, right or wrong, that women have been threatened and watched, in the dragonade district. I might be, under some circumstances[,] a dangerous inmate, and it would be too late to move out of the way when the lash would be raised, not over me personally but over my nearest and dearest.
>
> All these things considered, had I not better stay away?[90]

She had chosen exile. But exile need not impose silence. It had imposed the contrary upon Edward Hyde, relegated to the island of Jersey and to France, created earl of Clarendon by the Restoration which brought him home again. He had begun his *History of the Rebellion* when in exile; compelled to flee abroad again, deserted by an ungrateful king, the earl had written his own life, then again taken up the *History* and combined the two into the great work by which he is known. With him Louisa McCord shared a divided country, a civil war, a lost cause; she shared his aspiring eloquence and ambition of fame. She stood mute. The cause which Clarendon served was not permanently lost; he presumed that right and time would restore it, and he saw it restored; though himself ruined a second time, he knew that the cause remained, and would provide the audience for his writings meant to understand his past. "I have described the triumph of barbarism and religion," said Edward Gibbon, hopeful, or not diffident, of that triumph being reversed in his own times.[91] For Louisa McCord there was not hope of reversal or restoration. She had not departed with her stepson Russell McCord to Brazil, still a slaveholding society; she had talked of the Hawaiian Islands and had decided upon Canada—and Russell McCord soon returned. "I would like it said," wrote her daughter of a notice to introduce a posthumous selection of Mrs. McCord's verse, "that [her] son's death and the failure

90. LSM to Langdon Cheves III, April 6, July 11 [1876], to Augustine T. Smythe, Charlottesville, Nov. 14 [1871].

91. Edward Gibbon, *The History of the Decline and Fall of the Roman Empire,* ed. J. B. Bury, 7 vols. (1909–14 ed.; rpt. New York, 1974), 7:321.

of the cause she loved so well ended her life. After that she only waited patiently for the welcome release."[92]

"My world is dead and in the past." That was written after the last of the occupying troops had been withdrawn from her state; Wade Hampton III was governor of a South Carolina which many supposed to have shaken off the horrors of defeat. It made no difference to Mrs. McCord. Yet, if her world was dead, so was her father no less, and he was worth a memorial, though a written memorial had to be pressed upon her. Her world received no word. At Second Manassas, "my all was at stake."[93] The mother had written that, and the daughter of the father whom she had sought to re-create in the son; daughter and mother had dedicated *My Dreams* and *Caius Gracchus.* Together, daughter and mother killed the poet, the dramatist, the defender of a society who, seeing it destroyed, might have composed its dirge, or, better, its tragedy and its record. To us are left the gathered pieces of her work—reminiscent, perhaps, not of an antique Rome sacked and dismantled by barbarians and Christians, but rather of the Carthage of Queen Dido, its cranes swaying idly, its towers unfinished, a city abandoned in the building of it by its mistress whom an unworthy object has enraptured, then deserted to revenge and despair.[94]

At the beginning there was poetry, and ambition. Her state, and her South, came crowding in: at once anger with their enemies and dismay at the folly of their friends. Determination, struggling with helplessness in her essays, was distracted, choked off, by failing eyesight and the deaths of husband, brothers, father, son, by hopes overthrown in war and a savage peace. Then ruin, memory, memorial, the stark obelisk and tardy bust. Befitting a Roman and Cornelia, the death of Louisa McCord was without ease or complaint. Near the last, her daughter, leaning above her, said that likely she would not live: was she willing to see the end? "Willing, my child? *Glad* . . . glad to rest."

92. Louisa McCord Smythe to William Porcher Miles, Charleston, Feb. 26, 1880, printed in *PSE,* app. 3, pp. 483–84.

93. LSM to Preston Powers [May 29, 1878], to Mary Chesnut, Oct. 18, 1863; also to Augustine T. Smythe, April 28, 1863: "My all is gone"; chap. 5 above, *Caius Gracchus* 5.1.186–87 (Licinia to Cornelia): "Do you not love your son? . . . / He is your all on earth!"

94. Vergil *Aeneid* 4.86–89 = Dryden's translation, 4.123–28:

> Mean time the rising Tow'rs are at a stand:
> No Labours exercise the youthful Band:
> Nor use of Arts, nor Toils of Arms they know;
> The Mole is left unfinish'd to the Foe.
> The Mounds, the Works, the Walls, neglected lye,
> Short of their promis'd height that seem'd to threat the Sky.

BIBLIOGRAPHY

INDEX

Bibliography

MANUSCRIPT SOURCES

Charleston County, S.C.
  Probate Court Records

Manuscript Department, William R. Perkins Library, Duke University, Durham, N.C.
  Rachel S. Cheves Papers
  Ann Heatly Reid Lovell Papers

Henry E. Huntington Library, San Marino, Calif.
  Francis Lieber Papers

Library of Congress
  William Lowndes Papers

Orangeburg County, S.C.
  Mesne Conveyance Records

Peabody Institute, Baltimore
  John Pendleton Kennedy Papers

Historical Society of Pennsylvania, Philadelphia
  Edward Carey Gardiner Collection, Henry C. Carey Section
  Gratz Collection

Richland County, S.C.
  Mesne Conveyance Records

Archives of American Art, Smithsonian Institution, Washington, D.C.
  Hiram Powers and Powers Family Papers

South Carolina Department of Archives and History, Columbia
  Will of David James McCord

South Carolina Historical Society, Charleston
  Langdon Cheves I Papers
  Langdon Cheves III Papers
  Dulles-Cheves-McCord-Lovell Papers
  Smythe-McCord-Stoney Collection
  Smythe-Stoney-Adger Papers

South Caroliniana Library, University of South Carolina, Columbia
  Cheves Family Papers
  Francis Lieber Papers
  Snowden-Bennett Collection

James Henley Thornwell Papers
Williams-Chesnut-Manning Families Manuscripts
Louisa McCord Smythe. "Recollections of Louisa Rebecca Hayne McCord (Mrs. Augustine T. Smythe)" (typescript)

Southern Historical Collection, Library of the University of North Carolina at Chapel Hill
William Porcher Miles Papers
Pettigrew Family Papers

Virginia Historical Society, Richmond
Preston Family Papers

State Historical Society of Wisconsin, Madison
Lyman C. Draper Manuscripts

PUBLISHED SOURCES

Anderson, Mary Crow, ed. *Two Scholarly Friends: Yates Snowden–John Bennett Correspondence, 1902–1932*. Columbia, S.C., 1993.

Angell, James Burrill. *The Reminiscences of James Burrill Angell*. New York, 1912.

Barnwell, John. *Love of Order: South Carolina's First Secession Crisis*. Chapel Hill, N. C., 1982.

[Bass, Robert Duncan.] "McCord, Louisa Susanna Cheves." In *DAB*.

Bennett, Susan Smythe, comp. "The Cheves Family of South Carolina." *SCHM* 35 (1934): 79–95, 130–52.

———, comp. "The McCords of McCords' Ferry, South Carolina." *SCHM* 34 (1933): 177–93.

Bleser, Carol, ed. *Secret and Sacred: The Diaries of James Henry Hammond, a Southern Slaveholder*. New York, 1988.

The Book of Common Prayer. New York, 1992.

Burke, Edmund. *Letter to a Noble Lord* and *First Letter on a Regicide Peace*. 1796. In *The Writings and Speeches of Edmund Burke*. Vol. 9, pt. 1, *The Revolutionary War, 1794–1797*, and pt. 2, *Ireland*, ed. R. B. McDowell, pp. 145–264. Oxford, 1991.

Conrad, Susan Phinney. *Perish the Thought: Intellectual Women in Romantic America, 1830–1860*. New York, 1976.

Cooper, Thomas, and David James McCord, eds. *The Statutes at Large of South Carolina*. 10 vols. Columbia, S.C., 1836–41.

Daly, Louise Haskell. *Alexander Cheves Haskell: The Portrait of a Man*. Intro. Lee A. Wallace, Jr. Rev. rpt. of 1934 ed. Wilmington, N.C., 1989.

Davidson, Chalmers Gaston. *The Last Foray: The South Carolina Planters of 1860, A Sociological Study*. Columbia, S.C., 1971.

Davidson, James Wood. *The Living Writers of the South*. New York, 1869.

De Bow, James Dunwoody Brownson. *The Industrial Resources, etc. of the Southern and Western States. . . .* 3 vols. New Orleans, 1853.

Duyckinck, Evert A., and George L. Duyckinck. *Cyclopaedia of American Literature.* 2 vols. New York, 1856.

Eacker, Susan A. "'A Dangerous Inmate' of the Antebellum South: Louisa McCord on Gender and Slavery." In *Essays on Southern Writers and Their Worlds,* ed. Christopher Morris and Steven Reinhardt. Walter Prescott Webb Memorial Lectures, vol. 29. College Station, Tex., forthcoming.

Eaton, Clement. *The Mind of the Old South.* Rev. ed. Baton Rouge, La., 1967.

Fladeland, Betty. *Men and Brothers: Anglo-American Antislavery Cooperation.* Urbana, Ill., 1972.

Forrest, Mary [Julia D. Freeman]. *Women of the South Distinguished in Literature.* New York, 1861.

Fox-Genovese, Elizabeth. *Feminism without Illusions: A Critique of Individualism.* Chapel Hill, N.C., 1991.

———. *Within the Plantation Household: Black and White Women of the Old South.* Chapel Hill, N.C., 1988.

Fraser, Jessie Melville. "Louisa C. McCord." M.A. thesis, University of South Carolina, 1919.

Genovese, Eugene D., and Elizabeth Fox-Genovese. "Slavery, Economic Development, and the Law: The Dilemma of the Southern Political Economists, 1800–1860." *Washington and Lee Law Review* 41, no. 1 (Winter 1984): 1–29.

Gillespie, Neal C. *The Collapse of Orthodoxy: The Intellectual Ordeal of George Frederick Holmes.* Charlottesville, Va., 1972.

Hale, Sarah Josepha. *Woman's Record; or, Sketches of All Distinguished Women, from the Creation to* A.D. *1854.* 2d ed. rev. New York, 1855.

Hampton, A. F., ed. *A Divided Heart: Letters of Sally Baxter Hampton, 1853–1862.* Spartanburg, S.C., 1980.

Hart, John Seely. *The Female Prose Writers of America.* Philadelphia, 1852.

Haskell, John Cheves. *The Haskell Memoirs.* Ed. Gilbert E. Govan and James W. Livingood. New York, 1960.

Hollinger, David A., and Charles Capper, eds. *The American Intellectual Tradition.* 2d ed. 2 vols. New York, 1993.

Hubbell, Jay B. *The South in American Literature, 1607–1900.* Durham, N.C., 1954.

Huff, Archie Vernon, Jr. *Langdon Cheves of South Carolina.* Columbia, S.C., 1977.

Irving, Washington. *The Complete Works of Washington Irving. Letters.* Vol. 1, 1802–23. Ed. R. M. Aderman et al. Boston, 1978.

Jenkins, William Sumner. *Pro-Slavery Thought in the Old South.* Chapel Hill, N.C., 1935.

Jones, Norrece T., Jr. *Born a Child of Freedom, Yet a Slave: Mechanisms of Control and Strategies of Resistance in Antebellum South Carolina.* Hanover, N.H., and London, 1990.

LaBorde, Maximilian. *History of the South Carolina College. . . .* Columbia, S.C., 1859.

Lounsbury, Richard C., ed. *Louisa S. McCord: Political and Social Essays.* Publications of the Southern Texts Society. Charlottesville, Va., 1995.

———. "*Ludibria Rerum Mortalium:* Charlestonian Intellectuals and Their Classics." In *Intellectual Life in Antebellum Charleston,* ed. Michael O'Brien and David Moltke-Hansen, pp. 325–69. Knoxville, Tenn., 1986.

McCord, David James. "Africans at Home." *SQR*, n.s., 10 (July 1854): 70–96.

———. "American Institutions—the Monroe Doctrine—Intervention—etc." *De Bow* 15 (Dec. 1853): 584–95.

———. "The Anatomy of the Navigation Laws." *SQR* 16 (Jan. 1850): 416–44.

———. "Barhydt's Industrial Exchanges." *SQR* 15 (July 1849): 460–83.

———. "California Gold." *SQR*, n.s., 5 (April 1852): 301–21.

———. "Civil Liberty and Self-Government." *SQR*, n.s., 9 (April 1854): 300–332.

———. "The Federal Constitution." *Southern Review* 2 (Nov. 1828): 432–54.

———. "How the South Is Affected by Her Slave Institutions." *De Bow* 11 (Oct. 1851): 349–63.

———. "Lieber's Political Ethics." *SQR* 12 (Oct. 1847): 464–504.

———. "Life of a Negro Slave." *SQR*, n.s., 7 (Jan. 1853): 206–27.

———. "Memphis Convention." *SQR* 10 (Oct. 1846): 377–417.

———. "Mr. Clay and the American System." *SQR* 10 (July 1846): 174–227.

———. "Navigation Laws." *SQR*, n.s., 1 (April 1850): 48–75.

———. "Pennsylvania Iron Memorial." *SQR*, n.s., 6 (July 1852): 1–22.

———. "Political Economy—Manufactures." *SQR* 9 (April 1846): 392–433.

———. "Political Elements." *SQR*, n.s., 10 (Oct. 1854): 383–431.

———. "Practical Effects of Emancipation." *De Bow* 18 (April and May 1855): 474–96, 591–602.

———. *Reports of Cases Determined in the Constitutional Court of South Carolina: Being a Continuation of Nott and McCord's Reports.* 4 vols. Columbia, S.C., 1822–30.

———. "Slavery and the Abolitionists." *SQR* 15 (April 1849): 165–223.

———. "What Is Fair and Equal Reciprocity?" *De Bow* 15 (Nov. 1853): 433–47.

"McCord, Mrs. Louisa Susannah Cheves." In *The South in the Building of the Nation,* ed. Julian A. C. Chandler et al., 12:132. Richmond, 1909.

McCurry, Stephanie. "The Two Faces of Republicanism: Gender and Proslavery Politics in Antebellum South Carolina." *Journal of American History* 78 (1992): 1245–64.

McGowan, Clelia P. "Louisa S. McCord (1810–1879)." In *Library of Southern Literature,* ed. Edwin Alderman and Joel Chandler Harris, 8:3505–7. New Orleans, 1907.

Manly, Louise. *Southern Literature from 1579–1895: A Comprehensive Review, with Copious Extracts and Criticisms.* Richmond, 1895.

May, Caroline. *The American Female Poets, with Biographical and Critical Notices.* Philadelphia, 1848.

Meats, Stephen, and Edwin T. Arnold, eds. *The Writings of Benjamin F. Perry.* 3 vols. Spartanburg, S.C., 1980.

Meriwether, Anne Blythe. "McCord, Louisa Cheves." In *Encyclopedia of the Confederacy,* ed. Richard N. Current, 3:969. New York, 1993.

Nott, Henry Junius, and David James McCord. *Reports of Cases Determined in the Constitutional Court of South Carolina.* 2 vols. Columbia, S.C., 1820–21.

O'Brien, Michael, ed. *All Clever Men, Who Make Their Way: Critical Discourse in the Old South.* Fayetteville, Ark., 1982; 2d ed., Athens, Ga., 1992.

——, ed. *An Evening When Alone: Four Journals of Single Women in the South, 1827–67.* Publications of the Southern Texts Society. Charlottesville, Va., 1993.

Oliphant, Mary C. Simms, et al., eds. *The Letters of William Gilmore Simms.* 6 vols. Columbia, S.C., 1952–82.

Pease, William H., and Jane H. Pease. *James Louis Petigru: Southern Conservative, Southern Dissenter.* Athens, Ga., 1995.

Plutarch. *The Lives of the Noble Grecians and Romans.* The Dryden Translation, rev. Arthur Hugh Clough. 2 vols. New York, 1992.

Rable, George C. *Civil Wars: Women and the Crisis of Southern Nationalism.* Urbana, Ill., 1989.

Read, Thomas Buchanan, ed. *The Female Poets of America.* Philadelphia, 1849.

Sargent, Epes, ed. *Harper's Cyclopaedia of British and American Poetry.* New York, 1881.

"S.C. Birthday." Charleston *News and Courier.* Dec. 3, 1945.

Smythe, Louisa McCord. *For Old Lang Syne: Collected for My Children.* Charleston, S.C., 1900.

Stockton, David. *The Gracchi.* Oxford, 1979.

Stowe, Harriet Beecher. *Uncle Tom's Cabin or, Life among the Lowly.* New York, 1991.

[Tardy, Mary T., ed.] *The Living Female Writers of the South.* 1872. Rpt. Detroit, 1978.

Thorp, Margaret Farrand. *Female Persuasion: Six Strong-Minded Women.* 1949. Rpt. n.p., 1971.

——. "McCord, Louisa Susannah Cheves." In *Notable American Women, 1607–1950: A Biographical Dictionary,* ed. Edward T. James et al., 2:450–52. Cambridge, Mass., 1971.

Trent, William P. *William Gilmore Simms.* Boston and New York, 1892.

United Daughters of the Confederacy, South Carolina Division. *South Carolina Women in the Confederacy,* ed. Mrs. Thomas Taylor et al. 2 vols. Columbia, S.C., 1903–7.

Watson, Charles S. *Antebellum Charleston Dramatists.* University, Ala., 1976.

Wauchope, George Armstrong, ed. *The Writers of South Carolina.* Columbia, S.C., 1910.

Wise, Stephen R. *Gate of Hell: Campaign for Charleston Harbor, 1863.* Columbia, S.C., 1994.

Woodward, C. Vann, ed. *Mary Chesnut's Civil War.* New Haven, 1981.

——, and Elizabeth Muhlenfeld, eds. *The Private Mary Chesnut: The Unpublished Civil War Diaries.* New York, 1984.

Wunder, Richard P. *Hiram Powers: Vermont Sculptor, 1805–1873.* 2 vols. Newark, N.J., 1991.

Index

A. NAMES

When a name is followed by more than one page reference, annotation is signified by boldface type. Characters in Caius Gracchus *are indexed only when annotated or when discussed elsewhere.*

B. AUTHORS